VENICE

THE ROUGH GUIDE

Other guides available in this series

Amsterdam
Barcelona & Catalunya
Berlin
Brazil
Brittany & Normandy
Bulgaria
California & the West Coast
Canada
Crete
Cyprus
Czech & Slovak Republics
Egypt
Europe
Florida
France
Germany
Greece
Guatemala & Belize
Holland, Belgium & Luxembourg
Hong Kong
Hungary
Ireland
Israel
Italy
Kenya
Mediterranean Wildlife
Mexico
Morocco
Nepal
New York
Nothing Ventured
Paris
Peru
Poland
Portugal
Prague
Provence
Pyrenees
San Francisco
Scandinavia
Sicily
Spain
St Petersburg
Thailand
Tunisia
Turkey
Tuscany & Umbria
USA
West Africa
Women Travel
Zimbabwe & Botswana

Forthcoming titles

Australia
Corsica
England & Wales
Scotland

Rough Guide Credits

Text Editor: Jonathan Buckley
Series Editor: Mark Ellingham
Editorial: Martin Dunford, John Fisher, Jack Holland, Greg Ward, Kate Berens, Jules Brown
Publicity: Richard Trillo
Production: Susanne Hillen, Gail Jammy, Andy Hilliard, Vivien Antwi, Melissa Flack, Alan Spicer
Finance: Celia Crowley

Acknowledgements

Both authors are grateful to all those who have written in with comments on the Rough Guide to Venice over the past two years, particularly Linda Hart, Sue Downes, John Hults, Elizabeth Hughes, [illegible] A. Armstrong and Enid Gowie. Thanks also to Barry Curtis, Mike Ivy, Bruce Moffat, Michele Topper, [illegible] Nathalie Brooke at Venice in Peril, Gill Hedley at the British Council, and Ellen Sarewitz for proof-reading, Gail for typesetting, and Melissa and Contour Publishing, Cromford, for work on the maps. Above all, for up-to-the-minute information on the Veneto, we are indebted to **Brenda Keatley**. Individually, we would like to thank:

Jonathan – Sergio Fragiacomo, Baldessare de'Gasperi, Luigi and Maria-Luisa Benedetti, and Eliane Reggiori.

Hilary – Louise Schwartz and Mick Hargreaves; Franco Donaggio for insights into life on the lagoon; Roberto Longo, Mapi and Liri for hospitality, friendship and enthusiastic exposés; Matteo, Sandro and the rest of the drummers for entertainment during Carnevale, Gabriella Balbinot; and Sandro Sartori.

This edition published in 1993 by Rough Guides Ltd, 1 Mercer Street, London WC2H 9QJ.
Distributed by Penguin Books, 27 Wrights Lane, London W8 5TZ.
Previous edition published by Harrap Columbus Ltd.

Printed in the United Kingdom by Cox & Wyman Ltd (Reading).
Typography and **original design** by Jonathan Dear and The Crowd Roars.
Illustrations throughout by Edward Briant.

416pp.
Includes index.

British Library Cataloguing in Publication Data
A catalogue record for this book is available from the British Library.

ISBN 1-85828-036-2

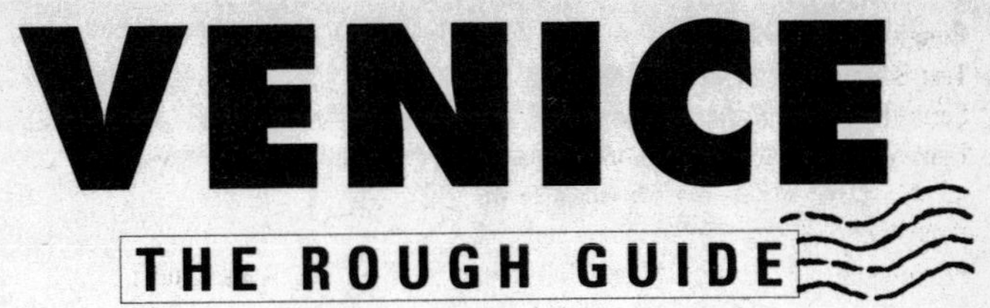

Written and researched by
Jonathan Buckley and Hilary Robinson

THE ROUGH GUIDES

The Contents

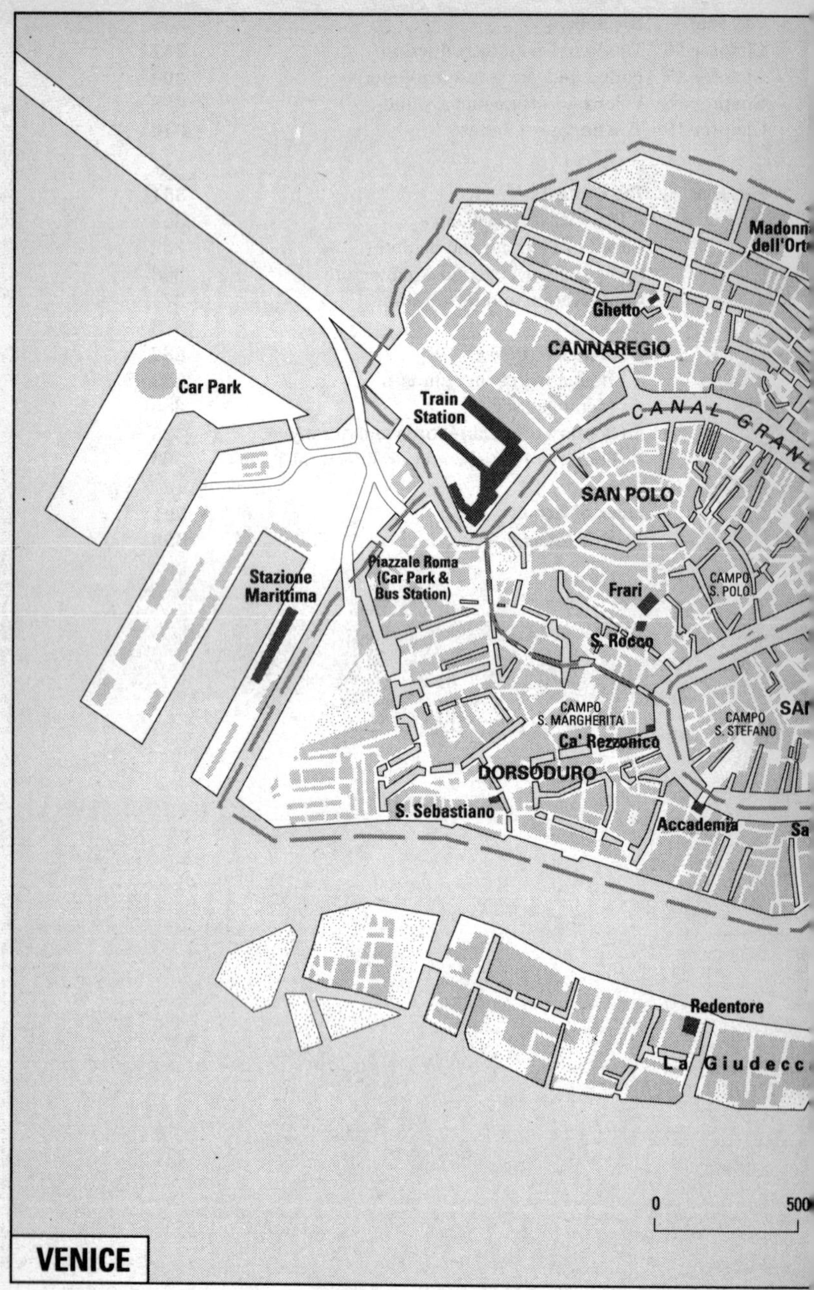

Madonna dell'Orto
Ghetto
CANNAREGIO
Car Park
Train Station
CANAL GRANDE
SAN POLO
Stazione Marittima
Piazzale Roma (Car Park & Bus Station)
CAMPO S. POLO
Frari
S. Rocco
CAMPO S. MARGHERITA
CAMPO S. STEFANO
Ca' Rezzonico
DORSODURO
S. Sebastiano
Accademia
Redentore
La Giudecca
0
VENICE

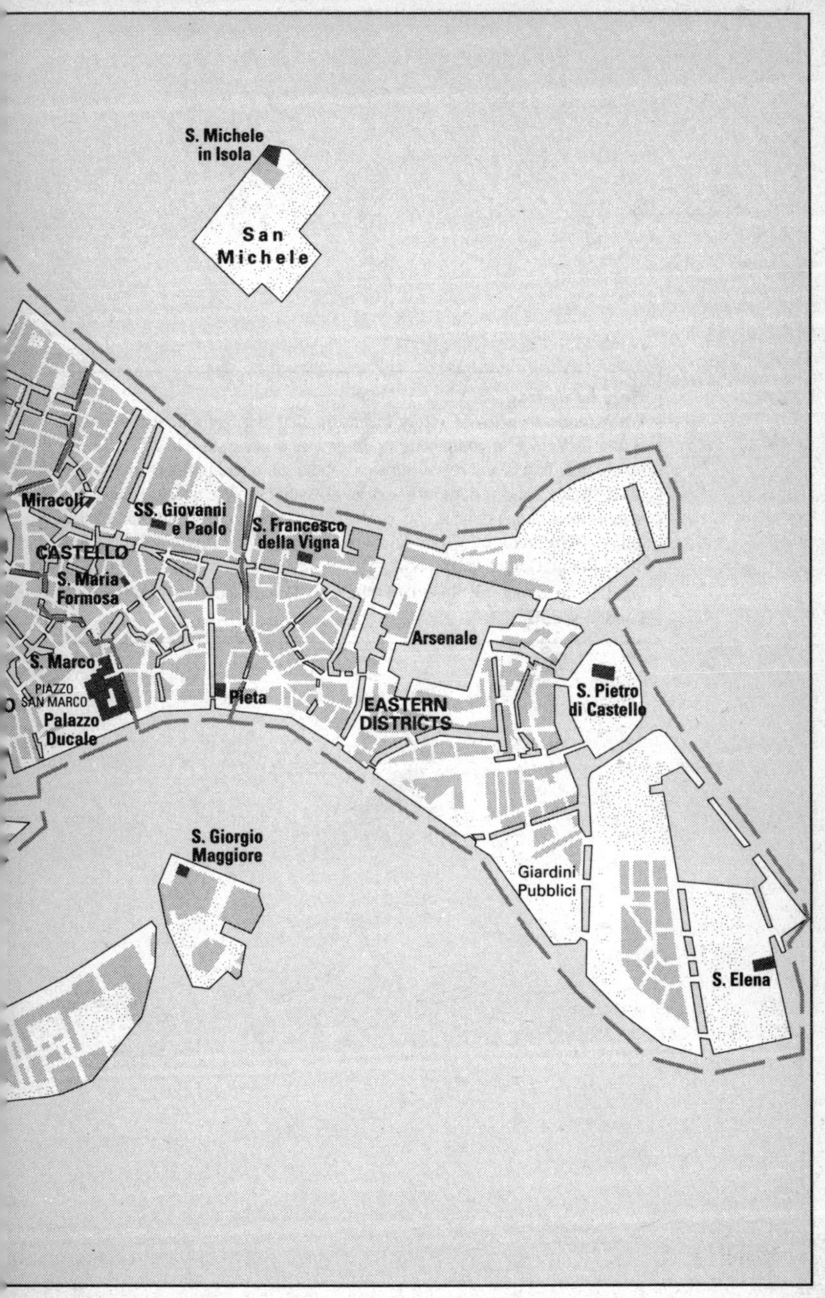
S. Michele
in Isola
San
Michele
Miracoli
SS. Giovanni
e Paolo
S. Francesco
della Vigna
CASTELLO
S. Maria
Formosa
Arsenale
S. Marco
PIAZZO
SAN MARCO
Pieta
EASTERN
DISTRICTS
S. Pietro
di Castello
Palazzo
Ducale
S. Giorgio
Maggiore
Giardini
Pubblici
S. Elena

Help us update

We've gone to a lot of effort to ensure that this edition of the Rough Guide to Venice is completely up-to-date and accurate. However, things do change: hotels and restaurants come and go, opening hours are notoriously fickle, and prices are extremely volatile. We'd appreciate any suggestions, amendments or contributions for future editions of the guide. We'll credit all letters and send a copy of the new edition (or any other Rough Guide) for the best.

Send them along to: Jonathan Buckley, Rough Guides, 1 Mercer St, London WC2H 9QJ.

Introduction

Depicted and described so often that its image has become part of the European collective consciousness, **Venice** can initially create the slightly anticlimactic feeling that everything looks exactly as it should. The water-lapped palaces along the Canal Grande are just as the brochure photographs made them out to be, Piazza San Marco does indeed look as perfect as a film set, and the panorama across the water from the Palazzo Ducale is precisely as Canaletto painted it. The sense of familiarity soon fades, however, as details of the scene begin to catch the attention – a strange carving high on a wall, a boat being manoeuvred round an impossible corner, a window through which a painted ceiling can be seen. And the longer one looks, the stranger and more intriguing Venice becomes.

Founded fifteen hundred years ago on a cluster of mudflats in the centre of the lagoon, Venice rose to become Europe's main trading post between the West and the East, and at its height controlled an empire that spread north to the Dolomites and over the sea as far as Cyprus. As its wealth increased and its population grew, the fabric of the city grew ever more dense. Very few parts of the hundred or so islets that compose the historic centre are not built up, and very few of its closely knit streets bear no sign of the city's long lineage. Even in the most insignificant alleyway you might find fragments of a medieval building embedded in the wall of a house like fossil remains lodged in a cliff face.

The melancholic air of the place is in part a product of the discrepancy between the grandeur of its history and what the city has become. In the heyday of the Venetian Republic, nearly 200,000 people lived in Venice, not far short of three times its present population. Merchants from Germany, Greece, Turkey and a host of other countries maintained warehouses here; transactions in the banks and bazaars of the **Rialto** dictated the value of commodities all over the continent; in the dockyards of the **Arsenale** the workforce was so vast that a warship could be built and fitted out in a single day; and the **Piazza San Marco** was perpetually thronged with people here to set up business deals or report to the Republic's government. Nowadays it's no longer a living metropolis but rather the embodiment of a fabulous past, dependent for its survival largely on the people who come to marvel at its relics.

The monuments which draw the largest crowds are the **Basilica di San Marco** – the mausoleum of the city's patron saint – and the **Palazzo Ducale** – the home of the doge and all the governing councils. Certainly these are the most dramatic structures in the city: the first a mosaic-clad emblem of Venice's Byzantine origins, the second perhaps the finest of all secular Gothic buildings. Every parish rewards exploration, though – a roll-call of the **churches** worth visiting would feature over fifty names, and a list of the important paintings and sculptures they contain would be twice as long. Two of the distinctively Venetian institutions known as the **Scuole** retain some of the outstanding examples of Italian Renaissance art – the **Scuola di San Rocco**, with its dozens of pictures by Tintoretto, and the **Scuola di San Giorgio degli Schiavoni**, decorated with a gorgeous sequence by Carpaccio.

Although many of the city's treasures remain in the buildings for which they were created, a sizeable number have been removed to one or other of Venice's **museums**. The one that should not be missed is the **Accademia**, an assembly of Venetian painting that consists of virtually nothing but masterpieces; other prominent collections include the museum of eighteenth-century art in the **Ca' Rezzonico** and the **Museo Correr**, the civic museum of Venice – but again, a comprehensive list would fill a page.

Then, of course, there's the inexhaustible spectacle of the streets themselves, of the majestic and sometimes decrepit palaces, of the hemmed-in squares where much of the social life of the city is conducted, of the sunlit courtyards that suddenly open up at the end of an unpromising passageway. The cultural heritage preserved in the museums and churches is a source of endless fascination, but you should discard your itineraries for a day and just wander – the anonymous parts of Venice reveal as much of the city's essence as the highlighted attractions. Equally indispensible for a full understanding of Venice's way of life and development are expeditions to the **northern and southern islands** of the lagoon, where the incursions of the tourist industry are on the whole less obtrusive.

Venice's hinterland – the **Veneto** – is historically and economically one of Italy's most important regions. Its major cities – **Padua**, **Vicenza** and **Verona** – are all covered in the guide, along with many of the smaller towns located between the lagoon and the mountains to the north. Although rock-bottom hotel prices are almost unheard of in the affluent Veneto, the cost of accommodation on the mainland is appreciably lower than in Venice itself, and it might be worth your while becoming a vacation commuter from Treviso, Padua or Vicenza in order to keep costs down. To get the most out of the less accessible sights of the Veneto it's definitely necessary to base yourself for a day or two somewhere other than Venice – perhaps in the northern town of Bassano or in the more central Castelfranco.

When to go

Venice's tourist season is very nearly an all-year affair. **Peak season** is from **April to October**, when hotel rooms are virtually impossible to come by at short notice; if possible give the central part of this period a miss, and at all costs don't try to stay in July and August, when the crowds are at their fullest, the climate becomes oppressively hot and clammy, and many of the restaurants close down anyway. The other two popular spells are the **Carnevale** (leading up to Lent) and the weeks on each side of **Christmas**; again, hotels tend to be heavily booked, but at least the authentic life of the city isn't submerged during these festive periods, as it is by the summer inundation.

For the ideal combination of comparative peace and pleasant climate, the two or three weeks **immediately preceding Easter** is perhaps the best time of year. The days should be mostly mild – though the weather can be capricious – and finding accommodation won't present insuperable problems. Climatically the months at the end of the high season are somewhat less reliable: some **November** days are so clear that the Dolomites seem to start on the edge of the mainland, while others bring fogs that make it difficult to see from one bank of the Canal Grande to the other. However, the desertion of the streets in winter is magical, and the sight of the Piazza under floodwater is unforgettable. This **aqua alta**, as Venice's seasonal flooding is called, is an increasingly common occurrence between November and March, and you should be prepared for at least a couple of inconvenient days in the course of a two-week visit in winter. Duck-boards enable people to move dry-footed around the busiest parts of the city, but some low-lying areas – such as around Campo San Polo – become impassable to anyone without gumboots, and on certain freakish days the water rises so high that boats can be rowed along some of the streets.

If you want to see the city at its quietest, **January** is the month to go – take plenty of warm clothes, though, as the winds of the Adriatic can be savage, and you should be prepared to spend a while looking for a room, as many of the cheaper hotels close down for the really slack period.

Average temperature and rainfall

	Temp °C (°F)	Rainfall mm (in)
January	3.8 (38)	58 (2)
April	12.6 (54)	77 (3)
July	23.6 (74)	37 (1)
October	15.1 (59)	66 (3)

Part 1

The Basics

Getting to Venice from the UK and Ireland

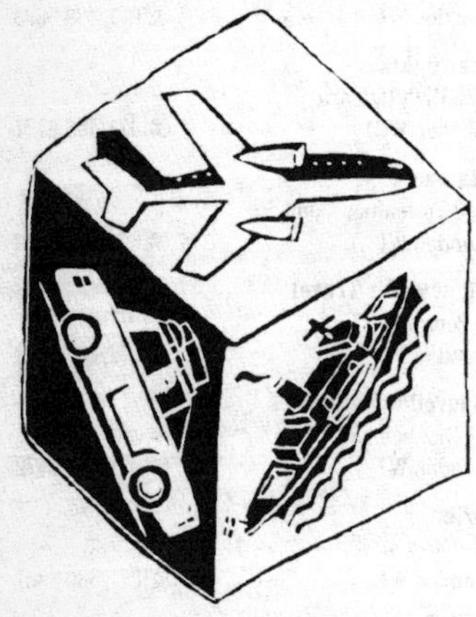

By far the most convenient way to get to Venice from the UK and Ireland is by plane, with plenty of weekly flights from London throughout the year. Rail tickets are very little cheaper than charter flights, though they do give you the option of breaking your journey along the way.

Flights

Direct flights take a few minutes over two hours from London. Many charters go to **Treviso**, 30km to the north of Venice, while scheduled services go to the more convenient Marco Polo airport, 13km from the centre of the city, on the edge of the lagoon (see p.25 for details of arrival at both airports).

Scheduled flights are operated daily from Heathrow by *Alitalia* and *British Airways*, whose best deals are the special-offer tickets sold within 7 days of departure, subject to availability. (The names given to these tickets change every few months – *Seatsale* is the current name of the *BA* ones.) Prices begin at around £180, no refund is payable in the event of cancellation, and your stay must cover at least one Saturday. **APEX** tickets, the next cheapest seats available to all customers, cost from around £265 in low season to a high-season (July–Sept) peak of around £320 – about half the price of a full-price economy class scheduled ticket. The conditions attached to APEX tickets are that the full amount must be paid at least two weeks before departure, and again you must be away for at least one Saturday; only 50 percent of the price will be returned if the ticket is cancelled, and if you want to change its date, you have to upgrade the ticket. The **student** rates offered by both airlines range from around £200 to £250, and are subject to APEX conditions.

Charter flights – operated by *LAI*, *Skybus* and *Italy Sky Shuttle* – are considerably less expensive than APEX, though they tend to subdivide the year into a bewildering league table of slack periods, semi-peaks, high peaks and so forth. With high-season charters selling for as little as £220, seats can be hard to come by in the height of summer, so don't leave it till the last moment. In the quietest months, a return can be picked up easily for as little as £120. You can get charter flights direct from the companies themselves (see box below), or from one of the numerous **agencies** which deal with charter flights (see box below) – and these agencies can often undercut even the charter price by selling off the seats unsold by charter companies and package holiday firms. If you scout around, a pre-Easter flight to Venice can be found for a touch under £100, going up to £150 in summer. Sources are numerous: look in the classified sections of the Sunday newspapers (*The Sunday Times* especially) and, if you live in London, *Time Out* magazine or the *Evening Standard*.

Even cheaper than this is a hybrid arrangement offered by *Italy Sky Shuttle* (the "Air Coach") and by Skybus ("Special Breaks"), involving an outward journey **to Venice by plane**, returning **by coach from Milan**. In low season a return costs as little as £75, and in high season it costs just under £100, but these deals are hedged by various conditions – for example, with the "Air Coach" you have to confirm your return in person

Airlines

Alitalia
27 Piccadilly
London W1 ☎ 071/602 7111

British Airways
156 Regent Street
London W1 ☎ 071/434 4700

Charter Companies

Italy Sky Shuttle
227 Shepherds Bush Rd
London W6 ☎ 081/748 1333

LAI
185 King's Cross Rd
London WC1 ☎ 071/837 8492

Skybus
24 Earls Court Gardens
London SW5 ☎ 071/373 6055

Agencies

CampusTravel
52 Grosvenor Gardens
London SW1 ☎ 071/730 3402
Also with branches in Bristol, Cambridge, Oxford and Edinburgh

Council Travel
28a Poland St
London W1 ☎ 071/287 3377

CTS Travel
44 Goodge St
London W1 ☎ 071/637 5601

Euro-City Tours
314–316 Vauxhall Bridge Rd
London SW1 ☎ 071/828 8361

Flight File
49 Tottenham Court Rd
London W1 ☎ 071/323 1515

Flightfinders
19 Old Court Place
London W8 ☎ 071/938 3933

Inter-Air
Liberty House, 222 Regent St
London W1 ☎ 071/439 6633

Italflights
125 High Holborn
London WC1 ☎ 071/405 6771

Italone
200 Tottenham Court Rd
London W1 ☎ 071/637 1284

Mundus Air Travel
5 Peter St
London W1 ☎ 071/437 2272

Nouvelles Frontières
11 Blenheim St
London W1 ☎ 071/629 7772

Orion
320 Regent St
London W1 ☎ 071/580 8267

STA Travel
86 Old Brompton Rd
London SW7;
117 Euston Rd
London NW1 ☎ 071/937 9921
Also with branches in Bristol, Cambridge, Oxford and Manchester

at the Milan office, with "Special Breaks" you have to stay exactly 6 nights in Italy, and the coaches for both services run no more frequently than twice a week.

An **"open-jaw"** return is something to consider if you're intending to explore Italy beyond the Veneto. It's generally calculated simply be adding together the charter price to each destination then dividing the sum by two. Finally, Venice's high accommodation costs can make a package deal an attractive proposition, as the preferential hotel rates given to the holiday firms might offset the slightly higher price of the flight (see below).

Packages

Many of Venice's hotels have cheap-rate block-booking arrangements with the larger companies. The brochures are normally dominated by three- and four-star hotels, but there might be a choice of lower-cost rooms as well. You can expect to pay from around £400 per person per week for a three-star double room in low season; the same deal in high season will cost at least £50 more.

If you can find a particularly conscientious travel agent, they might contact the package company for you to find out if any of the hotels have rooms cheaper than advertised – something they're more likely to do in the winter months. Special offers do crop up from time to time, but very rarely between April and October. You might, though, come across early-summer reduced packages to Padua or Vicenza, both near enough to Venice for you to commute from them.

Specialist Operators

Citalia
3 Lansdowne Rd
Croydon ☎081/686 5533

Italia Tours
241 Euston Rd
London ☎071/383 3886

Italian Escapades
227 Shepherds Bush Rd
London W6 ☎081/748 2661

Magic of Italy
227 Shepherds Bush Rd
London W6 ☎081/748 7575

Serenissima Travel
21 Dorset Square
London NW1 ☎071/730 9841

Sunvil Holidays
7 Upper Square, Old Isleworth
Middlesex TW7 7BJ ☎081/568 4499

Time Off
2a Chester Close
Chester St
London SW1 ☎071/235 8070

Train

An ordinary **return train ticket** from London to Venice costs £160 and the journey takes 27 hours, via Paris, Turin and Milan; the ticket is valid for two months. Under-26s can get a tiny reduction on this same route by buying a **BIJ youth ticket**; if travelling from outside London they can arrange discount add-on fares for the journey to and from the capital – or, alternatively, qualify for reduced-price tickets if they join the train at the Channel ports.

Another option for under-26s is the **Eurotrain** *Venice Explorer*, which costs £185, has the same validity as an ordinary return, and offers the advantage of returning by a route different from the outward trip. Leaving twice daily, the Venice Explorer goes out via Harwich, the Hook of Holland, Amsterdam, Cologne, Munich, Innsbruck and Verona, and returns via Milan, Paris and one of the French channel ports (either Dieppe, Boulogne or Calais) – total one-way travelling time is around 48hr.

If a trip to Venice and the Veneto is only part of a longer exploration of the continent, under-26s might consider investing in an **InterRail pass**, which for £249 gives you one month's unlimited rail travel throughout Europe, plus discounts of up to 50 percent on cross-Channel services and British Rail trains. It's available from all main British Rail stations and youth/student travel agencies, and you need to have been resident in Europe for at least six months to qualify for one.

Rail agencies in the UK

International Rail Centre
Victoria Station
London SW1 ☎071/834 2345

Eurotrain
52 Grosvenor Gardens
London SW1 ☎071/730 8518

To minimalise the discomfort of the trip, it's well worth **reserving a seat** (about £2) or even a **couchette bed** (about £10) for at least part of the journey. You should do both well in advance.

These tickets and passes are available at London's Victoria Station (from where all the trains depart), at *STA* or *Campus* (see box above), or direct from Eurotrain (see box below). For details of passes for use solely within Italy, see p.260.

Of course, the most glamorous mode of transport from London to Venice is the **Venice Simplon-Orient-Express**, which departs from

Cross-Channel Ferries

Hoverspeed
Maybrook House
Queens Gardens
Dover CT17 9UQ ☎0304/240 202

P&O European Ferries
Channel House
Channel View Road ☎0304/203 388
Dover CT17 9TJ or ☎081/575 8555

Sally Line
Argyle Centre
York Street
Ramsgate, Kent CT11 9DS ☎0843/595 522
81 Piccadilly
London W1V 9HF ☎071/858 1127

Stena Sealink
Charter House, Park Street
Ashford
Kent TN24 8EX ☎0233/647 047

Victoria up to twice weekly from March 25 to November 4, meandering through Paris, Zurich, Innsbruck and Verona in just over 30 hours. If you're undeterred by a price tag of around £900 per person for a double berth and cordon bleu meals, you can get the latest brochure from *Venice Simplon-Orient-Express Ltd*, 20 Upper Ground, SE1 (☎071/620 0003). As a special inducement, the company offers a free flight to Venice if you book an Orient Express seat from Venice to London.

Coach

Travelling to Venice and back by **coach** will appeal only to those with phobias about planes and trains. *National Express Eurolines* (☎071/730 0202) run a summer-only service once a week from their Victoria terminal; the journey takes around 27hr and the ticket costs around £130, with a small reduction for under-25s and students. Outside peak season, the best you can do is the once-weekly *Eurolines* coach from London to Milan, which is a few pounds cheaper than the Venice service and a couple of hours quicker.

Driving

There's not really a lot of sense in taking a car to water-bound Venice, but you might want to consider driving there if you're going to take in a lot of the Veneto – though bear in mind that petrol is extremely expensive in Italy. The most handy cross-Channel **ferry** links are between Dover and Calais or Boulogne (with *Hoverspeed*, *P&O* or *Stena Sealink*), Folkestone and Boulogne (*Stena Sealink*), or Ramsgate and Dunkerque (*Sally Line*). Once on the continent the Alpine route is the shortest as the crow flies, but can be pretty arduous; most drivers make for the south of France and then switch east into northern Italy. Any travel agent can provide up-to-date cross-Channel schedules and make advance bookings, which in season are essential. For details on car rental and on the Italian rules of the road, see p.262.

Getting to Venice from Ireland

No airline offers direct flights from Ireland to Italy – the cheapest way of flying to Venice from Ireland is to get to London and then catch a Venice-bound plane from there. There are numerous daily flights **from Dublin**, operated by *Ryanair*, *Aer Lingus* and *British Midland* – the cheapest are *Ryanair*, which cost from around IR£60 for a return to Luton or Stansted, though the cost of the bus and underground journeys across London may make the total cost greater than *Aer Lingus* or *British Midland* fares to Heathrow. **From Belfast**, there are *British Airways* and *British Midland* flights to Heathrow, but the cheapest service is the *Britannia Airways* run to Luton, at around £70 return.

From Dublin you can slightly undercut the plane's price by getting a **Eurotrain** ticket (IR£45 return), but from Belfast you'll save nothing by taking the train and ferry. For the best youth/student deals from either city, go to *USIT* (see box below).

Airlines and Agencies in Ireland

Aer Lingus
42 Grafton St
Dublin 2 ☎01/794 764
46 Castle St
Belfast ☎0232/245 151

British Airways
9 Fountain Centre
College St
Belfast ☎0232/240 522.

British Midland
54 Grafton St
Dublin 2 ☎01/798 733
Suite 2, Fountain Centre
College St
Belfast ☎0232/225 151

Britannia Airways
no reservations office in Ireland – bookings from Luton Airport,
Luton, Beds ☎0582/424 155

Ryan Air
College Park House
20 Nassau St ☎01/797 444
Dublin 2 or ☎01/770 444

USIT, 19–21 Aston Quay
O'Connell Bridge
Dublin 2 ☎01/679 8833
Fountain Centre
College St
Belfast ☎0232/324 073

Getting to Venice from North America and Australia

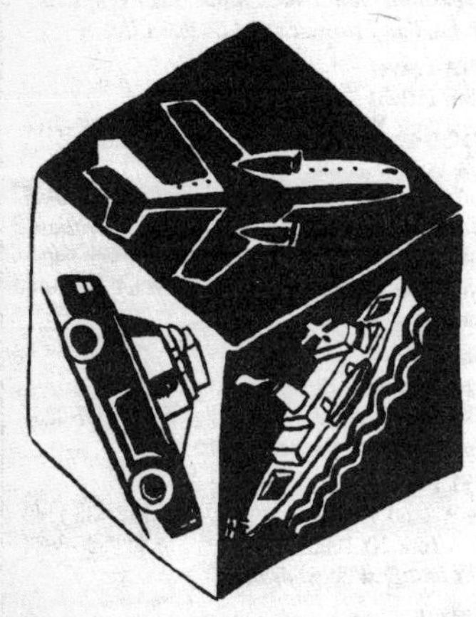

There are no direct flights to Venice from the US or Canada: you have to fly to Rome or Milan, from both of which there are plenty of connecting flights – or rail services, if you want to cut costs. From Australia and New Zealand again the best you can do is fly to Rome or Milan.

Flights From North America

Scheduled fares from North America to Italy are at their lowest from around the end of October to the end of March, excluding Christmas: in this **low season** you will be able to get various attractive offers from the airlines as they try to fill seats that might otherwise remain empty. Fares increase somewhat in the **shoulder season** – April and May, and September and October – then peak in the **high season**, from June to the end of August. Throughout the year it is more expensive to fly at weekends rather than during the week. On all the airlines the cheapest fares are usually **Apex** or **SuperApex** tickets, which come loaded with restrictions: you must book well in advance, normally at least three weeks; there is often a minimum and maximum stay, usually a minimum of a week and a maximum of 30 days; and the tickets are often unchangeable and non-refundable once you have booked them. Scheduled fares charged by the airlines don't vary all that much, so you should base your choice on timings, routes, ticket restrictions or the airline's reputation. It's a long flight, something like 9 hours from New York, Boston and the eastern Canadian cities, 12 hours from Chicago, and 15 hours from Los Angeles, so it's as well to be fairly comfortable and to arrive at a sociable hour.

Alitalia flies the **widest choice of routes between the USA and Italy**, flying direct every day from New York, Boston, Miami, Chicago and Los Angeles to Milan and Rome. As for American-based airlines, *Delta Airlines* flies daily to the same cities from New York, Chicago and Los Angeles; *Trans World Airlines* flies daily from New York, and around four times a week from Los Angeles; *United Airlines* flies direct from Washington once daily.

At the time of writing, the cheapest widely available round-trip ticket from New York or Boston to Rome, travelling midweek in low season, will cost in the region of $650, rising to around $700 during the shoulder season, and to about $950 during the summer. Travelling on a weekend will normally cost you around $50 more, and you should also add on $20 or so for taxes. Flights from LA work out about $200 on top of these round-trip fares; from Miami and Chicago, add on about $100. You can, however, sometimes get **special scheduled deals** that start at around $400 round trip from New York to Rome, flying midweek in low season, through around $650 during the shoulder season and rising to about $750 in the peak months – again adding on another $50 if you want to travel on a weekend, plus the usual taxes.

The only airline to fly direct to Italy **from Canada** is *Alitalia*, which flies from Toronto and Montréal to Rome. Its low-season Apex **fare** costs Can$899 midweek, rising to around Can$1200 in high season. Always add on at least Can$40 in taxes. Fares from both cities are the same.

Airlines in North America

Alitalia
666 Fifth Ave ☎212/582-8900
New York, NY 10103 or 800/223-5730
2055 Peel St
Montréal, PQ H3A 1V8 ☎514/842-5201
120 Adelaide St West,
Toronto, ON M5H 2E1 ☎416/363-2001

Delta Airlines
Hartsfield Atlanta International
Airport ☎404/765-5000
Atlanta, GA 30320 or ☎800/241-4141

Trans World Airlines
100 South Bedford Rd ☎212/290-2141
Mount Kisco, NY 10549 or 800/892-4141

United Airlines
PO Box 66100
O'Hare International Airport ☎312/952-4000
Chicago, IL 60666 or 800/538-2929

Rail Addresses

CIE Tours International
108 Ridgedale Ave ☎201/292-3438
Morristown, NJ 07690 or 800/522-5258

Rail Europe
226–230 Westchester Ave ☎914/682-2999
White Plains, NY 10604 or 800/438-724
Branches in Santa Monica, San Francisco, Fort Lauderdale, Chicago, Dallas, Vancouver, Montréal.

Discount Flight Agents, Travel Clubs and Consolidators

Access International
101 West 31st St, Suite 104
New York, NY 10001 ☎800/TAKE-OFF
Consolidator with good East Coast and central US deals.

Council Travel
205 E 42nd St
New York, NY 10017 ☎212/661-1450
Head office of the nationwide US student travel organization. Branches in San Francisco, LA, Boston and numerous other cities.

Encore Short Notice
4501 Forbes Blvd ☎301/459-8020
Lanham, MD 20706 or 800/638-0830
East Coast travel club.

Interworld
3400 Coral Way
Miami, FL 33145 ☎305/443-4929
Southeastern US consolidator.

Moment's Notice
425 Madison Ave
New York, NY 10017 ☎212/486-0503
Travel club that's good for last-minute deals.

Nouvelles Frontières
12 E 33rd St
New York, NY 10016 ☎212/779-0600
800 bd de Maisonneuve Est
Montréal, PQ H2L 4L8 ☎514/288-9942
Main US and Canadian branches of the French discount travel outfit. Other branches in LA, San Francisco and Québec City.

STA Travel
48 E 11th St
New York, NY 10003 ☎212/477-7166
166 Geary St, Suite 702
San Francisco, CA 94108 ☎415/391-8407
Main US branches of the originally Australian and now worldwide specialist in independent and student travel. Other offices in LA, Boston and Honolulu.

Stand Buys
311 W Superior St
Chicago, IL 60610 ☎800/331-0257
Good Midwestern travel club.

TFI Tours
34 W 32nd St ☎212/736-1149
New York, NY 10001 or 800/825-3834
The best East Coast deals.

Travac
1177 N Warson Rd
St Louis, MO 63132 ☎800/872-8800
Good central US consolidator.

Travel Avenue
180 N Jefferson ☎312/876-1116
Chicago, IL 60606 or 800/333-3335
Discount travel agent.

Travel Brokers
50 Broad St
New York, NY 10004 ☎800/999-8748
New York travel club.

Travel Cuts
187 College St
Toronto, ON M5T 1P7 ☎416/979-2406
Main office of the Canadian student travel organization. Many other offices nationwide.

Travelers Advantage
49 Music Square
Nashville, TN 37203 ☎800/548-1116
Reliable travel club.

Unitravel
1177 N Warson Rd
St Louis, MO 63132 ☎800/325-2222
Reliable consolidator.

Worldwide Discount Travel Club
1674 Meridian Ave
Miami Beach, FL 33139 ☎305/534-2082

Discount Flights

You can of course bypass the airlines altogether and go straight to a **travel agent**, who will often be able to at least match any special deals the airlines are offering. Check the Sunday newspapers' travel sections, which are always advertising discounted fares, or consult a **youth and student specialist** like *Council Travel* or *STA*, who often have the best deals, and not just for students (see box below). Another option is to contact a **discount travel club** – organisations which specialise in selling off the unsold seats of travel agents for bargain rates, often at up to half the original price, though you usually have to be a member to get the best deals. You could also try a ticket **consolidator**, who sells the unsold seats direct from airlines, though bear in mind that discounts are usually not as high as with travel clubs and you may not get the exact flight you want.

Packages and Organised Tours

Dozens of companies offer package tours to Venice and the Veneto, ranging from full-blown luxury escorted tours to simple flight-plus-accommodation deals. As with packages from the UK, this can often be a way of saving money, as the big tour companies get discounted rates from many Venetian hotels, and fly-drive deals are worth investigating if you're going to tour the Veneto for a while. However, Venice is just about the most expensive destination in Europe: you can reckon on paying around $3000 for a fourteen-day package.

Travelling via Great Britain

It might be a good idea to transit **via Britain**, since there's a broad range of well-priced flights available to London from North America, and a wide choice of onward flights from London (see p.3). If you're interested in seeing more of Europe en route to Venice, travelling **by train** from Britain may be appealing). If you're under 26, a range of youth fares is available, including **BIJ youth tickets** and **Explorer** tickets (see p.5), which have to be bought in Britain, or – the most attractive option – a **Eurail Youthpass**, which gives unlimited travel in seventeen countries and costs $508 for one month or $698 for two. It must be bought before leaving home, as must the other kinds of Eurailpass; they can be bought from youth specialists (*STA*, *Council*, *Travel Cuts* etc), and from *CIE* or *Rail Europe* (see box below for addresses). For over-26s there's the standard **Eurailpass**, giving 15 days' first-class travel for $460, 21 days' for $598, 1 month's for $728, 2 months' for $998, or 3 months' for $1260. The **Eurail Flexipass** entitles you to a number of days' first-class travel within a two-month period: 5 days for $298; 10 days for $496; 15 days for $676; the under-26s' version of this card, the **Eurail Youth Flexipass**, costs $220, $348 and $474 respectively. If you're travelling in a group, it might be worth buying the **Eurail Saverpass**, which for $390 per person gives 15 days' first-class travel for 2 or more people travelling together – or 3 or more from April to September. Finally, the **Eurail Drive Pass**, valid for any 7 days within a period of 2 months, gives you 4 days' first-class rail travel plus 3 days' car rental for $289, with options for additional days at heavy discounts.

Australians and Canadians can also buy *Eurail* passes; again they must be purchased before arrival in Europe.

Getting to Venice From Australasia

There are no direct flights from Australia or New Zealand to Venice – the best you can do is fly from Sydney, Melbourne or Auckland to Rome, and then take a train or internal flight from there. (The Rome–Venice train ticket will cost around L50,000 one way, the flight around L200,000). Two airlines run **from Australia** – *Qantas* and *Garuda Indonesian Airways* – and their fares are pretty well the same, rising from about Aus$1700 in low season to about Aus$2200 in high season. **From New Zealand**, return flights to Rome with *Garuda or Thai Airways International* cost from around NZ$2300 in low season to a peak of NZ$2900.

The best agent in both Australia and New Zealand is the long-established **STA**, with branches all over both countries (see box below).

STA Head Offices

Australia
1st Floor, 224 Faraday St
Carlton 3053, Melbourne ☎03/347 4711

New Zealand
10 High St
Auckland ☎09/309 9723

Red Tape and Visas

British citizens can enter Italy and stay as long as they like on production of either a full passport or a one-year British Visitor's Passport, available over the counter at post offices. Similarly unrestricted access is granted to all EC nationals, whereas citizens of the United States, Canada, Australia and New Zealand are limited to stays of three months, though they, too, need only a valid passport. All other nationals should consult the relevant embassies about visa requirements.

Legally, you're required to register with the police within three days of entering Italy. This will be done for you if you're staying in a hotel (this is why you have to surrender your passport on arrival), but if you're on a self-catering trip you should register at the *Questura* (HQ of the state police). It used to be the case that nobody bothered too much about this formality, but in recent the years the police have begun to be more pedantic with backpacking types in Venice. So if you think you might look like the sort of person a Venetian policeman might deem undesirable, get registered (see p.252 for the address of the Questura).

Italian Embassies and Consulates

UK
38 Eaton Place
London SW1 ☎071/235 9371

6 Melville Crescent
Edinburgh 3 ☎031/226 3631

111 Piccadilly
Manchester ☎061/228 7041

Ireland
63–65 Northumberland Rd
Dublin ☎01/601 744

7 Richmond Park
Belfast ☎0232/668 854

USA
690 Park Ave
New York ☎212/737 9100

12400 Wilshire Blvd, Suite 300
Lo Angeles ☎213/826 6207

Canada
136 Beverley St
Toronto ☎416/977 1566

Australia
61–69 Macquarie St
Sydney 2000, NSW ☎02/2478 442

509 St Kilda Rd
Melbourne ☎03/867 5744

New Zealand
34 Grant Rd
Wellington ☎04/7473 5339

Information and Maps

Virtually every Veneto town has a **tourist office**. Their usefulness is variable: some will hand out maps, hotel lists and additional leaflets on special events, whereas others will reply to whatever questions you have but offer next to nothing in the way of printed material. As a general rule, the bigger the town, the better the service, though some smaller places clearly feel they have to try harder. Before you leave, it's worth dropping in at the nearest **Italian State Tourist Office** (ENIT) to pick up some maps and brochures. Don't overload yourself, though – not only can most of the material be picked up in Venice, but the practical information such as accommodation prices is often out of date in the offices outside Italy.

ENIT offices abroad

UK: 1 Princes St,
London W1 ☎071/408 1254
open Mon–Fri 9am–2.30pm

Ireland
47 Merrion Square
Dublin 2 ☎01/766 397

US
500 N. Michigan Ave
Chicago, IL 60611 ☎312/644-0990

630 5th Ave
New York, NY 10111 ☎212/245-4822

Suite 801, 360 Post St
San Francisco, CA 94108 ☎415/392-6206

Canada
1 Place Ville Marie, Suite 1914
Montréal
Québec, H3B 2E3 ☎514/866-7667

Australia/New Zealand
an Australia office is due to open in 1993; it will also act as the ENIT office for New Zealand

Map Outlets in the UK and North America

London

Daunt Books, 83 Marylebone High St, W1 ☎071/224 2295

National Map Centre, 22–24 Caxton St, SW1 ☎071/222 4945

Stanfords, 12–14 Long Acre, WC2 ☎071/836 1321

The Travellers' Bookshop, 25 Cecil Court, WC2 ☎071/836 9132

Chicago

Rand McNally, 444 North Michigan Ave, IL 60611 ☎312/321-1751

New York

The Complete Traveler Bookstore, 199 Madison Ave, NY 10016 ☎212/685-9007

Rand McNally, 150 East 52nd St, NY 10022 ☎212/758-7488

Traveler's Bookstore, 22 West 52nd St, NY 10019 ☎212/664-0995

San Francisco

The Complete Traveler Bookstore, 3207 Filmore St, CA 92123

Rand McNally, 595 Market St, CA 94105 ☎415/777-3131

Seattle

Elliot Bay Book Company, 101 South Main St, WA 98104 ☎206/624-6600

Toronto

Open Air Books and Maps, 25 Toronto St, M5R 2C1 ☎416/363-0719

Vancouver

World Wide Books and Maps, 1247 Granville St

Maps

If you're going to explore Venice in depth, a really comprehensive map is a must. The tourist office's free map is useful for general orientation, but omits too many alleyways and buildings to be of any use for intensive investigation. The **most accurate map of Venice** is that produced by the *Touring Club Italiano:* consisting of a large-scale foldout map, a larger-scale mini-atlas of the city and a directory of street names, it comes in a neat plastic folder and will cost you around £12. It's difficult to obtain outside Venice, but in Britain you can sometimes find it at *Stanford's* (see box below). Equally clear, and almost as reliable, is the *Hallwag* 1:5500 plan of the city, which has the distinct advantage of costing around a third of the *TCI*'s price. If you don't want the fuss of unfolding and refolding a large single sheet every time you inadvertently stray into a cul-de-sac, the ingeniously designed *Falkplan* is very handy. The map published by *Litografia Artistica Cartografica* includes a detailed plan of the islands of the northern lagoon; as a map of the city itself, though, it's inferior to the *Hallwag* and *TCI* productions.

Costs and Money

There is no getting round the fact that Venice is the most expensive city in Italy. If you're on the least luxurious of expeditions – camping, walking wherever possible, cooking your own food – it would just about be possible to get by for less than £20/$34 a day. Assuming, though, that you stay in a one-star hotel, eat out in the evenings, and go to a museum each day, your minimum would be nearly twice that amount. Even in the dead of winter there are few double rooms in Venice costing less than £15 per person, and a strict diet of coffee and croissant in the mornings, a picnic at lunchtime and pizza in the evening will account for another £15 at least. Add onto this the cost of the odd entrance fee and boat ticket, and you've passed the £35/$53 mark before you know it. Allowing for the occasional excursion onto the mainland and other contingencies, it's reasonable to budget for a **basic outlay of £50/$75** per day for a summer trip to Venice. However, if you want to enjoy the occasional special meal or do a bit of shopping without worrying that your money will run out at the end of your holiday, you should set aside that amount as your spending money, **not counting accommodation costs**. And don't forget that, as ever, costs are higher for the person travelling alone: for single rooms, you'd be doing well to find anything lower than £20 in summer or £15 out of season.

Currency and Banks

The Italian unit of **money** is the **Lira** (plural *Lire*), always abbreviated as L: the rate right now is around L2200 to the pound sterling. You get notes for L1000, L2000, L5000, L10,000, L50,000 and L100,000; and coins for L50, L100, L200 and L500. Smaller denomination coins still float around and you might get given them as change.

It's an idea to have at least some Italian money for when you arrive, but you are limited to taking in no more than L400,000 in cash. The easiest and safest way to carry extra money is as **travellers' cheques**, available for a small commission (1 percent of the amount ordered) from any high-street bank, whether or not you have an account there. The most widely accepted are *American Express*, followed by *Visa* and *Thomas Cook* – most banks will issue you with one of these three. You'll usually pay a small commission, too, when you **exchange money** using travellers' cheques – unless you go to an *American Express* office or agency. Alternatively, most banks can issue current account holders with a **Eurocheque card** and chequebook, with which you can get cash from virtually all banks; you'll pay a few pounds service charge a year but usually no commission on transactions. The major **credit or charge cards** – *Visa* and *American Express* – are accepted in most of Venice's shops, hotels and banks; *Access* (*Mastercard*) comes a poor third, certainly as far as getting cash advances from banks is concerned. There are also an increasing number of **automatic cash machines** which you can use with a *Eurocheque* card or credit card and a PIN number.

If you run out of money, the quickest way to get **money sent out** is to contact your bank at home and have them wire the cash to the nearest bank. Branches and agencies of *Thomas Cook* and *American Express* can also wire money for a small fee; often their service is virtually instantaneous.

Banking hours vary slightly from town to town, but generally banks are open Monday to Friday from 8.30am to 1.20pm and 3 to 4pm. *American Express* and *Thomas Cook* offices are open longer hours, and in the largest towns you'll find exchange kiosks that stay open late, often at the train station. As a rule, though, the kiosks offer pretty bad rates – the only places where you'll get less for your money are the exchange desks of the biggest hotels.

Health and Insurance

EC nationals can take advantage of Italy's health services under the same terms as the residents of the country. You'll need form E111, which in theory you can get by applying on form SA30 by post, one month in advance, to any DSS office in Britain. In practice it can often be issued over the counter at a main DSS office. Citizens of other countires should make sure that their insurance policy covers all eventualities. No vaccinations are required for entry to Italy.

Doctors and Pharmacies

If you need treatment, go to a **doctor** (*médico*), taking your E111 with you if you're an EC citizen: this should enable you to get free treatment and prescriptions for medicines at the local rate. If you're looking for repeat medication, take any empty bottles or capsules with you to the doctors – the brand-names often differ. An Italian **pharmacist** (*farmacia*) is well qualified to give you advice on minor ailments, and to dispense prescriptions. A rota of *Farmacie di Túrno* ensures that there's always a chemist open all night: every *farmacia* should display the address of the nearest night chemist on its door – or you can ring ☎192 for information. If you get taken **seriously ill**, hunt out the nearest hospital and go to the *Pronto Soccorso* (casualty) section, or phone ☎113 and ask for *ospedale* or *ambulanza*. For the address of the Venice hospital, see p.252; other major hospitals are given in the relevant town accounts, under "Listings".

Dental treatment is expensive and is not covered by the Italian health service; private insurance is the only way to avoid getting seriously out of pocket, and even then you'll have to pay on the spot and claim later.

Insurance

The high cost of medical treatment makes travel insurance essential if you're a non-EC citizen, and the risks of theft or other unforeseen setbacks make it highly advisable even if you are. **UK citizens** can ask about policies at any bank or travel agency, or use a specialist, low-priced firm like *Endsleigh* (97 Southampton Row, London WC1; ☎071/436 4451), which offers two weeks' basic cover for around £20.

Before purchasing any insurance, **US and Canadian** citizens should check what you have already, whether as part of a family or student policy – you may find yourself covered for medical expenses and loss or damage to valuables while abroad. Bank and charge **accounts** often have certain levels of medical or other insurance included, as do **home owners' or renters'** insurance. Only after exhausting these possibilities might you want to contact a specialist travel insurance company; your travel agent should be able to recommend one – *Travelguard* and *The Travelers* are good policies.

A most important thing to keep in mind – and a source of major disappointment to would-be claimants – is that none of the currently available North American policies insures against **theft** while overseas. These travel policies apply only to items lost from, or damaged in, the custody of an identifiable, responsible third party, ie hotel porter, airline, luggage consignment, etc.

For medical treatment and drugs, keep all the bills and claim the money back later. If you have anything stolen (including money), register the loss immediately with the police, as without their report you won't be able to claim. The department you should go to is once again the *Questura* (see p.252).

Opening Hours and Holidays

Basic hours for most shops and small businesses in the Veneto are Monday to Saturday from 8 or 9am to around 1pm, and from around 4pm to 7 or 8pm, though an increasing number of offices work to a more standard European 9 to 5pm day. Everything closes on Sunday except bars and restaurants and a few pasticcerie which stay open until lunchtime.

Many **churches** open in the early morning, around 7 or 8am for mass and close around noon, and open again at 4 or 5pm, closing at 7pm; more obscure ones will only open for early morning and evening services; some only opcn on Sunday and on religious holidays. Wherever possible, the opening hours of churches are given in the guide. One problem you'll face is that many churches and monuments are either completely or partly **closed for restoration** (*chiuso per restauro*): at any one time dozens of projects are in progress all over Venice (see *Contexts*), and it's impossible to predict which buildings will be under wraps in the near future – all that can be said with any degree of certainty is that you'll find restorers at work in parts of the Basilica di San Marco and the Palazzo Ducale. (For the latest opening hours of all of Venice's museums, see p.32.) The museum **entry charges** quoted in the guide are the full adult charge – bear in mind that some museums give student discounts and visitors from EC countries who can prove they are aged **under 18 or over 60** are entitled to **free admission** to all state-owned museums.

Other disrupting factors are **national holidays**. Everything, except bars and restaurants, will be closed on the following dates:

January 1

January 6 (Epiphany)

Good Friday

Easter Monday

April 25 (Liberation Day and St Mark's Day)

May 1 (Labour Day)

August 15 (Assumption of the Blessed Virgin Mary)

November 1 (*Ogni Santi*; 'All Saints')

December 8 (Immaculate Conception of the Blessed Virgin Mary)

December 25

December 26

In addition, many shops and businesses close or work shorter hours for the local festival of the *Salute* on November 21 (see p.245).

Post and Phones

Post offices are generally open from Monday to Saturday from around 8am until 6.30pm, but smaller towns won't have a service on a Saturday. **Stamps** can be bought in *tabacchi*, too, as well as in some gift shops in the larger towns. **Postal rates** to Britain are L750 for a letter, L700 for a postcard; to North America the rates are L1150 and L1050 respectively. The Italian postal service is one of the tardiest in Europe – if your letter is urgent, consider spending the extra L3750 for the express service. Letters can be sent **poste restante** to any Italian town, by addressing them "Fermo Posta" followed by the name of the town. Mail will be sent to the central post office; when picking something up take your passport, and make sure they check under middle names and initials – and every other letter when all else fails – as filing is diabolical.

Public **telephones** come in various forms, often with clear instructions printed on them in English as well as Italian. In the major towns the most common type of phone accepts L100, L200, and L500 coins, as well as **phone cards** (*carte telefoniche*), available for L5000 and L10,000 from *tabacchi* or newsagents. In the cities you'll find booths that take phone cards only, but there's always a phone that takes coins nearby, usually adjacent. You can make **international calls** from any booth that accepts cards, and from any other booth labelled *interurbano*; the minimum charge for an international call is L2000. In the south and in smaller towns in the north you'll see more of the old-fashioned phones that take the same coins, or the tokens known as a *gettoni* (L200) – they are available from *SIP* offices (see below), *tabacchi*, bars and some newsagents, and are also in common use as currency. If you can't find a phone box, **bars** will often have a phone you can use (look for the red phone symbol), though these tend only to take *gettoni*.

The cheapest way to make international calls is to get hold of a **BT Chargecard** or the card issued by **AT&T Direct Service**. Both cards are free, and they work in the same way – just ring the company's international operator (*BT* ☎ 172 0044; *AT&T* ☎ 172 1011), who will connect you free of charge and add the cost of the connected call to your domestic bill. Another alternative is to find a **SIP office** (the state phone company), where you make your call from a kiosk and pay for your call afterwards. Some bars have this facility, too – it's called a *cabina a scatti*. Finally, you also make metered calls from higher-geared hotels, but will cost you at least 25 percent more, unless you make the call using a BT or AT&T charge card.

For direct **international calls from Italy**, dial the country code (given below), the area code (minus its first 0), and finally the subscriber number.

UK: 0044

IRELAND: 00353

US & CANADA: 001

AUSTRALIA: 0061

NEW ZEALAND: 0064

Calling Italy from abroad, dial 010 39 then the area code (the major Veneto towns are listed below), then the subscriber number. If calling **long distance within Italy**, dial 0 immediately before the area code.

Padua 49

Treviso 422

Venice 41

Verona 45

Vicenza 444

Phone **charges** are **highest** from Monday to Friday between 8am and 1pm; the **lowest** tariff is between 11pm and 8am on weekdays, and from 2.30pm on Saturday to 8am on Monday.

To make an international **reversed charge** call, ring the international operators at *BT* or *AT&T* (see above), who will connect your call free of charge, even if you don't have a charge card.

Police and Trouble

Venice has a few districts where you might think twice about walking unaccompanied late at night with a wallet stuffed full of lire (over towards Sant'Elena, for example), but in comparison with most Italian cities this is a sedate little place, and attacks on tourists are virtually unknown. **Pickpockets** on crowded vaporetti are the chief threat to the visitor, followed by the city's **cat burglars**, who are renowned for their ingenuity – so never leave the window of your hotel room open when you're out, even if you think only Spiderman could possibly get in through it. The mainland Veneto towns are generally tamer than their southern counterparts, though the rougher zones of Verona and Padua have their practitioners of the art of scooter-propelled **bag-snatching**.

If the worst happens, you'll be forced to have some dealings with the **police**, who come in many forms. Most innocuous are the Polizia Urbana or town police, who are mainly concerned with directing the traffic and punishing parking offences. The Guardia di Finanza, often heavily armed and screaming ostentatiously through the streets (and sometimes the canals), are interested in smuggling, tax evasion and other crimes of that ilk. Most conspicuous are the **Carabinieri** and **Polizia Statale**; no one knows what distinguishes their roles, apart from the fact that the *Carabinieri* are organised along military lines, and are a branch of the armed forces. The two forces are meant to act as a check and counter-balance to each other: a fine theory, but it results in a lot of time-wasting and rivalry in practice. In the event of **theft**, you'll need to report it at the headquarters of the *Polizia Statale*, the **Questura**; we've included the Questura address in the various city listings. If your passport goes astray, you'll also need to report to your nearest embassy or consulate – they are listed on p.252.

Although the streets of Venice are safer than those of any other major city in the country, **sexual harassment** can still a problem for a woman travelling on her own – the hustlers from the various glass factories are notoriously pushy with foreign women. The Venetian male might not be as aggressive in his attentions as some of his compatriots, but he can still be a pain in the neck. Walking alone at night at anything less than a determined pace, the odds are that you'll be approached at least once. Complete indifference is generally the most effective policy, but you may find it difficult to emulate the glacial brush-off that comes as second nature to many Italian women. A mouthful of Anglo-Saxon will often do the trick, but if he persists, *lasciátemi in pace* ("leave me alone") should see him off.

Emergencies

In an **emergency**, note the following national emergency telephone numbers.

☎ 112 for the police (*Carabinieri*).

☎ 113 for any emergency service (*Soccorso Pubblico di Emergenza*).

☎ 115 for the fire brigade (*Vigili del Fuoco*).

☎ 116 for road assistance (*Soccorso Stradale*).

Disabled Travellers

Although a few bridges are now fitted with wheelchair lifts, Venice presents problems for anyone who is not able-bodied. The islands that make up the city are joined by bridges that are usually steeply stepped, and getting in and out of the water buses can be hazardous if the water level is low or the canals are choppy, despite the helpfulness of the conductors. Wheelchair users should avoid the *motoscafi* – lines 2, 4 and 5 – as they have just a small platform around the pilot's cabin, the main passenger area being below deck level, down steep steps.

Two organisations that may be worth contacting before arriving in Venice are **ANFAS** (Frari, San Polo 3080/N; ☎719.020), which is a charitable organisation for the disabled, and **Progetto "Veneziapertutti"** (Università d'Architettura, Tolentini, Santa Croce), which is staffed by a team of disabled architects and planners. "Veneziapertutti" ("Venice for All") has produced a map grading the accessibility of different islands of the city – it's on display on some of the major vaporetto stops (train station, Rialto, Accademia and San Marco) and at the information office at Piazzale Roma.

In **Britain**, the best sources of information are *Radar*, 25 Mortimer Street, London W1 (☎071/637 5400), and *Mobility International*, 228 Borough High St, London SE11 (☎071/403 5688); a list of tour operators specialising in holidays for the disabled is available from the Italian State Tourist Office. In the **US**, you can get information and advice from *Mobility International USA*, PO Box 3551, Eugene, OR 97403 (☎503/343-1284), or the *Society for Advancement of Travel for the Handicapped*, 347 Fifth Ave, Suite 610, New York, NY 10016 (☎212/447-7284).

The City

Chapter 1

Introducing the City

The historic centre of Venice is made up of 118 islands, most of which began life as a micro-community, each with a parish church or two, and a square for public meetings. Though many Venetians maintain a strong attachment to their particular part of the city, the autonomy of these parishes has been eroded since the days when traffic between them moved by water. Some 400 bridges now tie the islands together, forming an amalgamation that's divided into six large administrative districts known as **sestieri**, three on each side of the Canal Grande.

The *sestiere* of **San Marco** is the zone where the majority of the essential sights are clustered, and is accordingly the most expensive and most crowded district of the city. On the east it's bordered by **Castello**, and on the north by **Cannaregio** – both of which become more residential, and poorer and quieter, the further you go from San Marco. On the other bank the largest of the *sestieri* is **Dorsoduro**, which stretches from the fashionable quarter at the tip of the Canal Grande, south of the Accademia gallery, to the docks in the west. **Santa Croce**, named after a now demolished church, roughly follows the curve of the Canal Grande from Piazzale Roma to a point just short of the Rialto, where it joins the commercially most active of the districts on this bank – **San Polo**.

To the uninitiated, the boundaries of the *sestieri* can seem utterly perplexing, and they are of little use as a means of structuring a guide. So, although in most instances this guide uses the name of a *sestiere* to indicate broadly which zone of the city we're in, the boundaries of our sections have been chosen for their practicality and do not, except in the case of *San Marco*, follow the city's official divisions. Most of the *sestiere* of Santa Croce, for example, is covered in the *San Polo* chapter, with the remnant covered in *Dorsoduro*, as the *sestiere* has no focal point for the visitor and very few sights.

Addresses

Within each *sestiere* the buildings are numbered in a sequence that makes sense solely to the functionaries of the post office – it's possi-

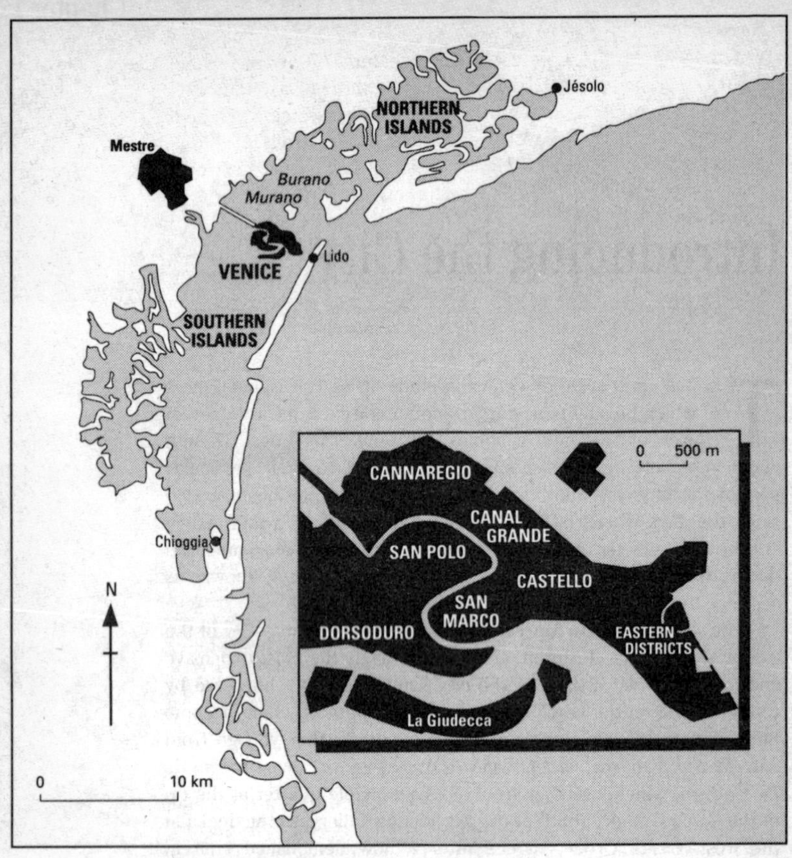

ble to find houses facing each other which have numbers separated by hundreds. Venetian **addresses** are conventionally written as the street name followed by the *sestiere* followed by the number – eg Calle Vallaresso, San Marco 1312. Sometimes, though, the *sestiere* is placed before the street, and sometimes the street is omitted altogether, which makes the place impossible to find. To maximise the convenience of the guide, we've listed hotels, restaurants and bars under subheads which correspond to our chapter divisions. However, wherever a full postal address is given in the guide, obviously the *sestiere* name is the one given; thus in a few instances you will find a place listed under a subhead which does not correspond to the postal address – for example, a bar on the edge of the eccentrically defined *sestiere* of Cannaregio may appear under the heading *Castello*.

Names

Venetians have idiosyncratic **names** for features of the townscape. A canal is a **rio**, and an alleyway that cuts through a building is a **sottoportico** or **sottoportego**, to give its dialect version. These are the straightforward ones. A street in Venice is generally a **calle**, but a major street might be a **ruga**, an old street might be a **salizzada**, a small street may be a **ramo**, a street alongside a body of water is a **fondamenta** (or a **riva** if it's really big), and a street formed by filling in a canal is customarily a **rio terrà**. A square is a usually a **campo** (there's only one piazza), but it might be a **campiello** if it's tiny, or a **piscina** if it was formed by filling in a place where boats used to turn, or a **corte** if it's more a courtyard than a square.

The Venetian **dialect** version of **proper names** adds a further twist to the visitor's bewilderment. For example, the Italian name Giuseppe here becomes Isepo, Eustachio becomes Stae, and Giovanni becomes Zuan. Things get even worse when two names appear together – thus Giovanni e Paolo becomes Zanipolo, and Sant'Ermagora e Fortunato somehow becomes San Marcuolo. As a final refinement, the Italian name is often used alongside the dialect name, of which there may be another variant – thus, on the wall outside the naval museum a sign tells you that the spot on which you're standing is called Campo S. Biagio or Campo S. Blasio or Campo S. Biasio. We've generally used the standard Italian names, with the dialect version in brackets wherever it's a name in common use.

Arriving in Venice

Millions of visitors pour into Venice each year, most of them funnelled through a pair of airports that are not geared to deal with such heavy traffic. Arriving by train and coach is painless – but driving into Venice is unmitigated hell in summer, and just plain expensive in winter.

By Air

If you are arriving **by air**, you'll touch down either at **Treviso**, 30km inland from Venice, or at Marco Polo airport, on the outskirts of Venice itself. The former is used by **charter** companies, many of whom provide a coach link from the airport into Venice. If such a service isn't provided, take the #6 bus from right outside the arrivals building into Treviso (30min), from where there are regular coach and train connections to Venice. Tickets must be bought before you get onto the bus – the bar across the road sells them.

All **scheduled** flights and some charters arrive at **Marco Polo**. Motor launches are timetabled to meet incoming scheduled flights, and if you're on a package holiday the cost of transport to the city centre might be already be covered. If it's not, don't take to the water: the launches are exorbitant, as are the water-taxis that hang around touting for trade – you'll not pay less than L80,000. The cost-conscious alternatives are to take one of the *ATVO* (*Azienda Trasporti Veneto Orientale*) **buses** that are also scheduled to meet incoming and outgoing flights (L5000), or to wait for the next *ACTV* (*Azienda del Consorzio Trasporti Veneziano*) **bus #5**, which runs every half-hour and costs just L1000 (plus a small supplement for large pieces of luggage). There's a ticket office in the airport, but beware that they'll sell you a ticket for the *ATVO* rather than the *ACTV* bus unless you make your preference clear.

By road and rail

People arriving **by car** must leave their vehicle either on the mainland or try for the car parks of Venice itself – either at **Piazzale Roma** or at the ever-expanding **Tronchetto**, Europe's largest car park. Piazzale Roma is well connected with the main water-bus services (see below), while from Tronchetto you can take the #84 or the summer-only #34 to the San Marco area, or the #17 direct to the Lido. Prices at these two vary according to the time of year, the length of stay and the size of car, but it's never a cheap option (from L30,000 per day), and in summer the tail-backs can be horrendous. Best to use the open-air **San Giuliano** car park at Mestre or the one at **Fusina**; both operate only in summer, at Easter and during the Carnevale, and *ACTV* buses connect both with central Venice.

Arriving **by train, coach or bus**, you simply get off at the end of the line. The **Piazzale Roma** bus station and **Santa Lucia** train station are just five minutes' walk from each other, at the top of the Canal Grande, and both well served by *vaporetto* services to the core of the city (see below). The **left luggage** office at the train station charges L1500 per item per 24 hours; when things get frenetic, they open a separate left luggage office for larger pieces of luggage, also at the station.

Information

The main **tourist office** is under the Piazza's arcades, at the end farthest from the Basilica (Mon–Sat summer 8.30am–7pm; winter 8.30am–2pm; ☎522.6356); smaller offices operate at the train station (daily 8am–9pm; ☎715.016) and on the Lido at Gran Viale 6 (daily summer 8.30am–7.30pm; winter 8.30am–1pm; ☎765.721). The free map distributed by these offices is fine for general orientation, but not much else. Far more useful is the English–Italian magazine *Un Ospite di Venezia*, produced weekly in summer and monthly in winter, which gives up-to-date information on exhibitions, special events and *vaporetto* timetables – it's free from the main office, and from the receptions of the posher hotels.

The Venice city telephone code is ☎041.

If you're aged between fourteen and twenty-nine, the tourist offices can also issue you with a **Carta Giovani**, which entitles you to discounts at some shops and restaurants, all of which are detailed in a leaflet that comes with the card. The card is free – all you need is a passport photo.

Getting around the city

Venice has two interlocking street systems – the canals and the pavements – and contrary to what you might expect, you'll be using the latter for most of the time. Apart from services #1 and the seasonal #34, which cut through the city along the Canal Grande, the water-buses skirt the city centre, connecting points on the periphery and the outer islands. In many cases the speediest way of getting around is **on foot**. Distances between major sights are extremely short (you can cross the whole city in an hour), and once you've got your general bearings you'll find that navigation is not as daunting as it seems at first.

The water-buses

A **water-bus** is the quickest way of getting between far-flung points, and even in cases where it might be quicker to walk, a canal trip is sometimes the more pleasant way of covering the distance. The lack of clear numbering on many of the boats is confusing at first, and the *ACTV* map of the lagoon transport system seems at first glance to resemble the wiring diagram of a telephone exchange, but in fact the routes are pretty straightforward.

There are two basic types of boat: the **vaporetti**, which are the lumbering workhorses used on the Canal Grande stopping service and other slow routes, and the **motoscafi**, smaller vessels employed on routes where a bit of speed is needed. **Tickets** are available from most landing stages, from *tabacchi* and from shops displaying the *ACTV* sign, with a flat-rate fare for any one journey on any one route. In the remoter parts of the city, you may not be able to find anywhere to buy a ticket, particularly after working hours; as tickets bought on board are subject to a surcharge, and there's a hefty spot-fine for not having a valid ticket, it's a good idea to keep a reserve supply. **Fares** are generally L2200 for a *vaporetto* service, L3300 for a *motoscafo*.

ACTV produces three **tourist tickets**, none of them valid on the #2 service: a **24-hour** ticket (L12,000); a **three-day** ticket (L17,000); and a **three-day "Giovani"** ticket (L13,000), available to all holders of a Carta Giovani. If you think you'll be making more than half a dozen trips, it's worth investing in a **Carta Venezia**. This

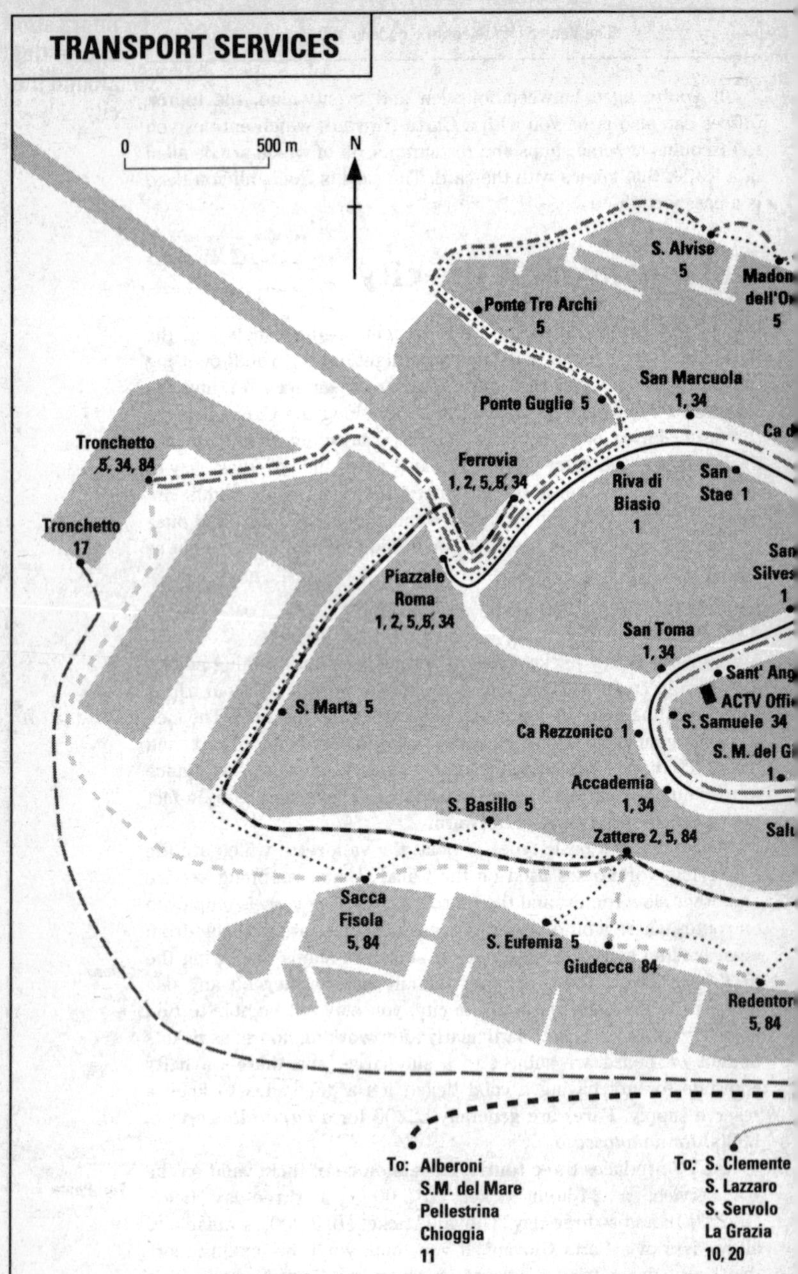
TRANSPORT SERVICES
0
500 m
N
S. Alvise
5
Ponte Tre Archi
5
San Marcuola
1, 34
Ponte Guglie 5
Tronchetto
5, 34, 84
Ferrovia
1, 2, 5, 5, 34
Riva di
Biasio
1
San
Stae 1
Tronchetto
17
Piazzale
Roma
1, 2, 5, 5, 34
San Toma
1, 34
S. Marta 5
ACTV Offi
S. Samuele 34
Ca Rezzonico 1
Accademia
1, 34
S. Basillo 5
Zattere 2, 5, 84
Sacca
Fisola
5, 84
S. Eufemia 5
Giudecca 84
5, 84
To: Alberoni
S.M. del Mare
Pellestrina
Chioggia
11
To: S. Clemente
S. Lazzaro
S. Servolo
La Grazia
10, 20

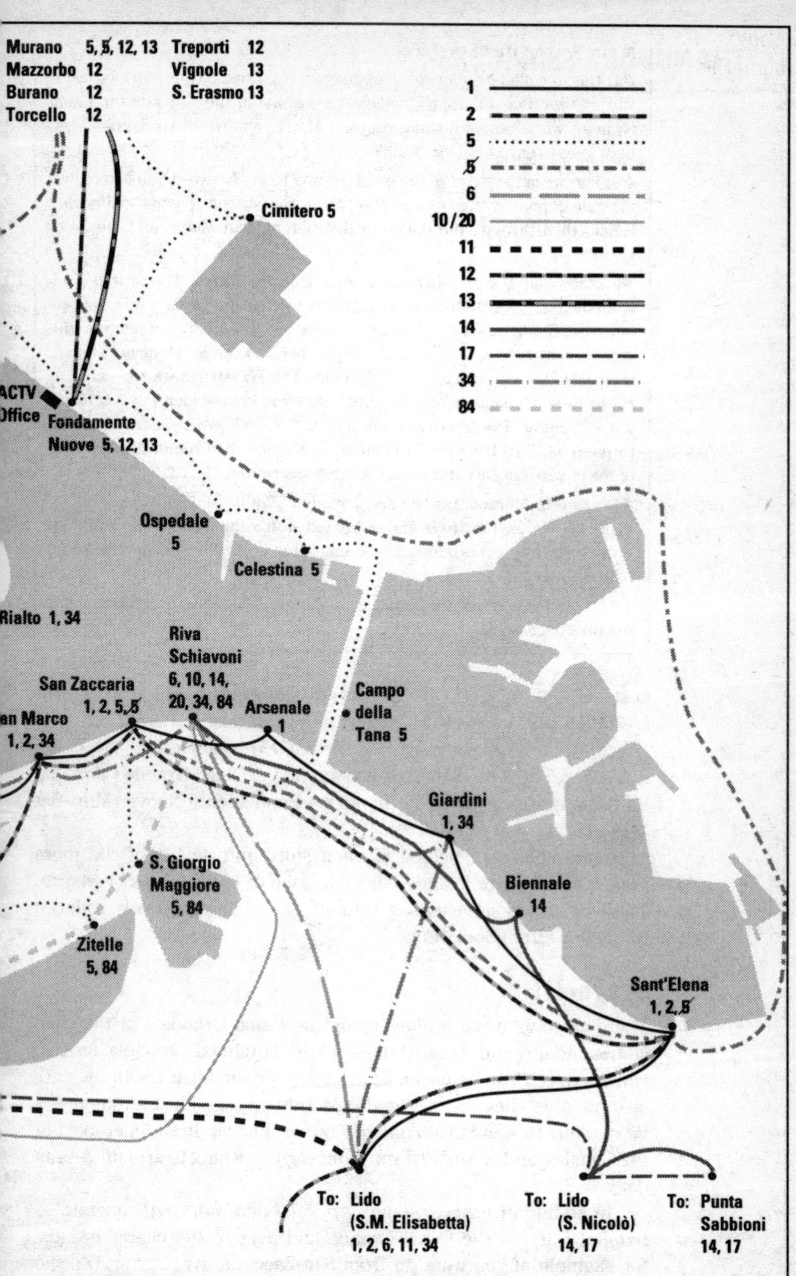
Murano 5, 5̸, 12, 13
Mazzorbo 12
Burano 12
Torcello 12
Treporti 12
Vignole 13
S. Erasmo 13
1
2
5
5̸
6
10/20
11
12
13
14
17
34
84
Cimitero 5
ACTV Office
Fondamente Nuove 5, 12, 13
Ospedale 5
Celestina 5
Rialto 1, 34
Riva Schiavoni 6, 10, 14, 20, 34, 84
San Zaccaria 1, 2, 5, 5̸
San Marco 1, 2, 34
Arsenale 1
Campo della Tana 5
Giardini 1, 34
S. Giorgio Maggiore 5, 84
Biennale 14
Zitelle 5, 84
Sant'Elena 1, 2, 5̸
To: Lido (S.M. Elisabetta) 1, 2, 6, 11, 34
To: Lido (S. Nicolò) 14, 17
To: Punta Sabbioni 14, 17

Main Water-Bus Services

#1: the so-called *accelerato*, perversely the slowest of the water buses; it starts at the Piazzale Roma, calls at all but one of the stops on the Canal Grande, works its way along the San Marco waterfront to Santa Elena, then goes over to the Lido. L2200.

#2: known as the *diretto*, the quickest way to get between San Marco and Piazzale Roma or the train station; from the station it goes to Piazzale Roma, then through the docks to the Záttere, San Marco and the Lido. L3300.

#5: known as the *circolare*, this comes in two forms. The *destra* goes from the Fondamente Nuove, through the Arsenale to San Zaccaria, zigzags between Giudecca and the Záttere, goes up to Piazzale Roma and the station, along the Canale di Cannaregio, back to the Fondamente Nuove, then over to the cemetery and Murano. The *sinistra* does the same in reverse – so if you jump on a #5, make sure you know which way round the city it's going. The *barrato* version of the #5 (shown by a 5 with a bar through it), runs from the Tronchetto to Murano then round the east side of the city to San Zaccaria, where it turns and retraces its route. L2200.

#12: runs to Murano, Burano and Torcello. L3300.

#34: known as the *turistico*; a limited-stop summer service from the Tronchetto car parks along the Canal Grande and across to the Lido. L2200.

#84: shuttles between the Tronchetto, Záttere, Giudecca, San Giorgio and the Riva degli Schiavoni. L2200.

costs L8000, is valid for three years and entitles you to travel for L1000/L1200 on all *ACTV* water- and road-buses. Take a passport photo and your passport to the *ACTV* head office in Corte dell'Albero, near the Sant'Angelo stop on the Canal Grande (Mon–Sat 8.30am–1pm), or the *ACTV* booth on Fondamente Nuove (Mon–Sat 1–6pm).

Timetables are posted at each stop, and details of the more important lines are included in each issue of *Un Ospite di Venezia*. The city centre services run through the night, at greatly reduced frequency after about 1am.

Traghetti

There are only three bridges along the Canal Grande – at the train station, Rialto and Accademia – so the **traghetti** (gondola ferries) which cross it can be useful time-savers. Costing just L500, they are also the only cheap way of getting a ride on a gondola – though it's *de rigueur* to stand in a *traghetto* rather than sit. In summer most of the Canal Grande *traghetti* run from early morning to around 7–9pm daily.

In addition to these, some *vaporetti* and *motoscafi* operate as *traghetti* across the Canal Grande and over to the nearer islands: for example, if you want go from San Zaccaria over to San Giorgio Maggiore, you need only pay the lower *traghetto* fare. If your journey is a single-stop trip across a body of water, check if a *traghetto* fare applies – it'll be shown on the tariff list on the ticket booth.

Gondolas

The **gondola** is no longer a form of transport but rather an adjunct of the tourist industry. To hire one costs L70,000 an hour for up to five passengers, rising to L90,000 per hour between 8pm and 8am; you pay an extra L35,000 for every additional 25 minutes. Further hefty surcharges will be levied should you require the services of an on-board accordionist or tenor – and a surprising number of people do, despite the strangulated voices of most of the aquatic warblers. Even though the tariff is set by the local authorities, it's been known for some gondoliers to try to extort even higher rates than these – if you do decide to go for a ride, establish the charge before setting off.

To minimise the chances of being ripped off by a private individual making a few million lire on the side, only take a boat from one of the following **official gondola stands**: west of the Piazza at Calle Vallaresso, Campo San Moisè or Campo Santa Maria del Giglio; immediately north of the Piazza at Bacino Orseolo; outside the *Danieli* hotel on Riva degli Schiavoni; at the train station; at Piazzale Roma; on the Molo, in front of the Palazzo Ducale; at Campo Santa Sofia, near the Ca' d'Oro; at San Tomà, to the east of the Frari; or by the Rialto Bridge on Riva Carbon.

Taxis

Venice's **water-taxis** are sleek and speedy vehicles that can penetrate all but the shallowest of the city's canals. Unfortunately their use is confined to all but the owners of the deepest pockets, for they are possibly the most expensive form of taxi in western Europe: the base rate is L27,000 for seven minutes, then L450 for every extra fifteen seconds (*sic*). All sorts of additional surcharges are levied as well – L3100 for each extra person if there are more than four people in the party; L2200 for each piece of luggage over 50cm long; L8500 for a ride between 10pm and 7am. And if you call a taxi by phone (which is the only way of getting one unless you happen to find one in the process of disgorging its passengers), it will have L8000 on the clock when it arrives. The number to ring is ☎522.2303 or ☎523.2326.

Museums and monuments

The opening hours listed below are the latest available times for the high season. Bear in mind that in winter some sights open slightly earlier and the great majority close considerably earlier than they do in summer – and that high-season times are prone to sudden, inexplicable alterations.

Museums and monuments

An asterisk after the price indicates that a concessionary rate is available for holders of a student card or similar; visitors from EC countries who can prove they are aged under 18 or over 60 are entitled to free admission at all state-owned museums. Visitors excluded from these categories can still save a bit of money by investing in a **Biglietto Cumulativo**, which for L16,000 allows you one visit to each of the following fee-charging attractions: Palazzo Ducale, Museo Correr, Ca'Pésaro, Ca'Rezzonico and Museo Vetrario (Murano). It's available at each of these museums, and at the Museo Guidi, Palazzo Mocenigo and Casa Goldoni.

Accademia Mon–Sat 9am–1.30pm, Sun 9am–12.30pm; L8000; ☎522.2247.

Basilica di San Marco:

Museo Marciana and Loggia dei Cavalli daily 9.45am–5.30pm; L2000.

Pala d'Oro Mon–Sat 9.45am–5.30pm, Sun 1.30–5.30pm; L2000.

Tesoro Mon–Sat 9.45am–5.30pm, Sun 1.30–5.30pm; L2000.

Ca' d'Oro Tues–Sat 9am–1.30pm, Sun 9am–12.30pm; L4000; ☎523.8790.

Campanile di San Giorgio Maggiore daily 9am–noon & 2.30–5pm; L2000; ☎528.9900.

Campanile di San Marco daily 9.30am–8pm; L3000; ☎522.4064.

Casa Goldoni Mon–Sat 8.30am–1.30pm; free; ☎523.6353.

Cattedrale di Torcello daily 10am–12.30pm & 2–5pm; L1500*; ☎730.084.

Convento di San Francesco del Deserto daily 9–11am & 3–5pm; donation; ☎528.6863.

Collezione Peggy Guggenheim 11am–6pm, plus Sat 6–9pm; closed Tues; L7000*, Sat free after 6pm; ☎520.6288.

Frari Mon–Sat 9am–noon & 2.30–6pm, Sun 3–5.30pm; L1000, free Sun.

Monastero Mekhitarista (San Lazzaro degli Armeni) daily 3–5pm; donation; ☎526.0104.

Museo Archeologico Mon–Sat 9am–2pm, Sun 9am–1pm; L4000; ☎522.5978.

Museo Civico Correr 9am–7pm; closed Tues; L5000*; ☎552.5625.

Museo Comunità Ebraica 10am–7pm; closed Sat; L3000; ☎715.359.

Museo d'Arte Moderna (Ca' Pésaro) Tues–Sun 9am–7pm; L3000; ☎721.127.

Museo dell'Estuario di Torcello Tues–Sun 10am–12.30pm & 2–5.30pm; L3000; ☎730.761.

Museo del Settecento Veneziano (Ca' Rezzonico) 9am–7pm; closed Fri; L5000*; ☎522.4543.

Museums and monuments

Museo Diocesiano daily 10.30am–12.30pm; free; ☎522.9166.

Museo Dipinti Sacri Bizantini Mon–Sat 9am–1pm & 2–5pm; L4000; ☎522.6581.

Museo di Storia Naturale Tues–Sun 9am–1pm; L8000*; ☎524.0885.

Museo Fortuny Tues–Sun 9am–7pm; L6000; ☎520.0995.

Museo Guidi Tues–Sun 10am–noon & 3–7pm; free.

Museo Orientale (Ca' Pésaro) Tues–Sat 9am–2pm, Sun 9am–1pm; L4000; ☎524.1173.

Museo Storico Navale Mon–Sat 9am–1pm; L2000; ☎520.0276.

Museo Vetrario (Murano) 9am–7pm; closed Wed; L5000*; ☎739.586.

Palazzo Ducale daily 9am–6pm; L8000*; ☎522.4951.

Palazzo Mocenigo: archive and costume collection Tues & Wed 8.30am–1.30pm; apartments Sat 8.30am–1.30pm; free.

Pinacoteca Querini-Stampalia Tues–Sun 10am–12.30pm; L5000; ☎522.5235.

Raccolta d'Arte Vittorio Cini summer only Tues–Sun 1–6pm; L5000; ☎521.0755.

Scuola dei Merletti di Burano Tues–Sat 9am–6pm, Sun 10am–4pm; L5000*; ☎730.034.

Scuola di San Giorgio degli Schiavoni Tues–Sat 9.30am–12.30pm & 3.30–6.30pm, Sun 11am–12.30pm; L4000*; ☎522.8828.

Scuola Grande dei Carmini Mon–Sat 9am–noon & 3–6pm; L5000; ☎528.9420.

Scuola Grande di San Rocco daily 9am–5.30pm; L6000*; ☎523.4864.

Chapter 2

San Marco

Enclosed by the lower loop of the Canal Grande, the *sestiere* of **San Marco** – a rectangle smaller than 1000m by 500m – has been the nucleus of Venice from the start of the city's existence. When its founders decamped from the coastal town of Malamocco to settle on the safer islands of the inner lagoon, the area now known as the **Piazza San Marco** was where the first rulers built their citadel – the **Palazzo Ducale** – and it was here that they established their most important church – the **Basilica di San Marco**. Over the succeeding centuries the Basilica evolved into the most ostentatiously rich church in Christendom, and the Palazzo Ducale grew to accommodate and celebrate a system of government that endured for longer than any other republican regime in Europe. Meanwhile, the setting for these two great edifices developed into a public space so dignified that no other square in the city was thought fit to bear the name "piazza" – all other Venetian squares are *campi* or *campielli*.

Nowadays the Piazza is basically what keeps the city solvent. Fifty percent of Venice's visitors make a beeline for this spot, spend a few hours and a few thousand lire here, then head for home without staying even for one night. For those who do hang around, San Marco has multitudinous ways of easing the cash from the pockets: the plushest hotels are concentrated in this *sestiere*; the most elegant and exorbitant cafés spill out onto the pavement from the Piazza's arcades; the most extravagantly priced seafood is served in this area's restaurants; and the swankiest shops in Venice line the Piazza and the streets radiating from it – interspersed with dozens of hugely profitable souvenir suppliers.

And yet, small though this *sestiere* is, it harbours plenty of refuges from the assaults of commerce. Even within the Piazza you can escape the crush, as the **Correr** Museum is rarely crowded and the excellent **archaeological museum** barely sees a soul. The Renaissance church of **San Salvatore** – only a few minutes' walk from the Piazza – and the Gothic **Santo Stefano** are both magnificent and comparatively neglected buildings, while **San Moisè**, **Santa**

Maria Zobenigo and the **Scala del Bovolo** rank among the city's most engaging oddities. On the fringes of the *sestiere* you'll find two of Venice's major exhibition spaces: the immense **Palazzo Grassi**, where the city's prestige art shows are held, and the **Museo Fortuny**, which as well as staging special events also contains a permanent collection of work by the designer Mariano Fortuny.

THE PIAZZA

When the first Palazzo Ducale was built, in the ninth century, the area now occupied by the **Piazza San Marco** was an islet known as Morso. Two churches stood here – San Teodoro and San Geminiano – but most of the land was covered by the orchard of the nuns of San Zaccaria. It was in the late twelfth century, under the direction of **Doge Sebastiano Ziani**, that the land was transformed into a public space – the canal connecting the waterways to the north with the Bacino di San Marco was filled in, the canalside San Geminiano was demolished (a plaque close to the Campanile marks where it stood) and a replacement built at the far end. The general shape of the Piazza hasn't changed much since Ziani's scheme, but most of the buildings you see today, excluding the Basilica and the Campanile, date from the great period of urban renewal which began at the end of the fifteenth century and went on for much of the following hundred years.

"The finest drawing room in Europe" was how Napoleon described the Piazza, but less genteel phrases than Napoleon's might seem appropriate on a summer afternoon, as your ears are battered by the competing café orchestras blasting out selected melodies from the Lloyd-Webber oeuvre, and your sightlines are repeatedly blocked. You can take some consolation from the knowledge that the crowds and the racket are maintaining a long tradition. The Piazza has always been crowded, and foreigners have always made up a sizeable proportion of the crowds – long before the tourist industry got into its stride, the swarms of foreign merchants and travellers in the Piazza were being cursed as "the monsters of the sea", to quote one disgruntled native.

If anything, life on the Piazza is less diverse nowadays than it used to be. From the foundation of the city, this area was used by traders (the slave market was here until the end of the ninth century) and as the city grew, so the range of activities taking place on the Piazza multiplied: by the end of the fifteenth century butchers and grocers had established their pitches, moneylenders and notaries had set up kiosks nearby, and makeshift stages for freak shows and masques were regular additions to the scene.

By the eighteenth century the Piazza might have become a touch more decorous, but it was certainly no emptier. One English visitor characterised the throng as "a mixed multitude of Jews,

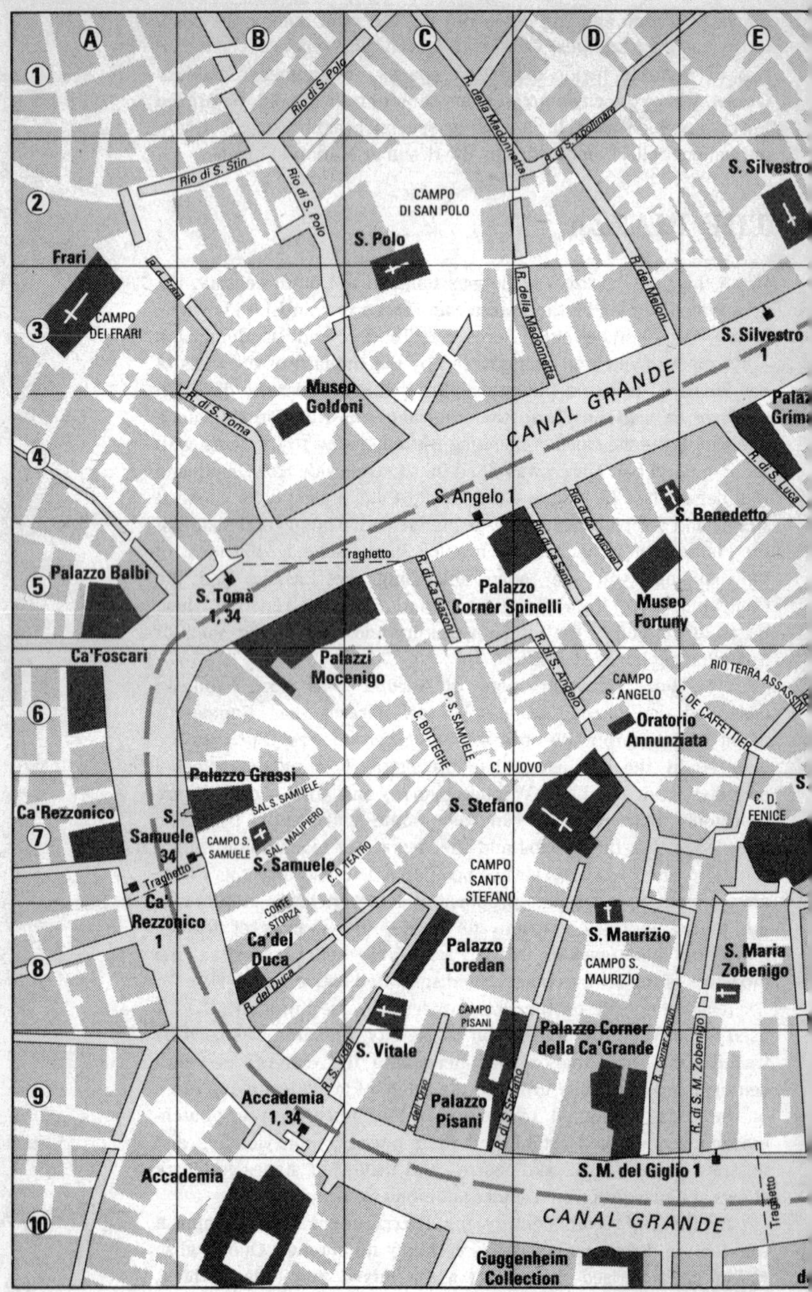
A
B
C
D
E
1
2
3
4
5
6
7
8
9
10
Rio di S. Polo
R. della Madonnetta
R. di S. Apollinare
Rio di S. Stin
Rio di S. Polo
CAMPO
DI SAN POLO
S. Silvestro
S. Polo
Frari
R. d. Frari
CAMPO
DEI FRARI
R. della Madonnetta
R. dei Meloni
S. Silvestro
1
CANAL GRANDE
Museo
Goldoni
R. di S. Tomà
Palazzo
Grimani
R. di S. Luca
S. Angelo 1
Rio di Ca Michiel
S. Benedetto
Rio di Ca Santi
Traghetto
R. di Ca Garzoni
Palazzo Balbi
S. Tomà
1, 34
Palazzo
Corner Spinelli
Museo
Fortuny
Ca'Foscari
Palazzi
Mocenigo
R. di S. Angelo
RIO TERRA ASSASSINI
CAMPO
S. ANGELO
C. DE CAFFETTIER
P. S. SAMUELE
C. BOTTEGHE
Oratorio
Annunziata
C. NUOVO
Palazzo Grassi
SAL. S. SAMUELE
S. Stefano
C. D.
FENICE
Ca'Rezzonico
S.
Samuele
34
CAMPO S.
SAMUELE
SAL. MALIPIERO
S. Samuele
C. D. TEATRO
Traghetto
Ca'
Rezzonico
1
CAMPO
SANTO
STEFANO
CORTE
STORZA
Ca'del
Duca
R. del Duca
Palazzo
Loredan
S. Maurizio
CAMPO S.
MAURIZIO
S. Maria
Zobenigo
CAMPO
PISANI
Palazzo Corner
della Ca'Grande
S. Vitale
R. S. Vidal
R. Corner Zaguri
R. di S. M. Zobenigo
Accademia
1, 34
R. dell'Orso
Palazzo
Pisani
R. di S. Stefano
S. M. del Giglio 1
Traghetto
Accademia
CANAL GRANDE
Guggenheim
Collection

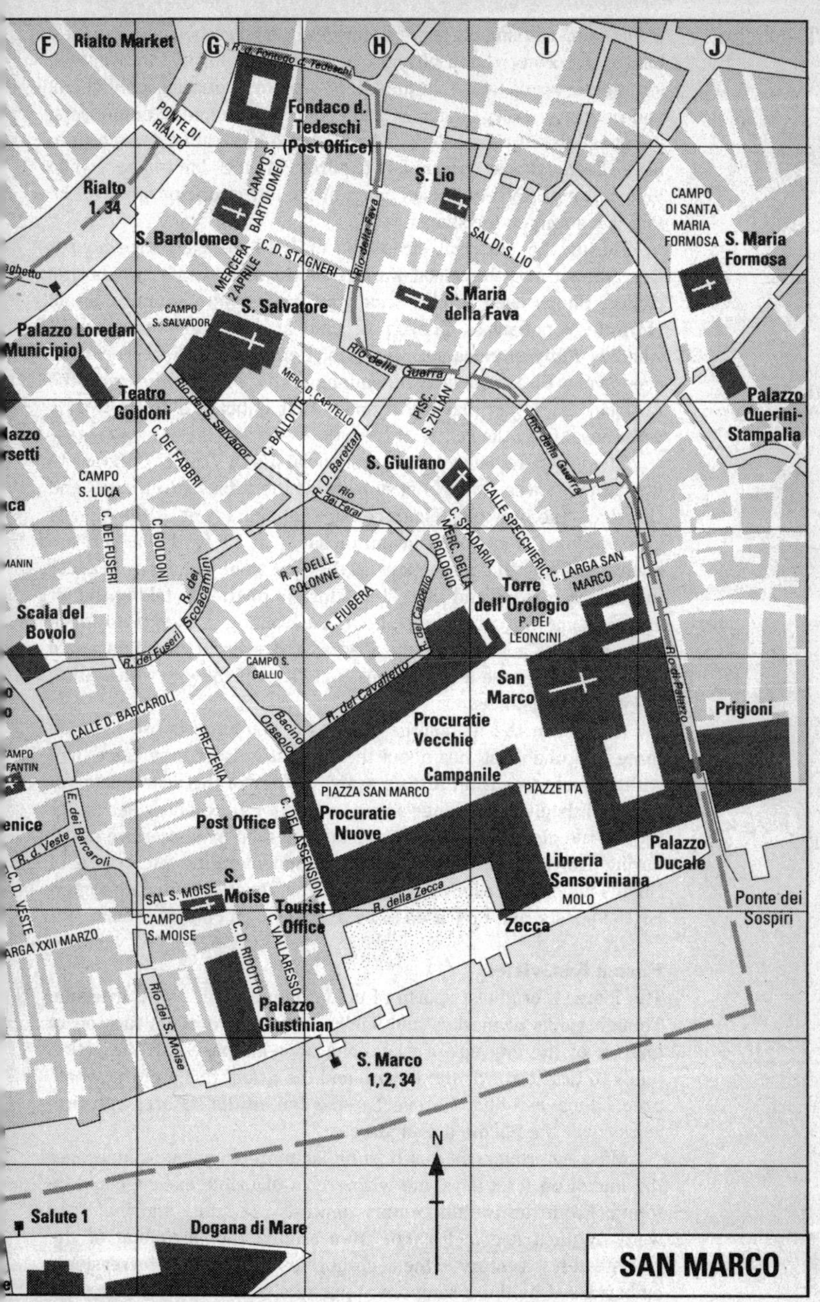
F
G
H
I
J
Rialto Market
R. d. Fontego d. Tedeschi
Fondaco d. Tedeschi (Post Office)
PONTE DI RIALTO
Rialto 1, 34
CAMPO S. BARTOLOMEO
S. Bartolomeo
S. Lio
SAL DI S. LIO
Rio della Fava
C. D. STAGNERI
MERCERIA 2 APRILE
CAMPO DI SANTA MARIA FORMOSA
S. Maria Formosa
S. Maria della Fava
CAMPO S. SALVADOR
S. Salvatore
Palazzo Loredan (Municipio)
Rio della Guerra
Teatro Goldoni
MERC. D. CAPITELLO
PISC. S. ZULIAN
Rio del S. Salvador
C. BALLOTTE
Palazzo Querini-Stampalia
C. DEI FABBRI
CAMPO S. LUCA
R. D. Barettari
S. Giuliano
Rio della Guerra
Rio dei Ferai
CALLE SPECCHIERI
C. SPADARIA
MERC. DELLA OROLOGIO
C. DEI FUSERI
C. GOLDONI
R. dei Scoacamini
R. T. DELLE COLONNE
C. FIUBERA
R. del Capello
C. LARGA SAN MARCO
Torre dell'Orologio
P. DEI LEONCINI
Scala del Bovolo
R. dei Fuseri
CAMPO S. GALLIO
San Marco
Rio di Palazzo
Prigioni
CALLE D. BARCAROLI
R. del Cavalletto
Bacino Orseolo
Procuratie Vecchie
FREZZERIA
Campanile
PIAZZA SAN MARCO
PIAZZETTA
Post Office
C. DEL ASCENSION
Procuratie Nuove
R. d. Veste
E. dei Barcaroli
Palazzo Ducale
Libreria Sansoviniana
SAL S. MOISE
S. Moise
Tourist Office
R. della Zecca
MOLO
CAMPO S. MOISE
C. D. RIDOTTO
C. VALLARESSO
Zecca
Ponte dei Sospiri
Rio dei S. Moise
Palazzo Giustinian
S. Marco 1, 2, 34
N
Salute 1
Dogana di Mare
SAN MARCO

Turks, and Christians; lawyers, knaves, and pick-pockets; mountebanks, old women, and physicians; women of quality, with masks; strumpets barefaced . . . a jumble of senators, citizens, gondoliers, and people of every character and condition". Jugglers, puppeteers, sweet-sellers, fortune-tellers and a host of other stallholders seem to have been almost perennial features of the landscape, while Venetian high society passed much of the day in one or other of the Piazza's dozen coffee shops.

During the Austrian occupation of 1814–66 the coffee houses were drawn into the social warfare between the city's two hostile camps. Shops used by the occupying troops were shunned by all patriotic Venetians – *Quadri* became an Austrian coffee house, whereas *Florian* remained Venetian. Certain prominent Venetians even went to the length of shunning the Piazza whenever the Austrian band was playing, a policy that entailed a thrice-weekly withdrawal from the centre of the city.

The Piazza remains the pivot of social life in Venice. Contrary to first appearances, today's customers at the tables of *Florian* and *Quadri* – the only eighteenth-century survivors – or at the equally intimidating *Lavena*, the favourite haunt of Richard Wagner, are almost as likely to be Venetians as they are to be outsiders. Wander through at midday and there'll be clusters of friends taking the air and chatting away their lunch-hour; the evening *passeggiata* inevitably involves a circuit of the Piazza; and even at midnight you'll almost certainly see a few groups rounding off the day with a stroll across the flagstones.

A note on the ubiquitous **pigeons** – you can choose between three improbable stories about their origins: either they came here with the refugees from Attila's army; or they're the descendants of caged birds given to a doge's wife in an attempt to cheer her up; or they're the distant relatives of pigeons released by successive doges during Holy Week, in a ceremony commemorating the return of Noah's dove. Whatever their ancestry, the Venetians appear to cherish the beasts, and they used to be fed daily by a council official.

Piazza festivities

The Piazza's brightest splash of colour comes from the **Carnevale**. Though gangs of masked and wildly costumed revellers turn every quarter of the city into a week-long open-air party, all the action tends to drift towards the Piazza, and the grand finale of the whole proceedings is a huge Shrove Tuesday ball in the square, with fireworks over the Bacino di San Marco.

Mass entertainments used to be far more frequent, taking over the Piazza on feast days and whenever a plausible excuse could be found. From the twelfth century onwards pig hunts and bullfights were frequent spectacles, but from around the beginning of the seventeenth century the authorities became increasingly embarrassed by these sanguinary pursuits, and they were relegated

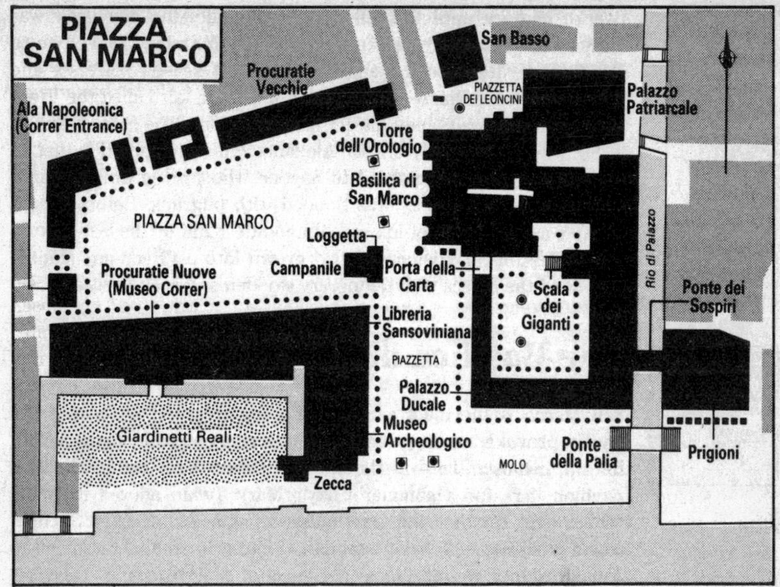

to other squares in the city. The bloodsports were succeeded by gymnastic performances known as **Labours of Hercules**, in which teams of young men formed human pyramids and towers on platforms that were often no more than a couple of planks resting on a pair of barrels. Military victories, ducal elections and visits from heads of state were commonly celebrated with **tournaments** and pageants – a three-day tournament was held in the Piazza in 1364 after the recapture of Crete, with guest appearances by a gang of English knights on their way to create bedlam in the Holy Land, and in 1413 the election of Doge Tommaso Mocenigo was marked by a tournament that was watched by 70,000 people. Mocenigo also initiated the post-electoral ritual of carrying the new doge shoulder-high round the Piazza while he distributed coins to the populace.

The major religious festivals were the occasion for lavish celebrations, the most spectacular of which was the **Procession of Corpus Domini**, a performance meticulously recorded in a painting by Gentile Bellini in the Accademia. Regrettably, not all of Venice's holy processions achieved the solemn dignity captured in Bellini's picture – in 1513 one stately progress went wrong when a row broke out over which group had the right to enter the Piazza first, a disagreement that rapidly escalated into an almighty punch-up.

But no festivities were more extravagant than those of **Ascension Day**, and it was in the wake of Ascension that the Piazza most closely resembled the modern tourist enclave. From the twelfth century until the fall of the Republic, the day itself was marked in Venice by the ceremony of **The Marriage of Venice to the Sea**, a ritual which inaugurated a short season of feasts and sideshows in the Piazza, culminating in a trade fair called the **Fiera della Sensa** (*Sensa* being dialect for Ascension). The Fiera began in 1180, when, as a result of Pope Alexander III's proclamation that an indulgence would be granted to anyone who prayed in San Marco during the year, the city was flooded with pilgrims. Before long it became a cornucopia of luxury commodities, and by the last century of the Republic's existence it had grown into a fifteen-day shindig that filled the Piazza with temporary wooden shops and arcades.

Although San Marco is open from 6.30am on most days, tourists are asked not to enter before 9.30am. Admission fees totalling L5000 are charged for certain parts of the church. Sections of the Basilica will almost certainly be under restoration; current long-term projects include the Cappella Zen and Baptistery.

The Basilica di San Marco

San Marco is the most exotic of Europe's cathedrals, and it has always provoked strong reactions. To Herman Melville it was beautiful and insubstantial – as though "the Grand Turk had pitched his pavilion here for a summer's day"; Mark Twain adored it for its "entrancing, tranquilizing, soul-satisfying ugliness"; Herbert Spencer found it loathsome – "a fine sample of barbaric architecture"; but to John Ruskin it was the most gorgeous of holy places, a "treasure-heap . . . a confusion of delight". The Basilica is certainly confusing, increasingly so as you come nearer and the details emerge, but some knowledge of the building's background helps bring a little order out of chaos.

The history of the Basilica

All over Venice you see images of the lion of Saint Mark holding a book on which are carved the text "Pax tibi, Marce evangelista meus. Hic requiescet corpus tuum" ("Peace be with you Mark, my Evangelist. Here shall your body rest"). These supposedly are the words with which Saint Mark was greeted by an angel who appeared to him on the night he took shelter in the lagoon on his way back to Rome. This **legend of Saint Mark's annunciation** was adopted as fact in order to overcome the discrepancy between the first Venetians' notion of their spiritual pedigree – as successors of the shattered Roman Empire and as the first state to be founded as a Christian community – and the inglorious fact that the settlement of the lagoon islands had begun as a scramble to get out of the path of Attila the Hun. Having thus assured themselves of the sacred ordination of their city, the proto-Venetians duly went about fulfilling the angelic prophecy. In **828** a pair of merchants called Buono Tribuno da Malamocco and Rustico da Torcello **stole the body of Saint Mark** from its tomb in Alexandria, and having smuggled the corpse past the Muslim guards by hiding it in a consignment of pork (or so the story goes), brought it back to Venice and presented it to the doge.

THE BASILICA DI SAN MARCO

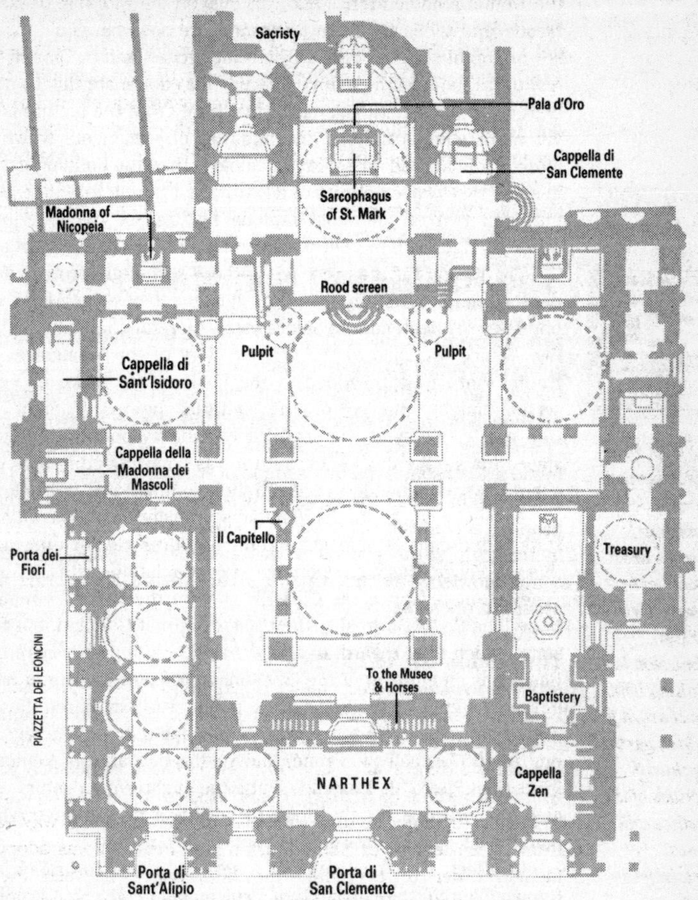

Work began immediately on a shrine to house the relic; modelled on Constantinople's Church of the Twelve Apostles, it was consecrated in 832. In 976 a riot provoked by the tyrannous Doge Pietro Candiano IV reduced the Palazzo Ducale to a pile of ashes and ruined the Basilica too; Candiano was murdered at the church's entrance. A replica was built in its place, to be in turn superseded by a **third church in 1063–94**. It is this third Basilica, embellished by the succeeding centuries, that you see now.

The combination of ancient structure and later decorations is, to a great extent, what makes San Marco so bewildering: for example, the Gothic pointed arches and carvings on the roof-line of the main facade (mostly early fifteenth-century) are not what you'd expect to see on top of squat, rounded Byzantine arches, and the garish seventeenth- to nineteenth-century mosaics that dominate this front must be the worst aesthetic mismatch in all Italy. But the picture is made yet more complicated by the addition of ornaments which were looted from abroad, are sometimes older than the building itself and in some cases have nothing to do with the Church. Into the last category fall two of the most famous features of the exterior: the porphyry figures of the **Tetrarchs** and the **horses of San Marco**.

The reason for the presence of these seemingly profane decorations is simple: the doge was the lieutenant of Saint Mark, as the pope was the lieutenant of Saint Peter – therefore anything that glorified Venice was also to the greater glory of the Evangelist. Every trophy that the doge added to the Basilica was proof of Venice's secular might and so of the spiritual power of Saint Mark. Conversely, the saint was invoked to sanctify political actions and state rituals – the doge's investiture was consecrated in the church, and military commanders received their commissions at its altar.

As can be imagined, the Venetians' conception of their city as the state with the purest lineage, and the often cynical use they made of this self-image, was not conducive to good relations with the Vatican. "They want to appear as Christian before the world," commented Pope Pius II, "but in reality they never think of God and, but for the state, which they regard as a deity, they hold nothing sacred." The Basilica is an emblem of the city's maverick position, for at no time in the existence of the Venetian Republic was San Marco the cathedral of Venice – it was the doge's chapel, and only became the cathedral in 1807, when the French moved the Patriarch of Venice here from San Pietro di Castello. Until the eighteenth century it was common practice for the doge to advertise his proprietorship by hanging his coat of arms on the front of the building.

In effect, the Venetians ran a semi-autonomous branch of the Roman Church: the Patriarch of Venice could convene a synod only with the doge's permission, bishops were nominated by the Senate, priests were appointed by a ballot of the parish and had to be of Venetian birth, and the Inquisition was supervised by the Republic's own, less draconian, doctrinal office. Inevitably, there were direct clashes with the papacy; for the story of the most serious, the interdict of 1606, see p.138.

The exterior of the Basilica

Shortly after becoming the architectural custodian (*Proto Magister*) of San Marco in 1529, Jacopo Sansovino set about strengthening the building and replacing some of its deteriorating decoration, a procedure that resulted in the removal of around thirty percent of the church's mosaics. On the main facade, the only mosaic to survive this and subsequent restorations is the scene above the **Porta di Sant'Alipio** (far left) – *The Arrival of the Body of St Mark*. Made around 1260, it features the earliest known image of the Basilica. In the lunette below the mosaic are fourteenth-century bas-reliefs of the symbols of the Evangelists; the panels comprising the door's architrave are fifth-century; and the door itself dates from 1300. The next door is from the same period, and the reliefs on the arch are thirteenth-century; the mosaic of *Venice Worshipping St Mark*, however, is an eighteenth-century effort.

The worst and the best aspects of the facade are to be found above the **central entrance**: the former being the nineteenth-century mosaic of the *Last Judgement*, the latter the **Romanesque carvings** of the arches. Begun with the innermost arch in the 1220s and completed about a century later, these are among the outstanding sculptural works of their time, but about one visitor in a thousand spares them a glance, despite their recently restored sparkle. **Inner arch**: underside – animals, Earth and Ocean; outer face – fighting figures (the savage antithesis of Venetian civilisation?). **Middle arch**: underside – the months and signs of the Zodiac; outer – Virtues and Beatitudes. **Outer arch**: under – the trades of Venice; outer – Christ and prophets. The carved panel in the lunette, *The Dream of St Mark*, is also thirteenth-century, but the door – known as the **Porta di San Clemente** – is 700 years older, and is thought to have been a gift from the Byzantine emperor Alexius Comnenus.

The fourth portal follows closely the model of the second; the mosaic of the fifth is similarly an eighteenth-century job, but the marble decoration is a mixture of eleventh- to thirteenth-century carvings, except for the architrave panel of *Christ Blessing*, a remnant of the second Basilica, built after the 976 fire.

Of the six marble panels between the entrance arches, only the Roman bas-relief of *Hercules and the Erymanthean Boar* isn't a twelfth- or thirteenth-century piece. The terrace running across the facade above them was the spot from which the doge and his guests watched the festivities in the Piazza; the mosaics on this level all date from the early seventeenth century, and the huge blank window was occupied by a Byzantine screen until a fire in 1419 destroyed everything except the four half-columns. The roof-line's encrustation of Gothic pinnacles, kiosks, figures and ornamental motifs was begun in 1385 under the direction of the **Dalle Masegne** family, the leading sculptors in Venice at that period, and was continued through the early part of the following century by various Tuscan and Lombard artists, of whom **Nicolo Lamberti** and his son **Pietro** were the most proficient.

To see the real **horses of San Marco** you have to go into the church – these are modern replicas.

The north and south facades

In the 1860s and 1870s an extensive and controversial **restoration** of the Basilica was begun, a scheme which would probably have finished with the rearrangement of the main facade. An international protest campaign, supported by Ruskin, forced the abandonment of the project soon after it had reached the Piazzetta corner of the west front, and the damage caused to that section was largely reversed in later years. The **north and south facades**, though, were altered irrevocably by the restorers, who replaced the old polychromatic marble panels with badly fitted sheets of grey stone, creating an effect described by an English stonemason in 1880 as resembling "a dirty lime wash on a white plastered wall".

The **north side** of San Marco, the last to be completed (in the first half of the thirteenth century), is studded with panels from a variety of sources – they include a seventh- or eighth-century relief showing the Apostles as twelve lambs, and a tenth-century piece illustrating Alexander the Great's mythical attempt to reach heaven by harnessing a pair of griffons to his chariot. The entrance on this side, the **Porta dei Fiori**, is thirteenth-century (the tomb of **Daniele Manin** is a bit further on); and most of the sculpture on the upper part is by the **Lamberti**.

Jutting out between the **south facade** and the entrance to the Palazzo Ducale is the wall of the Treasury, thought by some to be a remnant of the **first palace of the doges** and the chamber in which the body of Saint Mark was first placed after its arrival in Venice. The screen fragments (*plutei*) set into the walls date from the ninth to the eleventh centuries.

Sometimes the heads of freshly dispatched villains were mounted on the **Pietra del Bando**, the stump of porphyry against the corner of the Basilica; a more benign service was done on the day the Campanile collapsed, when it stopped the avalanche of bricks from hitting the church. Its routine use was as one of the two stones from which the laws of the Republic were proclaimed (the other is at the Rialto). The stone was brought back from Acre in 1256, following Venice's victory over the Genoese there; the two square pillars near to it – Syrian works dating from the fifth century – were filched from Constantinople during the Fourth Crusade.

A number of tales centre on the group of porphyry figures set into the angle of the Treasury. Thomas Coryat tells a version in which four Albanian brothers plot against each other for the possession of the cargo their ship is carrying, and end up poisoning each other. But the most popular version turns them into a gang of Saracens who raided the Treasury and then contrived to murder each other in a squabble over the spoils – hence, like the figures on the Torre dell'Orologio, they're often nicknamed "The Moors". More properly they're known as the **Tetrarchs**, as in all likelihood they're a fourth-century Egyptian work depicting Diocletian and the three colleagues with whom he ruled the unravelling Roman Empire –

peculiar adornments for a church, bearing in mind Diocletian's prowess as a persecutor of Christians.

The narthex

From the Piazza you pass into a vestibule called the **narthex**, which once, before the partitioning of the baptistery and the Cappella Zen, bracketed the entire west end of the church. The intricately patterned stonework of the narthex **floor** is mostly eleventh- and twelfth-century, and one fragment of it is especially significant: the small white lozenge set into the floor in front of the main entrance is said to mark the spot on which the Emperor Frederick Barbarossa knelt before Pope Alexander III on August 23, 1177. Prior to this, the empire and the papacy had been at each other's throats, and this symbolic reconciliation in the portal of San Marco clinched one of Venice's greatest diplomatic triumphs.

Most of the **mosaics** on the domes and arches constitute a series of **Old Testament scenes** which complements the New Testament iconography in the main body of the church. Predominantly thirteenth-century, the mosaics were begun in the dome on the far right, with scenes from *Genesis* (c.1230 but much restored, as indicated by the inset red lines), and executed in a continuous series right round the narthex. The *Genesis* dome is followed by: **first arch** – *Noah and the Flood* (note the preferential treatment handed out to the lion); in the **bay in front of main door** – double tier of niches containing the **oldest mosaics in San Marco**, a group showing *The Madonna with Apostles and Evangelists* (c.1065); **second arch** – end of *Life of Noah*, and a strikingly vivid *Tower of Babel*; **second dome** – *Story of Abraham* and four tondi of *Prophets*; **third arch** – *SS. Alipio and Simon* and tondo of *Justice*; **third, fourth and fifth domes** – *Story of Joseph*; **sixth dome** – *Story of Moses*.

Given the enormous complexity and scale of the Basilica's mosaics, this account is necessarily sketchy; if you want a more thorough guide, go for The Mosaics of St Mark's *in the Electa Artistic Guides series, which is often on sale at the kiosk in the narthex.*

Three doges and one dogaressa have tombs in the narthex. That of **Vitale Falier**, the doge who consecrated the Basilica in 1094, two years before his death, is the **oldest funerary monument in Venice** – it's at the base of the first arch. The others are of Felicità, wife of Doge Vitale Michiel (1101; second arch), Doge Bartolomeo Gradenigo (1342; under third dome) and Doge Marin Morosini (1253; under fourth dome). Two other doges besides these are buried in the narthex, but nobody has a clue where.

The Museo Marciano, the Loggia and the horses

On the right of the main door from the Narthex into the body of the church (made in 1113–18 and based on the Basilica's main door) is a steep staircase up to the **Museo Marciano** and the **Loggia dei Cavalli**. Apart from giving you an all-round view which it's difficult to tear yourself away from, the Loggia is also the best place from which to inspect the Gothic carvings of the facade – but the reason

The Museo Marciano is open daily 9.45am–5.30pm; L2000.

THE MOSAICS OF SAN MARCO

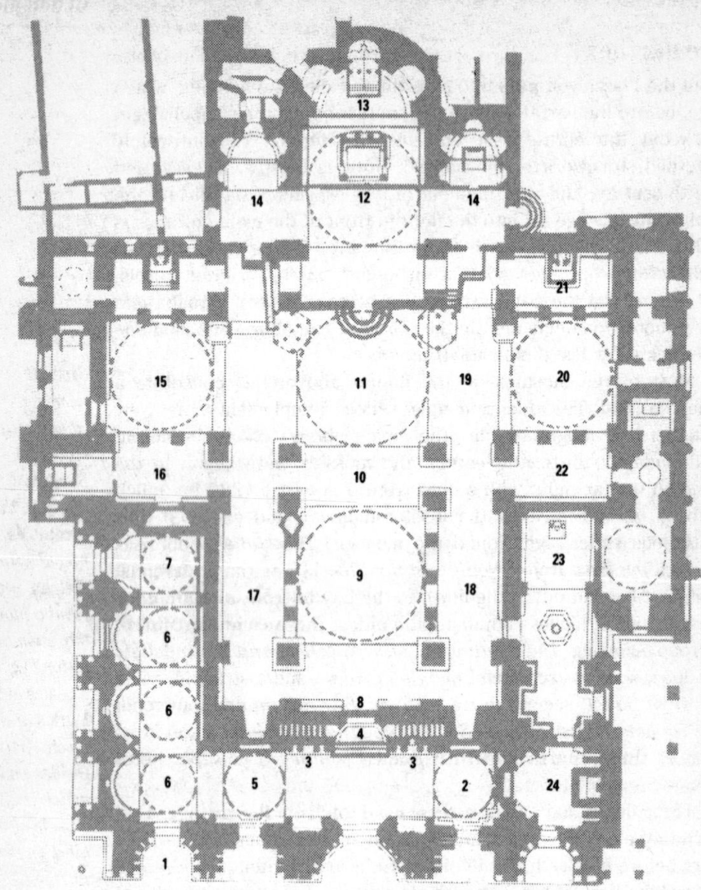

1. Arrival of the Body of St. Mark
2. The Creation
3. Noah
4. Madonna, Apostles & Evangelists
5. Abraham
6. Joseph
7. Moses
8. Christ, the Virgin and St. Mark
9. Dome of Pentecost
10. From the Betrayal to the Resurrection
11. Dome of the Ascension
12. Dome of Emmanuel
13. Christ Pantocrator and Patron Saints
14. Lives of St. Mark and St. Peter
15. Dome of St. John
16. Life of the Virgin
17. Christ and Prophets
18. Virgin and Prophets & Agony in the Garden
19. Life of Christ
20. Dome of St. Leonard
21. Parables and Miracles
22. The 'Inventio'
23. The Lives of Christ & John the Baptist
24. Life of St. Mark

most people haul themselves up the steps is to see the **horses of San Marco**.

The original horses have been removed to a room attached to the Museo, allegedly to protect them from the risks of atmospheric pollution, although some cynics have insisted that the rescue mission had less to do with any danger to the horses than with the marketing strategies of Olivetti, who sponsored the operation. In fact, it's quite likely that the condensation produced by thousands of exhaling tourists make the air in this confined space more corrosive than any acids floating around outside.

Thieved from the hippodrome of Constantinople in 1204, the horses spent a few years in front of the Arsenale before being installed on the terrace of the Basilica. So close did the association become between them and the people who had stolen them, that the Genoese in 1378 didn't boast that they would tame the lion of Saint Mark, but rather that they would "bridle those unbridled horses". The statues are almost certainly Roman works of the second century, and are the only *quadriga* (group of four horses harnessed to a chariot) to have survived from the classical world. Made from a bronze that contains an unprecedently high percentage of copper, they were cast in two parts, the junction being masked by their collars; medallions used to hang round their necks, but they were missing when the horses returned to Venice in 1815 after an eighteen-year sojourn on the Champs Élysées. The marks on the horses' skins are not the result of mistreatment – it's now thought that the scratches and the partial gilding were added at the time of their creation in order to catch the sun.

The small **Museo Marciano** is a miscellany of mosaic fragments, carvings, vestments and so forth from the church. The most interesting exhibits are the wooden cover for the Pala d'Oro, painted in 1345 by **Paolo Veneziano** and his sons, and the cycle of ten tapestries of *The Life of Christ* made around 1420 to designs by **Nicolò di Pietro** – but as likely as not they'll be under lock and key.

The interior of the Basilica

With its undulating floor of patterned marble, its plates of eastern stone on the lower walls, and its 4000 square metres of mosaic covering every other inch of wall and vaulting, the golden **interior** of San Marco achieves a hypnotic effect. Whether you look down or up, some decorative detail will catch your eye, drawing you into the narratives of its mosaics, or the geometric complexities of its pavements. One visit is not enough: there's too much to take in at one go, and the shifting light reveals some parts and hides others as the day progresses – at noon you might have to peer through the murk to see a patch of wall which two hours later could as bright as a projected picture. The only way to do it justice is to call in for at least half an hour at the beginning and end of a couple of days.

The mosaics

The majority of the **mosaics** were in position by the middle of the thirteenth century, but scenes were added right down to the eighteenth century, most of the later work being carried out to replace damaged early sections. An adequate guide to them would take volumes: this is only a key to the highlights. The mosaics in the nave, transepts and presbytery are dealt with first; the mosaics in the chapels come into the entries on those chapels. The complex shape of the Basilica makes it most convenient to locate the various features by points of the compass, with the high altar marking the east.

On the **west wall, above the door** – *Christ between the Virgin and St Mark* (thirteenth century, restored). **West dome** – *Pentecost* (early twelfth century); the paired figures between the windows represent the diverse nations in whose languages the Apostles spread the Word after Pentecost. **Arch between west and central domes** – *Betrayal of Christ, Crucifixion, Marys at the Tomb, Descent into Limbo, Incredulity of Thomas* (all late twelfth century except the *Marys*, which is a fifteenth-century copy); these are among the most inventive of all the ancient mosaics, both in terms of their richness of colour and their presentation of the intense drama of the events.

The **central dome**, a dynamic composition of concentric circles, depicts the *Ascension, Virgin with Angels and Apostles, Virtues and Beatitudes, Evangelists, Four Allegories of the Holy Rivers* (late twelfth century except *St Mark* and *St Matthew*, which are mid-nineteenth century); the four allegorical figures shown watering the earth are almost certainly a coded reference to the Christian destiny of the city built on water.

East dome – *Religion of Christ Foretold by the Prophets* (early to mid-twelfth-century; tondo of Christ restored c.1500). A *Christ Pantocrator* (1506, based on twelfth-century figure) blesses the congregation from the position in the **east apse** traditionally occupied by such figures in Byzantine churches; between the windows below stand the *Four Patron Saints of Venice*, created around 1100 and thus among the earliest works in San Marco. **Arches above north and south singing galleries** (ie linking chancel to side chapels) – *Acts from the Lives of St Peter and St Mark* (early twelfth century, altered in nineteenth century); this sequence, mingled with *Scenes from the Life of St Clement*, is continued on the end walls, but is obscured by the organs.

North transept: **dome** – *Acts of St John the Evangelist* (early to mid-twelfth century); **arch to west of dome** (continued on upper part of adjacent wall) – *Life of the Virgin, Life of the Infant Christ* (late twelfth to early thirteenth century); **arch at north end of transept** (above Cappella di San Isidore) – *Miracles of Christ* (late twelfth to early thirteenth century). On **wall of north aisle** – five mosaic tablets of *Christ with the Prophets Hosea, Joel, Micah and Jeremiah* (c.1210–30). This series is continued on the **wall of south**

aisle with figures of *The Virgin, Isaiah, David, Solomon and Ezekiel*; above these five is the large and complex *Agony in the Garden* (early thirteenth century); Mark's Gospel tells us that Christ fell on the ground in the Garden of Gethsemane, Matthew describes him falling on his face, and Luke writes that he simply knelt down – the mosaic thus shows Christ in three different positions.

South transept: dome (the *Dome of St Leonard*) – *SS. Nicholas, Clement, Blaise and Leonard* (early thirteenth century), with *St Dorothea* (thirteenth century), *St Erasma* (fifteenth century), *St Euphamia* (fifteenth century) and *St Thecla* (1512) in the **spandrels**. The formality of the mosaics in the **arch between dome and nave** – *Scenes from the Life of Christ* (early twelfth century) – makes a striking contrast with the slightly later scenes on the church's central arch; the depiction of Christ's temptation is especially beautiful, showing the protagonists suspended in a field of pure gold. **Arch above Altar of the Sacrament** – *Parables and Miracles of Christ* (late twelfth century or early thirteenth); **arch in front of Gothic window** – *SS. Anthony Abbot, Bernardino of Siena, Vincent Ferrer and Paul the Hermit* (1458); **west wall of transept** – *Rediscovery of the Body of St Mark* (second half of thirteenth century).

This last picture refers to a miraculous incident known as the *Inventio* (or "Rediscovery"). In 1094 the body of Saint Mark, having been so well hidden during the rebuilding of the Basilica in 1063 that nobody could find it again, interrupted the service of consecration by breaking through the pillar in which it had been buried. The actual pillar is to your right as you enter the sanctuary, and the very place at which the Evangelist's arm appeared is marked by a marble and mosaic panel.

The sanctuary and the Pala d'Oro

Steps lead from the south transept up to the **sanctuary**, via the **Cappella di San Clemente**, where most of the sculpture is by the **Dalle Masegne** family. On the fronts of the singing galleries next to the rood screen are eight **bronze panels** of *Scenes from the Life of St Mark* by **Sansovino** (1537), who also executed the figures of *The Evangelists* on the balustrade of the high altar. The other four figures, *The Doctors of the Church*, are seventeenth-century pieces.

The sanctuary is open Mon–Sat 9.45am–5.30pm, Sun 1.30–5.30pm; L2000.

Officially the remains of Saint Mark lie in the sarcophagus underneath the altar, but it's quite likely that the body was actually destroyed in the fire of 976. The altar **baldachin** is supported by four creamy **alabaster columns** carved with mostly indecipherable scenes from the lives of Christ and His Mother; the date of the columns is a matter of intense argument – estimates fluctuate between the fifth and the thirteenth centuries.

Behind the altar, and usually enveloped by a scrum, is the most precious of San Marco's treasures, the astonishing **Pala d'Oro** – the "golden altar screen". Commissioned in 976 in Constantinople, the

Pala was enlarged, enriched and rearranged by Byzantine goldsmiths in 1105, then by Venetians in 1209 to incorporate some of the less cumbersome loot from the Fourth Crusade, and again (finally) in 1345. The completed screen, teeming with jewels and minuscule figures, holds 83 enamel plaques, 74 enamelled roundels, 38 chiselled figures, 300 sapphires, 300 emeralds, 400 garnets, 15 rubies, 1300 pearls and a couple of hundred other stones. Such is the delicacy of the work that most of the subjects depicted on the screen are impossible to make out if you don't have 40/20 vision, and you need an encyclopaedic knowledge of medieval iconography to decipher every episode. Basically, at the top there's the Archangel Michael surrounded by medallions of saints, with *The Entry into Jerusalem*, *The Crucifixion*, *The Resurrection*, *Ascension*, *Pentecost* and *The Death of the Virgin* to the sides; below, a *Christ Pantocrator* is enclosed by a host of angels, prophets and saints, and on three sides of the border there are scenes from the lives of Christ and Saint Mark. Eighteen small panels representing profane subjects (set into lower part of frame, separated by tiny figures) survive from the first Pala.

Before leaving the sanctuary, take a look at **Sanovino**'s door to the sacristy (invariably shut) – it incorporates portraits of Titian (top left) and Sansovino himself (under Titian's head).

The treasury

The treasury is open Mon–Sat 9.45am–5.30pm, Sun 1.30–5.30pm; L2000.

Tucked into the corner of the south transept is the door of the **treasury**, installed in a thick-walled chamber which is perhaps a vestige of the first Palazzo Ducale. This dazzling warehouse of chalices, icons, reliquaries, candelabra and other ecclesiastical appurtenances is an unsurpassed collection of Byzantine silver and gold work. Particularly splendid are a twelfth-century Byzantine incense burner in the shape of a domed church, and a gilded silver Gospel cover from Aquileia, also made in the twelfth century. Much of the treasury's stock owes its presence here to the great Constantinople robbery of 1204, and there'd be a lot more of the same on display if the French occupation force of 1797 hadn't given Venice a taste of its own medicine by helping itself to a few cartloads. To be fair to the Venetians, they at least gave the stuff a good home – the French melted down their haul, to produce a yield of 55 gold and silver ingots.

The sanctuary attached to the treasury, in which are stored over 100 reliquaries, is hardly ever open to the public.

The baptistery and the Cappella Zen

The **baptistery**, entered from the south aisle, was altered to its present form by **Doge Andrea Dandolo** (d. 1354), whose tomb (facing the door) was Ruskin's favourite monumental sculpture in the city. It was Dandolo who ordered the creation of the baptistery **mosaics** of *Scenes from the Lives of Christ and John the Baptist*, works in which the formality of Byzantine art is blended with the anecdotal observation of the Gothic. "The most beautiful symbolic design of the Baptist's death that I know in Italy," wrote Ruskin. The tomb of Dandolo's predecessor, Doge Giovanni Soranzo (d. 1328) is on the right as you come in, and **Jacopo Sansovino** – who designed the enormous font – lies beneath a slab at the eastern end. The huge granite block at the altar is said to have been brought back from Tyre in 1126; more fancifully, it's also claimed as the stone from which Christ delivered the Sermon on the Mount.

In the **Cappella Zen**, adjoining the baptistery, there's an object of similar mythical potency – a bas-relief of the Virgin that is supposed to have been carved from the rock from which Moses struck water. As its rich decoration indicates, the portal from the chapel into the narthex used to be the entrance from the Piazzetta; this portico was enclosed in 1504–21 to house the tomb of Cardinal Giambattista Zen, whose estate was left to the city on condition that he was buried within San Marco. The two **mosaic angels** alongside the Virgin on top of the doorway are twelfth-century; the mosaics below are early fourteenth-century and the small statues between them date from the thirteenth. The mosaics on the **vault** show *Scenes from the Life of St Mark* (late thirteenth century, but restored). The Cappella Zen is sometimes known as the *Chapel of the Madonna of the Shoe*, taking its name from the *Virgin and Child* by **Antonio Lombardo** (1506) on the high altar.

Stonework, carvings and icons

Back in the main body of the Basilica, make sure you give the **pavement** a good look – laid out in the twelfth and thirteenth centuries, it's a constantly intriguing patchwork of abstract shapes and religious symbols. Of the church's other marvels, the next three paragraphs are but a partial list.

The **rood screen** is surmounted by a silver and bronze **cross** (1394) and marble figures of *The Virgin, St Mark and the Apostles* (also 1394) by **Jacobello and Pietro Paolo Dalle Masegne**. The **pulpits** on each side of the screen were assembled in the early fourteenth century from assorted panels, some of them taken from Constantinople; the new doge was presented to the people of Venice from the right-hand one.

Venice's most revered religious image is the tenth-century **Icon of the Madonna of Nicopeia**, in the chapel on the east side of the north transept; until 1204 it was one of the most revered in Constantinople, where it used to be ceremonially carried at the head of the emperor's army. At the north end of this transept is the **Cappella di Sant'Isidoro**: the mosaics, which have scarcely been touched since their creation in the mid-fourteenth century, depict scenes from the life of the saint, whose remains were grabbed from Chios by Doge Domenico Michiel in 1125. A beautiful mid-fifteenth-century mosaic cycle of *Scenes from the Life of the Virgin*, one of the earliest Renaissance works in Venice, is to be seen in the adjacent **Cappella della Madonna dei Mascoli**, which takes its name from the male confraternity that took it over in the seventeenth century. (The Sant'Isidore chapel is often closed; the Mascoli chapel is reserved for confessions but can be seen easily from outside.)

Against the west face of the end pillar on the north side of the nave stands **Il Capitello**, a tiny chapel fabricated from a variety of rare marbles to house the *Crucifix* on the altar; the painting arrived in Venice the year after the Nicopeia icon (and came from the same source), and in 1290 achieved its exalted status by spouting blood after an assault on it. Finally, the **galleries** merit a perusal from below (visitors are rarely allowed to walk round them): the parapets facing the aisle consist of reliefs dating from between the sixth and the eleventh century, some of them Venetian, some Byzantine. They weren't designed as catwalks, as they now appear: this is what was left when the women's galleries over the aisles were demolished in the late twelfth century to let more light into the building, after some windows had been bricked over to make more surfaces for mosaics. Apart from this, no major structural change has been made to the interior of San Marco since its consecration in 1094.

The Palazzo Ducale

Architecturally, the **Palazzo Ducale** is a unique mixture: the style of its exterior, with its geometrically patterned stonework and continuous tracery walls, can only be called Islamicised Gothic, whereas courtyards and much of the interior are based on Classical forms – a blending of influences that led Ruskin to declare it "the central building of the world". Unquestionably, it is the finest secular building of its era in Europe, and the central building of Venice. The Palazzo Ducale was far more than the residence of the doge – it was the home of all of Venice's governing councils, its law courts, a sizeable number of its civil servants and even its prisons. All power in the Venetian Republic and its domains was controlled within this one building.

The exterior of the Palazzo Ducale

Like San Marco, the Palazzo Ducale has been rebuilt many times. The original fortress, founded at the start of the ninth century, was razed by the fire of 976, and fire destroyed much of its replacement in 1106. The third palace was habitable within ten years, and was extended and altered frequently over the next couple of centuries. But it was with the construction of a new hall, parallel to the waterfront, for the Maggior Consiglio that the Palazzo began to take on its present shape. Work began in 1340, and the hall was inaugurated in 1419; then, three years later, it was decided to extend the new building along the Piazzetta, and to carry on in the same style. One feature

THE PALAZZO DUCALE

SECONDO PIANO NOBILE

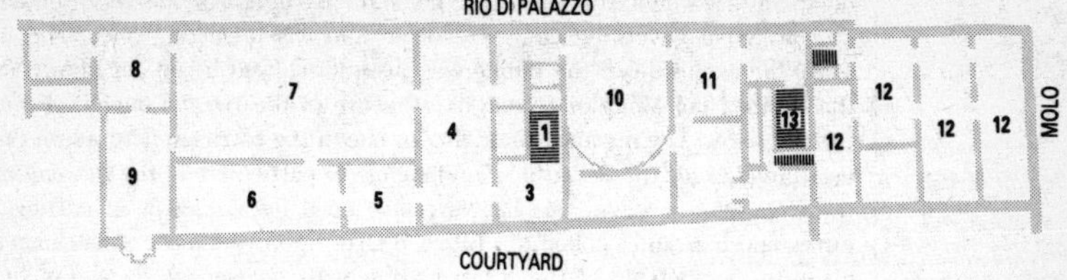

1. Scala D'Oro
2. Doge's Apartments
3. Atrio Quadrato
4. Sala delle Quattro Porte
5. Anticollegio
6. Sala del Collegio
7. Sala del Senato
8. Anti-chapel
9. Chapel
10. Sala del Consiglio dei Dieci
11. Sala della Bussola
12. Armoury
13. Scala dei Censori
14. Andito del Maggior Consiglio
15. Sala della Quarantia Civil Vecchia
16. Sala del Guariento
17. Sala del Maggior Consiglio
18. Sala del Quarantia Civil Nuova
19. Sala dello Scrutinio

PRIMO PIANO NOBILE

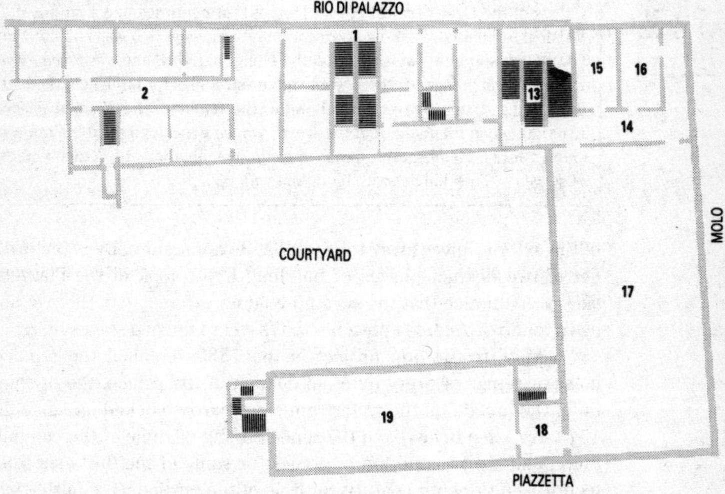

The Government of Venice

Virtually from the beginning, the **government of Venice** was dominated by the merchant class, despite the existence, in the early years, of nominally democratic assemblies in which the general male populace was represented. The principal governing council evolved into a self-electing body, and in 1297 the exclusion of the public was institutionalised by an act known as the **Serrata del Maggior Consiglio** (Closure of the Great Council). From then onwards, any man not belonging to one of the patrician families on the list compiled for the *Serrata* was ineligible to participate in the running of the city. After a while, this list was succeeded by a register of patrician births and marriages called the **Libro d'Oro**, upon which every patrician's claim to membership of the elite was based. By the second decade of the next century, the constitution of Venice had reached a form that was to endure until the coming of Napoleon; its civil and criminal code, defined in the early thirteenth century, was equally resistant to change.

What made the political system stable was its web of counterbalancing councils and committees, and its exclusion of any youthful element. Most patricians entered the Maggior Consiglio at 25 (although a group of younger high-fliers was admitted annually) and could not expect a middle-ranking post before 45; from the middle ranks to the top was another long haul – the average age of the doge from 1400 to 1600 was 72. As promotion was dependent upon a network of supporters in the elderly and conservative upper ranks, a situation was created in which, as Marin Sanudo wrote in the sixteenth century, "anyone who wishes to dissent must be mad".

However, although Venice's domestic history can seem placid to the point of tedium, backstage politics were as sordid a business as anywhere else. Cabals of the **Case Grandi** (Great Houses) for centuries had a stranglehold on most influential positions, corruption in various guises was endemic, and voting conspiracies were constantly being hatched and thwarted. Even within the *Case Grandi* there were vicious struggles for influence, the battle lines being drawn between the **Longhi**, the families who claimed descent from the city's founders, and the **Curti**, whose genealogical tables ran a bit short. An outside observer, exposed to the machinations of Venice's rulers, observed – "They kill not with blood but with ballots".

of the exterior gives away the fact that its apparent unity is the product of two distinct phases of building: if you look at the Piazzetta side, you'll notice that the seventh column is fatter than the rest and has a tondo of *Justice* above it – that's where the two stages meet.

A huge restoration project in the 1880s entailed the replacement or repair of every external column of the palace, the opening up of the arcade on the waterfront side (partly blocked up since the 1574 fire – see below) and the repositioning of some of the columns there, and the substitution of copies for some of the thirty-six fourteenth- and fifteenth-century **capitals** of the portico. (It's fairly obvious which are the copies.) Ruskin is at his most fanciful when writing about these carvings, which for him exemplify the transition from the purity of the Gothic (see the heads of children on the fourth capital from the *Drunkenness of Noah*) to the vulgar decadence of the Renaissance (compare the fifteenth-century children,

The seeming compliance of the 98 percent of the population that was shut out from active politics is largely explained by the economic cohesion of the city: its governors were also its businessmen and its chief employers, so were unlikely to adopt policies damaging to the financial interests of themselves and their workforce. The paternalism of the Venetian system helped keep things quiet too – the public health measures and emergency plans for bad harvest years were admired throughout Europe. And when, on the odd occasion, the bosses did contemplate measures that would have been unpopular outside the council chambers, there is plenty of evidence that "the murmuring in the city" quickly put them right. In 1510, for example, a massive demonstration in the Piazza persuaded the government that they should imprison the defeated general whose arrest the people were demanding.

The doge

Regarding the **doge**, it's a common misunderstanding that he was a mere figurehead, confined to his palace under a sort of luxurious house arrest. It's true that there were numerous restrictions on his activities – all his letters were read by censors, for example, and he couldn't receive foreign delegations alone – but these were steps taken to reduce the possibility that an ambitious leader might exploit his office, and they didn't always succeed. Whereas his colleagues were elected for terms as brief as a month, the doge was **elected for life** and sat on all the major councils of state, which at the very least made him extremely influential in steering policy. The dogeship was the monopoly of old men not solely because of the celebrated Venetian respect for the wisdom of the aged, but also because a man in his seventies will have fewer opportunities to abuse the unrivalled powers of the dogeship. So it was that in 1618 a certain Agostino Nani, at 63 the youngest candidate for the dogeship, feigned a life-threatening decrepitude to enhance his chances of getting the job. A neat summary of the doge's position was made by **Girolamo Priuli**, an exact contemporary of Sanudo – "It is true that if a doge does anything against the Republic, he won't be tolerated; but in everything else, even in minor matters, he does as he pleases."

second from the Porta della Carta – "capable of becoming nothing but perfumed coxcombs"); if you've got a copy of *The Stones of Venice*, take it with you to the Palazzo Ducale – for all its dottiness, it's still the best guide to the sculpture.

The interventions of restorers are less obtrusive on the late fourteenth-century to early fifteenth-century **corner sculptures**: by the Ponte della Paglia – *Archangel Raphael* and *Drunkenness of Noah*; Piazzetta corner – *Archangel Michael* and *Adam and Eve*; Basilica corner – *Archangel Gabriel* and *Judgement of Solomon*. Some see these pieces as a cogent sequence, illustrating justice (Solomon) and the counterbalancing qualities of severity (expulsion of Adam and Eve) and compassion (Noah's sons) needed for its administration; Ruskin, naturally, saw things slightly differently – whereas the humble Gothic mind dwells on the frailty of mankind (Noah's intemperance, Adam and Eve's disobedience), the

The Palazzo Ducale

vainglorious Renaissance celebrates Solomon's God-like wisdom. The **balconied window** on the lagoon side is another contribution from the **Dalle Masegne** family (1404); the corresponding window on the Piazzetta facade is a mid-sixteenth-century imitation.

The principal entrance to the Palazzo is the **Porta della Carta**, its name deriving perhaps from the archives kept nearby, or from the clerks' stalls around it. Commissioned in 1438 by **Doge Francesco Fóscari** from **Bartolomeo and Giovanni Bon**, this is one of the most ornate Gothic works in the city. Many of its carvings used to be painted and gilded, and the lack of colour isn't the only respect in which the Porta della Carta differs nowadays from its original state – the figures of Fóscari and his attendant lion are nineteenth-century replicas. The fifteenth-century pieces were smashed to bits in 1797 by the head of the stonemasons' guild, who offered to do Napoleon a favour by removing from his sight all images of the lion of Saint Mark. Luckily, his iconoclastic career seems to have ended soon after it began.

The Arco Fóscari and the courtyard

The passageway into the Palazzo ends under the **Arco Fóscari**, also commissioned from the Bons by Doge Fóscari but finished a few years after his death by **Antonio Rizzo** and **Antonio Bregno**. Rizzo's *Adam* and *Eve*, the best of the Arco Fóscari sculptures, have been replaced by copies – the originals, along with the original of Bandini's late sixteenth-century statue of Francesco Maria I della Rovere (on the courtyard side), are on show inside. In 1483 yet another fire demolished most of the wing in front of you, and led to more work for Rizzo – he designed the enormous, over-ornamented staircase called the **Scala dei Giganti**, and much of the new wing. Underneath the lion at the top of the staircase is the spot where the new doge was crowned with the jewel-encrusted cap called the *zogia*; the ungainly figures of *Neptune* and *Mars* were sculpted in 1566 by **Sansovino**. Reconstruction of the east wing continued under **Pietro Lombardo**, **Spavento** and **Scarpagnino** (who created the *Senators' Courtyard* to the left of the staircase), and finally (c.1600) **Bartolomeo Monopola**, who finished the facade overlooking the Rio di Palazzo and completed the courtyard by extending the arcades along the other two sides.

The interior

The Palazzo Ducale is open daily: summer 9am–6pm, winter 9am–4pm; L8000.

Several sections of the Palazzo Ducale can be dealt with fairly briskly. The building is clad with paintings by the hectare, but a lot of them are just wearying exercises in self-aggrandisement (no city in Italy can match Venice for the narcissism of its art), and if you take away the paintings, there's not much left to some of the rooms. But it seems wilful not to visit so integral a part of the city, and there are parts you will not want to rush. For this reason a visit needs to be timed carefully. In high season scores of tour groups are being propelled round the place by multilingual guides for much of the day. If you want any control over what you get a look at, buy your ticket within half an hour of opening, or within ninety minutes of closing.

A word of warning. As with San Marco, restoration work is always taking place somewhere in the Palazzo Ducale, and there is rarely any indication before you go in as to how much of the building is under wraps, so prepare to be disappointed – you are almost certain to come across scaffolding and plywood barriers at some point.

To the Sala delle Quattro Porte

Sansovino's **Scala d'Oro**, with its stuccoes by Vittoria (c.1558), takes you from the upper arcade to the **primo piano nobile** and the **doge's apartments**. Exhibitions are often held here, and the doors are likely to be locked if there isn't a show on. All the furniture and much of the decoration have been stripped from this floor, but some of the rooms have ornate ceilings and fireplaces, installed when the Lombardo family were in charge of rebuilding this part of the palace. The finest is in the first room, the **Sala degli Scarlatti** (probably named after the scarlet robes of the doge's attendants), which has a fireplace by **Antonio and Tullio Lombardo**, a bas-relief by **Pietro Lombardo** over the door and a gilded ceiling from 1505.

The Scala d'Oro continues up to the **secondo piano nobile**, ending in the **Atrio Quadrato**, which has a ceiling painting of *Justice* by Tintoretto. This small anteroom opens into the first of the great public spaces, the **Sala delle Quattro Porte**. Before 1574 this room was the meeting place of the Collegio (see below), but in that year a fire gutted this portion of the building, necessitating a major programme of reorganisation and decoration. (Three years later an even worse blaze destroyed the hall of the Maggior Consiglio and other rooms around it – this is why the Palazzo Ducale contains so few paintings that predate the 1570s.) After the repairs the Sala delle Quattro Porte was where ambassadors awaited their summons to address the doge and his councillors. **Tintoretto**'s ceiling frescoes, most of which are allegories of the Veneto cities subservient to the Republic, are in a generally woeful condition. The painting opposite the entrance is a reasonably accurate record of the show put on to welcome Henry III of France when he arrived in the city a few weeks before the fire of '74 – by all accounts one week of Venetian hospitality put the young king into a lifelong daze. The easel painting at the far end of the room – *Venus Receiving the Homage of Neptune* by **Giambattista Tiepolo** – can be seen at closer range when the itinerary doubles back through here.

The Anticollegio and Collegio

As regards the quality of its decorations, the next room – the **Anticollegio** (the inner waiting room) – is one of the richest in the

Palazzo Ducale. It has looked like this only since the early eighteenth century, though – after the 1574 fire it was decked out with tapestries and gilded leather, a Venetian speciality. Four pictures by **Tintoretto** hang on the door walls: *Vulcan's Forge, Mercury and the Graces, Bacchus and Ariadne* and *Minerva Dismissing Mars* (all c.1578); it almost goes without saying that these pictures were open to a propagandist reading – eg Ariadne = Venice, Bacchus = Adriatic. Facing the window wall is **Veronese**'s characteristically and incongruously benign *Rape of Europa* – "the brightest vision that ever descended upon the soul of a painter," sighed Henry James.

Thoroughly humbled by now, the emissaries to Venice were ultimately admitted to the **Sala del Collegio**. Presiding over the Senate and deciding the agenda it would discuss, the full Collegio was the cabinet of Venetian politics, and consisted of the doge, six ducal councillors, the three heads of the judiciary, and sixteen *Savi* (senators with special responsibility for maritime, military and governmental affairs). The **Signoria**, Venice's highest executive body, was the inner council of this inner council, comprising the Collegio minus the *Savi*. In Ruskin's opinion, in no other part of the palace could you "enter so deeply into the heart of Venice" as in the Sala del Collegio, but his observation referred not to the mechanics of Venetian power but to the luscious cycle of ceiling paintings by **Veronese**. Outstanding is *Venice Triumphant*, the central panel above the throne. Veronese also produced the picture on the wall over the throne – *Doge Sebastiano Venier Offering Thanks to Christ for the Victory of Lépanto*, in which, as is so often the case in Venetian state-sponsored art, the Son of God is obliged to share top billing.

The Sala del Senato

The room next door – the **Sala del Senato** – was where most major policies, both domestic and foreign, were determined. It was also where the ambassadors of Venice delivered their reports on the countries in which they had served. These *relazioni* were essential to the formation of foreign policy, and a Venetian nobleman did his career prospects no harm by turning in a detailed document; few, however, equalled the conscientiousness of the sixteenth-century ambassador to France whose speech to the Senate kept them in their seats for two whole days. The Senate originally comprised sixty councillors invited to take the higher office by the doge (hence the alternative name *Sala dei Pregadi*, from *pregati*, meaning "invited") but eventually grew to contain almost three hundred officials under the doge's chairmanship. A motley collection of late sixteenth-century artists, Tintoretto and his pupils prominent among them, produced the mechanically bombastic decoration of the walls and ceiling. Tintoretto's personal touch is most evident in the picture above the throne: *Descent from the Cross, with doges Pietro Lando and Marcantonio Trevisan*. (Sometimes the doors to the side of the throne are open – they lead to the doge's chapel and its anteroom; only the marble *Virgin and Child* by Sansovino, in the former, is of interest.)

The Sala del Consiglio dei Dieci and Sala della Bussola

After recrossing the Sala delle Quattro Porte you enter the **Sala del Consiglio dei Dieci**, the room in which all matters relating to state security were discussed. The Council of Ten was established in 1310 in response to the revolt of disaffected nobles led by Bajamonte Tiepolo – and the secrecy and the speed of its deliberations, and the fact that it allowed no defence counsel, soon made it the most feared of the Republic's institutions. Its members held office for one year and their number was supplemented by the doge and the ducal councillors – which meant, confusingly, that the Ten were never fewer than seventeen. In the sixteenth century the Ten became even stronger as a result of the War of the League of Cambrai, when places on the Senate were taken by a bunch of social climbers as reward for the loans they'd made for the war effort. The men of the *Case Grandi* (see p.54) retaliated by increasing the power of the bodies they could still control – the Collegio and the Ten. Only in the seventeenth century, when the power of the old families was weakened by the sale of places on the Maggior Consiglio, did the Senate revert to being the nucleus of the Venetian state. Of the paintings here, the finest are a couple of **Veronese** panels on the ceiling, painted at the age of 25 – *Juno Offering Gifts to Venice* and *Old Man in Oriental Costume with Young Woman*. The central panel is a copy of a Veronese original that was packed off to the Louvre by Napoleon's army and has never made it back.

The unfortunates who were summoned before the Ten had to await their grilling in the next room, the **Sala della Bussola**; in the wall is a *Bocca di Leone* (Lion's Mouth), one of the boxes into which citizens could drop denunciations for the attention of the Ten and other state bodies. Nobody could be convicted without corroborating evidence, and all anonymous accusations were rejected, but nonetheless the legend spread throughout Europe that one word to the Ten was tantamount to a death sentence. The door in the corner leads to the office of the Three Heads of the Council of Ten, which in turn leads to the State Inquisitors' room, then on to the torture chamber and finally the prisons – a doleful route that can be followed on the *Itinerari Segreti* (see p.62). As for the decoration, the last sentence of the previous paragraph applies.

The armoury and the Andito del Maggior Consiglio

From the landing, steps lead up to the four rooms of the **armoury**, consisting in part of weapons assembled for the defence of the Palazzo Ducale, and in part of specially commissioned pieces and gifts from foreign rulers. You don't need an interest in militaria to be impressed by some of the items, such as the unique fourteenth-century beaked helmet in room 1, or the white armour given to Henry IV of France in 1603 (room 2). But if any section of the Palazzo is going to be shut because of staff shortages, this is it.

The **Scala dei Censori** takes you back to the second floor; here you go along the **Andito del Maggior Consiglio** (Lobby of the Great Council) past the **Sala della Quarantia Civil Vecchia**, the seat of the civil court, and the **Sala del Guariento**, the old ammunition store, containing the remnants of a fourteenth-century fresco by Guariento which used to be in Sala del Maggior Consiglio. The veranda at the end now houses the sculptures by **Rizzo** and Bandini from the Arco Fóscari; allegedly, the Duke of Mantua offered to buy Rizzo's *Eve* for her weight in gold, but for once the Venetians found it within themsleves to resist the lure of huge sums of money.

The Sala del Maggior Consiglio

Now comes the stupendous **Sala del Maggior Consiglio**, the assembly hall of all the Venetian patricians eligible to participate in the running of the city. By the mid-sixteenth century 2500 men were entitled to sit here, but frequently as few as half that number were present. This was the forum of the so-called *giovani*, the younger men on the bottom rung, and it was here that the voice of the populace filtered into the system. Technically, the Maggior Consiglio had little direct impact on government as it voted directly only on administrative legislation, and for much of the time the *giovani* kept fairly quiet in order to stay on the right side of the power-brokers. But if the bosses did something that alienated the majority of the underlings, the Maggior Consiglio was able to make things awkward, because the electoral process for nearly all state officials, including the doge, began here. Its last political act was the vote of May 12, 1797, when it put an end to Venice's independence by voting to accept Napoleon's constitution.

The disastrous fire of December 1577 destroyed the paintings by Bellini, Titian, Carpaccio, Veronese and others which had lined this room; most of the replacements have the sole merit of covering a lot of space. There are, of course, notable exceptions. The immense *Paradiso*, begun at the age of 77 by **Tintoretto** and completed by his son Domenico, is an amazing feat of pictorial organisation and a perfect work for its setting; the cast of 500 figures is arrayed in the ranks ordained by Dante in Canto XXX of his *Paradiso*. Two of the **ceiling panels** are well worth a crick in the neck – *The Apotheosis of Venice*, a late work by Veronese (large oval above tribune), and *Venice Welcoming the Conquered Nations* by Palma il Giovane (large oval at opposite end).

Tintoretto was commissioned to replace the room's **frieze of portraits** of the first 76 doges (the series continues in the Sala dello Scrutinio), but in the event his son (with assistants) did the work. On the Piazzetta side the sequence is interrupted by a painted black veil, marking the place where **Marin Falier** would have been honoured had he not conspired against the state in 1355 and (as the lettering on the veil says) been beheaded for his crime. After two years spent in the city, Byron wrote that Falier's black veil was for him the city's most memorable image.

Falier remains the most celebrated of Venice's errant leaders, but he is far from being alone in the ranks of the disgraced – by the end of the twelfth century about half the doges had been killed, exiled or simply run out of office. Nor is he the only eminent Venetian to be posthumously vilified in such a manner: for instance, under the arcade of the Palazzo Ducale you'll find a plaque perpetuating the dishonour of Girolamo Loredan and Giovanni Contarini, exiled for abandoning a fort to the Turks. In the Venetian republic, where staunch service to the state was regarded as a duty, the backsliders were the ones singled out for special treatment, and the city is almost devoid of public monuments to its great statesmen.

For more on the treason of Marin Falier, see p.144.

The Sala della Quarantia Civil Nuova and Sala dello Scrutinio

The door at the far end opens into the **Sala della Quarantia Civil Nuova**, where civil cases involving Venetian citizens outside the city were heard; it retains the only examples of Venetian gilt leatherwork left in the building, though nothing really grabs the attention. From here you pass into the **Sala dello Scrutinio**, the room in which votes by the Maggior Consiglio were counted and certain electoral committees met. The system for electing the doge was highly complex. In a nutshell: 30 men were selected by lot from the Maggior Consiglio; they reduced themselves by lot to 9 members; they elected 40, who reduced themselves to 12, who elected 25, who reduced themselves to 9, who elected 45, who reduced themselves to 11, who elected 41, who finally elected the doge by at least 25 votes. This rigmarole could last quite a while, you might think, and you'd be right – it took a minimum of five days, and in the record-breaking 1615 election the last stage alone went to 104 ballots, and lasted 24 days. And this intricately democratic machinery was in fact extremely undemocratic – everyone had an equal chance of getting through the first lottery, but only those with a lot of friends and hangers-on could expect to be nominated to the decisive committees. Perhaps to ensure that the electoral colleges kept their minds on the job, the decoration of the room is stunningly dreary; among the celebrations of great moments in Venetian military history there is just one decent picture – *The Conquest of Zara*, a late **Tintoretto** painting (first on right). The frieze of the last 42 doges was begun by assistants of Tintoretto and continued by contemporaries of each of the doges.

The prisons and the loggia

Sometimes visits are directed down the staircase from the Sala dello Scrutinio, but more often you have to backtrack through the Sala del Maggior Consiglio to the Scala dei Censori, following it down to to the **Ponte dei Sospiri** (Bridge of Sighs) and the **Prigioni** (Prisons). The bridge was built in 1600 by Antonio Contino, and takes its popular name from the sighs of the prisoners who shuffled through its corridor. In reality, though, not a lot of sighing went on here. Before the construction of these cells in the early seventeenth century, prisoners were kept in the **Piombi** (the Leads), under the roof of the Palazzo Ducale, or in the **Pozzi** (the Wells) in the bottom two storeys. This new block was occupied mainly by petty criminals – political prisoners were still incarcerated in the Piombi, and a few hard cases went to the Pozzi.

After recrossing the bridge, you leave the building through the offices of the **Avogaria**, the officers who, from the sixteenth century onwards, prepared the documents for the courts. Before leaving the building altogether, take a turn round the upper **loggia** of the palace, reached by a staircase on the Piazzetta side of the courtyard – it's a good place from which to look at the Porta della Carta, and a relatively peaceful vantage point for the Bacino di San Marco. Folklore has it that the two reddish columns on the Piazzetta side were crimsoned by the blood of traitors, whose tortured corpses were hung here for public edification; certainly this is the spot where Filippo Calendario, one of the Palazzo Ducale's architects, was quartered for abetting the conspiracy of Marin Falier.

In its middle section the loggia widens out, and on some of the columns you'll see painted coats of arms of the ducal families: this is where the guilds of Venice were invited to display their wares after the coronation of the dogaressa – if you look carefully you'll find the word *spaderi* on one of them, marking the sword-makers' pitch.

The Itinerari Segreti

If you want to see the rooms in which the day-to-day administration of Venice took place, take the **Itinerari Segreti del Palazzo Ducale**, a ninety-minute guided tour through the warren of offices and passageways that interlocks with the public rooms of the building. The guide speaks only Italian, but if you can understand even a little of the language, then go – few guided tours can be more enjoyable.

The myriad councils and committees of Venice required a vast civil service, which was staffed by men drawn from the social class immediately below the patriciate – the *cittadini originarii*. (To be accepted into this class of full citizens one had to have lived in Venice for 25 years and never engaged in manual labour.) Roaming through the shadow-palace in which these functionaries carried out their duties, you begin to understand why, for all the Palazzo Ducale's extravagant show of democratic rectitude, the Venetian republic aroused in many people the sort of dread a police state inspires.

The tour begins with the chambers of the **Chancellery**, the tiny rooms in which all acts of state were drafted and tabulated, then passes through the eighteenth-century Hall of the Chancellery, lined with cabinets for filing state documents. From here it's onward into the belly of the beast, through the judiciary's suites and into a high-ceilinged den where a rope hangs between two tiny wooden cells – the idea being that their two occupants, hearing the screams of the suspended victim, would need no further encouragement to talk. Paintings by Veronese, Tintoretto and Hieronymus Bosch provide a civilising gloss in the **Sala dei Tre Capi** – for the Heads of the Council of Ten – and the **Sala degli Inquisitori** – for the officers who investigated charges of treason.

After these, you're led up into the roof, to see the timber-lined **Piombi**. By the standards of the day they are not too grim, but there's a typically Venetian touch of refined malevolence – the doors have a superfluity of locks, just so that the noise of turning keys and slamming bolts would impress upon the inmate the finality of his incarceration. A few recalcitrant cases were not deterred – you're shown the cell from which Casanova escaped in 1775, by burrowing through the floor. Under the rafters there's a museum of Venetian history that deserves more time than is allotted for it, but you do have time to be stunned by the views from the portholes in the roof. And if you wondered, when you were in the Sala del Maggior Consiglio, how the ceiling stayed up with no visible means of support, all is revealed near the end.

The Itinerari Segreti begin daily except Wed at 10am and noon (sometimes more frequently), and cost L8000; tickets must be booked at least two days in advance, by phoning ☎522.4951.

The Campanile and the clock tower

The **Campanile** began life as a combined lighthouse and belltower in the early tenth century, when what's now the Piazzetta was the city's harbour. Modifications were made continually up to 1515, the year in which Bartolomeo Bon the Younger's rebuilding was rounded off with the positioning of a golden angel on the summit. Each of its five bells had a distinct function: the *Marangona*, the largest, tolled the beginning and end of the working day; the *Trottiera* was a signal for members of the Maggior Consiglio to hurry to the council chamber; the *Nona* rang midday; the *Mezza Terza* announced a session of the Senate; and the smallest, the *Renghiera* or *Maleficio*, gave notice of an execution.

The Campanile opens daily at 9.30am and closes between 3.30 and 8pm, depending on season; L3000.

The Campanile played another part in the Venetian penal system – "persons of scandalous behaviour" ran the risk of being subjected to the *Supplizio della Cheba* (Torture of the Cage), which involved being stuck in a crate which was then hoisted up the south face of the tower; if you were lucky you'd get away with a few days swinging in the breeze, but in some cases the view from the Campanile was the last thing the sinner saw. A more cheerful diversion was provided by the *Volo dell'Anzolo* (or *del Turco* – Flight of the Angel or Turk), a stunt which used to be performed each year at the end of the Carnevale, in which an intrepid volunteer from the Arsenale would slide on a rope from the top of the Campanile to the first-floor loggia of the Palazzo Ducale, and there present a bouquet to the doge.

To the people of Venice, the Campanile's most significant contribution to the history of the city was made on July 14, 1902, the day on which, at 9.52am, the tower succumbed to the weaknesses caused by recent structural changes, and fell down. (At some postcard stalls you can buy faked photos of the very instant of disaster.) The collapse was anticipated and the area cleared, so there were no human casualties; the only life lost was that of an incautious cat called Mélampyge (named after Casanova's dog, apparently). What's more, the bricks fell so neatly that San Marco was barely scratched and the Libreria lost just its end wall. The town councillors decided that evening that the Campanile should be rebuilt "dov'era e com'era" (where it was and how it was), and a decade later, on St Mark's Day 1912, the new tower was opened, in all but minor details a replica of the original.

At 99m, the Campanile is the tallest structure in the city, and from the top you can make out virtually every building, but not a single canal – almost as surprising as the view of the Dolomites, which on clear days seem to be in Venice's back yard. Among the many who have marvelled at the panorama are Galileo, who demonstrated the telescope from here; Goethe, who had never before seen the sea; and the Emperor Frederick III, whose climb to the top was achieved with a certain panache – he rode his horse up the tower's internal ramp. The ready access granted to the tourist is a modern privilege – the Venetian state used to permit foreigners to ascend only at high tide, when they would be unable to see make out the elusive channels through the lagoon, which were crucial to the city's defence.

The collapse of the Campanile of course pulverised the **Loggetta** at its base, but somehow it was pieced together again, mainly using material retrieved from the wreckage. **Sansovino**'s design was for a building that would completely enclose the foot of the Campanile, but only one quarter of the plan was executed (in 1537–49). Intended as a meeting place for the city's nobility, it was soon converted into a guardhouse for the *Arsenalotti* (workers from the Arsenale) who patrolled the area when the Maggior Consiglio was sitting, and in the last years of the Republic served as the room in which the state lottery was drawn. The bronze figures in niches are also by Sansovino (Pallas, Apollo, Mercury and Peace), as is the terracotta group inside (although the figure of St John is a modern facsimile); the three marble reliefs on the attic are, as ever, allegories of the power and beneficence of the *Serenissima* (the Most Serene Republic): Justice = Venice, Jupiter = Crete, Venus = Cyprus.

The Torre dell'Orologio and Piazzetta dei Leoncini

The Campanile and the clock tower

The other tower in the Piazza, the **Torre dell'Orologio** (Clock Tower) was built between 1496 and 1506, the central portion being by **Mauro Coducci** and the wings possibly by Pietro Lombardo. (The three ornate **flagstaff bases** between the Campanile and the Torre were made at the same time – 1505 – by **Leopardi**, the sculptor who finished the Colleoni monument.) A gruesome popular tale relates that the makers of the clock's elaborate mechanism, Paolo and Carlo Rainieri, slaved away for three years at their project, only to have their eyes put out so that they couldn't repeat their engineering marvel for other patrons. In fact the Venetians were suitably grateful and gave the pair a generous pension – presumably too dull an outcome for the city's folklorists.

The tower's roof terrace supports the two bronze wild men known as "The Moors", because of their dark patina; they were cast in the Arsenale in 1497. A seemingly interminable restoration prevents you from taking the internal stairs past the innards of the clock, but the view can't compete with the Campanile's, and you can watch the Moors strike the hour perfectly well from the ground. If you're in Venice on Epiphany or during Ascension week, you'll witness the clock's star turn – on the hour the Magi, led by an angel, troop out and bow to the figure of the Madonna.

To your right as you face the Torre is the **Piazzetta Giovanni XXIII**, familiarly known as **dei Leoncini**, after the two eighteenth-century marble lions – if you can't see them immediately, it's because they're smothered in children. Facing San Marco's flank is **San Basso**, a deconsecrated church now used for exhibitions, and at the far end is the nineteenth-century **Palazzo Patriarcale**, home of the Patriarch of Venice. The Palazzo contains the banqueting hall in which the doge used to entertain official guests and, once a year, the *Arsenalotti*; a corridor, now demolished, ran from the hall, through San Marco and into the Palazzo Ducale.

The Procuratie

Away to the left, from the Clock Tower, stretches the **Procuratie Vecchie**, once the home of the **Procurators of San Marco**, whose responsibilities included the upkeep of San Marco and the administration of the other government-owned properties. Never numbering more than nine, the procurators were second in position only to the doge, who himself was generally drawn from their ranks. With the doge and the Grand Chancellor – the head of the civil service – they shared the distinction of being the only state officials elected for life.

From the time of Doge Ziani, the procurators and their attendant bureaucracies were installed on this side of the Piazza, but the present building was begun around 1500 by **Coducci**, continued after a fire in 1512 by **Bartolomeo Bon the Younger** and completed

The Procuratie

c.1532 by **Sansovino**. Much of the block earned rents for the city coffers, the upper floors housing some of the choicest apartments in town and the ground floor being leased to shopkeepers and craftsmen.

Within a century or so, the procurators were moved across the Piazza to new premises. Sansovino, who had only recently completed the old offices, proposed a development that involved knocking down a pilgrims' hospice, along with the unsightly shacks around it. The **Procuratie Nuove** were eventually built between 1582 and 1640, first to designs by **Scamozzi**, and then under Longhena's control. Napoleon's stepson Eugène Beauharnais, the Viceroy of Italy, appropriated the quarters for use as a royal palace, and then discovered that the accommodation lacked a ballroom. His solution had the true, gossamer Napoleonic touch to it: he demolished Sansovino's church of San Geminiano, which had taken up part of the third side of the Piazza, and connected the Procuratie Nuove and Vecchie with a wing containing the essential facility. Generally known as the **Ala Napoleonica**, the building is topped by a gallery of Roman emperors – there are no prizes for guessing whose effigy was meant to fill the gap in the middle.

The Museo Correr

The Museo Correr is open 9am–7pm; closed Tues; L5000.

The majority of the rooms in the Ala Napoleonica and Procuratie Nuove have been occupied since 1923 by the **Museo Correr**, the civic museum of Venice. An immense and sometimes turgid triple-decker collection which nobody could digest in its entirety, it incorporates a picture gallery that more than makes up for the duller stretches.

The first floor is given over to the **historical collection**, only sporadically enlightening unless your Italian is good or you have a pretty wide knowledge of Venetian history already. The collection of Venetian coins from the ninth century to the end of the Republic is impressive, as are some of the pieces of ducal regalia and depictions of state ceremonies, but really this part of the Correr is downhill all the way once you're past the pieces by **Canova** in the first couple of rooms – including the group that made his name, *Daedalus and Icarus*, sculpted at the age of twenty-one. The figures of *Orpheus and Eurydice*, placed just outside the door to room 1, were created even earlier.

Things improve sharply on the floor above, where you come to the **Quadreria** picture gallery. It may be no rival for the Accademia's collection, but it sets out clearly the evolution of painting in Venice from the thirteenth century to around 1500 (though not all of its pictures are by Venetians), and does contain some gems. Ones to seek out are the *Pietà* by **Cosmè Tura** (room 7), the *Transfiguration* and *Dead Christ Supported by Angels* by **Giovanni Bellini** (room 13), and a couple of **Carpaccios** – the

Portrait of a Young Man in a Red Hat, and the painting of two terminally bored women that is usually known as *The Courtesans* (room 15). The subjects of this last picture are in fact a couple of late fifteenth-century bourgeois ladies dressed in a style at which none of their contemporaries would have raised an eyebrow. Their perilous platform shoes (*ciapine*) served a twin function: they kept the silks and satins out of the mud, and they enabled the wearer to circumvent the sumptuary laws, which naively attempted to limit the volume of expensive materials used in dresses by forbidding trailing hems.

At room 19 the Quadreria turns into a display of ceramics, most of them hideous, but in the very last rooms (often closed) there's a more appealing exhibition of small bronzes, household objects and other examples of the applied arts in Venice, featuring pieces by **Tullio Lombardo**, **Riccio** and **Vittoria**, and the original blocks, plus a print, of **Jacopo de'Barbari's** astonishing **aerial view of Venice**, engraved in 1500. The final part of the Correr, the **Museo del Risorgimento** (also on the second floor) is rarely open, a fact which should grieve only worshippers of **Daniele Manin** – five of its fifteen rooms are given over to the brief rebellion he led against the Austrians.

The Piazzetta and the Molo

For much of the Republic's existence, the **Piazzetta** – the open space between San Marco and the waterfront – was the area where the councillors of Venice would gather to scheme and curry favour. Way back in the earliest days of the city, this patch of land was the garden – or *broglio* – of the San Zaccaria convent: this is the probable distant source of the English word "imbroglio". But as well as being a sort of open-air clubhouse, the Piazzetta played a crucial part in the penal system of Venice.

Those found guilty of serious crime by Venice's courts were often done away with in the privacy of their cells; for public executions the usual site was the pavement between the **two granite columns** on the **Molo**, as this stretch of the waterfront is called. Straightforward hanging or decapitation were the customary techniques, but refinements were available to certain offenders, such as the three traitors who, in 1405, were buried alive, head down. Even this was mild by comparison with an execution that goes some way to explaining the reputation for barbarity that the Venetian system had abroad: the victim was taken to a raft over in the west of the city, where he was mutilated and burned until almost dead, then tied to a horse and hauled through the streets to the columns, where he was at last given the *coup de grâce*. The last person to be executed here was one Domenico Storti, condemned to death in 1752 for the murder of his brother. Superstitious Venetians avoid passing between the columns.

The columns should have a companion, but the third one fell off the barge on which they were being transported and has remained submerged somewhere off the Piazzetta since around 1170. The columns themselves were purloined from the Levant, whereas the figures perched on top are bizarre hybrids. The statue of **Saint Theodore** – the patron saint of Venice when it was dependent on Byzantium – is a modern copy; the original was a compilation of a Roman torso, a head of Mithridates the Great (first century BC) and miscellaneous bits and pieces. The **winged lion** on the other column is a 3000-kilo bronze beast that is documented as having been restored in Venice as far back as 1293. Of numerous successive repairs the most drastic was in 1815, when its wings, paws, tail and back were recast, to rectify damage done by the French engineers who, in the course of arranging its return from Paris, broke it into twenty pieces. Scientific analysis for its most recent restoration revealed that the lion is composed of a patchwork of ancient metal plates, but its exact provenance remains a mystery – the latest favoured theory is that it was originally part of a Middle Eastern monument made around 300 BC.

The Libreria Sansoviniana

The Piazzetta is framed by two outstanding buildings – the Palazzo Ducale on one side and the **Libreria Sansoviniana** or Biblioteca Marciana on the other. Sansovino's contemporaries regarded the Libreria as one of the supreme designs of the era: Palladio remarked that it was "perhaps the richest and most ornate building to be created since the times of ancient Greece and Rome". Venice had an opportunity to establish a state library in the fourteenth century, when Petrarch left his priceless collection to the city – but the beneficiaries somehow mislaid the legacy, which gives you some idea of the importance of literature in Venetian culture. In the end, the impetus to build the library came from the bequest of Cardinal Bessarion, who left his celebrated hoard of classical texts to the Republic in 1468. Bessarion's books and manuscripts were housed in San Marco and then the Palazzo Ducale, but finally it was decided that a special building was needed.

Sansovino got the job, and in 1537 the site was cleared of its hostels, slaughterhouse and bakery, thus turning the Campanile into a freestanding tower. Construction was well advanced when, in December 1545, the project suffered a minor setback: frost got into the vaulted ceiling of the main hall and brought it crashing down. Charged with incompetence, Sansovino was thrown into prison, and it took some determined pleading by his cronies – Titian among them – to get him out. Upon being allowed back on the job he took notice of conventional wisdom, which argued that vaults really weren't a terrific idea in a place where the land keeps shifting, and stuck a flat ceiling in its place, with a wooden vault attached, to keep up appearances. The library was finished in 1591, two decades after Sansovino's death.

The **main hall** of the original library, one of the most beautiful rooms in the city, is covered with paintings by **Veronese**, **Tintoretto** and others; the anteroom has a **Titian** ceiling panel. (Items from the library's collection – such as the *Grimani Breviary* of 1500, and Fra' Mauro's 1459 map of the world, are sometimes displayed, but the rooms are currently being rearranged.) Permission to see the hall, and the grand **staircase** stuccoed by **Vittoria**, can be obtained from the director's office at the main library (no. 13a), though you'll have to convince the people on the front desk that you're no idle tourist, and be prepared to come back at a time convenient to the library (visits permitted Mon–Fri 9am–1pm). It's worth the effort.

The Museo Archeologico

The Museo Archeologico is open Mon–Sat 9am–2pm, Sun 9am–1pm; L4000.

The entrance to the **Museo Archeologico** is also in the loggia of the Libreria, at no. 17. The core of the museum is Cardinal Domenico Grimani's bequest of Greek and Roman sculpture, which was given to the city in 1523 and exercised a powerful influence on the artists of Renaissance Venice. His collection of fourth- and fifth-century BC statues, including an amazing *Persephone*, is the highlight of the visit. Of the Roman pieces, the second-century bust presumed to be of Vitellius is the most striking. In many cities a collection of classical works as comprehensive as this one would merit the strongest recommendation; but in Venice it's hard to feel guilty about leaving it for a rainy day. At some point in the future the museum will be uprooted and transported over to the Grimani palace at Santa Maria Formosa, but the shift doesn't seem to be imminent.

The Zecca and the Giardinetti Reali

Attached to the Library, with its main facade to the lagoon, is Sansovino's first major building in Venice, the **Zecca** or Mint. Constructed in stone and iron to make it fireproof (most stonework in Venice is just skin-deep), it was built between 1537 and 1545 on the site occupied by the mint since the thirteenth century, when it was moved from a factory near the Rialto bridge. Some of the finance for the project was raised on the Venetian colony of Cyprus, by selling the island's slaves their liberty. By the beginning of the fifteenth century the city's prosperity was such that the Venetian gold ducat was in use in every European exchange, and Doge Tommaso Mocenigo could look forward to the day when the city would be "the mistress of all the gold in Christendom". In later years the ducat became known as the *zecchino*, source of the word "sequin". The rooms of the Mint are now part of the library.

Beyond the Zecca, and behind a barricade of postcard and toy gondola sellers, is a small public garden – the **Giardinetti Reale** –

created by Eugène Beauharnais on the site of the state granaries as part of his improvement scheme for the Procuratie Nuove. It's the nearest place to the centre where you'll find a bench and the shade of a tree, but in summer it's about as peaceful as a school playground. On the far side of the gardens is that rare thing in Venice – a public toilet. The boarded-up building at the foot of the nearby bridge is the Casino da Caffè, another legacy of the Napoleonic era, now in the process of conversion into a tourist office.

OUT FROM THE PIAZZA

From the Piazza the bulk of the pedestrian traffic flows **north to the Rialto** along the **Mercerie**, the most aggressive shopping mall in Venice and the part of the city which comes closest to being devoid of magic. Apart from the church of **San Giuliano** – one of Venice's lesser eccentricities – only the stately **San Salvatore** provides a diversion from the spotlights and price tags until you come to the **Campo San Bartolomeo**, the forecourt of the Rialto bridge and the locals' favoured spot for an after-work drink and chat. Another lively square at the end of the day is the **Campo San Luca**, within a minute's stroll of the bar at *Al Volto*, the best-stocked *enoteca* in town. Secreted in the folds of the alleyways are the old Armenian quarter and the spiralling **Scala del Bovolo** – featured on a thousand postcards, but actually seen by a minority of visitors. And slotted away in a tiny square close to the Canal Grande you'll find the most delicate of Venice's museum buildings – the Palazzo Pésaro degli Orfei, home of the **Museo Fortuny**.

Leaving the Piazza **by the west side**, through the colonnade of the Ala Napoleonica, you enter another major shopping district, but one which presents a contrast to the frenetic and tawdry Mercerie: here the clientele are drawn almost exclusively from the city's well-heeled, or from the four-star tourists staying in the hotels that overlook the end of the Canal Grande. To a high proportion of visitors, this part of the city is just **the route to the Accademia** – many pass through with their noses buried in their maps, and hardly break step before they reach the bridge over the Canal Grande. It's true that none of the first-division attractions are here and that much of the northern part of the area offers little but the pleasure of wandering through its alleyways, but there are things to see apart from the latest creations from Milan and Paris – the extraordinary Baroque facades of **Santa Maria Zobenigo** and **San Moisè**, for instance, or the graceful **Santo Stefano**, which rises at the end of one of the largest and most attractive squares in Venice. And two of the city's most stylish artistic venues lie within this district: **La Fenice**, an opera house so opulent as to be almost a parody of the genre; and the **Palazzo Grassi**, an exhibition centre with the highest production values in Italy.

North from the Piazza

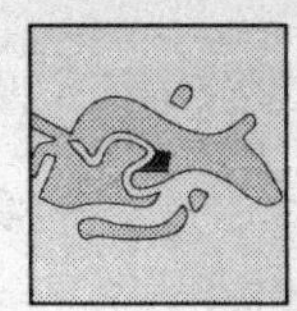

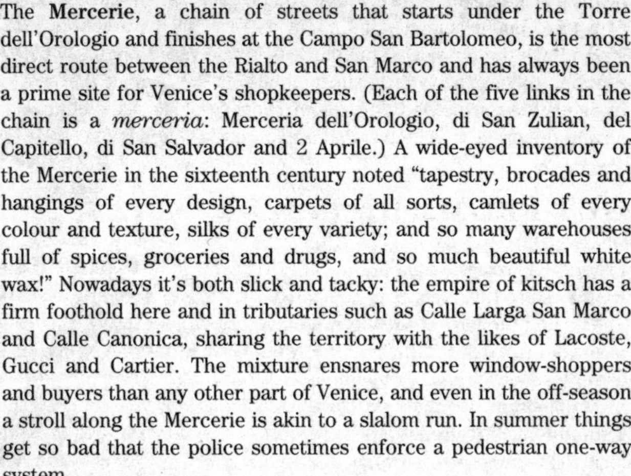

The **Mercerie**, a chain of streets that starts under the Torre dell'Orologio and finishes at the Campo San Bartolomeo, is the most direct route between the Rialto and San Marco and has always been a prime site for Venice's shopkeepers. (Each of the five links in the chain is a *merceria*: Merceria dell'Orologio, di San Zulian, del Capitello, di San Salvador and 2 Aprile.) A wide-eyed inventory of the Mercerie in the sixteenth century noted "tapestry, brocades and hangings of every design, carpets of all sorts, camlets of every colour and texture, silks of every variety; and so many warehouses full of spices, groceries and drugs, and so much beautiful white wax!" Nowadays it's both slick and tacky: the empire of kitsch has a firm foothold here and in tributaries such as Calle Larga San Marco and Calle Canonica, sharing the territory with the likes of Lacoste, Gucci and Cartier. The mixture ensnares more window-shoppers and buyers than any other part of Venice, and even in the off-season a stroll along the Mercerie is akin to a slalom run. In summer things get so bad that the police sometimes enforce a pedestrian one-way system.

For those immune to the charms of consumerism there are only a couple of things to stop for between the San Marco end of the Mercerie and the church of San Salvatore. Over the Sottoportego del Cappello (first left after the Torre) is a relief known as **La Vecia del Morter** – the Old Woman of the Mortar. The event it commemorates happened on the night of June 15, 1310, when the occupant of this house, an old woman named Giustina Rossi, looked out of her window and saw a contingent of Bajamante Tiepolo's rebel army passing below. Possibly by accident, she knocked a stone mortar from her sill, and the missile landed on the skull of the standard-bearer, killing him outright. Seeing their flag go down, Tiepolo's troops panicked and fled back towards the Rialto. (Scores of other rebels were killed in the Piazza – those ringleaders who survived the carnage were punished with execution or exile.) Asked what she would like as her reward for her patriotic intervention, Giustina requested permission to hang the Venetian flag from her window on feast days, and a guarantee that her rent would never be raised; both requests were granted.

Further on is the church of **San Giuliano** (or San Zulian), rebuilt in the mid-sixteenth century with the generous aid of the physician **Tommaso Rangone**. His munificence and intellectual brilliance are advertised by the inscriptions on the facade – freshly scrubbed thanks to money from the Venice in Peril fund – and by **Sansovino**'s portrait statue above the door. Inside, the central panel of the ceiling, *St Julian in Glory* by **Palma il Giovane** and assistants, is a cut above the man's general standard; over the first altar on the right is a late work by **Veronese** – *Pietà with SS. Roch, Jerome and Mark*;

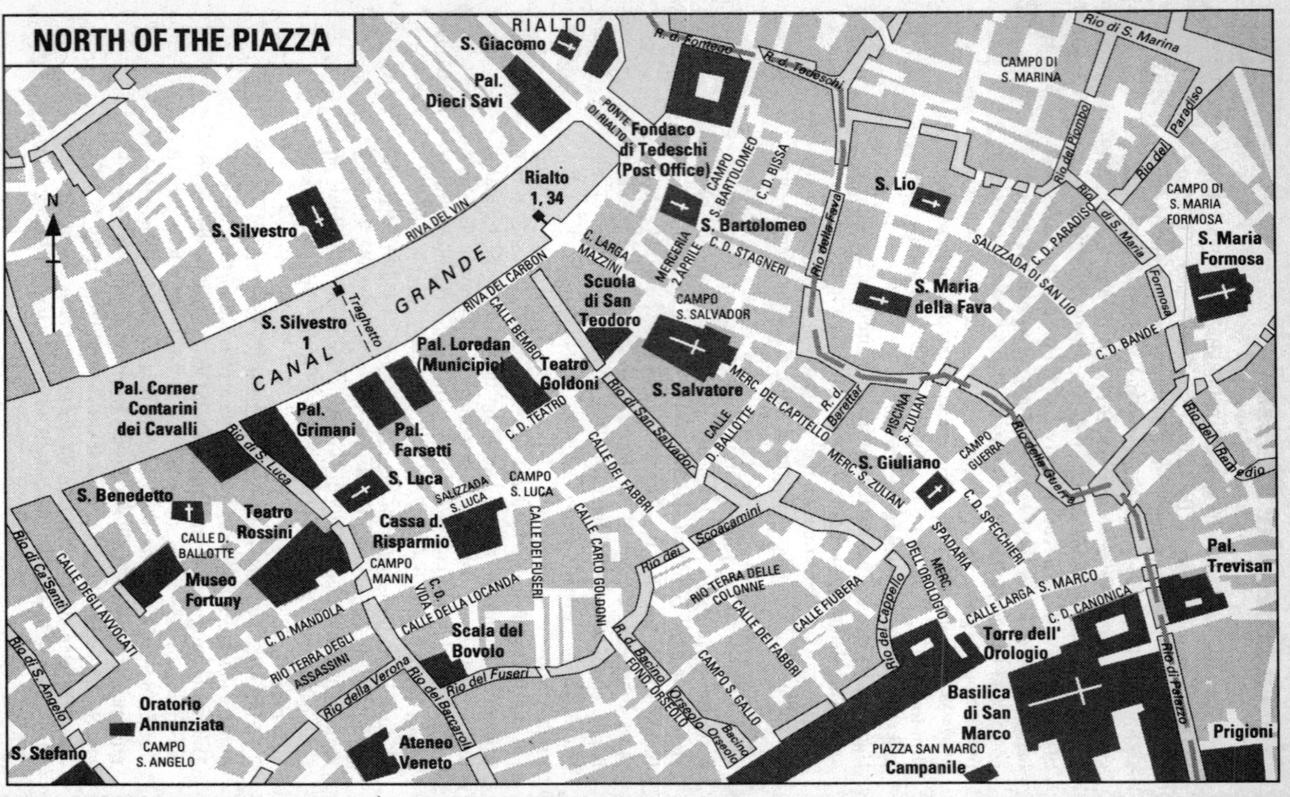
NORTH OF THE PIAZZA
RIALTO
S. Giacomo
Pal. Dieci Savi
N
S. Silvestro
RIVA DEL VIN
Rialto 1, 34
PONTE DI RIALTO
Fondaco di Tedeschi (Post Office)
R. d. Fontego
R. d. Tedeschi
CAMPO DI S. MARINA
Rio di S. Marina
Rio del Paradiso
Rio del Piombo
Rio di S. Maria
CAMPO DI S. MARIA FORMOSA
S. Maria Formosa
Formosa
S. Lio
C. D. BISSA
CAMPO S. BARTOLOMEO
S. Bartolomeo
C. D. STAGNERI
MERCERIA 2 APRILE
C. LARGA MAZZINI
Rio della Fava
S. Maria della Fava
SALIZZADA DI SAN LIO
C. D. PARADISO
C. D. BANDE
GRANDE
CANAL
Traghetto
S. Silvestro 1
RIVA DEL CARBON
CALLE BEMBO
Scuola di San Teodoro
CAMPO S. SALVADOR
S. Salvatore
Pal. Loredan (Municipio)
Teatro Goldoni
Pal. Corner Contarini dei Cavalli
Pal. Grimani
Pal. Farsetti
C. D. TEATRO
Rio di San Salvador
MERC. DEL CAPITELLO
R. d. Barettar
CALLE D. BALLOTTE
PISCINA S. ZULIAN
Rio della Guerra
Rio del Remedio
Rio di S. Luca
S. Luca
S. Benedetto
Teatro Rossini
SALIZZADA S. LUCA
CAMPO S. LUCA
CALLE DEI FABBRI
Cassa d. Risparmio
MERC. S. ZULIAN
S. Giuliano
CAMPO GUERRA
C. D. SPECCHIERI
SPADARIA
MERC. DELL'OROLOGIO
Scoacamini
Rio dei
CALLE D. BALLOTTE
Museo Fortuny
CAMPO MANIN
C. D. VIDA
CALLE DEI FUSERI
CALLE CARLO GOLDONI
RIO TERRA DELLE COLONNE
CALLE DEI FABBRI
CALLE FIUBERA
Rio del Cappello
CALLE LARGA S. MARCO
C. D. CANONICA
Pal. Trevisan
Rio di Ca' Santi
CALLE DEGLI AVVOCATI
C. D. MANDOLA
CALLE DELLA LOCANDA
RIO TERRA DEGLI ASSASSINI
Scala del Bovolo
Rio del Fuseri
R. d. Bacino
FOND. ORSEOLO
CAMPO S. GALLO
Orseolo
Bacino Orseolo
Torre dell' Orologio
Rio di Palazzo
Rio di S. Angelo
Rio della Verona
Rio dei Barcaroli
Oratorio Annunziata
CAMPO S. ANGELO
S. Stefano
Ateneo Veneto
Basilica di San Marco
PIAZZA SAN MARCO
Campanile
Prigioni

and in the chapel to the left of the chancel there are ceiling stuccoes by **Vittoria**, and three pieces by **Campagna** – terracotta figures of *The Virgin* and *The Magdalen*, and a marble altar panel (all from c.1583).

Obscure corners are to be discovered even in the vicinity of this main avenue. Very close to San Giuliano is the heart of the old Armenian quarter: take the bridge that comes into the Campo San Zulian opposite the church, into Calle Fiubera, and then take the first right – Calle degli Armeni. Under the *sottoportego* is the door to the best-hidden church in Venice, **Santa Croce degli Armeni**, which was founded as an oratory in 1496 and rebuilt as the community's church in 1688. Nowadays the congregation is small, and the most visible Armenian community is the one on the island of San Lazzaro.

For more on the Armenians of Venice, see p.215.

San Salvatore and its campo

At the far end, the Mercerie veers right at the church of **San Salvatore**. The newly restored facade, applied in 1663, is less interesting than the interior, which was begun around 1508 by Spavento and continued by Tullio Lombardo and Sansovino. It's cleverly designed in the form of three domed Greek crosses placed end to end, thus creating the longitudinal layout required by the religious orders while paying homage to the centrally planned churches of Byzantium and, of course, to the Basilica di San Marco.

In the middle of the right-hand wall stands the **tomb of Doge Francesco Venier**, designed by Sansovino, who also sculpted the figure of *Faith* on the right; this was possibly his last sculpture. To the left hangs **Titian**'s *Annunciation* (1566), signed *"Fecit, fecit"*, supposedly to emphasise the wonder of his continued creativity; its ungainly angel is often held to be the fault of assistants. A scrap of paper on the rail in front of the picture records the death of the artist on August 25, 1576. The end of the right transept is filled by the **tomb of Caterina Cornaro**, one of the saddest figures in Venetian history. Born into one of Venice's pre-eminent families, she became Queen of Cyprus by marriage, and after her husband's death was forced to surrender the strategically crucial island to the doge. On her return to Venice she was led in triumph up the Canal Grande, as though her abdication had been entirely voluntary, and then was presented with possession of the town of Ásolo as a token of the city's gratitude. She died in 1510 and was given a heroine's funeral in the Apostoli church, her body being removed to San Salvatore, and this tomb erected, at the end of the century.

For more on Caterina Cornaro, see p.335.

The **altarpiece**, a *Transfiguration* by **Titian** (c.1560), covers a fourteenth-century silver reredos, and if you ask the sacristan nicely, he'll lower the picture to reveal it. In front of the main altar, a glass disc set into the pavement allows you to see a recently unearthed merchant's tomb, with badly damaged decoration by Titian's brother Francesco. Your coin to illuminate the

Tranfiguration also lights up an excellent painting from the workshop of Giovanni Bellini – *The Supper at Emmaus*. Finally, the third altar of the left aisle, the altar of the sausagemakers' guild, was designed by Vittoria, who sculpted its figures of *Saint Roch* and *Saint Sebastian*.

Next door to the church is the former monastery, now the local headquarters of the phone company; the man at the desk might allow you a look at the beautiful **cloisters**, attributed to Sansovino. Overlooking the campo is the home of the last of the major *scuole* to be established, the **Scuola di San Teodoro**, which was founded 1530; the facade was designed in 1655 by Sardi, the architect responsible for the front of San Salvatore. After several years as a cinema, it's now a general purpose exhibition hall, but the shows hardly ever live up to their setting. The column in the centre of the campo is a memorial to the revolt of 1848–49, and was placed here on the fiftieth anniversary of the insurrection.

Campo San Bartolomeo

The **Campo San Bartolomeo**, terminus of the Mercerie, is at its best in the evening, when it's as packed as any bar in town – the hum of voices can be picked up from a hundred metres away. To show off their new wardrobe the Venetians take themselves off to the Piazza, but Campo San Bartolomeo is the spot to head for if they just want to meet friends and talk. For a crash course in the Venetian character, hang around the statue of the playwright Goldoni at around 7pm. A handful of functional bars are scattered about, but it's really the atmosphere you come for.

The restoration of the **church of San Bartolomeo** has been going on for years, but has progressed far enough for the building to be opened for the occasional exhibition. For the foreseeable future, though, its notable paintings – organ panels by Sebastiano del Piombo – will remain in the Accademia; its most famous picture, the altarpiece painted by Dürer in 1505 at the request of the German merchant Christopher Fugger, long ago migrated to Prague. In the sixteenth century this area would have been swarming with men like Dürer's patron, as the base for the German traders was the **Fondaco dei Tedeschi**, now the main post office, at the far end of the campo.

For more on the Fondaco dei Tedeschi, see p.181.

Campo San Luca and around

If the crush of San Bartolomeo is too much for you, you can retire to the **Campo San Luca** (past the front of San Salvatore and straight on), another open-air social centre, but not as much of a pressure-cooker as San Bartolomeo. From Campo San Luca, Calle Goldoni is a direct route back to the Piazza, via the Bacino Orseolo – the city's major gondola depot, and one of the few places where you can admire the streamlining and balance of the boats without being hassled by their owners. Calle dei Fuseri leads down to the smart Frezzeria (its name derived from the arrow-makers who worked there), which takes you in one direction to La Fenice and in the other to the area just west of the Piazza.

Unusually, the church of **San Luca** is not on the campo named after it, but on a *campiello* some way off, down Salizzada San Luca, then right and then left. Somewhere in the church is buried a writer whose name would have been known to all Venetians in the mid-sixteenth century – **Pietro Aretino**. Nicknamed "The Scourge of Princes", Aretino milked a hefty income from the rulers of a dozen states, who coughed up either in response to his flattery or out of terror at the damage that his tongue could do. So adept was he at juggling his various sponsors that he managed simultaneously to be on the payroll of Emperor Charles V and his enemy King Francis I of France. With Sansovino and Titian (who painted his portrait many times and used him as a model for Pontius Pilate) he formed a clique that dominated artistic circles in the city and made life intolerable for anyone they didn't like – both Lorenzo Lotto and Pordenone suffered at their hands. Aretino's notoriety rested as much on his dubious morals as on his scurrilous poetry and brilliant letters (which were a Venetian bestseller); some idea of the man is given by the popular story that he died as a result of his uncontrollable laughter at a filthy story about his own sister. Today there's not even a tombstone left to mark his existence. The church itself is a drab nineteenth-century reconstruction, and its one picture of any importance – *The Virgin and St Luke* by **Veronese** (on the high altar) – is ruined.

Campo Manin and the Scala del Bovolo

Apart from Pietro Aretino and the altogether more proper Cardinal Bembo, Renaissance Venice produced virtually no writers – and yet it was the greatest printing centre in Italy. By the second half of the sixteenth century there were over one hundred presses in Venice, and their output was more than three times greater than that of Rome, Florence and Milan added together. The doyen of Venetian printers was **Aldus Manutius**, publisher of the very first pocket editions of the classics, whose workshop stood on the edge of **Campo Manin**, on the site occupied by Pier Luigi Nervi's Cassa di Risparmio building. Founded in 1490, the Aldine Press employed teams of printers, die-cutters, proof-readers and compositors, but was always on the lookout for casual labour, as the sign over the door made clear – "Whoever you are, Aldus earnestly begs you to state your business in the fewest words possible and begone, unless, like Hercules to weary Atlas, you would lend a helping hand. There will always be enough work for you and all who pass this way." Erasmus once grudgingly did a stint here, when the Aldine workshop was producing an edition of his *Proverbs*.

North from the Piazza

The square was enlarged in 1871 to make room for the monument to **Daniele Manin**, the lawyer who led the revolt of 1848–49; his statue looks towards his house, alongside the left-hand bridge. Under Manin's control the provisional government of Venice was run with exemplary efficiency – a legislative assembly was set up, a new currency printed, and even a newspaper was circulated. In the course of the Austrian blockade Venice became the first city ever to be bombarded from the air, when explosives attached to balloons were floated over the city. The damage caused by this ploy was not too substantial, but inevitably the resistance was short-lived, and on August 23, 1849, weakened by hunger and disease, the Venetians surrendered. Manin and the other leaders of the uprising died in exile.

On the wall of the alley on the south side of Campo Manin, a sign directs you to the staircase known as the **Scala del Bovolo** (a *bovolo* is a snail shell in Venetian dialect). External staircases, developed originally as a way of saving space inside the building, were a common feature of Venetian houses into the sixteenth century, but this specimen, dating from around 1500, is the most flamboyant variation on the theme. The collection of well-heads in the garden (the oldest is eleventh-century) is one of the spots where cat lovers are certain to be able to observe the scrawny Venetian species.

The Museo Fortuny and San Benedetto

The Museo Fortuny is open Tues–Sun 9am–7pm; L6000.

The fifteenth-century Palazzo Pésaro degli Orfei, now the **Museo Fortuny**, is close at hand, hidden away in a campo you'd never accidentally pass – take either of the bridges out of the Campo Manin, turn first right, and keep going. Born in Catalonia, **Mariano Fortuny** (1871–1949) is famous chiefly for the body-clinging silk dresses he created, which were so finely pleated that they could be threaded through a wedding ring, it was claimed. However, Fortuny was also a painter, architect, engraver, photographer, theatre designer and sculptor, and the contents of this rickety and atmospheric palazzo reflect his versatility, with ranks of exotic landscapes, symbolist scenes, come-hither nudes, terracotta portrait busts, stage machinery and so forth. That said, you'll probably come out thinking that he's best known for what he was best at – and lamenting the fact that the museum doesn't contain any of the sexy frocks. The top floor houses a collection of paintings by Virgilio Guidi (1892–1983), about which the kindest comment would be that they are generally no worse than Fortuny's. Design and photography exhibitions are often held here, and as a rule are more interesting than the permanent displays – if the show's good, you'll have to queue, as the palace is so fragile that only 75 people at a time are allowed in.

The church of **San Benedetto** – founded in the eleventh century, rebuilt 1685 – gangs up with Fortuny's house to overwhelm the little square. It has a few good pictures: *St Sebastian* by Strozzi (second altar on right); two paintings of *St Benedict* by Mazzoni (over the doors to the side of the high altar); and *St Francis of Paola* by Giambattista Tiepolo (first altar on left). Finding this church open is a matter of pot-luck – late afternoon is normally a good bet.

West of the Piazza

Heading west from the Piazza, on the road to the Accademia, you soon pass on the left the **Calle del Ridotto**, named after the most notorious of Venice's gambling dens, which operated from 1638 to 1774 in the Palazzo Dandolo (no. 1332). Gamblers of all social classes were welcome at the Ridotto's tables – as long as they wore masks – but most of the clients came from the nobility. The consequent damage to the financial resources of the Venetian upper class became so great that the government was finally forced to close the joint. There was, though, no shortage of alternative houses in which to squander the family fortune – in 1797 there were 136 gambling establishments in the city. The modern visitor to Venice can experience the frisson of self-induced bankruptcy by nipping into *Harry's Bar*, right by the landing stage in the nearby Calle Vallaresso, and ordering a *Bellini* (prosecco and fruit juice) and one of Harry's fabled sandwiches. Hemingway did some celebrated boozing here, but only the wealthiest inebriates should contemplate emulating him.

San Moisè and Calle Larga XXII Marzo

San Moisè is open daily 3.30–7pm.

The first church you come across on this route is **San Moisè**, runaway winner of any poll for the ugliest church in Venice. (Its neighbour, the *Hotel Bauer-Grünwald*, would corner several votes for the Worst Building in All Categories.) The church's name means "Saint Moses", the Venetians here following the Byzantine custom of canonising Old Testament figures. Its facade sculpture, featuring a species of camel unknown to zoology, was created in 1668 by **Heinrich Meyring**, known locally as Enrico or Arrigo; and if you think this bloated display of fauna and flora is in questionable taste, wait till you see the miniature mountain he carved as the main altarpiece, representing *Mount Sinai with Moses Receiving the Tablets*. In the sacristy you'll find a fine example of comparatively restrained proto-Baroque – a bronze altar panel of the *Deposition* by Niccolò and Sebastiano Roccatagliata.

If you're looking for an escritoire for your drawing room, an oriental carpet for the reception area, a humble Dutch landscape, a new Kenzo outfit, or simply an exquisite piece of leather, then you'll probably find what you're after on the broad **Calle Larga XXII Marzo**, which begins over the canal from San Moisè. Many of the streets off the western side of the Piazza are similarly dedicated to the beautification of the prosperous and their dwellings, with names such as Versace, Armani and Missoni lurking round every corner.

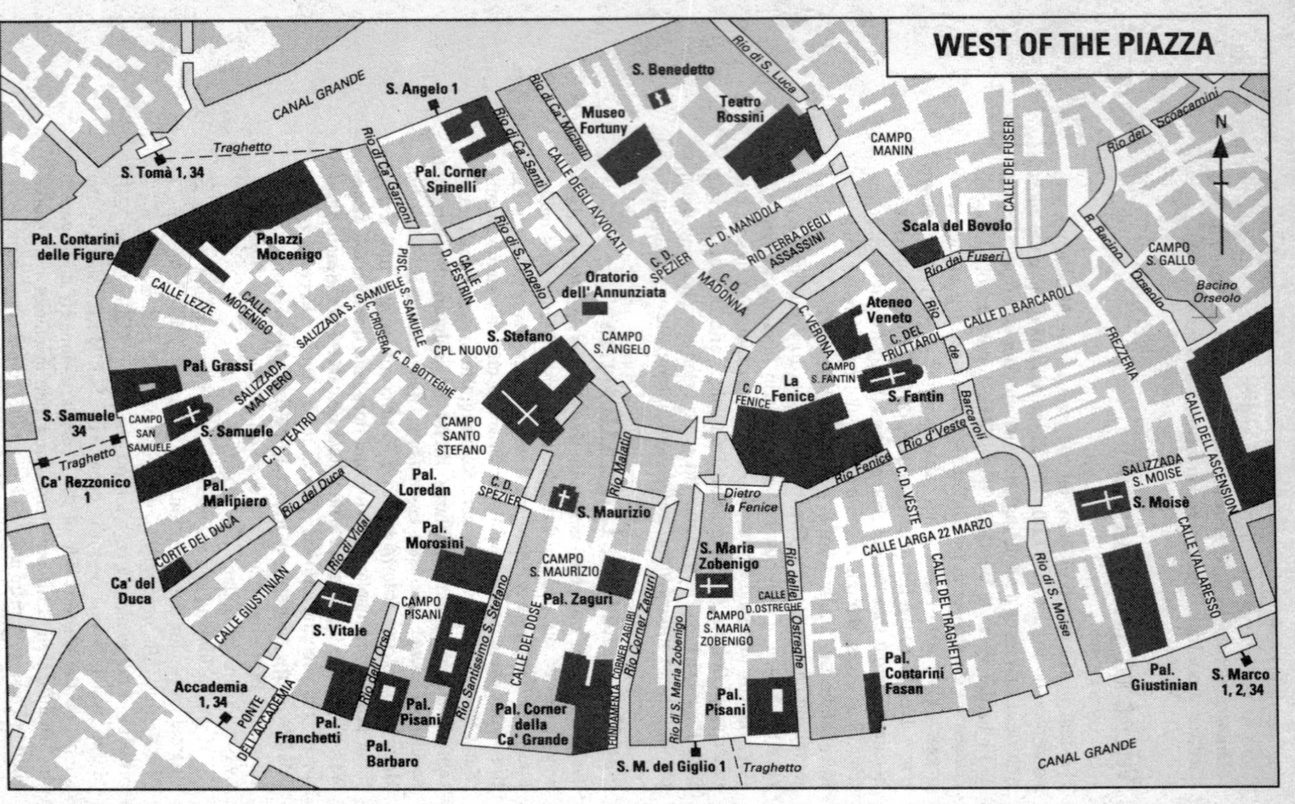
WEST OF THE PIAZZA
N
CANAL GRANDE
S. Angelo 1
Traghetto
S. Tomà 1, 34
Rio di Ca' Garzoni
Pal. Corner Spinelli
Rio di Ca' Santi
Rio di Ca' Michiel
S. Benedetto
Museo Fortuny
Teatro Rossini
Rio di S. Luca
CAMPO MANIN
CALLE DEI FUSERI
Rio dei Scoacamini
R. Bacino
CAMPO S. GALLO
Orseolo
Bacino Orseolo
Pal. Contarini delle Figure
Palazzi Mocenigo
CALLE DEGLI AVVOCATI
Rio di S. Angelo
CALLE D. PESTRIN
PISC. S. SAMUELE
C. D. MANDOLA
RIO TERRA DEGLI ASSASSINI
Scala del Bovolo
Rio dei Fuseri
C. D. SPEZIER
C. D. MADONNA
Oratorio dell' Annunziata
CALLE LEZZE
CALLE MOCENIGO
SALIZZADA S. SAMUELE
C. CROSERA
CPL. NUOVO
S. Stefano
CAMPO S. ANGELO
C. VERONA
Ateneo Veneto
Rio
C. DEL FRUTTAROL
de
CALLE D. BARCAROLI
FREZZERIA
Pal. Grassi
SALIZZADA MALIPIERO
C. D. BOTTEGHE
CAMPO S. FANTIN
S. Fantin
C. D. FENICE
La Fenice
CALLE DELL ASCENSION
S. Samuele 34
CAMPO SAN SAMUELE
S. Samuele
C. D. TEATRO
CAMPO SANTO STEFANO
Barcaroli
Rio d'Veste
Traghetto
Ca' Rezzonico 1
Pal. Malipiero
Rio del Duca
Pal. Loredan
C. D. SPEZIER
Rio Malatin
Rio Fenice
C. D. VESTE
SALIZZADA S. MOISE
S. Moisè
S. Maurizio
Dietro la Fenice
CALLE LARGA 22 MARZO
CORTE DEL DUCA
Rio di Vida
Pal. Morosini
CAMPO S. MAURIZIO
S. Maria Zobenigo
Rio delle Ostreghe
Rio di S. Moise
CALLE VALLARESSO
Ca' del Duca
CALLE GIUSTINIAN
CAMPO PISANI
Pal. Zaguri
CALLE D. OSTREGHE
CALLE DEL TRAGHETTO
S. Vitale
Rio Santissimo S. Stefano
CALLE DEL DOSE
FONDAMENTA CORNER ZAGURI
Rio Corner Zaguri
CAMPO S. MARIA ZOBENIGO
Pal. Contarini Fasan
Pal. Giustinian
S. Marco 1, 2, 34
Accademia 1, 34
PONTE DELL'ACCADEMIA
Rio dell' Orso
Pal. Pisani
Rio di S. Maria Zobenigo
Pal. Pisani
Pal. Franchetti
Pal. Barbaro
Pal. Corner della Ca' Grande
S. M. del Giglio 1
Traghetto
CANAL GRANDE

Campo San Fantin and La Fenice

West from the Piazza

Halfway along the Calle Larga XXII Marzo, on the right, the Calle del Sartor da Veste takes you over a canal and into **Campo San Fantin**. The church of **San Fantin**, begun in 1507 by Scarpagnino, is notable for its graceful domed apse, built in 1549–63 to plans by Sansovino. On the far side of the campo is the home of the **Ateneo Veneto**, a cultural institution which organises some of Venice's more arcane exhibitions. The building was formerly occupied by a confraternity whose main service to the community was to comfort those sentenced to death – hence the name by which it was generally known: the Scuola della Buona Morte. Part of the *scuola*'s collection of works of art has been dispersed, but pieces by Veronese and Alessandro Vittoria, among others, are still in the building; if you ask at the door in Calle della Verona you might be allowed a look, but the request could well be met with a reminder that the building is private property.

The square is dominated by the **Teatro la Fenice**, Venice's oldest and largest theatre. **Giannantonio Selva**'s gaunt Neoclassical design was not deemed a great success on its inauguration on December 26, 1792, but nonetheless very little of the exterior was changed when the place had to be rebuilt after a fire in 1836. More extensive changes were made to the interior, a luxuriant late-Empire confection of gilt, plush and stucco; smile sweetly and the doorman might be persuaded to let you look in at the 1500-seat auditorium. La Fenice has seen some significant musical events this century – Stravinsky's *The Rake's Progress* and Britten's *The Turn of the Screw* were both premiered here – but the music scene was more exciting in the nineteenth century, when, in addition to being the first opera house to produce several operas by Rossini, Bellini and Verdi, it became the focal point for protests against the occupying Austrian army. Favourite forms of nationalist expression included bombarding the stage with bouquets in the colours of the Italian tricolour, and yelling "Viva Verdi!" at strategic points in the performance – the composer's name being the acronym for *Vittorio Emanuele, Re d'Italia* (Vittorio Emanuele, King of Italy).

Santa Maria Zobenigo and San Maurizio

Back on the main road to the Accademia, another extremely odd church awaits – **Santa Maria Zobenigo**. It was actually consecrated as Santa Maria del Giglio (. . . of the Lily), but its alternative title – derived from the name of the Jubanico family, who founded it in the ninth century – is more commonly used. You can stare at the front of this church all day and still you won't find a single unequivocally Christian image. The main statues are of the five Barbaro brothers, who financed the rebuilding of the church in 1678; Virtue, Honour, Fame and Wisdom hover at a respectable distance; and relief maps at eye level depict the towns distinguished with the brothers' presence in the course of their military and diplomatic careers. Antonio Barbaro – the central figure and chief benefactor of the church – was not rated quite so highly by his superiors as he was by himself: he was dismissed from Francesco Morosini's fleet for incompetence. The interior, full to bursting with devotional pictures and sculptures, overcompensates for the impiety of the exterior. A *Madonna and Child* in the sacristy is implausibly attributed to Rubens, but the eighteenth-century *Stations of the Cross* by various artists in the body of the church have a better claim on your attention, as do the *Evangelists* by **Tintoretto** behind the altar. The detached one-storey shop right by the church occupies the stump of the campanile, pruned to its present dimensions in 1774.

The tilting campanile of Santo Stefano (see below) soon looms into view over the vapid church of **San Maurizio**, a collaboration between Giannantonio Selva and Antonio Diedo, secretary of the Accademia. The inside of the church has nothing to recommend it, and the exterior is overshadowed by the fifteenth-century **Palazzo Zaguri**, on the campo's east side. This district is the antiques centre of Venice and from time to time the Campo San Maurizio is taken over by an antiques and bric-a-brac fair. The nostalgia industry has a permanent representative on the square in the shape of *V. Trois*, where they sell the Fortuny-designed fabrics manufactured over on La Giudecca.

If you wander off the campo down Calle del Dose you'll come to a short *fondamenta* on the Canal Grande, with fabulous views of its lower reach. Continuing along the Accademia route, at the beginning of Calle del Piovan stands a diminutive building that was once the **Scuola degli Albanesi**; it was established in 1497 and the reliefs on the facade date from shortly after that. In 1504 Carpaccio produced a cycle of *Scenes from the Life of the Virgin* for the *scuola*, and the pictures remained here even after the declining Albanian community led to the disbanding of the confraternity in the late eighteenth century; it wasn't until 1808, when the baker's guild that had moved into the building was itself scrapped, that the series was broken up. The bits that remained in Venice are now in the Correr collection and the Ca' d'Oro.

Stop for a second on the bridge just after the Scuola, and look down the canal – you'll see that it runs right under the east end of Santo Stefano, the only church in Venice to have quite so intimate a relationship with the city's waterways.

Campo Santo Stefano

The church of Santo Stefano closes one end of the next square – **Campo Santo Stefano**. Large enough to hold several clusters of tourists, a few dozen café tables plus a kids' football match or two, the campo is always lively but never feels crowded; provided you're willing to do battle against the rapacious pigeons, a picnic can be spread around the well-head or the base of the statue of Risorgimento idealogue Nicolò Tommaseo – and there's an additional inducement to sit down for a while in the form of *Paolin*, purveyors of the city's ultimate pistachio ice cream. One of the city's sunniest spots, this used to be one of its bloodiest – it was a popular bullfighting arena until 1802, when the collapse of a bank of seats killed a number of spectators and provoked an absolute ban on such events.

The campo has an alias – Campo Francesco Morosini – that comes from a former inhabitant of the palazzo at no. 2802, at the Canal Grande end of the square. The last doge to serve as military commander of the Republic (1688–94), **Francesco Morosini** became a Venetian hero with his victories in the Peloponnese, as is attested by the triumphal arch built in his honour in the Palazzo Ducale's Sala dello Scrutinio, and the exhaustive documentation of his career in the Correr Museum. But to those few non-Venetians to whom his name means anything at all, he's known as the goon who lobbed a missile through the roof of the Parthenon, detonating the Turkish gunpowder barrels that had been stored there. He then made matters even worse by trying to prise some of the decoration off the half-wrecked temple, shattering great chunks of statuary in the process. Morosini and Venice didn't come back from that campaign empty-handed though – the Arsenale gate is guarded by two of his trophies.

San Vitale and the Palazzo Pisani

Right at the end of the campo, past the elongated **Palazzo Loredan** (originally fifteenth century but rebuilt around 1540; facade towards Santo Stefano added in 1618), stands the deconsecrated church of **San Vitale** (or Vidal). It's now a private art gallery, but has somehow hung onto a painting by **Carpaccio** of *San Vitale and other Saints*, which you can just about see over the screens erected for the temporary exhibitions. If the facade of the church seems strangely familiar, that's because it's a slavish replica of San Giorgio Maggiore's.

Campiello Pisani, at the back of Morosini's house, is effectively a forecourt to the **Palazzo Pisani**, one of the biggest houses in the city, and now the Conservatory of Music. Work began on it in the early seventeenth century, continued for over a century, and at last was brought to a halt by the government, who decided that the Pisani, among the city's richest banking families, were getting ideas above their station. Had the Pisani got their way, they wouldn't have stopped building until they reached the Canal Grande.

The church of Santo Stefano

As a building, the church of **Santo Stefano** – founded in the thirteenth century, rebuilt in the fourteenth and altered again in the first half of the fifteenth – is notable for its Gothic doorway and beautiful **ship's keel roof**, both of which belong to the last phase of building. The airy and calm interior is one of the most pleasant places in Venice to just sit and think, but it also contains some major works of art. The **tomb of Giacomo Surian**, on the entrance wall, was designed and carved in the final decade of the fifteenth century by Pietro Lombardo and his sons. Less easily overlooked is the **tomb of Francesco Morosini**: it's the oversized bronze badge in the centre of the nave. A more discreet funerary monument – Canova's stele for Giovanni Falier (1808) – is in the baptistery (door off left aisle), but this part of the church is usually locked. The major **paintings** are in the sacristy: a *Holy Family* by Palma il Vecchio, and *The Agony in the Garden*, *The Last Supper* and *The Washing of the Disciples' Feet*, three late works by Tintoretto.

You can walk round the **cloister** (far door in left aisle), even though it's been appropriated by government offices, to see the **tomb of Doge Andrea Contarini**, head of state when the Venetians took on the Genoese at Chioggia. The weather long ago wiped out the frescoes by Pordenone that used to cover much of the walls – a few scraps are preserved in the Ca' d'Oro. Pordenone was for a while Titian's main rival in the city, and such was his fear of the great man and his cronies that he invariably turned up to work here with daggers and swords hanging from his belt. No assault actually occurred, but there has been plenty of bloodshed within the church precincts – so much, in fact, that the place has had to be reconsecrated half a dozen times.

Premature death on a terrible scale accounts for the peculiar raised pavement of nearby **Campo Novo**, off Calle del Pestrin: formerly the churchyard of Santo Stefano, it was used as a burial pit during the catastrophic plague of 1630, and such was the volume of corpses interred here that for health reasons the site remained closed to the public from then until 1838.

Campo Sant'Angelo

A door leads from the cloister of Santo Stefano into the **Campo Sant'Angelo** (or Anzolo), a square almost as capacious as Campo Morosini, but which usually feels more like a crossroads than a meeting place. It's bounded by some fine buildings, however, including two magnificent fifteenth-century palaces: the **Palazzo Gritti** and, facing it, the **Palazzo Duodo**, home of the composer Cimerosa, who died there in 1801. The minuscule **Oratorio dell'Annunziata** – founded in the tenth century, rebuilt in the twelfth and once the home of the Scuola dei Sotti ("of the Lame") – contains a sixteenth-century crucifix and an *Annunciation* by the omnipresent Palma il Giovane. No trace remains of Sant'Angelo church, but it's still remembered as a leading player in one of Venice's great architectural cock-ups. By 1445 the lean of the church's campanile had become so severe that urgent measures were deemed necessary to right it. It was discovered that there was a builder in Bologna who had made such problems his speciality, and so he was brought on to the case.

The expert fixed it so the tower was as straight as a pine tree; the scaffolding was taken down; a banquet was held to honour the engineering genius; and the next morning the whole thing keeled over.

Palazzo Grassi and Ca' del Duca

From opposite the entrance to Santo Stefano church, Calle delle Botteghe and Crosera go up to Salizzada San Samuele; a left turn takes you past the house in which **Paolo Veronese** lived his final years, and on to **Campo San Samuele**. Built in the late twelfth century and not much altered since, the **campanile** of the church is one of the oldest in the city. The church itself was founded in the previous century but was largely reconstructed in the late seventeenth century; there are fifteenth-century frescoes by Paduan artists in the apse, but the building is generally more absorbing when there's a show on at the Palazzo Grassi, at which times it becomes an annexe for showing videos and slides.

San Samuele is dwarfed by the glitzy **Palazzo Grassi**, which in 1984 was bought by Fiat and converted into a cultural centre. No expense was spared in realising the plans drawn up by Gae Aulenti, the fashionable architect of Paris's Musée d'Orsay, and the refurbished palace now stages the flashiest exhibitions you'll ever see. Grassi blockbusters have ranged from the Celts to Futurism, with perhaps the biggest hit being *I Fenici* (The Phoenicians), for which the glazed courtyard was filled with an artificial sand dune, every wall was painted with illustrative maps and diagrams, and a full-colour catalogue as heavy as a paving stone was produced. Reviewed by papers from all over Europe, *I Fenici* was visited by thousands of people who came to Venice solely to see it, and the show has left a permanent mark on the city landscape – many of the designs in the windows of the jewellers and mask-makers were plundered from its exhibits. As the numbers allowed inside the building at one time are strictly limited, a show at the Grassi can turn the campo into the city's most crowded spot.

From San Samuele a fairly straightforward chain of alleys leads back to Campo Morosini (follow the trail of "Palazzo Grassi" signs). On the corner of the first of these – Calle Malipiero – is a plaque marking the birthplace of one of the paltry band of world-famous native Venetians: **Giovanni Giacomo Casanova**. Both his parents were actors, and the family lived within a stone's throw of one of Venice's main theatres, the San Samuele, which until its demolition in the nineteenth century stood in the adjoining Calle del Teatro.

The Ca' del Duca can be visited by appointment April–Oct Mon, Wed & Fri 9.30am–12.30pm, Sat 3–6pm; ring ☎538.7903.

A right turn just before the Rio del Duca, into Corte del Duca, brings you to the **Ca' del Duca**, home of the **Raccolte d'Arte Orientale e di Porcellane**, Venice's most obscurely located museum. It combines two small collections of Oriental art and European porcelain, both of high quality, but neither of sufficient general interest to make a visit a top priority.

Chapter 3

Dorsoduro

There were not many places among the lagoon's mudbanks where Venice's builders could be confident that their work wouldn't slide down into the water, but **Dorsoduro** was one of them; its name translates as "hard back", and it occupies just about the firmest land in the city. Some of the finest minor domestic architecture in Venice is concentrated here, and in recent years many of the area's best houses have been bought up by industrialists and financiers from elsewhere in northern Italy, investing in permanent or merely weekend havens from their places of work. The top-bracket colony is, however, pretty well confined to a triangle defined by the Accademia, the Punta della Dogana and the Gesuati. Stroll up to the area around Campo Santa Margherita and the atmosphere is quite different, in part because of the proximity of the university.

Even if your stay's so short that you've time only for the brightest highlights, you should give a day to Dorsoduro. The **Gallerie dell'Accademia**, replete with masterpieces from each phase in the history of Venetian painting, is the area's essential port of call, and figures on most itineraries as the place to make for when the Piazza's sights have been done. **Santa Maria della Salute**, the grandest gesture of Venetian Baroque and a prime landmark when looking across the water from the Molo, is architecturally the major religious building of the district – but in terms of artistic contents it takes second place to **San Sebastiano**, the parish church of **Paolo Veronese**, who decorated much of its interior. **Giambattista Tiepolo**, the master colourist of a later era, is well represented at the **Scuola Grande dei Carmini**, and for an overall view of Tiepolo's cultural milieu there's the **Ca' Rezzonico**, home of Venice's museum of eighteenth-century art and artefacts. Unusually for Venice, art of the twentieth century is also in evidence – at the **Guggenheim Collection**, which is at least the equal of the city's public collection in the Ca' Pésaro. And yet despite all these attractions the district as a whole is remarkably quiet – most tourists step across the Accademia bridge, whirl through the gallery, then cross back over the Canal Grande again.

As with San Polo, the area designated by the chapter title is slightly more extensive than the *sestiere* of the same name, because in order to simplify the scheme of the city it incorporates a portion of the Santa Croce *sestiere* – for the visitor, the most arbitrary and confusing of Venice's divisions. For our purposes Dorsoduro stretches from the Punta della Dogana and the Salute west to the docks of the Stazione Maríttima, and north to Piazzale Roma (technically in Santa Croce).

The Accademia

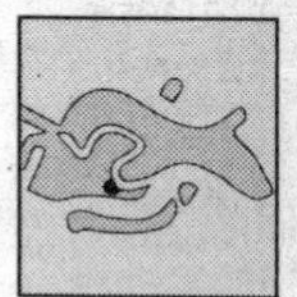

The fame of Venice's school of art, the **Accademia di Belle Arti**, nowadays has nothing to do with the reputation of its staff or pupils – it's been going steadily downhill since the lively days of '68 – and everything to do with the attached **Gallerie dell'Accademia**, one of Europe's finest specialised art collections. A Napoleonic decree of 1807 moved the Accademia to its present site and instituted its galleries of Venetian paintings, a stock drawn largely from the city's suppressed churches and convents.

The Accademia is open Mon–Sat 9am–1.30pm, Sun 9am–12.30pm; L8000.

Parts of the premises themselves were formerly religious buildings: the church of **Santa Maria della Carità** (rebuilt by **Bartolomeo Bon** 1441–52) and the **Convento dei Canonici Lateranensi** (built by **Palladio** in 1561 but not completed) were both suppressed in 1807. The third component of the Accademia used to be the **Scuola della Carità**, founded in 1260 and the oldest of the six Scuole Grande; the Gothic building dates from 1343, but has an eighteenth-century facade. There is talk now of moving the school to another site, allowing the Gallerie to expand here.

The Accademia is the third component – with San Marco and the Palazzo Ducale – of the triad of obligatory tourist sights in Venice, but admissions are restricted to batches of 180 people at a time. Accordingly, if you're there in high summer and don't want to wait, get to the door before 9am.

To the early Renaissance

The first room of the Accademia's generally chronological arrangement is the fifteenth-century former chapter house of the Scuola (with its original gilded ceiling), now filled with pieces by the earliest-known individual Venetian painters. The icon-like Byzantine-influenced figures of **Paolo Veneziano** (first half of the fourteenth century) are succeeded by the Gothic forms of his follower **Lorenzo Veneziano** – look at the swaying stances of his figures and the emphasis on the sinuous lines of the drapery.

Room 2 is given over to large altarpieces from the late fifteenth century and early sixteenth century, including works by **Giovanni Bellini, Cima da Conegliano** and **Vittore Carpaccio**. All of these paintings appear to have slightly warped perspectives: this is

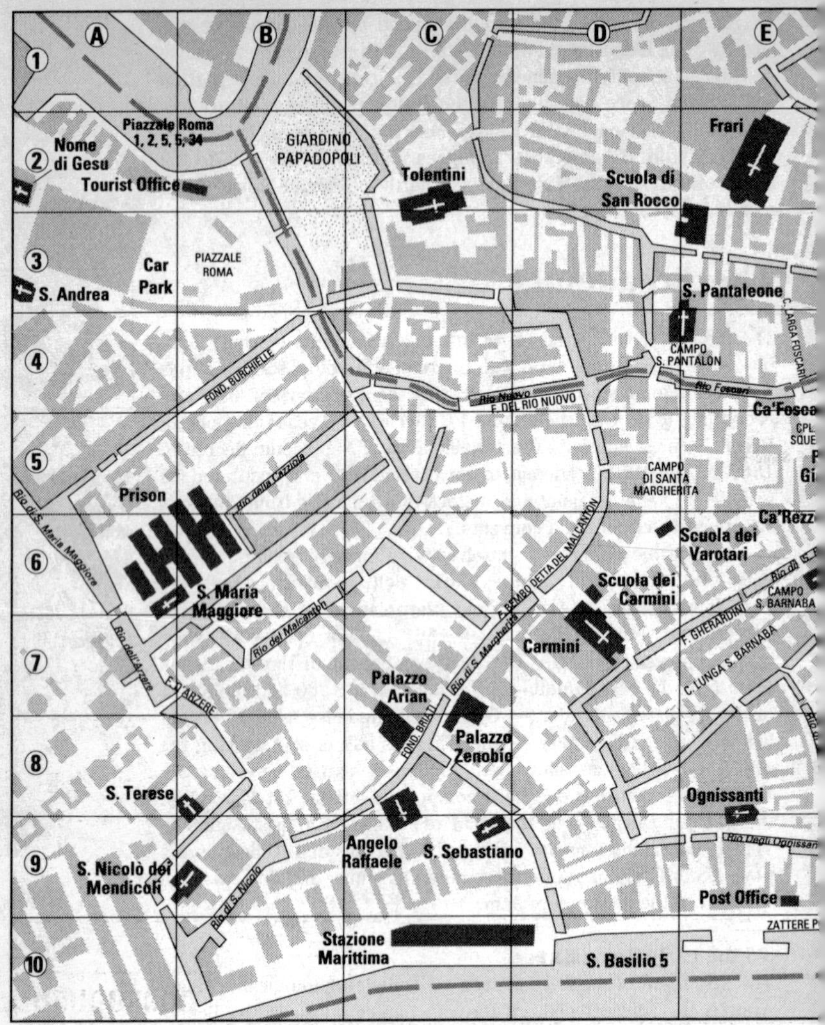

because they were intended to be placed above head height – a fact that the Accademia's picture-hangers have not taken into consideration. Carpaccio's strange *Crucifixion and Glorification of the Ten Thousand Martyrs of Mount Ararat* is the most gruesome painting in the room, and the most charming is by him too: *The Presentation of Jesus in the Temple*, with its pretty, wingless, lute-playing angel.

The beginnings of the Venetian obsession with the way in which forms are defined by light (as differentiated from the Florentines'

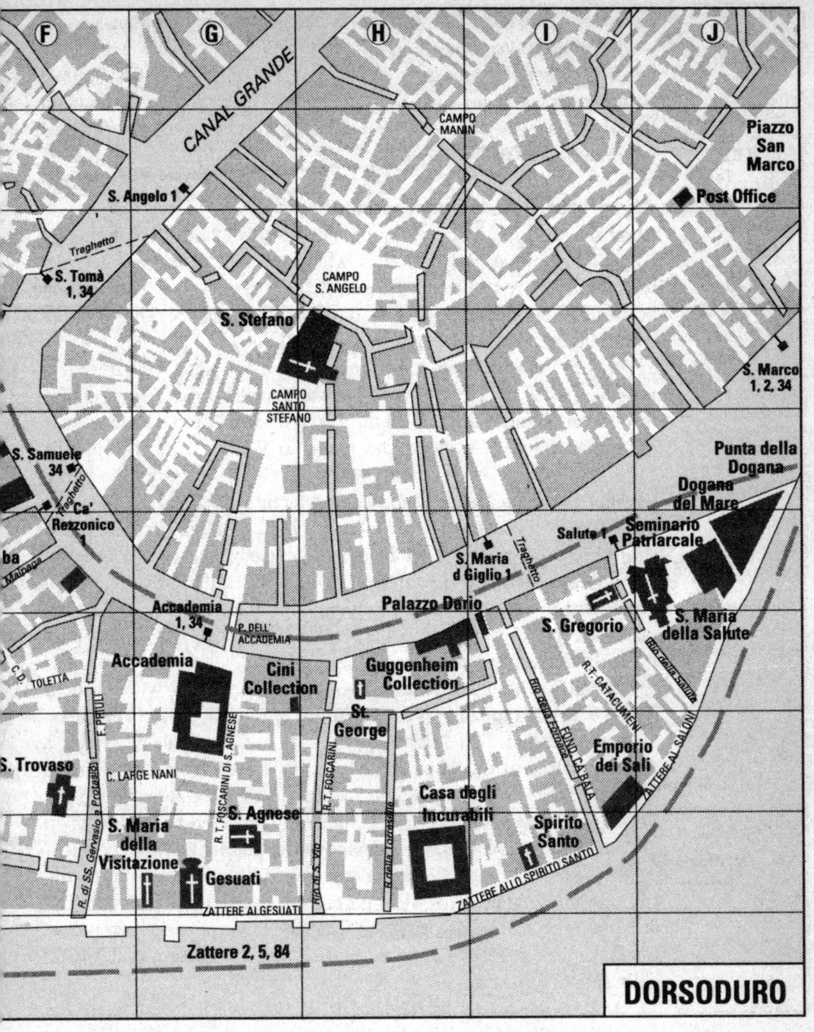

more geometrical notions of form) and the emergence of the characteristically soft and rich Venetian palette are seen in **rooms 3, 4 and 5**, the last two of which are a high point of the Accademia. Almost all of the small paintings here would alone be worth a detour, but outstanding are an exquisite *St George* by **Mantegna** (c.1466), a series of *Madonnas* and a *Pietà* by **Giovanni Bellini**, and two pieces by the most mysterious of Italian painters, **Giorgione** – his *Portrait of an Old Woman* and the so-called

Tempest (c.1500). The former is an urgent and compassionate study of mortality (the inscription means "with time"), while the latter resists all attempts to deduce its meaning – the first known painting to have no historical, religious, mythological or factual basis, it seems to have been as perplexing to Giorgione's contemporaries as it is to us.

Tintoretto, Titian and Veronese

Rooms 6 to 8 mark the entry of the heavyweights of the Venetian High Renaissance, the period in which the cult of the artist really took hold, with painters cultivating their reputations and writers boosting their favourites while damning their rivals. These works would be the prize of many other collections, but here they are just appetisers for what's to come. Jacopo Robusti, alias **Tintoretto**, is represented by an *Assumption*; Tiziano Vecellio, alias **Titian**, comes in with an unenthralling *John the Baptist*; and Paolo Caliari, better known as **Paolo Veronese** (he came to Venice from Verona), is represented by a neck-cricking series of ceiling panels. In the parallel suite of rooms the most compelling pictures is the *Young Man in his Study* by **Lorenzo Lotto** (c.1528), a portrait in which the subject's gaze manages to be simultaneously sharp and evasive. Lotto was eventually driven from Venice by the vindictiveness of Titian and his entourage; presumably a happier life was led by the unknown follower of Titian who produced the beguiling *Tobias and the Angel* nearby .

Room 6 is in effect the ante-room to **room 10**, one whole wall of which is needed for *Christ in the House of Levi* by **Paolo Veronese**. Originally called *The Last Supper* – being a replacement for a Titian painting of the same subject which was destroyed by a fire in the refectory of San Zanipolo – this picture brought down on Veronese the wrath of the Inquisition, who objected to the inclusion of "buffoons, drunkards, Germans, dwarfs, and similar indecencies" in the sacred scene. (What really raised their hackles was the German contingent, who were perceived by the Holy Office as the incarnation of the Reformation menace.) Veronese's insouciant response was simply to change the title, an emendation that apparently satisfied his critics.

Among the works by **Tintoretto** is the painting that made his reputation: *The Miracle of the Slave* (1548), showing Saint Mark's intervention at the execution of a slave who had defied his master by travelling to the Evangelist's shrine. Comparison with Gentile Bellini and Carpaccio's unruffled depictions of miraculous events in rooms 20–21 (see below) makes it easy to understand the sensation caused by Tintoretto's whirling, brashly coloured scene. The legend of Venice's patron saint is further elaborated by his dreamlike *The Translation of the Body of St Mark* (see entry on the Basilica for the story of the "translation" – ie theft) and *St Mark Saving a Saracen* (both from the 1560s), and *The Dream of St Mark*

(1570), which is largely by his son **Domenico**. Tintoretto's love of physical and psychological drama, the energy of his brush-strokes, and the sometimes uncomfortable originality of his colours and poses, are all displayed in this group. (And all over Venice you can see how his concentration on dramatic highlights and his use of gesture spawned a shoal of imitators whose clichéd contortions of pose and expression covered oceans of canvas.) Opposite is **Titian**'s highly charged *Pietà* (1576), painted for his own tomb in the Frari; the immediacy of death is expressed in the handling of the paint, here scratched, scraped and dolloped onto the canvas not just with brushes but with the artist's bare hands. It was completed after Titian's death by Palma il Giovane, as the inscription explains.

The eighteenth century

A major shift occurs in **room 11**. In one part there's more from **Veronese** and **Tintoretto**, including a *Creation of the Animals* which features a few species which must have followed the unicorn into extinction, and the sumptuous *Madonna dei Camerlenghi* (1566), showing the city's treasurers hobnobbing with the Mother of Our Saviour – the facial types are still seen in Venice today. Elsewhere in the room hang pieces by **Giambattista Tiepolo**, including the only two pieces to have survived the destruction of the Scalzi's ceiling in 1915. Although some of the side rooms contain a few decent sixteenth- and seventeenth-century pieces, the chief interest of the generally dull section that follows is provided by eighteenth-century painters. **Giambattista Piazzetta**'s extraordinary *The Fortune-Teller* (1740), in **room 16a**, is also known as *The Enigma*, although the woman is offering the least enigmatic sexual invitation you'll ever see on canvas; some interpreters see it as a satirical allegory, showing how once-glorious Venice now behaved towards the rest of the world. In **room 17** there's the Accademia's only piece that's certainly by **Canaletto**, accompanied by **Guardi**'s views of Venice, **Pietro Longhi**'s documentary interiors and a series of portraits by **Rosalba Carriera**, one of the very few women shown in the collection. Carriera's work established the use of pastel as a medium in its own right, rather than as a preparation for oil paint, and her moving *Self-Portrait in Old Age*, done at a time when her sight was beginning to fail, is a high point of her work.

To the Miracles of the Relic of the Cross

The top part of the Carità church now forms **room 23**, which houses works mainly from the fifteenth and early sixteenth centuries, the era of two of Venice's most significant artistic dynasties, the **Vivarini** and **Bellini** families. Of the pieces by the Vivarini – **Antonio**, his brother **Bartolomeo** and his son **Alvise** – the most striking is Alvise's *Santa Chiara* (1485–90). **Giovanni Bellini** is represented by four workshop-assisted triptychs (painted for this church in the 1460s), and his brother **Gentile** by the intense portrait of *The Blessed Lorenzo Giustinian* (1445). One of the oldest surviving Venetian canvases and Gentile's earliest signed work, it was possibly used as a standard in processions, which would account for its tatty state.

There's more from Gentile over in **room 20**, which is entirely filled by the cycle of *The Miracles of the Relic of the Cross*. The work was produced by various artists between 1494 and 1501, and was commissioned by the Scuola Grande di San Giovanni Evangelista to extol the holy fragment it had held since 1369. Gentile's *Procession of the Relic in the Piazza* (1496), executed the year the Torre dell'Orologio was started (and with artistic licence shifting the campanile to the right), is perhaps the best-known image of the group; the devotional moment is easily missed – the bare-headed man in a red cloak kneeling as the relic passes him is one Jacopo de' Salis, praying for his son's recovery from a fractured skull. In *The Recovery of the Relic from the Canal of San Lorenzo* (1500) Gentile shows Andrea Vendramin, Grand Guardian of the Scuola, retrieving the relic from the spot where it had floated after being knocked into the water during a procession; the fourth figure from the left in the group of donors in the right foreground is alleged to be a self-portrait, and Caterina Cornaro is portrayed on the far left.

A wealth of anecdotal detail adds historical veracity to **Carpaccio**'s *Cure of a Possessed Man* (1494). Set by the Rialto (and showing one of the wooden precursors of the present bridge), its cast of characters includes turbanned Turks and Arabs, Armenian (or Greek) gentlemen in tall brimmed hats, an African gondolier, a woman beating carpets on an *altana* and a man repairing a roof; the miracle – the cure of a lunatic – is happening on the first floor of the building on the left. **Giovanni Mansueti**'s *Miracle of the Relic in Campo San Lio* (1494) shows what happened at the funeral of a dissolute and impious member of the confraternity: the relic refused to allow itself to be carried into the church for his service. Each window has a woman or child in it, witnessing the shame of the old reprobate. The reason for all these anecdotal details and the marginalising of the miracles was not a lack of piety but quite the reverse: the miracle was authenticated by being depicted in the documentary context of teeming everyday life.

Carpaccio's St Ursula paintings – and Titian's Presentation

Another remarkable cycle fills **room 21** – **Carpaccio**'s *Story of Saint Ursula*, painted for the Scuola di Sant'Orsola at San Zanipolo in 1490–94. A superlative exercise in pictorial narrative, the paintings are especially fascinating to the modern viewer as a meticulous record of domestic architecture, costume, the decorative arts, and even ship design in Venice at the close of the fifteenth century – and a scrupulous recent renovation has further increased their lustre. The legend is that a British prince named Hereus proposed marriage to Ursula, a Breton princess, who accepted on two conditions: that Hereus convert to Christianity, and that he should wait for three years, during which time he should accompany Ursula and her company of 11,000 virgins on a pilgrimage to Rome. The conditions were accepted, and the eventual consequence was that Ursula and her troop were massacred by the Huns near Cologne – as she had been forewarned by an angel in a dream.

After this room, you leave the Accademia through the former *albergo* of the Scuola; **Titian**'s *Presentation of the Virgin* (1539) occupies the wall over the door, the place for which it was painted – and the triptych by **Antonio Vivarini** and **Giovanni d'Alemagna** (1446) similarly hangs where it always has.

Eastern Dorsoduro

Along the east flank of the Accademia runs the wide Rio Terrà Foscarini, named after **Senator Antonio Foscarini**, victim of the Venetian judicial system's most notorious gaffe; he lived at no. 180–181, but the house was radically altered in the nineteenth century. The street cuts down almost as far as the Záttere, but for the direct route to the mouth of the Canal Grande you turn left along Calle Nuova a Sant'Agnese, one of the district's main shopping streets.

For the story of Antonio Foscarini, see p.183.

The Cini and Guggenheim collections

Just before the Rio San Vio you pass the Palazzo Cini (no. 864), once the home of the industrialist Vittorio Cini (founder of the Fondazione Cini on San Giorgio Maggiore) and now occupied by the **Raccolta d'Arte Vittorio Cini**. Although Cini's private collection contains a miscellany of valuable manuscripts, porcelain and other artefacts, the substance of the museum is its gathering of Tuscan paintings, including pieces by Bernardo Daddi, Filippo Lippi, Piero di Cosimo and Pontormo. It also occasionally hosts special exhibitions – keep an eye out for posters.

The Cini collection is open summer Tues–Sun 1–6pm; L5000.

A meatier aesthetic experience is provided by the **Peggy Guggenheim Collection**, installed in the peculiarly modernistic fragment of the quarter-built Palazzo Venier dei Leoni, a bit farther down the Canal Grande. In the early years of this century the leading lights of the Futurist movement came here for the parties thrown by the dotty Marchesa Casati, who was fond of stunts like setting wild cats and apes loose in the palazzo garden, among plants sprayed lilac for the occasion.

Peggy Guggenheim, a considerably more discerning patron of the arts, moved into the palace in 1949; since her death in 1979 the Guggenheim Foundation has looked after the administration of the place, and has turned her private collection into one of the city's glossiest museums. It's a generally top-quality assembly of twentieth-century art, touching on most of the major modern movements.

The Guggenheim collection is open 11am–6pm, plus Sat 6–9pm; closed Tues; L7000, free Sat 6–9pm.

Prime pieces include Brancusi's *Bird in Space* and *Maestra*, De Chirico's *Red Tower* and *Nostalgia of the Poet*, Max Ernst's *Robing of the Bride*, several of Joseph Cornell's boxes, sculpture by Laurens and Lipchitz, and works by Malevich and Schwitters; other artists include Picasso, Braque, Chagall, Pollock, Duchamp, Giacometti, Picabia and Magritte. The watergates are often closed to protect public decency from the erection flaunted by the rider of Marino Marini's *Angel of the Citadel*, out on the terrace.

The Salute and around

After the wrought iron and greenery of the tiny **Campo Barbaro** (from where you can see the Gothic back half of the Palazzo Dario – see p.188) a handful of glass workshops and furnaces lie in wait for the more monied Guggenheim clientele. From the next open space an underpassage burrows alongside the Gothic church of San Gregorio (now a restoration centre) towards the Campo della Salute, where the dazzle off the water and the white stone of the Salute can give the eyeballs quite a jolt after the gloom of the tunnel.

The Salute is open daily 8am–noon & 3–5pm.

In 1630–31 Venice was devastated by a plague which exterminated nearly 95,000 of the lagoon's population – one person in three. In October 1630 the Senate decreed that a new church would be dedicated to Mary if the city were saved, and the result was the **Salute** (*salute* meaning "health"), or Santa Maria della Salute, to use its full title. Resting on a platform of over 100,000 wooden piles, the Salute took half a century to build; its architect, **Baldessare Longhena**, was only 26 years old when his proposal was accepted. He lived just long enough to see it finished – he died in 1682, one year after completion.

Each year on November 21 (the feast of the Presentation of the Virgin) the Signoria processed from San Marco to the Salute for a service of thanksgiving, crossing the Canal Grande on a pontoon bridge laid from Santa Maria del Giglio. The Festa della Madonna della Salute is still a major event on the Venetian calendar, with thousands of people making their way over the water in the course of the day to pray for, or give thanks for, their health.

The form of the Salute owes much to the plan of Palladio's Redentore – the obvious model for a dramatically sited votive church – and to the repertoire of Marian symbolism. The octagonal plan and eight facades allude to the eight-pointed Marian star for example, while the huge dome represents Mary's crown and the centralised plan is a conventional symbol of the Virgin's womb. Its decorative details are saturated with coded references: the inscription in the centre of the mosaic floor, "Unde Origo, Inde Salus" (From the Origins came Salvation) refers to the coincidence of Mary's feast day and the legendary date of Venice's foundation – March 25, 421; the Marian rosary is evoked by the encircling roses.

Eastern Dorsoduro

Less arcane symbolism is at work on the **high altar**, where the Virgin and Child rescue Venice (kneeling woman) from the plague (old woman); in attendance are Saint Mark and Saint Lorenzo Giustiniani, first Patriarch of Venice. The Byzantine painting, a little uneasy in this Baroque opulence, was brought to Venice in 1672 by Francesco Morosini, never a man to resist the opportunity for a bit of state-sanctioned theft.

For more on Francesco Morosini, see p.81.

The most notable paintings in the Salute are the **Titian** pieces brought from the suppressed church of Santo Spirito in 1656, and now displayed in the sacristy (L1000): an early altarpiece of *St Mark Enthroned with SS. Cosmas, Damian, Sebastian and Roch* (the plague saints), three violent ceiling paintings of *David and Goliath*, *Abraham and Isaac* and *Cain and Abel* (1540s), and eight late *tondi* of the Doctors of the Church (Jerome, Augustine, Gregory and Ambrose) and the Evangelists. Tintoretto has included himself in the dramatis personae of his *Marriage at Cana* (1561) – he's the first Apostle on the left. Nearby is a fine *Madonna* by Palma il Vecchio, one of the sixteenth century's more placid souls.

The Manfrediana and the Dogana di Mare

Longhena was also the architect of the **Seminario Patriarcale**, within which lurks one of the city's more ramshackle museums. The collection of tombstones and sculptural pieces around the cloister, many of them trawled from suppressed religious foundations, was thrown together in the early years of the nineteenth century; it was augmented soon after by the **Pinacoteca Manfrediana**, a motley collection of artworks incorporating items as diverse as paintings by Antonio Vivarini and Paolo Veronese, and portrait busts by Alessandro Vittoria, Gian'Lorenzo Bernini and Antonio Canova. It's years since the museum was last opened to the public on a regular basis, but if you give them a call (☎522.5558) it might be possible to arrange a visit.

On the point where the Canal Grande and the Giudecca canal merge stands the **Dogana di Mare** (Customs House), another late seventeenth-century building. The figure which swivels in the wind on top of the Dogana's gold ball is said by most to represent Fortune, though others identify it as Justice. From the tip of Dorsoduro, the Punta della Dogana, is one of the city's great panoramas.

Along the Záttere

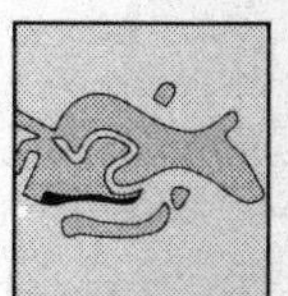

Known collectively as the **Záttere**, the sequence of waterfront pavements between the Punta della Dogana and the Stazione Maríttima are now a popular place for a stroll or an *al fresco* pizza, but were formerly the place where most of the bulky goods coming into Venice were unloaded onto floating rafts called *záttere*. A fair quantity of cargo was carted into the state-run and highly lucrative

Magazzini del Sale (Salt Warehouses), the vast low structure near the Punta della Dogana. In the tenth century the Venetians established a regional monopoly in salt production by destroying the rival town of Comacchio, near the Po delta; some 44,000 tons of salt, most of it made in salt pans near Chioggia, could be stored in this one building, a stock-pile that represented at its peak nearly ten percent of the state's income. It's now a boathouse.

The Gesuati to San Trovaso

The Gesuati is open Mon–Sat 8–10am & noon–6.30pm, Sun 8am–6.30pm.

There's an appealing mix of architectural exteriors on the eastern reaches of the Záttere: the fifteenth-century facade of **Spirito Santo** church, the pink **Casa degli Incurabili** (once one of Venice's four main hospitals, now a children's home), and the Veneto-Byzantine church of **Sant'Agnese**, begun in the twelfth century but much remodelled since then. However, the first building to break your stride for is the church of the **Gesuati** or Santa Maria del Rosario. Built in 1726–43, this was the first church designed by **Giorgio Massari**, an architect whose work combines Rococo preciousness with a more robust classicism – here his creation forms a sort of counterpoint to the Redentore, over the water. He often worked with **Giambattista Tiepolo**, who painted the Gesuati's three ceiling panels of *Scenes from the Life of St Dominic* (1737–39) and the first altarpiece on the right, *The Madonna and Child with SS. Catherine of Siena, Rose and Agnes* (c.1740).

Santa Maria della Visitazione, a couple of doors down, is entered through the gateway of the attached educational institute; the only part of the interior as attractive as its Lombardesque facade is the sixteenth-century **ceiling**, with panels painted by Umbrian artists. The lion's-mouth letter box to the right of the facade was for the use of residents with complaints relating to health and sanitation; a complaint sent to the authorities in 1498 resulted in punishment for tradesmen who had sold oil which was full of "immonditie e sporchezi" (filth and dirt) – syphilitic patients had been immersed in it as a cure.

San Trovaso is open Mon–Sat 8–11am & 4–6pm, Sun 8.30am–6.30pm.

For more on the the Nicolotti and the Castellani see p.96.

Don't bother consulting your dictionary of saints for the dedicatee of **San Trovaso** church – the name's a baffling dialect version of Santi Gervasio e Protasio. Since its tenth-century foundation the church has had a chequered history, falling down once, and twice being destroyed by fire; this is the fourth incarnation, built in 1584–1657. There are two facades, one at the traditional "west" end, the other on the "south" side – legend says that this church was the only neutral ground between the Nicolotti and the Castellani factions, who celebrated intermarriages and other services here, but entered and departed by separate doors. It's a large dark church, best visited in the morning if you want a decent view of its pictures. **Tintoretto**'s last works, both of which were finished by his son Domenico and other assistants, hang on each side of the choir: *The*

Gondolas

Gondolas may be far less numerous than they used to be (a total of 10,000 operated on the canals of sixteenth-century Venice) but the tourist industry ensures steady employment for a few *squeri*, as the gondola yards are called. A display in the Museo Storico Navale takes you through the construction of a gondola, but no abstract demonstration can equal the fascination of a working yard, and the most public one in Venice is the **squero di San Trovaso**, just on the Záttere side of San Trovaso church. Another *squero* is tucked away on the Rio dell'Avogaria, a short distance west of here.

The earliest mention of a gondola is in a decree of 1094, but the vessel of that period bore little resemblance to today's streamlined thoroughbred. As late as the thirteenth century the gondola was a twelve-oared beast with an iron beak – an adornment that evolved into the saw-toothed projection called the **ferro**, which fronts the modern gondola. (The precise significance of the *ferro*'s shape is unclear – traditon has it that the six main prongs symbolise the six *sestieri*, with the backward-facing prong representing La Giudecca.) Over the next two centuries the gondola shrank to something near its present dimensions, developed multicoloured coverings and sprouted the little chair on carved legs that it still carries. The gondola's distinctive oarlock, an elaborately convoluted lump of walnut or pear wood known as a **forcola**, which permits the long oar to be used in eight different positions, reached its definitive form at this time too.

By the sixteenth century the gondola had become a mode of social ostentation, with gilded prows, fantastically upholstered *felzi* (cabins), cushions of satin and silk, and hulls decked out with a profusion of embroidery, carvings and flowers. Sumptuary laws were introduced to quash this aquatic one-upmanship, and though some of them had little effect, one of them changed the gondola's appearance for good – since an edict of 1562 gondolas have been uniformly black, a livery which prompted Shelley to compare them to "moths of which a coffin might have been the chrysalis".

There's been little alteration in the gondola's dimensions and contruction since the end of the seventeenth century: the only significant changes have been adjustments of the gondola's asymmetric line to compensate for the weight of the gondolier – a characteristic that's particularly noticeable when you see the things out of water. All gondolas are 10.87 metres long and 1.42 metres wide at their broadest point, and are assembled from seasoned mahogany, elm, oak, lime, walnut, fir, cherry and larch. Each *squero* turns out only about four new gondolas a year, at a cost of around twenty million lire; most are destined for the private lakes of foreign millionaires.

Adoration of the Magi and *The Expulsion from the Temple* (1594). In the chapel right of the altar is *St Crysogonus on Horseback* by Michele Giambono (c.1450), Venice's main practitioner of the International Gothic style; and next to the south door you'll find a marble altar-front carved with angels – dated around 1470, it's one of the first Renaissance low reliefs produced in Venice.

San Sebastiano and beyond

At the end of the Záttere the barred gates of the Stazione Marittima deflect you away from the waterfront and towards the church of **San Sebastiano**. The parish church of **Paolo Veronese**, it contains a group of resplendent paintings by him that gives it a place in his career comparable to that of San Rocco in the career of Tintoretto. But in contrast to San Rocco, this is the most dejected of Venice's first-rank cultural monuments. A terse note on the door explains that the church can't afford a custodian (opening hours are thus a matter of guesswork), and the interior is in a perpetual state of disarray, with dusty tarpaulins and bits of scaffolding occupying various corners.

Veronese was still in his twenties when, thanks largely to his contacts with the Verona-born prior of San Samuele, he was asked to paint the ceiling of the **sacristy** with a *Coronation of the Virgin* and the *Four Evangelists* (1555); once that commission had been carried out, he decorated the **nave ceiling** with *Scenes from the Life of St Esther*. His next project, the dome of the chancel, was later destroyed, but the sequence he and his brother Benedetto then painted on the walls of the church and the nun's choir at the end of the 1550s has survived in pretty good shape. In the following decade he executed the last of the pictures – those around the **high altar** and on the **organ shutters**. Other riches include a late **Titian** of *St Nicholas* (on the right as you enter), and the early sixteenth-century majolica pavement in the chapel to the left of the chancel – in front of which is Veronese's tomb slab.

Angelo Raffaele

Angelo Raffaele is open daily 7.30am–noon & 5–6pm.

Across the campo, the seventeenth-century church of **Angelo Raffaele** – so dilapidated it seems to be held upright by the two huge war memorials on the canal facade – has an organ loft decorated by one or other of the **Guardi** brothers (nobody's sure which). In the campo behind the church is a well-head built from the bequest of Marco Arian, who died of the Black Death in 1348, an outbreak which he blamed on contaminated water. The **Palazzo Arian**, on the opposite bank of the canal, was built in the second half of that century and is adorned by one of the finest and earliest Gothic windows in Venice.

San Nicolò dei Mendicoli

San Nicolò dei Mendicoli is open daily 10am–noon & 4.30–7.30pm.

Although it's located on the edge of the city, the church of **San Nicolò dei Mendicoli** is one of Venice's oldest churches, traditionally predated only by San Giacomo di Rialto. It gave its name to the *Nicolotti*, a working-class faction whose frequently violent rivalry with the equivalent faction from the other side of the city – the *Castellani*, from San Pietro di Castello – added a bit of spice to life from the fourteenth century right down to the nineteenth. The titular head of the *Nicolotti* was the so-called *Gastaldo* or the *Doge dei Nicolotti*, whose election by the parishioners was followed by a ceremonial greeting from the Republic's doge.

Founded in the seventh century, San Nicolò dei Mendicoli has been rebuilt and altered at various times, and was last restored by Venice in Peril in the 1970s. (If you've seen Nic Roeg's *Don't Look Now*, the church might seem familiar – this was the church that Donald Sutherland was restoring.) Its Veneto-Byzantine campanile dates from the end of the twelfth century, but more intriguing is the fifteenth-century porch, a type of construction once common in Venice and often used as makeshift accommodation for penurious nuns. The oldest parts of the **interior** – whose floor is a good foot below the level of the canals – are the twelfth-century apse and nave columns; the large wooden statue of Saint Nicholas is a mid-fifteenth-century piece, possibly from the workshop of Bartolomeo Bon.

The church of **Santa Teresa**, on the other side of the canal, is now permanently closed, and there's no reason to set foot on the island on which it stands, as it's a grim zone of warehouses, docks and gasometers.

Northern Dorsoduro

The vast, elongated **Campo Santa Margherita**, ringed by houses that date back as far as the fourteenth century, is the social heart of Dorsoduro, many of whose inhabitants come here daily to stock up at the market stalls. Students from the nearby university hang out in the campo's bars, and the place as a whole – with its herbalist, wholefood store and handpainted clothes shop – has a vaguely alternative feel. The church that gives the campo its name was closed in 1810, for a while functioned as a cinema, and is now being restored; the dragons that feature so prominently in the decorative stonework on and around the church relate to the legend of Saint Margaret, who emerged unscathed after the dragon that had swallowed her exploded. Isolated at the fish stall end of the campo stands the **Scuola dei Varotari** (tanners' guild), bearing an eroded relief of the Madonna with members of the *scuola*.

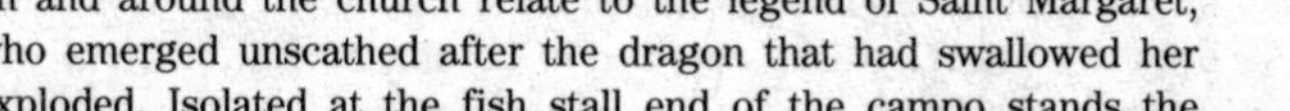

The Carmini and around

Just off Campo Santa Margherita's southwest tip is the **Scuola Grande dei Carmini**, built in the 1660s, probably to plans by Longhena, and effectively a showcase for the art of **Giambattista Tiepolo**, who in the 1740s painted the ceiling of the upstairs hall. *St Simon Stock Receiving the Scapular from the Madonna* is the central panel; the four *Virtues* in the corners were such a hit with Tiepolo's clients that he was instantly granted membership of the Scuola.

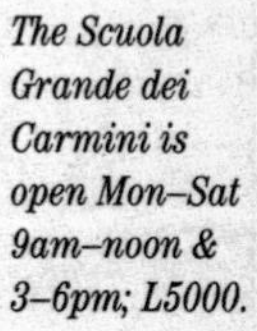

The Scuola Grande dei Carmini is open Mon–Sat 9am–noon & 3–6pm; L5000.

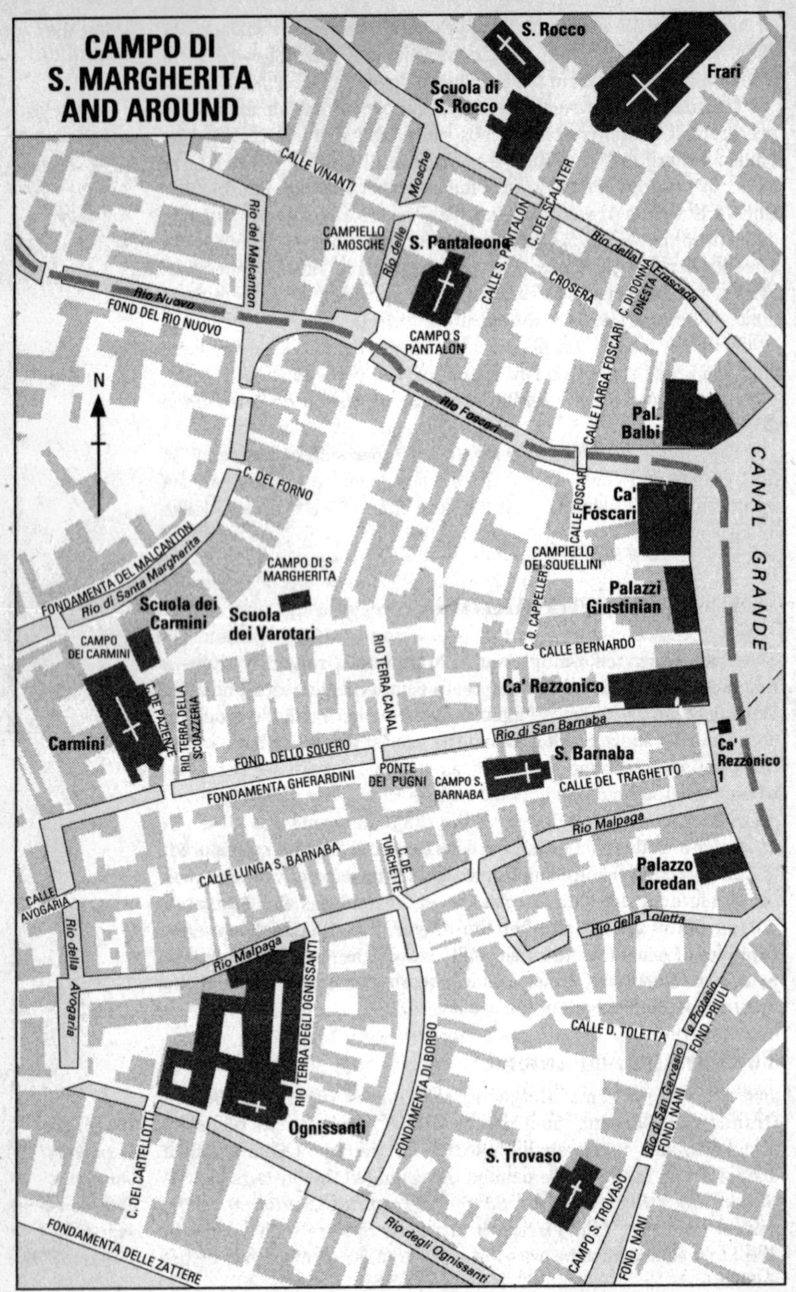
CAMPO DI
S. MARGHERITA
AND AROUND
S. Rocco
Frari
Scuola di
S. Rocco
CALLE VINANTI
Mosche
Rio del Malcanton
CAMPIELLO
D. MOSCHE
Rio delle
S. Pantaleone
CALLE S. PANTALON
C. DEL SCALATER
Rio della Frescada
CROSERA
C. DI DONNA ONESTA
Rio Nuovo
FOND DEL RIO NUOVO
CAMPO S
PANTALON
CALLE LARGA FOSCARI
N
Rio Foscari
Pal.
Balbi
CANAL GRANDE
C. DEL FORNO
CALLE FOSCARI
Ca'
Fóscari
CAMPIELLO
DEI SQUELLINI
FONDAMENTA DEL MALCANTON
Rio di Santa Margherita
CAMPO DI S
MARGHERITA
Palazzi
Giustinian
Scuola dei
Carmini
Scuola
dei Varotari
C. D. CAPPELLER
CAMPO
DEI CARMINI
RIO TERRA CANAL
CALLE BERNARDO
Ca' Rezzonico
C. DE PAZIENZE
RIO TERRA DELLA SCOAZZERIA
Carmini
Rio di San Barnaba
FOND. DELLO SQUERO
S. Barnaba
Ca'
Rezzonico
1
PONTE
DEI PUGNI
CAMPO S.
BARNABA
FONDAMENTA GHERARDINI
CALLE DEL TRAGHETTO
Rio Malpaga
C. DE
TURCHETTE
CALLE LUNGA S. BARNABA
Palazzo
Loredan
CALLE
AVOGARIA
Rio della Avogaria
Rio della Toletta
Rio Malpaga
RIO TERRA DEGLI OGNISSANTI
e Protasio
FOND. PRIULI
CALLE D. TOLETTA
Rio di San Gervasio
FOND. NANI
FONDAMENTA DI BORGO
Ognissanti
S. Trovaso
C. DEI CARTELLOTTI
CAMPO S. TROVASO
FOND. NANI
Rio degli Ognissanti
FONDAMENTA DELLE ZATTERE

The **Carmini** church is a collage of architectural styles, with a sixteenth-century facade, a Gothic side doorway which preserves several Byzantine fragments, and a fourteenth-century basilican interior. A dull series of Baroque paintings illustrating the history of the Carmelite order covers a lot of space inside, but the second altar on the right has a *Nativity* by Cima da Conegliano (before 1510), and Lorenzo Lotto's *St Nicholas of Bari* (1529) hangs on the opposite side of the nave.

Northern Dorsoduro

The Carmini church is open daily 7.30am–noon & 4.30–7pm.

The most imposing building on Fondamenta del Soccorso (leading from Campo dei Carmini towards Angelo Raffaele) is the **Palazzo Zenobio**, built in the late seventeenth century when the Zenobio family were among the richest in Venice. It's been an Armenian college since 1850, but visitors are sometimes allowed to see the ballroom, one of the richest eighteenth-century interiors in Venice. In the late sixteenth century a home for prostitutes who wanted to get off the game was set up at no. 2590 – the chapel of Santa Maria del Soccorso – by **Veronica Franco**, a renowned ex-courtesan who was as famous for her poetry and her artistic salon as she was for her sexual allure; both Michel de Montaigne and King Henry III of France were grateful recipients of samples of her literary output.

(**Between here and Piazzale Roma** lies a predominantly residential area that constitutes the largest completely uninteresting sector of central Venice. Santa Maria Maggiore, the only church before you reach the bus station, is now part of the city **prison**. The fifteenth-century church of **Sant'Andrea della Zirada**, in the lee of the Piazzale's multi-storey car park, is closed for restoration and only has its Baroque altar to recommend it anyway; and the diminutive Neoclassical **Nome di Gesù**, cringing underneath the flyover, has absolutely nothing going for it.)

San Barnaba

Cutting down the side of the Carmini church takes you over the Rio di San Barnaba, along which a *fondamenta* runs to San Barnaba. Just before the end of the *fondamenta* you pass the **Ponte dei Pugni**, the main link between San Barnaba and Santa Margherita, and one of several bridges with this name. Originally built without parapets, they were the sites of mass fist-fights between the *Castellani* and *Nicolotti*; this one is inset with marble footprints marking the starting positions. By the early eighteenth century these punch-ups had become so violent that they were finally banned, and less bloody forms of competition, such as regattas, were encouraged instead. Pugilists have now been replaced by tourists taking shots of the photogenic San Barnaba grocery barge moored at the foot of the bridge.

The damp-ridden **San Barnaba** church, built in 1749, has a small *Holy Family* attributed to Veronese and a trompe l'oeil ceiling painting of *St Barnabas in Glory* by Constantino Cedini, a follower of Tiepolo. At the time of the church's construction the parish was

San Barnaba is open daily 7.30am–noon & 4.30–7pm.

swarming with so-called *Barnabotti*, impoverished noble families who moved into the area's cheap lodgings to eke out their meagre incomes. Forbidden as members of the aristocracy to practise a craft or run a shop, some of the *Barnabotti* supported themselves by selling their votes to the mightier families in the Maggior Consiglio, while others resigned themselves to subsistence on a paltry state dole. Visitors to the city often remarked on the incongruous sight of its silk-clad beggars – the nobility of Venice were obliged to wear silk, regardless of their ability to pay for such finery.

The Ca' Rezzonico

The Ca' Rezzonico is open 9am–7pm; closed Fri; L5000.

The eighteenth century, the period of Venice's political senility and moral degeneration, was also the period of its last grand flourish in the visual and decorative arts, so it's not entirely surprising that the city's most opulent museum should be the **Museo del Settecento Veneziano** – the Museum of the Venetian Eighteenth Century. Culled from dozens of different buildings but arranged so that you seem to be walking through the best-appointed palace in town, rather than through an array of exhibits, the collection spreads through most of the enormous **Ca' Rezzonico**, which the city authorities bought in 1934 specifically as a home for the museum.

Most of the decorations and furnishings in the Ca' Rezzonico are genuine items, and where originals weren't available the eighteenth-century ambience has been preserved by using almost indistinguishable modern reproductions. Sumptuary laws in Venice restricted the quantities of silk, brocade and tapestry that could be draped around a house, so legions of painters, stuccoists, cabinetmakers and other such applied artists were employed to fanfare the wealth of their patrons to the world. The work they produced is certainly not to everyone's taste, but even if you find most of the museum's contents frivolous or grotesque, the frescoes by the Tiepolo family and Pietro Longhi's affectionate Venetian scenes should justify the entrance fee.

A man in constant demand in the early part of the century was the Belluno sculptor-cum-woodcarver **Andrea Brustolon**, much of whose output consisted of wildly elaborated pieces of furniture. A few of his pieces are displayed in the chandeliered ballroom at the top of the entrance staircase, and elsewhere on this floor there's an entire roomful of them, including the *Allegory of Strength* console. Featuring Hercules underneath, two river gods holding four vases and a fifth vase held up by three black slaves in chains, this is a creation that makes you marvel at the craftsmanship and wince at the ends to which it was used.

The less fervid imaginations of **Giambattista Tiepolo** and his son **Giandomenico** are introduced in room 2 with the ceiling fresco celebrating Ludovico Rezzonico's marriage into the hugely powerful Savorgnan family in 1758. This was quite a year for the Rezzonico clan, as it also brought the election of Carlo Rezzonico as Pope Clement XIII; the son of the man who bought the uncompleted palace and finished its construction, Carlo the pontiff was notorious both for his rampant nepotism and for his prudery – he insisted that the Vatican's antique nude statuary be made more modest by the judicious application of fig leaves. Two other Tiepolo ceilings enliven the rooms overlooking the Canal Grande on each side of the main *portego* (an *Allegory of Merit* by Giambattista and Giandomenico, and *Nobility and Virtue Triumphing over Perfidy*, a solo effort by the father), but you have to wait until the last suite of rooms (on the second floor) to see the museum's most engaging Tiepolo productions – Giandomenico's sequence of **frescoes from the Villa Zianigo** near Mestre, the Tiepolo family home. With the exception of the pieces from the villa's chapel, which date from 1749, the frescoes were painted towards the end of the century, at a time when their satirical playfulness was going out of fashion. *The New World* shows a crowd turned out in its best attire to watch a Sunday peepshow; another room is devoted to the antics of *Pulchinello*, the ancestor of our Mr Punch; and typically good-humoured centaurs and satyrs lark around on nearby walls.

Rosalba Carriera's pastels get a good area of wall space to themselves on the first floor and she crops up again in the more intimate rooms of the second floor, where the furnishings include a full suite of green and gold lacquer pieces – one of the finest surviving examples of Venetian chinoiserie. The only two canal views by **Canaletto** on show in public galleries in Venice are on this storey, as are Francesco Guardi's scenes of high society in the parlour of San Zaccaria's convent and the gambling rooms of the Ridotto. Technically less adroit than Guardi's work, **Pietro Longhi**'s wide-ranging paintings of life in eighteenth-century Venice – including a version of the famous *Rhinoceros* – have more than enough curiosity value to make up for their shortcomings in execution. Visitors at Carnevale time will recognise several of the festival's components in the Longhi room: the beak-like *volto* masks, for example, and the little doughnuts called *frittelle*, an essential part of the Carnevale scene.

The low-ceilinged rooms of the third floor contain yet more Longhi paintings, but the main point of clambering upstairs is to see the **pharmacy** and **puppet theatre**. A sequence of wood-panelled rooms full of the appropriate furniture, ceramic jars and glass bottles, the pharmacy has to be viewed through windows, rather like peering into the set of a Longhi picture. The puppets are fairly unremarkable specimens, each about one foot high, but their very ordinariness makes their survival remarkable in itself.

From the Ca' Rezzonico, the quickest route up to the Rialto takes you across the herringbone-patterned pavement of the Campiello dei Squellini, past the entrance to the main university building and over the Rio Fóscari – whereupon you're in the *San Polo* section.

For the background to the university building – the Ca' Fóscari – and the neighbouring Palazzi Giustinian, see p.187.

Chapter 4

San Polo

Bounded on one side by the Rio Nuovo–Rio di Ca' Fóscari (the waterways dug under Mussolini's instructions from Piazzale Roma to the Volta del Canal) and on the others by the upper loop of the Canal Grande, the area covered by this chapter is composed of the entire **San Polo** *sestiere*, the greater part of the *sestiere* of Santa Croce and a couple of slivers of Dorsoduro. This jigsaw is not as baffling as it at first appears. There are two main routes through the district, each following approximately the curve of the Canal Grande – one runs between the Rialto and the Scalzi bridge, the other takes you in the opposite direction from the Rialto, down towards the Accademia. Virtually all the essential sights lie on, or just off, one of these two routes, and once you've become familiar with these the exploration of the streets and squares between them can be attempted with only a minimal risk of feeling that you'll never see friends and family again. Wherever you are in this area, you cannot be more than a couple of minutes' well-navigated walk from one of the two roads to the Rialto.

As far as the day-to-day life of Venice is concerned, the focal points of the district are the sociable open space of **Campo San Polo** and the **Rialto** area, once the commercial heart of the Republic and still the home of a **market** that's famous far beyond the boundaries of the city. The bustle of the stalls and the unspoilt bars used by the porters are a good antidote to cultural overload. Nobody, however, should miss the extraordinary pair of buildings in the southern part of San Polo: the colossal Gothic church of the **Frari**, embellished with three of Venice's finest altarpieces, and the **Scuola Grande di San Rocco**, decorated with an unforgettable cycle of paintings by Tintoretto.

In the northern part of the district, Venice's **modern art, oriental and natural history museums** are clustered together on the bank of the Canal Grande – the first two sharing one of the city's most magnificent palaces and the third installed in the former headquarters of the Turkish merchants. As ever, numerous treasures are also scattered among the minor churches – for example in **San**

Cassiano, **San Simeone Grande** and **San Pantaleone**. Lastly, if you're in search of a spot in which to sit for an hour and just watch the world go by, head for the **Campo San Giacomo dell'Orio**, one of Venice's better-kept secrets.

From the Rialto to the Ponte degli Scalzi

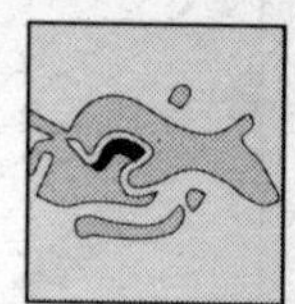

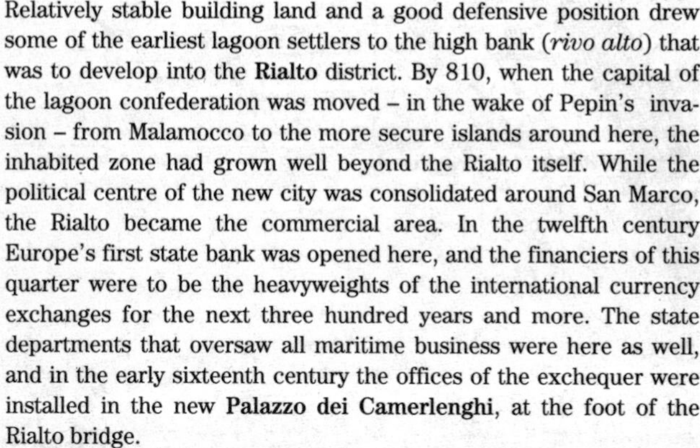

Relatively stable building land and a good defensive position drew some of the earliest lagoon settlers to the high bank (*rivo alto*) that was to develop into the **Rialto** district. By 810, when the capital of the lagoon confederation was moved – in the wake of Pepin's invasion – from Malamocco to the more secure islands around here, the inhabited zone had grown well beyond the Rialto itself. While the political centre of the new city was consolidated around San Marco, the Rialto became the commercial area. In the twelfth century Europe's first state bank was opened here, and the financiers of this quarter were to be the heavyweights of the international currency exchanges for the next three hundred years and more. The state departments that oversaw all maritime business were here as well, and in the early sixteenth century the offices of the exchequer were installed in the new **Palazzo dei Camerlenghi**, at the foot of the Rialto bridge.

The connection between wealth and moral turpitude was exemplified by the Rialto, which was almost as famous for its fleshpots as for its cashboxes. A sixteenth-century survey showed that there were about 3,000 patrician women in the city, but well over 11,000 prostitutes, the majority of them based in the banking quarter. One Rialto brothel, the *Casteletto*, was especially esteemed for the literary, musical and sexual talents of its staff, and a perennial Venetian bestseller was the *Catalogue of the Chief and Most Renowned Courtesans of Venice*, a directory that told you everything you needed to know, right down to prices. If Thomas Coryat's report of 1608 is anything to go by, the courtesans were seen in some quarters as the city's main attraction – "So infinite are the allurements of these amorous Calypsoes that the fame of them hath drawn many to Venice from some of the remotest parts of Christendome."

The Market

It was through the **markets of the Rialto** that Venice earned its reputation as the bazaar of Europe. Virtually anything could be bought or sold here: Italian fabrics, precious stones, silver plate and gold jewellery, spices and dyes from the Orient. Trading had been going on here for over 400 years when, in the winter of 1514, a fire destroyed everything in the area except the church. (Most of the wells and canals were frozen solid, so the blaze burned virtually

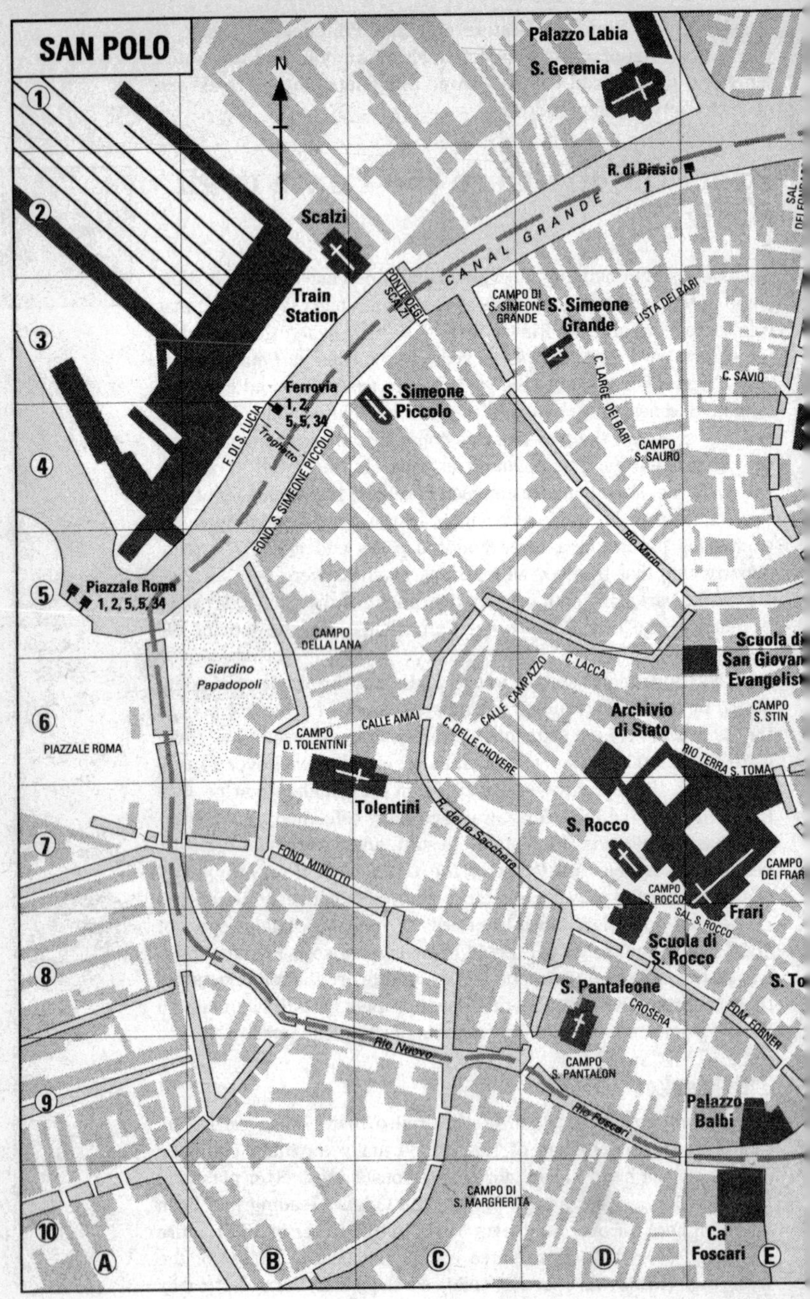
SAN POLO
N
Palazzo Labia
S. Geremia
R. di Biasio 1
Scalzi
Train Station
CANAL GRANDE
PONTE DEGLI SCALZI
CAMPO DI S. SIMEONE GRANDE
S. Simeone Grande
LISTA DEI BARI
C. LARGA DEI BARI
C. SAVIO
Ferrovia 1, 2, 5, 5, 34
S. Simeone Piccolo
F. DI S. LUCIA
Traghetto
FOND. S. SIMEONE PICCOLO
CAMPO S. SAURO
Rio Marin
Piazzale Roma 1, 2, 5, 5, 34
CAMPO DELLA LANA
Giardino Papadopoli
C. LACCA
CALLE CAMPAZZO
Scuola di San Giovan Evangelist
Archivio di Stato
CAMPO S. STIN
CAMPO D. TOLENTINI
CALLE AMAI
C. DELLE CHOVERE
PIAZZALE ROMA
RIO TERRA S. TOMA
Tolentini
R. de la Sacchera
S. Rocco
FOND. MINOTTO
CAMPO DEI FRARI
CAMPO S. ROCCO
Frari
SAL. S. ROCCO
Scuola di S. Rocco
S. Pantaleone
CROSERA
S. To
FDM. FORNER
Rio Nuovo
CAMPO S. PANTALON
Rio Foscari
Palazzo Balbi
CAMPO DI S. MARGHERITA
Ca' Foscari
1
2
3
4
5
6
7
8
9
10
A
B
C
D
E

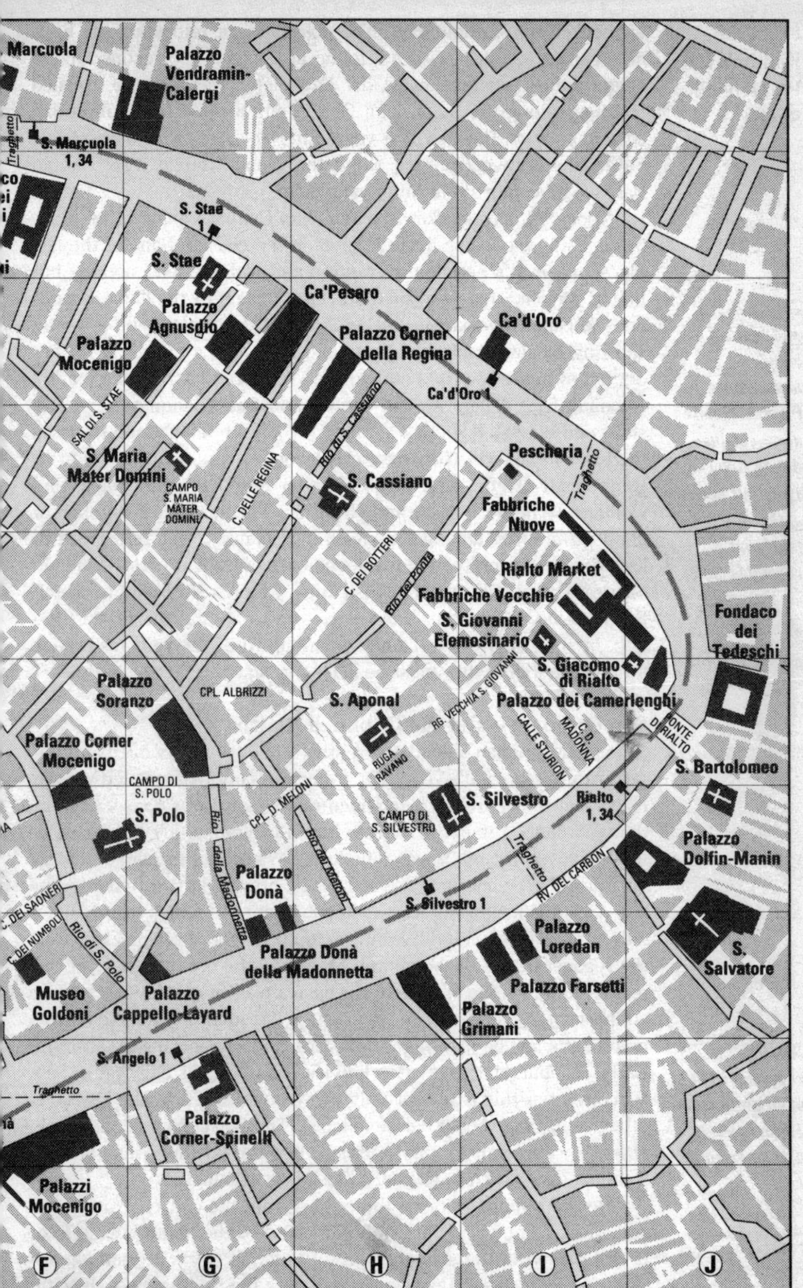

Marcuola
Palazzo Vendramin-Calergi
Traghetto
S. Marcuola 1, 34
S. Stae 1
S. Stae
Palazzo Agnusdio
Ca'Pesaro
Palazzo Mocenigo
Palazzo Corner della Regina
Ca'd'Oro
Ca'd'Oro 1
SAL DI S. STAE
Rio di S. Cassiano
S. Maria Mater Domini
CAMPO S. MARIA MATER DOMINI
C. DELLE REGINA
Pescheria
Traghetto
S. Cassiano
Fabbriche Nuove
C. DEI BOTTERI
Rio del Ponte
Rialto Market
Fabbriche Vecchie
S. Giovanni Elemosinario
Fondaco dei Tedeschi
S. Giacomo di Rialto
Palazzo Soranzo
CPL. ALBRIZZI
S. Aponal
RG. VECCHIA S. GIOVANNI
Palazzo dei Camerlenghi
CALLE STURION
C. D. MADONNA
PONTE DI RIALTO
Palazzo Corner Mocenigo
RUGA RAVANO
S. Bartolomeo
CAMPO DI S. POLO
CPL. D. MELONI
CAMPO DI S. SILVESTRO
S. Silvestro
Rialto 1, 34
S. Polo
Rio della Madonnetta
Rio dei Meloni
Traghetto
Palazzo Dolfin-Manin
Palazzo Donà
RV. DEL CARBON
S. Silvestro 1
C. DEI SAONERI
C. DEI NUMBOLI
Rio di S. Polo
Palazzo Loredan
S. Salvatore
Palazzo Donà della Madonnetta
Palazzo Farsetti
Museo Goldoni
Palazzo Cappello-Layard
Palazzo Grimani
S. Angelo 1
Traghetto
Palazzo Corner-Spinelli
Palazzi Mocenigo
F
G
H
I
J

unchecked for a whole day.) The possibility of relocating the business centre was discussed but found little favour, so reconstruction began almost straight away: the **Fabbriche Vecchie** (the arcaded buildings along the Ruga degli Orefici and around the Campo San Giacomo) were finished five years after the fire, with Sansovino's **Fabbriche Nuove** (running along the Canal Grande from Campo Battisti) following about thirty years later.

The Pescheria and most of the larger wholesalers at the Rialto close down for the day at around 1pm, but many of the smaller fruit and vegetable stalls keep normal shop hours.

Today's Rialto market is tamer than that of Venice at its peak, but it's still one of the liveliest spots in the city, and one of the few places where it's possible to stand in a crowd and hear nothing but Italian spoken. There's a shoal of trinket sellers by the church, gathered to catch the tourists as they spill off the bridge, and a strong showing of glass junk, handbags and "Venezia" sweatshirts further on, but swing to the right and you're in the true heart of the market – mainly fruit sellers around the **Campo San Giacomo**, vegetable stalls and butcher's shops as you go through to the **Campo Battisti**, then the **Pescheria** (fish market) beyond. Around the junction of **Ruga degli Orefici** and **Ruga Vecchia San Giovanni** you'll find wonderful cheese kiosks, and the Ruga Vecchia has a number of good *alimentari* among the kitsch merchants. If you're in need of liquid refreshment, the old-fashioned bars of Calle do Mori–Calle do Spade (by San Giovanni Elemosinario), which keep hours to match the working day of the Rialto porters, are among the best in the city. In short, if you can't find something to excite your taste buds around the Rialto, they must be in a sorry state.

San Giacomo – and the Gobbo di Rialto

A popular Venetian legend asserts that the city was founded at noon on Friday, March 25, 421 AD; from the same legend derives the claim that the church of **San Giacomo di Rialto** was consecrated in that year, and is thus **the oldest church in Venice**. It might actually be the oldest, though it was rebuilt in 1071, about the same time as San Marco's reconstruction. Parts of the present structure date from this period – the interior's six columns of ancient Greek marble have eleventh-century Veneto-Byzantine capitals – and it seems likely that the reconstruction of the church prompted the establishment of the market here. On the outside of the apse a twelfth-century inscription addresses the merchants of the Rialto – "Around this temple let the merchant's law be just, his weights true, and his promises faithful." Early Venetian churches often had lean-to porticoes like that of San Giacomo, but this is one of only two examples left in the city (the other being San Nicolò dei Mendicoli). The inaccuracy of the clock above – a fifteenth-century addition, like the portico – has been a standing joke in Venice since the day it was installed.

San Giacomo is supposed to be open daily from 10am to noon, and sometimes is.

On the opposite side of the campo from the church crouches a stone figure known as the **Gobbo di Rialto** or the Rialto hunchback. It was carved in the sixteenth century and supports a granite platform from which state proclamations were read simultaneously with their announcement from the Pietra del Bando, beside San Marco; it had another role as well – certain wrongdoers were sentenced to run the gauntlet, stark naked, from the Piazza to the Gobbo.

From the Rialto to the Ponte degli Scalzi

From San Giovanni Elemosinario to the Ca' Pésaro

Once past the Pescheria, you're into a district which quickly becomes labyrinthine even by Venetian standards. A stroll between the Rio delle Beccarie and the Rio di San Zan Degolà will satisfy any addict of the picturesque – you cannot walk for more than a couple of minutes without coming across a workshop crammed into a ground-floor room or a garden spilling over a canalside wall.

The barn-like church of **San Cassiano** is a building you're bound to pass as you wander out of the Rialto. The thirteenth-century campanile is the only appealing aspect of the exterior, and the interest of the interior lies mainly with its three paintings by **Tintoretto**: *The Resurrection*, *The Descent into Limbo* and *The Crucifixion* (all 1565–68). The first two have been mauled by restorers, but the third is one of the most startling pictures in Venice – centred on the ladder on which the executioners stand, it's painted as though the observer were lying in the grass at the foot of the Cross.

San Cassiano is open daily 9.45–11.30am & 4.30–7pm; no tourists allowed on Sun.

Campo San Cassiano was the site of the **first public opera house** in the world – it opened in 1637, at the peak of Monteverdi's career. Long into the following century Venice's opera houses were among the most active in Europe; around 500 works received their first performances here in the first half of the eighteenth century.

A sign directs you from the campo over the right-hand bridge towards the Ca' Pésaro, home of the modern art and oriental collections, but before you reach it you'll pass the back of the **Palazzo Corner della Regina**, now the home of the Biennale archives. There's a small selection of works from past shows on display, which you can see after signing in at the desk; access to the Biennale libraries (books, magazines and videos) is at the discretion of the curators, but should be no problem for anyone with an interest.

A diversion down Corte Tiossi from Calle Tiossi brings you to **Santa Maria Mater Domini**, an early sixteenth-century church of disputed authorship – Mauro Coducci and Giovanni Buora are the leading candidates. The rescue of this building is one of Venice in Peril's proudest achievements; now protected by a totally reconstructed roof, the crisp white and grey interior boasts an endearing *Martyrdom of St Christina* by **Vincenzo Catena** (second altar on the right), showing a flight of angels plucking the saint from Lago di Bolsena, into whose waters she had been hurled with a millstone for an anchor. Few works by the elusive Catena have survived, and it is not even certain what he did for a living. He seems to have been a successful spice trader, and thus may have been a businessman who painted for recreation; alternatively he may have been an artist who subsidised himself through commercial dealings – he is mentioned

Santa Maria Mater Domini is open daily 10am–noon & 3–5pm.

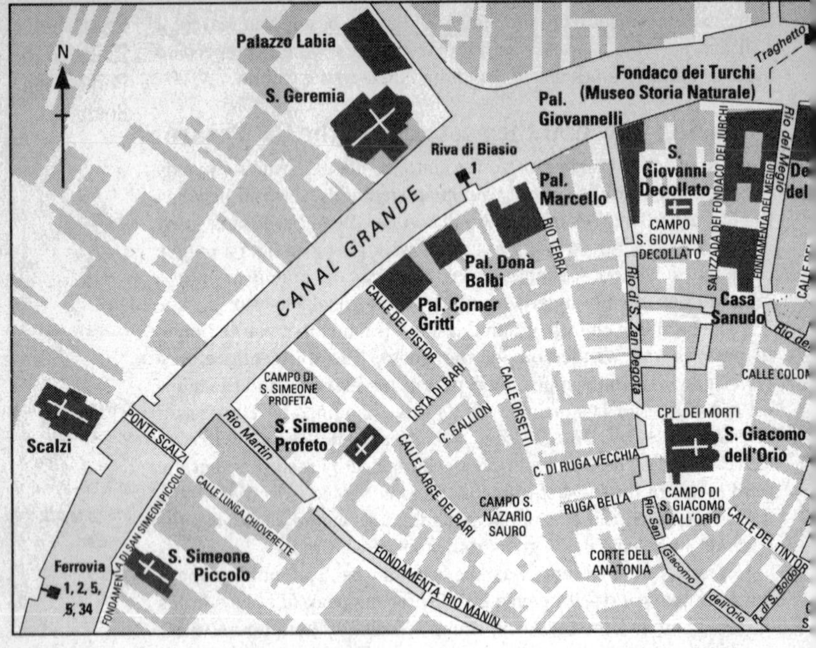

on the reverse of one of Giorgione's paintings as a "colleague". On the opposite side of the church you'll find one of the city's less powerful Tintoretto paintings, a *Discovery of the Cross*.

The small **Campo Santa Maria Mater Domini** would have to be included in any anthology of the hidden delights of Venice; it's a typically Venetian miscellany – a thirteenth-century house (the Casa Zane), a few ramshackle Gothic houses, an assortment of stone reliefs of indeterminate age, a fourteenth-century well-head in the centre, a couple of bars, and an ironsmith's workshop tucked into one corner.

Back at the end of Calle Tiossi, in front of you on the other side of the bridge as you turn right for the Ca' Pésaro, is the late fourteenth-century **Palazzo Agnusdio**, which takes its name not from the family that lived there but from the *patera* of the mystic lamb over the watergate.

The Museo d'Arte Moderna is open Tues–Sun 9am–7pm; L3000.

The **Ca' Pésaro** was bequeathed to the city at the end of the last century by the Duchessa Felicità Bevilacqua La Masa, who stipulated in her will that it should provide studio and exhibition space for impoverished young artists. Subsequent machinations put paid to the Duchess's enlightened plans, and in place of the intended living arts centre the city acquired the **Museo d'Arte Moderna**. Pieces bought from the Biennale formed the foundation of the collection, which consists predominantly of work by Italian artists,

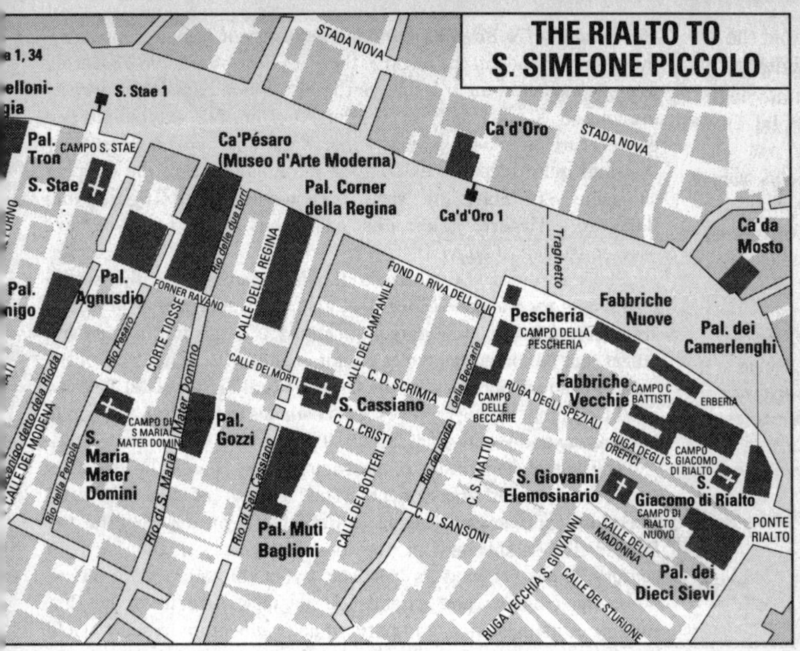

many of whom will be unfamiliar (and not surprisingly, you might think in some cases); the wax sculptures of the nineteenth-century Milanese artist **Medardo Rosso** are the main revelation. Of the major names you'd expect to come across, Klimt, Kandinsky, Matisse and Klee get a look in – but it's not an outstanding selection. The **Museo Orientale**, on the palace's top floor, is built round the hoard of artefacts amassed by the Conte di Bardi during a long Far Eastern voyage in the last century. The jumble of lacquer work, armour, screens, weaponry and so forth is likely to perplex and tire all but the initiated.

The Museo Orientale is open Tues–Sat 9am–2pm, Sun 9am–1pm; L4000.

From San Stae to the Museo di Storia Naturale

Continuing along the line of the Canal Grande from the Ca' Pésaro, Calle Pésaro takes you over the Rio della Rioda, and so to the seventeenth-century church of **San Stae** (a contraction of San Eustachio); its Baroque facade, enlivened by precarious statues, was added around 1710. Repairs to the *marmorino* (pulverised marble) surfaces of the interior have made San Stae as bright as an operating theatre. In the chancel there's a series of paintings from the beginning of the eighteenth century, the pick of which are *The Martyrdom of St James the Great* by Piazzetta (low on the left), *The Liberation of St Peter* by Sebastiano Ricci (same row) and *The*

Martyrdom of St Bartholomew by Giambattista Tiepolo (opposite). In the first chapel on the left side there's a bust of Antonio Foscarini, wrongly executed for treason, as the inscription explains. Normally the church is open daily from 10am to 1pm, but exhibitions and concerts are often held here, so expect variations in the hours.

For the story of Antonio Fóscarini, see p.183.

Until quite recently, exhibitions were also held in the building alongside San Stae, the early seventeenth-century **Scuola dei Battiloro e Tiraoro** (goldsmiths' guild), but it now seems to have been consigned to oblivion.

Halfway down the salizzada flanking San Stae is the seventeenth-century **Palazzo Mocenigo**, the main apartments of which are decorated with late eighteenth-century frescoes by Guarana and others, but the paintings really are for cognoscenti only. Parts of the palazzo are now occupied by the **Centro Studi di Storia del Tessuto e del Costume**, whose archives and costumes are open to the public on Tuesday and Wednesday from 8.30am to 1.30pm.

The Palazzo Mocenigo apartments are open Sat 8.30am–1.30pm; free.

The signposted route to the train station passes the deconsecrated and almost permanently shut church of **San Giovanni Decollato**, or San Zan Degolà in dialect – it means "St John the Beheaded". Established in the opening years of the eleventh century, it has retained its basilican layout through several alterations; the columns and capitals of the nave date from the first century of its existence, and parts of its fragmentary frescoes could be of the same age. Some of the paintings are certainly thirteenth-century, and no other church in Venice has frescoes that predate them. San Giacomo dell' Orio's sacristan might get you in; otherwise you just have to hope that the door is left unlocked during the preparations for the concerts that take place here.

The **Museo di Storia Naturale** is right by the church, in the **Fondaco dei Turchi**. Top-billing exhibits are the remains of a thirty-seven-foot-long ancestor of the crocodile and an Ouranosaurus, both dug up in the Sahara in 1973; of stricter relevance to Venetian life is the display relating to the lagoon's marine life, and a pre-Roman boat dredged from the silt.

The Museo di Storia Naturale is open Tues–Sun 9am–1pm; L8000. For an entry on the building itself, see p.185.

From San Giacomo dell'Orio to San Simeone Piccolo

Unless you've got restless kids to keep quiet, in which case a twelve-metre crocodile could come in handy, your time would be better spent at **San Giacomo dell'Orio**, a couple of minutes from the Fondaco dei Turchi. Standing in a shaded campo which, despite its size, you could easily miss if you weren't looking for it, the church has a fascinating **interior**, an agglomeration of materials and styles from the thirteenth century to the sixteenth. Founded in the ninth century and rebuilt in 1225 – the approximate date of the campanile – San Giacomo was remodelled on numerous subsequent occasions. Its **ship's keel roof** dates from the fourteenth century; the massive

San Giacomo dell'Orio is open daily 7.30am–noon & 5–8pm.

From the Rialto to the Ponte degli Scalzi

columns, made stockier by frequent raisings of the pavement, are a couple of hundred years older. Two of the columns – behind the pulpit and in the right transept – were brought to Venice by the fleet returning from the Fourth Crusade; the latter, an extraordinary chunk of *verde antico*, was compared by the excitable Gabriele d'Annunzio to "the fossilized compression of an immense verdant forest". The shape of the main apse betrays its Byzantine origins, but the inlaid marbles were placed there in the sixteenth century. The altarpiece, *Madonna and Four Saints*, was painted by Lorenzo Lotto in 1546, shortly before he left the city complaining that the Venetians had not treated him fairly. The church's principal paintings are on the ceiling of the **new sacristy** (opened by the sacristan): *Faith* and *The Doctors of the Church* by Veronese. Among the other pictures here is Francesco Bassano's *St John the Baptist Preaching* – the spectator on the far left, in the red hat, is Titian.

San Giacomo dell'Orio is plumb in the middle of an extensive residential district, much of which is as close to bland as you can get in Venice. Don't, though, leave out the church of **San Simeone Profeta** (or Grande) – remarkable for its reclining **effigy of Saint Simeon** (to the left of the chancel), a luxuriantly bearded, larger than lifesize figure, whose half-open mouth disturbingly creates the impression of the moment of death. It was sculpted in 1317 by **Marco Romano**, and is the only example of his work in Venice. On the left immediately inside the door, there's a run-of-the-mill *Last Supper* by **Tintoretto**. Originating in the tenth century, the church has been often rebuilt – most extensively in the eighteenth century, when the city sanitation experts, anxious about the condition of the plague victims who had been buried under the flagstones in the 1630 epidemic, ordered the whole floor to be relaid. Close by the church, the Riva di Biasio allows a short walk on the bank of the Canal Grande, with a view across the water of San Geremia.

San Simeone Profeta is the last stop before the Scalzi bridge. Immediately after the bridge rises the green dome of the early eighteenth-century **San Simeone Piccolo**; closed since time immemorial, the mouldering church nowadays functions chiefly as a pigeonloft.

From the Rialto to San Tomà

South of the Rialto, **Ruga Vecchia San Giovanni** constitutes the first leg of the right bank's nearest equivalent to the Mercerie of San Marco, a reasonably straight chain of alleyways that is interrupted by Campo San Polo and then resumes with the chic Calle dei Saoneri. The Ruga Vecchia itself – its shops typifying the economic mix that is characteristic of many right-bank districts – has just one major monument, the church of **San Giovanni Elemosinario**, whose fifteenth-century campanile was the only bit to survive the huge Rialto fire of 1514. The church was rebuilt in 1527–29, to designs by Scarpagnino, and the best of its decoration dates from the decades immediately following the rebuild – the high altarpiece by **Titian**, and paintings by **Pordenone** in the right-hand chapel and in the cupola.

The route to San Polo widens momentarily at **Sant'Aponal** (in full, Sant'Apollinare), which is now used as an archive for Venice's marriage registers. Its most interesting feature is on the outside anyway – the *Crucifixion and Scenes from the Life of Christ* (1294), in the tabernacle over the door. Venetian legend has it that Pope Alexander III, on the run in 1177 from the troops of Emperor Frederick Barbarossa, found refuge close to Sant'Aponal; over the entrance to the Sottoportego della Madonna (to your left as you face the church facade), a plaque records his plight and promises a perpetual plenary indulgence to anyone saying a Pater Noster and Ave Maria on the spot.

Slip down Calle Sbianchesini from Sant'Aponal (towards the Canal Grande), and you come to the nondescript church of **San Silvestro**. It deserves a visit for Tintoretto's *Baptism of Christ*, one of his simplest paintings. Opposite the church, at no. 1022, is the Palazzo Valier, where Giorgione died in 1510.

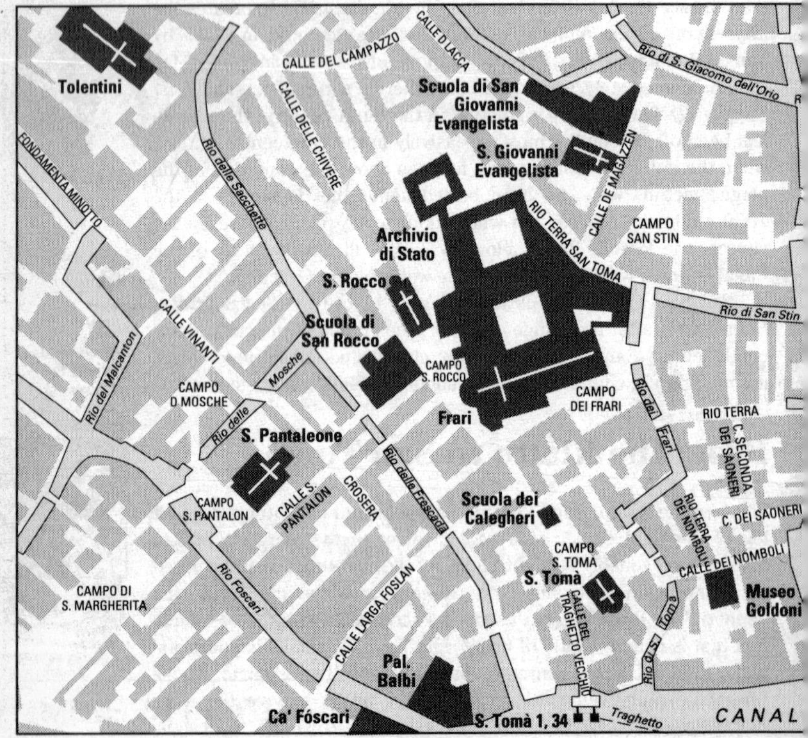

Campo San Polo

From the Rialto to San Tomà

The largest square in Venice after the Piazza, the **Campo San Polo** is the best place in the area to sit down and tuck into a bagful of supplies from the Rialto market. Most of the traffic passes down the church side, leaving a huge area of the campo free for those in no hurry to get a bit of sun, and for the budding Paolo Rossis of the parish to practise their ball skills. In earlier times it was the site of weekly markets and occasional fairs, as well as being used as a bull-fighting arena and parade ground.

Several palaces overlook the campo, the most impressive of which is the double **Palazzo Soranzo**, built between the late fourteenth and mid-fifteenth centuries, over the square from the church. This might seem an exception to the rule that the main palace facade should look onto the water, but in fact a canal used to run across the campo just in front of the Soranzo house. Casanova gained his introduction to the Venetian upper classes through a senator who lived in this palace; he was hired to work as a musician in the house and so impressed the old man that he was adopted as his son.

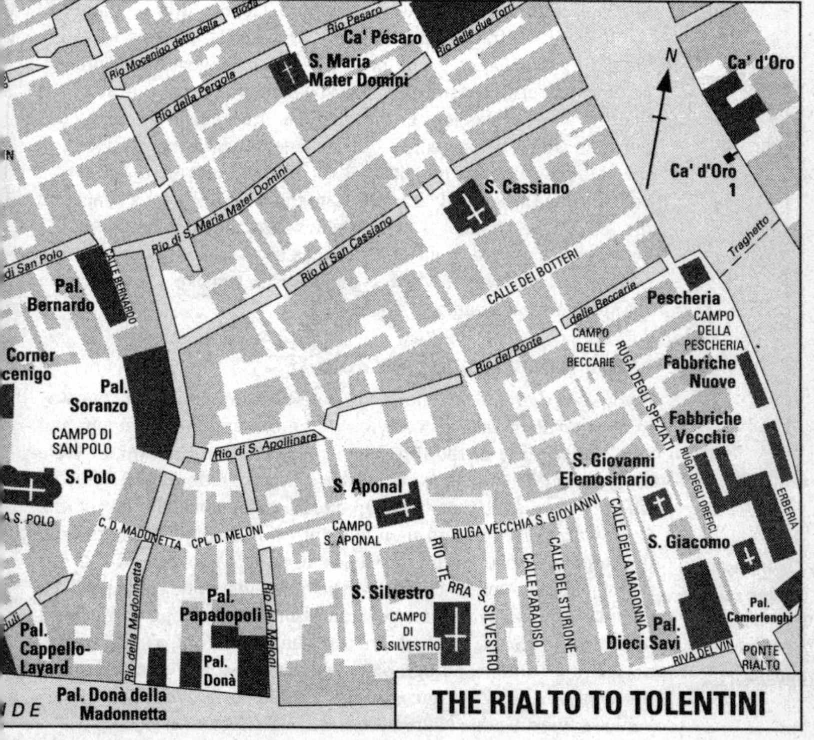

On the same side as the church, but in the opposite corner, is the **Palazzo Corner Mocenigo**, designed around 1550 by Sanmicheli – the main facade is visible from the bridge beyond the church. In 1909 **Frederick Rolfe** (Baron Corvo) became a tenant here, an arrangement that came to an abrupt end the following year when his hosts discovered that the manuscript he was working on – *The Desire and Pursuit of the Whole* – was a vitriolic satire directed at them and their acquaintances. Rolfe was given the alternative of abandoning the libellous novel or moving out; he moved out, contracted pneumonia as a result of sleeping rough and became so ill he was given the last rites – but he managed to pull through, and lived for a further three disreputable years.

San Polo church

San Polo is open Mon–Sat 7.30am–noon & 4–7pm, Sun 8am–12.15pm.

Restoration carried out in the early nineteenth century made a thorough mess of the fifteenth-century Gothic of **San Polo** church, which was established as far back as the ninth century. The beautiful main doorway, possibly by **Bartolomeo Bon**, survives from the first church. The bleak interior is worth a visit for a superior *Last Supper* by **Tintoretto** (on the left as you enter) and a cycle of the *Stations of the Cross* by **Giandomenico Tiepolo** in the Oratory of the Crucifix (entrance under organ). This series, painted when the artist was only twenty, may persuade you to amend a few preconceptions about Giandomenico, but you still can't resist the suspicion that his interest was less in the religious drama than in the society portraits which fill the edges of the stage. Back in the main part of the church, paintings by Giambattista Tiepolo and Veronese are to be found on the second altar opposite the door and in the chapel on the left of the chancel – neither shows the artist at his best. The detached campanile, built in 1362, has a couple of twelfth-century lions at its base, one of which is playing with a snake, the other with a severed human head.

South from Campo San Polo

If you turn right halfway down Calle dei Saoneri, you're on your way to the Frari (see below); carry on to the end and then turn left, and you'll soon come to the fifteenth-century **Palazzo Centani**, in Calle dei Nomboli. This was the birthplace of **Carlo Goldoni** (1707–93), of whom it was said that he adopted the indigenous theatre of the Commedia dell'Arte, and then killed it off. Goldoni's plays are still the staple of theatrical life in Venice, and there's no risk of running out of material – allegedly, he once bet a friend that he could produce one play a week for a whole year, and won. The building now houses the *Istituto di Studi Teatrali* and the **Museo Goldoni**, a small collection of first editions, autograph papers and theatrical paraphernalia; the display is less diverting than the building itself, which has one of Venice's finest Gothic courtyards and a beautiful well-head.

The Museo Goldoni is open Mon–Sat 8.30am–1.30pm; free.

The parish of San Tomà is the base of many of Venice's best silver- and goldsmiths, but **San Tomà** church, a few yards past Goldoni's house, is now a sad, broken-backed structure encased in scaffolding. In the days when the Venetians were known as the sharpest relic-hunters around, San Tomà was the city's bumper depository, claiming to possess some 10,000 sacred bits and pieces, and a dozen intact holy corpses. At the other end of the campo, the facade of the **Scuola dei Calegheri** (shoemakers' guild), has a relief by Pietro Lombardo (1478), showing Saint Mark healing the cobbler Ananias; the building is now used as an exhibition venue.

From the Rialto to San Tomà

A **vaporetto and traghetto stage** – one of the transport system's most useful time-savers – is at the back of the church, midway between the Rialto and Accademia bridges.

The Frari district

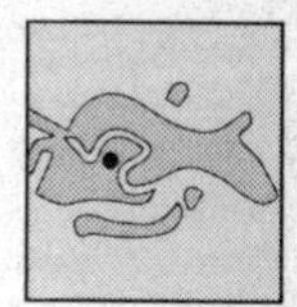

For a rapid survey of the summit of Venetian painting in its golden age, your first stop after the Accademia should be the constellation of buildings a few alleys west of San Polo – the **Frari**, the **Scuola Grande di San Rocco** and **San Rocco** church. The genesis of Ruskin's obsession with Venice was a visit to the Scuola, where a pictorial interpretation of the life of Christ by **Tintoretto** flows through the entire building; and if you can take yet more after the intensity of the Scuola's cycle, the church next door contains further works by him. A trio of magnificent altarpieces by **Bellini** and **Titian** are the principal treasures of the Frari, but even if these don't strike a chord there's bound to be something among the church's assembly of paintings, sculptures and monuments that'll get it onto your list of Venetian highlights.

Santa Maria Gloriosa dei Frari

San Zanipolo and **Santa Maria Gloriosa dei Frari** – abbreviated to the **Frari** – are the twin Gothic giants of Venice: from the campanile of San Marco they can be seen jutting above the rooftops on opposite sides of the Canal Grande, like a pair of destroyers amid a flotilla of yachts. The Franciscans were granted a plot of land here around 1250, not long after the death of their founder, but almost no sooner was the first church completed (in 1338) than work began on a vast replacement – a project which took well over a hundred years. The campanile, one of the city's landmarks and the tallest after San Marco's, was finished in 1396.

The Frari is open Mon–Sat 9.30am–noon & 2.30–6pm, Sun 3–5.30pm; L1000, free on Sun.

Admirers of northern Gothic are unlikely to fall in love at first sight with this mountain of brick. Only a few pieces of sculpture relieve the monotony of the exterior: on the **west front**, there's a figure of *The Risen Christ* by **Vittoria**, and a *Virgin* and *St Francis* from the workshop of **Bartolomeo Bon**; an impressive early fifteenth-century Tuscan relief of the *Madonna and Child with*

Angels is set into the side of the left transept. As is so often the case in Venice, though, the outside of the church is a misleadingly dull prelude to a remarkable interior.

Titian's altarpieces

Paradoxically, Venice is under-endowed with paintings by **Titian**, its most illustrious artist: apart from the Accademia and the Salute, the Frari is the only building in Venice with more than a single first-rate work by him. One of these – the **Assumption** – you see almost immediately as you look towards the high altar through the monks' choir. (The choir itself was built in the late fifteenth century, with a marble screen by Bartolomeo Bon and Pietro Lombardo; it's the only one left in Venice that occupies a site in the nave.)

A piece of compositional and colouristic bravura for which there was no precedent in Venetian art – for one thing, no previous altarpiece had been taller than it was wide – the *Assumption* nevertheless fits its surroundings perfectly. The spiralling motion of the Apostles and the Virgin complements the vertical movement of the surrounding architecture, an integration that is strengthened by the coincidence between the division of the painting's two major groupings and the division of the windows in the chancel. It seems to have disconcerted the friars for whom it was painted, but nonetheless was instantly recognised as a major work. **Marin Sanudo**, whose *Diaries* are an essential source for historians of the Republic, somehow wrote 58 volumes containing scarcely a mention of any Venetian artist – yet even he refers to the ceremony on May 19, 1518, at which the picture was unveiled.

The other Titian masterpiece here, the **Madonna di Ca' Pésaro** (to the left of the door), was completed eight years after the *Assumption* and was equally innovative in its displacement of the figure of the Virgin from the centre of the picture. The altarpiece was commissioned by Bishop Jacopo Pésaro, who managed to combine his episcopal duties with a military career; in 1502 he had led a successful naval campaign against the Turks – hence the prisoners being dragged in, behind the kneeling figure of Pésaro himself, to meet the Redeemer and His Mother. Pésaro's tomb, with an effigy, is to the right (c.1547).

The chapels, chancel and sacristy

A doorway next to the Pésaro monument leads into the **Cappella Emiliani**, which has a fifteenth-century marble altarpiece by followers of Jacobello Dalle Masegne. The **Cappella Corner** (end of left transept, often locked) contains a painting by Bartolomeo Vivarini, *St Mark Enthroned* (1474), and, on the font, a figure of *St John the Baptist* by Sansovino (1554).

St Ambrose and other Saints, the last painting by **Alvise Vivarini**, the nephew of Bartolomeo, is in the adjoining chapel. Overpopulated with meticulously drawn but lifeless figures, it was

THE FRARI

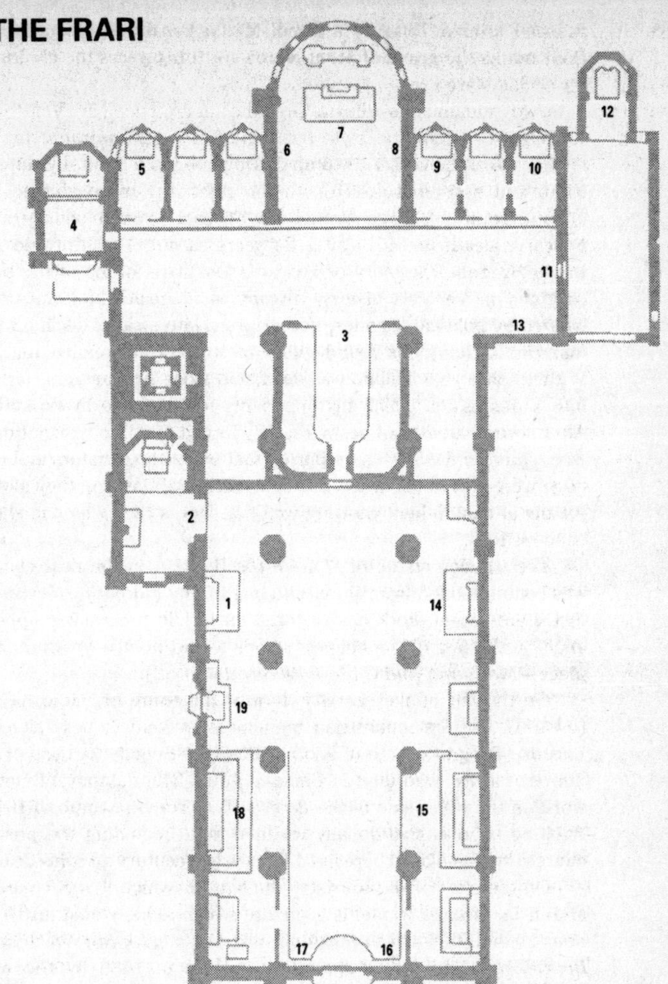

1. 'Madonna di Ca' Pésaro'
2. Cappella Emiliani
3. Monks' Choir
4. Cappella Corner
5. Vivarini and Basaiti's 'St. Ambrose'
6. Tomb of Doge Niccolo Tron
7. Titian's 'Assumption'
8. Tomb of Doge Francesco Fóscari
9. Donatello's 'St. John'
10. Bartolomeo Vivarini Altarpiece
11. Tombs of Paolo Savelli, Benedetto Pésaro and Beato Pacifico
12. The Bellini Altarpiece
13. Tomb of Jacopop Marcello
14. Vittoria's 'St. Jerome'
15. Titian's Monument
16. Tomb of Alvise Pasqualino
17. Tomb of Pietro Bernardo
18. Mausoleum of Canova
19. Tomb of Doge Giovanni Pésaro

finished around 1503 by a pupil, Marco Basaiti. A plaque in the floor marks the **grave of Monteverdi**, for thirty years the choirmaster of San Marco.

Two monuments illustrating the emergence in Venice of Renaissance sculptural style flank the Titian *Assumption*: on the left the proto-Renaissance **tomb of Doge Niccolò Tron**, by Antonio Rizzo and assistants (1476); on the right, the more archaic and chaotic **tomb of Doge Francesco Fóscari**, carved shortly after Fóscari's death in 1457 (after 34 years as doge) by **Antonio and Paolo Bregno**. The story of Fóscari's last days is one of the most poignant in Venice's history. Already in ill health and constantly harried by political enemies, Fóscari went into a rapid decline when his son, Jacopo, was found guilty of treason and exiled for life. Within half a year Jacopo was dead, and Doge Fóscari sank further into a depression which his opponents lost no time in exploiting. After several months of pressure, they forced him into resignation; a week later he died. It was reported that when the senators and new doge were told of his death, during mass in the Basilica, they looked guiltily at each other "knowing well that it was they who had shortened his life".

The wooden statue of *St John the Baptist*, in the next chapel, was commissioned from **Donatello** in 1438 by Florentine merchants in Padua; recent work has restored its luridly naturalistic appearance. In the last of the chapels stands a Bartolomeo Vivarini altarpiece – *Madonna and Child with Saints* (1482).

On the left of the **sacristy door** is the **tomb of Paolo Savelli** (c.1406), the first equestrian monument in Venice; next along is **Lorenzo Bregno**'s tomb of another Pésaro – Benedetto, head of the Venetian army, who died in Corfu in 1503. The flamboyant Gothic work on the other side of the door is the terracotta **tomb of Beato Pacifico**, who is traditionally credited with beginning the present church; he was placed here in 1437, nearly a century after his death.

On the altar of the **sacristy** (the site for which it was created), and in its original frame, is a picture which alone would justify an hour in the Frari – the *Madonna and Child with SS. Nicholas of Bari, Peter, Mark and Benedict*, painted in 1488 by **Giovanni Bellini**. Gazing at this picture is like looking into a room that's soaked in a warm dawn light; in the words of Henry James – "it is as solemn as it is gorgeous and as simple as it is deep". From the sacristy there's occasional access to the **chapter house**, with its tomb of Doge Francesco Dandolo (c.1340); the painting above it by **Paolo Veneziano** contains what is probably the first portrait of a doge ever painted from life.

The rest of the church

Back in the right transept, on the west wall, there's the very odd **tomb of Jacopo Marcello**, supported by small stooping figures (c.1485, probably by Giovanni Buora). High on the wall round the corner is something far less florid but equally strange – a plain black coffin which is said to have been meant for the body of the *condottiere* **Carmagnola**, who, having shown a suspicious reluctance to earn his money against the Milanese (his former employers), was executed after a dodgy treason trail in 1432. Carmagnola is now in Milan, and another tenant occupies the coffin.

Facing the Pésaro altarpiece stands one of **Alessandro Vittoria**'s best marble figures – *St Jerome*, for which Titian was reputedly the model. The house-sized tomb further along is the bombastic **monument to Titian**, built in the mid-nineteenth century on the supposed place of his burial. He died in 1576, in around his ninetieth year, a casualty of the plague; such was the esteem in which Titian was held, he was the only victim to be allowed a church burial in the course of the outbreak, one of the most terrible in the city's history.

The delicate statuettes on the water stoups against the last columns, facing each other across the nave, are *St Anthony of Padua* and *St Agnes* by Campagna (1609). The **tomb of Procurator Alvise Pasqualino**, to the left of the door, is attributed to Lorenzo Bregno, whose death in 1523 preceded his client's by five years. Ordering your tomb in advance was not an unusual practice: **Pietro Bernardo** (died 1538), whose tomb (possibly by Tullio Lombardo, who died in 1532) is on the other side of the door, did the same thing – although the finished article was rather more humble than he had intended. In his will he specified, among other provisions, that his epitaph should be cut in letters legible from 25 paces, and should be accompanied by an epic poem of 800 stanzas, extolling the Bernardo family. His executors seem to have wriggled out of these clauses, and out of another that ordered that a monastic choir should sing psalms in front of his tomb on the first Sunday of every month until Judgement Day.

The marble pyramid with the troop of mourners is the **Mausoleum of Canova**, erected in 1827 by pupils of the sculptor, following a design he himself had made for the tombs of Titian and Maria Christina of Austria. Only the artist's heart is actually entombed here – most of the body was interred at Possagno, but his right hand is somewhere in the Accademia.

For more on Canova, see p.333.

On your way out you'll be stopped in your tracks by what is surely the most grotesque monument in the city; this is the tomb of yet another Pésaro – **Doge Giovanni Pésaro** (1669). The architecture is usually attributed to Longhena; for the gigantic ragged-trousered Moors and decomposing corpses, a German sculptor called Melchiorre Barthel must take the blame.

The state archive

At the fall of the Republic the Franciscan monastery attached to the church was taken over for use as the **Archivio di Stato** (State Archive). Its documents, cramming more than three hundred rooms, relate to the Council of Ten, the courts, the embassies, the Arsenale, the *scuole* – to every aspect of Venetian public life – and go back as far as the ninth century. From time to time the archive puts on an exhibition of material dredged from the shelves; the shows habitually sound unenthralling, but if you're at all interested in the city's past you should get something from them.

The Scuola Grande di San Rocco

The Scuola Grande di San Rocco is open daily: summer 9.30am–5.30pm; winter 10am–1pm; L6000.

Venice may not tell you much about Titian's work that you didn't already know, but in the case of **Tintoretto** the situation is reversed – until you've been to Venice, and in particular the **Scuola Grande di San Rocco**, you haven't really seen him. "As regards the pictures which it contains, it is one of the three most precious buildings in Italy," wrote Ruskin, and although the claim's open to argument, it's not difficult to understand why he resorted to such hyperbole. (His other votes were for the Sistine Chapel and the Campo Santo at Pisa – the latter was virtually ruined in World War II.) The concentration and restlessness of Tintoretto's paintings won't inspire unqualified enthusiasm in everyone: Henry James, though an admirer, found the atmosphere of San Rocco "difficult to breathe". But even those who prefer their art at a lower voltage will find this an overwhelming experience.

From its foundation in 1478 the special concern of this particular *scuola* was the relief of the sick – a continuation of the Christian mission of its patron saint, Saint Roch (Rocco) of Montpellier. The Scuola had been going for seven years when the body of the saint was brought to Venice from Germany, and the consequent boom in donations was so great that in 1489 it acquired the status of *Scuola Grande*. The intervention of Saint Roch was held to be especially efficacious in cases of bubonic plague, an illness from which he himself had been rescued by angelic assistance (which is why the churches of Venice are littered with paintings of the saint pointing to a sore on his thigh). When, in 1527, the city was hit by an outbreak of plague the Scuola's revenue rocketed to record levels as gifts poured in from people hoping to secure Saint Roch's protection against the disease. In 1515 the Scuola had commissioned a prestigious new headquarters from **Bartolomeo Bon the Younger**, but for various reasons the work had ground to a halt within a decade; the fattened coffers naturally prompted a second phase of building, and from 1527 to 1549 the scheme was taken over by **Scarpagnino**.

When the scaffolding came down in 1560, the end product was incoherent and lopsided. Not that the members of the Scuola would have been bothered for long: within a few years the decoration of the interior was under way, and it was this decoration – **Tintoretto**'s cycle of more than fifty major paintings – that secured the confraternity's social standing. An opportunistic little trick won the first contract for Tintoretto. In 1564 the Scuola held a competition to decide who should paint the inaugural picture for the recently completed building. The subject was to be *The Glorification of St Roch*, and four artists were approached for proposals: Salviati, Zuccari, Veronese and Tintoretto. On the day for submissions the first three duly presented their sketches; Tintoretto, though, had painted a finished panel and persuaded a sidekick to rig it up, hidden by a veil, in the very place in which the winning picture was to be installed – the centre of the ceiling in the Sala dell'Albergo. A rope was pulled, the picture revealed, and the commission, despite the opposition's fury, was given to Tintoretto. Further commissions ensued, which were to occupy much of his time until 1587.

The Sala dell'Albergo

The narrative sequence of the cycle begins with the first picture in the lower room – the *Annunciation*. But to appreciate Tintoretto's development you have to begin in the smaller room on the upper storey – the **Sala dell'Albergo**. This is dominated by the stupendous *Crucifixion* (1565), the most compendious image of the event ever painted. Henry James made even greater claims for it: "Surely no single picture in the world contains more of human life; there is everything in it." Ruskin was reduced to a state of dumbfounded wonder – his loquacious commentary on the San Rocco cycle concludes with the entry: "I must leave this picture to work its will on the spectator; for it is beyond all analysis, and above all praise."

The other works in the room inevitably suffer from such company, but several of them reward close attention. On the entrance wall are *The Way to Calvary*, *Christ Crowned with Thorns* and *Christ before Pilate*. The easel painting of *Christ Carrying the Cross* has been attributed to Giorgione but now is generally thought to be an early Titian; from about 1510 until 1955 it was displayed in the church of San Rocco, where it was revered as a miraculous image. The other easel painting is probably by a pupil of Giorgione.

The chapter house and lower hall

Tintoretto finished work in the Sala dell'Albergo in 1567, and after a pause of eight years started on the main upper hall – the **chapter house**. The three large panels of the **ceiling** – *Moses Striking Water from the Rock*, *The Miracle of the Brazen Serpent* and *The Miraculous Fall of Manna* – were the first part to be painted, and their Old Testament subjects are coded declarations of the Scuola's charitable programme, with their references to the alleviation of physical suffering.

The New Testament scenes around the **walls** defy every convention of perspective, lighting, colour and even anatomy, an amazing feat of sustained inventiveness from a mind that was never content with inherited ideas, and rarely content with his own. On the **left wall** (as you face the altar) – *Nativity*, *Baptism*, *Resurrection*, *Agony in the Garden*, *Last Supper*; on the **right wall** –

Temptation of Christ, *Miracle at the Pool of Bethesda*, *Ascension*, *Raising of Lazarus*, *Miracle of the Loaves and Fishes*. On the **end wall** by the Sala dell'Albergo – *St Roch* and *St Sebastian*; on the **altar** – *The Vision of St Roch* (1588, with his son, Domenico); on **easels to the side of the altar** – an *Annunciation* by **Titian**, a *Visitation* by Tintoretto, *Hagar, Ishmael and an Angel* and *Abraham and an Angel*, both by Giambattista Tiepolo, and a portrait by Tintoretto, often wrongly called a self-portrait.

The trompe l'oeil **carvings** underneath the paintings were done in the late seventeenth century by **Francesco Pianta** – not far from the altar, opposite the stairs, you'll find a caricature of the irascible Tintoretto, with a jarful of paint-brushes. The painter's short temper was notorious – for instance, when a group of senators, seeing him at work on the *Paradiso* in the Palazzo Ducale, observed that some of his rivals painted more slowly and more carefully, he's said to have replied that this was possibly because they didn't have to contend with such stupid onlookers.

The paintings in the **Lower Hall** were created between 1583 and 1587, when Tintoretto was in his late sixties. The violent *Annunciation*, with the Archangel crashing into the room pursued by a tornado of cherubim, is followed by *Adoration of the Magi*, *Flight into Egypt*, *Massacre of the Innocents*, *St Mary Magdalen*, *St Mary of Egypt*, *Circumcision* and *Assumption*. The landscapes in the *Flight into Egypt* and the meditative depictions of the two saints are among the finest Tintoretto ever painted.

The church of San Rocco

Yet more Tintorettos are to be found in the neighbouring **church of San Rocco**, built in 1489–1508 to designs by **Bartolomeo Bon the Younger**, but altered extensively in the eighteenth century. On the right wall of the nave you'll find *St Roch Taken to Prison*, and below it *The Pool of Bethesda*; only the latter is definitely by Tintoretto. Between the altars on the other side are a couple of good pictures by **Pordenone** – *St Christopher* and *St Martin*. Four large paintings by Tintoretto hang in the chancel, but they're usually either lost in the gloom or glazed with sunlight: the best (both painted in 1549) are *St Roch Curing the Plague Victims* (lower right) and *St Roch in Prison* (lower left). The two higher pictures are *St Roch in Solitude* and *St Roch Healing the Animals* – the second is a doubtful attribution.

San Pantaleone

For a quick dose of frivolity to leaven the day, pop round to the waterside pavement at the back of the Scuola di San Rocco; on the far side of the canal there's a house decked out with scores of toy windmills in all shapes and colours, evidently planted by someone for whom the Sixties never ended.

Cross over the bridge to the left and you hit the teeming Crosera San Pantalon, the atmosphere in whose shops, cafés and bars has a lot to do with the proximity of the university. Between this street and the Rio di Ca' Fóscari stands the church of **San Pantaleone**, which possesses a picture by **Antonio Vivarini and Giovanni d'Alemagna** (*Coronation of the Virgin*, in the Chapel of the Holy Nail, to left of chancel) and **Veronese**'s last painting, *St Pantaleone Healing a Boy* (second chapel on right). San Pantaleone was credited with medicinal capabilities only slightly less awesome than San Rocco's, and Veronese's scene emphasises the miraculous nature of his power (he spurns the offered box of potions) and the impotence of non-Christian treatment (symbolised by the limbless figure of Asclepius, the classical god of medicine).

The Frari district

San Pantaleone is open daily 8–11.30am & 4.30–7pm.

The church can also boast of having the most melodramatic **ceiling** in the city: *The Martyrdom and Apotheosis of St Pantaleone*. Painted on sixty panels, some of which actually jut out over the nave, it kept **Gian Antonio Fumiani** busy from 1680 to 1704. Sadly, he never got the chance to bask in the glory of his labours – he died in a fall from the scaffolding from which he'd been working.

San Giovanni Evangelista to the Tolentini

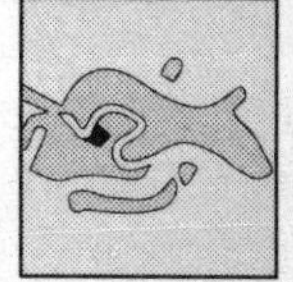

Another of the Scuole Grandi nestles in a line of drab buildings very near to the Frari – the **Scuola di San Giovanni Evangelista**, founded in 1261 by one of the many flagellant confraternities that sprang up at that time. The quickest way to get to it is to take the bridge facing the Frari's facade, turn left and then left again, then second right into Calle del Magazzen – the *scuola* is halfway down on the left.

This institution's finest hour came in 1369, when it was presented with a **relic of the True Cross**, an item that can be seen to this day in the first-floor **Oratorio della Croce**. The miracles effected by the relic were commemorated in the Oratory by a series of paintings by Carpaccio, Gentile Bellini and others, now transplanted to the Accademia.

Nowadays the delights of the Scuola are architectural. The **courtyards** are something of a composite: the mid-fifteenth-century facade of the Scuola incorporates two mid-fourteenth-century reliefs, and the **screen** of the outer courtyard was built in 1481 by **Pietro Lombardo**. The latter is one of Venice's pleasantest surprises – approached from the train station direction it just looks like any old brick wall, but round the other side it reveals itself to be as delicate a piece of marble carving as any church interior could show. Inside, a grand **double staircase** built by **Coducci** in 1498 rises to the main hall and the Oratorio; the climb is more enjoyable than its culmination, as the hall is clad with lifeless paintings, many showing scenes from the life of Saint John, most of them by Domenico

Tintoretto. The Scuola is open Monday to Friday 9.30am to 12.30pm; ring for admission – they might balk at letting you into the Oratorio, but there shouldn't be any problem about getting a look at the Coducci bits, unless one of the Scuola's frequent conferences is in progress.

The church of San Giovanni Evangelista is one of the select band of religious buildings in Venice that are of no interest whatsoever.

The Tolentini and the Giardino Papadopoli

The Tolentini is open daily 7.45am–noon & 4.30–7pm.

Calle della Lacca–Fondamenta Sacchere–Calle Amai is a dullish but uncomplicated route from San Giovanni Evangelista to San Nicolò da Tolentino – alias the **Tolentini**. A portentous church begun in 1590 by Palladio's follower Scamozzi, it was finished in 1714 by the addition of a freestanding portico – the first in Venice – designed by Andrea Tirali. Among the scores of seventeenth-century paintings, just two stand much chance of becoming lodged in the memory. The first is a *St Jerome* by Johann Lys, on the wall outside chancel, to the left; it was painted in 1628, just two years before German-born Lys died of the plague, aged just thirty-three. The other is *St Lawrence Giving Alms* by Bernardo Strozzi, round the corner from the Lys painting. Up the left wall of the chancel swirls the best Baroque monument in Venice: the **monument to Francesco Morosini**, created in 1678 by a Genoese sculptor, Filippo Parodi. That's Francesco Morosini, Patriarch of Venice, on no account to be confused with Francesco Morosini, Doge of Venice 1688–94, buried in Santo Stefano – though that Francesco Morosini did present the Tolentini with the banner of the Turkish general whom he had trounced in the Morea in 1685.

If fatigue is setting in and you need a pit-stop, the **Giardino Papadopoli**, formerly one of Venice's biggest private gardens but now owned by the city, is just over the Rio dei Tolentini. In winter you may have to make do with the pavement, because the park's often shut then.

Chapter 5

Cannaregio

Within the northernmost section of Venice, **Cannaregio**, you pass from one urban extreme to another in a matter of minutes, the time it takes to get away from the hubbub of the train station and the hustle of the Lista di Spagna – the tawdriest street in Venice – and into the backwaters away from the Canal Grande. There may no longer be any signs of the bamboo clumps that were the source of the *sestiere*'s name (*canna* means "reed"), but in all of Venice you won't find as many village-like parishes as in Cannaregio, and exploring them at any time of year you'll be well away from the crowds.

Imprisoned in the very centre of Cannaregio is the **Ghetto**, the first place in the world to bear that name, and one of Venice's most evocative areas. The pleasures of the rest of Cannaregio are generally more a matter of atmosphere than of specific sights, but there are some special buildings to visit too: **Madonna dell'Orto**, with its astonishing Tintoretto paintings; **Sant'Alvise** and the **Palazzo Labia**, the first remarkable for canvases by Giambattista Tiepolo, the second for the same artist's frescoes; the **Ca' d'Oro**, a gorgeous Canal Grande palace housing a fine collection of paintings and carving; and the **Gesuiti**, a Baroque creation in the northeastern part of the district which boasts perhaps the weirdest interior in the city.

From the train station to San Giobbe

The area around Venice's train station is one in which nearly every visitor sets foot but very few actually investigate. Nobody could pretend that it's one of the city's enticing spots, but it does repay a saunter. The station building itself is a functional 1950s effort, but the rail link to the mainland was opened in the 1840s; within a few years the expansion of traffic had made it necessary to demolish Palladio's church of Santa Lucia, the building from which the station's name is taken.

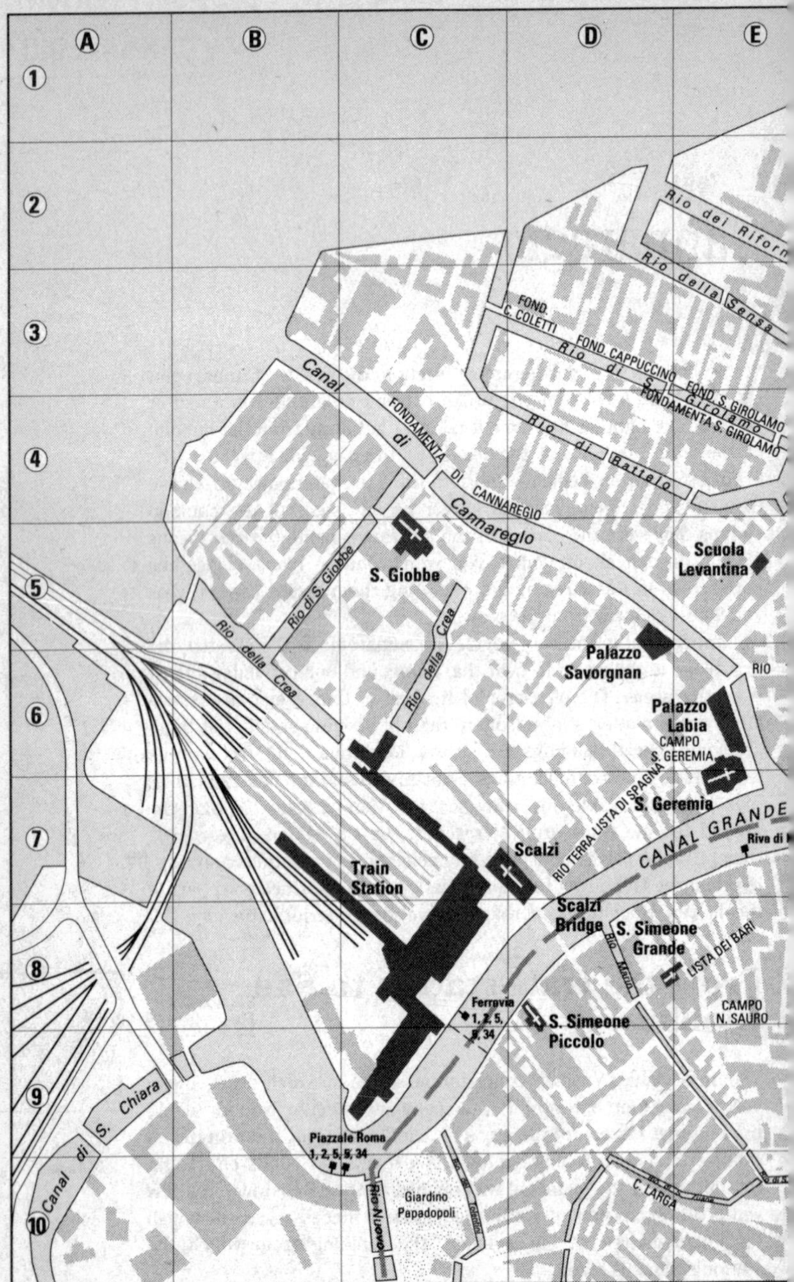
A
B
C
D
E
1
2
3
4
5
6
7
8
9
10
Rio dei Riform
Rio della Sensa
FOND. C. COLETTI
FOND. CAPPUCCINO
Rio di S. Girolamo
FOND. S. GIROLAMO
FONDAMENTA S. GIROLAMO
Rio di Battelo
Canal di Cannaregio
FONDAMENTA DI CANNAREGIO
Scuola Levantina
S. Giobbe
Rio di S. Giobbe
Rio della Crea
Rio della Crea
Palazzo Savorgnan
RIO
Palazzo Labia
CAMPO S. GEREMIA
RIO TERRA LISTA DI SPAGNA
S. Geremia
CANAL GRANDE
Scalzi
Train Station
Scalzi Bridge
S. Simeone Grande
LISTA DEI BARI
Rio Marin
CAMPO N. SAURO
Ferrovia 1, 2, 5, 5, 34
S. Simeone Piccolo
Canal di S. Chiara
Piazzale Roma 1, 2, 5, 5, 34
Rio Nuovo
Giardino Papadopoli
C. LARGA

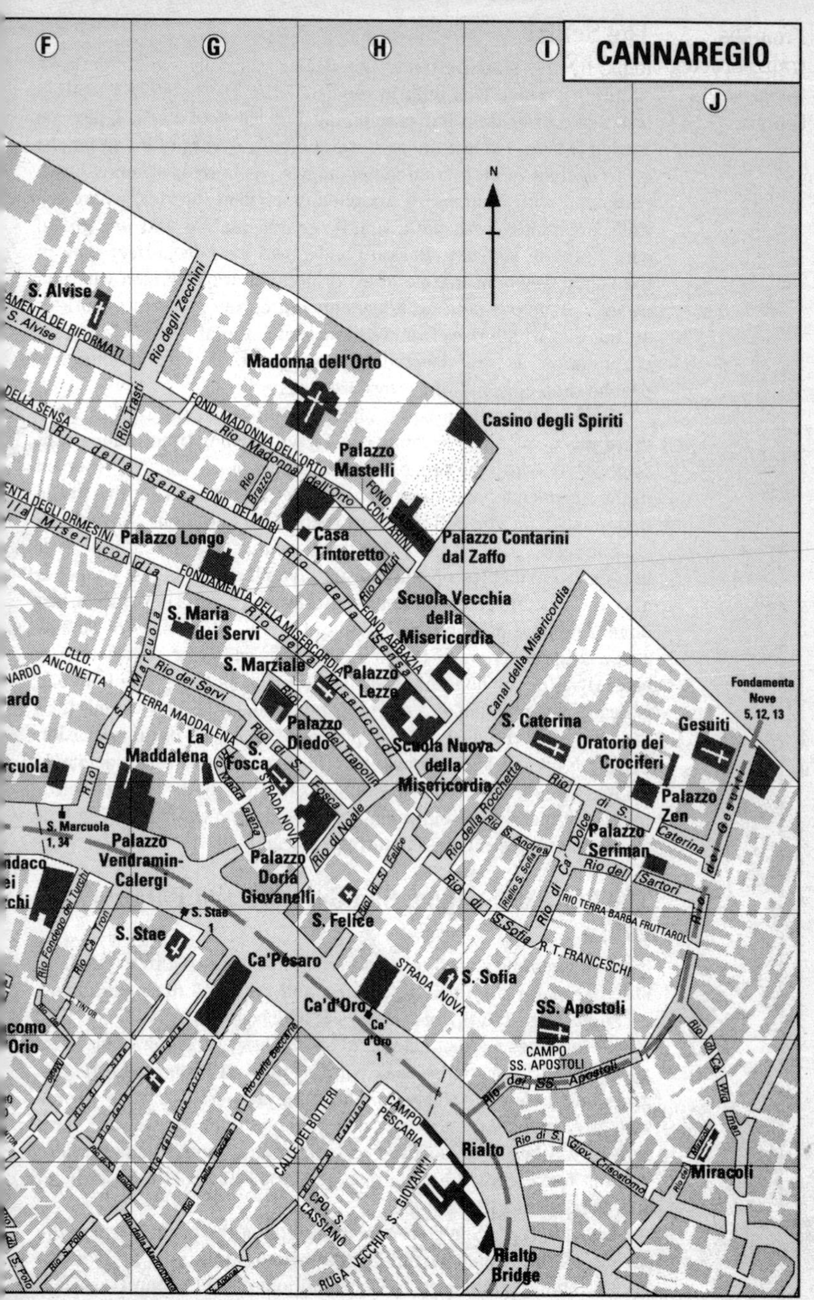
CANNAREGIO
F
G
H
I
J
N
S. Alvise
Madonna dell'Orto
Casino degli Spiriti
Palazzo Mastelli
Casa Tintoretto
Palazzo Contarini dal Zaffo
Palazzo Longo
S. Maria dei Servi
Scuola Vecchia della Misericordia
S. Marziale
Palazzo Lezze
Palazzo Diedo
Scuola Nuova della Misericordia
S. Caterina
Oratorio dei Crociferi
Gesuiti
Fondamenta Nuove 5, 12, 13
Palazzo Zen
Palazzo Seriman
La Maddalena
S. Fosca
Palazzo Vendramin-Calergi
S. Marcuola 1, 34
Palazzo Doria Giovanelli
S. Felice
S. Stae
S. Stae 1
Ca'Pésaro
Ca'd'Oro
Ca' d'Oro 1
S. Sofia
SS. Apostoli
CAMPO SS. APOSTOLI
CAMPO PESCARIA
Rialto
Rialto Bridge
Miracoli
CALLE DEI BOTTERI
RUGA VECCHIA S. GIOVANNI
CPO. S. CASSIANO
STRADA NOVA
Canal della Misericordia
Rio degli Zecchini
Rio Trasti
FOND. MADONNA DELL'ORTO
Rio Madonna dell'Orto
Rio della Sensa
FOND. DEI MORI
Rio Brazzo
FOND. CONTARINI
Rio della Misericordia
FONDAMENTA DELLA MISERICORDIA
Rio dei Servi
TERRA MADDALENA
Rio di S. Fosca
Rio di Noale
Rio della Rocchetta
Rio di S. Sofia
RIO TERRA BARBA FRUTTAROL
R.T. FRANCESCHI
Rio dei SS. Apostoli
Rio di S. Giov. Crisostomo
Rio Fondego dei Turchi
Rio Cà Tron
FOND. ABBAZIA
Rio di Cà Dolce
Rio del Sartori
Rio dei Gesuiti
CLLO. ANCONETTA
S. Alvise
FONDAMENTA DEI RIFORMATI
DELLA SENSA
FONDAMENTA DEGLI ORMESINI

From the train station to San Giobbe

The Scalzi

Right by the station stands the **Scalzi** (formally Santa Maria di Nazareth), which was built in the 1670s for the barefoot ("scalzi") order of Carmelites, but is anything but barefoot itself. Giuseppe Sardi's facade – at last under restoration after years of being fenced off to protect mortals from falling angels – is fairly undemonstrative compared with **Baldessare Longhena**'s opulent interior, where the walls are plated with dark, multi-coloured marble and overgrown with Baroque statuary. Ruskin condemned it as "a perfect type of the vulgar abuse of marble in every possible way, by men who had no eye for colour, and no understanding of any merit in a work of art but that which rises from costliness of material, and such powers of imitation as are devoted in England to the manufacture of peaches and eggs out of Derbyshire spar".

Before an Austrian bomb plummeted through the roof in 1915 there was a splendid **Giambattista Tiepolo** ceiling to introduce a bit of good taste into the proceedings; a couple of scraps are preserved in the Accademia, and some wan frescoes by the man survive in the first chapel on the left and the second on the right. As well as containing a pair of huge candlesticks that are about the most impressive examples of Murano glass you'll see, this last chapel is also the resting place of **Lodovico Manin** (d.1802), Venice's last doge. The bare inscription – "Manini Cineres" (the ashes of Manin) – is a fair reflection of the low esteem in which he was held. His chief rival for the dogeship wailed "a Friulian as doge! The Republic is dead!" when Manin was elected, and although Lodovico can't take the blame for the death of independent Venice, he did on occasion display a certain lack of backbone. In response to French demands he meekly surrendered his insignia of office to be burned on a bonfire in the Piazza, and when later called upon to swear an oath of allegiance to Austria, he fell down in a dead faint.

The Lista di Spagna, San Geremia and Palazzo Labia

Foreign embassies used to be corralled into this area to make life a little easier for the Republic's spies, and the **Lista di Spagna** takes its name from the Spanish embassy which used to be at no. 168. (*Lista* indicates a street leading to an embassy.) It's now completely given over to the tourist trade with shops and stalls, bars, restaurants and hotels all plying for the same desperate trade – people who are spending one day "doing Venice", or those who have arrived too late and too tired to look any farther. Whether you're hunting for a trinket, a meal or a bed, you'll find better elsewhere, and usually cheaper.

The church of **San Geremia**, at the end of the Lista, is where the travels of **Saint Lucy** eventually terminated – martyred in Syracuse in 304, she was stolen from Constantinople by Venetian Crusaders in 1204, then ousted from her own church in Venice by the railway board in the mid-nineteenth century. Lucy's response to an unwanted suitor who praised her beautiful eyes was to pluck out the offending organs, a display of otherworldliness which led to her adoption as the patron saint of eyesight and, logically enough, of artists. Her dessicated body, wearing a lustrous silver mask, lies behind the altar, reclining above a donations box that bears the prayer "Saint Lucy, protect my eyes". Nothing else about the church is of interest, except the twelfth-century **campanile**, one of the oldest left in the city.

From the train station to San Giobbe

The **Palazzo Labia**, next door to San Geremia, was built in 1720–50 for a famously extravagant Spanish family by the name of Lasbias, who had bought their way into the *Libro d'Oro* (the register of the nobility) for the obligatory 100,000 ducats in the middle of the previous century. Their taste for conspicuous expenditure wasn't lessened by the cost of the house – a party here once finished with a member of the Labia family hurling the gold dinner service from the window into the canal and declaiming the worst-ever Venetian pun: "L'abia o non l'abia, sarò sempre Labia" (Whether I have it or whether I have it not, I will always be a Labia). The impact of the gesture is somewhat lessened by the rumour that fishing nets had been placed in the canal so the service could be retrieved under cover of darkness.

The Palazzo Labia is open Wed, Thurs & Fri 3–4pm; for an appointment ring ☎ 781.111.

No cost was spared on decoration either, and no sooner was the interior completed than **Giambattista Tiepolo** was hired to cover the walls of the ballroom with **frescoes** depicting the story of Anthony and Cleopatra. (The architectural trompe l'oeil work is by another artist – Gerolamo Mengozzi Colonna.) Restored to something approaching their original freshness after years of neglect and some damage in the last war, this is the only sequence of Tiepolo paintings in Venice that is comparable to his narrative masterpieces in such mainland villas as the Villa Valmarana near Vicenza (see p.301). RAI, the Italian radio and TV company, now owns the palace, but they allow visitors in for a few hours each week; the public can also attend the concerts that are recorded here – for free tickets ask at the door or phone to reserve in advance.

The San Giobbe district

The Palazzo Labia's longest facade overlooks the **Canale di Cannaregio**, the main entrance to Venice before the rail and road links were constructed; if you turn left along its *fondamenta* rather than going with the flow over the the Ponte delle Guglie, you'll be virtually alone by the time you're past the late seventeenth-century **Palazzo Savorgnan**. This was the home of one of Venice's richest families – indeed so great was the Savorgnans' social clout that the Rezzonico family marked their intermarriage by getting Tiepolo to paint a fresco celebrating the event in the Ca' Rezzonico. Beyond

From the train station to San Giobbe

San Giobbe is open daily 10am–11.30am & 4.30–5.30pm.

the palazzo, swing left at the Ponte dei Tre Archi (Venice's only multiple-span bridge) and you're at the church of **San Giobbe**, like San Moisè an example of Venice's habit of canonising Old Testament figures.

"So went Satan forth from the presence of the Lord and smote Job with sore boils from the sole of his foot unto his crown," records the Bible. Job's physical sufferings – sanctioned by the Almighty in order to test his faith – greatly endeared him to the Venetians, who were regularly afflicted with malaria, plague and a plethora of water-related diseases, and in the fourteenth century an oratory dedicated to him was founded here. Antonio Gambello began a Gothic replacement in the mid-fifteenth century, but the specially interesting parts of the building are its exquisitely carved doorway and chancel, early Renaissance works by **Pietro Lombardo**, whose first Venetian project this was.

Gambello's church was a commemoration of a recent visit by the great preacher Saint Bernardino of Siena, an eminent member of the Observant Franciscans; the Franciscans' wide-ranging organisation explains the presence of non-Venetian elements such as the roundels and tiles from the Florentine **della Robbia** workshop in the Cappella Martini (second chapel on left). The tomb slab in the centre of the chancel floor is that of **Doge Cristoforo Moro**, the donor of the new building; a satirical leaflet about Moro may have been a source for Shakespeare's *Othello*, even though – as the portrait in the sacristy shows – Moro bore no racial similarity to the Moor of Venice. San Giobbe's altarpieces by Bellini and Carpaccio have been removed to the damp-free environment of the Accademia; the parishioners might not weep if a crowbar were taken to the ludicrous lions on the tomb of the magnificently named **Renato de Voyer de Palmy Signore d'Argeson**.

North of San Giobbe

At the top of the *fondamenta* to the north of San Giobbe, looking over the lagoon to the mainland, is the Macello Pubblico (municipal slaughterhouse), built by the hygiene-conscious Austrians in 1843 and adorned with ox-skulls. Now used by rowing clubs, its future is the subject of some discussion and has been for some time – Le Corbusier designed a hospital for the site in 1964, but the plan was shelved in the face of local opposition to the demolition of the building, opposition with which the architect himself sympathised.

On the opposite side of the Canale di Cannaregio, on the south side of the Ponte dei Tre Archi, stands the **Palazzo Surian**, once the French embassy. **Jean-Jacques Rousseau** lived here in 1743–44 as secretary to an indolent boss: "The French who lived in Venice would never have known that there was a French ambassador resident in the city, had it not been for me," he wrote. His *Confessions* record the political bickerings of his time here, and a number of discreditable sexual adventures. At the far northern end of this *fondamenta* you'll find one of the few new building projects in central Venice – a new **housing development** which elegantly combines modern architectural techniques with elements of Venetian vernacular style, such as the characteristic flowerpot chimneys.

From the train station to San Giobbe

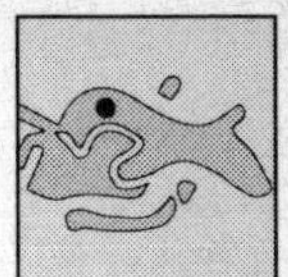

The Ghetto

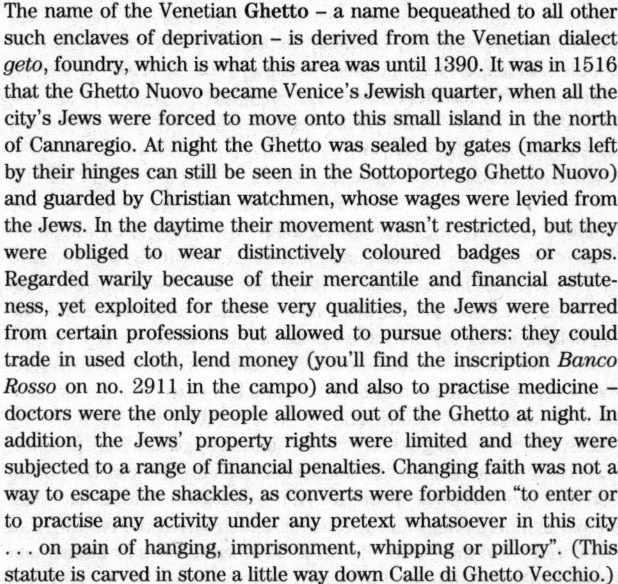

The name of the Venetian **Ghetto** – a name bequeathed to all other such enclaves of deprivation – is derived from the Venetian dialect *geto*, foundry, which is what this area was until 1390. It was in 1516 that the Ghetto Nuovo became Venice's Jewish quarter, when all the city's Jews were forced to move onto this small island in the north of Cannaregio. At night the Ghetto was sealed by gates (marks left by their hinges can still be seen in the Sottoportego Ghetto Nuovo) and guarded by Christian watchmen, whose wages were levied from the Jews. In the daytime their movement wasn't restricted, but they were obliged to wear distinctively coloured badges or caps. Regarded warily because of their mercantile and financial astuteness, yet exploited for these very qualities, the Jews were barred from certain professions but allowed to pursue others: they could trade in used cloth, lend money (you'll find the inscription *Banco Rosso* on no. 2911 in the campo) and also to practise medicine – doctors were the only people allowed out of the Ghetto at night. In addition, the Jews' property rights were limited and they were subjected to a range of financial penalties. Changing faith was not a way to escape the shackles, as converts were forbidden "to enter or to practise any activity under any pretext whatsoever in this city . . . on pain of hanging, imprisonment, whipping or pillory". (This statute is carved in stone a little way down Calle di Ghetto Vecchio.)

Yet the fact remains that Venice was one of the few states to tolerate the Jewish religion, and the Ghetto's population was often swelled by refugees from more oppressive societies. Jews expelled from Spain and Portugal in the 1490s came here, as did Jews later displaced from the Veneto by the Habsburg army during the War of the League of Cambrai, and from the eastern Mediterranean by the Ottoman Turks. Venice's burdensome protection was entirely pragmatic, however, as is shown by two conflicting responses to Church interference: when criticised by the Inquisition for not burning enough Jews as heretics, Venetian leaders replied that non-Christians logically could not commit heresy; yet when Pope Julius II ordered the destruction of the Talmud in 1553, the Signoria obligingly arranged a bonfire of Jewish books in the Piazza.

The Ghetto looks quite different from the rest of Venice, as a result of the overcrowding that remained a problem even after the Jewish population was allowed to spread into the **Ghetto Vecchio** (1541) and the **Ghetto Nuovissimo** (1633). As buildings in the Ghetto were not allowed to be more than one-third higher than in the rest of Venice, storeys were made as low as possible in order to fit in the maximum number of floors; seven is the usual number – the first high-rise blocks. The gates of the Ghetto were finally torn down by Napoleon in 1797, but it wasn't until the city's unification with the Kingdom of Italy in 1866 that the Jews achieved equal status with their fellow citizens.

Present-day Venice's Jewish population of around 600 (compared to the Ghetto's peak of around 5000) is dispersed all over the city, but the Ghetto is still the centre of the community, with offices and a library in Calle Ghetto Vecchio, a nursery, an old people's home, a small kosher restaurant, and a baker of unleavened bread, in Calle del Forno.

The scole and the campo

Each wave of Jewish immigrants, while enriching the overall cultural environment of the city (Venetians of all religions frequented the Ghetto's salons), also maintained their own synagogues with their distinctive rites: the **Scola Tedesca** (for German Jews) was founded in 1528, the **Scola al Canton** (probably Jews from Provence) in 1531–32, the **Scola Levantina** (eastern Mediterranean) in 1538, the **Scola Spagnola** (Spanish) at an uncertain date in the later sixteenth century, and the **Scola Italiana** in 1575. Since the Jews were disqualified from the profession of architect and forbidden to use marble in their buildings, the *scole* tend to have oddly Christian interiors, thickly adorned with gilt and stucco. Funded by particularly prosperous trading communities, the Scola Levantina and the Scola Spagnola are the most lavish of the synagogues (the latter, redesigned by Longhena, greatly influenced the look of the others), and these can be viewed with the Scola Tedesca in an informative and multilingual guided tour that leaves on the half-hour from the **Museo Comunità Ebraica** in Campo del Ghetto Nuovo. The museum's collection consists mainly of silverware, sacred objects, textiles and furniture.

The Museo Ebraica is open 10am–7pm in high season, with shorter hours for the rest of the year; closed Sat; L3000, or L7000 with guided tour.

In the northern corner of the campo is a reminder of the ultimate suffering of the Jewish people: a series of seven reliefs by **Arbit Blatas**, with a poem by André Tranc, commemorating the 202 Venetian Jews deported to the death-camps in 1943 and 1944.

Northern Cannaregio

Land reclamation and the consolidation of the lagoon's mudbanks has been a continuous process in Venice since the time of the first settlers, but the contours of the city have been modified with particular rapidity in the last hundred years or so. As its long straight canals and right-angled alleyways suggest, much of northern Cannaregio has come into existence comparatively recently: the Sacca di San Girolamo, for example, was reclaimed in the first half of this century to provide working-class housing of a higher standard than in much of the rest of the city.

In the area **northwest from the Ghetto**, inland from the Sacca, there's nothing to ferret out: the tiny seventeenth-century church of the Cappuccine (open for services) faces the equally dull but bigger and uglier (and closed) San Girolamo, a church once used by the Austrians as a steam-powered flour mill, with the campanile converted to a chimney. **Northeast of the Ghetto**, though, is one of the most attractive domestic quarters of Venice: its long fondamente dotted with food shops, bars and trattorias, and the colourful juxtapositions of walls, shutters, water and boats composing a scene like Henry James's evocation of the essence of Venice – "a narrow canal in the heart of the city – a patch of green water and a surface of pink wall . . . a great shabby facade of Gothic windows and balconies – balconies on which dirty clothes are hung and under which a cavernous-looking doorway opens from a low flight of slimy water-steps".

Sant'Alvise to Campo dei Mori

For all the apparent rationality of the city's layout in this district, the church of **Sant'Alvise** is fairly tricky to get to, standing as it does on an island with no eastward land connection with the rest of the city. Dedicated to Saint Louis of Toulouse (Alvise being the Venetian version of Louis/Luigi), the church was commissioned in the 1380s by Antonia Venier, daughter of Doge Antonio Venier, after the saint appeared to her in a vision. It has recently undergone restoration work, as has the chancel's immense *Road to Calvary* by **Giambattista Tiepolo**, which now looks as if it should reek of fresh paint. His *Crown of Thorns* and *Flagellation*, slightly earlier works, hang on the right-hand wall of the nave. Under the nun's choir are eight small tempera paintings, familiarly known as "The Baby Carpaccios" since Ruskin assigned them to the painter's precocious childhood; they're not actually by Carpaccio, but were produced around 1470, when he would indeed have been just an infant. The extraordinary seventeenth-century trompe l'oeil **ceiling** is by Antonio Torri (the architectural work) and Paolo Ricchi (the religious scenes).

To get from Sant'Alvise to Madonna dell'Orto you can either squander a few lire on a one-stop vaporetto hop, or cross over the canal to the Fondamenta della Sensa, the main street immediately to the south. One bridge after the early fifteenth-century **Palazzo Michiel** (the French embassy at the time of Henry III's visit), the *fondamenta* opens out at the **Campo dei Mori**, a square whose name possibly comes from the proximity of the now extinct Fondaco degli Arabi (Arabs' warehouse). There is another explanation: the four thirteenth-century **statues** around the campo are popularly associated with a family of twelfth-century merchants

For more on the Mastelli brothers' house, see opposite.

called the Mastelli brothers, who used to live in the palace into which two of the figures are embedded – they hailed from the Morea (the Peloponnese), and hence were known as *Mori*. Venice's more malicious citizens used to leave denunciations at the feet of "Sior Antonio Rioba" (the statue with the rusty nose), and circulate vindictive verses signed with his name.

Just beyond the campo is the elegant fifteenth-century house where **Tintoretto** lived for the last two decades of his life (1574–94), accompanied by one of his daughters, **Marietta**. Supremely skilled as a painter, and a fine musician and singer too, Marietta was married off to a man who preferred his wife to produce portraits of his colleagues and his friends instead of painting more ambitious works. She died aged 34, four years before her father, her career having epitomised the restriction of women's talents to genres compatible with a life of domestic conformity. None of her paintings is on public show in Venice, though some scholars have detected her touch in some of her father's large-scale works.

Madonna dell'Orto

Madonna dell'Orto is open daily 9am–noon & 3–7pm; closes 5pm in winter.

Marietta, her father, and her brother Domenico are all buried in **Madonna dell'Orto**, the family's parish church and arguably the superlative example of ecclesiastical Gothic in Venice. Ferrymen for the northern islands used to operate from the quays near here, and the church was founded in the name of Saint Christopher, their patron saint, some time around 1350. It was popularly renamed after a large stone *Madonna* by **Giovanni de'Santi**, found in a nearby vegetable garden (*orto*), began working miracles; brought into the church in 1377, the heavily restored figure can still be seen in the Cappella di San Mauro.

The main figure on the **facade** is a fifteenth-century *St Christopher* by the Florentine **Nicolò di Giovanni**, and was the first major sculptural project in the restoration programmes that began after the 1966 flood. (It's now the turn of the figures on the crest of the facade – hence the scaffolding.) **Bartolomeo Bon**, formerly credited with the *St Christopher*, designed the portal in 1460, shortly before his death. The **campanile**, finished in 1503, is one of the most notable landmarks when approaching Venice from the northern lagoon.

Restoration work in the 1860s made a right mess of the **interior**, ripping up memorial stones from the floor, for instance, and destroying the organ, once described as the best in Europe. Partial reversal of the damage was achieved in the 1930s, when some overpainting was removed from the Greek marble columns, the fresco work and elsewhere, and in 1968–69 the whole building was given a massive overhaul.

An amusing if implausible tale explains the large number of **Tintoretto** paintings here. Having added cuckold's horns to a portrait of a doge that had been rejected by its subject, Tintoretto allegedly took refuge from his furious ex-client in Madonna dell'Orto; the doge then offered to forget the insult if Tintoretto agreed to decorate the church, figuring it would keep him quiet for a few years. The painter was in fact out and about again within six months, most of which time must have been spent on the epic numbers on each side of the choir: *The Last Judgement*, described by Ruskin as the only painting ever to grasp the event "in its Verity . . . as they may see it who shall not sleep, but be changed", and *The Making of the Golden Calf*, in which the carriers of the calf have been speculatively identified as portraits of Giorgione, Titian, Veronese and the artist himself, and Aaron (pointing on the right) as Sansovino.

There could hardly be a sharper shift of mood than that from the apocalyptic temper of *The Last Judgement* to the reverential tenderness of *The Presentation of the Virgin* (end of right aisle), which makes a fascinating comparison with Titian's Accademia version of the incident. It's by a long way the best of the other Tintorettos, but most are interesting: *The Vision of the Cross to St Peter* and *The Beheading of St Paul* flank an *Annunciation* by Palma il Giovane in the chancel; four *Virtues* (the central one is anonymous) are installed in the vault above; and *St Agnes Reviving Licinius* stands in the fourth chapel on the left. Two major figures of the early Venetian Renaissance – **Cima da Conegliano** and **Giovanni Bellini** – are represented by a *St John the Baptist and Other Saints* (first altar on right) and a *Madonna and Child* (first chapel on the left) respectively.

To the Scuole della Misericordia

Diagonally south of the church, the **Palazzo Mastelli** looks across the canal, its facade a sort of architectural album featuring a Gothic top-floor balcony, thirteenth-century Byzantine fragments set into sixteenth-century work below, a bit of a Roman altar set into a column by the corner, and a quaint little relief of a man leading a laden camel – hence the alternative title, Palazzo del Cammello.

On the canal's north side stand the seventeenth-century **Palazzo Minelli Spada** and, one of the many palaces owned by the vast Contarini clan, the sixteenth-century **Palazzo Contarini dal Zaffo**. Numerous though they once were, the last male of the Contarini line died in 1836, thus adding their name to the roll-call of aristocratic dynasties that vanished in the nineteenth century. Lack of money almost certainly accounts for their extinction – already impoverished by loans made to the dying Republic and by the endless round of parties, the Venetian aristocracy were finally bankrupted by the Napoleonic and Austrian occupations, and so, no longer having money for dowries and other related expenses, simply chose not to marry.

The Casino degli Spiriti, in the garden of the Palazzo Contarini dal Zaffo, is covered on p.141, as it can only be seen from the far side of the Sacca della Misericordia.

Northern Cannaregio

Crossing the canal at the Sacca della Misericordia, you quickly come to the *fondamenta* leading to the defunct **Abbazia della Misericordia** and the **Scuola Vecchia della Misericordia**; neither is particularly lovely, and the latter's proudest adornment – Bartolomeo Bon's relief of the *Madonna della Misericordia* – is exiled in London's Victoria and Albert Museum. The complex is now used as a restoration centre. When the Misericordia became a Scuola Grande in the sixteenth century its members commissioned the huge **Scuola Nuova della Misericordia** (on the far side of the bridge), a move which benefitted Tintoretto, who set up his canvases in the upper room of the old building to work on the *Paradiso* for the Palazzo Ducale. Begun in 1532 by Sansovino but not opened until 1589, the new block was never finished; today a part of it serves as a gym, and strolling past at dusk you'll probably hear the thump of basketballs against the walls. Its neighbour is the **Palazzo Lezze**, another project by Longhena.

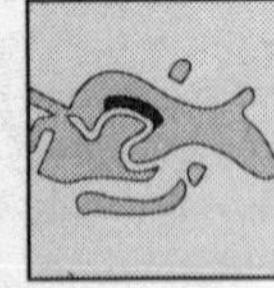

Southern Cannaregio

If you follow the main route east from the station, crossing the Canale di Cannaregio by the Guglie bridge, you come onto the shopping street of **Rio Terrà San Leonardo**. Like the Lista di Spagna, this thoroughfare follows the line of a former canal, filled in during the 1870s by the Austrians as part of a scheme to rationalise movement round the north bend of the Canal Grande. (The name "Rio Terrà", prefixed to many alleyways in Venice, signifies a pavement that was once a waterway.) The continuation of the route to the Rialto bridge – the Strada Nova – was by contrast created by simply ploughing a line straight through the houses that used to stand there.

Rio Terrà Cristo, on the south of Rio Terrà San Leonardo just before the market stalls of the Campiello dell'Anconetta, runs down to Giorgio Massari's church of **San Marcuola** (1728–36), whose unfinished brick front is as clear a landmark on the Canal Grande as the facade of the Palazzo Vendramin-Calergi, which stands a little to the east of it. The tiered ledges and sockets of the exterior, intended for marble cladding but now crammed with pigeons, are a more diverting sight than the inside, where statues of the church's two patron saints by Gian Maria Morleiter, and an early *Last Supper* by Tintoretto (left wall of the chancel) are the only things to seek out. Those apart, the main interest in the church is a story about one of its priests. He was once foolish enough to announce from the pulpit that he didn't believe in ghosts, and that "where the dead are, there they stay"; that night all the corpses buried in the church rose from their graves, dragged him from his bed and beat him up. Incidentally, the church's name is perhaps the most baffling of all the Venetian diminutives – it's somehow derived from Santi Ermagora e Fortunato.

The Maddalena district

Southern Cannaregio

The parish to the east of Campiello dell'Anconetta is centred on the little Neoclassical church of **La Maddalena** (1760), set back from the main street on its own small campo. Its designer, the unprolific **Tomasso Temanza**, was more noted as a theoretician than as an architect, and his *Lives of the Most Famous Venetian Architects and Sculptors* (modelled on Vasari's *Lives of the Artists*) remains the classic text for those interested in the subject. A couple of twists and turns away from La Maddalena is the land entrance of the **Palazzo Vendramin-Calergi**, where a plaque records the death of Richard Wagner here in 1883; the surprisingly tatty entrance is as far as you'll get unless your wallet's full and your attire impeccable, because it's now the winter home of the Casino. It is one of just four licensed casinos in Italy – but Venetian residents are forbidden to gamble here.

For more on the Palazzo Vendramin-Calergi, see p.180.

Back on the main drag, a nineteenth-century monument of **Paolo Sarpi** (see box below) fronts the unmemorable church of **Santa Fosca**, close to which is the oldest chemist's shop in Venice, the *Farmacia di Santa Fosca*, with seventeenth-century wood panelling and furniture. Antiquarians might also investigate the early fifteenth-century **Palazzo Donà Giovanelli**, just to the east of the church. Now owned by an auctioneers, it's sometimes open for pre-sale viewings, an experience as interesting for the authentic decorations of the palace as for the collectables on show.

The western part of the island immediately north of Santa Fosca is occupied by the **Palazzo Diedo**, scene of a peculiar incident in 1606. An astrologer named Benedetto Altavilla rushed in to tell its owner that the stars had revealed to him that a quantity of gunpowder had been stacked feloniously under the Sala del Maggior Consiglio. The Council of Ten duly found the explosives, but suspected, not unreasonably, that Altavilla had put them there. Shaved and shorn, in case his hair gave him occult strength, the astrologer was tortured to unconsciousness and then hanged, protesting throughout his ordeal that the stars had told him everything. On the canal bank opposite Palazzo Diedo stands **San Marziale**, where, if you're in town on one of the rare days when this church is open, you'll see **Sebastiano Ricci**'s ceiling paintings, a set of works that made his reputation in the city. Those who haven't acquired the taste will get more of a buzz from the dotty Baroque high altar, depicting Saint Jerome at lunch with a couple of associates – Faith and Charity.

Most of the island to the west of San Marziale is occupied by the remnants of the church and ex-convent of **Santa Maria dei Servi**. When the church was demolished in 1812, some of its monuments were thrown away and others were shuffled around Venice – such as Doge Andrea Vendramin's tomb, now in Santi Giovanni e Paolo; the ruins themselves were offered to Ruskin, who turned the deal down.

Paolo Sarpi and the Excommunication of Venice

Unswerving moral rectitude and fierce intellectual rigour are not qualities that come first to mind when considering most of the public men of Venetian history, but both were exemplified by the Servite priest **Fra' Paolo Sarpi**, one of Venice's titanic figures. Author of a magisterial history of the Council of Trent, discoverer of the mechanics of the iris of the eye and a partner in Galileo's optical researches, Sarpi is best known as the adviser to the Venetian state in its row with the Vatican at the start of the seventeenth century. Although Venice's toleration of non-Christians was a cause of recurrent friction, the area of greatest discord was the Republic's insistence on separating the sovereignty of the Church and that of the State – "The Church must obey the State in things temporal and the latter the former in things spiritual, each maintaining its proper rights," to quote Sarpi himself.

Matters came to a head when Venice restricted the amount of money that monasteries on the mainland could return to Rome from their rents and marketing and then imprisoned two priests found guilty in secular courts of secular crimes. Pope Paul V's demand for the return of the priests and the repeal of the monastic legislation was firmly rebuffed, and the upshot was a **papal interdict** in April 1606, forbidding all religious services in Venice. Excommunication for the entire city then followed. In retaliation, Venice booted out the Jesuits and threatened with exile or death any priests who didn't ignore the interdict – a priest in Padua who insisted that the Holy Spirit had moved him to obey the pope was informed by the Council of Ten that the Holy Spirit had already moved them to hang any who disagreed with them. Sarpi and the dauntless Doge Leonardo Donà maintained their closely argued defiance of Rome until French mediation brought about a resolution which in fact required no compromises from the Venetians. The moral authority of Rome was diminished forever. Six months later, Sarpi was walking home past Santa Fosca when he was set upon by three men and left for dead with a stiletto in his cheek; the assassins failed, though – Sarpi eventually died naturally on January 15, 1623.

The Strada Nova

Continuing east from Santa Fosca, you pass the church of **San Felice** – rebuilt in the 1530s, savagely renovated in the last century, and now very much a local place of worship. One local curiosity: at the far end of the *fondamenta* going up behind the church is the only parapet-less bridge left in the main part of Venice. It leads to a private door. Once over the canal that's crossed by this oddity, you're on the **Strada Nova**, a brisk, broad and basic shopping street where you can buy anything from delicious home-made cakes to surgical trusses.

The Ca' d'Oro

Nearly halfway along the Strada an inconspicuous calle leads down to the **Ca' d'Oro** (House of Gold), the showpiece of domestic Gothic architecture in Venice and home of one of the city's most varied art collections, the **Galleria Giorgio Franchetti**. Built for procurator Marino Contarini between 1425 and 1440, the palace takes its name from its Canal Grande **facade**: incorporating parts of the thirteenth-century palace that used to stand here, this was highlighted in gold leaf, ultramarine and vermilion – materials which, as the three most expensive pigments of the day, spectacularly publicised the wealth of its owner. The house's cosmetics have now worn off, but the facade has at least survived unaltered, whereas the rest of the Ca' d'Oro was badly abused by later owners. After the dancer Maria Taglioni had finished her home improvements, Ruskin lamented that it was "now destroyed by restorations", and today, despite the subsequent structural repairs, the interior of the Ca' d'Oro is no longer recognisable as that of a Gothic building. The staircase in the **courtyard** is an original feature, though – ripped out by Taglioni, it was reacquired and reconstructed by Franchetti, who likewise put back the well-head by Bartolomeo Bon (1427). There's a display on the restoration of the building in a room to the side of the first-floor loggia.

Southern Cannaregio

The Ca' d'Oro is open Mon–Sat 9am–1.30pm, Sun 9am–12.30pm; L4000.

The gallery's main attraction is undoubtedly the *St Sebastian* painted by **Mantegna** shortly before his death in 1506, now installed in a chapel-like alcove on the first floor. Many of the big names of Venetian art are here, too, but the canvases by Titian and Tintoretto are not among their best, and Pordenone's fragmentary frescoes from Santo Stefano require a considerable feat of imaginative reconstruction, as do the remains of Giorgione and Titian's work from the Fondaco dei Tedeschi. You'll get more out of pieces from less elevated artists – **Tullio Lombardo**'s beautifully carved *Young Couple* shows him on top form, and Biagio d'Antonio da Firenze's *The Story of Lucrezia* reminds us that for a long time suicide was one of the few "honourable" responses a woman could have to rape. **Andrea di Bartolo**'s fine *Coronation of the Virgin* shows one way in which the impossible female ideal was maintained. Keep an eye out also for an anonymous *Madonna and Child* in the midst of the Flemish collection, a sixteenth-century English alabaster polyptych of *Scenes from the Life of St Catherine*, and a case of Renaissance medals containing fine specimens by **Gentile Bellini** and **Pisanello**, to name just two.

Santa Sofia and Santi Apostoli

A little further down the Strada Nova, opposite a campo bordering the Canal Grande but camouflaged by house fronts, is the entrance to the small church of **Santa Sofia**, which contains sculptures of four saints by followers of Antonio Rizzo. At the eastern end of the Strada you come to the Campo dei Santi Apostoli, an elbow on the road from the Rialto to the train station, with the church of **Santi Apostoli**, a dark and frequently renovated building last altered substantially in the eighteenth century. The **campanile** was finished in 1672 – and soon afterwards, according to James (Jan) Morris, "an old and simple-minded sacristan" fell from it, "but was miraculously caught by the minute hand of the clock, which, slowly revolving to six o'clock, deposited him safely on a parapet".

Santi Apostoli is open daily 7.30–11.30am & 5–7.30pm.

The **Cappella Corner**, off the right side, is the most interesting part of the interior – attributed to Mauro Coducci, its altarpiece is the *Communion of St Lucy* by Giambattista Tiepolo (1748). One of the inscriptions in the chapel is to Caterina Cornaro, who was buried here before being moved to San Salvatore; the tomb of her father Marco (on the right) is probably by Tullio Lombardo, who also carved the peculiar plaque of Saint Sebastian in the chapel to the right of the chancel, which makes him look as if he has a tree growing out of his head.

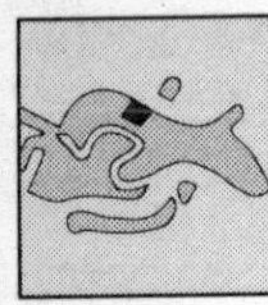

The Gesuiti district

The Gesuiti is open daily 10am–noon & 5–7pm.

The major monument of the northeastern corner of Cannaregio is **Santa Maria Assunta**, commonly known simply as the **Gesuiti**. Built for the Jesuits in 1714–29, six decades after the foundation here of their first monastery in Venice, the church was clearly planned to make an impression on a city that was habitually mistrustful of the order's close relationship with the papacy. Although the disproportionately huge facade clearly wasn't the work of a weekend, most of the effort went into the stupefying **interior**, where green and white marble covers every wall and stone is carved to resemble swags of damask – the result is jaw-dropping. Unless you're a devotee of Palma il Giovane (in which case make for the sacristy), the only painting to seek out is the *Martyrdom of St Lawrence* on the first altar on the left; painted by **Titian** in 1558, it's a night scene made doubly difficult to see by the lighting arrangements.

The Oratorio dei Crociferi is open Fri–Sun: April–June & Oct 10am–noon; July–Sept 4.30–6.30pm; free.

Almost opposite the church is the **Oratorio dei Crociferi**, reopened in 1984 after thorough restoration of **Palma il Giovane**'s *Scenes from the History of the Order of the Crociferi* (1583–91). The paintings show Palma's technique at its subtlest, and the richness of the colours is a good advertisement for modern cleaning techniques. There's not much else to look at in the immediate vicinity. Titian use to live in Calle Larga dei Botteri (no. 5179–83), across the Rio dei Gesuiti – but the house has been rebuilt and the building of the Fondamente Nuove (see below) did away with the waterside garden where he entertained such exalted clients as Henry III of France.

A short distance to the west, past the huge sixteenth-century Palazzi Zen, the church of **Santa Caterina** comes into view. Another restoration scheme is in progress here: the fourteenth-century ship's keel ceiling, destroyed by fire in 1978, has now been rebuilt, but the building belongs to a school and is thus out of bounds.

The Fondamente Nuove

The long waterfront to the north of the Gesuiti, the **Fondamente Nuove**, is the point at which the vaporetti leave the city for San Michele, Murano and the northern lagoon. On a clear day you can follow their course as far as the distant island of Burano, and you might even be treated to the startling sight of the white crags of the Dolomites, apparently hanging in the sky over the Veneto. Being relatively new, this waterfront isn't solidly lined by buildings like its counterpart in the south of the city, the Záttere. The one house of interest is the **Palazzo Donà delle Rose** on the corner of the Rio dei Gesuiti. Architecturally the palace is an oddity, as the main axis of its interior runs parallel to the water instead of at ninety degrees; the cornerstone was laid in 1610 by **Doge Leonardo Donà** (Paolo Sarpi's boss), who died two years later from apoplexy after an argument with his brother about the house's layout. It's one of the very few Venetian residences still owned by the family for whom it was built.

From the northern tip of the Fondamente the sixteenth-century **Casino degli Spiriti** can be seen across the inlet known as the Sacca della Misericordia. A *casino* (little house) – a suite set aside for private entertainments – was a feature of many Venetian palaces, and a few were set up in separate pavilions in the grounds. This is one of only two surviving examples of the latter, yet it's best known not for its architectural rarity but for the ghost story that's sometimes said to be the source of its name. A certain noblewoman took her husband's best friend as a lover, and this is where they would meet. At her paramour's sudden death she began to pine away, and shut herself in the *casino* to die. No sooner had she exhaled her last breath than the ghost of her lover came in, raised her from the bed and, pushing the nursemaid to one side, made off with her. Whether they turned up in another city under assumed names is not recorded.

Chapter 6

Castello

Bordering San Marco on one side and spreading across the city from Cannaregio in the west to the housing estates of Sant'Elena in the east, **Castello** is the most amorphous of the *sestieri*. So unwieldy is this district that somewhat altered boundaries have been used in laying out our guide. In the west, this chapter starts off from the waterway that cuts round the back of Santi Apostoli to the northern lagoon, rather than following the zigzagging border of the *sestiere*. In the east we've stopped at a line drawn north from the landmark **Pietà** church; the atmospherically distinct area beyond this boundary is covered in the next chapter.

Even after this rationalisation, the area covered by this chapter is an amalgamation of disparate units rather than an area with an overall identity. Its points of interest are evenly distributed, but in terms of its importance and its geographical location, Castello's central building is the immense Gothic church of **Santi Giovanni e Paolo** (or **Zanipolo**), the pantheon of Venice's doges. A couple of minutes away stands **Santa Maria dei Miracoli**, the city's most refined architectural miniature, which in turn is close to the often-overlooked **San Giovanni Crisostomo**. The museums covered in this chapter lie in the southern zone – the **Querini-Stampalia** picture collection, the museum at **San Giorgio dei Greci**, and the **Museo Diocesano**'s sacred art collection. This southern area's dominant building is the majestic **San Zaccaria**, a church that has played a significant part in the history of the city – as has nearby **Santa Maria Formosa**, on the liveliest and friendliest square in Castello. Busier still is the southern waterfront, the **Riva degli Schiavoni**, Venice's glamorous promenade.

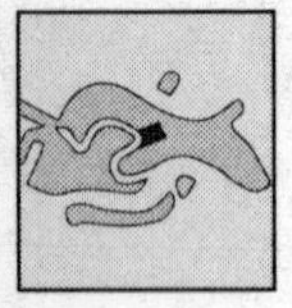

San Giovanni Crisostomo to the Miracoli

On the western edge of Castello, a couple of minutes' walk north of the post office, stands **San Giovanni Crisostomo** (John the Golden-

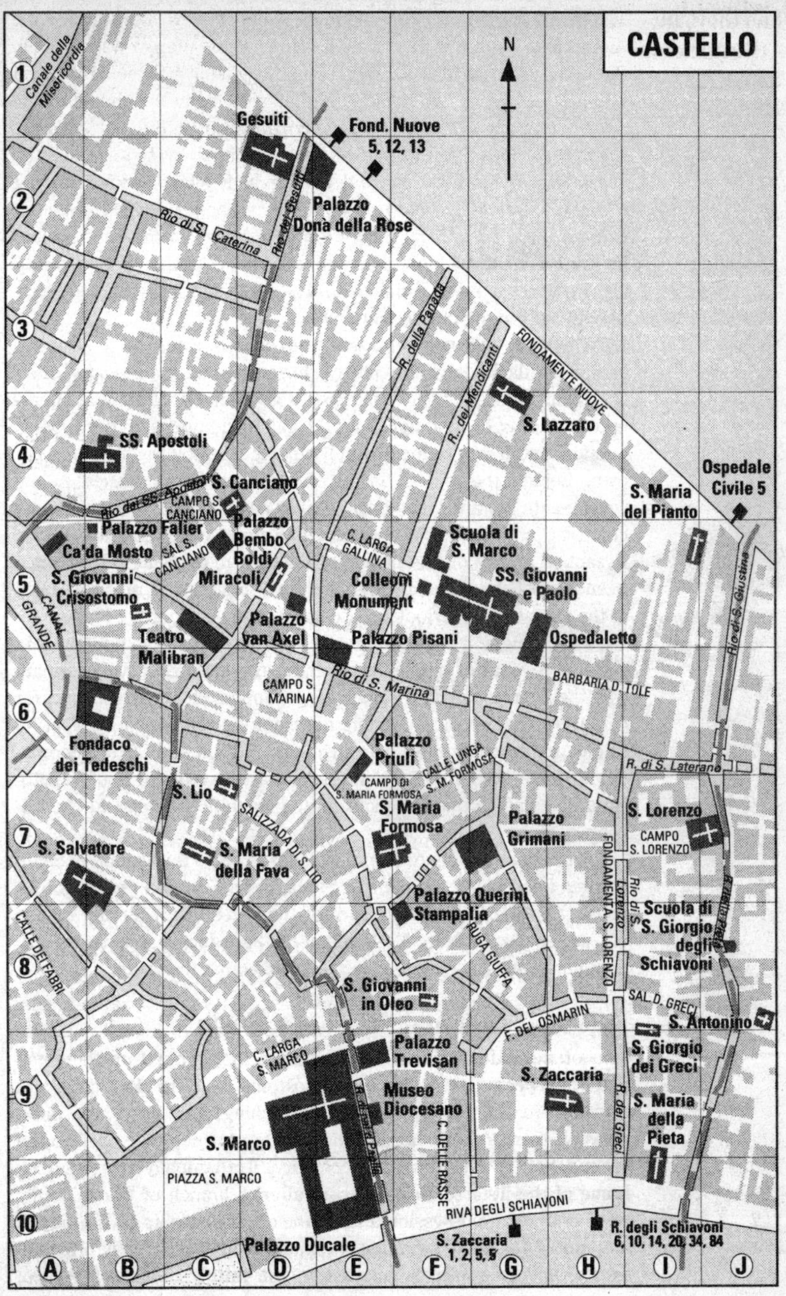

CASTELLO
N
Canale della Misericordia
Gesuiti
Fond. Nuove
5, 12, 13
Palazzo
Donà della Rose
Rio di S. Caterina
Rio dei Gesuiti
R. della Panada
R. dei Mendicanti
FONDAMENTE NUOVE
S. Lazzaro
SS. Apostoli
S. Canciano
Rio dei SS. Apostoli
CAMPO S. CANCIANO
Palazzo Falier
Palazzo
Bembo
Boldi
Ca'da Mosto
SAL. S. CANCIANO
Miracoli
S. Giovanni
Crisostomo
CANAL GRANDE
C. LARGA GALLINA
Scuola di
S. Marco
Colleoni
Monument
SS. Giovanni
e Paolo
S. Maria
del Pianto
Ospedale
Civile 5
Rio di S. Giustina
Palazzo
van Axel
Palazzo Pisani
Ospedaletto
Teatro
Malibran
CAMPO S. MARINA
Rio di S. Marina
BARBARIA D. TOLE
Fondaco
dei Tedeschi
Palazzo
Priuli
CAMPO DI S. MARIA FORMOSA
CALLE LUNGA S. M. FORMOSA
R. di S. Laterano
S. Lio
SALIZZADA DI S. LIO
S. Maria
Formosa
Palazzo
Grimani
S. Lorenzo
CAMPO S. LORENZO
S. Salvatore
S. Maria
della Fava
FONDAMENTA S. LORENZO
Rio di S. Lorenzo
Palazzo Querini
Stampalia
RUGA GIUFFA
Scuola di
S. Giorgio
degli
Schiavoni
CALLE DEI FABRI
S. Giovanni
in Oleo
SAL. D. GRECI
F. DEL OSMARIN
S. Antonino
C. LARGA S. MARCO
Palazzo
Trevisan
S. Giorgio
dei Greci
S. Zaccaria
Museo
Diocesano
S. Maria
della
Pieta
R. dei Greci
C. DELLE RASSE
S. Marco
PIAZZA S. MARCO
RIVA DEGLI SCHIAVONI
Palazzo Ducale
S. Zaccaria
1, 2, 5, 5
R. degli Schiavoni
6, 10, 14, 20, 34, 84
1
2
3
4
5
6
7
8
9
10
A
B
C
D
E
F
G
H
I
J

San Giovanni Crisostomo to the Miracoli

Mouthed), named after the eloquent Archbishop of Constantinople. An intimate church with a compact Greek-cross plan, it was possibly the last project of Mauro Coducci, and was built between 1497 and 1504. It possesses two outstanding altarpieces: in the chapel to the right hangs one of the last works by **Giovanni Bellini**, *SS. Jerome, Christopher and Louis of Toulouse*, painted in 1513 when the artist was in his eighties; and on the high altar, **Sebastiano del Piombo**'s gracefully heavy *St John Chrysostom with SS. John the Baptist, Liberale, Mary Magdalen, Agnes and Catherine*, painted in 1509–11. On the left side is a marble panel of the *Coronation of the Virgin* by Tullio Lombardo, a severe contrast with the more playful stuff in the nearby Miracoli.

The calle virtually opposite the church leads to a secluded campiello flanked by the partly thirteenth-century **Palazzo Lion-Morosini**, whose external staircase is guarded by a little lion apparently suffering from indigestion; the campiello opens onto the Canal Grande, and if you're lucky you'll be able to enjoy the view on your own. Behind the church is the **Teatro Malibran**, opened in the seventeenth century, rebuilt in 1920 as a venue for ballet, opera and concerts, and currently undergoing a protracted restoration. The Byzantine arches on the facade of the theatre are said to have once been part of the house of **Marco Polo**'s family, who probably lived in the tatty place overlooking the canal at the back of the Malibran.

Polo's memoir *Il Milione* (1298), detailing his experiences in seventeen years of service throughout the empire of Kublai Khan, was the first account of Asian life to appear in the West, and for centuries was the most reliable description available in Europe. Its title is preserved by the **Corte Prima del Milion** and **Corte Seconda del Milion** – the latter is an interesting architectural mix of Veneto-Byzantine and Gothic elements, with a magnificently carved twelfth-century arch.

From here the Ponte Marco Polo leads off to the Campo di Santa Marina; keep going straight for Santa Maria Formosa (see p.155) – pausing on the Ponte del Cristo for the seventeenth-century facade of the Palazzo Marcello-Pindemonte-Papadopoli (attributed to Longhena) and the Gothic Palazzo Pisani across the water.

Palazzo Falier and the Ca' da Mosto

Two of the oldest houses in Venice are to be found on the small patch between San Giovanni Crisostomo and the Rio dei Santi Apostoli. At the foot of the bridge arching over to Campo Santi Apostoli there's the **Palazzo Falier**, parts of which date back to the second half of the thirteenth century. Traditionally this was the home of the ill-fated **Doge Marin Falier**, a branch of whose family was certainly in possession at the time of his dogeship (1354–55). A man noted for his unswerving rectitude, Falier was greatly offended by the licence routinely allowed to the unruly nobles of Venice;

when a lenient punishment was given to a young nobleman who had insulted Falier, his wife and her ladies, he finally went right off the rails and hatched a conspiracy to install himself as the city's benevolent despot – a plot into which he conscripted the overseer of the Arsenale and Filippo Calendario, one of the architects of the Palazzo Ducale. Their plan was discovered and Falier, admitting the conspiracy, was beheaded on the very spot on which he had earlier been invested as doge.

Interlocking with the Falier house is the equally ancient **Ca' da Mosto**, reached through the passage on the right – though the best view of it is from the deck of a vaporetto. This was the birthplace of **Alvise da Mosto** (1432–88), a Venetian merchant-explorer who threw in his lot with Portugal's Henry the Navigator and went on to discover the Cape Verde Islands. The popular *Albergo del Leon Bianco* occupied these premises for a long time; among its guests were J.M.W. Turner, who had himself rowed up and down the Canal Grande while he scribbled in his notebook, and two German officers who in 1716 fought a duel in the courtyard and contrived to skewer each other to death.

There's an unusual memorial to Marin Falier in the Palazzo Ducale – see p.60.

Santa Maria dei Miracoli

Inland from these palaces, beyond the dull San Canziano, stands the church which Ruskin paired with the Scuola di San Marco as "the two most refined buildings in Venice" – **Santa Maria dei Miracoli**, always known simply by the last word of its name.

It was built in the 1480s to house a miracle-working image of the Madonna – it was credited with the revival of a man who'd spent half an hour at the bottom of the Giudecca canal and of a woman left for dead after being stabbed. Financed by gifts left at the painting's nearby shrine, the church was most likely designed by **Pietro Lombardo;** certainly he and his two sons **Tullio** and **Antonio** oversaw the construction, and the three of them executed much of the carving. Richness of effect takes precedence over classical correctness on the **exterior**: pilasters are placed close together along the sides to create the illusion of longer walls, for example, and Corinthian pilasters are placed below Ionic (in defiance of classical rules) so that the viewer can better appreciate the former's more elaborate detailing. Venetian folklore has it that the materials for the multi-coloured marble cladding and inlays, typical of the Lombardi, were the surplus from the decoration of the Basilica di San Marco.

The marble-lined **interior** contains some of the most intricate decorative sculpture to be seen in Venice. The *Annunciation* and half-length figures of two saints on the balustrade at the altar end are thought to be by Tullio; the rest of the carvings at this end are arguable between the two brothers and their father. Ruskin was rather distressed by the children's heads carved to the side of the steps – "the man who could carve a child head so perfectly must

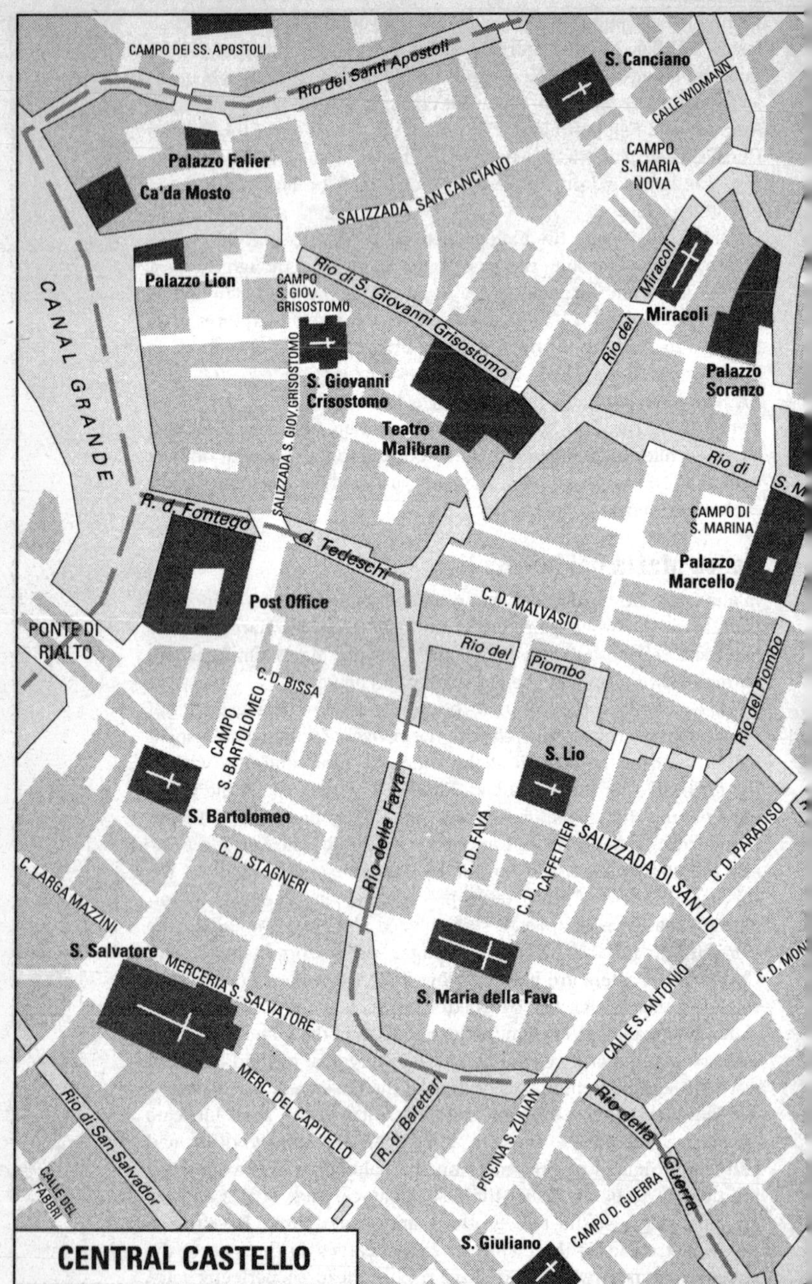

CAMPO DEI SS. APOSTOLI
Rio dei Santi Apostoli
S. Canciano
CALLE WIDMANN
CAMPO
S. MARIA
NOVA
Palazzo Falier
Ca'da Mosto
SALIZZADA SAN CANCIANO
Palazzo Lion
CAMPO
S. GIOV.
GRISOSTOMO
Rio di S. Giovanni Grisostomo
Miracoli
Rio dei
Miracoli
CANAL GRANDE
S. Giovanni
Crisostomo
SALIZZADA S. GIOV. GRISOSTOMO
Teatro
Malibran
Palazzo
Soranzo
Rio di
CAMPO DI
S. MARINA
Palazzo
Marcello
R. d. Fontego
d. Tedeschi
Post Office
C. D. MALVASIO
PONTE DI
RIALTO
Rio del
Piombo
Rio del Piombo
C. D. BISSA
CAMPO
S. BARTOLOMEO
S. Lio
Rio della Fava
S. Bartolomeo
C. D. FAVA
C. D. CAFFETTIER
SALIZZADA DI SAN LIO
C. D. PARADISO
C. D. STAGNERI
C. LARGA MAZZINI
S. Salvatore
MERCERIA S. SALVATORE
S. Maria della Fava
CALLE S. ANTONIO
MERC. DEL CAPITELLO
R. d. Barettari
PISCINA S. ZULIAN
Rio della Guerra
Rio di San Salvador
CALLE DEL FABBRI
CAMPO D. GUERRA
S. Giuliano
CENTRAL CASTELLO

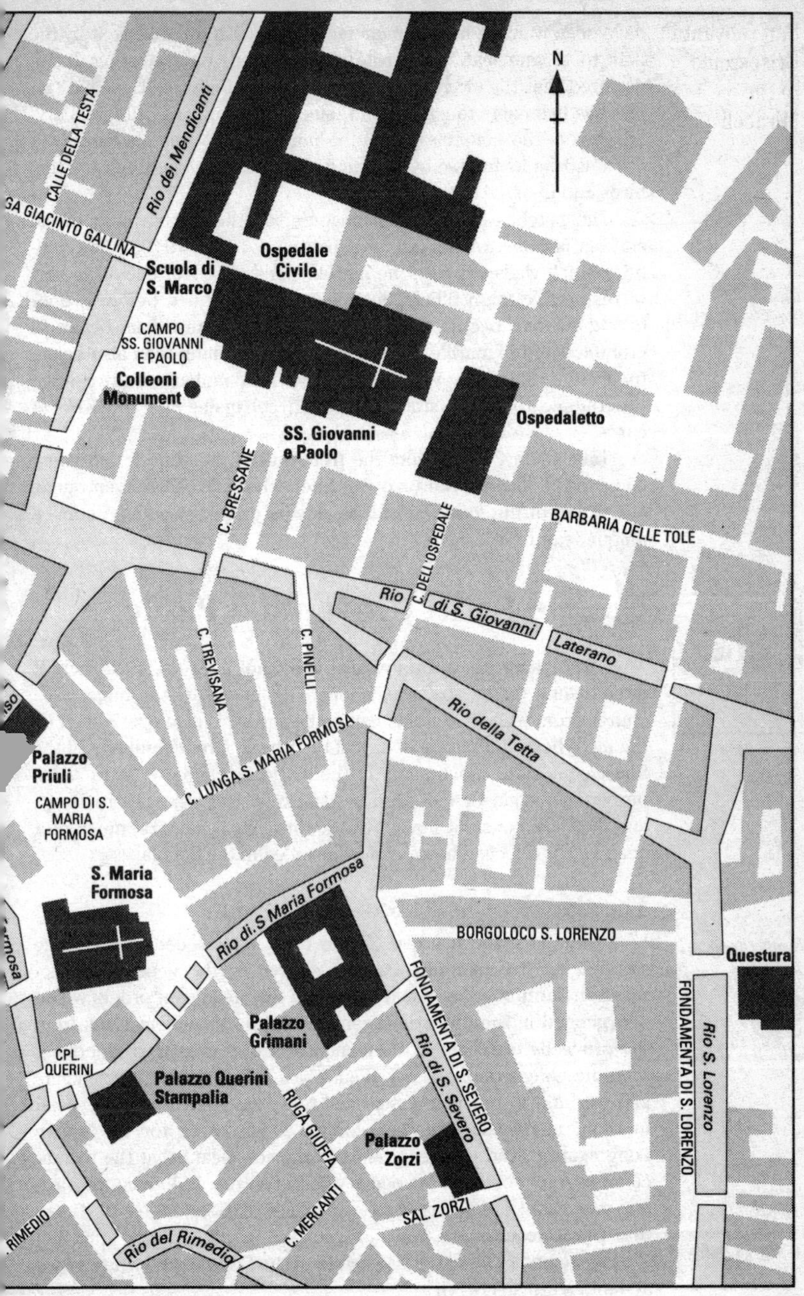
N
CALLE DELLA TESTA
Rio dei Mendicanti
GA GIACINTO GALLINA
Scuola di
S. Marco
Ospedale
Civile
CAMPO
SS. GIOVANNI
E PAOLO
Colleoni
Monument
Ospedaletto
SS. Giovanni
e Paolo
C. BRESSANE
C. DELL'OSPEDALE
BARBARIA DELLE TOLE
Rio
di S. Giovanni
Laterano
C. TREVISANA
C. PINELLI
Rio della Tetta
C. LUNGA S. MARIA FORMOSA
Palazzo
Priuli
CAMPO DI S.
MARIA
FORMOSA
S. Maria
Formosa
Rio di. S Maria Formosa
BORGOLOCO S. LORENZO
Questura
FONDAMENTA DI S. SEVERO
Rio di S. Severo
FONDAMENTA DI S. LORENZO
Rio S. Lorenzo
Palazzo
Grimani
CPL.
QUERINI
Palazzo Querini
Stampalia
RUGA GIUFFA
Palazzo
Zorzi
SAL. ZORZI
C. MERCANTI
RIMEDIO
Rio del Rimedio

San Giovanni Crisostomo to the Miracoli

have been wanting in all human feeling, to cut it off, and tie it by the hair to a vine leaf," he wrote; Ezra Pound, on the other hand, declared that the siren figures were so beautifully realised that "no one has been able to carve them" since. Extraordinary filigree carving covers the columns below the nun's choir – the sacristan will demonstrate its finesse by inserting a cocktail stick between the tiny birds and the face of the columns.

The patches of crystalline material on the marble both inside and out are due to overzealous repair work in the 1970s: the crumbling brick walls between the marble skins were stuffed with a sort of restorative foam filling, but the holes were filled before proper drying-out had occurred. The result was that the bricks began to crumble and the marble stuck fast to the new filling then also began to disintegrate. Save Venice Inc. have now embarked on a huge programme to try to stop the church collapsing like a house of cards.

Take Calle Castelli from the front end of the church and you'll come to the **Palazzo Soranzo-van Axel**, whose fine Gothic entrance, at the end of the *fondamenta*, retains its original wooden door – a unique feature in Venice.

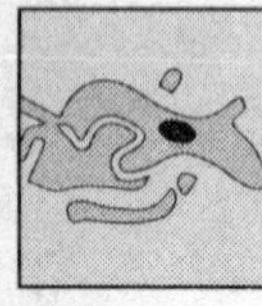

Campo Santi Giovanni e Paolo

After the Piazza, the **Campo Santi Giovanni e Paolo** is the richest monumental public space in Venice. Dominated by the huge brick church from which it gets its name, the square is also overlooked by the most beautiful facade of any of the Scuole Grandi and one of the finest equestrian monuments in the world. A couple of bars and a perpetual gaggle of ball-playing kids keep the atmosphere lively, and there's a constant flow of traffic through the square, much of it heading for the civic hospital now installed in the Scuola.

The church of Santi Giovanni e Paolo

Santi Giovanni e Paolo is open daily 7am–12.30pm & 3.30–7.30pm.

Like the Frari, the massive Gothic brick edifice dedicated to the twinned **Santi Giovanni e Paolo** – slurred by the Venetian dialect into **San Zanipolo** – was built for one of the mendicant orders which bourgeoned in the fourteenth century. Supporting themselves from the proceeds of begging, the mendicants were less inward-looking than the older orders, basing themselves in large urban settlements and working to relieve the sick and the poor. Reflecting this social mission, mendicant churches contain a vast area for the public congregation, and this requirement of space meant that the mendicants typically built on the edges of city centres. In Venice the various mendicant orders are scattered outside the San Marco *sestiere*: the **Dominicans** here, the Franciscans at the Frari and San Francesco della Vigna, the Carmelites at the Carmini and the Servites at Santa Maria dei Servi.

SANTI GIOVANNI E PAOLO (SAN ZANIPOLO)

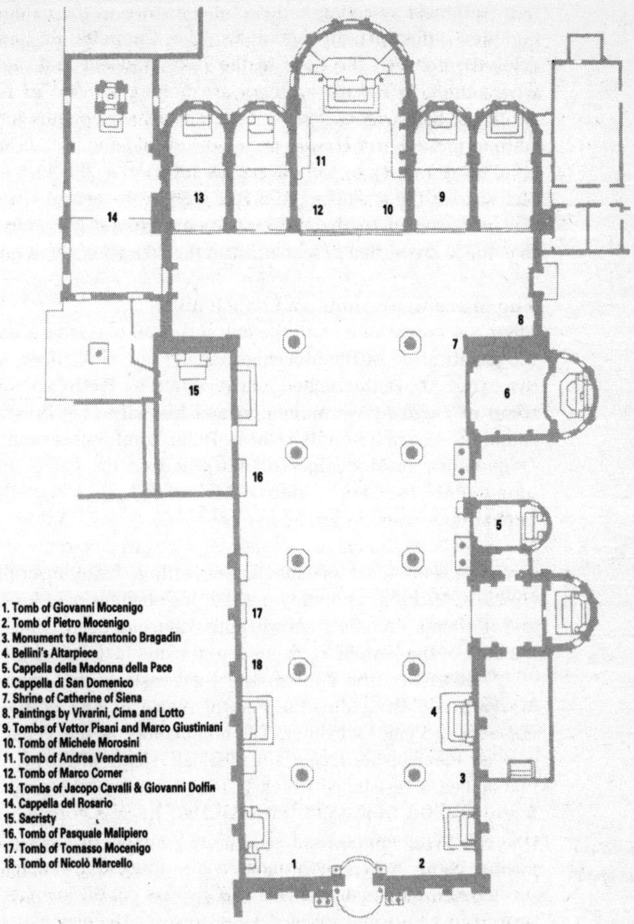

The first church built on this site was begun in 1246 after **Doge Giacomo Tiepolo** was inspired by a dream to donate the land to the Dominicans; but that version was soon demolished to make way for this larger building, begun in 1333, though not consecrated until 1430. Tiepolo's simple sarcophagus is outside, on the left of the door, next to that of his son **Doge Lorenzo Tiepolo** (d.1275); both tombs were altered after the Bajamonte Tiepolo revolt of 1310, when the family were no longer allowed to display their old crest and had to devise a replacement. The **doorway**, flanked by Byzantine reliefs, is thought to be by **Bartolomeo Bon**, and is one of the major transitional Renaissance works in the city; apart from that, the most arresting architectural feature of the exterior is the complex brickwork of the **apse**. The **Cappella di Sant'Orsola** (closed), between the door to the right transept and the apse, is where the two **Bellini** brothers are buried; it used to house the Scuola di Sant'Orsola, the confraternity which commissioned from Carpaccio the *Saint Ursula* cycle now installed in the Accademia.

The simplicity of the cavernous **interior** – 290 feet long, 125 feet wide at the transepts, 108 feet high in the centre – is offset by the profusion of tombs and monuments around the walls; twenty-five doges are buried here, but it can feel like all of them must be.

The Mocenigo tombs and south aisle

There's scarcely an inch of the entrance wall that isn't given over to the glorification of the Mocenigo family, one of Venice's top-notch dynasties. Above the niched pair of saints by Pietro Lombardo, the **tomb of Doge Alvise Mocenigo and his wife** (1577) wraps itself round the doorway; on its right is Tullio Lombardo's **monument to Doge Giovanni Mocenigo** (d.1485); and on the left is the superb **monument to Doge Pietro Mocenigo** (d.1476), by Pietro Lombardo, with assistance from Tullio and Antonio. Pietro Mocenigo's sarcophagus, supported by warriors representing the three Ages of Man, is embellished with a Latin inscription (*Ex Hostium Manibus*) pointing out that his enemies paid for the tomb, and a couple of reliefs showing his valorous deeds, including the handing of the keys of Famagusta to the doomed Caterina Cornaro.

For more on Caterina Cornaro, see p.335.

Next to the first altar of the right aisle is the **monument to Marcantonio Bragadin**, the central figure in one of the grisliest episodes in Venice's history. The commander of the Venetian garrison at Famagusta during the Turkish siege of 1571, Bragadin marshalled a resistance which lasted eleven months until, with his force reduced from 7000 men to 700, he was forced to sue for peace. Given guarantees of safety, the Venetian officers entered the enemy camp, whereupon most were dragged away and cut to pieces, whilst Bragadin himself had his ears cut off in an assault that proved to be a foretaste of days of torture. His eventual execution was appalling – chained to a stake on the public scaffold, he was slowly flayed alive in front of the Pasha. His skin, stuffed with straw, was then mounted on a cow and paraded through the streets, prior to being hung from the bowsprit of the admiral's galley for the return voyage to Constantinople. Later the skin was brought back to Venice, and today it sits in that urn high up on the wall.

Giovanni Bellini's painting for the first altar went up in smoke some years ago, but his marvellous polyptych of *SS. Vincent Ferrer, Christopher and Sebastian* (on the third altar) has come through the centuries in magnificent fettle, although it has lost the

Campo Santi Giovanni e Paolo

image of God the Father which used to accompany the upper-level *Annunciation* and *Pietà*. The oozing effigy reclining below is of Tommaso Caraffini, confessor and biographer of Saint Catherine of Siena.

The next chapel but one, the **Cappella della Madonna della Pace**, is named after its Byzantine Madonna, brought to Venice in 1349 and attributed with amazing powers; above the chapel entrance the figures of Doge Bertucci Valier (d.1658), Doge Silvestro Valier (d.1700) and Silvestro's wife, Dogaressa Elizabetta Querini (d.1708), are poised like actors taking a bow.

St Dominic in Glory, the only ceiling panel in Venice by Giambattista Piazzetta, Giambattista Tiepolo's tutor, covers the vault of the neighbouring **Cappella di San Domenico**, alongside which is a tiny shrine containing the **foot of Saint Catherine of Siena**. Born in 1347 as the youngest of 25 children, Catherine manifested early signs of uninhibited piety – wearing hair shirts, sleeping on bare boards, and crashing up and down stairs on her knees, saying a Hail Mary on each step. She died in 1380 and her body promptly entered the relic market – most of it is in Rome, but her head is in Siena, a foot here, and other lesser relics are scattered about Italy.

The south transept and the chancel

San Zanipolo's best paintings are clustered in the **south transept**: Alvise Vivarini's *Christ Carrying the Cross* (1474), a *Coronation of the Virgin* attributed to Cima da Conegliano and Giovanni Martini da Udine, and Lorenzo Lotto's *St Antonine* (1542). As payment for his work Lotto asked only for his expenses and permission to be buried in the church; presumably the first part of the deal went through all right, but Lotto soon afterwards quit the backbiting of Venice's artistic circles, and eventually died in Loreto, where he was buried.

Much of the right wall of the second apsidal chapel – the **Cappella della Maddalena** – is taken up with a twentieth-century reconstruction of the **monument to Admiral Vettor Pisani**. Pisani's role in the victory over the Genoese at Chioggia in 1380 – a campaign in which he was mortally wounded – is neatly summed up by John Julius Norwich: "it would perhaps be an exaggeration to say that he saved Venice single-handed; the fact remains that she would not have survived without him". The tomb supported by what look like the heads of giant elves, is of another sea captain, Marco Giustiniani (d.1346).

For more on Vettor Pisani, see p.214.

The **chancel** is one of the high points of funerary art in Venice. **Doge Michele Morosini**, who ruled for four months before dying of plague in 1382, is buried in the tomb at the front on the right, a work which in Ruskin's eyes marked a fault-line in European civilisation, showing as it does "not only the exactly intermediate condition in style between the pure Gothic and its final Renaissance corruption, but, at the same time, the exactly intermediate condition of feeling between the pure calmness of early Christianity, and the boastful pomp of the Renaissance faithlessness". The fallen Renaissance world is represented by the tomb of **Doge Andrea Vendramin** (d.1478), diagonally opposite from Morosini's, which was moved here in 1818 from the church of the Servi. The sculptor (probably Tullio Lombardo) carved only the half of the figure that could be seen from below, an act which Ruskin condemned as being of "such utter coldness of feeling as could only consist with an extreme of intellectual and moral degradation". Next to it is the Gothic tomb of **Doge Marco Corner** (d.1368), which was hacked about to make way for its neighbour.

The north transept and north aisle

Of the **tomb of Jacopo Cavalli** (d.1384), on the right of the final chapel in the north transept, Ruskin scornfully remarked: "I find no especial reason for the images of the Virtues, especially that of Charity, appearing at his tomb, unless it be this: that at the siege of Feltre, in the war against Leopold of Austria, he refused to assault the city because the senate would not grant his soldiers the pillage of the town." As if in response, the Virtues are no longer in place; the frescoes around the tomb are by Titian's nephew, Lorenzo Vecellio. On the left is the tomb of **Doge Giovanni Dolfin** (d.1361) who was besieged by the Hungarians in Trieste when elected in 1356, and had to charge through enemy lines under cover of darkness in order to take up the post.

The **Cappella del Rosario**, at the end of the north transept, was built 1582 and dedicated to the victory over the Turkish fleet at Lépanto, which happened on the feast-day of the Madonna of the Rosary, October 7, 1571. In 1867 a fire destroyed its paintings by Tintoretto, Palma il Giovane and others, as well as Giovanni Bellini's *Madonna* and Titian's *Martyrdom of St Peter*, San Zanipolo's two most celebrated paintings, which were in here for restoration; arson by anti-Catholics was suspected, but nothing was ever proved. A lengthy twentieth-century restoration made use of surviving fragments and installed other pieces such as **Veronese**'s ceiling panels of *The Annunciation*, *The Assumption* and *The Adoration of the Shepherds*, and the other *Adoration* by him on the left of the door.

In the north aisle, Bartolomeo Vivarini's *Three Saints* (1473), a portion of a dismantled polyptych, is the first thing to grab your eye. Busts of Titian, Palma il Vecchio and Palma il Giovane look down from over the sacristy door, forming the monument which the last of the three designed for himself. After the sacristy, the rest of the aisle is stacked with monuments, the first of which is that of **Doge Pasquale Malipiero** (d.1462) – created by **Pietro Lombardo**, it's one of the earliest in Renaissance style in Venice. After the equestrian monument of the *condottiere* **Pompeo Giustiniani** (aka *Braccio di Ferro* – Iron Arm) comes the **tomb of Doge Tommaso Mocenigo** (d.1423) by Pietro di Nicolò Lamberti and Giovanni di Martino, followed by another Pietro Lombardo monument, for **Doge**

Nicolò Marcello (d.1474), just before the altar with the copy of Titian's *Martyrdom of St Peter*. Three eminent Venetians of a more recent time – the Risorgimento heroes Attillo and Emilio Bandiera and Domenico Moro – are commemorated alongside; they're also honoured by having a square named after them (see p.168). On the last altar is a somewhat over-dramatic figure of *St Jerome* by Alessandro Vittoria (1576).

Around the church

The *condottiere* **Bartolomeo Colleoni**, celebrated by the great **equestrian statue** outside Santi Giovanni e Paolo, began his wayward career in Venice's army in 1429 after a spell in the pay of Naples, and for a while took orders from Gattamelata, who's commemorated in Padua by Donatello's superb monument. In the succeeding years Colleoni defected to Milan, was imprisoned there, escaped, re-enlisted for Venice, fled once again, and finally joined the Republic's ranks for good in 1455 – whereupon Venice suffered an outbreak of peace which resulted in his being called upon to fight on just one occasion during the last twenty years of his life. Resisting several lucrative offers from France and Rome, he settled into a life of prosperous leisure, and when he died in 1475 he left a legacy of over 100,000 ducats to the Venetian state. But there was a snag to this bequest: the Signoria could have the money only if an equestrian monument to him were erected in the square before San Marco – an unthinkable proposition to Venice's rulers, with their cult of anonymity. The problem was circumvented with a fine piece of disingenuousness, by which Colleoni's will was taken to allow the state to claim his money if his statue were raised before the Scuola di San Marco, rather than the Basilica.

Andrea Verrocchio won the commission for the monument in 1481, and difficulties cropped up in this stage of the proceedings, too. Verrocchio was preparing the figure of the horse for casting when he heard that another artist was being approached to sculpt the rider. Insulted, he smashed up his work and returned to Florence in a rage, to be followed by a decree forbidding him on pain of death to return to Venice. Eventually he was invited back, and was working again on the piece when he died in June 1488. The Signoria then hired **Alessandro Leopardi** to finish the work and produce the plinth for it, which he gladly did – even signing his own name on the horse's girth, and taking the self-bestowed title *del Cavallo*. According to Marin Sanudo, when the monument was finally unveiled in 1496 all of Venice came to marvel at it. Don't run away with the notion that Colleoni was a dead ringer for Klaus Kinski – this isn't a portrait (Verrocchio never met his subject), but rather an idealised image of steely masculinity. And talking of masculinity, Thomas Coryat noted that the name Colleoni "doth signify a testicle", but sadly did not speculate further.

Campo Santi Giovanni e Paolo

An entirely different spirit of that age is manifested by Colleoni's backdrop, the **Scuola Grande di San Marco,** which since its suppression in the early nineteenth century has provided a sumptuous facade and foyer for the Ospedale Civile. The **facade** was started by Pietro Lombardo and Giovanni Buora in 1487 and finished in 1495 by Mauro Coducci; taken as a whole, the perspectival panels by **Tullio and Antonio Lombardo** might not quite create the intended illusion, but they're some of the most charming sculptural pieces in Venice. The **interior** was radically altered by the Austrians in 1819 but partly reconstructed using some original bits; if you ask at the desk they might let you into the upstairs library, which still has its early sixteenth-century ceiling, and the church of **San Lazzaro dei Mendicanti** (open mornings only), which contains a Veronese and an early Tintoretto – but bear in mind that this is a hospital like any other, so be discreet.

Another hospital block is attached to Longhena's church of the **Ospedaletto** (or Santa Maria dei Derelitti), beyond the east end of the church. The leering giants' heads and overripe decorations of its facade drew Ruskin's wrathful attention – "it is almost worth devoting an hour to the successive examination of five buildings as illustrative of the last degradation of the Renaissance. San Moisè is the most clumsy, Santa Maria Zobenigo the most impious, San Eustachio the most ridiculous, the Ospedaletto the most monstrous, and the head at Santa Maria Formosa the most foul." The much less extravagant interior, recently restored, has a series of eighteenth-century paintings high on the walls above the arches, one of which – *The Sacrifice of Isaac* – is an early **Giambattista Tiepolo** (fourth on the right). The adjoining music room, frescoed in the eighteenth century, is sometimes open – or just pop your head round the door if you hear a rehearsal in progress.

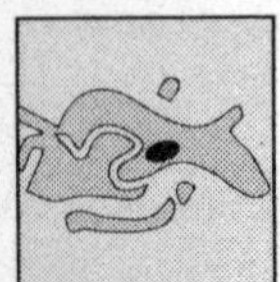

Campo Santa Maria Formosa and around

The spacious **Campo di Santa Maria Formosa**, virtually equidistant from the Piazza, San Zanipolo and the Ponte di Rialto, is a major confluence of routes on the east side of the Canal Grande, and one of the most attractive and atmospheric squares in the city. Its fruit and vegetable stalls may be less numerous than those of the Rialto, but they're very nearly as fertile, and their owners are generally readier to pass the time of day with you. It's also a regular pitch for sellers of antiquarian bits and pieces, their tables laden with the harvest of a few attic clearances. A number of elegant buildings border the square, the most enigmatic of which is the sixteenth-century **Palazzo Priuli**, which has been closed up for some time, although someone pays its rates and post is sometimes delivered there. The Partito Democratico della Sinistra occupies the red building alongside – a more appropriate symbolism before the break-up of its precursor, the Italian communist party.

The church of Santa Maria Formosa

Santa Maria Formosa is open daily 8.30am–12.30pm & 5–7pm.

The uniquely named **Santa Maria Formosa** was founded in the seventh century by San Magno, Bishop of Oderzo, who was guided by a dream in which he saw the Madonna *formosa* – a word which most closely translates as buxom and beautiful. In 944 it gained a place in the ceremonials of Venice when a group of its parishioners rescued some young women who had been abducted from San Pietro in Castello (see p.173); as a reward, the doge thereafter visited the church each year, when he would be presented with a straw hat to keep the rain off and wine to slake his thirst. The hat given to the last doge can be seen in the Museo Correr.

Mauro Coducci, who rebuilt the church in 1492, followed quite closely the original Greek-cross plan, both as an evocation of Venice's Byzantine past and as a continuation of the tradition by which Marian churches were centrally organised to symbolise the womb. A dome was frequently employed as a reference to Mary's crown; this one was rebuilt in 1922 after an Austrian bomb had destroyed its predecessor in World War I.

There are two **facades** to the church. The one facing the canal was built in 1542 in honour of the military leader Vincenzo Cappello (d.1541); Ruskin, decrying the lack of religious imagery on this facade, identified Santa Maria Formosa as the forerunner of those churches "built to the glory of man, instead of the glory of God". The decoration of the other facade, constructed in 1604, is a bit less presumptuous, as at least there's a figure of the Virgin to accompany the three portrait busts of other members of the Cappello clan. Ruskin reserved a special dose of vitriol for the **mask** at the base of the Baroque campanile: "huge, inhuman and monstrous – leering in bestial degradation, too foul to be either pictured or described . . . in that head is embodied the type of the evil spirit to which Venice was abandoned." Pompeo Molmenti, the most assiduous chronicler of Venice's socio-cultural history, insists that the head is both a talisman against the Evil Eye and a piece of clinical realism, portraying a man with the same rare congenital disorder as disfigured the so-called Elephant Man.

The church contains two good paintings. Entering from the canal side, immediately on the right is **Palma il Vecchio's** *St Barbara* (1522–24), praised by George Eliot as "an almost unique presentation of a hero-woman, standing in calm preparation for martyrdom, without the slightest air of pietism, yet with the expression of a mind filled with serious conviction". Having added a third window to her two-windowed bathroom to symbolise the Trinity, and generally displayed an intolerable Christian recalcitrance, Saint Barbara was hauled up a mountain by her exasperated father and there executed. On his way down, the man was struck down by lightning, a fate which turned Barbara into the patron saint of soldiers, the terrestrial agents of violent sudden death. This is why Palma's painting stands in the former chapel of the Scuola dei Bombardieri, and shows her treading on a cannon.

Bartolomeo Vivarini's *Triptych of the Madonna of the Misericordia* (1473), once the church's high altarpiece, is now in a nave chapel on the same side of the church as the *St Barbara*. It was paid for by the congregation of the church, and some of the figures under the Madonna's cloak are believed to be portraits of the parishioners. Such images of the merciful Madonna, one of the warmest in Catholic iconography, can be seen in various forms throughout the city – there's another example a few minutes' walk away, on the route to the Rialto bridge.

Santa Maria to the Rialto

Either of the two bridges on the canal side of Santa Maria Formosa will take you onto the busy Salizzada di San Lio, a direct route to the Rialto that has one of the best *pasticcerie* in Venice (*Il Golosone*) and a handy supermarket. Calle del Paradiso, off to the right as you head towards the Rialto, is a pocket of almost untouched Gothic Venice, overlooked at one end by an early fifteenth-century arch showing the *Madonna della Misericordia*: unusually, she's sheltering a single person – the arch's donor. The coats of arms on the arch are those of the Fóscari and Mocenigo families, who owned the adjoining buildings.

San Lio church is notable for its ceiling panel of the *The Apotheosis of St Leo* by **Giandomenico Tiepolo**, and for the chapel to the right of the high altar, which was designed by the Lombardi and contains a *Pietà* possibly by Tullio Lombardo; there's also a low-grade Titian on the first altar on the left. Unfortunately the church is usually closed, for lack of money to pay a custodian.

A diversion south from San Lio down Calle della Fava brings you to the church of **Santa Maria della Fava**, whose peculiar name derives from a sweet cake called a *fava* (bean), once an All Souls' Day speciality of a local baker, and still a seasonal treat. Canova's tutor Giuseppe Bernardi (known as Torretto) carved the statues in niches along the nave; on the first altar on the right stands Giambattista Tiepolo's early *Education of the Virgin* (1732), and on the other side of the church there's *The Madonna and St Philip Neri*, painted five years earlier by Giambattista Piazzetta, the most influential painter in early eighteenth-century Venice.

The Querini-Stampalia and Museo Diocesano

Some of the most impressive palaces in the city stand on the island immediately to the south of Santa Maria Formosa; turn first left off Ruga Giuffa and you'll be confronted by the land entrance of the gargantuan sixteenth-century **Palazzo Grimani**, but for a decent view of the exterior you have to cross the Rio San Severo, which also runs past the Gothic **Palazzo Zorzi-Bon** and Coducci's neighbouring **Palazzo Zorzi**.

Campo Santa Maria Formosa and around

If, instead of taking Ruga Giuffa, you take the alley that follows the south wall of Santa Maria Formosa, you pass into the Campiello Querini, forecourt of the Renaissance **Palazzo Querini-Stampalia**. From 1807 to 1850 this was the home of the Patriarch of Venice, and on August 3, 1849, was besieged by indignant Venetians when the patriarch refused to support resistance to Austrian rule. It now houses one of the city's more recondite collections, the **Pinacoteca Querini-Stampalia**. Although there are a batch of Renaissance pieces – such as Palma il Vecchio's marriage portraits of *Francesco Querini* and *Paola Priuli Querini* (for whom the palace was built), and Giovanni Bellini's *Presentation in the Temple* – the general tone of the collection is set by the culture of eighteenth-century Venice, a period to which much of the palace's decor belongs. The winningly inept pieces by **Gabriel Bella**, piled high in the first room, form a comprehensive record of Venetian life in that century, and genre paintings by **Pietro and Alessandro Longhi**, a few rungs up the aesthetic ladder, feature prominently later on. All in all, unless you've a voracious appetite for the art of Venice's twilight decades, the Querini-Stampalia isn't going to thrill you.

The Querini-Stampalia is open Tues–Sun 10am–12.30pm; L5000.

South of the Querini-Stampalia lies the crumbly, deconsecrated church of **San Giovanni in Oleo**, now housing the **Museo Guidi**, a contemporary gallery with a predilection for the output of Sunday painters. Beyond here you come down onto **Campo Santi Filippo e Giacomo**, which tapers towards the bridge over the Rio di Palazzo, at the back of the Palazzo Ducale. The sixteenth-century **Palazzo Trevisan-Cappello**, on one side of the foot of the bridge, was once the home of Bianca Cappello, who was sentenced to death in her absence for eloping to Florence with her lower-class lover. All was forgiven when she later dumped her hapless swain for Francesco de'Medici, with whom she stayed until their joint death in 1587. They may have been poisoned, which rather embarrassed the Venetians, who couldn't publicly mourn their "daughter of the Republic" for fear of offending the couple's unknown but probably influential killer.

The Museo Guidi is open Tues–Sun 10am–noon & 3–7pm; free.

On the other side a short *fondamenta* leads to the early fourteenth-century cloister of **Sant'Apollonia**, the only Romanesque cloister in the city. Fragments from the Basilica di San Marco dating back to the ninth century are displayed here, and a miscellany of sculptural pieces from other churches are on show in the adjoining **Museo Diocesano d'Arte Sacra**, where the permanent collection consists of a range of religious artefacts and paintings gathered from churches which have closed down or entrusted their possessions to the safety of the museum. In addition, works temporarily removed for restoration are often installed here for a while, which gives the museum an edge of unpredictability.

The Museo Diocesano is open daily 10.30am–12.30pm; free.

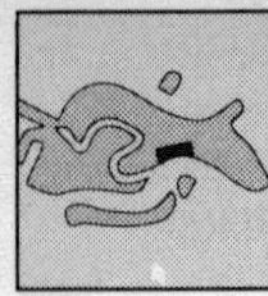

San Zaccaria to San Giorgio dei Greci

The Salizzada di San Provolo, leading east out of Campo Santi Filippo e Giacomo runs straight to the elegant **Campo San Zaccaria**, a spot with a chequered past. The convent attached to the church was notorious for its libidinous goings-on – a state of affairs not so surprising if you bear in mind that many of the nuns were incarcerated here either because they were too strong-willed for their families or because their fathers couldn't afford a dowry. On one occasion officials sent to put a stop to the nuns' amorous liaisons were pelted with bricks by the residents, but behaviour was customarily more discreet: Venice's upper classes supplied the convent with several of its novices, and the nuns' parlour became one of the city's most fashionable salons, as Guardi's painting of it in the Ca' Rezzonico shows.

There's a gory side to the area's history as well. In 864 **Doge Pietro Tradonico** was murdered in the campo as he returned from vespers, and in 1172 **Doge Vitale Michiel II**, having not only blundered in peace negotiations with the Byzantine empire but also brought the plague back with him, was murdered as he fled for the sanctuary of San Zaccaria. Michiel's assassins disappeared into Calle delle Rasse, between the Palazzo Ducale and San Zaccaria, and it was later decreed that only wooden buildings should be built there, to make it easier to flatten the hideout of any future doge-assassin. The decree wasn't contravened until 1948.

The church of San Zaccaria

San Zaccaria is open daily 10am–noon & 4–6pm.

Founded in the ninth century as a shrine for the body of Zaccharias, father of John the Baptist, the church of **San Zaccaria** was rebuilt in 1444–1515, forming an unusually harmonious mix of Gothic and Renaissance styles. (Zaccharias is still here, under the second altar on the right.) Started by **Antonio Gambello**, the reconstruction was finished after Gambello's death (1481) by **Mauro Coducci**, who took over the **facade** from the first storey upwards – hence its resemblance to San Michele. The interior's notable architectural feature is its **ambulatory**: unique in Venice, it might have been built to accommodate the procession of the doges' Easter Sunday visit, a ritual that began after the convent had sold to the state the land that was to become the Piazza.

The church is stuffed with seventeenth- and eighteenth-century paintings, all of them outshone by **Giovanni Bellini**'s large *Madonna and Four Saints* (1505), on the second altar on the left; you might think that the natural light is enough, but drop a coin into the light-box and you'll see what you were missing. Further up the left aisle, by the sacristy door, is the tomb of **Alessandro Vittoria** (d.1608), including a self-portrait bust; he also carved the *St*

Zaccharias and *St John the Baptist* for the two holy water stoups, and the now faceless *St Zaccharias* on the facade above the door.

The small fee payable to enter the **Cappella di Sant'Atanasio** and **Cappella di San Tarasio** is well worth it. The former – containing **Tintoretto**'s early *The Birth of St John the Baptist* and some fifteenth-century stalls – was rebuilt at the end of the sixteenth century. Only in the latter does it become obvious that the chapels occupy much of the site of the old church; three wonderful *anconas* (composite altarpieces) by **Antonio Vivarini and Giovanni d'Alemagna** (1443) are the highlight, but you can also make out the decayed frescoes by Andrea del Castagno and Francesco da Faenza in the vault, while panels set into the floor reveal mosaics of the ninth and twelfth centuries. Downstairs is the spooky and perpetually waterlogged ninth-century crypt, the burial place of eight early doges.

The Riva degli Schiavoni

The broad **Riva degli Schiavoni**, stretching from the edge of the Palazzo Ducale to the canal just before the Arsenale entrance, is constantly thronged during the day, with an unceasing flow of promenading tourists and passengers hurrying to and from its vaporetto stops. It's at its best in the evening, when the crowds have dwindled and the sun goes down over the Salute. The name is a vestige of an ignominious side of the Venetian economy, as *schiavoni* denotes both slaves and the Slavs who in the early days of Venice provided most of the human merchandise. By the early eleventh century the Slavs were becoming extensively Christianised and so came to be regarded as too civilised for such treatment; in succeeding centuries the slave trade turned to Greece, Russia and Central Asia for its supplies, until the fall of Constantinople in 1453 forced a switch of attention to the black populations of Africa.

Now colonised by the aristocracy of the hotel trade, the Riva has long been one of Venice's smart addresses. **Petrarch** and his daughter lived at no. 4145 in 1362–67, and **Henry James** stayed at no. 4161, battling against the constant distractions outside to finish *The Portrait of a Lady*. George Sand, Charles Dickens, Proust, Wagner and the ever-present Ruskin all checked in at the **Hotel Danieli** (the former Palazzo Dandolo), which nowadays attracts the likes of Tina Turner and others with stratospheric income levels; and at the other end of the musical spectrum, Monteverdi's *Proserpina Rapita* was first performed here – one of the earliest opera productions. The *Danieli*'s nondescript extension, built in 1948, was the first transgression of the 1172 ban on stone buildings on this spot (see above).

The Pietà

Looking east from the Molo, the main eyecatcher – rising between the equestrian monument to King Vittorio Emanuele II and the tugboats berthed in the distance – is the white facade of **Santa Maria**

della Visitazione, known less cumbersomely as **La Pietà. Vivaldi** wrote many of his finest pieces for the orphanage attached to the church, where he worked as violin-master (1704–18) and later as choirmaster (1735–38). Such a success did the orchestra and choir of the Pietà become that some unscrupulous parents tried to get their progeny into its famous ranks by foisting them off as orphans.

The Pietà is open daily 10am–noon & 5–7pm

During Vivaldi's second term **Giorgio Massari** won a competition to rebuild the church, and it's probable that the composer advised him on acoustic problems such as the positioning of the double choir on the entrance wall and two along the side walls. He may also have suggested adding the vestibule to the front of the church, as insulation against the background noise of the city. Building eventually began in 1745 (after Vivaldi's death), and when the interior was completed in 1760 (the facade didn't go on until 1906) it was regarded more as a concert hall than a church. You get some idea of the showiness of eighteenth-century Venice from the fact that whereas this section of the Riva was widened to give a grander approach to the building, Massari's plans for the orphanage were shelved owing to lack of funds.

The Pietà is still one of Venice's main music venues, and just about the only times you can get a peek inside is when the box office is open – and even then the entrance is usually barred by a rope. The newly restored white and gold interior, looking like a wedding cake turned inside out, is crowned by a ceiling painting of *The Glory of Paradise* by **Giambattista Tiepolo**, who also painted the ceiling above the high altar.

The Greek quarter

A couple of minutes' walk north of La Pietà the campanile of **San Giorgio dei Greci** lurches spectacularly canalwards. The **Greek** presence in Venice was strong from the eleventh century, and became stronger still after the Turkish seizure of Constantinople. This mid-fifteenth-century influx of Greek speakers provided a resource which was exploited by the city's numerous scholarly publishing houses, and greatly enriched the general culture of Renaissance Venice: the daughter of the *condottiere* Gianfrancesco Gonzaga, for example, is known to have written perfect Greek at the age of ten. At its peak, the Greek community numbered around 4000, some of whom were immensely rich: a Greek merchant murdered in Venice in 1756 left 4,000,000 ducats to his daughters, a legacy which was said to have made them the richest heiresses in Europe.

The church was built in 1539–61 to a Sansovino-influenced design by **Sante Lombardo**; the cupola and campanile came later in the century. Inside, the Orthodox architectural elements include a *matroneo* (women's gallery) above the main entrance and an iconostasis (or rood screen) that completely cuts off the high altar.

The icons on the screen are a mixture of works by a sixteenth-century Cretan artist called **Michael Danaskinàs**, and a few Byzantine pieces dating back as far as the twelfth century.

San Zaccaria to San Giorgio dei Greci

Permission to found an Orthodox church was given at the end of the fifteenth century, and a Greek college and *scuola* were approved at the same time. The college, redesigned in the 1670s by **Longhena**, is now home to the *Hellenic Centre for Byzantine and Post-Byzantine Studies*, custodian of Venice's Greek archives. The Scuola di San Nicolò dei Greci houses the **Museo Dipinti Sacri Bizantini**, a collection of predominantly fifteenth- to eighteenth-century icons, many of them by the *Madoneri*, the school of Greek and Cretan artists working in Venice in that period. Although many of the most beautiful of these works maintain the compositional and symbolic conventions of icon painting, it's fascinating to observe the impact of Western influences – one or two of the artists achieve a synthesis, while others clearly struggle to harmonise the two worlds.

The Museo Dipinti Sacri Bizantini is open Mon–Sat 9am–1pm & 2–5pm; L4000.

The area to the north of San Giorgio dei Greci is more interesting for its associations than its sights. The unfinished and hangar-like **San Lorenzo** – undergoing a slow restoration – was where Marco Polo was buried, but his sarcophagus went astray during sixteenth-century rebuilding. Gentile Bellini's *Miracle of the Relic of the Cross*, now in the Accademia, depicts an extraordinary incident that once occurred in the Rio di San Lorenzo – for the story, see p.90.

Chapter 7

The Eastern Districts

For all that most visitors see of Venice's **eastern districts**, the city may as well peter out a few metres to the east of the Palazzo Ducale, and at first glance any map of the city would seem to justify this neglect. Certainly the sights are thinly spread, and a huge bite is taken out of the area by the pools of the **Arsenale**, for a long time the largest manufacturing site in Europe, but now little more than a decoratively framed blank space.

Yet the slab of the city immediately to the west of the Arsenale contains places that shouldn't be ignored – the Renaissance **San Francesco della Vigna**, for example, and the **Scuola di San Giorgio degli Schiavoni**, with its endearing cycle of paintings by **Carpaccio**. And although the mainly residential area beyond the Arsenale has little to offer in the way of cultural monuments other than the ex-cathedral of **San Pietro di Castello** and the church of **Sant'Elena**, it would be a mistake to leave the easternmost zone unexplored. Except in the summer of odd-numbered years, when the **Biennale** sets up shop in the specially built pavilions behind the **Giardini Pubblici** and elsewhere in the neighbourhood, few visitors stray into this latter area – and there lies one of its principal attractions. And the whole length of the waterfront gives spectacular panoramas of the city, with the best coming last: from near the Sant'Elena landing stage you get a view that takes in the Palazzo Ducale, the back of San Giorgio Maggiore and La Giudecca, the tiny islands of La Grazia, San Clemente, Santo Spirito, San Servolo and San Lazzaro degli Armeni, and finally the Lido. A picnic here, having stocked up at the shops and stalls of Via Garibaldi, is guaranteed to recharge the batteries.

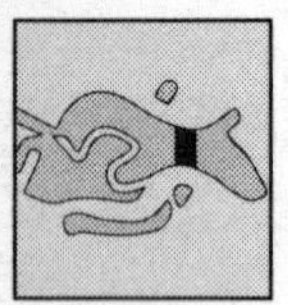

San Francesco della Vigna to the waterfront

If you continue **east from San Zanipolo**, you might soon begin to feel that you've roamed into one of Venice's drabber districts. The church of Santa Maria del Pianto, so prominent on the city's maps, turns out to be an abandoned hulk, and is barely visible over its surrounding wall. Cross the Rio di Santa Giustina and you're confronted by the shabby church of the same name; it's now part of a school. Follow the *fondamenta* down to the mouth of the canal, and to your right you'll get a view of the gasworks' rusting remains. But it's not all decay and dereliction – carry on east for just a minute more, and a striking Renaissance church blocks your way.

San Francesco della Vigna to the waterfront

San Francesco della Vigna

The ground occupied by **San Francesco della Vigna** has a hallowed place in the mythology of Venice, as according to tradition it was around here that the angel appeared to Saint Mark to tell him that the lagoon islands were to be his final resting place. (The angel's words – "Pax tibi" and so forth – remained unchanged on the book held by Venice's symbolic lion until Napoleon substituted the rubric "To the Rights of Men and Citizens" on official proclamations; "at last he's turned the page," remarked an anonymous wag.) Some time after the alleged annunciation the area was cultivated as a vineyard, and when the land was given to the Franciscans in 1253 as a site for a new church, the vines were immortalised in their church's name.

San Francesco della Vigna is open daily 7–11.45am & 4.45–7pm.

Begun in 1534, to a design by **Sansovino**, the present building was much modified in the course of its construction. **Palladio** was brought in to provide the **facade** (1568–72), a feature that looks like something of an afterthought from the side, but which must have been quite stunning at the time, when the only other all-white Istrian stone facade in Venice would have been that of San Michele. The **interior** was altered by a humanist scholar monk, **Fra' Francesco Zorzi**, who rearranged the proportions along philosophically approved lines and generally amended its acoustic and decorative design. The calculated Renaissance improvements and cold colouring make the church less welcoming than the two great mendicant churches of San Zanipolo and the Frari, despite its less belittling dimensions; however, there are some fine works of art here, for whose essential light-boxes you should take a pocketful of coins.

Close to the door there's a trio of interesting pieces – a triptych attributed to Antonio Vivarini (on the entrance wall) and bronze figures of *St Francis* and *John the Baptist* by Alessandro Vittoria (on the water stoups). Some of Venice's wealthiest families contributed to the cost of building San Francesco by paying for family chapels: the third on the right belonged to the **Contarini**, and contains memorials to a pair of seventeenth-century Contarini doges; the next is the **Badoer** chapel (with a *Resurrection* attributed to Veronese); and after that comes the chapel of the **Barbaro** family. The Barbaro ancestral device – a red circle on a white field – was granted in the twelfth century after a particularly revolting act by the Admiral Marco Barbaro: in the thick of battle he cut off a

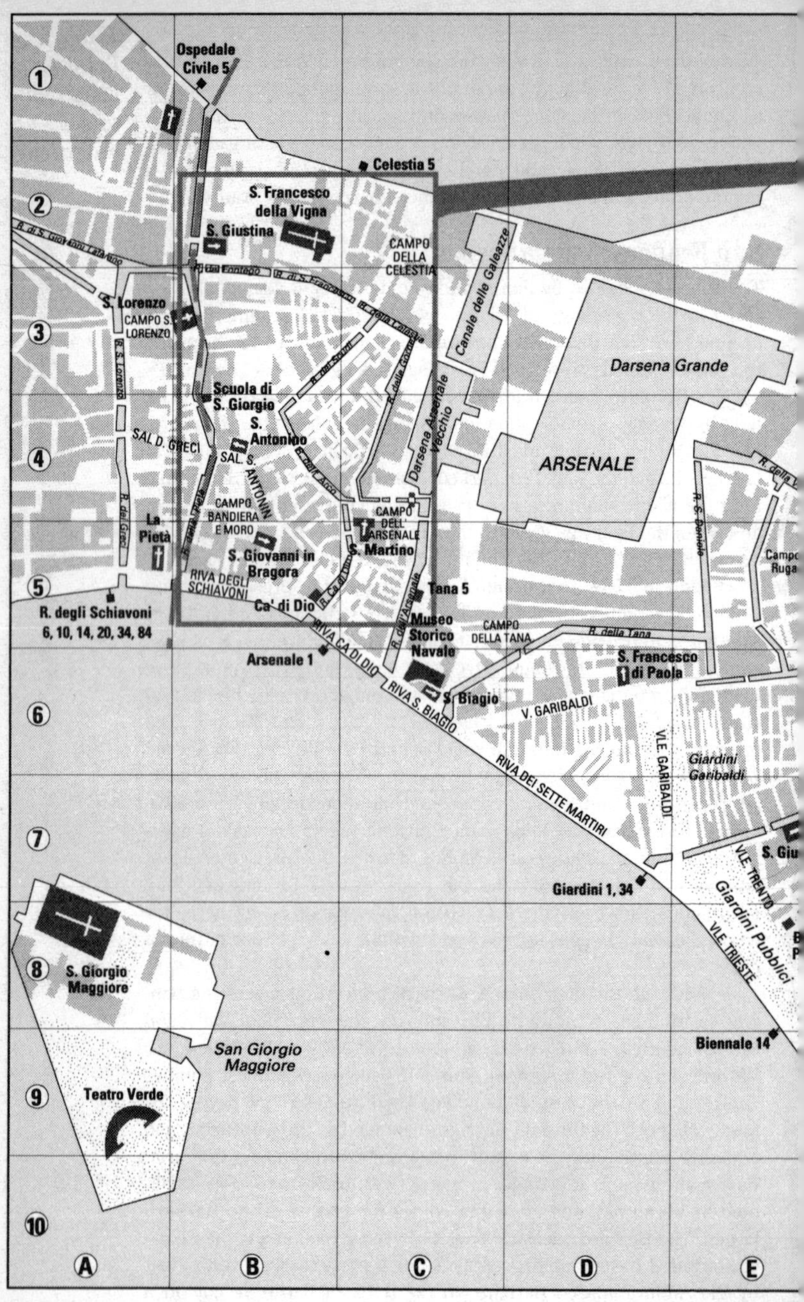
Ospedale Civile 5
Celestia 5
S. Francesco della Vigna
S. Giustina
CAMPO DELLA CELESTIA
S. Lorenzo
CAMPO S. LORENZO
Canale delle Galeazze
Darsena Grande
Scuola di S. Giorgio
S. Antonino
Darsena Arsenale Vecchio
SAL. D. GRECI
SAL. S. ANTONIN
ARSENALE
CAMPO BANDIERA E MORO
CAMPO DELL' ARSENALE
La Pietà
S. Giovanni in Bragora
S. Martino
RIVA DEGLI SCHIAVONI
Tana 5
R. degli Schiavoni 6, 10, 14, 20, 34, 84
Ca' di Dio
Museo Storico Navale
CAMPO DELLA TANA
R. della Tana
Arsenale 1
RIVA CA DI DIO
S. Francesco di Paola
RIVA S. BIAGIO
S. Biagio
V. GARIBALDI
VLE. GARIBALDI
Giardini Garibaldi
RIVA DEI SETTE MARTIRI
Giardini 1, 34
VLE. TRENTO
Giardini Pubblici
VLE. TRIESTE
S. Giorgio Maggiore
San Giorgio Maggiore
Biennale 14
Teatro Verde
1
2
3
4
5
6
7
8
9
10
A
B
C
D
E

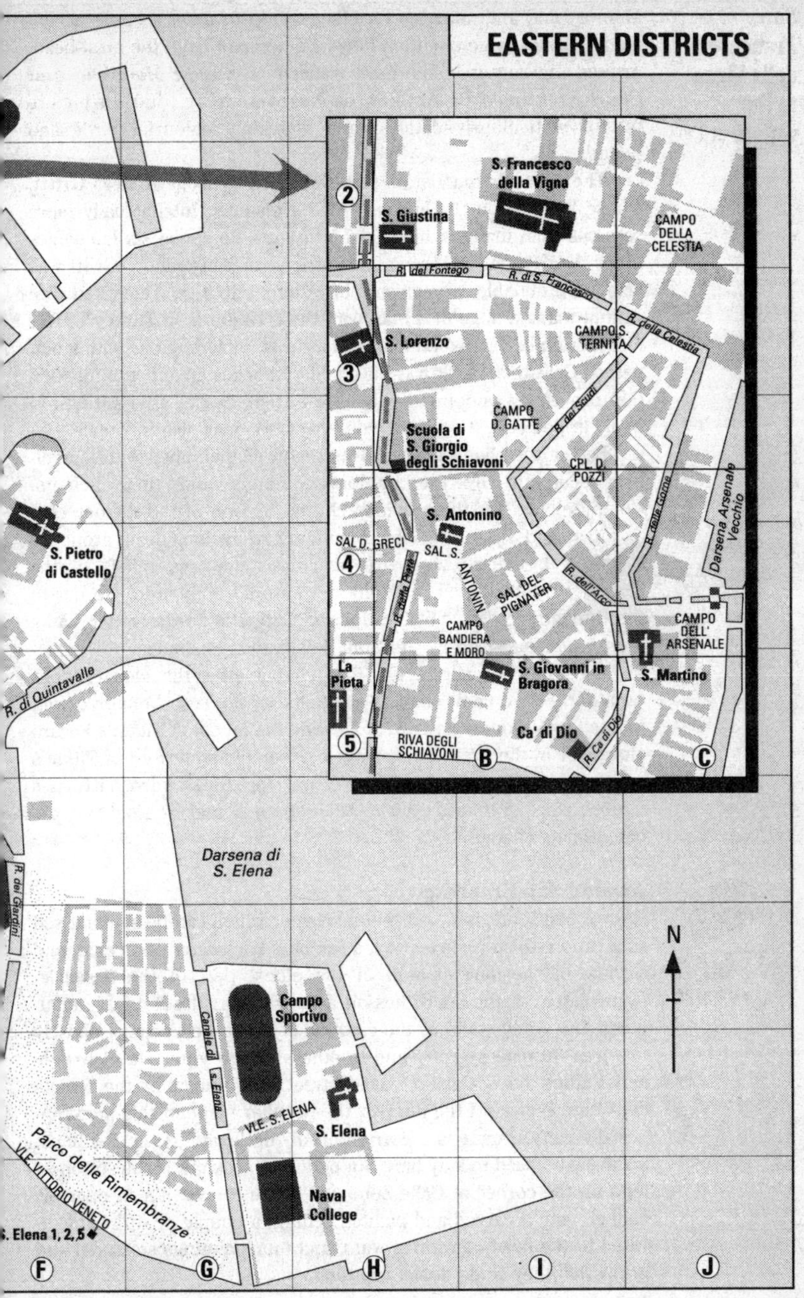
EASTERN DISTRICTS
S. Francesco della Vigna
S. Giustina
CAMPO DELLA CELESTIA
R. del Fontego
R. di S. Francesco
R. della Celestia
CAMPO S. TERNITA
S. Lorenzo
CAMPO D. GATTE
R. dei Scudi
Scuola di S. Giorgio degli Schiavoni
CPL. D. POZZI
S. Antonino
R. delle Gorne
Darsena Arsenale Vecchio
SAL D. GRECI
SAL. S. ANTONIN
R. della Pietà
SAL DEL PIGNATER
R. dell'Arco
CAMPO BANDIERA E MORO
CAMPO DELL' ARSENALE
S. Martino
S. Giovanni in Bragora
La Pieta
Ca' di Dio
R. Ca di Dio
RIVA DEGLI SCHIAVONI
S. Pietro di Castello
R. di Quintavalle
Darsena di S. Elena
R. dei Giardini
Campo Sportivo
Canale di s. Elena
VLE. S. ELENA
S. Elena
Naval College
Parco delle Rimembranze
VLE. VITTORIO VENETO
S. Elena 1, 2, 5
N
2
3
4
5
B
C
F
G
H
I
J

Moor's hand and used the bleeding stump to draw a circle on the man's turban, which he then flew as a pennant from the mast-head. Around the corner in the right transept is a large *Madonna and Child Enthroned* by **Antonio da Negroponte** (c.1450), a picture full of meticulously detailed and glowingly colourful birds and plants.

The church's foundation stone was laid by **Doge Andrea Gritti**, whose tomb is on the left wall of the chancel. Intellectually more versatile than many in his social stratum – he spoke six languages other than Italian and was a close friend of Sansovino – Gritti was also a formidable womaniser, of whom one rival remarked "we cannot make a doge of a man with three bastards in Turkey". After his election he carried on making bastards, including one with a nun named Celestina, but it was his equally Rabelaisian appetite for food that proved his undoing: he died on Christmas Eve after eating too many grilled eels. It's still a traditional Christmas dish in Venice.

Left of the chancel is the **Giustiniani** chapel, lined with marvellous sculpture by the **Lombardo** family and their helpers. Commissioned for the previous church by one of the Badoer clan and installed here after the rebuilding, they include a group of *Prophets* by Pietro Lombardo and assistants and reliefs of the *Evangelists* attributed to Tullio and Antonio Lombardo. Go out to the fifteenth-century cloisters for the **Cappella Santa**, which has a *Madonna and Child* by Giovanni Bellini and assistants.

Back in the church, the first chapel after the cloister door (another Giustiniani chapel) contains a *Sacred Conversation*, painted by **Veronese** in 1562, following the model of Titian's Pésaro altarpiece in the Frari. Michelangelo, often characterised as Titian's antithesis, was the partial inspiration for **Alessandro Vittoria**'s figures of *St Anthony Abbot*, *St Sebastian* and *St Roch*, in the penultimate chapel.

Around San Francesco

East of San Francesco is a remote corner which can be summarised as a vaporetto stop (*Celestia*), a scummy backwater of a canal, and a view of the sinister wall of the oldest part of the Arsenale. Immediately to the south lies an area which is destitute of monuments but could stand as the epitome of domestic Venice – densely textured, in places grotty and in others picturesque. The Salizzada and Campo delle Gatte ("paved street and square of the female cats") are typical of the district; the peculiar name of this unexceptionally catty avenue is a corruption of "de legate", from the papal legates who used to stay here. An oddity to seek out is the sottoportego on the corner of Calle Zorzi and Corte Nuova: it's an open-air chapel, with a carved and painted ceiling, a couple of shrines dedicated to the dead of various wars, and four paintings so flaked and grimy that they could depict anything.

San Giorgio degli Schiavoni

If there's one building in Venice that can be guaranteed to provide affectionate memories, it's the **Scuola di San Giorgio degli Schiavoni**, home of a brilliant cycle of pictures by the most seductive of Venetian artists, **Vittore Carpaccio**. Venice's relations with the Slavs (*schiavoni*) were not always untroubled – the city's slave markets were originally stocked with captured Slavs, and in later centuries the settlements of the Dalmatian coast were a harassment to Venetian shipping. By the mid-fifteenth century, though, Venice's Slavic inhabitants – many of them sailors and merchants – were sufficiently established for a *scuola* to be set up in order to protect their interests. After several years of meeting in the church of San Giovanni di Malta, the *scuola* built itself a new headquarters on the church's doorstep at the start of the sixteenth century, and summoned Carpaccio to brighten up the first-storey hall. Painted from 1502 to 1508, after the Accademia's St Ursula cycle, Carpaccio's pictures were moved downstairs when the building was rearranged in 1551, and the interior has scarcely changed since.

San Francesco della Vigna to the waterfront

The Scuola di San Giorgio degli Schiavoni is open Tues–Sat 9.30am–12.30pm & 3.30–6.30pm, Sun 11am–12.30pm; L4000.

The cycle illustrates mainly the lives of the Dalmatian patron saints – George, Tryphone and Jerome. The scenes depicted are: *Saint George and the Dragon*; *The Triumph of St George*; *St George Baptising the Gentiles* (George had rescued the princess of of Selene, daughter of the royal couple being baptised); *The Miracle of St Tryphone* (the dainty little basilisk is a demon just exorcised from the daughter of the Roman emperor Gordianus); *The Agony in the Garden*; *The Calling of Matthew*; *St Jerome Leading the Lion to the Monastery*; *The Funeral of St Jerome*; and *The Vision of St Augustine* (he was writing to Saint Jerome when a vision told him of Jerome's death). The *Madonna and Child* altarpiece is by **Benedetto Carpaccio**, Vittore's son, while the panelled upstairs hall is decorated with early seventeenth-century paintings in honour of various brethren of the *scuola*, some of which are almost surreal in their composition.

From Sant'Antonino to the waterfront

The frequently closed church of **Sant'Antonino**, the next stop south along the *fondamenta* from San Giorgio, is an unenticing seventeenth-century effort housing nothing except a picture by Carpaccio's not over-talented teacher, but has some good stories attached to it. It enshrined the body of a certain Saint Sabus from the mid-thirteenth century until 1965, when Pope Paul VI returned the relic to the the monastery in Istanbul whence it had been stolen by a future doge; for all that time the monks had been meeting disconsolately every night at their saint's empty sarcophagus. The emblems of Saint Anthony Abbot are a pig and a bell, and this church once kept a sty of belled and notoriously unruly pigs – though it's not clear if this was some sort of tribute to their patron.

The campanological swine were allowed to roam the parish unfettered, but eventually they so annoyed the locals that in 1409 their freedom was curtailed by a sumptuary edict. "Saint Anthony loved a pig" is still a Venetian saying, used to express a lack of surprise at an odd occurrence. And finally, James (Jan) Morris records that in 1819 an elephant escaped from a visiting menagerie and took refuge in Sant'Antonino; having cornered the hapless beast, its pursuers shot it.

San Giovanni in Brágora

Salizzada Sant'Antonin curves down to the quiet **Campo Bandiera e Moro**, named after the Venetians Attillo and Emilio Bandiera and Domenico Moro, who in 1844 were executed for leading an abortive revolt against the Bourbons. The Bandiera brothers were born at no. 3610, and all three are buried together in San Zanipolo. Next door to the Bandiera house is the campo's handsomest building, the fifteenth-century Palazzo Gritti Badoer; it was a ruin in Ruskin's day (and "inhabited by the lowest orders," he added snootily) but has since been renovated as a hotel.

San Giovanni in Brágora is open daily 8.30–11.30am & 5–7pm.

Across the square stands **San Giovanni in Brágora**, probably best known to Venetians as the baptismal church of Antonio Vivaldi. Begun in 1475, about the same time that San Michele was finished and only six years before the Miracoli was started, this simple Gothic building shows no sign of the arrival of Renaissance architecture in Venice. But one can trace the inception of a more sophisticated Renaissance aesthetic in its best paintings: a triptych by **Bartolomeo Vivarini**, in the chapel to the left of the chancel (1478); a *Resurrection* by **Alvise Vivarini**, to the left of the sacristy door (1498); and a *Baptism* by **Cima da Conegliano**, behind the high altar (1494). The body of Saint John the Almsgiver, stolen from Alexandria in 1247, lies in the second chapel on the right, though the Venetian church dedicated to him – San Giovanni Elemosinario – is way over in the Rialto.

San Martino to the waterfront

A group of Paduan refugees are said to have founded a church on the site of the nearby **San Martino** in 593, which would give it one of Venice's longest pedigrees; Sansovino designed the present Greek-cross building in around 1540. To get a decent perusal of **Domenico Bruni**'s distortedly perspectival ceiling painting (seventeenth-century) you have to lie on your back in the very middle of the church, more or less where most of **Doge Francesco Erizzo** (d.1646) is buried; his heart is in the Basilica di San Marco.

San Martino is open daily 11am–noon & 6–7pm.

South of San Martino, the short stretch of waterfront west of the canal that cuts through the Arsenale takes its name from the **Ca' di Dio**, which stands on the far side of the Rio di San Martino. Founded in the thirteenth century as a hospice for pilgrims and Crusaders, it was extended in 1545 by Sansovino – his new wing, with its profusion of chimneys, is visible from the bridge. The building at the eastern end of the Riva Ca' di Dio, decorated with a frieze of little marble peaks, is the **Forni Pubblici** (1473), the bakery which supplied the ships leaving the Arsenale with ship's biscuit, the last stage in the preparations for sailing (see below for more).

The Arsenale

A corruption of the Arabic *darsin'a* (house of industry), the very name of the **Arsenale** is indicative of the strength of Venice's links with the eastern Mediterranean, and the workers of these dockyards and factories were the foundations upon which the city's maritime supremacy rested. Visiting dignitaries were often as astonished by the industriousness of the Arsenale as by the opulence of the Canal Grande. At the beginning of the fourteenth century Dante came to Venice twice (once as ambassador from Ravenna), and was so impressed by what he saw on his first mission that he evoked the sight in a famous passage of the *Inferno*, in which those guilty of selling public offices are tortured in a lake of boiling pitch like the caulkers' vats in the Arsenale.

The development of the Arsenale commenced in the early years of the twelfth century, and by the middle of that century a state monopoly in the construction of galleys was established here. By the third decade of the fifteenth century it had become the base for some 300 shipping companies, operating around 3000 vessels of 200 tons or more; at its peak, the wet and dry docks, the rope and sail factories, the ordnance depots and gunpowder mills employed a total of 16,000 men – equal to the population of a major town of the period.

In *The City in History*, Lewis Mumford credits the Venetians with the invention of "a new type of city, based on the differentiation and zoning of urban functions, separated by traffic ways and open spaces", and cites the island of Murano and the Arsenale as Europe's first examples of industrial planning. Of these two, the Arsenale most closely resembled a modern factory complex. Construction techniques in the Arsenale were the most sophisticated of their time; one awestruck visitor in the fifteenth century recorded the Venetians' production-line process for equipping their warships, in which the vessels were towed past a succession of windows, to collect ropes, sails, armaments, oars and all their other supplies (ending with barrels of hard biscuits), so that by the time they reached the lagoon the vessels were fully prepared for battle. The productivity of the wharves was legendary: at the height of the conflict with the Turks in the sixteenth century, one ship a day was being added to the Venetian fleet. On the occasion of the visit of Henry III of France in 1574, the lads from the Arsenale put on a bravura performance – in the time it took the king and his hosts to work their way through a state banquet in the Palazzo Ducale, the *Arsenalotti* assembled and made seaworthy a ship sturdy enough to bear a crew plus a cannon weighing 16,000 pounds.

To an extent, the governors of the city acknowledged their debt to the workers of the Arsenale. They were a privileged group within the Venetian proletariat, acting as watchmen at the Palazzo Ducale whenever the Maggior Consiglio was in session, carrying the doge in triumph round the Piazza after his inauguration, and serving as pallbearers at ducal funerals. By the standards of other manual workers they were not badly paid either, although the 50 ducats which was the typical wage of a master shipwright in the early sixteenth century should be set against the 40,000 ducats spent by Alvise Pisani, one of the most powerful politicians of the period, on the weddings of his five daughters. The *Arsenalotti* were also less docile than most of their fellow artisans, and were responsible for a number of strikes and disturbances. A dramatic protest took place in 1569, when a gang of 300 *Arsenalotti* armed with axes smashed their way into the hall of the Collegio to present their grievances to the doge in person.

The growth and decline of the Arsenale

Expansion of the Arsenale was particularly rapid in the fourteenth century and continued into the sixteenth – **Sanmicheli**'s covered dock for the state barge (the *Bucintoro*) was built in 1544–47, for example, and **da Ponte**'s gigantic rope factory – the *Corderia* or **Tana** – in 1579. (The greater part of the *Tana* runs along the Rio della Tana; a single room 316m long – not far off twice the length of the Piazza – it provides an extraordinary exhibition space for the *Aperto* section of the Biennale.) By that time, though, the maritime strength of Venice was past its peak: Vasco da Gama had rounded the Cape of Good Hope in 1497, thus opening a direct sea route to the East; the New World routes were growing; and there was the perpetual threat of the ever stronger Turkish empire. The shrinkage of the Venetian mercantile fleet was drastic – between 1560 and 1600 the volume of shipping registered at the Arsenale was halved. Militarily as well, despite the conspicuous success at Lépanto (1571), Venice was on the wane, and the reconquest of the Morea (Peloponnese) at the end of the seventeenth century was little more than a glorious interlude in a long story of decline. When **Napoleon** took over the city in 1797 he burned down the docks, sank the last *Bucintoro* and confiscated the remnant of the Venetian navy, sailing off with it to attempt the invasion of Ireland. After the failure of that expedition the fleet was taken back to the Mediterranean, only to be destroyed by Nelson at the battle of Aboukir.

Under Austrian occupation the Arsenale was reconstructed, and it stayed in continuous operation until the end of 1917 when, having produced a number of ships for the Italian navy in World War I, the dockyards were dismantled to prevent them being of use to the enemy forces which seemed likely to invade the lagoon. Since then it has been used by the navy for storage and repairs, and as a venue for part of the Biennale, but plans exist to extend the Museo Storico Navale into the Arsenale buildings and to convert other parts into sports halls.

The Arsenale buildings

There is no public access to the Arsenale. You can get a look at part of it, however, from the bridge connecting the Campo Arsenale and the Fondamenta dell'Arsenale; a better view can be had by taking the vaporetto #5, which cuts through the oldest part of the complex, taking you past Sanmicheli's *Bucintoro* building, alongside which is the mouth of the Darsena Grande.

The main **gateway** to the Arsenale was the first structure in Venice to employ the classical vocabulary of Renaissance architecture. Built by **Antonio Gambello** in 1460 (but incorporating, at ground level, Veneto-Byzantine capitals of the twelfth century), it consists of a triumphal arch topped by a less precisely classical storey – a design that was possibly intended to create the illusion that the entrance to the Arsenale was an amalgam of a genuine Roman edifice and more modern Venetian building. You'll notice that the Lion of Saint Mark is holding a closed book, perhaps because the book's traditional inscription – "Pax tibi . . ." – was thought to be too pacific for this context; the statue above his head, *Santa Justina* by **Campagna**, was put there in 1578.

The **four lions** outside the gateway feature in coffee-table books on Venice almost as frequently as the San Marco horses, and, like the horses, they are stolen goods. Exactly when the two furthest on the right were grabbed isn't known, but they probably came from the Lion Terrace at Delos, and date from around the sixth century BC; the left-hand one of the pair (with the prosthetic head) was positioned here to mark the recapture of Corfu in 1716 – the other was in place slightly earlier. The larger pair aren't as enigmatic: they were swiped from Piraeus in 1687 by Francesco Morosini, after the reconquest of the Morea. The blurred and incomprehensible inscription on the shoulder and side of the lion on the left of the gate (which started life as an ancient Greek fountain) is a piece of runic graffiti, the handiwork of a Norse mercenary serving with the army hired by the Byzantine emperor in the eleventh century to suppress a rebellion of his Greek subjects.

For more on Morosini, see p.81.

The Museo Storico Navale and San Biagio

Nearby, on the other side of the Rio dell'Arsenale, is the **Museo Storico Navale**, most of which is housed in a former granary. Documenting every conceivable facet of Venice's naval history, the museum is another loose baggy monster like the Correr, but a selective tour is an essential supplement to a walk round the Arsenale

The Museo Storico Navale is open Mon–Sat 9am–1pm; L2000.

district – and it's laid out far better than the Correr, with bilingual captions on many of the exhibits. Improbable though it sounds, the models of Venetian craft – from the gondola to the 224-oar fighting galley and the last *Bucintoro* – will justify the entrance fee for most people. It was common practice in the Venetian shipyards to build their boats not from scale drawings but from models, and the most meticulous pieces in the collection (on the first floor) are the functional models retrieved from the yards after Napoleon's arsonists had done their work.

At ground level there's a miscellany of armaments and a room dedicated to Angelo Emo, the last admiral of the Republic – including a monument by Canova. Models of more recent ships take up much of the second floor; the third has a large display on the evolution of the gondola and a roomful of models of Far Eastern vessels. The top storey's installation, illustrating the part played by Sweden in the maritime history of Venice, is not as eccentric as you might think, but is nonetheless strictly for specialists. About 250 metres along the *fondamenta* is the second section of the museum, the **Padiglioni delle Navi** – a vast shed full of craft with Venetian connections.

The church of **San Biagio**, alongside the main museum block, was the Greek community's church before San Giorgio dei Greci, and took on its present municipal office appearance after an eighteenth-century refit. It's now the naval chapel and is rarely open – no great loss, as apart from **Giovanni Ferrari**'s reclining statue of Admiral Angelo Emo (1792), there's nothing much in it. Tucked behind the church is the concrete bunker known as Palasport (or Palazzetto dello Sport), the city's main indoor sports hall, used for handball and basketball matches.

Beyond the Arsenale

The Riva San Biagio is the only land route into the districts to the east of the Arsenale, but once over the wide bridge that traverses the Rio della Tana you have to make a choice. By following the waterfront you'll pass the main public gardens of Venice before finally reaching the somewhat isolated church of Sant'Elena. Opt for the less picturesque Via Garibaldi, and you're on your way to the church of San Pietro di Castello, the major monument of this part of the city.

To San Pietro di Castello

In 1808 the greater part of the canal connecting the Bacino di San Marco to the broad northeastern inlet of the Canale di San Pietro was filled in to form what is now **Via Garibaldi**, the widest street in the city and the busiest commercial area in the eastern district. (The pattern of the pavement shows clearly the course of the former canal.) The bars, *pasticcerie* and *alimentari* of Via Garibaldi are as good as most of those in the more comfortable areas of the city, are generally quite a bit cheaper, and are far less likely to treat you as a tedious occupational hazard. Roaming through the alleyways and squares of the vicinity, it's possible to forget for a while that you're in the most commercialised city in the country.

There's just a couple of spots of cultural or historical significance along Via Garibaldi. The first house on the right was for a time the home of the navigators **John and Sebastian Cabot**, explorers respectively of Newfoundland and Brazil in the late fifteenth century and early sixteenth. The church of **San Francesco di Paola**, opposite the entrance to the tree-lined alley that glories in the name Giardini Garibaldi, has a painting by Giandomenico Tiepolo on its cornice. A far more impressive sight awaits if you walk beyond the market stalls on the right-hand side of the street, which becomes the Fondamenta di Sant'Anna: this takes you onto the Ponte di Quintavalle, and so to the island of San Pietro.

The island of San Pietro di Castello

Originally named **Castello**, after a castle that used to stand here (built by either the Romans or the first "Venetian" settlers), the island of **San Pietro** was one of the very first of parts of central Venice to be occupied. Nowadays this is a run-down district where the repairing of boats is the main occupation, yet it was once the ecclesiastical centre of Venice. By 775 the settlement here had grown sufficiently to be granted the foundation of a bishopric under the authority of the Patriarch of Grado. Within the next half-century Castello joined the immediately surrounding islands to form Rivoalto, the embryonic city of Venice. From the beginning, the political and economic power was concentrated in the distant Rialto and San Marco districts, and the relationship between the church and the geographically remote rulers of the city was never to be close. In 1451 the first **Patriarch of Venice** was invested, but still his seat remained at Castello, and succeeding generations of councillors and senators showed no inclination to draw the father of the Venetian church into the centre of power. San Pietro di Castello remained the cathedral of Venice, emblematically marooned on the periphery of the city, until 1807, when the Patriarch was at last permitted to install himself in San Marco – ten years after the Republic had ceased to exist.

One of the major Venetian festivals – the Festival of the Marys – had its origin in an incident that occurred here in the tenth century. A multiple marriage in the church was interrupted by a posse of Slav pirates, who carried away the brides and their substantial dowries. Men from the parish of Santa Maria Formosa led the pursuit, which succeeded in retrieving the women. To celebrate their safe return, every year two girls were chosen from each *sestiere* to be married in a single ceremony at San Pietro, the weddings being followed by an eight-day junket that culminated at Santa Maria Formosa on the Day of the Purification of Mary – the day on which the brides had been kidnapped.

Beyond the Arsenale

San Pietro di Castello is open daily: winter 8am–noon & 3–6pm; summer 8am–noon & 4.30–7pm.

As with the Arsenale, the history of San Pietro is more interesting than what you can see. A church was raised here as early as the seventh century, but the present **San Pietro di Castello** was built nearly a millennium later. A new facade was designed in the mid-sixteenth century by **Palladio**, but the work was not carried out until the end of the century, and the executed project was a feeble version of the original scheme. Similarly, the interior is an early seventeenth-century derivation from a plan by Palladio, and is unlikely to convince any Ruskinite that classicism has something to it after all. Nor will the paintings put a skip in your stride: best of the bunch are *SS. John the Evangelist, Peter and Paul*, a late work by Veronese (left aisle), and the altarpiece by Luca Giordano in the Cappella Vendramin (left transept). The Vendramin chapel and the high altar were both designed by Longhena; take a look as well at the Cappella Lando (left aisle), which has a fifth-century mosaic fragment and a bust of San Lorenzo Giustiniani, the first Patriarch of Venice, by a follower of Antonio Rizzo. The most unusual feature of the church is the so-called **Throne of Saint Peter** (right aisle), a marble seat made in the thirteenth century from an Arabic funeral stone cut with texts from the Koran.

The **campanile**, one of the most precarious in the city, was rebuilt by Mauro Coducci in the 1480s, and was the first tower in Venice to be clad in Istrian stone. Its original cupola was replaced with the present one in 1670.

The public gardens and Sant'Elena

Stretching from Via Garibaldi to the Rio di Sant'Elena, the arc of green spaces formed by the **Giardini Garibaldi, Giardini Pubblici** and **Parco delle Rimembranze** can usually be relied on to provide a remedy for the claustrophobia that overtakes most visitors to Venice at some point. The first of the three is really little more than a short-cut from Via Garibaldi to the Giardini Pubblici, which Eugène Beauharnais created by draining a swamp and demolishing a batch of monastic buildings.

For more on the Biennale, see p.243.

Largely obscured by the trees are the rather more extensive grounds belonging to the **Biennale**, closed off to the public except when the arts shindig is in progress, in the summer of odd-numbered years. Various countries have built permanent pavilions for their Biennale representatives, forming a unique twentieth-century architectural colony; the best of the buildings are the Austrian pavilion, built by Josef Hoffman in the 1930s, the Finnish pavilion, created by Alvar Aalto in the 1950s, and the Netherlands pavilion, designed by arch-modernist Gerrit Thomas Rietveld, also in the 1950s. Naturally enough, the biggest pavilion is the Italian one – five times larger than the next largest, it was completely redesigned in 1989, giving it a glossier finish than most of its neighbours.

If you want to squeeze every last drop from the eastern districts, call in at the church of **San Giuseppe di Castello** (or San Isepo), to the north of the Giardini Pubblici – a gateway from the gardens opens onto a street just yards from the church. It houses Alessandro Vittoria's monument to Procurator G. Grimani (in the chancel), and a vast **monument to Doge Marino Grimani**, designed in the late sixteenth century by Vincenzo Scamozzi, with reliefs and figures by Campagna (left side).

The island of **Sant'Elena**, the city's eastern limit, was greatly enlarged during the Austrian administration, partly to furnish accommodation and exercise grounds for the occupying troops. Much of the island used to be covered by a meadow, a favourite recreation area in the last century, but the strip of park along the waterfront is all that's left of it, houses having been built on the rest. Still, the walk out here is the nearest you'll get to country pleasures in central Venice, and the **church of Sant'Elena**, approached between the concrete walls of the naval college and the football stadium, is worth a visit.

A church was erected here in the thirteenth century, following the acquisition of the body of Saint Helena, Constantine's mother. It was rebuilt in 1435 but from 1807 to 1928 it was abandoned, except for a spell as an iron foundry, when the campanile was coverted into a chimney. The spartan Gothic interior has recently been restored, as have the cloister and campanile – the latter so zealously that it now looks exactly like a chimney. The main attraction is the **doorway** to the church, an ensemble created in the 1470s by **Antonio Rizzo** and incorporating the **monument to Vittore Cappello**, showing the admiral kneeling before Saint Helena.

Chapter 8

The Canal Grande

Known to the locals as the *Canalazzo*, the **Canal Grande** is Venice's high street, and divides the city in half, with three *sestieri* to the west and three to the east. Only three bridges cross it – at the station, Rialto and Accademia – but traversing the city is not quite the complex procedure it might seem, as a number of *traghetti* operate along the canal, ferrying people from one bank to the other. The Canal Grande is almost four kilometres long and

---

The Palaces of the Canal Grande

The majority of the most important palaces in Venice stand on the Canal Grande – and all have their main facades on the canalside. It's not the case, however, that the Canal Grande was Venice's sole smart address; each parish had its important families, and the palaces of those families were the pivots of each parish. The Canal Grande has a lot of palaces because it cuts through a lot of parishes.

Virtually all the surviving Canal Grande palaces were built over a span of about 500 years, and in the course of that period the **basic plan** varied very little. The typical Venetian palace has an entrance hall (the *andron*) on the ground floor, and this runs right through the building; it is flanked by storage rooms. Above comes the mezzanine floor – the small rooms on this level were used as offices or, from the sixteenth century onwards, as libraries or living rooms. On the next floor – often the most extravagantly decorated – you find the *piano nobile*, the main living area, arranged as suites of rooms on each side of a central hall (*portego*), which runs, like the *andron*, from front to back. The plan of these houses can be read from the outside of the palace, where you'll usually see a cluster of large windows in the centre of the facade, between symmetrically placed side windows. Frequently there is a second *piano nobile* above the first – this generally would have been accommodation for relatives or children (though sometimes it was the main living quarters); the attic would have been for servants' rooms or storage.

The Venetian taste for surface **decoration** was as durable as this general palace plan. Just as the facades of the older palaces were adorned with carved panels and slabs of coloured marble, so the later ones were studded with reliefs and heraldic devices, and sometimes were frescoed. Underneath their decorative skins, nearly all the palaces are made of **brick**, which is

---

varies in width between thirty and seventy metres; it is, however, surprisingly shallow, at no point much exceeding five metres. In the fourteenth century an earthquake pulled the plug out and the entire contents drained away – for the best part of a fortnight Venice's finest waterway was an avenue of slime.

The section that follows is principally a guide to the Canal Grande palaces – the churches and other public buildings that you can see from the vaporetto are covered in the appropriate geographical sections. You'd need an amazing reading speed and a rubber neck to do justice to the Canal Grande in one run, though; even these edited highlights cover around fifty buildings (less than a third of the total). Try to allow for several trips, and don't miss the experience of a nocturnal boat ride – the romance of Venice at night survives even the din of a vaporetto.

The Left Bank

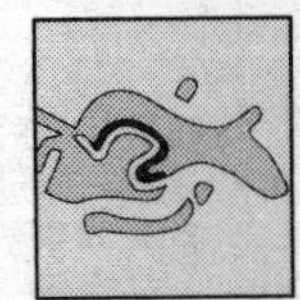

If you come into Venice by train, your first sight of the Canal Grande will be from the upper stretch of its left bank, with the vaporetto landing-stages directly in front. To the left is the **Ponte degli Scalzi**,

cheaper, lighter and easier to obtain in the Veneto than building stone. Obviously mud-banks are not the stablest of bases, so the builders' usual procedure was to drive oak piling into the mud as a foundation, and then consolidate this with a superstructure of planks and cement. Between this "raft" and the brickwork, they often placed a damp-course of highly resistant Istrian stone.

A couple of features of the Venetian skyline call for explanation. The bizarre **chimneys** were designed to function as spark-traps – fire being a constant hazard in a city where the scarcity of land inevitably resulted in a high density of housing. (The development of Venice has been punctuated by terrible fires – notably at the Rialto, San Marco and, at least four times, the Palazzo Ducale.) The **roof-level platforms** (*altane*) you'll see here and there had a variety of uses: drying laundry and bleaching hair being two of the most common. For the latter operation, the women of Renaissance Venice wore wide-brimmed crownless straw hats, which allowed them to get the sun on their hair while keeping it off their complexions.

The frequency with which the same **family names** recur can be confusing. More than ten palaces bear the Contarini name, for example, and at one time there were around thirty. Intermarriage between families is one reason for this – dynastic marriages were often marked by grafting the new relatives' surname onto the house's original name. The other main explanation is the fact that under Venetian law the eldest son was not the sole heir – the sons of wealthy patricians would often, upon receiving their shares of the father's estate, set up their own branches of the family in houses in other parts of the city. This did not always involve commissioning a new building; palaces were regularly bought and sold within the patriciate, and the transaction often resulted in another double-barrelled palace name.

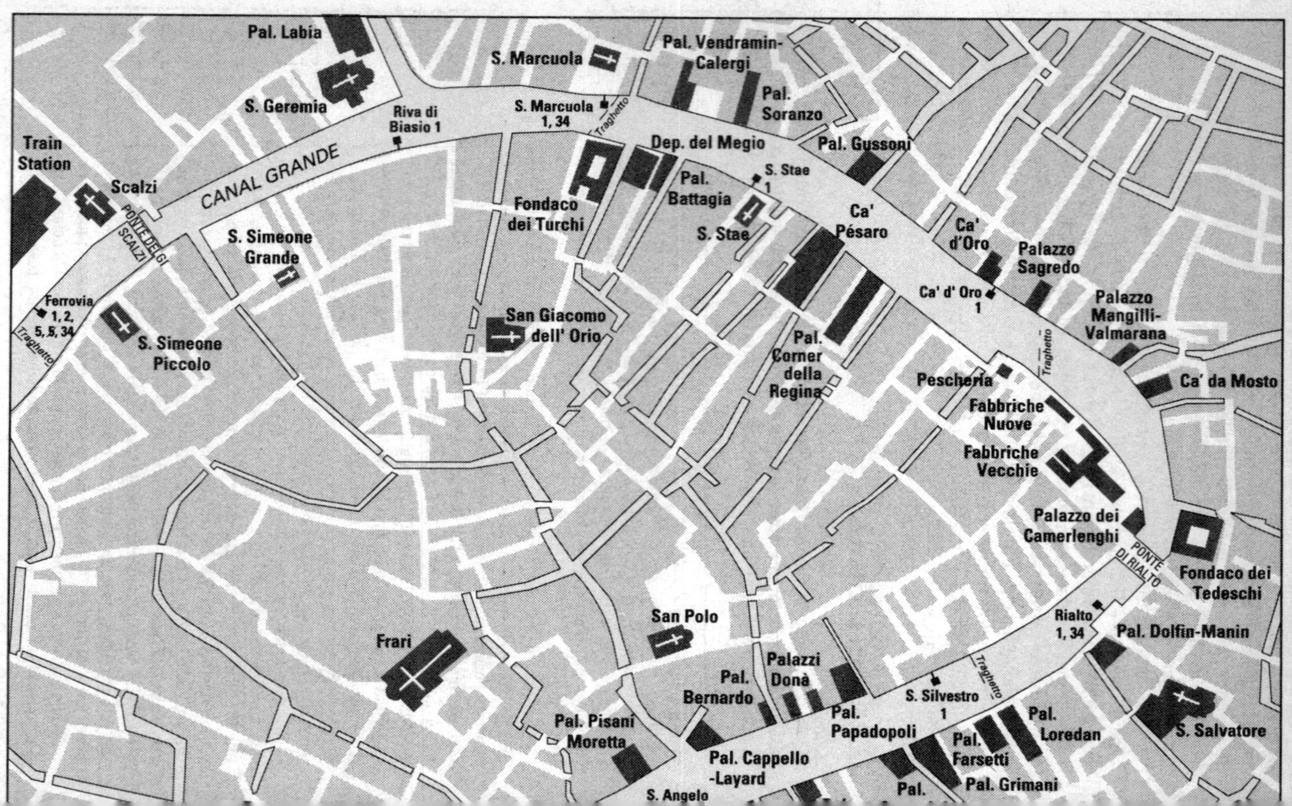

Pal. Labia
S. Geremia
S. Marcuola
Pal. Vendramin-Calergi
Pal. Soranzo
Riva di Biasio 1
S. Marcuola 1, 34
Traghetto
Train Station
Scalzi
CANAL GRANDE
PONTE DEGLI SCALZI
Dep. del Megio
Pal. Gussoni
Pal. Battagia
S. Stae 1
S. Stae
Fondaco dei Turchi
Ca' Pésaro
Ca' d'Oro
Palazzo Sagredo
S. Simeone Grande
Ca' d' Oro 1
Palazzo Mangilli-Valmarana
Ferrovia 1, 2, 5, 5, 34
Traghetto
San Giacomo dell' Orio
S. Simeone Piccolo
Pal. Corner della Regina
Traghetto
Pescheria
Ca' da Mosto
Fabbriche Nuove
Fabbriche Vecchie
Palazzo dei Camerlenghi
PONTE DI RIALTO
Fondaco dei Tedeschi
San Polo
Rialto 1, 34
Pal. Dolfin-Manin
Frari
Palazzi Donà
Pal. Bernardo
Traghetto
S. Silvestro 1
Pal. Pisani Moretta
Pal. Papadopoli
Pal. Loredan
S. Salvatore
Pal. Farsetti
Pal. Cappello -Layard
Pal. Grimani
S. Angelo
Pal.

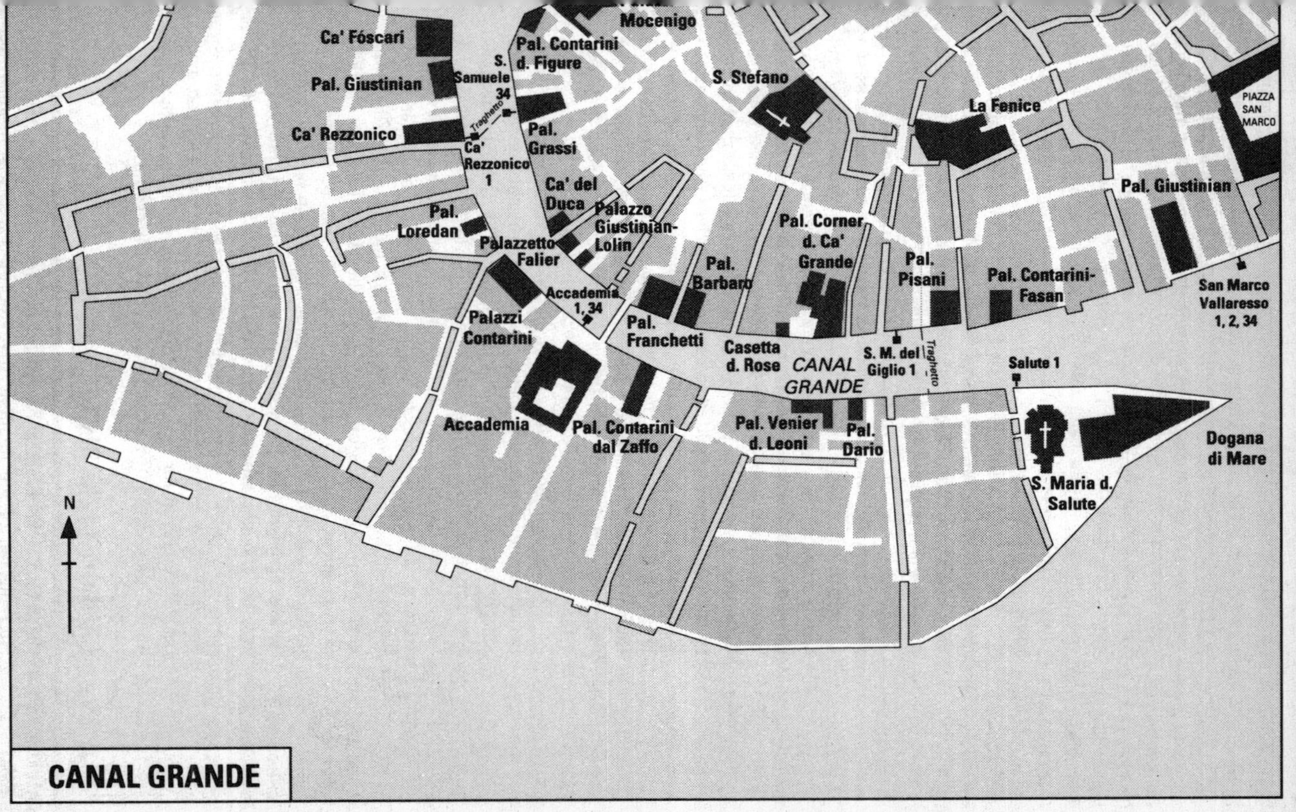
Mocenigo
Ca' Fóscari
Pal. Contarini d. Figure
S. Samuele 34
Pal. Giustinian
S. Stefano
La Fenice
PIAZZA SAN MARCO
Traghetto
Ca' Rezzonico
Pal. Grassi
Ca' Rezzonico 1
Ca' del Duca
Pal. Giustinian
Pal. Loredan
Palazzo Giustinian-Lolin
Pal. Corner d. Ca' Grande
Palazzetto Falier
Pal. Barbaro
Pal. Pisani
Pal. Contarini-Fasan
Accademia 1, 34
San Marco Vallaresso 1, 2, 34
Palazzi Contarini
Pal. Franchetti
Casetta d. Rose
S. M. del Giglio 1
Traghetto
Salute 1
CANAL GRANDE
Accademia
Pal. Contarini dal Zaffo
Pal. Venier d. Leoni
Pal. Dario
Dogana di Mare
S. Maria d. Salute
N
CANAL GRANDE

successor of an iron structure put up by the Austrians in 1858–60; like the one at the Accademia, it was replaced in the early 1930s, to give the new steamboats enough clearance. The boat passes two churches, the **Scalzi** and **San Geremia**, before the first of the major palaces comes into view – the **Palazzo Labia** (completed c.1750). The main facade of the building stretches along the Canareggio canal, but from the Canal Grande you can see how the side wing wraps itself round the campanile of the neighbouring church – such interlocking is common in Venice, where maximum use has to be made of available space.

The ballroom of the Palazzo Labia contains frescoes by Tiepolo, which can be seen by appointment; *see p.129.*

Not far beyond the unfinished church of **San Marcuola** stands the **Palazzo Vendramin-Calergi**, begun by Mauro Coducci at the very end of the fifteenth century and finished in the first decade of the sixteenth, probably by Tullio Lombardo. This is the first Venetian palace to be influenced by the classically based architectural principles of Leon Battista Alberti, and is frequently singled out as the Canal Grande's masterpiece. The round-arched windows enclosing two similar arches are identifying characteristics of Coducci's designs. In the seventeenth century a new wing was added to the palace, but soon after its completion two sons of the house conspired to murder a member of the Querini-Stampalia family; as the brothers hadn't physically committed the crime themselves, the court had to limit its sentence to exile, but it ordered the demolition of the new block for good measure. The most famous subsequent resident was Richard Wagner, who died here in February 1883; the size of the palace can be gauged from the fact that his rented suite of fifteen rooms occupied just a part of the mezzanine level.

The **Palazzo Soranzo**, a bit further along, dates from the same period as the Vendramin-Calergi; appealing in itself, it gives you an idea of the originality of Coducci's design. The **Palazzo Gussoni-Grimani della Vida**, on the near side of the Rio di Noale, was rebuilt to Sanmicheli's designs in the middle of the sixteenth century. From 1614 to 1618 it was occupied by the English consul Sir Henry Wotton, at the time of whose residence the facade of the palace was covered with frescoes by Tintoretto – they have long since faded. Wotton spent much of his time running a sort of import–export business: when he wasn't buying paintings to ship back to England he was arranging for Protestant texts to be brought into Venice, a city he thought ripe for conversion. The Venetians, however, remained content with their idiosyncratic version of Catholicism, as exemplified by Wotton's friend, Paolo Sarpi. In Britain, Wotton is best remembered for his rueful definition of an ambassador – "an honest man sent to lie abroad for the good of his country".

For more on Paolo Sarpi, see p.138.

Ca' d'Oro to the Rialto

For more on the Ca' d'Oro, see p.138.

The next palace of interest is the most beguiling on the canal – the **Ca' d'Oro**. (*Ca'* is an abbreviation of *Casa* – house. It was only after the fall of the Republic that the title *Casa* was dropped in favour of *Palazzo*.) Incorporating fragments of a thirteenth-century palace that once stood on the site, the Ca' d'Oro was built in the 1420s and 1430s, and acquired its nickname – "The Golden House" – from the gilding that used to accentuate much of its carving.

The facade of the **Palazzo Sagredo**, on the near side of the Campo Santa Sofia, is an overlay of different periods, and a good demonstration of the Venetian custom of adapting old buildings to current needs and principles. The tracery of the *piano nobile* is fourteenth-century, and clearly later than the storeys below; the right wing, however, seems to belong to the fifteenth century.

On the near corner of the Rio dei Santi Apostoli stands the **Palazzo Mangilli-Valmarana**, built in the eighteenth century for the English consul, Joseph Smith, who was one of the chief patrons of Canaletto. More interesting is the **Ca' da Mosto**, close to the Rio's opposite bank. The arches of the first floor and the carved panels above them are remnants of a thirteenth-century Veneto-Byzantine building, and thus are among the oldest structures to be seen on the Canal Grande. Alvise da Mosto, discoverer of the Cape Verde Islands, was born here in 1432; by the end of that century it had become the *Albergo del Lion Bianco*, and from then until the last century the palace was one of Venice's most popular hotels.

As the canal turns, the **Ponte di Rialto** comes into view. The huge building before it is the **Fondaco dei Tedeschi**, once headquarters of the city's German merchants. On the ground floor their cargoes were weighed, packaged and stored; the upper storeys contained a refectory and around sixty bedrooms, many of which were rented on an annual basis by the biggest firms. The German traders were the most powerful foreign grouping in the city, and as early as 1228 they were leased a building on this central site. In 1505 the Fondaco burned down, and was rebuilt by Spavento and Scarpagnino; Giorgione and Titian, who had helped the firefighters on the night of the blaze, were then commissioned to paint the exterior walls. The remains of their contribution are now in the Ca' d'Oro. The Fondaco has been renovated several times since the sixteenth century, and is now the main post office.

The famous **bridge** superseded a succession of wooden and sometimes unreliable structures – in 1444 a forerunner collapsed under the weight of the crowd gathered to watch the wedding procession of the Marquis of Ferrara; and one of Carpaccio's *Miracles of the True Cross*, in the Accademia, shows you what the next drawbridge looked like. The decision to construct a stone bridge was taken in 1524, and over the following sixty years proposals by Michelangelo, Vignola, Sansovino and Palladio were considered and rejected. Eventually the job was awarded to the aptly named **Antonio da Ponte**, whose top-heavy design was described by Edward Gibbon as "a fine bridge, spoilt by two rows of houses upon it". Until 1854, when the first Accademia bridge was built, this was the only point at which the Canal Grande could be crossed on foot.

From the Rialto to the Volta del Canal

Immediately before the next *rio* is Sansovino's first palace in Venice, the **Palazzo Dolfin-Manin**. It dates from the late 1530s, a period when other projects by Sansovino – the Libreria, the Zecca and the Loggetta – were transforming the centre of the city. The public passageway (*sottoportego*) running under the facade is a feature common to many Venetian houses. Lodovico Manin, the last doge of Venice, lived there – he had the interior rebuilt, so the facade is the only bit entirely by Sansovino.

The **Palazzo Loredan** and the **Palazzo Farsetti**, standing side by side at the end of the Fondamenta del Carbon, are heavily restored Veneto-Byzantine palaces of the thirteenth century. The former was the home of **Elena Corner Piscopia**, who in 1678 graduated from Padua University, so becoming the first woman ever to hold a university degree. The two buildings are now occupied by the town hall.

Work began on the **Palazzo Grimani** (on the near side of the Rio di San Luca) in 1559, to designs by Sanmicheli, but was not completed until 1575, sixteen years after his death. Ruskin, normally no fan of Renaissance architecture, made an exception for this colossal palace, calling it "simple, delicate, and sublime". A Venetian folktale attributes the scale of the palace to a thwarted passion: it's said that the young man who built it was in love with a woman from the Coccina-Tiepolo palace over the way, but was turned away by her father who wanted someone wealthier for his offspring. The suitor's revenge was to humiliate the father by building a palace which had windows bigger than the main doorway at the Coccina-Tiepolo.

The **Palazzo Corner Contarini dei Cavalli**, on the other side of the *rio*, was built around 1445; the "cavalli" part of the name comes from the horses on the crest of the facade's coat of arms. The pink **Palazzo Benzon**, just before the next canal, was where the most fashionable salon of early nineteenth-century Venice used to meet – regular guests included Byron, Thomas Moore, Ugo Foscolo and Canova. Their hostess, Contessa Querini-Benzon, was celebrated in a song that still occupies a place in the gondoliers' repertoire – "La Biondina in Gondoleta" (The Blonde in a Gondola). The **Palazzo Corner-Spinelli**, on the far side of the Rio di Ca' Santi, is another work by Coducci; it dates from 1490–1510, so preceding his more monumental Palazzo Vendramin-Calergi.

Four houses that once all belonged to the Mocenigo family stand side by side on the **Volta del Canal**, as the Canal Grande's sharpest turn is known: the **Palazzo Mocenigo-Nero**, a late sixteenth-century building; the double **Palazzo Mocenigo**, built in the eighteenth century as an extension to the Nero house; and the **Palazzo Mocenigo Vecchio**, a Gothic palace remodelled in the seventeenth century.

One of the great Venetian scandals centres on the first of the four. In 1621 Lady Arundel, wife of one of King James's most powerful courtiers, became its tenant; before long it was rumoured that the house was being visited by **Antonio Foscarini**, a former ambassador from Venice to England, whose term in London had ended with an abrupt recall home and a three-year stay in prison under suspicion of treason. On that occasion Foscarini had finally been cleared, but now there were renewed allegations of treacherous behaviour, and the Council of Ten quickly shifted into top gear. Foscarini was arrested, interrogated and, twelve days later, executed. Lady Arundel instantly demanded an audience with the doge, the result of which was a public declaration that she had not been involved in any plot; and within a few months the Council of Ten had conclusive evidence that Foscarini had been framed. The men who had accused him were put to death, and Foscarini's body was exhumed and given a state funeral.

The Left Bank

Byron and his menagerie – a dog, a fox, a wolf and a monkey – lived in the Mocenigo-Nero palace for a couple of years. Much of his time was taken up with a local baker's wife called Margarita Cogni, the most tempestuous of his mistresses – her reaction to being rejected by him was to attack him with a table knife and then, having been shown the door, hurl herself into the Canal Grande. The Palazzo Mocenigo Vecchio is supposed to be haunted by the ghost of the philosopher-alchemist Giordano Bruno, whose betrayal by Giovanni Mocenigo in 1592 led ultimately to his torture and execution.

The neighbouring building is the early sixteenth-century **Palazzo Contarini delle Figure** – the *figure* are the almost invisible figures above the water entrance. It was begun by Spavento and completed by Scarpagnino, a combination previously employed on the Fondaco dei Tedeschi and the Palazzo Ducale.

To the Palazzo Giustinian

The vast and pristine palace round the *Volta* is the **Palazzo Grassi**, built in 1748–72 by Massari, who supervised the completion of the Ca' Rezzonico on the opposite bank. Its first owners were accepted into the ranks of the nobility in return for a hefty contribution to the war effort against the Turks in 1718. Nowadays it's owned by Fiat – hence the sparkling renovation – and is used as an exhibition and conference centre.

For more on the Palazzo Grassi, see p.83.

On the edge of the first canal after the campo of San Samuele stands the **Ca' del Duca**. Commissioned in the mid-fifteenth century from Bartolomeo Bon, it was left unfinished in 1461 when the Corner family sold it to Francesco Sforza, Duke of Milan (from whom it takes its name) – the wedge of rusticated masonry gives some idea of the sort of fortified look the Corners had in mind. In 1514 Titian had a studio here. Across the *rio* there's the tiny

Palazzetto Falier, a reworked Gothic house of the fifteenth century, chiefly remarkable for its two roofed terraces. Although they used to be quite common, very few examples of this feature (called a *liagò*) have survived. Next door is one of Longhena's earliest projects, the **Palazzo Giustinian-Lolin** (1623).

As the larger vaporetti couldn't get under the iron **Ponte dell' Accademia** built by the Austrians in 1854, it was replaced in 1932 by a wooden one – a temporary measure that has become permanent. At the foot of the bridge, on the far side, is the huge fifteenth-century **Palazzo Franchetti**; repaired and enlarged at the end of the nineteenth century, it's often cited as one of the city's most heavy-handed pieces of restoration work.

On the opposite side of the Rio dell'Orso are the twinned **Palazzi Barbaro**; the house on the left is early fifteenth-century, the other late seventeenth-century. Henry James, Monet, Whistler, Browning and John Singer Sargent were among the luminaries who stayed in the older Barbaro house as guests of the Curtis family in the late nineteenth century. James wrote *The Aspern Papers* here, and used it as a setting for *The Wings of a Dove*; so attached was he to the place that when given the opportunity of buying a home in Venice at a very reasonable price, he decided he would rather go on living here as a lodger.

Soon after the short fondamenta comes the tiny **Casetta delle Rose**, where Canova once had his studio and D'Annunzio lived during World War I. The Casetta lies in the shadow of one of the Canal Grande's most imposing buildings – Sansovino's **Palazzo Corner della Ca' Grande**. The palace that used to stand here was destroyed when a fire lit to dry out a stock of sugar in the attic ran out of control, an incident that illustrates the dual commercial-residential function of many palaces in Renaissance Venice. Sansovino's replacement, commissioned by the nephew of Caterina Cornaro, was built from 1545 onwards. The rustication of the lower storey – a distinctive aspect of many Roman and Tuscan buildings of the High Renaissance – makes it a prototype for Longhena's Ca' Pésaro and Ca' Rezzonico.

The heavily restored fifteenth-century **Palazzo Pisani**, now the *Gritti Hotel*, looms over the Santa Maria del Giglio landing stage – John and Effie Ruskin stayed here in 1851, the year *The Stones of Venice* began to appear in print. Squeezed into the line of buildings that follows is the narrow **Palazzo Contarini-Fasan**, a mid-fifteenth-century palace with unique wheel tracery on the balconies. It's popularly known as "the house of Desdemona", but although the model for Shakespeare's heroine did live in Venice, her association with this house is purely sentimental. The last major building before the *Giardinetti Reali* is the fifteenth-century **Palazzo Giustinian**; now the HQ of the Biennale offices and the tourist board, in the last century it was one of the plushest hotels in town, its registers being signed by the likes of Verdi, Ruskin and Proust.

The Right Bank

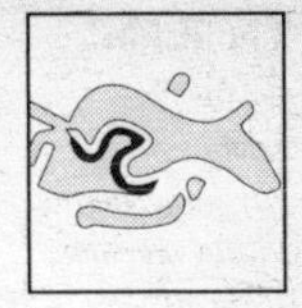

Arriving in Venice by road, you come in on the right bank of the Canal Grande at Piazzale Roma, opposite the train station. Orientation is initially difficult, with canals heading off in various directions and no immediate landmark; it's not until the vaporetto swings round by the train station that it becomes obvious that this is the city's main waterway.

Having passed the green-domed church of **San Simeone Piccolo**, the end of the elongated campo of **San Simeone Grande** and a procession of nondescript buildings, you come to the **Fondaco dei Turchi** (opposite San Marcuola). A private house from the early thirteenth century until 1621 (including spells when it was used as a guesthouse for VIPs), the building was then turned over to the Turkish traders in the city, who stayed here until 1838. By the 1850s it was in such a terrible state that a campaign for its restoration was started, with Ruskin at the helm; the city undertook the repair, but the result was judged nearly as bad an eyesore as the ruin had been, and has had few admirers since. There's hardly an original brick left in the building, but whatever the shortcomings of the work, the building's towers and long water-level arcade give a reasonably precise, if schematic, picture of what a Veneto-Byzantine palace would have looked like. One of the sarcophagi underneath the portico belongs to the family of the disgraced Marin Falier. The Fondaco housed the Correr collection from 1880 to 1922, and now contains the natural history museum.

For more on Marin Falier see p.60; for the natural history museum, see p.110.

The crenellated structure next along from the Fondaco is the fifteenth-century **Depositi del Megio** (public granary); its neighbour is another palace by Longhena – the **Palazzo Belloni-Battagia** (1647–63). Longhena's client experienced severe cash-flow problems not long after the house was finished, a consequence of simultaneously building the house and buying his way into the pages of the *Libro d' Oro* (the register of the nobility), and so was obliged to rent the place out rather than live in it himself.

A short distance down the canal, after the church of **San Stae**, stands a far more impressive Longhena building – the thickly ornamented **Ca' Pésaro**, bristling with diamond-shaped spikes and grotesque heads. Three houses had to be demolished to make room for this palace and its construction lasted half a century – work started in 1652 and finished in 1703, long after Longhena's death. Unusually, the Ca' Pésaro has a stone-clad side facade: most houses in Venice have plain brick sides, either because of the cost of stone, or because of the possibility that a later building might be attached.

The Ca' Pésaro contains the Galleria d' Arte Moderna and the Museo Orientale – see p.108.

The next large building is the **Palazzo Corner della Regina**, built in 1724 on the site of the home of Caterina Cornaro, Queen of Cyprus, from whom the palace takes its name. The base of the Biennale archives, it was formerly the *Monte di Pietà* (municipal pawnshop).

The Right Bank

For more on the Rialto markets, see p.103.

Beyond, there's nothing especially engrossing until you reach the **Rialto markets**, which begin with the neo-Gothic fish market, the **Pescheria**, built in 1907; there's been a fish market here since the fourteenth century. The older buildings which follow it, the **Fabbriche Nuove di Rialto** and (set back from the water) the **Fabbriche Vecchie di Rialto** are by Sansovino (c.1550) and Scarpagnino (c.1520) respectively. The large building at the base of the Rialto bridge is the **Palazzo dei Camerlenghi** (c.1525), the former chambers of the Venetian exchequer. Debtors could find themselves in the cells of the building's bottom storey – hence the name *Fondamenta delle Prigioni* for this part of the canalside. At the foot of the Rialto Bridge, on the other side, were the offices of the state finance ministers, in Scarpagnino's **Palazzo dei Dieci Savi**.

From the Rialto to the Volta del Canal

From the Rialto down to the *Volta del Canal* the right bank is of more sporadic interest. The **Palazzo Papadopoli** (aka **Palazzo Coccina-Tiepolo**), on the far side of Rio dei Meloni, was built in the 1560s; the Venetian mercantile class rarely wanted adventurous designs for their houses, and the conservative Papadopoli palace, with its emphasis on blank wall spaces broken up with applied decoration, was to prove extremely influential. (Contrast it with the contemporaneous Grimani palace, on the opposite side of the Canal Grande.) The adjacent **Palazzo Donà** and **Palazzo Donà della Madonnetta** (named after the fifteenth-century relief on the facade) date from the twelfth and thirteenth centuries; they have been frequently altered, but some original features survive, notably the main windows.

The tracery of the mid-fifteenth-century **Palazzo Bernardo** (across the Rio della Madonnetta), among the most beautiful on the Canal Grande, is copied from the loggia of the Palazzo Ducale – you'll find echoes of the pattern all over the city. The sixteenth-century **Palazzo Cappello-Layard**, on the edge of the wide Rio San Polo, was the home of the English ambassador Sir Henry Layard, whose astuteness assured that the British public profited from the destitution of Venice in the last century. His collection of nineteen major Venetian paintings, picked up for a song, were left to the National Gallery in London. Another of the National's masterpieces – Veronese's *The Clemency of Alexander* – was bought in 1857 from the **Palazzo Pisani della Moretta** (mid-fifteenth-century), second along on the other side of the rio.

The cluster of palaces at the *Volta* constitutes one of the city's architectural glories. The **Palazzo Balbi**, on the near side of the Rio di Ca' Fóscari, is the youngest of the group, a proto-Baroque design executed in the 1580s to plans by Alessandro Vittoria, whose sculpture is to be found in many Venetian churches. Nicolo Balbi is reputed to have been so keen to see his palace finished that he moored a boat alongside the building site so that he could watch the work progressing – and died of a chill caught by sleeping in it. Had Frank Lloyd Wright got his way, the Palazzo Balbi would have acquired a new neighbour in the 1950s, but local opposition, orchestrated from the Balbi palace, scuppered the scheme.

On the opposite bank stands the **Ca' Fóscari** (c.1435), which Ruskin thought "the noblest example in Venice" of late Gothic architecture. The largest private house in Venice at the time of its construction, it was the home of one of the more colourful figures of Venetian history, Doge Francesco Fóscari, whose extraordinarily long term of office (thirty-four years) came to an end with his forced resignation. When Henry III of France passed through Venice on his way to his coronation in 1574, it was at the Ca' Fóscari that he was lodged. After a banquet for which all sumptuary laws had been suspended and at which the tables had been set with utensils and decorative figures made from sugar to Sansovino's designs, Henry reeled back here to find his rooms decked out with silks and cloth of gold, and lined with paintings by Bellini, Titian, Veronese and Tintoretto. Venice's university now owns the building.

For more on Doge Fóscari, see p.118.

Adjoining it are the **Palazzi Giustinian**, a pair of palaces built in the mid-fifteenth century for two brothers who wanted attached but self-contained houses. In the twelfth century the Giustinian family was in danger of dying out, and such was the panic induced in Venice by the thought of losing one of its most illustrious dynasties (it traced its descent from the Emperor Justinian), that papal permission was sought for the young monk who was the one surviving male of the clan to be released from his vows in order to start a family. The pope gave his consent, a bride was found, and twelve Giustinians were propagated; his duty done, the father returned to his monastery, and his wife went off to found a convent on one of the remoter islands of the lagoon. For a while one of the Palazzi Giustinian was **Wagner**'s home. Finding the rooms inimical to the creative process he made a few improvements such as hanging the walls with red cloth and importing his own bed and grand piano from Zurich. Having made the place comfortable, he settled down, flirted with the idea of suicide, and wrote the second act of *Tristan und Isolde*. Venice also supplied him with inspiration for the final part of his masterpiece – the long horn motif that begins the third act was based on the nocturnal calls of the gondoliers.

From the Ca' Rezzonico to the Dogana di Mare

A little farther on comes Longhena's **Ca' Rezzonico**, as gargantuan as his Ca' Pésaro, but less aggressive. It was begun in 1667 as a commission from the Bon family, but their ambition exceeded their financial resources, and not long after hiring Giorgio Massari to complete the upper part they were obliged to sell the still unfinished palace to the Rezzonico, a family of Genoese bankers. Despite

The Ca' Rezzonico houses the Museo del Settecento Veneziano – see p.100.

having lashed out 100,000 ducats to buy their way into the *Libro d'Oro* (at a time when 1000 per annum was a comfortable income for a noble), the new owners could afford to keep Massari employed on the completion of the top floor, and then to tack a ballroom and staircase onto the back. Among its subsequent owners was Pen Browning, whose father Robert died here in 1889; and both Whistler and Cole Porter stayed here briefly.

After a couple of canals you pass the **Palazzo Loredan dell' Ambasciatore**, opposite the Ca' del Duca. Taking its name from the Austrian embassy that used to be here, it was built in the fifteenth century, and is notable mainly for the figures in niches on the facade, which possibly came from the workshop of Antonio Rizzo. On the far side of the next canal, the Rio di San Trovaso, stand the **Palazzo Contarini-Corfu** and the **Palazzo Contarini degli Scrigni**. The "Corfu" bit of the first name derives either from the fact that a Contarini was once a military commander on that island, or from the name of a family that lived in the parish before the Contarini crew. The two palaces form a single unit: the Scrigni was built in 1609 as an extension to the Corfu, a fifteenth-century Gothic house. A similar operation was carried out at the Palazzi Barbaro (opposite, just after the Accademia bridge), with less jarring results.

Yet another Contarini palace stands a few yards past the Accademia bridge – the **Palazzo Contarini-Polignac**. This branch of the Contarini family made itself rich through landholdings around Jaffa, and the dialect version of that place-name is the source of the alternative name for the palace: Contarini dal Zaffo. The facade, which was applied to the Gothic building in the late fifteenth century, represents a transitional phase between the highly decorative style associated with the Lombardi and their imitators (see the Palazzo Dario, below) and the classicising work of Coducci.

The unfinished **Palazzo Venier dei Leoni** (soon after the Campo San Vio) would have been the largest palace on the canal, but its construction, begun in 1759, never progressed further than the first storey – hence its alternative name, **Palazzo Nonfinito**. Its abandonment was almost certainly due to the ruinous cost, but there's a tradition which says the project was stopped by the objections of the Corner family across the water, who didn't want their sunlight blocked by a house that was bigger than theirs. The stump of the building and the platform on which it is raised (itself an extravagant and novel feature) are occupied by the Guggenheim collection of modern art.

For an entry on the Guggenheim collection, see p.91.

The one domestic building of interest between here and the end of the canal is the miniature **Palazzo Dario**, the next building but one after the Palazzo dei Leoni. Compared by Henry James to "a house of cards that hold together by a tenure it would be fatal to touch", the palace was built in the late 1480s not for a patrician family but for a member of the middle ("citizen") class – a chancery secretary named Giovanni Dario; it was later owned by the Rolling

Stones' manager. The multi-coloured marbles of the facade are characteristic of the work of the Lombardo family, and the design may actually be by the founder of that dynasty, Pietro Lombardo. Two doors down, the technicolour **Palazzo Salviati** was built in 1924 by the glassmakers of the same name; perhaps the nastiest building on the canal, its emetic decoration is a foretaste of what awaits you in the glass showrooms of Murano.

The focal point of this last stretch of the canal is Longhena's masterpiece, **Santa Maria della Salute** – it's dealt with in the *Dorsoduro* chapter, as is the **Dogana di Mare** (Customs House), the Canal Grande's full stop.

The Right Bank

For the entries on the Salute and the Dogana di Mare, see p.92–93.

Chapter 9

The Northern Islands

The islands lying to the north of Venice – **San Michele**, **Murano**, **Burano**, **Torcello** and **San Francesco del Deserto** – are the places to visit when the throng of tourists in the main part of Venice becomes too oppressive, or when the stone pavements and ravines of brick become wearying and you want to enjoy the smell of plants growing. An excursion through this part of the lagoon will reveal the origins of the glass and lace work touted in so many of the city's shops, and give you a glimpse of the origins of Venice itself.

To get to the islands, the main **vaporetto stop** is the **Fondamente Nuove**. The **vaporetto #5** (*circolare destra* or *circolare sinistra* – right or left circular) runs about every fifteen minutes from here to **San Michele** and **Murano**. If you're hopping onto the *circolare* elsewhere in the city, be careful: take the *destra* if you are at the station or on the Canale di Cannaregio, and the *sinistra* if you are on Giudecca or just down from San Marco at San Zaccaria – the round trip from the station to the Fondamente Nuove the wrong way can take a good hour. For **Torcello** and **Burano** there is the **vaporetto #12**, which leaves every hour to ninety minutes, depending on time of day, and takes forty minutes to reach Burano, from where it's a short hop to Torcello; this can also be caught from Murano, but only from the *Faro* landing stage.

If you take this journey at low tide the reason for the route markers (*bricole*) will be apparent: over half the lagoon is *laguna morta*, and only covered at high tide. Nowadays it's virtually impossible to hire a boat to explore the lagoon independently, as so many enthusiastic visitors became stranded on the mud flats that the novelty of rescuing them wore off years ago.

San Michele

A church was founded on **San Michele**, the innermost of the northern islands, in the tenth century, and a monastery was established in the thirteenth. Its best-known resident was Fra Mauro (d.1459),

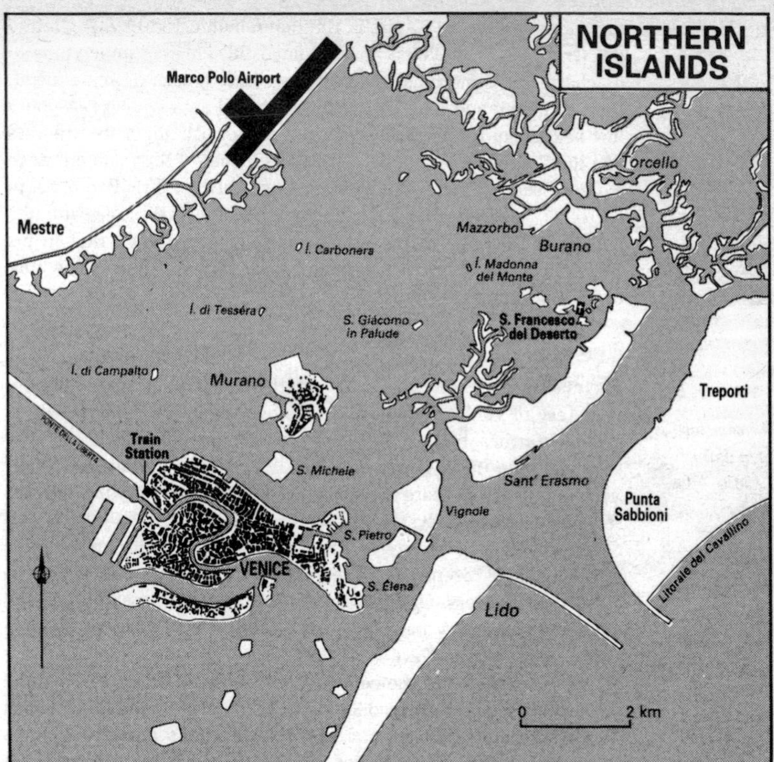

whose map of the world – the most accurate of its time – is now one of the most precious possessions of the Libreria Sansoviniana. The monastery was suppressed in the early nineteenth century, but in 1829, after a spell as an Austrian prison for political offenders, it was handed back to the Franciscans, who look after the church and the cemetery to this day.

The high brick wall around the island gives way by the landing stage for the elegant white facade of **San Michele in Isola**, designed by **Mauro Coducci** in 1469. With this building Coducci quietly revolutionised the architecture of Venice, advancing the principles of Renaissance design in the city and introducing the use of Istrian stone as a material for facades. Easy to carve yet resistant to water, Istrian stone had long been used for damp courses, but never before had anyone clad the entire front of a building in it; after the construction of San Michele, most major buildings in Venice were given an Istrian veneer.

The **interior** of the church has the air of being well and constantly used, with a scent which is a mixture of fresh flowers, incense and a little hint of the cypress trees. Attached on the left is the dainty hexagonal **Cappella Emiliana**, built c.1530 by **Guglielmo dei Grigi**, and completely marble lined. Ruskin was impervious to its charm: "It is more like a German summer-house, or angle-turret, than a chapel, and may be briefly described as a bee-hive set on a low hexagonal tower, with dashes of stonework about its windows like the flourishes of an idle penman." In front of the main entrance a floor plaque marks the final resting place of **Fra Paolo Sarpi** (d.1623), Venice's principal ideologist during the tussle with the papacy at the start of the seventeenth century; buried first in his Servite monastery, Sarpi's remains were removed here when that order was suppressed in 1828.

For more on Paolo Sarpi, see p.138.

The cemetery

The main part of the island, through the cloisters, is covered by the **cemetery** of Venice, established here by a Napoleonic decree which forbade further burials in the centre of the city. Space is at a premium, and the majority of Venetians lie here in cramped conditions for just ten years or so, when their bones are dug up and removed to an ossuary, and the land recycled. Thus the boats to the cemetery release a steady procession of people coming to tend the graves of their recently dead relatives, and the main part is always ablaze with flowers. Only those who can afford to lease a plot stay longer; a still empty mausoleum is engraved *La Famiglia Antony Quinn*, but most here are Venetians.

The cemetery is open daily 8.15am–4pm.

At the entrance to the cemetery you can pick up a small plan of the various sections. Most dilapidated is the **protestant** section (no. XV), where any admirers can find **Ezra Pound's grave** – a crude slab with his name on it, but missing the epitaph he wrote for himself:

Ezra Pound
Got around
He was born in Hailey
But he was buried in San Michele
not the terzo cielo
but socially meglio

(not the third heaven, but socially the best). Adjoining is the **Greek and Russian Orthodox** area (no. XIV), including the simple gravestones of **Igor and Vera Stravinsky** – Stravinsky was given a funeral service in San Zanipolo, the highest funeral honour the city can bestow – and the more elaborate tomb for **Serge Diaghilev**. (There is a separate Jewish cemetery over on the Lido.) Fans of **Frederick Rolfe** (Baron Corvo) can reach his disconsolate memorial by going through the gap in the wall-graves to the right of sections M and N, then doubling back behind section M: he's up on the top row of block 13. The most poignant section is C, for **infants**, behind which are piled the discarded crosses of dug-up graves, many still hung with dead flowers.

Murano

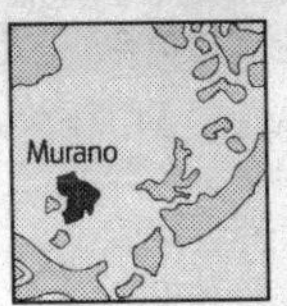

In 1276 the island of **Murano** became a self-governed enclave within the Republic, with its own judiciary, its own administration and a *Libro d'Oro* to register its nobility. By the early sixteenth century Murano had 30,000 inhabitants, and was a favourite summer retreat for Venice's upper classes, who could lay out gardens here which were far more extensive than those in the cramped centre of the city. The Mocenigo family had a house here, and Caterina Cornaro often stayed at her family's palace. The intellectual life of the island was especially healthy in the seventeenth century, when literature, philosophy, the occult and the sciences were discussed in the numerous small *accademie* that flourished here. In the same century the mint on Murano was granted the privi-

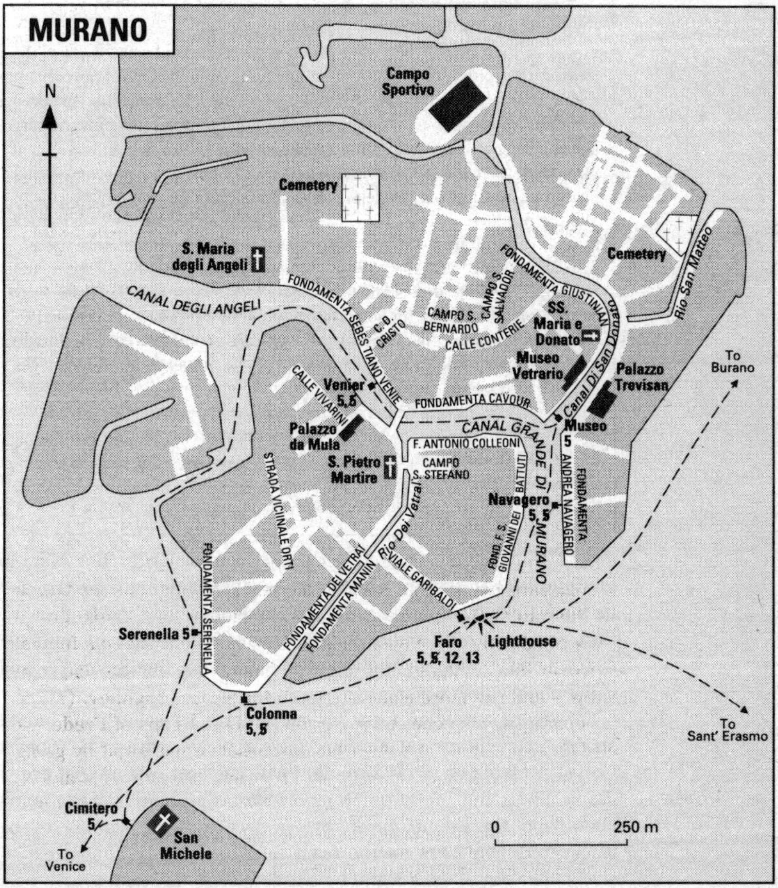

MURANO
N
Campo Sportivo
Cemetery
S. Maria degli Angeli
CANAL DEGLI ANGELI
FONDAMENTA SEBES TIANO VENIER
C. D. CRISTO
CAMPO S. BERNARDO
CAMPO S. SALVADOR
CALLE CONTERIE
FONDAMENTA GIUSTINIAN
Cemetery
Rio San Matteo
SS. Maria e Donato
Museo Vetrario
Palazzo Trevisan
Canal Di San Donato
To Burano
CALLE VIVARINI
Venier 5, 5
Palazzo da Mula
FONDAMENTA CAVOUR
CANAL GRANDE DI MURANO
Museo 5
F. ANTONIO COLLEONI
S. Pietro Martire
CAMPO S. STEFANO
FOND. DEI BATTUTI
FONDAMENTA ANDREA NAVAGERO
STRADA VICINALE ORTI
Rio Dei Vetrai
Navagero 5, 5
FOND. F. S. GIOVANNI DEI
FONDAMENTA SERENELLA
FONDAMENTA DEI VETRAI
FONDAMENTA MANIN
VIALE GARIBALDI
Serenella 5
Faro 5, 5, 12, 13
Lighthouse
Colonna 5, 5
To Sant' Erasmo
Cimitero 5
To Venice
San Michele
0 250 m

Venetian Glass

The glass furnaces were moved to Murano from Venice as a safety measure in 1291, and thenceforth all possible steps were taken to keep the secrets of the trade locked up on the island. Although Muranese workers had by the seventeenth century gained some freedom of movement, for centuries prior to that any glass-maker who left Murano was hunted down as a traitor. Various privileges reduced the temptation to rove – unlike other artisans, the glass-blowers were allowed to wear swords, and from 1376 the offspring of a marriage between a Venetian nobleman and the daughter of a glass-worker were allowed to be entered into the *Libro d'Oro*, unlike the children of other cross-class matches. Normal principles of justice were sometimes waived for the glass-blowers – on one occasion a man who had committed a murder and then fled Murano was accepted back without punishment once his father had hinted to the city's governors that his son might set up a furnace in Mantua.

A fifteenth-century visitor judged that "in the whole world there are no such craftsmen of glass as here", and the Muranese were masters of every aspect of their craft. They were producing spectacles by the start of the fourteenth century, monopolised the European manufacture of mirrors for a long time (and continued making larger mirrors than anyone else even after the monopoly had gone), and in the early seventeenth century became so proficient at making coloured crystal that a decree was issued forbidding the manufacture of false gems out of glass, as many were being passed off as authentic. Understatement has never been a characteristic of Murano produce: in 1756 Lady Mary Wortley Montague was wonderstruck by a set of furniture made entirely in glass, and earlier this century the less favourably impressed H.V. Morton longed "to see something simple and beautiful", adding that sixteenth-century customers felt the same way "when, looking around for something to take home, they were repelled by drinking-glasses in the shape of ships, whales, lions and birds". Murano kitsch extends to all price categories, from the mass-produced nicknacks sold for a couple of thousand lire, through to monstrosities such as Peggy Guggenheim's pieces based on figures from the works of Picasso – specially commissioned by her, they are on show in that bastion of modernist art, the Guggenheim Collection. Plenty of Murano's furnaces are open to the public; entry is free, on the assumption that you will then want to buy something, though you won't be pressed too hard to do so.

lege of forging the tribute medals known as *oselle*. But Murano nowadays owes its fame entirely to its **glass-blowing industry**, and its main fondamente are crowded with shops selling the fruit of the furnaces, most of it repulsive and some of it laughably pretentious. Don't despair, though: Murano does have other things to offer and is definitely worth a visit.

If you're setting off for a day in the northern islands, and intend spending lunchtime on Murano, take a picnic. Although Thomas Coryat declared in 1611 "here did I eate the best oysters that ever I did in all my life", food on Murano today is nothing to write home about and there's no cheap but perfect trattoria waiting to be discovered. The bars on the main *fondamente* are almost exclusively male out of season and tourist-dominated in season.

Around the island

From the vaporetto you step onto the Fondamenta dei Vetrai, traditionally the core of the glass industry (as the name suggests) and now the principal tourist trap. Towards the far end is the Dominican church of **San Pietro Martire**, one of only two churches still in service on the island (compared with seventeen when the Republic fell in 1797). Begun in 1363 but largely rebuilt after a fire in 1474, its main interest lies with its paintings, which are lit by an annoying system that entails a lot of running about with a lot of coins. Save most of your change for the large and elegant *Madonna and Child with St Mark, St Augustine and Doge Barbarigo* (1488) by **Giovanni Bellini**, hanging on the right wall; a second Bellini (an *Assumption*) is at present being restored. On the opposite side of the church are two pieces by **Veronese** – *St Agatha in Prison* and *St Jerome in the Desert*. The Cappella del Sacramento, to the left of the main altar, was originally dedicated to the angels and contains four paintings of personable representatives of the heavenly host. Also worth a look is the sacristy, where characters such as Nero, Caesar, Socrates, Pythagoras, Castor and Pollux, Herod and Pontius Pilate are depicted in seventeenth-century carved panels, along with scenes from the life of John the Baptist.

Just round the corner is the main bridge, the **Ponte Vivarini**, a few yards beyond which is the **Palazzo da Mula**, a Gothic palace altered in the sixteenth century, one of the few surviving examples of a Venetian summer residence on Murano. Many of the other palaces were demolished during the nineteenth century.

The Museo Vetrario

A left turn on the far side of the bridge comes to a dead end at the most recently closed of Murano's churches, **Santa Maria degli Angeli**, in whose convent Casanova had an amorous experience involving many changes of costume.

The Museo Vetrario is open 9am–7pm; closed Wed; L5000.

Turn right along Fondamenta Cavour and you'll soon come to the seventeenth-century Palazzo Giustinian, facing the sixteenth-century Palazzo Trevisan across the canal. Home of the Bishop of Torcello until his diocese was joined to Venice in 1805, the Palazzo Giustinian now houses the **Museo Vetrario**. Featuring pieces dating back to Roman times and examples of Murano glass from the fifteenth century onwards, the museum exerts a fascination even if you can't read the Italian of the perfunctory labels – how *did* the aristocracy manage to drink in the seventeenth century? A separate display, with captions in English this time, covers the history of Murano glass techniques – look out for the extraordinary *Murine in Canna*, the method of placing different coloured rods together to form an image in cross-section.

Hang on to your ticket as it will also get you into the recently opened **Modern and Contemporary Glass Museum** on Fondamenta

Manin (opposite Fondamenta Vetrai; same opening hours), where you'll see pieces of functional glassware that try to look like modernist sculptures, and one or two modernist sculptures that look like giant pieces of functional ware. But there are some interesting works: the baby by Alfredo Borbini which looks as though it's carved from lava, for instance, or the mirror with gold leaf by Piero Fornasetti.

Santi Maria e Donato

Santi Maria e Donato is open daily 8am–noon & 4–7pm.

The other Murano church, and the main reason for visiting the island today, is **Santi Maria e Donato**. It was founded in the seventh century but rebuilt in the twelfth, and is one of the lagoon's best examples of Veneto-Byzantine architecture – the ornate **rear apse** being particularly fine. Originally dedicated to the Virgin, the church was re-dedicated in 1125 when the relics of Saint Donatus were brought here from Cephalonia by **Doge Domenico Michiel**, who also picked up the remains of Saint Isidore and the stone on which Jesus stood to preach to the men of Tyre – both of which are now in the Basilica di San Marco. Saint Donatus once slew a dragon simply by spitting at it – the four splendid bones hanging behind the altar are allegedly from the unfortunate beast.

The glory of the interior is its **mosaic floor** (dated 1141 in the nave), a beautiful weave of abstract patterns and figures – an eagle carries off a deer; two roosters carry off a fox, slung from a pole. The floor was extensively restored in 1977, a process illustrated in a photographic display; proceeds from the sale of the guide to the church help finance further work. Apart from the twelfth-century **mosaic of the Madonna** in the apse, the features that invite perusal are the fifteenth-century ship's-keel roof, the sixth-century pulpit and the Veneto-Byzantine capitals.

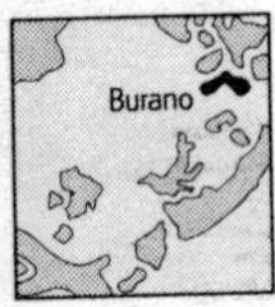

Burano – and San Francesco del Deserto

After Murano, the next stop for the #12 boat is at the small island of **Mazzorbo**, a densely populated town a couple of centuries ago, before it became a place of exile for disgraced noblemen, whereupon the undisgraced citizens decamped for homes elsewhere in the lagoon. Nowadays Mazzorbo doesn't amount to much more than a few scattered villas, a lot of grassy space, a handsome new housing development and the unremarkable church of Santa Caterina. You can either get off the boat here, and walk round Mazzorbo to the sixty-metre footbridge to Burano, or continue on the boat to the main Burano stop.

After the peeling plaster and eroded stonework of the other lagoon settlements, the brightly painted houses of **Burano** come as something of a surprise; once symbolic, the colours are now used in

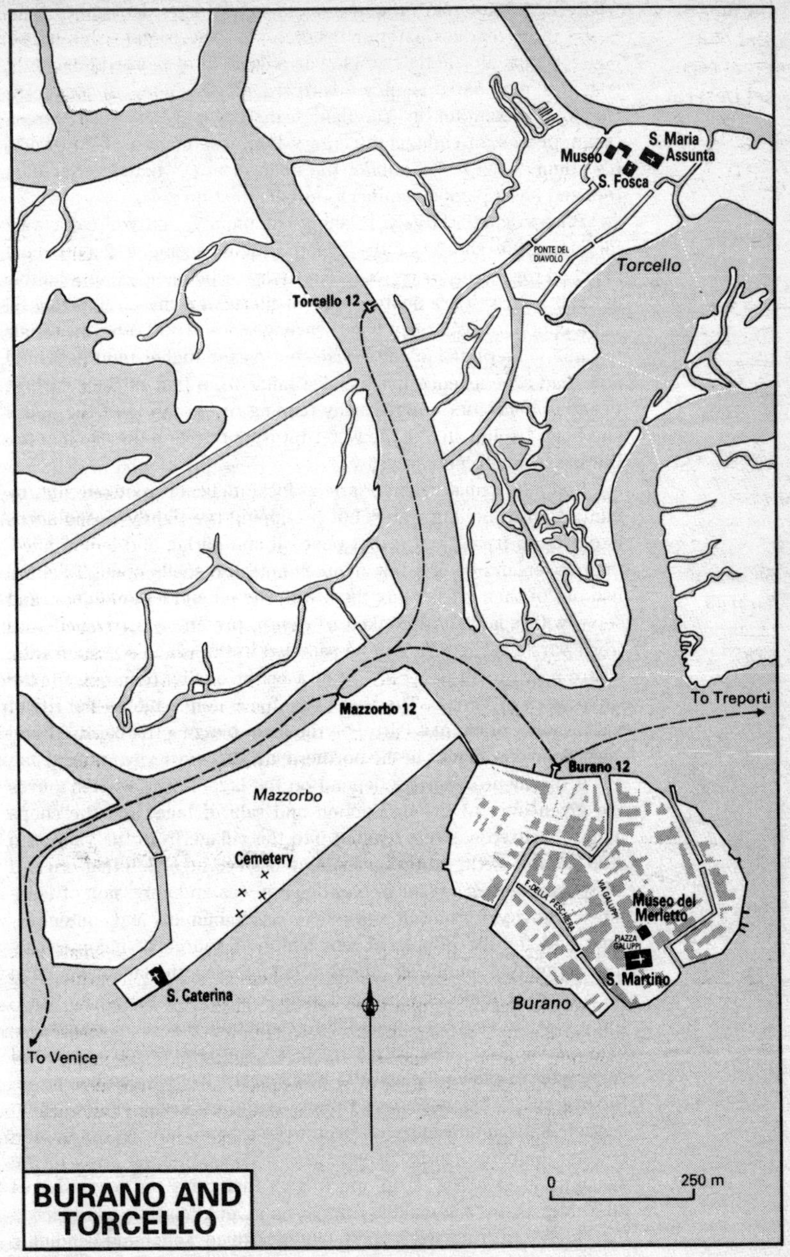
S. Maria
Assunta
Museo
S. Fosca
PONTE DEL
DIAVOLO
Torcello
Torcello 12
Mazzorbo 12
To Treporti
Burano 12
Mazzorbo
Cemetery
F. DELLA PESCHERIA
VIA GALUPPI
Museo del
Merletto
PIAZZA
GALUPPI
S. Martino
S. Caterina
Burano
To Venice
0
250 m
BURANO AND
TORCELLO

whatever fashion takes the occupants' fancy. A resident called Bepe is the most fearless exterior decorator on the island – his house, covered in a constantly changing arrangement of painted diamonds, triangles and bars, is in a courtyard off the alley opposite the *Galuppi* restaurant in Via Baldessare Galuppi, the main street. (Galuppi was an eighteenth-century Buranese composer, known to his admirers as *Il Buranello*; the main piazza is named after him, too, and has a plaque commemorating him at no. 24.)

Burano is still largely a fishing community, and you can't walk far along the shores of the island without seeing a fishing boat beached for repair, or nets laid out to dry or be mended, or a jumble of crab boxes. It's a solitary way of life under any circumstances, but a couple of fishermen have scavenged wood and other materials to build vulnerable-looking houses out on the higher mud flats, and now lead an existence not too dissimilar from that of their earliest Venetian ancestors – perpetually tending to the fabric of the house and boat, fishing among the water-birds, and selling the catch at the Burano or Rialto *pescherie*.

Vongole (small clams) are a local delicacy, cooked not by immersion in boiling water, but by tipping the tightly-closed shells into a large frying pan of hot olive oil and garlic; add lemon juice, then cover and cook a few minutes until the shells open. Take the fish out of their shells, mix them with the oil and lemon liquor, and serve with spaghettini cooked *al dente*, preferably garnished with fresh parsley. The dish can be sampled in the island's **restaurants**, where a meal will generally be of a better quality than one for the same price in Venice. The best place for a simple bite is the HQ of the former Communist Party, on the main piazza – the cheapest and most delicious snacks in the northern lagoon.

For more on Burano's restaurants, see p.235.

If the men of Burano depend on the lagoon, the women's lives are given over to the production and sale of **lace**, and the shops lining the narrow street leading into the village from the vaporetto stop are full of the stuff. Lacemaking used to be a skill that crossed all social boundaries: for noblewomen it was an expression of feminine creativity; for nuns it was an exercise in humility and contemplation; and for the poorest it was simply a source of income. (It's interesting that, unlike all other crafts in Venice, the lacemakers had no *scuola* or guild to represent them – perhaps because its workforce was exclusively female.) Its production was once geographically diverse, too – **Dogaressa Morosina Morosini** set up a large and successful workshop near Santa Fosca in the late sixteenth century, for instance – but nowadays Burano is the exclusive centre. Much sentimentalised nonsense has been written about how "every Burano cottage doorway has its demure lace-maker, stitching away in the sunshine, eyes screwed up and fingers flickering", to quote James (Jan) Morris. In fact, making Burano-point and Venetian-point lace is extremely exacting work, both highly skilled and mind-bendingly repetitive, taking an enormous toll on the eyesight. Each woman specialises in one particular stitch, and as there are seven stiches in all, each piece is passed from woman to woman during its construction. An average-size table centre requires about a month of work.

The skills of lacemaking are still taught at Burano's **Scuola dei Merletti**, in Piazza Baldessare Galuppi. The school was opened in 1872, when the indigenous crafting of lace had declined so far that it was left to one woman, Cencia Scarpariola, to transmit the necessary skills to a younger generation of women. Pieces produced here are displayed in the attached museum, along with specimens dating back to the sixteenth century; after even a quick tour you'll have no problems distinguishing the real thing from the machine-made and imported lace that fills the Burano shops.

The church of **San Martino**, with its drunken campanile, contains a fine *Crucifixion* by Giambattista Tiepolo.

Burano – and San Francesco del Deserto

The Scuola dei Merletti is open Tues–Sat 9am–6pm, Sun 10am–4pm; L5000.

San Martino is open daily 7am–noon & 3–7pm.

San Francesco del Deserto

While on Burano, try to get to across to the island of **San Francesco del Deserto**. This will mean negotiating either for a taxi (prohibitively expensive) or for someone to row you across in a *sándolo*, when the charge will vary with the time of year and the disposition of the person you ask – on some days the San Francesco shuttle is the virtual monopoly of a churlish father and son double act. Expect to pay upwards of L10,000 per person if there's a group of four or more. An added complication is the Buranese dialect, which has even fewer consonants than the Venetian.

Saint Francis ran aground here in 1220 and decided to build a chapel and cell on the island. Jacopo Michiel, the owner of the island, gave it to the Franciscans soon after the saint's death, and apart from deserting it for a while in the fifteenth century because of malaria, and being pushed out in the nineteenth century by the military, they have been here ever since. The present chapel was built over the original one in the fifteenth century, and was lovingly and simply restored in 1962, uncovering some of the original floor and foundations. Nine friars live here, some in retreat, and a few young men stay for a year before becoming Franciscan novices. With its birdsong, its profusion of plants and its cypress-scented air, the monastery is the most tranquil place in the lagoon.

Visitors are shown round the island of San Francesco del Deserto daily 9–11am & 3–5.30pm; a few thousand lire should be left as a donation.

Torcello

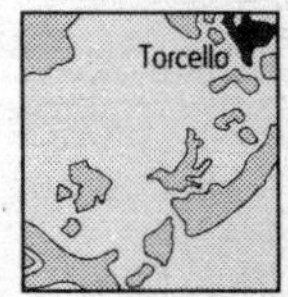

Some of John Ruskin's purplest prose was prompted by the sight of **Torcello**: "Mother and daughter, you behold them both in their widowhood – Torcello and Venice", his elegy for the island begins. The place has certainly come full circle. Settled by the very first refugees from the mainland in the fifth century, it became the seat of the Bishop of Altinum in 638 and in the following year its cathedral – the oldest building in the lagoon – was founded. By the fourteenth century its population had peaked at around 20,000, but Torcello's canals were now silting up and the ascendancy of Venice was imminent. By the end of the fifteenth century Torcello was largely deserted – even the bishop lived in Murano – and today only about one hundred people remain in residence, their numbers swelled by thousands of tourists, and by the ever-increasing ranks of stallholders eager to sell lace and glass to the summer boatloads.

Santa Maria dell'Assunta

Santa Maria dell'Assunta is open daily 10am–12.30pm & 2–5pm; L1500.

The main reason for a visit is to see Venice's first cathedral and the serenest building in the lagoon – the **Cattedrale di Santa Maria dell'Assunta**. A Veneto-Byzantine building dating substantially from 1008, the cathedral has evolved from a church founded in the seventh century, of which the crypt and the circular foundations in front of the **Baptistery**'s doors have survived. The first major transformation of the church occurred in the 860s, the period to which the **facade and portico** belong (though they were altered in later centuries). For the most unusual features of the exterior, go down the right side of the cathedral, where the windows have eleventh-century **stone shutters**. Ruskin described the view from the campanile as "one of the most notable scenes in this wide world" – you'll have to take his word for it, as the tower's now too shaky to open.

The dominant tones of the **interior** come from the watery green-grey marble of its columns and panelling, which cast a cool light on the richly patterned eleventh-century **mosaic floor**. (Look for the two wooden panels which lift to reveal portions of the church's first floor.) On the semi-dome of the apse a stunning twelfth-century **mosaic of the Madonna and Child**, the figures isolated in a vast field of gold, looks down from above a **frieze of the Apostles** of the previous century. Below the window, at the Madonna's feet, is an image of **Saint Heliodorus**, the first Bishop of Altinum, whose remains were brought here by the earliest settlers. It makes an interesting comparison with the gold-plated face mask on his sarcophagus in front of the high altar, another seventh-century vestige. His original Roman sarcophagus is placed to one side nearby. Mosaic work from the ninth and twelfth centuries adorns the chapel to the right of the high altar, while the other end of the cathedral is dominated by the tumultuous **mosaic of the Apotheosis of Christ and the Last Judgement** – created in the twelfth century, but renovated in the nineteenth. Have a good look, too, at the **rood screen**, where paintings of *The Virgin and Apostles* are supported by eleventh-century columns and finely carved translucent marble panels; and if you go through the chapel to the left of the altar, you can take a look at the waterlogged ancient crypt.

Santa Fosca is open the same hours as Santa Maria; same ticket.

Santa Fosca and the Museo dell'Estuario

Torcello's other church, **Santa Fosca**, was built in the eleventh and twelfth centuries for the body of the saint, brought to Torcello from

Libya some time before 1011 and now resting under the altar. Much restored, the church retains the Greek-cross form and a fine exterior apse; the bare interior, with beautiful marble columns and elegant brick arches, exudes a calmness which no number of visitors can quite destroy.

In the square outside sits the curious **chair of Attila**, perhaps once the throne of Torcello's judges in its earliest days. Local folklore has it that if you sit in it, you will be wed within a year – you have been warned. Behind it, the well-laid out **Museo dell'Estuario** includes thirteenth-century beaten gold figures, jewellery, mosaic fragments (including pieces from the cathedral's *Last Judgement*, in which the hands of several artists can be distinguished) and a mish-mash of pieces relating to the history of the area. A major archaeological survey was carried out by a Polish team in the 1960s, but it's possible still to find pot shards as you wander off looking for a picnic spot. And anything more ambitious than a picnic is really not on – there are a couple of **bars** near the parapetless Ponte del Diavolo, but the restaurants are overpriced – especially the one owned by the *Cipriani*.

The Museo dell'Estuario is open Tues–Sun 10am–12.30pm & 2–5.30pm; L3000.

Chapter 10

The Southern Islands

The section of the lagoon to the south of the city, enclosed by the long islands of the **Lido** and **Pellestrina**, has far fewer outcrops of solid land than the northern half. Once past San Giorgio Maggiore and La Giudecca, and clear of the smaller islands beyond, you could look in the direction of the mainland and think you were out in the open sea – an illusion strengthened by the sight of tankers making their way across the lagoon to the port of Marghera. On the other hand, the shallowness of most of the lagoon is brought home to you with a jolt when you happen upon a fisher-

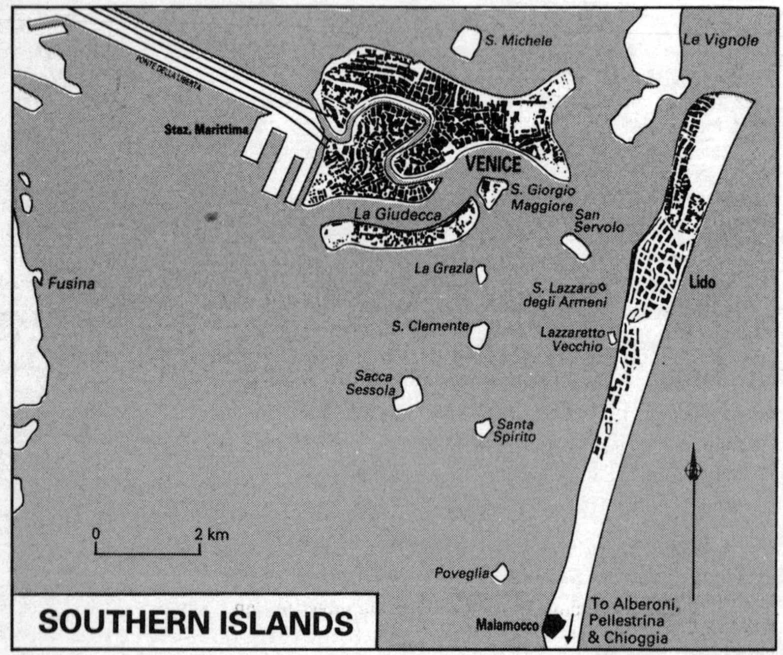

man standing on a barely submerged sandbank a long way from the shore – a spectacle that initially prompts thoughts of the Second Coming.

The nearer islands are the more interesting: the Palladian churches of **San Giorgio** and **La Giudecca** are among Venice's most significant Renaissance monuments, while the alleyways of the latter are full of reminders of the city's manufacturing past. The Venetian tourist industry began with the development of the **Lido**, which has now been eclipsed by the city as a holiday destination, yet still draws thousands of people to its beaches each year, many of them Italians. A visit to the Armenian island, **San Lazzaro degli Armeni**, makes an absorbing afternoon's round trip, and if you've a bit more time to spare you could undertake an expedition to the fishing town of **Chioggia**, at the southern extremity of the lagoon. The farther-flung settlements along the route to Chioggia may have seen more glorious days, but the voyage out from the city is a pleasure in itself.

San Giorgio Maggiore

San Giorgio Maggiore is open daily 9am–noon & 2.30–6pm.

Palladio's church of **San Giorgio Maggiore**, facing the Palazzo Ducale across the Bacino di San Marco, is one of the most prominent and familiar of all Venetian landmarks. It is a startling building, whose isolation almost forces you to have an opinion as to its architectural merits. Ruskin didn't much care for it: "It is impossible to conceive a design more gross, more barbarous, more childish in conception, more servile in plagiarism, more insipid in result, more contemptible under every point of rational regard." Goethe, on the other hand, sick of the Gothic art that was to Ruskin the index of spiritual health, gave thanks to Palladio for purging his mind of medieval clutter.

Designed in 1565, but only completed in 1610, San Giorgio Maggiore was a greatly influential solution to the chief problem of Renaissance church design: how to use Classical forms in a structure that, with its high central nave and lower aisles, had no precedent in Classical culture. Palladio's answer was to superimpose two temple fronts: the nave being defined by an upper pediment supported by gigantic Composite columns, and the aisles by lower half-pediments resting on Corinthian pilasters. Inside, the relationship between the major Composite order and the minor Corinthian is maintained, so unifying the facade of the church and its interior. The scale of Palladio's forms and his use of shadow-casting surfaces ensures that the design of the facade retains its clarity across the water.

The interior

The Venetians were the first to cover church interiors with white stucco, and the technique is used to dazzling effect in San Giorgio Maggiore – "Of all the colours, none is more proper for churches

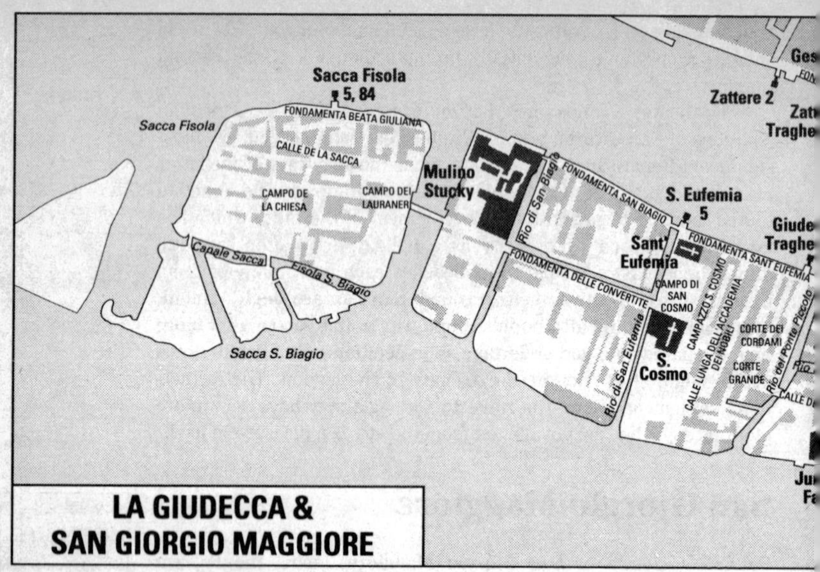

than white; since the purity of colour, as of the life, is particularly gratifying to God," wrote Palladio. It's hard to imagine how anyone could remain totally unimpressed by the interior's finely calculated proportions and Counter-Reformation austerity, but in Ruskin's opinion, only the paintings inside justified the effort of opening the door.

The first altar on the right has an *Adoration of the Shepherds* by **Jacopo Bassano**, which is followed by an alarming late fifteenth-century Crucifix – not, as the label says, by Brunelleschi, but by an anonymous Venetian artist. Most of the other pictures are from the workshop of **Tintoretto**, with two outstanding pictures by the master in the chancel: *The Last Supper*, perhaps the most famous of all Tintoretto's works, and *The Fall of Manna*, one of the few depictions of the event to dwell on the fact that the shower was not a single miraculous deluge but rather a supply that continued for forty years. They were painted as a pair in 1592–94 – the last two years of the artist's life – to illustrate the significance of the Eucharist to the communicants at the altar rail. A *Deposition* of the same date, in the Cappella dei Morti (through the door on the right of the choir), may well be Tintoretto's last completed painting. The carnage-strewn picture alongside is a photograph of Carpaccio's *St George and the Dragon*, painted several years after the equally gruesome version in the Scuola di San Giorgio degli Schiavoni. (The original is in a private room elsewhere in the building.)

There are few pieces of woodwork in Venice more impressive than the **choirstalls** of San Giorgio Maggiore. Decorated with scenes

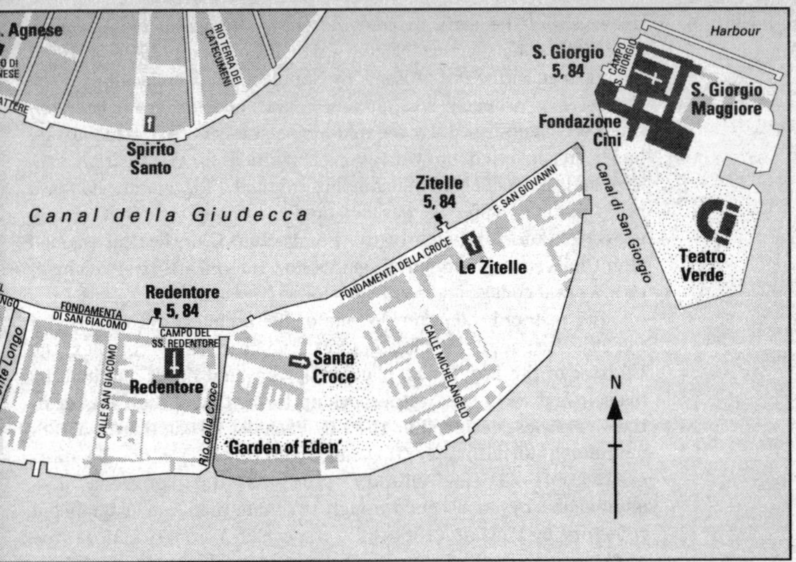

from the life of St Benedict, they were carved in the late 1590s, as the church was being completed; the bronze figures of *St George* and *St Stephen* on the balustrade are by **Niccolò Roccatagliata** (1593), who also made the florid candlesticks at the entrance to the chancel. Apart from Roccatagliata's pieces, the best sculptures in the church are the *Evangelists* by **Vittoria**, incorporated into the **tomb of Doge Leonardo Donà**, on the west wall. A close friend of Paolo Sarpi and Galileo, the scholarly Donà was the redoubtable leader of Venice at the time of the Interdict of 1602. The Papal Nuncio was sent packing by him with the lofty dismissal – "We ignore your excommunication: it is nothing to us. Now think where our resolution would lead, were our example to be followed by others."

The campanile of San Giorgio is open daily 9am–noon & 2.30–5pm; L2000.

The door on the left of the choir leads to the **campanile**; rebuilt in 1791 after the collapse of its predecessor, it rivals that of San Marco as the best vantage point in the city.

The monastery – and the harbour

Since the early ninth century there's been a church on this island, and at the end of the tenth century the lagoon's most important Benedictine monastery was established here. Both church and monastery were destroyed by an earthquake in 1223, but were rebuilt straight away, and subsequently renovated and altered several times. Cosimo de' Medici stayed at the monastery in 1433, during his exile from Florence, and it was with his assistance that the monastic library was set up; by the end of the century the Benedictines of San Giorgio Maggiore had become renowned for their erudition. With the upheavals of the early nineteenth century things changed rapidly. When the conclave that elected Pope Pius VII met here in 1800, having been turfed out of Rome by Napoleon, the confiscation of the monastery's property had already begun, and six years later the order was suppressed. By the mid-nineteenth century the monastery had been converted into workshops and offices for the Austrian artillery, and the decline of the complex continued for another hundred years until, in 1951, it was acquired by Count Vittorio Cini and converted into the home of the **Fondazione Giorgio Cini** (named after Cini's son), an organisation that now runs an arts research institute, a naval college and a craft school on the island.

The restored monastery is one of the architectural wonders of the city. Two adjoining cloisters form the heart of the complex: the **Cloister of the Bay Trees**, planned by Giovanni Buora and built by his son Andrea in the two decades up to 1540; and the **Cloister of the Cypresses**, designed in 1579 by Palladio. Inside, there's a 128-metre-long **dormitory** by Giovanni Buora (c.1494), a **double staircase** (1641–43) and **library** (1641–53) by Longhena and, approached by an ascent through two ante-rooms, a magnificent **refectory** by Palladio (1560–62) – for which Veronese's *Marriage at Cana*, now in the Louvre, was painted. Exhibitions are regularly held at the Fondazione (often solemn and bookish affairs), and the open-air Teatro Verde is occasionally used for plays and concerts. It's always possible to visit the monastery at other times by ringing for an appointment (☎528.9900); if you just turn up unannounced, a word with the custodian could do the trick if he's not feeling harassed or you can convince him of an unquenchable interest in Palladian architecture.

The little **harbour** on the other side of the church was expanded during the second French occupation of 1806–15, when Napoleon decided to accord the island the status of a free port, in emulation of the tariff-free port of Trieste. A professor of architecture at the Accademia designed the two diminutive lighthouses in 1813.

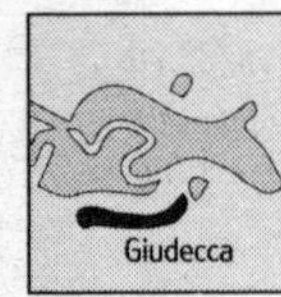

La Giudecca

In the earliest records of Venice the chain of islets now called **La Giudecca** was known as Spina Longa, a name clearly derived from its shape. The modern name might refer to the Jews (*Giudei*) who were based here from the late thirteenth century until their removal to the Ghetto, or to the disruptive noble families who, from the ninth century, were shoved into this district to keep them out of mischief (*giudicati* means "judged"). Before the Brenta River became the prestigious site for summer abodes, La Giudecca was where the wealthiest aristocrats of early Renaissance Venice built their villas. Michelangelo, self-exiled from Florence in 1529, consoled himself in the gardens of this island, traces of which remain on its south side. The most extensive of La Giudecca's surviving private gardens, the so-called *Garden of Eden* (at the end of the Rio della Croce), is bigger than any other in Venice – larger even than the public Giardini Papadopoli, at the head of the Canal Grande. Its name refers not to its paradisical properties but to a certain Mr Eden, the English gardener who planted it.

Giudecca was also the city's **industrial** inner suburb: Venice's public transport boats used to be made here; an asphalt factory and a distillery were once neighbours on the western end; and the matting industry, originating in the nineteenth century, kept going until 1950. However, the present-day island is a potent emblem of Venice's loss of self-sufficiency in the twentieth century. The clock and watch firm Junghans, formerly one of La Giudecca's major employers, nowadays occupies only part of its 1940s factory, which stands like a Fritz Lang film-set between Rio del Ponte Lungo and Rio del Ponte Piccolo. Plans have been announced to close it down completely, and a similar fate seems to await the *Fortuny* factory, manufacturer of luxury fabrics for the past century. On the south side, the boatyards and fishing quays are interspersed with half-abandoned factories, roofless sheds and a miscellany of other ruins. Even the public face of La Giudecca, the side facing the rest of the city, presents a stark economic contrast: at the western edge is the derelict neo-Gothic fortress of the Mulino Stucky flour mill, the largest industrial wreck in Venice (see below), and at the other stands the *Cipriani*, the city's most expensive hotel.

Swathes of La Giudecca are now purely residential areas, but one result of the partial decline is that artists, theatre co-operatives and other groups have moved into a number of the redundant buildings. Their presence isn't especially visible, though, and in the bars along the main *fondamenta* you're still more likely to overhear complaints about the day's lousy catch, or the closure of another factory.

The Zitelle and the Redentore

The first vaporetto stop after San Giorgio Maggiore is in front of the tiny church of the **Zitelle**, built in 1582–86 from plans worked out some years earlier by Palladio, albeit for a different site. In the eighteenth century the convent attached to the church was renowned for the delicacy of the lace produced by the young girls who lived in its hostel. The **Casa de Maria**, to the right of the Zitelle, is an inventive reworking of Venetian Gothic, built as a studio by the painter Mario de Maria in 1910–13. Its diaper-pattern brickwork, derived from that of the Palazzo Ducale, is the only example of its kind in Venetian domestic building.

The Zitelle is open Sun morning only.

La Giudecca's main monument, beyond the tug-boats' mooring and the youth hostel (once a granary), is the Franciscan church of the **Redentore**, designed by **Palladio** in 1577. In 1575–76 Venice suffered an outbreak of plague which killed nearly 50,000 people –

The Redentore is open daily 7.30am–noon & 3.30–7pm.

virtually a third of the city's population. The Redentore was built by the Senate in thanks for Venice's deliverance, and every year until the downfall of the Republic the doge and his senators attended a mass here to renew their declaration of gratitude, walking to the church over a pontoon bridge from the Zattere. The *Festa del Redentore* has remained a major event on the Venetian calendar – celebrated on the third Sunday of July, it's marked by a general procession over the temporary bridge and a huge fireworks display on the previous evening. A large number of people spend the night out on the water, partying with friends on board their boats.

Palladio's commission called for a church to which there would be three distinct components: a choir for the monks to whom the church was entrusted, a tribune around the altar for the dignitaries of the city, and a nave with side-chapels for the humbler worshippers. The architect's scheme, in which the tribune forms a circular chapel which opens into the nave and blends into the choir through a curved screen of columns, is the most sophisticated of his church projects, as well as the one most directly evolved from the architecture of ancient Rome (the Imperial baths in particular). Unfortunately, the present state of the Redentore makes an appreciation of its subtleties a bit of an effort – the plasterwork is dowdy, statues with fairy-light haloes clutter the place and a rope prevents visitors going beyond the nave. The best paintings in the church, including a *Madonna with Child and Angels* by **Alvise Vivarini**, are in the sacristy (ask the sacristan), alongside a gallery of eighteenth-century wax heads of illustrious Franciscans, arranged in glass cases all round the room, in various attitudes of agony and ecstasy.

Sant'Eufemia and the factories of La Giudecca

For more on Fortuny, see p.76.

Sant'Eufemia is open Mon–Sat 9am–noon & 6–7pm, Sun 7am–12.30pm.

Beyond the **Fortuny** factory, where they still make some of the fabrics designed by the founder of the company (albeit under threat of closure), the church of **Sant'Eufemia** shelters in the lee of the immense Mulino Stucky. Founded in the ninth century and often rebuilt, it's one of Venice's most engaging stylistic discords: late sixteenth-century portico, nave and aisles still laid out as in the original basilica (with some eleventh-century columns and capitals), stucco work and painted decoration in eighteenth-century boudoir mode. It has one good painting, immediately on your right as you go in: *San Rocco and Angel* (with lunette of *Madonna and Child*), the central panel of a triptych painted in 1480 by **Bartolomeo Vivarini**.

The **Mulino Stucky** got to look the way it does in 1895–96, after Giovanni Stucky brought in a German architect, Ernst Wullekopf, to convert and expand the premises of his flour mill. Planning permission for the brick bastion which Wullekopf came up with was obtained by the simple expedient of threatening to sack all the workers if the okay were withheld by the council. By the beginning of this century Stucky had become one of the richest men in the city, and in 1908 he bought one of the Canal Grande's less discreet houses, the Palazzo Grassi. He didn't enjoy his occupancy for long, though – in 1910 one of his employees murdered him at the entrance to the train station. With the development of the industrial sector at Marghera after World War I, the Mulino Stucky went into a nose dive, and in 1954 it closed. Since then its future has been a perenially contentious issue – plans are afoot to convert it into housing but there doesn't seem to be any likelihood of action in the short term.

There's not much point in going past the Stucky building: **Sacca Fisola**, the next island along, is all modern flats, bordered on one side by boatyards and on the other by the site at which waste is mixed with silt to form the basic material of land reclamation in the lagoon.

For a taste of the economic past and present of La Giudecca, double back along the waterfront and then turn down the Fondamenta del Rio di Sant'Eufemia; a circuitous stroll from the run-down Campo di San Cosmo to the Rio Ponte Lungo will take you through the core of Giudecca's **manufacturing district**. The interior of the island on the other side of the Rio Ponte Lungo is not so densely built up, with a fair amount of open space (even vegetable gardens) around the Redentore and the husk of Santa Croce church (built c.1510 and long ago deconsecrated). Frustratingly, hardly any of La Giudecca's alleyways lead down to the lagoon on the south side; if you want a view across the water in that direction, it's best to take Calle Michelangelo, which comes onto the main *fondamenta* between the Zitelle and the youth hostel.

The Lido

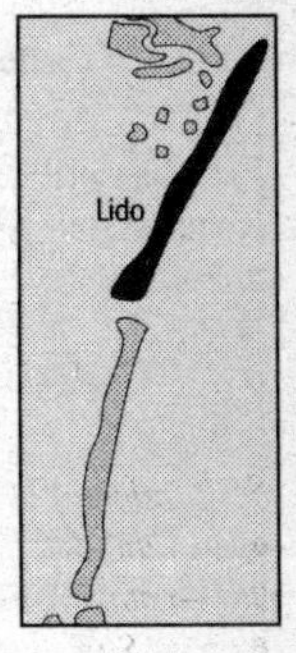

The shores of the Lido have seen some action in their time: in 1202 a huge French army, assembled for the Fourth Crusade, cooled its heels on the beaches while its leaders haggled with the Venetians over the terms for transport to the East; Henry III of France was welcomed here in 1574 with fanfares and triumphal monuments made in his honour; and every year, for about eight centuries, there was the hullaballoo of Venice's **Marriage to the Sea**.

This ritual, the most operatic of Venice's state ceremonials, began as a way of commemorating the exploits of Doge Pietro Orseolo II, who on Ascension Day of the year 1000 set sail to subjugate the pirates of the Dalmatian coast. (Orseolo's standard, by the way, possibly featured the first representation of what was to become the emblem of Venice – the Lion of Saint Mark with its paw on an open book.) According to legend, the ritual reached its definitive form after the Venetians had brought about the reconciliation of Pope Alexander III and Frederick Barbarossa in 1177; the grateful

Alexander is supposed to have given the doge the first of the gold rings with which Venice was married to the Adriatic. It's more likely that the essential components of the ritual – the voyage out to the Porto di Lido in the *Bucintoro* with an escort of garlanded vessels, the dropping of the ring into the brine "In sign of our true and perpetual dominion", and the disembarkation for a solemn mass at the church of San Nicolò al Lido – were all fixed by the middle of the twelfth century. Unless you steadfastly shun all the public collections in Venice, you're bound to see at least one painting of the ceremony during your stay. Nowadays the mayor, patriarch and a gaggle of other VIPs annually enact a sad facsimile of the grand occasion. And in case you're thinking of launching a salvage operation for all those gold rings, a fifteenth-century traveller recorded that – "After the ceremony, many strip and dive to the bottom to seek the ring. He who finds it keeps it for his own, and, what's more, lives for that year free from all the burdens to which dwellers in that republic are subject."

In the twelfth century the Lido was an unspoilt strip of land, and it remained so into the last century. Byron used to gallop his horses across the fields of the Lido every day, and as late as 1869 Henry James could decribe the island as "a very natural place". Before the

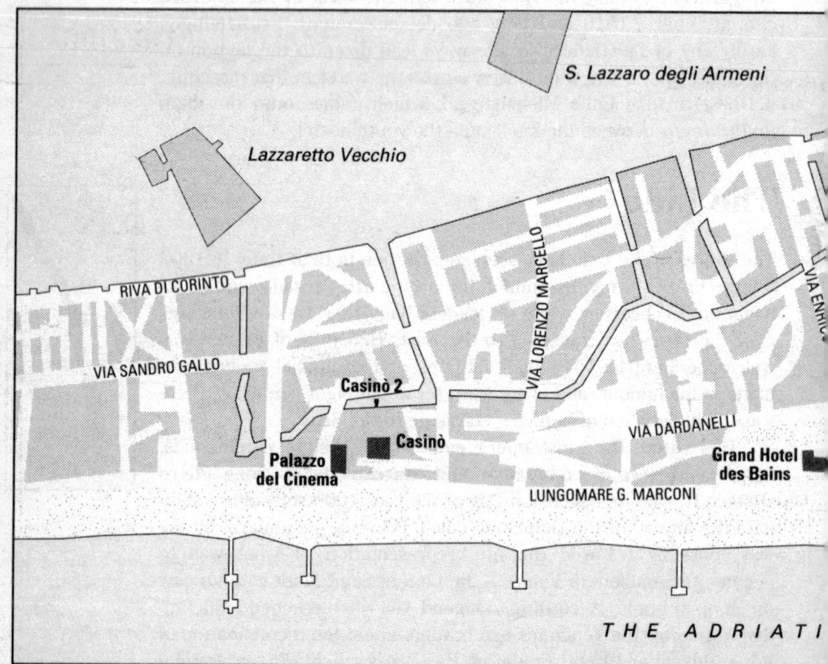

nineteenth century was out, however, it had become the smartest **bathing resort** in Italy, and although it's no longer as chic as it was when Thomas Mann installed von Aschenbach, the central figure of *Death in Venice*, as a guest at the Lido's *Grand Hotel des Bains*, there's less room on its beaches now than ever before. But unless you're staying at one of the flashy hotels that stand shoulder to shoulder along the seafront, or are prepared to pay a ludicrous fee to hire one of their beach hutches for the day, you won't be allowed to get the choicest Lido sand between your toes.

If you're the sort of person who regards access to the sea as a God-given right, then you'll have to content yourself with the ungroomed **public beaches** at the northern and southern ends of the island – though why anyone should want to jeopardise his or her health in the filthy waters of this stretch of the Adriatic is one of the great imponderables. (The traffic is the other health hazard of the Lido. Just as the Venetians were once regarded as the worst riders in Italy, they are now ranked as its most inept drivers.) The northern beach is fifteen minutes' walk from the vaporetto stop at Piazzale Santa Maria Elisabetta; the southern one, right by the municipal golf course, necessitates a bus journey from the Piazzale, and is consequently less of a crush.

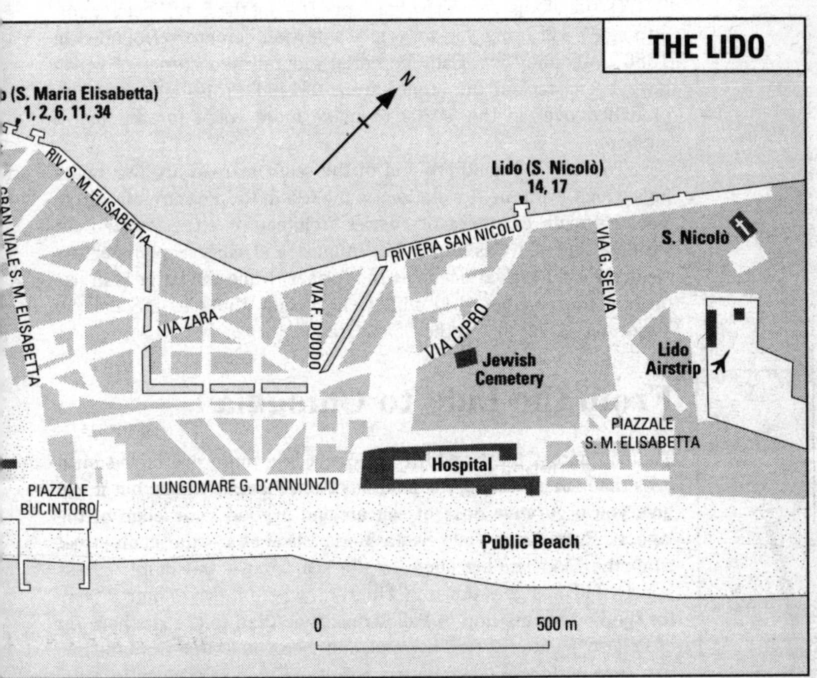

The monuments of the Lido

In the vicinity of the Piazzale, one building alone – the **Fortezza di Sant'Andrea** – is of interest, and you have to admire that from a distance, across the Porto di Lido. The principal defence of the main entrance to the lagoon, it was designed by **Sanmicheli**; work began on it in 1543, in the face of some scepticism as to whether the structure would be strong enough to support the Venetian artillery. The doubters were silenced when practically all the cannons to hand in the Arsenale were brought out to the Fortezza and fired simultaneously from its terraces, with no harmful effects except to the eardrums. The church and Benedictine monastery of **San Nicolò**, from where you get a good view of the Fortezza, were founded in 1044, when there wasn't so much as a brick wall in the area. The doge and his entourage used to visit this church twice a year: on Ascension Day, after the acquatic wedding service, and on the feast day of St Nicholas of Myra (aka Santa Claus), whose body, so the Venetians claimed, had rested here since it was stolen from the Norman port of Bari in 1099. In fact the theft never happened – the Venetian raid on Bari was a classic piece of disinformation, devised to score points off the Normans, and the grand display on the saint's day was a propagandist sham. The present church is notable only for its seventeenth-century choir stalls.

A stroll along the nearby Via Cipro (facing the San Nicolò vaporetto stop) will bring you to Venice's **Jewish cemetery** (founded in 1386). Adjoining is a Catholic burial ground, in a corner of which have been stacked the stones from the old Protestant cemetery, ploughed over in the 1930s to make more room for the Lido's airstrip.

Towards the southern end of the seafront road are two buildings which, with the fire station on the Rio di Ca' Fóscari, constitute Venice's main examples of Fascist architecture – the **Palazzo del Cinema** and the **Casinò**. In late August and early September the **Venice Film Festival** occupies the former, while the latter is in use only in the summer – in winter the action shifts to the Palazzo Vendramin-Calerghi, on the Canal Grande.

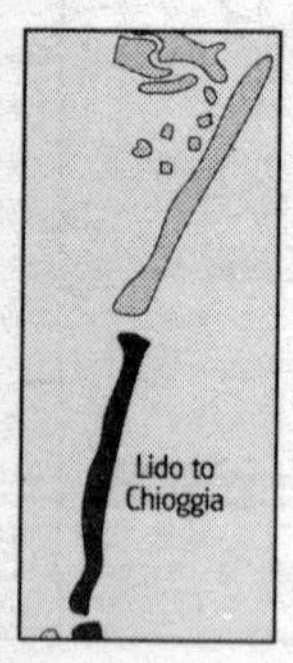

From the Lido to Chioggia

The trip across the lagoon to **Chioggia** is a more protracted business than simply taking the land bus from Piazzale Roma, but it will give you a curative dose of salt air and a good knowledge of the lagoon. From Gran Viale Santa Maria Elisabetta – the main street from the Lido landing stage to the sea front – the more or less hourly #11 bus goes down to **Alberoni**, where it drives onto a ferry for the five-minute hop to Pellestrina; the 10km to the southern tip of Pellestrina are covered by road, and then you switch from the bus to a steamer for the 25-minute crossing to Chioggia. The entire journey takes about eighty minutes, and costs L4900 – but be sure to check the timetable carefully at Gran Viale Santa Maria Elisabetta – not every #11 goes all the way to Chioggia.

Malamocco and Pellestrina

The fishing village of **Malamocco**, about 5km into the expedition, is the successor of the ancient settlement called Metamauco, which in the eighth century was the capital of the lagoon confederation. In 810 the town was taken by **Pepin**, son of Charlemagne, and there followed one of the crucial battles in Venice's history, when Pepin's fleet, endeavouring to reach the islands of Rivoalto (forerunner of Venice), became jammed in the mudbanks and was swiftly pounced upon. After the battle the capital was promptly transferred to the safer islands of Rivoalto, and in 1107 the old town was destroyed by a tidal wave. The new town has a place in the bloodier footnotes of later Venetian history – the **Canal Orfano**, close to the Malamocco shore, was the spot where some of those condemned by the Council of Ten were bound, gagged, weighted and thrown overboard by the executioner. Malamocco's most appealing building – the church's scaled-down replica of the Campanile of San Marco – can be seen without getting off the bus.

The most ferocious defenders of the lagoon in the war against Pepin came from the small island of **Poveglia**, just off Malamocco. Once populous enough to have a practically independent administration, it suffered greatly in the war against Genoa (see below) and went into a steep decline immediately after, becoming little more than a fort. For much of this century it was a hospital island, but since the closure of the hospital in the late 1960s it has been abandoned.

Fishing and the production of fine pillow-lace are the mainstays of life in the village of **Pellestrina**, which is strung out along nearly a third of the ten kilometres of the next island. There's one remarkable structure here, but you get the best view of it as the boat crosses to Chioggia. This is the **Murazzi**, the colossal walls of Istrian boulders, 4km long and 14m thick at the base, which were constructed at the sides of the Porto di Chioggia to protect Venice from the battering of the sea. The maintenance of the water level in the lagoon has always been a preoccupation of Venetian life: very early in the city's development, for example, the five gaps in the *lidi* (the Lido–Chioggia sand bars) were reduced to the present three to strengthen the barrier against the Adriatic and to increase the dredging action of the tides through the three remaining *porti*. In time a special state official, the *Magistrato alle Acque*, was appointed to supervise the management of the lagoon, and the Murazzi were the last major project undertaken by the *Magistrato*'s department. Devised as a response to the increased flooding of the early eighteenth century, the Murazzi took 38 years to build, and remained unbreached from 1782, the year of their completion, until the flood of November 1966.

Chioggia

Chioggia was the scene, in 1379, of the most serious threat to Venice since Pepin's invasion, when the Genoese, after copious shedding of blood on both sides, took possession of the town. Venice at this time had two outstanding admirals: the first, Vettor Pisani, was in prison on a charge of military negligence; the second, Carlo Zeno, was somewhere off in the East. So serious was the threat to the city that Pisani was promptly released, and then put in command of the fleet that set out in December – with the doge himself on board – to blockade the enemy. Zeno and his contingent sailed over the horizon on the first day of the new year and there followed months of siege warfare, in the course of which the Venetian navy employed shipboard cannons for the first time. (Casualties from cannonballs were as high on the Venetian as on the Genoese side, and some crews refused to operate these suicidal weapons more than once a day.) In June 1380, with medieval Chioggia in ruins, the enemy surrendered, and from then until the arrival of Napoleon's ships the Venetian lagoon remained impregnable.

Modern Chioggia is the second largest settlement in the lagoon after Venice, and one of Italy's busiest fishing ports. Lorenzetti describes the *Chioggiotti* as "extremely individual types and among the most expert and intrepid sailors of the Adriatic", but those with insufficient time to plumb the depths of the local character will probably find Chioggia one of the less charming towns of the region. With the exception of a single church, you can see everything worth seeing in a hour's walk along the **Corso del Popolo**, the principal street in Chioggia's grid-iron layout. The exception is the church of **San Domenico**, which houses **Carpaccio**'s *St Paul*, his last known painting, plus a couple of pictures by **Leandro Bassano**; you get to it by taking the bridge to the left of the Chioggia landing stage and going straight on until you can't go any further.

The boat puts you down at the **Piazzetta Vigo**, at the head of the Corso. The locals are reputedly touchy about the excuse for a lion that sits on top of the column here, a beast known to the condescending Venetians as the *Cat of St Mark*. Only the thirteenth-century campanile of the church of **San Andrea** (rebuilt in 1743) is likely to catch your eye before the street widens at the **Granaio**, a grain warehouse built in 1322 but got at by nineteenth-century restorers; the facade relief of the *Madonna and Child* is by Sansovino. Behind the Granaio is the **fish market**; open for business every morning except Monday, it's a treat for gourmet and marine biologist alike – make sure you don't arrive too late to see it.

From the Lido to Chioggia

In the Piazzetta Venti Settembre, immediately after the town hall, there's the church of the **Santissima Trinità**, radically altered in 1703 by Andrea Tirali and almost perpetually shut – the Oratory, behind the main altar, has an impressive ceiling set with paintings by followers of Tintoretto. **San Giacomo Apostolo**, a bit further on, has a sub-Tiepolo ceiling by local boy Il Chiozzotto, and a much venerated fifteenth-century Venetian painting known as the *Madonna della Navicella*. Soon you pass a house once occupied by the family of Rosalba Carriera and later by Goldoni (in Chioggia this counts as an important historical item), and then, on the opposite side of the road, just before the Duomo, the **Tempio di San Martino**, built immediately after the war of 1380. It's rarely open except for temporary exhibitions.

The **Duomo** was the first major commission for **Longhena**, who was called in to design a new church after the previous cathedral was burned down in 1623; the detached fourteenth-century campanile survived the blaze. The chapel to the left of the chancel contains half a dozen good eighteenth-century paintings, including one attributed to Tiepolo; except in freakish weather conditions they're all but invisible, a drawback which the over-sensitive might regard as a blessing in view of the subjects depicted – *The Torture of Boiling Oil*, *The Torture of the Razors*, *The Beheading of Two Martyrs*, and so on.

Buses run from the Duomo to **Sottomarina**, Chioggia's down-market answer to Venice's Lido. On the beaches of Sottomarina you're a fraction closer to nature than you would be on the Lido, and the resort does have one big plus – after your dip you can go back to the Corso and have a fresh seafood meal that's cheaper than any you'd find in Venice's restaurants and better than most.

The quickest way **back to Venice** is by bus from the Duomo or Sottomarina to Piazzale Roma, but it's a dispiriting drive, slightly dearer than the island-hop route, and only about twenty minutes quicker.

San Lazzaro degli Armeni and the minor islands

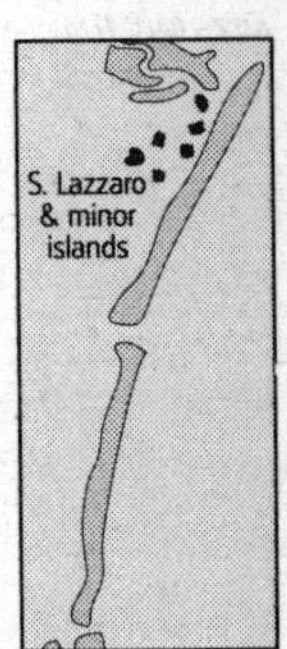

No foreign community has a longer pedigree in Venice than the Armenians. Their position in the economy of the city, primarily as tradesmen and money-lenders, was secure by the end of the thirteenth century, and for around five hundred years they have had their own church within a few yards of the Piazza, in the narrow Calle degli Armeni (see p.73). The Armenians are far less numerous now than formerly, and the most conspicuous sign of their presence is the Armenian island by the Lido, **San Lazzaro degli Armeni**, identifiable from the city by the onion-shaped summit of its campanile.

San Lazzaro degli Armeni and the minor islands

From the late twelfth century to the beginning of the seventeenth the island was a leper colony – hence *Lazzaro*, Lazarus being the patron saint of lepers – but the land was disused when in 1717 a Roman Catholic Armenian monastery was founded here by one Manug di Pietro. Known as **Mekhitar** ("The Consoler") he had been driven by the Turks from the religious foundation he had established with Venetian aid in the Morea. Within a few years the monks of San Lazzaro earned a wide reputation as scholars and linguists, a reputation that has persisted to the present. Today, Vienna has the only community outside the Soviet Union that can compare to Venice's as a centre of Armenian culture. (If you're wondering how the Armenians escaped suppression by the French, it's allegedly got something to do with the presence of an indispensible Armenian official in Napoleon's secretariat.)

The monastery's collection of precious manuscripts and books – the former going back to the fifth century – is a highlight of the visit, and you can expect the father who shows you round to be trilingual, at the very least. Reflecting the encyclopaedic interests of its occupants, the monastery is in places like a whimsically arranged museum, nowhere more so than in the old **library**, where a mummified Egyptian body is laid out near Canova's figure of Napoleon's infant son and a miscellany of letters and printed paraphernalia. Elsewhere you'll be shown antique writing instruments, pieces of pottery, firearms, a gallery of paintings by Armenian painters and a ceiling panel by the young Giambattista Tiepolo. The tour lingers in two smaller rooms: the cell occupied by Mekhitar (including the scourging chain found on the body after his death), and the room in which Byron stayed while lending a hand with the preparation of an Armenian–English dictionary. Finally you're led into a **printing and typesetting hall**, the nerve-centre of the polyglot press which has been operating here since 1789; it's all up-to-date machinery (in a side-office you can look over the shoulder of a monk setting Armenian texts on a computer screen) and the range of material produced here is enormous – everything from books to wine labels. You're expected to leave a donation as you leave, or buy something from the press – the old maps and prints of Venice are a bargain.

Visitors are received at San Lazzaro daily 3–5pm; take the #10 vaporetto from Riva degli Schiavone – you have to catch one just before 3pm to have any time on the island.

The "Hospital Islands"

San Lazzaro is the only minor island of the southern lagoon that's of interest to tourists. The boat out to San Lazzaro calls at **La Grazia**, successively a pilgrims' hostel, a monastery and now a hospital, and **San Servolo**, once one of the most important Benedictine monasteries in the region (founded in the ninth century), then a hospital for the insane, and now used by the Council of Europe's School of Craftsmanship. **San Clemente**, to the south of La Grazia, is another hospital island but is due to be closed down, a fate which overtook **Sacca Sessola**, the large hospital island to the southwest of San Clemente, in 1980.

A sports centre has been planned for the ex-ammunition factory on **Santo Spirito**, southeast of Sacca Sessola; until the mid-seventeenth century there was a monastery here, with a church redesigned by Sansovino, but when the order was suppressed most of its treasures, including paintings by Titian, were sent to the then unfinished Salute church on the Canal Grande, where they can now be seen. **Lazzaretto Vecchio** (south of San Lazzaro), at present a dogs' home, is also due to have a sports complex built on it; the site of a pilgrim's hostel from the twelfth century, the island took a place in medical history when, in 1423, it became the site of Europe's first permanent isolation hospital for plague victims.

7
ROW K SEAT 15

Venice Listings

Chapter 11

Accommodation

The virtually limitless demand for **accommodation** in Venice has pushed prices to such a level that it's possible to pay over L100,000 for a double room in a one-star hotel in high season. What's more, the **high season** here is longer than in anywhere else in the country – it is officially classified as running from March 15 to November 15 and then from December 21 to January 6, but many places don't recognise the existence of a low season any more. At any time during the official high season it's wisest to book your place well in advance, whether it's a hostel bed or a five-star suite, and for July and August it's virtually obligatory. Should you bowl into town unannounced in high summer, the booking offices (see below) may be able to dig out something in the hotels of mainland Mestre or way out in the lagoon at Cavallino (a half-hour boat ride), but rooms here would be nobody's free choice, which is why we have not included them in our listings. During the winter it's possible to bargain for a reduced-rate room, but many hotels – especially the cheaper ones – close down from November to February or even March, so you might have to put in a bit of leg-work before finding somewhere.

If you arrive with nowhere to stay and find that there's no space in any of the places listed in the following sections, there are plenty of **booking offices** that will hunt out a room for you: at the **train station** (daily 8am–9pm); on the **Tronchetto** (9am–8pm); in the multi-storey car park at **Piazzale Roma** (9am–9pm); at **Marco Polo airport** (summer 9am–7pm; winter noon–7pm); at the **autostrada's Venice exit** (8am–8pm). They only deal with hotels (ie no hostels) and take a deposit that's deductable from your first night's bill.

Hostels and hotels in this guide are classified into nine price categories. **Hostels** (categories ① & ②) are classified according to the **high-season cost per person per night**; the **hotel** categories refer to the **minimum** you can expect to pay for **a double room in high season**, excluding the cost of breakfast, which you might not be able to avoid. For the few weeks of the low season, you can expect prices to be around ten percent lower. In high season it is very unlikely that you will readily find a hotel room under category ⑤ in Venice itself – rooms in the lower ranges are confined to the less glamorous spots on the mainland.

① Under L20,000 per person.
② Over L20,000 per person.
③ Under L40,000 per room.
④ L40–60,000 per room.
⑤ L60–80,000 per room.
⑥ L80–100,000 per room.
⑦ L100–150,000 per room.
① L150–200,000 per room.
② Over L200,000 per room.

Accommodation

Hotels

Venice has around two hundred hotels, ranging from spartan one-star joints to five-star establishments charging a million lire a night, and what follows is a run-down on the best choices in all categories. Though there are some typical anomalies, the star system is a broadly reliable indicator of quality, but always bear in mind that you pay through the nose for your proximity to the Piazza. So if you want maximum comfort for your money, decide how much you can afford then look for a place outside the San Marco *sestiere* – after all, it's not far to walk, wherever you're staying.

Be warned that although **breakfast** should be optional, many hotels get round this regulation by simply refusing to take guests who don't want to pay a ludicrous extra charge for a jug of coffee and a puny croissant – breakfast at the humblest one-star can add L15,000 per person onto your bill. By law, the price of the room must be displayed on the back of its door; if it's not, or if the price doesn't correspond to what you're being charged, complain first to the management and then to the Questura (see p.252).

The sub-headings used below correspond to the chapter areas in which the hotels are to be found, while the addresses given are the full postal addresses. For the explanation as to how a place can be in the Dorsoduro district but not in the Dorsoduro chapter, see p.23. In the listings for hotels in central Venice, the phone number is followed by a grid reference to make it easy to locate the hotel; the marginal note tells you which map to consult.

The Venice city **telephone code** is ☎041.

San Marco

The grid references after the phone numbers relate to the map on p.36.

Ai Do Mori, Calle Larga San Marzo, S. Marco 658 ☎520.4817; I5. Very friendly, and situated a few paces off the Piazza, this is a top recommendation for budget travellers. When the 1993 refit is completed the top-floor room, with its private terrace looking over the roofs of the Basilica and the Torre dell'Orologio, will be one of the most attractive one-star rooms in the city. ⑤.

Al Gambero, Calle dei Fabbri, S. Marco 4687 ☎522.4384; G5. Large hotel in an excellent position a short distance off the north side of the Piazza; the rooms are plain but well maintained, and many of them overlook a canal that's on the standard gondola route from the Bacino Orseolo. Has more single rooms than many Venice hotels. Soon to be refurbished, but it will stay a one-star. ⑤.

Bauer Grünwald, Campo S. Moisè, S. Marco 1459 ☎520.7022; G8. Top-notch hotel, but to get the most for your money you have to stay in the thirteenth-century part, on the Canal Grande. The boxy modern part, on the campo, is unbeguiling. ⑨.

Boston, Calle dei Fabbri, S. Marco 848 (☎528.7665); G5. Large and efficient hotel on one of the main shopping streets. ⑧.

Casa Petrarca, Calle delle Colonne, S. Marco 4394 ☎520.0430; G5. The cheapest near the Piazza – but phone first, as they only have six rooms. Extremely hospitable, with English-speaking staff. ④.

Concordia, Calle Larga San Marzo, S. Marco 367 ☎520.6866; I5. This is the only hotel that actually looks onto the Piazza, which enables it to charge more than its rather characterless furnishings might justify. ⑧.

Europa e Regina, Calle Larga XXII Marzo, S. Marco 2159 ☎520.0477; F8. Run by the Ciga chain, which also owns the *Danieli* and the *Excelsior* over on the Lido. Considerably less expensive than either of those, it nonetheless commands stunning views from the mouth of the Canal Grande, and its terraces must be the most spectacular places to eat in the city. ⑨.

Fiorita, Campiello Nuovo, S. Marco 3457 ☎522.8043; C6. Just nine rooms, so again it's important to book. Welcoming management, and there's a nearby *traghetto* across the Canal Grande. ④.

Accommodation

Flora, Calle Larga XXII Marzo, S. Marco 2283/a ☎520.5844; F8. Some of the rooms are very cramped, but this three-star is close to the Piazza and has a pleasant little garden, too. ⑦.

Gritti Palace, S. Maria del Giglio, S. Marco 2467 ☎794.611; E9. One of Venice's most prestigious addresses, reeking of old regime opulence. Nothing under L500,000 per night. ⑨.

Kette, Piscina S. Moisè, S. Marco 2053 ☎520.7766; F7. A favourite with the upper-bracket tour companies, mainly on account of its quiet location, within a hop of La Fenice. ⑧.

La Fenice et des Artistes, Campiello Fenice, S. Marco 1936 ☎523.2333; E7. Favoured hangout of the opera crowd – performers and audience alike. ⑦.

Luna Baglioni, Calle Vallaresso, S. Marco 1243 ☎528.9840; G7. Established in the late fifteenth century, this claims to be the oldest hotel in the city, but it's been modernised almost to death. ⑨.

Monaco and Grand Canal, Calle Vallaresso, S. Marco 1325 ☎520.0211; G7. Very stylish hotel – try to get one of the ground-floor rooms, which look over to the Salute. Has a few rooms around L200,000 in summer, but most are double that. ⑨.

San Fantin, Campiello Fenice, S. Marco 1930/a ☎523.1401; E7. Bland little hotel, but right next to the opera house. ⑤.

San Salvador, Calle Galliazzo, S. Marco 5264 ☎528.9147; G2. Just off Campo S. Bartolomeo, with good views from some rooms. ④.

San Samuele, Piscina S. Samuele, S. Marco 3358 ☎522.8045; B7. A friendly place close to Palazzo Grassi, with rooms distinctly less shabby than some at this end of the market, if not exactly plush. ④.

Dorsoduro

The grid references after the phone numbers relate to the map on p.86.

Accademia Villa Maravegie, Fondamenta Bollani, Dorsoduro 1058 ☎521.0188; F7. Once the Russian embassy, this seventeenth-century villa has a devoted following, not least on account of its garden. To be sure of a room, get your booking in at least two months ahead. ⑦.

Agli Alboretti, Rio Terrà S. Agnese, Dorsoduro 884 ☎523.0058; G8. Very close to the Accademia, on a street shaded by trees. Avoid the murky room 19 and you can't go wrong. ⑥.

Alla Salute da Cici, Fondamenta Ca' Balà, Dorsoduro 222/8 ☎523.5404; I7. Pleasant canalside locale close to the Salute compensates for slightly brisk atmosphere. ⑤.

Antico Capon, Campo S. Margherita, Dorsoduro 3004 ☎528.5292; D5. Rooms are above a pizzeria-restaurant on an atmospheric square in the heart of the student district. ④.

Calcina, Záttere ai Gesuati, Dorsoduro 780 ☎520.6466; G9. Unpretentious and charismatic hotel in the house where Ruskin wrote much of *The Stones of Venice*. From some of the rooms you can gaze across to Giudecca's church of the Redentore, a building that gave the old man apoplexy. ⑤.

Messner, Rio Terrà dei Catacumeni, Dorsoduro 216 ☎522.7443; I7. Recently refurbished place close to the Salute vaporetto stop. ⑤.

Montin, Fondamenta di Borgo, Dorsoduro 1147 ☎522.7151; E8. Famed for its restaurant, recommended by everyone who stays there, though the food is on a different price-scale than the accommodation. Only seven rooms. ⑤.

Seguso, Záttere ai Gesuati, Dorsoduro 779 ☎528.6858; H9. There are no bad rooms here – those that don't face Giudecca overlook an attractive side-canal. Essential to book months ahead, as it's another one with a great word-of-mouth reputation. ⑤.

San Polo

The grid references after the phone numbers relate to the map on p.104.

Ai Due Fanali, Campo S. Simeone Grande, S. Croce 946 ☎718.344; D3. Modern and

Accommodation

quiet hotel, a short distance from the foot of the Scalzi bridge, on the opposite side from the train station. ⑤.

Al Gallo, Calle Amai, S. Croce 197/g ☎523.6761; C6. A few basic rooms over a pizzeria not far from the Tolentini church. ⑤.

Al Sole, Fondamenta Minotto, S. Croce 136 ☎523.2144; B7. Huge hotel in gorgeous Gothic palazzo on tiny canal. ⑦.

Alex, Rio Terrà Frari, S. Polo 2606 ☎523.1341; F7. One-star hotel decorated in Sixties style, but bearably so. The supermarket in front is useful for picnic preparations. ④.

Ca' Fóscari, Calle della Frescada, Dorsoduro 3888 ☎522.5817; E9. Tucked away in a micro-alley near S. Tomà. Quiet, well decorated and relaxed. Despite its size (10 rooms), you can sometimes find a room even when all others are booked out. ④.

Da Bepi, Fondamenta Minotto, S. Croce 160 ☎522.6735; B7. Run by the same family as keeps the *Casa Verardo* over in the Castello district, and has the same standards. ⑤.

Da Pino, Crosera S. Pantalon, Dorsoduro 3942 ☎522.3646; D8. By Venetian standards this is a very cheap hotel, and its location, in the district's main shopping street, could hardly be more convenient ④.

Falier, Salizzada S. Pantalon, S. Croce 130 ☎522.8882; D8. Neat little hotel close to San Rocco. ⑥.

San Cassiano-Ca' Favretto, Calle della Rosa, S. Croce 2232 ☎524.1768; H3. Well worth the money if you can get one of the rooms looking across the Canal Grande at the Ca' d'Oro. ⑦.

Stefania, Fondamenta Tolentini, S. Croce 181 ☎520.3757; B6. Decent one-star lodgings a few minutes from the Piazzale Roma; big rooms, some with bizarre murals. ④.

Sturion, Calle del Sturion, S. Polo 679 ☎523.6243; I6. Formerly one of Venice's choicest one-stars, the *Sturion* has now been completely overhauled, transforming it into an immaculate three-star. It's on a wonderful site a few yards from the Canal Grande, close to the Rialto, and is run by an exceptionally welcoming management. It's bound to be more popular now than ever, so book well in advance. ⑧.

Tivoli, Crosera S. Pantalon, Dorsoduro 3638 ☎524.2460; D8. The biggest cheap hotel in the immediate vicinity of the Frari and San Rocco, so often has space when the rest are full. ⑤.

Cannaregio

The grid references after the phone numbers relate to the map on p.126.

Al Gobbo, Campo S. Geremia, Cannaregio 312 ☎715.001; D6. Rather more genteel than most on the adjacent Lista di Spagna. ⑤.

Alle Guglie, Rio Terrà S. Leonardo, Cannaregio 1523 ☎717.351; E6. Minuscule place, with one bathroom between four rooms; the cheapest around. ④.

Adua, Lista di Spagna, Cannaregio 233/a ☎716.184; D7. Appalling decor but fairly humane prices. ⑤.

Bernardi Semenzato, Calle dell'Oca, Cannaregio 4366 ☎522.7257; I8. The owners of this recently upgraded place speak good English and are immensely helpful. ⑥.

Casa Carettoni, Lista di Spagna, Cannaregio 130 ☎717.231; D7. Probably the most comfortable one-star in the station area. ④.

Eden, Rio Terrà della Maddalena, Cannaregio 2357 ☎720.228; G6. Located in a characterful area about midway between the Rialto Bridge and the train station; has just eight rooms, so book ahead. ⑥.

Giorgione, Campo SS. Apostoli, Cannaregio 4587 ☎522.5810; I9. Modern, high-class hotel, with facilities that bear comparison with many far dearer ones. ⑧.

Guerrini, Lista di Spagna, Cannaregio 265 ☎715.333; D7. Just about as pleasant a hotel as you can find on the Lista itself. ⑤.

Accommodation

Rossi, Calle delle Procuratie, Cannaregio 262 ☎715.164; D6. In a quiet back-street off the Lista; rather functional but pleasant enough. ④.

San Geremia, Campo S. Geremia, Cannaregio 290 ☎716.245; D6. One to try if you're on your own, as it has some good single rooms. ④.

Villa Rosa, Calle Pésaro, Cannaregio 389 ☎716.569; C6. Excellent one-star secreted in the S. Giobbe district of Cannaregio, well away from the main traffic. ④.

Castello

The grid references after the phone numbers relate to the map on p.143.

Al Piave da Mario, Ruga Giuffa, Castello 4838 ☎528.5174; G8. Not the most picturesque of hotels, but frequented mainly by Italians, which must mean something. ④.

Bisanzio, Calle della Pietà, Castello 3651 ☎520.3100; I9. Very quiet and unshowy three-star hotel, right by Vivaldi's church. ⑦.

Canada, Campo S. Lio, Castello 5659 ☎522.9912; C7. Pristine two-star, with more single rooms than most. Book well in advance for the double room with a roof terrace. Amenable to bargaining in off-season. ⑥.

Caneva, Ramo della Fava, Castello 5515 ☎522.8118; C7. On the approach to the busy Campo S. Bartolomeo, yet very peaceful; has a private inner courtyard and overlooks the Rio della Fava. Not the most genial proprietors in town, though. ⑤.

Casa Verardo, Ruga Giuffa, Castello 4765 ☎528.6127; G8. Thought by many to be the best deal in the district, just a couple of minutes from San Marco. All rooms have a bath or shower. ⑤.

Corona, Calle Corona, Castello 4464 ☎522.9174; G8. Not far from the *Casa Verardo*, next door to a glassmaker's. Very friendly. ④.

Da Bruno, Salizzada S. Lio, Castello 5726 ☎523.0452; D7. Rooms are not the biggest you'll get for the money, but the location is excellent, on one of the principal routes to the Rialto. ⑤.

Danieli, Riva degli Schiavoni, Castello 4196 ☎522.6480; F10. No longer the most expensive hotel in Venice, but no other place can compete with the glamour of the *Danieli*. Balzac stayed here, as did George Sand, Wagner and Dickens. This magnificent Gothic palazzo affords just about the most sybaritic hotel experience on the continent – provided you book a room in the old part of the building, not the modern extension. Rooms cost around half a million lire. ⑨.

Doni, Fondamenta del Vin, Castello 4656 ☎522.4267; G9. Behind San Marco, heading towards San Zaccaria; most of the eleven rooms look over the Rio del Vin or over a courtyard. Cosy, with wooden floors instead of the usual stone. No private bathrooms. ⑤.

Londra Palace, Riva degli Schiavoni, Castello 4171 ☎520.0533; H10. The beautiful entrance area creates an aura of grandeur that some of the rooms don't live up to, but the majority of guests get a glorious view for a bill that comes midway between the average at the *Danieli* and the *Gabrielli Sandwirth*. ⑨.

Malibran, Corte Milion, Cannaregio 5864 ☎522.8028; C5. Comfortable three-star in an atmospheric cubby-hole of a square, where Marco Polo used to live. ⑦.

Paganelli, Riva degli Schiavoni, Castello 4182 ☎522.4324; G10. A wonderful place to stay, as long as you get one of the rooms on the lagoon side – the ones in the annexe look onto S. Zaccaria, which is a nice enough view, but not really in the same league. ⑤.

Rio, Campo SS. Filippo e Giacomo, Castello 4356 ☎523.4810; F9. A couple of minutes' walk from the Piazza, so a bargain in the circumstances. ④.

Scandinavia, Campo S. Maria Formosa, Castello 5240 ☎522.3507; F7. Sizeable and comfortable hotel on one of the city's most lively and spacious squares. ⑦.

Silva, Fondamenta del Rimedio, Castello 4423 ☎522.7643; E8. Overlooking a quiet canal to the north of San Marco. ⑤.

Accommodation

Wildner, Riva degli Schiavoni, Castello 4161 ☎522.7463; G10. Modest little two-star hotel that offers some of the lowest-priced views over to San Giorgio Maggiore. ⑥.

Eastern districts

The grid references after the phone numbers relate to the map on p.164.

Belvedere, Via Garibaldi, Castello 1636 ☎528.5148; C6. Far from the crowds, and usually with a room or two available, except in the height of summer. ④.

Gabrielli Sandwirth, Riva degli Schiavoni, Castello 4110 ☎523.1580; B5. Another converted Gothic palace, with a lovely courtyard. *Danieli*-style views across the Bacino di San Marco, for a fraction of the price. ⑦.

La Residenza, Campo Bandiera e Moro, Castello 3608 ☎528.5315; B4. Even though the rooms are a touch bare, this fourteenth-century palazzo is a mid-budget gem, occupying much of one side of a tranquil square just off the main waterfront. ⑥.

Sant'Anna, Corte del Bianco, Castello 269 ☎528.6466; E5. Good for families with children, as it has rooms for three or four people and is fairly near the Giardini Pubblici. Although it's in one of the remotest parts of the city, beyond the far end of Via Garibaldi, it's been discovered in recent years – so book well in advance. ⑥.

Toscana Tofanelli, Via Garibaldi, Castello 1650 ☎523.5722; C6. Spartan, but on a terrific site, and with a passable trattoria downstairs. Midnight curfew. ④.

Northern islands

Locanda Cipriani, Piazza S. Fosca 29, Torcello ☎730.150. Tiny and exclusive place, where Hemingway created *Across the River and into the Trees*. Half-board obligatory, sometimes full board . ⑨.

Raspo de Ua, Piazza Galuppi 560, Burano ☎730.095. The occupants of the other five rooms in this family hotel will probably be the only non-locals you'll see around here, once the daily rush has gone back to the city. ⑤.

Southern islands

Casa Frollo, Fondamenta Zitelle, Giudecca 50 ☎522.2723. Wonderful seventeenth-century palazzo that barely advertises the fact that it's a hotel. The place to stay if you want the spectacle of the views from Giudecca but can't afford the *Cipriani* and can't bear the hostel. Constantly under the threat of closure – so ring ahead if only to check that it still exists. ⑤.

Cipriani, Giudecca 10 ☎520.7744. The priciest and most decadent retreat in Venice – perks include butler service, jacuzzis in every suite, and Olympic-size swimming pool. Though guests can avail themselves of limitless complementary motorboat rides over to the city, it's not unknown for people to stay within the confines of the *Cipriani* for their entire stay. With prices rising to not far short of a million lire per night, it's not surprising they want to get every lira's worth. ⑨.

Des Bains, Lungomare Marconi 17, Lido ☎526.5921. Thomas Mann stayed here, rubbing shoulders with half the continent's aristocrats as he crafted *Death in Venice*. Set in its own park, this Art Deco extravaganza has over 200 rooms (from around L200,000) and, of course, exclusive rights to a slab of the Lido beach. ⑨.

Excelsior, Lungomare Marconi 41, Lido ☎526.0201. Built in the 1900s as the world's top resort hotel, the *Excelsior* is like something devised by Cecil B. de Mille, and is a favourite with film festival glitterati. Its private beach huts are so well appointed that your average visitor would be perfectly content with one of them as holiday accommodation. ⑨.

Quattro Fontane, Via delle Quattro Fontane 16, Lido ☎526.0227. By Lido standards, this is quite a humble establishment – the guests have to use public transport to get into the city, for example, rather than being able to summon a flunky in a private boat. But many people for whom money is no object prefer this quiet, antique-furnished villa to the more ostentatious competition. ⑨.

Hostels and institutions

Venice's hostels, most of which are run by religious foundations, are generally comfortable, well-run and inexpensive by Venetian standards – moreover, even in the high season they might well have a place or two to spare. Each year the tourist office produces a simple typed list of all hostel accommodation in the city; if the places listed below are full up, ask for a copy of it at the San Marco branch.

Archie's House, Rio Terrà S. Leonardo, Cannaregio 1814/b ☎720.884; map on p.126, F6. This cross between a hostel and a *pensione* has gone steeply downhill in recent years, but is still a favourite with many budget travellers, especially US college kids. No breakfast. ①.

Domus Cavanis, Rio Terrà Foscarini, Dorsoduro 912 ☎528.7374; map on p.86, G8. On the street going down the left of the Accademia. Catholic-run (ie separate male and female rooms); open June–Sept; single, double and triple rooms. ②.

Domus Civica, Calle Campazzo, S. Polo 3082 ☎721.103; map on p.104, D6. A student house in winter, open to women travellers June–July & Sept–Oct. A little awkward to find: it's off Calle della Lacca, to the west of San Giovanni Evangelista. Most rooms are double with running water; showers free; no breakfast; reception 7.30–11.30am; 11.30pm curfew. ②.

Foresteria Santa Fosca, Santa Maria dei Servi, Cannaregio 2372 ☎715.775; map on p.126, G5. Student-run hostel in the former Servite convent, with dorm beds and double rooms. Check-in 10am–noon & 7–9pm; 11.30pm curfew. Open July & Aug. ①.

Foresteria Valdese, S. Maria Formosa, Castello 5170 ☎528.6797; map on p.143, G6. Installed in a palazzo at the end of Calle Lunga S. Maria Formosa, with flaking frescoes and a large salon. Run by Waldensians, it's principally a hostel for grown-ups, with occasional school groups. Two large dorms, and a couple of rooms for two to four people. It also has a couple of self-catering flats for three to six people, usually heavily booked. Open for registration 11am–1pm and 6–8.30pm. ②.

Istituto Ciliota, Calle delle Muneghe, S. Marco 2976 ☎520.4888; map on p.36, C7. Welcoming but expensive mixed hostel-style accommodation, close to Campo S. Stefano. Open mid-June to mid-Sept. ②.

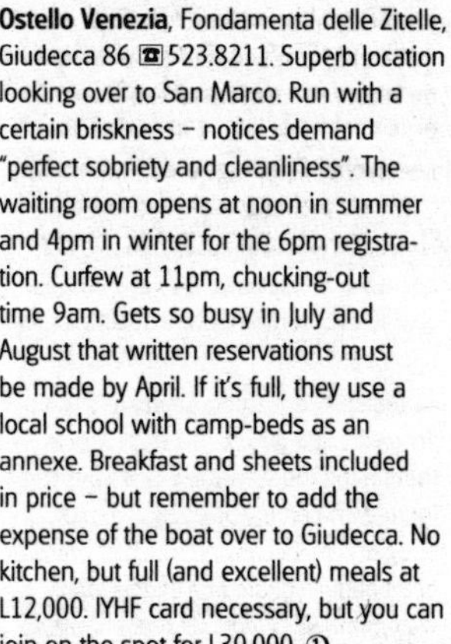

Ostello Venezia, Fondamenta delle Zitelle, Giudecca 86 ☎523.8211. Superb location looking over to San Marco. Run with a certain briskness – notices demand "perfect sobriety and cleanliness". The waiting room opens at noon in summer and 4pm in winter for the 6pm registration. Curfew at 11pm, chucking-out time 9am. Gets so busy in July and August that written reservations must be made by April. If it's full, they use a local school with camp-beds as an annexe. Breakfast and sheets included in price – but remember to add the expense of the boat over to Giudecca. No kitchen, but full (and excellent) meals at L12,000. IYHF card necessary, but you can join on the spot for L30,000. ①.

Suore Cannosiano, Fondamenta del Ponte Piccolo, Giudecca 428 ☎522.2157. Women-only hostel near the Sant'Eufamia vaporetto stop. Closed 8.30am–4pm. Curfew 10.30pm. ①.

Suore Mantellate, Calle Buccari, Castello 10 ☎522.0829; map on p.164; G9. Another convent-run women-only hostel, near Sant'Elena vaporetto stop. Closed Aug. ②.

Camping

There are no inexpensive campsites in the immediate area of Venice, but perhaps the most convenient are the pair on the grim road from the airport, which at least have the benefit of frequent bus connections to Piazzale Roma: the *Marco Polo* (L20,000 per person per night) and the friendlier *Leone di San Marco* (L16,000).

The **Litorale del Cavallino**, stretching from the Punta Sabbioni to Jésolo, has sites with a total of around 60,000 places, many of them quite luxurious. The vaporetto #14, from the Riva degli

Accommodation

Accommodation

Schiavoni to the Punta, stops close to *Marina di Venezia*, Via Montello 6 (April–Sept; ☎966.146; minimum stay 3 days). and *Miramare*, Lungomare Dante Alighieri 29 (April–Sept; ☎966.150). Most of the sites along the Cavallino shore cost around L15,000 for the pitch plus L5000 per person; when you've added on the fare for the forty-minute boat trip into the city you're not left with a particularly economical proposition.

The **Lido** is a shorter ride away, but its **San Nicolò** site, at Riviera San Nicolò 65 (☎767.415), has only 150 places; an International Camping Card is necessary.

There's a cheaper all-year site back on the mainland at **Fusina**, in Via Moranzani (☎547.055); in summer the #16 vaporetto connects Fusina to the city – at other times you have to get the bus to Mestre and change there. It has 1000 places.

Desperate travellers used to spread their sleeping bags on the forecourt of the train station in summer, an expedient that was banned in 1987. At that point the Scuola San Caboto (Cannaregio 1104/f; ☎716.629) opened its doors to take in the displaced *saccopelisti*, as they're called; its charges were lower than any campsite, but its existence was precarious – the tourist office at the station will tell you if San Caboto is still open.

Chapter 12

Eating and drinking

Nowhere is the damage done to Venice by mass tourism more apparent than in the city's **restaurants**, whose menus are becoming increasingly homogenised and standards increasingly slapdash. The reliably objective judges of the Accademia della Cucina recently ventured that it was "a rare privilege" to eat well in Venice, and there's more than an element of truth to Venice's reputation as a place where only the rich will get a first-rate meal. However, the picture is not entirely bleak for those on a tighter budget – some good-value restaurants do exist, it's just that they tend to be hidden away in the city's quieter places.

For a quick **snack**, pop into a bar and sample a couple of plump *tramezzini* (sandwiches), chasing them down with an *ombra*, the quick shot of wine that punctuates many a Venetian's working day. As is the case all over Italy, the division between **bars** and restaurants is often difficult to draw – some of the places listed below under "Restaurants" are in effect bars that have expanded their operation, while some of the "Bars" have basic sit-down areas for eating. With establishments that straddle both categories, we've listed them according to which aspect of the operation draws most of the customers.

As enticing as the city's bars are its **cafés** and **pasticcerie**, where a variety of waistline-threatening delicacies are on offer, and there aren't too many nicer things you can do to your taste buds than hit them with a coneful of **ice cream** from *Paolin* or *Nico*. Stocking up for an *al fresco* lunch, you'll be spoiled for choice at the stalls of the Rialto and the smaller **markets** pitched in a number of Venice's campi, whilst there's a host of tempting *alimentari* to supplement supplies.

Night owls have a fairly tough time of it in Venice. The locals seem to be a homely crowd, for whom a sociable end to the day usually means having a few friends round for a meal, perhaps after a brief call at the local bar. By 9.30pm most of the shutters have come down; all the places that stay open later are included in the box on p.237, but it's a pretty scrawny roll-call.

VENETIAN FOOD AND DRINK

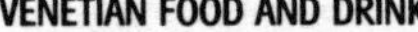

Venetian cuisine bears little trace of the city's past as Europe's trading crossroads, when spices from the East were among the most lucrative commodities sold in Venice's markets. Nowadays Venetian food is known for its simplicity, with plain pepper and salt as the principal means of gingering up a meal. **Fish and seafood** dominate the restaurant menus, the former being netted in the Adriatic and the rivers and lakes of the mainland, the latter coming from the lagoon and open sea. Prawns, squid and octopus are typical Venetian *antipasti* (usually served with a plain dressing of olive oil and lemon), as are Murano crabs and *sarde in saor* (marinated sardines). Dishes like eel cooked in Marsala wine, *baccalà* (salt cod) and *seppioline nere* (baby cuttlefish cooked in its own ink) are other Venetian

Eating and drinking

staples, but the quintessential dish is the **risotto**, made with rice grown along the Po valley. Apart from the seafood variety (*risotto bianco, risotto di mare* or *risotto dei pescatori*), you'll come across risottos that incorporate some of the great range of vegetables grown in the Veneto, and others that draw on such diverse ingredients as snails, tripe, quails and sausages.

Venetian **soups** are as versatile as their risottos, with *brodetto* (mixed fish) and *pasta e fasioi* (pasta and beans) being the most popular kinds. **Polenta** is another recurrent feature of Venetian meals; made by slowly stirring maize flour into boiling salted water, it's served as an accompaniment to a number of dishes, in particular liver (*fegato*), a special favourite in Venice.

Pastries and sweets are also an area of Venetian expertise. Look out for the thin oval biscuits called *baicoli*, the ring-shaped cinnamon-flavoured *bussolai* (a speciality of Burano), and *mandolato* – a cross between nougat and toffee, made with almonds. The Austrian occupation has left its mark in the form of the ubiquitous *strudel* and the cream- or jam-filled *krapfen* (doughnuts).

For a glossary of food and drink, see p.385.

Particular foods are traditional to certain **feast days**. During Carnevale you can buy small doughnuts known as *frittelle*, which come plain, *con frutta* (with fruit), *con crema* (confectioner's cream) or *con zabaglione* (which is made out of egg yolks and Marsala). During Lent there's an even greater emphasis on fish, and also on omelettes (*frittata*), often made with shrimps and wild asparagus; lamb is popular at Easter. On Ascension Day it's customary to have pig's trotter, either plain or stuffed, while for the feast of the Redentore (third Sunday in July) *sarde in saor* or roast duck are in order. Tiny biscuits called *fave* ("beans") fill the *pasticcerie* around All Saints' Day and All Souls' Day (November 1 & 2); on the feast of Saint Martin (November 11) you get biscuits or heavy quince jelly cut into the shape of the saint on his horse; and on the feast of the Madonna della Salute (November 21), it's traditional to have *castradina* (salted smoked mutton). On Christmas Eve many Venetians eat eel, usually grilled, though with variations from island to island; on Christmas Day the traditional dishes are roast turkey, veal, duck or capon.

Many of the **wines** of the Veneto will already be familiar, especially **Valpolicella** (red), **Bardolino** (red) and **Soave** (white) – the Veneto produces more DOC (*Denominazione di origine controllata*) wine than any other region, and this trio of Veronese wines comprise the bulk of exported quality Italian wine. Far more rarely exported is **Prosecco**, light, champagne-like wine from the area around Conegliano – don't miss a chance to sample Prosecco Rosé and the delicious **Cartizze**, the finest type of Prosecco. Wines from neighbouring Friuli are well worth exploring too: the most common reds are Pinot Nero, Refosco, Merlot and Cabernet, with Tocai, Pinot Bianco and Sauvignon the most common whites. **Grappa** is the local fire-water – associated particularly with the town of Bassano del Grappa, it's made from grapes, juniper berries or plums, and will take your head off if you don't exercise a degree of caution.

Apart from coffee in its manifold varieties, non-alcoholic drinks include *frullati*, a milk shake made with fruit; a freshly squeezed fruit juice is a *spremuta* and is usually *d'arancia* (orange), *pompelmo* (grapefruit), *limone* (lemon) or *mele* (apple).

Restaurants

Virtually every budget restaurant in Venice advertises a set-price **menu turistico**, which at its best will offer a choice of three or four dishes for each course. This can be a cheap way of sampling Venetian specialities, but the quality and certainly the quantity won't be up to the mark of an **à la carte** meal. As a general rule, value for money tends to increase with the distance from San Marco; plenty of restaurants within a short radius of the Piazza offer menus that seem to be reasonable, but you'll probably find the food unappetising, the portions tiny and the service abrupt. **Pizza** is a generally reliable stand-by here as elsewhere in Italy, but as a principle steer clear of the places in the immediate vicinity of the Piazza and Mercerie.

In the following listings, the term "inexpensive" means that you should be able to get a meal with a drink for under L25,000, including service and *coperto* (cover charge); "moderate" means L25,000–50,000; "expensive" means L50,000–80,000; and "very expensive" covers the rest. We've supplied the phone numbers for those places where **booking** is advisable. Wherever possible, we've also supplied the day of the week on which each restaurant is closed, but bear in mind that many restaurateurs take their annual holiday in August, and that quite a few close down in the dead weeks of January and early February.

San Marco

The grid references relate to the map on p.36.

Al Bacareto, Salizzada S. Samuele 3447; C6. Handy for the Palazzo Grassi. Best to eat standing here: excellent *risotto alla pescatore* (fisherman's risotto) and a glass of wine for around L10,000; sitting, a full meal will cost far more. Closed Sun. Inexpensive to moderate.

Al Conte Pescaor, Piscina S. Zulian 544 ☎522.1483; H3. Fine little fish restaurant that draws its custom mainly from the locals. Closed all Sun & Mon lunchtime. Expensive.

Al Theatro, Campo S. Fantin 1916 ☎522.1052; E6. This long-established bar-restaurant does a roaring trade before and after the performances at the Fenice – so the most pleasant mealtime is a summer mid-evening while there's a show on, when you can enjoy the outside tables in peace. Closed Mon. Moderate to expensive.

Bora Bora, Calle Stagneri; H2. Buzzing young pizzeria-restaurant, down an alley off Campo San Bartolomeo. Ten percent discount for *Rough Guide* readers. Closed Wed. Inexpensive.

Da Arturo, Calle degli Assassini 3656 ☎528.6974; E6. Celebrated as the only top-notch restaurant in Venice that doesn't serve fish. Closed Sun. Expensive.

Da Ivo, Ramo dei Fuseri 1809 ☎528.004; F5. As with 95 percent of Venice's restaurants, fish features at *Ivo*'s, but its reputation rests on its *bistecca* and other Tuscan dishes. Closed Sun. Expensive.

Da Raffaele, Fondamenta delle Ostreghe 2347 ☎523.2317; E9. Menu varies according to what's in season, so seafood gives way to meat in the autumn. Eat on the terrace rather than in the large Merrye Italie dining room. Closed Thurs. Expensive.

Do Forni, Calle dei Specchieri 468 ☎523.2148; I5. High-class Venetian restaurant with two dining rooms – one like an Orient Express cabin, the other in "farmhouse" style. Quality and prices are high in each. Closed Thurs. Very expensive.

Harry's Bar, Calle Vallaresso 1323 ☎523.6797; G8. Often described as the most reliable of the city's gourmet restaurants, though there are sceptics who think the place's reputation has more to do with glamour than cuisine – when the Film Festival is on, it's wall-to-wall starlets and paunchy producers. Closed Mon. Very expensive.

La Caravella, Calle Larga XXII Marzo 2396 ☎520.8901; F8. One of two restaurants inside the *Saturnia* hotel, the *Caravella* has an ambitious *nouvelle* pan-European menu, rated by many as the best in the city. Closed Wed. Very expensive.

Latteria Veneziana, Calle dei Fuseri; F5. Billed as Venice's sole vegetarian restaurant, this place tends to serve very small portions of the sort of food a carnivore rustles up when a cranky relative is due – but at least it's fairly cheap.

Rosticceria San Bartolomeo, Calle della Bissa 5423; H2. Downstairs it's a sort of glorified snack-bar, the meals starting from around L12,000 – the trick is to first grab a place at the long tables along the windows, then order from the counter. Good if you need to refuel quickly and cheaply, but can't face another pizza.

Eating and drinking

There's a less rudimentary restaurant upstairs, where prices are quite a bit higher and quality a touch better. Closed Mon. Inexpensive to moderate.

Vino Vino, Ponte delle Veste 2007; F7. Very close to the Fenice opera house, this place is primarily a wine bar (see p.236), but also serves quick, simple and relatively inexpensive meals. Closed all day Tues & Wed lunchtime.

Dorsoduro

The grid references relate to the map on p.86.

Alle Burchielle, Fondamenta Burchielle; B4. Simple neighbourhood trattoria, a minute's walk south of Piazzale Roma. Just ask for the day's special. Closed Mon. Moderate.

Alle Záttere, Fondamenta Záttere ai Gesuati; G9. Same sort of place as *Da Gianni*, but not quite as good. Go for the pizzas – *Primavera*, with vegetables, is recommended. Closed Tues. Inexpensive.

Al Profeta, Calle Lunga S. Barnaba 2689; E7. Popular and cheerful pizzeria. Closed Mon. Inexpensive.

Al Sole di Napoli, Campo Santa Margherita; D5. Cheap and very cheerful pizzeria – especially pleasant in summer, when its tables colonise the campo. Closed Thurs. Inexpensive.

Antico Capon, Campo S. Margherita; D5. Wide range of pizzas, including such novelties as gorgonzola and walnut. Closed Wed. Inexpensive.

Anzolo Raffael, Campo Angelo Raffaele 1722; C8. Unpretentious restaurant tucked in a corner of the *sestiere* where few tourists venture. Specialises in fish. Closed Mon & Tues. Moderate.

Da Bruno, Calle Lunga San Barnaba; E7. Friendly, very basic trattoria. Closed Sat & Sun. Inexpensive.

Da Gianni, Fondamenta Záttere; G9. Nicely sited restaurant-pizzeria. Closed Wed. Inexpensive.

Due Torri, Campo S. Margherita 3408; D5. Humblest of eateries, right next to the *Antico Capon*. Has a very small menu, and does most of its business at lunchtime, when the local workers drop in for a quick bite. Closed Sun. Inexpensive.

Isola Misteriosa, Rio Terrà Scozzera 2894; D6. Serves nice food but in small portions, and a touch overpriced. It's possible to sit and drink here when it's not full of people eating, and there's a stand-up bar. It appeals to those who wear sunglasses at midnight and never smile. Closed Thurs.

La Furatola, Calle Lunga S. Barnaba 2870 ☎520.8594; E7. Good seafood; a small place, so booking is advisable. Closed Wed evening & all Thurs. Expensive.

Montin, Fondamenta di Borgo 1147 ☎522.7151; E8. Very highly rated, but the quality is more erratic than you'd expect for the money; you'll pay in the region of L50,000 here for what would cost L30,000 in some places. It's always been a place for the literary/artistic set – Pound, Hemingway, Peggy Guggenheim and Visconti, for example – and the restaurant doubles as a commercial art gallery. Closed Tues & Wed. Expensive.

San Trovaso, Fondamenta Priuli 1016; F7. A restaurant-pizzeria which serves a menu of basic Venetian dishes at prices just a little higher than rock bottom. Closed Mon evening and all Tues. Inexpensive.

San Polo

The grid references relate to the map on p.104.

All'Anfora, Lista Vecchia dei Bari; D3. An unpretentious local restaurant that's open for breakfast coffee and still going late at night. Has a pizza list, but the trattoria list is not expensive and features dishes you might find in a Venetian home. The seafood risotto is good, as is the *spaghetti del doge*. Closed Fri. Moderate.

Alle Colonnette, Campiello del Piovan; E4. Nudging the church of San Giacomo dell'Orio, this little place is high on atmosphere, and serves good pizzas and basic trattoria fare. Closed Wed. Moderate.

Alla Madonna, Calle della Madonna 594 ☎523.3824; I6. Roomy, bustling seafood restaurant. Little finesse but good value, and refreshingly varied clientele. Closed Wed. Moderate.

Alla Rivetta, Campiello dei Meloni 1479; H6. Pleasant canalside trattoria between San Polo and Sant'Aponal. Closed Mon. Moderate.

Alla Zucca, Ponte del Megio; F3. Serves chiefly vegetarian dishes, and is patronised heavily by the city's students. Closed Sun. Inexpensive to moderate.

Alle Oche, Calle del Tintor 1459; F4. Excellent pizzeria on the south side of Campo S. Giacomo dell'Orio. Has about fifty varieties to choose from, so if this doesn't do you, nothing will; on summer evenings if you're not there by 8pm you may have to queue on the pavement. Closed Mon. Inexpensive.

Al Nono Risorto, Sottoportego de Siora Bettina 2338; H4. Busy pizzeria-restaurant just off Campo S. Cassiano; has a pleasant garden, but the staff can make outsiders feel uncomfortable. Closed Sun. Inexpensive.

Antica Bessetta, Calle Savio 1395 ☎523.687; E3. One of the best places in Venice to experience real Venetian home cooking. Closed Tues & Wed. Moderate.

Crepizza, Calle S. Pantalon 3757; D8. One of the city's trendiest eateries – excellent pizzas and crêpes, buzzing atmosphere. Closed Tues. Inexpensive.

Da Fiore, Calle del Scaleter 2202 ☎731.308; G6. Small restaurant off Campo San Polo; prides itself on its seafood and homemade bread. Definitely well above average. Closed Sun & Mon. Moderate to expensive.

Da Ignazio, Calle Saoneri 2749 F7. Unspoilt trattoria between the Frari and San Polo. Closed Sat. Moderate.

Da Sandro, Campiello dei Meloni; H6. Split-site pizzeria, with rooms on both sides of the campiello and tables on the pavement. Often frenetic, though not aggressively so. Closed Fri. Inexpensive.

Da Silvio, Calle San Pantalon 3748; D8. The best of the clutch of trattorias in this alley, with a reputation for its *tortellini*. Closed Sun. Moderate.

Donna Onesta, Calle della Madonna Onesta 3922; E8. Once a simple little trattoria, the *Donna Onesta* is going increasingly for the tourist market, with a corresponding drop in quality and rise in prices. Still better than many though. Closed Sun. Moderate.

Giardinetto, Fondamenta del Forner; E8. Big and slightly impersonal pizzeria-trattoria, with wide shaded courtyard. Popular with students. Closed Mon. Inexpensive.

La Regina, Calle della Regina 2331 ☎524.1402; G4. Specialises in hybrid Franco-Italian cuisine, and offers a *menu degustazione* as a way of sampling the kitchen's delights at slightly reduced cost. Closed Mon. Expensive.

Poste Vecie, Pescheria 1608 ☎721.822; I4. As you'd expect by the location next to the fish market, this superb restaurant – run by the owners of the *Regina* – is another place for connoisseurs of maritime dishes. Closed Tues evening & all Wed. Expensive.

San Tomà, Campo San Tomà 2864; E8. Outdoor tables on the campo and under a pergola out the back; pizzas are succulent, but the waiters have a reputation for hostility towards foreigners. Closed Tues. Inexpensive.

Cannaregio

The grid references relate to the map on p.126.

Ai Promessi Sposi, Calle dell'Oca 4367; I8. Bar-trattoria specialising in *baccalà* and other basic traditional fish recipes. Closed Tues. Inexpensive.

A La Vecchia Cavana, Rio Terrà SS. Apostoli 4624 ☎87.106; I8. Seafood is the staple at this, the poshest restaurant in the Cannaregio *sestiere*. Closed Tues. Expensive.

Al Bacco, Fondamenta degli Ormesini 3054 ☎717.493; F4. Like the *Antica Mola*,

Eating and drinking

Eating and drinking

further east along the canal, *Al Bacco* started life as a humble neighbourhood stop-off, but has grown into a fully fledged restaurant, with prices to match. It retains a rough-and-ready feel, but the food is distinctly classy. Closed Mon. Moderate.

Al Ponte, Rio Terrà Maddalena 2352; G6. Worth mentioning if only because they have the cheapest *menu turistico* on this main street. Closed Sun. Inexpensive.

Antica Mola, Fondamenta degli Ormesini 2800; F4. This family-run trattoria, near the Ghetto, is becoming more popular by the year. Good food, good value, and nice garden at the back. Closed Sat. Moderate.

Bruno, Fondamenta delle Cappuccine; D3. Very pleasant little canalside trattoria in deepest Cannaregio; tasty seafood at reasonable prices. Closed Sun. Moderate.

Casa Mia, Calle dell'Oca 4430; I8. Always heaving with locals, who usually go for the pizza list rather than the menu, though the standard dishes are reliable enough. Closed Tues. Inexpensive to moderate.

Paradiso Perduto, Fondamenta della Misericordia 2540; G5. Fronted by a popular bar, this place has a lively relaxed atmosphere, attracting students, arty types and the gay community. The bar opens around 7.30pm, the kitchen gets going at 8pm, and the doors close at midnight or later, depending on how things are going. Bar prices higher when live music is playing – usually Sunday. Closed Wed. Inexpensive to moderate.

Vesuvio, Rio Terrà Farsetti 1837; F5. Excellent wood-oven pizzas attract a full crowd every night. Inexpensive.

Vini da Gigio, Fondamenta S. Felice 3628; H7. Family-run wine bar-trattoria, where the menu changes daily and most of the customers are locals. Absolutely authentic and, by Venetian standards, excellent value. Closed Mon. Moderate.

Castello

The grid references relate to the map on p.143.

Aciugheta, Campo Santi Filippo e Giacomo 4357; F9. A bar with a pizzeria-trattoria next door. The closest spot to San Marco to eat without paying through the nose. Good bar-food to nibble or have as a meal. The name translates as "the little anchovy" and there are portraits of anchovies on the wall. Closed Wed. Inexpensive to moderate.

Al Giardinetto da Gianni, Barbaria delle Tolle 6418; H6. Small family-run trattoria-pizzeria with vine-swathed garden. Closed Mon. Inexpensive.

Alla Conchiglia, Fondamenta S. Lorenzo 4990; H8. Canalside pizzeria-trattoria, with low prices considering its proximity to the Piazza. Closed Wed. Inexpensive to moderate.

Alla Rivetta, Ponte San Provolo 4625; F9. Near Campo SS. Filippo e Giacomo. Excellent *sepie in nero*, best eaten *con polenta*. Closed Mon. Inexpensive to moderate.

Al Mascaron, Calle Lunga Santa Maria Formosa 5225; F7. Has an arty feel and interesting bar food, but definitely two types of clientele – Italians and non-Italians – with service to match. Has a good reputation among the locals though, and worth a try if you're confident. Closed Sun. Moderate.

Al Milion, Corte del Milion 5841; C5. Trattoria with bar that serves snacks. Wide selection of Veneto wines. Closed Wed. Moderate.

Da Remigio, Salizzada dei Greci 3416 ☎ 523.0089; I8. Brilliant local trattoria, serving gorgeous homemade gnocchi. Be sure to book – the locals pack this place every night. Closed Mon evening and Tues. Moderate.

Fiaschetteria Toscana, Salizzada S. Giovanni Crisostomo 5719 ☎ 528.5281; B5. The name means "Tuscan Wine Shop", but the menu is quintessentially Venetian. Highly rated for its food, the *fiaschetteria* also has an excellent wine list. Closed Tues, the week after Carnevale and two weeks in June or July. Expensive.

Malibran, Corte del Milion 5864; C5. Relatively smart trattoria-pizzeria. Closed Wed. Inexpensive.

Eastern districts

The grid references relate to the map on p.164.

Al Covo, Campiello della Pescaria ☎533.3812; B5. Located in a backwater to the east of Campo Bandiera e Moro, the innovative *Covo* opened in the mid-1980s, and its stock has been rising steadily since. Closed Tues & Wed. Moderate.

Al Marca, Via Garibaldi; D6. Has a filling *menu turistico*, which is more than can be said for some places on this street. Closed Sun. Moderate.

Da Franz, Fondamenta S. Isepo 754 ☎522.7505; E7. Lurking in an extremely unfashionable area to the north of the Giardini Pubblici, this is one of the choicest seafood kitchens in the city. Closed Mon. Expensive.

Da Paolo, Campo dell'Arsenale; C4. Tables outside in the summer, facing the Arsenale entrance. Good pizzas and *sarde in saor*; house wine not great. Closed Mon. Moderate.

La Corte Sconta, Calle del Pestrin 3886 ☎522.7024; B4. Wonderful seafood dishes and far better than average house wine. If your budget only stretches to one gourmet experience, blow your money here. Closed Sun & Mon. Moderate to expensive.

Toscana, Via Garibaldi 1650; C6. Plain, with a tiny menu, but all the dishes are good. Closes at 8pm. Closed Wed. Inexpensive.

Northern islands

Ai Pescatori, Via Galuppi 371, Burano ☎730.650. One of the top choices on Burano. Risotto and other fish dishes predominate. Closed Mon. Moderate to expensive.

Al Gatto Nero, Guideca 88, Burano. Plain local trattoria, just a few minutes' walk from the busy Via Galuppi, opposite the Pescheria. Closed Tues. Inexpensive to moderate.

Busa alla Torre, Campo S. Stefano 3, Murano ☎739.602. In the opinion of many, this place serves the best fish on Murano. Closed Sun. Moderate to expensive.

Da Romano, Via Galuppi 221, Burano ☎730.030. Huge old Burano restaurant with no lack of local devotees. Closed Wed. Moderate.

Locanda Cipriani, Torcello ☎730.757. Desperately modish and desperately overpriced offspring of *Harry's Bar*, though some may think the money well spent for the Torcello setting alone. Closed Mon & Tues. Very expensive.

Valmarana, Fondamenta Navagero 31, Murano. Humble trattoria with trellised garden at the back. Closed Wed. Inexpensive.

Southern islands

Altanella, Calle delle Erbe 270, Giudecca ☎522.7780. Highly recommended for its beautiful fish dishes and the terrace overlooking the island's central canal. Closed Mon & Tues. Moderate.

Bella Venezia, Calle Corona 51, Chioggia ☎400.500. A lot of people think that Chioggia's fish market sells better quality stuff than Venice's, and this is one of the best places to check out the truth of the claim. Closed Thurs. Moderate.

Do Mori, Fondamenta Sant'Eufemia 588, Giudecca ☎522.5452. Run by the former chef at *Harry's Bar*. Serves humble pizzas as well as classier fare, and everything is more democratically priced than at any of the other establishments bearing the "Harry" tag. Closed Sun. Moderate to expensive.

El Gato, Corso del Popolo 653, Chioggia ☎401.806. Another fine Chioggia fish restaurant, and less crowded than the *Bella Venezia*. Closed Mon. Moderate.

Bars and snacks

One of the most appealing aspects of Venetian social life is encapsulated in the phrase "andemo a ombra", which translates literally as an invitation to go into the shade, but is in fact an invitation for a drink – more specifically, a small

Eating and drinking

glass of wine, customarily downed in one. (The phrase is a vestige of the time when wines were unloaded on the Riva degli Schiavoni and then sold at a shaded kiosk at the base of the Campanile; the kiosk was shifted as the sun moved round, so as to stay in the shade.) Stand at a bar any time of the day and you won't have to wait long before a customer drops by for a reviving mouthful. Occasionally you'll come across a group doing a *giro de ombre*, the highly refined Venetian version of the pub-crawl; on a serious *giro* it's almost obligatory to stop at an *enoteca* – a bar where priority is given to the range and quality of the wines (for example, *Al Volto*).

Most bars serve some kind of **food**, their counters usually bearing trays of the fat little sandwiches called *tramezzini*. Devoid of natural fibre (even the crusts are removed) but stuffed with delicious fillings – eggs and mushrooms, eggs and anchovies, Parma ham and artichokes – they can cost anything from L1000 up to about L3000. At the older-style *osterie* there's often a choice of little snacks called *cicheti*, which you can either nibble at or heap up on a plate; the array will typically include *polpette* (small beef and garlic meatballs), *carciofini* (artichoke hearts), hard-boiled eggs, anchovies, *polipi* (baby octopus or squid), sun-dried tomatoes, peppers and courgettes cooked in oil. Some *osterie* also produce one or two more substantial dishes each day.

Take-away pizza is all over the place, though most of it is pretty miserable fare – *Cip Ciap*, in Castello, is the best source (see below).

San Marco

The grid references relate to the map on p.36.

Al Volto, Calle Cavalli 4081; E4. An *enoteca* in the true sense of the word – 1300 wines from Italy and elsewhere, some cheap, many not; good snacks, too. Closed Sun.

Devil's Forest, Calle Stagneri; H2. The liveliest bar in the vicinity of Campo San Bartolomeo, and Venice's most convincing facsimile of a British pub, with a good range of beers and a dartboard – though the food is a lot better than you'd find in most real pubs. Open till midnight every night except Monday.

Harry's Bar, Calle Vallaresso 1323; G8. Trendiest bar in town since time immemorial; famed in equal measure for its cocktails, its sandwiches and its celebrity league prices. Open 3pm–1am; closed Mon.

Osteria alle Botteghe, Calle delle Botteghe; C7. Sumptuous sandwiches, but most lunchtimes you need a shoehorn to get in the place. Closed Sun.

Osteria Terrà Assassini, Rio Terrà degli Assassini; E6. Very good range of wines and small selection of choice snacks and small meals. Closed Mon.

Vino Vino, Ponte delle Veste 2007; F7. Slightly posey wine bar, but it does stock over 100 wines. Open until midnight; closed Tues.

Dorsoduro

The grid references relate to the map on p.86.

Bar Novo, Calle Lunga S. Barnaba 2753; E7. Has a wide range of *cicheti* – a good place for a lunchtime snack after a tour of the Accademia. Closed Sat.

Cantina del Vino già Schiavi, Fondamenta Nani 992; F8. Great bar and wine shop opposite San Trovaso – do some sampling before you buy. Closed Sun.

Corner Pub, Calle della Chiesa 684; H7. Usually has a few hooray art history students from the home counties, but is authentically Venetian nonetheless. Open till 2am. Closed Tues.

Da Codroma, Fondamenta Briati 2540; C7. The kind of place you could sit for an hour or two with a beer and a book and feel comfortable. Interesting toasted sandwiches – brie with different sauces, for example. Shows work by local artists, and is a venue for poetry readings and live music. Open till 1am. Closed Thurs.

> **Late-night Bars**
> **Devil's Forest**, San Marco.
> **Harry's Bar**, San Marco.
> **Vino Vino**, San Marco.
> **Corner Pub**, Dorsoduro.
> **Da Codroma**, Dorsoduro.
> **Ai Canottieri**, Cannaregio.
> **Paradiso Perduto**, Cannaregio (see "Restaurants").
> **Leon d'Oro: Bar Gobbi**, Cannaregio.

San Polo

The grid references relate to the map on p.104.

Antico Dolo, Ruga Vecchia S. Giovanni 778; I5. Excellent osteria-style establishment, a good source of wine and snacks near the Rialto. Closed Sun.

Do Mori, Calle Do Mori 429; I5. Hidden just off Ruga Vecchia S. Giovanni, this is the best bar in the market area – a narrow, standing-only place, packed every evening with home-bound shopworkers, Rialto porters, and locals just out for a stroll. Delicious snacks and terrific atmosphere. Open 9am–1pm & 5–8pm; closed Wed afternoon and all Sun.

Do Spade, Sottoportego delle Do Spade 860; I5. Larger and a touch more genteel than the nearby *Do Mori* (it has tables), but very similar. Almost impossible to locate from a map – walk past the *Do Mori* and keep going as straight as possible. Open 9am–1pm & 5–8pm; closed Sun.

Gastronomia Aliani, Rugheta del Ravano 655; H6. First-class *alimentari*, serving luscious and expensive snacks. Closed Sun.

Soto Sopra, Calle S. Pantalon 3740; D8. Trendy hi-tech bar.

Cannaregio

The grid references relate to the map on p.126.

Ai Canottieri, Ponte Tre Archi; B4. Has live music occasionally, but as usual bar prices go up to pay the band. Has a restaurant section. Open till 1am every night except Sun.

Leon d'Oro: Bar Gobbi, Rio Terrà della Maddalena; G6. A pleasant family-run place on a main street, a couple of doors down from the flashier *Alla Maddalena*. Excellent thick hot chocolate; good range of sandwiches, with *osteria* food at the back. Open until 12.30am. Closed Fri.

Osteria ai Ormesini da Aldo, Fondamenta Ormesini 2710; F4. One of a number of bars on this long chain of *fondamante*, and a particularly pleasant spot for a lunchtime snack in the sun.

Osteria alla Ghiacciaia, Fondamenta di Cannaregio; C4. Small local bar with an impressive kitchen. One, inexpensive, main dish which changes daily. Tends to shut early. Closed Sun.

Osteria dalla Vedova, Calle del Pistor 3912; I8. Run by the same family for over a century. Mouthwatering selection of *cicheti*, good range of wines.

Train Station Buffet; Cannaregio; C8. A good place to fill up cheaply. Open 6am–10pm daily, with self-service buffet meals 11.30am–3pm & 6.30–9.30pm, and restaurant service 11.30am–3pm.

Castello

The grid references relate to the map on p.143.

Bar Penasa, Calle delle Rasse; F10. Possibly the best bar for a reviving measure after a tour of the Piazza – it's a few minutes' stroll from the Palazzo Ducale, off the Riva degli Schiavoni. Closed Wed.

Cip Ciap, Calle Mondo Nuovo 5799; E7. The widest range of take-out pizzas and pies – their spinach and *ricotta* pie is especially tasty and filling. Closed Thurs.

Cafés, pasticcerie and gelaterie

When **coffee** first appeared in Venice in 1640, imported by the Republic from the Levant, it was treated as a medicine; today it's a drug of which all Venetians need a fix several times a day. (Tea-drinkers will be horrified by the Venetian notion of their favoured beverage – often a jug of hot water with a tea-bag lying on

Eating and drinking

the saucer.) High-quality outlets range from the *Rosa Salva* chain, whose chilly ambience might not tempt you to hang around for longer than it takes to slug the coffee back, to the decadent old coffee houses of the Piazza, whose prices will prompt you to linger just so you can feel you've had your money's worth.

As with bars, if you **sit in a café** you will be charged more, and if you **sit outside** the bill will be even higher. Many **pasticcerie** also serve coffee, but will have at most a few bar-stools; they're all right for a swift caffeination before the next round of church-visiting, but not for a session of postcard writing or a longer recuperative stop. Elbow-room in the city's *pasticcerie* is especially restricted first thing in the morning, as the citizens pile in for a coffee and *cornetto* (croissant). You can also stop for a coffee at most of Venice's **gelaterie**, where the ice cream comes in forms that you won't have experienced before, unless you're a seasoned traveller in Italy.

General areas to find good cafés include **Campo Santa Margherita**, **Crosera San Pantalon** (running just south of San Rocco), **Campiello Meloni**, (between S. Polo and S. Aponal), **Calle della Bissa** (behind Campo S. Bartolomeo), **Salizzada San Giovanni Crisostomo**, the **Strada Nova** and its continuations towards the train station, and **Via Garibaldi**. In one way or another, the following specific places stand out from the rest.

San Marco

The grid references relate to the map on p.36.

Florian, Piazza San Marco 56–59; H7. Opened in 1720 by Florian Francesconi, and frescoed and mirrored in a passable pastiche of that period, this has long been the café to be seen in. A simple *cappuccino* will set you back around L10,000 if the band's performing, and you'll have to take out a mortgage for a cocktail. Closed Wed.

Latteria Veneziana, Calle dei Fuseri; F5. Recommended for its *cioccolata con panna* (hot chocolate with cream) and its selection of *frullati* (milkshakes with fresh fruit).

Marchini, Ponte San Maurizio 2769; D8. The most delicious and most expensive of Venetian *pasticciere*, where people come on Sunday morning to buy family treats. Indulge at least once.

Paolin, Campo Santo Stefano 2962; C7. Thought by many to be the makers of the best ice cream in Venice; certainly their pistachio is amazing, and the outside tables have one of the finest settings in the city. Closed Fri.

Quadri, Piazza San Marco 120–124; H6. In the same price league as *Florian*, but not quite as pretty. Austrian officers patronised it during the occupation, while the natives stuck with *Florian*, and it still has something of the air of being a runner-up in the society stakes. Closed Mon.

Rosa Salva, Campo San Luca (F4), Calle Fiubera (H5) and Merceria San Salvador (G3). Venice's premier catering chain: excellent coffee, but slightly surgical decor.

Dorsoduro

The grid references relate to the map on p.86.

Causin, Campo S. Margherita 2996; D5. Yet more home-made ice cream. Closed Sun.

Gian Carlo Vio, Rio Terrà Toletta 1192; F7. Great cakes – one to make for after the Accademia.

Il Caffè, Campo S. Margherita 2963; D5. Newish but old-fashioned café-bar with great views and so-so sandwiches.

Il Doge, Campo S. Margherita 3058; D5. Well-established *gelateria*. Open till midnight. Closed Mon.

Nico, Záttere ai Gesuati 922; G9. A high-point of a wander in the area, celebrated for an artery-clogging creation called a *gianduiotto* – ask for one *da passeggio* (to take out) and you'll be given a paper cup with a block of praline ice cream drowned in whipped cream. Closed Thurs.

Cannaregio

The grid references relate to the map on p.126.

Ca' d'Oro, Strada Nova 3843a; H8. Belt-loosening cakes. Closed Mon.

Caffè Costarica, Rio Terrà S. Leonardo; E6. Does delicious iced coffee.

Pasticceria Boscolo Anna, Campiello dell'Anconetta; F6. One of a chain of "Antichi pasticceri Venexiani", established in the 1930s and still going strong.

Castello

The grid references relate to the map on p.143.

Chiusso Pierino, Salizzada dei Greci 3306; I8. Another of the reliable "Antichi pasticceri Venexiani" group. Closed Wed.

Domenegati Eugenio, Calle Caffettier 6645; I6. Belongs to the same organisation as *Chiusso Pierino*, and does equally fine cakes. Closed Tues.

Il Golosone, Salizzada San Lio; D7. *Pasticceria* and bar with a glorious spread of cakes; does a delicious apple *spremute*. Closed Mon.

Giudecca

Harry's Dolci, Fondamenta S. Biagio 773. Hyper-refined cakes and other sweets; mass at the Redentore followed by a trip to *Harry's* is a Sunday morning ritual for many.

Food markets and shops

The campi, parks and canalside steps make picnicking a particularly pleasant alternative in Venice, and if you're venturing off to the outer islands it's often the only way of fuelling yourself. Supplies are always sold by weight (even bread): order by the *chilo, mezzo chilo* (kilo, half kilo) or the *etto* (100g). Bear in mind that food shops are generally open 8.30am–1pm and 4–7pm or thereabouts, and that the great majority are closed all day Sunday. And don't try to picnic in the Piazza – the by-laws against it are strictly enforced.

Open-air **markets** for fruit and vegetables are held in various squares every day except Sunday; check out **Santa Maria Formosa**, **Santa Margherita**, **Campiello dell'Anconetta**, **Rio Terrà San Leonardo** and the barge moored by **Campo San Barnaba**. The market of markets however is the one at the **Rialto**, where you can buy everything you need for an impromptu feast – wine, cheese (the best stalls in the city are here), fruit, salami, vegetables, and bread from nearby bakers or *alimentari* (delicatessens). The stalls of the Rialto **Erberia** (fruit and vegetables), arranged with wonderful colour sense, are laden at different times of the year with peaches, peppers, apples, artichokes, fresh herbs and salad leaves nameless in English – look out for the produce labelled "Sant'Erasmo", which is grown on the island of that name and is held by many locals to be the best quality. The Rialto market is open Monday to Saturday 8am–1pm, with a few stalls opening again in the late afternoon; the **Pescheria** (fish market) – of no practical interest to picnickers but a sight not to be missed – is closed on Monday as well.

Virtually every parish has its **alimentari** and most of them are good; one to single out, though, is *Aliani Gastronomia* in Ruga Vecchia S. Giovanni (San Polo) – scores of cheeses, meats and salads that'll have you drooling as soon as you're through the door. As you'd expect, the cheaper *alimentari* are those farthest from San Marco – such as the ones along Via Garibaldi, out beyond the Arsenale.

For **local wines**, Venice has three branches of a wine merchant called *La Nave d'Oro*: Calle Lunga S. Maria Formosa 5179 (Castello); Via Garibaldi 1133 (Eastern Districts); and Campo S. Margherita 2897 (Dorsoduro). A bar that sells **draught Veneto wine to take out** is to be found in deepest Dorsoduro, a few minutes' walk from San Nicolò dei Mendicoli at the northern end of Fondamenta dell'Arziere. The wine bars *Al Volto, Do Mori, Do Spade* and *Cantina del Vino* (see p236–37) boast comprehensive cellars, and many *alimentari* have an

Eating and drinking

Eating and drinking

impressive choice of wines – there's a marvellous selection in the one in Salizzada San Rocco, round the back of the Frari (San Polo).

Alternatively, you could get everything from one of Venice's well-hidden **supermarkets**. Most central is *Su.Ve.*, on the corner of Salizzada San Lio and Calle Mondo Nuovo (Castello); others are tucked between houses 3019 and 3112 on Campo Santa Margherita (Dorsoduro), on Rio Terrà Frari (San Polo) and Záttere Ponte Lungo, close to the docks (Dorsoduro). The last is the largest and cheapest. They have similar hours – approximately 8.30am–12.30pm and 3–7.30pm.

Chapter 13

Nightlife, the arts and festivals

As recently as just one generation ago Venice was a night city, where the residents of each parish set out tables on the street at the flimsiest excuse. Nowadays, with the pavements overrun by outsiders, the social life of the Venetians is more of an indoor business – a restaurant meal or a drink with friends might feature in most people's diary for the week, and a conversational stroll is certainly a favourite Venetian pastime, but home entertainment takes up most time and energy. That said, Venice's calendar of special events is pretty impressive, with the Carnevale, the Film Festival and the Biennale ranking among the continent's hottest dates. To find out what's on in the way of concerts and films, check *Un Ospite di Venezia*, a free bilingual magazine available from the tourist office and some hotels – it's produced weekly in peak season, monthly in winter. For news of events outside the mainstream, check the posters.

Music and theatre

Music in Venice, to all intents and purposes, means classical music – rock bands rarely come nearer than Padua, and big names stop at Verona. The top-bracket **music venues** are **La Fenice** on Campo S. Fantin (☎521.0161) and the **Teatro Goldoni** in Calle Goldoni (☎520.5422), both in the San Marco *sestiere*. The third-ranking Italian opera house after Milan's La Scala and Naples' San Carlo, La Fenice isn't quite as expensive as some other such establishments, but it isn't in the international first division any more either. Tickets start at about L15,000, though for the exciting stuff, such as a visit by the Kirov, you've about as much chance of a seat as you have of a private audience with the pope. In addition to the main auditorium, La Fenice contains the Sale Apollinee, a hall used for concerts of more limited appeal – recitals of Messiaen, for instance. Music performances at the Goldoni are somewhat less frequent than at La Fenice; the repertoire here isn't as straitlaced, with a jazz series cropping up every now and then. The Fenice and Goldoni box offices are both open 9.30am–12.30pm & 4–6pm.

Classical concerts are also performed at the **Palazzo Prigione Vecchie**, the **Scuola Grande di San Giovanni Evangelista** and the churches of **Santo Stefano**, the **Frari** and the **Pietà**. The last has excellent acoustics and is the most regularly used of the group, but the cheapest seats are in the same range as La Fenice's, which the quality of the concerts doesn't often justify. The state radio service records concerts at the **Palazzo Labia**, to which the public are admitted free of charge, as long as seats are reserved in advance (☎716.666).

For most of the year the *Goldoni* specialises in the works of the eponymous writer. Until restoration of the Malibran theatre is completed, the city has just one other **theatre**: the **Ridotto** in Calle Vallaresso (San Marco; ☎ 522.2939), which stages predominantly twentieth-century plays.

Up beat and down market from the theatre and classical concerts, some **bars** have live music: the main ones are *Paradiso Perduto* and *Ai Canottieri* in Cannaregio, and *Da Codroma* in Dorsoduro (see p.234, 236 & 237 for addresses). They don't charge for entrance, but a mark-up on the drinks pays for the bands.

Cinema

English-language films are the basic fare for Venice's moviegoers, but virtually every screening is dubbed rather than subtitled. If you fancy brushing up your Italian on a rainy night, the cinemas are as follows:

Accademia, Calle Corfù, Dorsoduro 1019 ☎ 528.7706. By the Accademia; mixture of general release and art-house films.

Centrale, Piscina da Frezzeria, San Marco 1659 ☎ 522.8201. Mainstream programmes.

Olimpia, Campo San Gallo, San Marco 1094 ☎ 520.5439. Just north of the Piazza; similar repertoire to the *Accademia*.

Ritz, Calle dei Segretaria, San Marco 617 ☎ 520.4429. By S. Giuliano; general release.

Rossini, Calle delle Muneghe, San Marco 4000 ☎ 523.0322. Facing church of S. Luca; general release.

The Film Festival

The **Venice Film Festival**, founded in 1932 as a propaganda showcase for Mussolini's hi-tech Italy, is the world's oldest and the most important in Europe after Cannes. Originally the festival had no competitive element, but with the creation of the *Leon d'Oro* (the Golden Lion) in 1949, the organisers created a focal point for the rivalries that beset this narcissistic business. Spike Lee is far from being the only director to feel slighted by a biased jury. In the student-orchestrated turmoil of 1968 the *Leon d'Oro* was deemed to be an insult to the workers of Venice, and it was only in 1980 that the trophy was reinstated. Now every Festival is beset with rows between directors of differing political persuasions and vehement disputes over the programming.

The Film Festival takes place on the Lido every year in **late August and early September**. Posters advertising the Festival's schedule appear weeks in advance, and the tourist office will have the festival programme a fair time before the event, as will the two cinemas where the films are shown – the main **Palazzo del Cinemà** on Lungomare G. Marconi (☎ 526.0188) and the **Astra** on Via Corfù (☎ 526.0289). Tickets are available for the general public, but you have to go along and queue for them on the day of performance; the *Carta Giovani* (see p.27) will get you a discount. Outside the festival season, the *Palazzo* and *Astra* are run as ordinary commercial cinemas.

Discos, clubs and casinos

There's only one mainstream **disco** in central Venice – *El Souk*, in Calle Corfù, two minutes' walk from the Accademia. It's a "Pub American Bar" from 10am to 8pm (closed Sat afternoon and Sun), and a disco from 10pm to 2 or 3am (closed Sun). Only those deemed by the doorman to be fit for admission get to pay the entrance charge of L15,000, a fee that includes the price of your first drink. In Calle Lionpardo, just off Rio Terrà San Leonardo (Cannaregio), there's a **women-only** disco, *La Casa Gialla* (Fri–Sun 7pm–late).

The much-hyped *Martini*, Campo S. Fantin (San Marco) is more of a smarmy nightclub, all plastic money and that'll do nicely sir (10pm–3.30am; closed Tues & Nov–Jan). There's also a tiny disco over on the Lido, *Nuova Acropolis*, Lungomare Marconi 22 (closed Tues); it's packed with the people who have spent the day on the Lido beaches. If these don't appeal, you'll have to hop over the causeway into miserable Mestre, whose identikit discos are listed in the local press.

If you're feeling flush and lucky, and can sport a neatly pressed Armani number, then you could roll along to the **Casinò** (daily 3pm–2.30am). From October to March it's at the Palazzo Vendramin-Calergi (Cannaregio) on the Canal Grande; in summer it migrates to the Lido's Palazzo del Casinò on Lungomare Marconi, served by the #2 vaporetto.

Special exhibitions – and the Biennale

As if the profusion of galleries, museums and picture-stuffed churches weren't enough, Venice boasts a phalanx of venues for **special exhibitions**. Listed below are the places where you'll find the first-rank shows, with an indication of the themes favoured by each venue – look in *Un Ospite di Venezia* for details of fringe events, and take note of advertising posters and banners.

Archivio di Stato (San Polo): Venetian history.

Ca' Pésaro (San Polo): modern art.

Fondazione Cini, on San Giorgio Maggiore (Southern Islands): art history.

Guggenheim (Dorsoduro): modern art.

Museo Correr (San Marco): specifically Venetian exhibitions in the main part of the building; other art shows in the Ala Napoleonica.

Museo Fortuny (San Marco): design and photography.

Museo Guidi (Castello): modern art – generally dreadful.

Palazzo Ducale (San Marco): art history, ethnology and archaeology.

Palazzo Grassi (San Marco): cultural themes, as diverse as Celtic civilisation and Futurist arts.

Querini-Stampalia (Castello): art history.

Scuola Grande di San Giovanni Evangelista (San Polo): photography, video, technology as applied to the arts.

Scuola Grande di San Teodoro (San Marco): modern and applied art – often tacky.

Contemporary private galleries in Venice are generally timorous affairs; again, look in *Un Ospite* for their latest offerings. A handful stand out against a background of dross, all of them in the *sestiere* of San Marco:

Bugno & Samueli, Campo San Fantin.
Capricorno, Calle dietro della Chiesa, near San Fantin.
Cavallino, Frezzeria.
Luce, Campiello della Fenice.
Santo Stefano, Campo Santo Stefano.
Traghetto, Campo Santa Maria del Giglio.

The Biennale

The Venice **Biennale**, Europe's most glamorous international forum for contemporary art, was first held in 1895 as the city's contribution to the celebrations for the silver wedding anniversary of King Umberto I and Margherita of Savoy. In the early years the exhibits were dominated by standard academic painting, despite the presence of such artists as Ensor, Klimt and Whistler. Since World War II, however, the Biennale has become a self-consciously avant-garde event, a transformation symbolised by the award of the major Biennale prize in 1964 to Robert Rauschenberg, the enfant terrible of the American art scene. The French contingent campaigned vigorously against the nomination of this New World upstart, and virtually every Biennale since then has been characterised by the sort of controversy that is now endemic in the publicity-addicted art circuit.

After years of occurring in even-numbered years, the Biennale has shifted back to being held **every odd-numbered year from June to September**, so that a centenary show can be held in 1995. It will continue to occupy its site in the Giardini Pubblici, with permanent pavilions for about forty countries plus space for a thematic international exhibition. Supplementing this central part of the Biennale is the *Aperto* ("Open"), a mixed exhibition showing the work of younger or less established artists – often more exciting than the main event. The *Aperto* takes over spaces all over the city: the salt warehouses on the Záttere, for instance, or the

Corderie in the Arsenale. In addition, various sites throughout the city host fringe exhibitions, installations and performances, particularly in the opening weeks. There are also plans to utilise the pavilions in even-numbered years by instituting an independent Biennale for **architecture**, a discipline whose practitioners have played an increasingly active role in the main Biennale – Aldo Rossi's floating *Teatro del Mondo*, for example, was the showstopper of the 1980 festival.

Exhibits from earlier years, plus a fabulous collection of magazines and catalogues from all over the world, are kept in the **archive** in the Palazzo Corner della Regina (close to Ca' Pésaro); entrance is free. The San Marco tourist office should be able to give you all the information you need, but if not try the Biennale administrative headquarters, in the Ca' Giustinian in Calle Vallaresso (San Marco).

Festivals

Venice enthusiastically celebrates a number of special days either not observed elsewhere in Italy, or, like the Carnevale, celebrated to a lesser extent. Although they have gone through various degrees of decline and revival, the form they take now is still related very strongly to their traditional character.

Carnevale

John Evelyn wrote of the 1646 Carnevale: "all the world was in Venice to see the folly and madness . . . the women, men and persons of all conditions disguising themselves in antique dresses, & extravagant Musique & a thousand gambols." Not much is different in today's Carnevale, for which people arrive in such numbers that the causeway from the mainland has sometimes had to be closed because the city has been too packed.

The origins of the Carnevale can be traced in the word itself: *carne vale*, a "farewell to meat" before the rigours of Lent – the same origin as the tamer British custom of eating pancakes on Shrove Tuesday. The medieval European carnival developed into a period when the world could be turned over – a time of licence for those normally constrained by rank, and a means of quelling discontent by a ritualised relinquishing of power. Venice's Carnevale can be related to the surrender of power on a wider scale, as the festival's heyday – the eighteenth century – coincided with the terminal decline of the Republic. The eighteenth-century Carnevale officially began on December 26, lasting for nearly two months until Shrove Tuesday; aspects of it, such as the wearing of masks, stretched into the rest of the year, until Carnevale unofficially continued for six months.

Today's Carnevale is limited to the **ten days leading up to Lent**, finishing on Shrove Tuesday with a masked ball for the glitterati, and dancing in the Piazza for the plebs. It was revived in 1979 by a group of non-Venetians, and soon gained support from the canny city authorities, who now organise various pageants and performances. (Details from the San Marco tourist office.) Apart from these events, Carnevale is very much a case of see and be seen. During the day people don costumes and go down to the Piazza to be photographed; parents dress up their kids; businessmen can be seen doing their shopping in the classic white mask, black cloak and tricorne hat. In the evening some congregate in the remoter squares, while those who have spent literally hundreds of pounds on their costumes install themselves in the windows of *Florian's* and pose for a while before making an exit with an adoring entourage. But you don't need to spend money or try to be "traditional" in your disguise: a simple black outfit and a painted face is enough to transform you from a spectator into a participant.

Masks are on sale throughout the year in Venice, but new mask and costume shops suddenly appear during Carnevale, when Campo San Maurizio sprouts a marquee with mask-making demonstrations and a variety of designs for sale. For the best stockists, see p.248.

La Sensa

The feast of **La Sensa** happens in May on the **Sunday after Ascension Day** – the latter being the day on which the doge enacted the wedding of Venice to the sea (see p.209). The ritual has recently been revived – a distinctly feeble procession which ends with the mayor and a gang of other dignitaries getting into a present-day approximation of the *Bucintoro* (the state barge) and sailing off to the Lido. Of more interest is the **Vogalonga** (long row), held on the same day. Open to any crew in any class of rowing boat, it covers a 32-kilometre course from the Bacino di San Marco out to Burano and back; the competitors arrive at the bottom of the Canal Grande anywhere between about 11am and 3pm.

Festa del Redentore

The **Festa del Redentore** is one of Venice's plague-related festivals, marking the end of the epidemic of 1576. Celebrated on the **third Sunday in July**, the day is centred on Palladio's church of the Redentore, which was built by way of thanksgiving for the city's escape. A bridge of boats is strung across the Giudecca canal to allow the faithful to walk over to the church, and on the Saturday night hundreds of people row out for a picnic on the water. The night ends with a grand fireworks display, after which it's traditional to row to the Lido for the sunrise.

The Regata Storica

Held on the **first Sunday in September**, the **Regata Storica** is the annual trial of strength and skill for the city's gondoliers and other expert rowers. It starts with a procession of richly decorated historic craft along the Canal Grande course, their crews all decked out in period dress. Bystanders are expected to join in the support for the contestants in the main event, and may even be issued with appropriate colours. Other *regate* are held throughout the year in various parts of the lagoon, the main ones being the **Regata di S. Zanipolo** (June), the **Regata di Pellestrina** (Aug) and the **Regata di Burano** (Sept).

La Salute

Named after the church of the Salute, the **Festa della Salute** is a reminder of the plague of 1630–31, which killed one third of the population of the lagoon. The church was built in thanks for deliverance from the outbreak, and every **November 21** since then the Venetians have processed over a pontoon bridge across the Canal Grande to give thanks for their good health, or to pray for sick friends and relatives. It offers the only chance to see the church as it was designed to be seen – with its main doors open and hundreds of people milling up the steps.

Chapter 14

Shopping

The torpor of Venice after dark is inversely proportional to the hustle of its shopping streets in the daytime, where vast sums are trawled daily from the tourists' pockets. It's easy to get the impression that Venice's shops are polarised at two extremes – geared either to the trinket trade or to expense-account fashion and accessories. The middle ground does exist, however, and it doesn't take too much ferreting around to find it: small workshops all over the city produce a range of reasonably priced items such as bags, masks and decorative papers; unusual prints and books are on sale in a number of shops; and there's even the odd bargain to be picked up amid the antique stalls.

Antiques

Although the antiques shops around **San Maurizio** and **Santa Maria Zobenigo** cater for the wealthier collectors, bargain hunters should be able to pick something up at the **antiques fairs** that crop up throughout the year in Campo San Maurizio, where the stalls groan under the weight of old books, prints, silverware and general bric-a-brac. (The tourist office will be able to tell you if one is due.) The traders in the **San Barnabà** district are also slightly down-market, running the kind of places where you could find a faded wooden cherub or an old picture frame.

The **auction house** in the Palazzo Giovanelli, near Santa Fosca (Cannaregio) is good for a browse on their viewing days, too, even if you can't afford to join in the bidding (see p.137).

Art materials

Should you want to add your own contribution to the stockpile of visual images of Venice, all the necessary materials can be bought in the city. The best-known supplier is *Testolino* on Fondamenta Orseolo, north of the Piazza, though *Seguso*, in nearby Calle dei Fabbri, is almost as good. Three other general suppliers are in Campiello di Ca' Zen on the north side of the Rio dei Frari (San Polo), at Crosera S. Pantalon 3954 (San Polo), and at Campo S. Margherita 2928 (Dorsoduro). *Pontini*, off Campo Anconetta (Cannaregio) sells stretched and primed canvases, while *Renato Burelli*, Calle Lunga San Barnaba (Dorsoduro) is the place to go for pigments, media with which to mix them and varnishes. Pigment is also sold on Burano, in a shop on Via Galuppi that has two numbers, 194 and 310; it's immediately recognisable by the old copper pots in the window.

Books

Alberto Bertoni, Rio Terrà degli Assassini, San Marco 3637/b. For remaindered and secondhand books, including a number of art-book bargains.

Cluva, Campo dei Tolentini, Santa Croce 197. Situated next to the university's architecture department, this unsurprisingly is the most comprehensive stockist of books on architecture.

Shopping

Fantoni, Salizzada S. Luca, San Marco 4121. For the glossiest, weightiest and most expensive art books.

Filippi Editore Venezia, Calle della Bissa (San Marco 5458) and Calle del Paradiso (Castello 5762). Has an amazing stock of books about Venice in Italian, and also produces a vast range of facsimile editions, including Francesco Sansovino's sixteenth-century guide to the city – the first city guide ever published.

Goldoni, Calle dei Fabbri, San Marco 4742. The best general bookshop in the city; also keeps an array of maps and posters.

Libreria della Toletta, Sacca della Toletta, Dorsoduro 1214. Sells reduced-price books, mainly in Italian, but some dual language and translations.

Libreria Serenissima, Merceria dell'Orologio, San Marco 739. Has an impressive selection of books on Venice in English and a good choice of maps.

Sangiorgio, Calle Larga XXII Marzo, San Marco 2087. A small but well-stocked art bookshop.

Sansovino, Bacino Orseolo, San Marco 84. Second only to *Fantoni* for books on art.

Clothes

As you'd expect, many of the top-flight Italian designers – Versace, Missoni, Valentino, Krizia, Armani – are represented in Venice, most of their outlets being clustered within a street or two of the Piazza. For those with wallets as deep as oil wells, the **Mercerie**, **Frezzeria**, **Calle Larga XXII Marzo** and the area around **La Fenice** are the most fruitful zones.

For good quality, moderately priced clothes, there's the inevitable *Benetton* and *Stefanel* (both in the Mercerie), and *Coin*, a national department store based in Venice. *Coin*'s home branch specialises in clothing, and is located between the Rialto and San Giovanni Crisostomo. The area **between Campo San Bartolomeo and Santi Apostoli** is well supplied with shops aimed at a young clientele, as is the line of streets running from **Ruga Vecchia San Giovanni to San Polo**, on the other side of the Canal Grande.

More idiosyncratic stuff is sold at *Lespritznuvo* on Campo S. Margherita (Dorsoduro), where they design, make up and decorate their own clothes. The wacky jackets at *Fiorella*, on Campo S. Stefano (San Marco), are beautifully made and wittily displayed – the mannequins have female bodies but their faces are modelled on portraits of the doges. *Aldo Strasse*, Campo S. Giustina detta da Barbara (Castello) is good for **trendy secondhand clothes** and some new pieces, too. You can buy mock gondolier's hats everywhere, but for the real McCoy, as well as the shirts, jackets and trousers, go to *Emilio Ceccato* in Sottoportego di Rialto (San Polo).

Glass

As with lace, for Venetian **glass** you're better off going to the main source of production, in this case **Murano**. The Piazza and its environs are prowled by well-groomed young characters offering free boat trips to the island – on account accept, as you'll be subjected to a relentless hard sell on arrival. If you are in the market, just take the vaporetto to the Colonna stop and follow your eyes: the most expensive and most pretentious shops are to the fore, the rest stretched out beyond. Pseudo-artistic ornaments, extortionately expensive tableware and ranks of eye-bruising kitsch – a life-size bush with a cast of glass parrots – make up the bulk of the stock. The further you wander from the landing-stage, the more likely you are to find nicer pieces. The pick of the showrooms for more portable glass objects are listed below: unless stated otherwise, they are on Murano.

For more on Murano glass, see p.194.

Barovier & Tosio, Fondamenta Vetrai 28. Family-run firm which can trace its roots back to the fourteenth century. Predominantly traditional designs.

Ercole Moretti, Fondamenta Navagero 42. Good for glass jewellery.

L'Isola, Salizzada San Moisè 1468 and Mercerie 723 (both San Marco). Showcase for the best modernist glassware.

Seguso, Ponte Vivarini 138. Renowned for its opaque, pseudo-antique glassware.

Shopping

Venini, Fondamenta Vetrai 50 (Murano) and Piazzetta dei Leoncini 314 (San Marco). One of the more adventurous producers, *Venini* often employs designers from other fields of the applied arts.

Jewellery

Al Canale, Ruga Rialto, San Polo. Ceramic jewellery.

Codognato, Calle dell'Ascensione, San Marco 1295. One of the city's most expensive outlets, selling everything from antique pieces through to Art Deco brooches and modern designs.

La Ciotola, Crosera S. Pantalon, S. Polo. Ceramic buttons, clips and earrings made on the premises.

Missiaglia, Piazza San Marco, San Marco 125. Peerless gold and silver work from a firm that has a good claim to be Venice's classiest.

Nardi, Piazza San Marco, San Marco 69–71. Coral, tortoiseshell, ebony and other environment-abusing materials are the keynote of Nardi's production. Also makes some less objectionable if similarly overwrought gold objects.

Oggetti d'Arte "M", Calle Brentana, San Marco 1689. Very expensive outlet for luscious jewellery derived from Art Nouveau designs, and for similarly expensive old-fashioned dresses and fabrics.

Paolo Scarpa, Merceria S. Salvador, San Marco 4850. Gallery-like shop specialising in "primitive" jewellery from all corners of the planet.

Totem, Rio Terrà Foscarini, Dorsoduro 878/b. African jewellery and Africa-inspired pieces by Venetian artisans.

Lace

For more on Burano lace, see p.199.

It's cheaper to buy **lace** on **Burano** than in the centre of Venice, but be warned that the cheapest stuff is machine-made and not from Burano either. The handmade work sold at the island's Scuola dei Merletti is expensive, though not to a degree that's disproportionate to the hours and labour that go into making it. If you want an inexpensive example of the work, a little butterfly goes for about L10,000. In **Venice** itself, the most impressive shop is *Jesurum* at Ponte Canonica, installed in a converted church at the rear of the Basilica di San Marco. Small hand-embroidered lace and linen gifts are sold at *Annelie*, Calle Lunga S. Barnaba (Dorsoduro).

Masks

Many of the Venetian masks on sale today are derived from the Carnevale of old: the ones representing characters from the *Commedia dell'Arte* (Pierrot, Harlequin, Columbine) for example, and the classic white half-mask called a *volto*, with a kind of beak over the mouth so the wearer could eat and drink. Although masks are worn only during the ten days of Carnevale, they are on sale all year round; most designs are conveyor-belt stuff which you'll soon recognise – for genuinely crafted examples, go to one of the following.

Emile Massaro, Calle Vitturi, San Marco 2934. Massaro sells his stuff to retailers all over the city – buy them at his workshop, near Campo Santo Stefano, and you'll save the mark-up.

Laboratorio Artigiano Maschere, Barbaria delle Tole, Castello 6657. Founded by Giorgio Clanetti, who is from a family of puppet-makers, this workshop is the place where the revival of traditional Venetian masks began.

Mondonovo, Rio Terrà Canal, Dorsoduro 3063. Just off Campo S. Margherita, this innovative workshop doubles as a theatrical costumier.

Paulo Vasques, Corte Lucatello, near San Giuliano; San Marco. Vasques paints his masks using painstaking traditional techniques.

Prints, cards and paper

The best range of **posters and inexpensive prints** is at *Antonio Porto* on Rio Terrà dei Nomboli (San Polo). *Goldoni* (see "Books") also carries a selection of posters. *Segno Grafico* on Campo S. Fantin (San Marco) is a print workshop and gallery that sells **hand-printed book-**

Shopping

lets and pamphlets, many of them related to the history of the city. For reprints of old topographical engravings of Venice at very moderate prices, visit the Armenian island of **San Lazzaro** (see p.215).

Postcards are on sale everywhere, though the fund of images isn't as imaginative as it could be. Just inside the Basilica di San Marco there's a stall selling a vast spread of good quality cards of the church and its mosaics, but Venice's museums are a letdown, usually offering a choice of a bare half dozen. For something a little more unusual try *Filippi Editore Venezia* (see "Books") or *ZWF* on Campiello Meloni (San Polo).

Most of the decorative **paper** on sale in Venice comes from Florence or is affiliated to or inspired by Florentine producers, but is none the worse for that. Shops selling these marbled papers, notebooks and so forth are all over the city; more idiosyncratic stuff is sold at the following places.

Alberto Valese, Salizzada S. Samueie, San Marco 3135. not only produces the most luscious marbled papers in Venice, but also transfers the designs onto silk scarves and a variety of ornaments; the marbling technique he uses is a Turkish process called ebrû – which is the name given to Valese's other branch, at Calle del Teatro, San Marco 1920, by the side of the Fenice.

Arcumbè, Ponte S. Barnaba, Dorsoduro 2806. Produces a style of patterned paper known as "cat's eye", using a process that involves mixing ink and algae.

Legatoria Piazzesi, Campiello della Feltrina, San Marco 2511. Located near Santa Maria Zobenigo, this is the only truly Venetian paper-producer left in the city, using old wooden blocks to produce some stunning hand-printed papers and cards; they do a nice line in pocket diaries, too.

Paolo Olbi, Calle della Mandola, San Marco 3653. The founder of this shop was largely responsible for the revival of paper marbling; today it sells a whole range of marbled stationery.

Polliero, Campo dei Frari, San Polo 2995. A bookbinding workshop that sells patterned paper as well as heavy, leather-bound albums of handmade plain paper.

Serigrafia Grafco, just off the west side of Campo S. Pantalon, Santa Croce 4/b. Patterns from Venetian textiles applied to paper and other materials.

Shoes and leather

As far as chic shoes, bags and wallets go, the shops around the **Mercerie** are not as expensive as they might first appear, and sales are a regular occurrence. *Zecchi*, right beside the Torre dell'Orologio, has some of the cheapest high-class leather footwear, and it's worth checking the windows at the other end of the Mercerie and round Sant'Aponal (San Polo). Velour slippers in a variety of colours are sold in a number of shoe shops and gift shops; perhaps derived from Commedia dell'Arte costume, they're made at *La Pantofola* in Calle della Mandola (San Marco).

If money is no object, go browsing between Calle dell'Ascensione and the far end of Calle Larga XXII Marzo, where names such as *Vogini, Bottega Veneta* and *Delmo* uphold the city's reputation as a market for immaculately produced leather goods. Superbly rugged handcrafted purses, bags and cases are sold by *Pietro Gradenigo*, whose one-man workshop is in Calle Seconda Saoneri (San Polo). Similar items can be found at a trio of shops in Dorsoduro – Salizzada Ca' Fóscari 3856, Campo Squellini 3234, and Campo S. Margherita 2946 – but *Gradenigo* is the best of the bunch.

Miscellaneous

If you can't be bothered to chase out to the islands to look for glass and lace, or traipse round Venice looking for out-of-the-way craft shops, try *Venziartigiana* in Calle Larga San Marco (San Marco), which sets itself up as the showcase for Venice's **craft-workers**. It's by no means fully representative, though, and even those it does represent are better stocked at their own bases.

All manner of small **hand-made gifts** in wood, tapestry and various other materials can be found at *Toti Campizi* in Calle Marcello, off Campo S. Marina (Castello). Jigsaw-like wooden objects – musical instruments, palace facades – are sold by *Signor Blum* on Campo San Barnaba (Dorsoduro) and Salizzada S. Samuele (San Marco). Somewhat stranger wooden creations are on sale from the workshop of Livio de Marchi, also in Salizzada S. Samuele; life-sized battered shoes and hanging items of underwear are among the more portable items, and if you have the transport you could take back a gigantic bundle of wooden asparagus. Model kits and elegantly drawn plans for **Venetian boats** are sold at *La Scialuppa*, Calle Seconda Saoneri (San Polo).

Lastly, aficionados of souvenir **kitsch** can have a field day around the main tourist traps, especially the Lista di Spagna (Cannaregio): plastic gondolas set against blurred photos and fixed in illuminated plastic frames; gondolas that play *O Sole Mio*, gondola cigarette-lighters . . . the list is endless.

Chapter 15

Directory

ACTV INQUIRIES For *ACTV* land buses ring ☎528.7886; for information on *ACTV* water buses, ring ☎700.310.

AIRLINES *Alitalia*, Salizzada San Moisè, San Marco 1463 ☎520.0355; *British Airways*, Riva degli Schiavoni, Castello 4191 ☎528.5026; *TWA*, Salizzada San Moisè, San Marco 1475 ☎520.3219.

AIRPORT INQUIRIES Marco Polo airport, ☎661.262.

AMERICAN EXPRESS The *American Express* office in Salizzada S. Moisè (a couple of minutes' walk west of the Piazza), is useful for changing cash or travellers' cheques out of office hours (Mon–Sat 8am–8pm; ☎520.0844).

BANKS Banks in Venice are concentrated on Calle Larga XXII Marzo (west of the Piazza), and along the chain or squares and alleyways between Campo San Bartolomeo and Campo Manin (in the north of the San Marco *sestiere*). There's not much to choose between them in terms of commission and exchange rates, and their hours are generally Mon–Fri 8.30am–1.30pm and 3–4pm. The main ones are as follows:

Banca Commerciale Italiana, Calle Larga XXII Marzo, San Marco 2188.

Banca d'America e d'Italia, Calle Larga XXII Marzo, San Marco 2216.

Banca d'Italia, Campo San Bartolomeo, San Marco 4799.

Banca Credito Italiano, Campo San Salvador, San Marco.

Banco Ambrosiano Veneto, Calle Goldoni, San Marco 4481.

Banco di Napoli, Campo San Gallo, Bacino Orseolo, San Marco 112.

Banco di Roma, Mercerie dell'Orologio, San Marco 191.

Banco San Marco, Calle Larga XXII Marzo, San Marco 383.

BEACHES The Lido has two public beaches, at the northern and southern extremities of the island. The southern is the less crowded; better still, go down to Sottomarina, in the south of the lagoon (see p.215).

CAR RENTAL At Marco Polo airport: *Autorent* ☎541.5675; *Avis* ☎541.5030; *Europcar* ☎541.5092; *International Rent-a-Car* ☎541.5540; *InterRent* ☎541.5570; *Mini Rent a Car* ☎541.5675. At Piazzale Roma: *Autorent* ☎520.4880; *Avis* ☎522.5825; *Europcar* ☎523.8616; *InterRent* ☎523.8558; *Mattiazzo* ☎520.5910. The cheapest rates are those offered by *Europcar*.

CHILDREN Children can get fatigued easily in Venice. If the various squares don't appeal as playgrounds, you could try the Giardini Pubblici or the Lido's beaches. A long boat trip often works wonders too, as does a visit to the city's aquarium (see the list of museums). Hotels normally charge around 30 percent extra to put a bed or cot in your room.

CIGARETTES You buy cigarettes (and tobacco) in shops called *tabacchi*, which distinguish themselves by a sign outside with a T on it. Historically, tobacco and salt were both state monopolies, sold only in *tabacchi* – salt's no longer

Directory

deemed so important, but cigarettes are still hard to track down anywhere else.

CONSULATES AND EMBASSIES The British consulate is in the Palazzo Querini, Accademia, Dorsoduro 1051 ☎522.7207. The nearest US consulate is in Milan, at Largo Donegani 1 ☎02/290.351. Travellers from Ireland, Australia, New Zealand and Canada should contact their Rome embassies: Irish embassy, Via Largo Nazareno 3 ☎06/678.2541; Australian Embassy, Via Alessandria 215 ☎06/832.721; New Zealand Embassy, Via Zara 28 ☎06/440.2928; Canadian Embassy, Via G. B. de Rossi 27 ☎06/841.5341.

ELECTRICITY The supply is 220 volts AC, but anything requiring 240V will work. Most plugs are two round pins: a travel plug is useful.

EMERGENCIES For all emergency services ring ☎113. Alternatively, dialling ☎112 puts you straight through to the *Carabinieri* (police) and ☎115 goes straight to the *Vigili del Fuoco* (fire brigade).

EXCHANGE There are clusters of exchange bureaux (*cambio*) where most tourists gather – near San Marco, the Rialto and the train station. Open late every day of the week, they can be useful in emergencies, but their rates of commission and exchange tend to be steep. The best rates are at *American Express* and the main banks (see opposite).

HOSPITAL *Ospedale Civile*, Campo Santi Giovanni e Paolo ☎520.5622.

LAUNDRIES In Salizzada del Pistor, Cannaregio 4553, near Santi Apostoli; or on Fondamenta Pescaria, Cannaregio 1269, off Rio Terrà San Leonardo.

LEFT LUGGAGE Train station left luggage desk open 24hr; L1500 per item.

LOST PROPERTY If you lose anything on the train or at the station, call ☎716.122 (ext. 3238); on the vaporetti call ☎780.310; and anywhere in the city itself call the town hall on ☎520.8844.

NEWSPAPERS You'll find the main national newspapers on any newsstand: *La Repubblica* is middle-to-left with a lot of cultural coverage; *Il Corriere della Sera* is authoritative and rather right-wing; *L'Unità* is the Communist Party organ; and *Il Manifesto*, a more radical left-wing daily. Venice's local papers are the *Gazzettino* and *Nuova Venezia* (good for listings). More widely read than any, however, is the pink *Gazzettino dello Sport*, essential for the serious sports fan. English and American newspapers can be found for around L2000 at the railway station, by the Calle dell'Ascensione post office and at various stands throughout the city – usually a day or two late.

PASSPORTS In the event of a lost passport, notify the Questura on Fondamenta San Lorenzo (☎520.3222) and then your consulate or embassy.

POLICE To notify police of a theft, report to the Questura (see above); in emergencies, ring ☎113.

PORTERS Porters tout for trade at Piazzale Roma and the train station, and at places in the city where luxury hotels are concentrated – such as Riva degli Sciavoni and Calle Larga XXII Marzo. Their charges are officially regulated, and range from around L1000 for carrying one piece of luggage over a distance not exceeding fifty metres, to around L10,000 for carrying up to two pieces between any two points.

POST OFFICES Venice's main post office is in the Fondaco dei Tedeschi, near the Rialto bridge. Any poste restante should be addressed to Fermo Posta, Fondaco dei Tedeschi, 80100 Venezia; it can be collected Mon–Sat 8.15am–6.45pm – take your passport with you. Stamps are on sale Mon–Sat 8.15am–7pm; the telegram service operates round the clock. The principal branch post offices are in Calle dell'Ascensione (Mon–Fri 8.10am–1.25pm, Sat 8.10am–noon) and at Záttere 1406 (same hours). Stamps can also be bought in *tabacchi*, as well as in some gift shops.

PUBLIC SHOWERS For L7000 you can have the use of a shower cubicle at an *Albergo Diurnale* – there's one off Calle dell'Ascensione and one at the train station (both open 9am–7.30pm). For a wash-basin and toilet the charge is L500.

Directory

PUBLIC TOILETS At the train station, at Piazzale Roma, on the west side of the Accademia bridge, by the Giardinetti Reali, off Campo San Bartolomeo, on Calle Erizzo (near S. Martino church) and a few other places; the charge is around L500. Toilets are to be found in all the city's bars as well – it's diplomatic to buy a drink before availing yourself of the facility, but it's not a legal requirement.

TELEPHONES Virtually all Venice's public call-boxes accept phone cards, but for lengthy long distance calls it's best to go to the two main SIP offices, where you can dial direct and be charged afterwards. The offices are at Piazzale Roma (daily 8am–9.30pm) and in the main post office building (daily 8am–8pm).

TIME Italy is always one hour ahead of Britain except for one week at the end of September when the time is the same. Italy is six hours ahead of Eastern Standard Time and nine hours ahead of Pacific Standard Time.

TRAIN INQUIRIES ☎715.555.

TRAVEL AGENTS *Bassani*, Calle Larga XXII Marzo, San Marco 2414 ☎520.8633; *CIT*, Piazza San Marco, San Marco 48 ☎528.5480; *Clementson*, Campo San Provolo, Castello 4709 ☎520.0466; *Kele & Teo*, Ponte dei Bareteri, San Marco 4930 ☎520.8722; *Ital Travel*, Calle dell'Ascensione, San Marco 72 ☎522.9111; *Sattis*, Bocca de Piazza, San Marco 1261 ☎528.5101. The best outlet for low-cost flights and rail tickets from Venice is *CTS*, Fondamenta del Tagliapiera, Dorsoduro 3252 ☎520.5660 – it's right by the university building.

Part 4

The Veneto

Chapter 16

The Veneto: an introduction

Taking its name – as does Venice itself – from the pre-Roman people known as the Veneti, the present-day region of the **Veneto** essentially covers the area that became the core of the Republic's mainland empire. Everywhere in the Veneto you'll find the imprint of Venetian rule. In **Belluno**, right under the crags of the Dolomites, the style of the buildings declares the town's former allegiance. A few kilometres away, the lion of Saint Mark looks over the central square of the hill town of **Feltre**, as it does over the market square of **Verona**, on the Veneto's western edge. On the flatlands of the Po basin (the southern border of the region) and on farming estates all over the Veneto, the elegant **villas** of the Venetian nobility are still standing.

Yet the Veneto is as diverse culturally as it is geographically. The aspects of Verona's urban landscape that make the city so attractive were created long before the expansion of Venice's *terra firma* empire, and in **Padua** – a university seat since the thirteenth century – the civilisation of the Renaissance displays a character quite distinct from that which evolved in Venice. Even in **Vicenza**, which reached its present form mainly during its long period of subservience, the very appearance of the streets is proof of a fundamental independence.

Nowadays this is one of Italy's wealthiest regions. Verona, Padua, Vicenza and **Treviso** are all major industrial and commercial centres, while intensive dairies, fruit farms and vineyards (around Conegliano and Verona especially) have made the Veneto a leading agricultural producer as well. Much of the Veneto's income is earned by the industrial complex of **Mestre** and **Marghera**, the grim concrete conurbation through which all road and rail lines from Venice pass before spreading out over the mainland. It's less a city than an economic life-support system for Venice, and the negative impression you get on your way through is entirely justified. Some people trim their holiday expenses by staying in Mestre's less

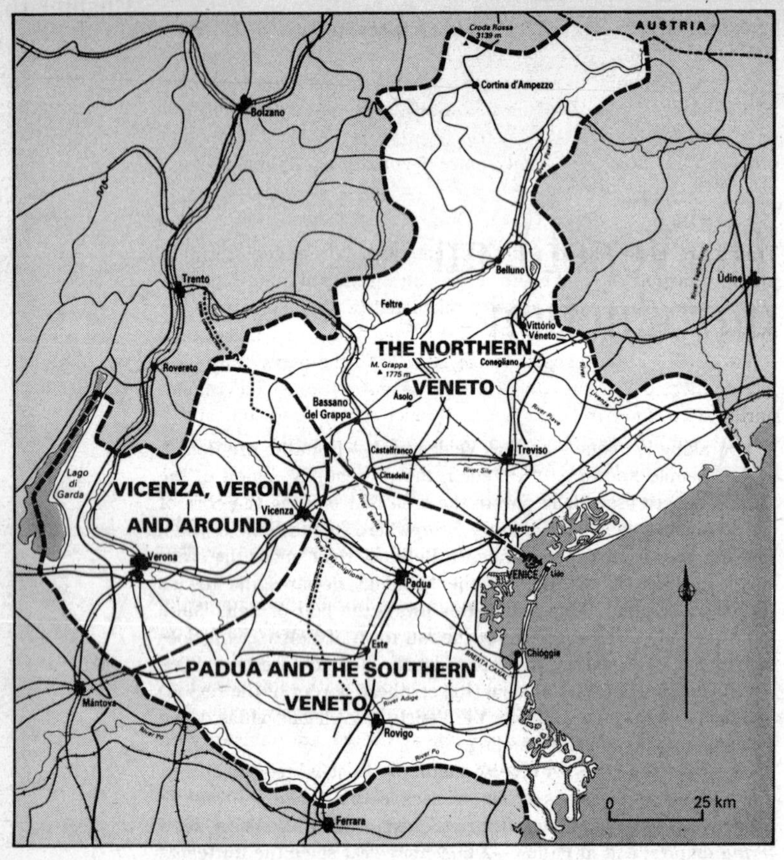

expensive hotels (Venice's tourist offices will supply addresses), but venturing further inland is a far more pleasurable cost-cutting exercise.

The administrative region of the Veneto actually extends right to the Austrian border, taking in the portion of the **Dolomites** known as the Cadore, the main town of which is Pieve di Cadore – Titian's birthplace. Further north still is Cortina d'Ampezzo, the swishest ski resort of the eastern Dolomites since it hosted the Winter Olympics in 1956. This whole area offers some of Italy's most sublime landscapes, but the mountains are quite distinct from Venice's immediate hinterland, and cannot really be visited on an excursion from the city. As the purpose of this section of the guide is to reveal the mainland sights and towns that can be seen on a day's excursion from Venice, its northern limit is Belluno.

Getting Around the Veneto

The Veneto's public transport system will easily get you to almost all the places covered in the following chapters, at generally low cost. In nearly all cases a day-trip from Venice is feasible, though obviously the larger towns need more than a day to do them justice.

By Train

Trains are generally the cheapest and most convenient form of public transport in the Veneto. Prices on the Italian State Railways (*Ferrovie dello Stato* or *FS*) are calculated by the kilometre – for instance, a second-class return ticket from Venice to Bassano, a round trip of 122km, costs around L8000. All the major towns are interconnected: one main line runs from Venice through Treviso and northwards, another through Castelfranco up to Bassano, and a third through Padua, Vicenza and Verona. Frequencies of services are given in the box below and in the text, but bear in mind that comments such as "every half-hour" are approximations – as with all Italian train services, there are occasional gaps in the schedule, typically occurring just after the morning rush-hour, when the gap between trains may be twice as long as normal.

There are now six types of train in Italy. Top of the range is the **ETR 450 "Pendolino"**, an exclusively first-class inter-city service on which your ticket includes seat reservation, newspapers and a meal. **Eurocity** trains connect the major Italian cities with centres such as Paris, Vienna, Hamburg and Barcelona, while **Intercity** trains link the Italian centres with each other; reservations are obligatory on both of these services, and a supplement in the region of 30 percent of the ordinary fare is payable. (Make sure you pay your supplement before getting on board – you'll have to cough up a far bigger surcharge to the conductor). **Espresso** trains are the common-or-garden long-distance expresses, calling only at larger stations; then come the **Diretto** trains, stopping at most stations; and lastly there are the **Locale** services, which stop at every place with a population higher than zero.

The main routes (*Espresso* and upwards) are covered by *FS*'s little national pocket book, *Principali Treni*, issued twice yearly and free from most railway stations, but if you're travelling extensively by train you should pick up the free *FS* leaflets detailing individual lines (readily available from the larger stations). Pay attention to the timetable notes, which may specify the dates between which some services run (*Si effetua dal . . . al . . .*), or whether a service is seasonal (*periódico*).

A word of warning. Some stations have now installed machines in which passengers should stamp their ticket immediately before embarking on the return leg of a journey. Look out for them at the end of the platform – if you fail to validate your ticket at a station

Main Veneto Train Services

Belluno to: Calalzo (10 daily; 1hr); Conegliano (15 daily; 1hr–1hr 30min); Vittorio Veneto (15 daily; 30min).

Conegliano to: Belluno (15 daily; 1hr–1hr 30min); Udine (30 daily; 1hr 15min); Venice (34 daily; 1hr); Vittorio Veneto (15 daily; 25min).

Monsélice to: Venice (6 daily; 50min); Padua (9 daily; 20min); Montagnana (9 daily; 25min); Este (9 daily; 10min).

Padua to: Bassano (10 daily; 1hr 5min); Belluno (12 daily; 2hr); Feltre (12 daily; 50min); Milan (25 daily; 2hr 30min); Monsélice (9 daily; 25min); Rovigo (hourly; 40min); Venice (every 30min; 35min); Verona (25 daily; 55min); Vicenza (25 daily; 20min).

Rovigo to: Venice (22 daily; 90min); Padua (22 daily; 40min).

Treviso to: Castelfranco Veneto (hourly; 25min); Cittadella (hourly; 35min); Udine (hourly; 1hr 10min–1hr 30min); Venice (30 daily; 30min); Vicenza (hourly; 1hr).

Venice to: Bassano (14 daily; 1hr); Belluno (1 daily; 2hr); Castelfranco Veneto (at least every 2hr; 50min); Conegliano (34 daily; 1hr); Milan (25 daily; 2hr 50min–3hr 50min); Monsélice (6 daily; 50min); Padua (every 30min; 35min); Rovigo (19 daily; 1hr–1hr 30min); Treviso (30 daily; 30min); Trieste (14 daily; 2hr 10min); Udine (hourly; 2hr); Verona (at least 25 daily; 1hr 30min); Vicenza (25 daily; 55min); Vittorio Veneto (4 daily; 1–2hr).

Verona to: Milan (30 daily; 1hr 40min); Padua (25 daily; 50min); Venice (25 daily; 90min); Vicenza (30 daily; 30min).

Vicenza to: Castelfranco (hourly; 40min); Cittadella (hourly; 30min); Milan (30 daily; 1hr 40min); Padua (25 daily; 20min); Thiene (hourly; 25min); Treviso (hourly; 1hr); Venice (25 daily; 55min); Verona (30 daily; 30min).

where these machines have been fitted, you'll be given a spot-fine in the region of L40,000.

Rail Passes and Discounts

The Europe-wide *InterRail* and *Eurail* passes (see pp.5 & 9) give unlimited travel on the *FS* network, though you'll be liable for supplements. These are the passes that are most likely to prove useful, but if you're flying to north Italy and then undertaking an intensive bout of rail travel, you might want to invest in one of the many passes exclusive to the *FS* system.

Travellers from the UK have a choice of three **Euro-Domino** passes for the Italian network – 3 days' unlimited rail travel for £100, 5 days' for £124, or 10 days' for £208. All these passes are available from the *International Rail Centre* or *Wasteels* (see box below).

In addition, there are three specific Italian passes, available at all the agencies listed in the box below, and at Venice train station – the only outlet in the Veneto. The **Biglietto turistico libera circolazione** is valid for unlimited travel on all *FS* trains, including *Intercity*; for 8 days its costs £88/$140, for 15 days £110/$172, for 21 days £126/$198, and for 30 days £152/$240. The **Flexi-Card** is similarly valid for all trains, and gives a certain number of days' travel within a certain period; for 4 days' travel in any 9-day period it costs £66/$105, for 8 days in 21 it costs £94/$150, and for 12 in 30 it costs £120/$190. With this card you must get the ticket office to validate the journey you're about to make before getting on the train. The **Chilométrico** ticket, valid for up to five people, gives 3000km worth of travel on a maximum of twenty separate journeys; it costs £90/$150, but you have to pay supplements on faster trains – and it's all but impossible to cover that sort of distance on an Italian holiday anyway.

There are two **discount cards** that come into their own if you're going to spend a long time in the country. For under-26s there's the **Cartaverde**, which is valid for one year, gives 20 percent discount on any fare, and costs L40,000; it's available from any main train station in Italy. Stations also issue the **Cartargento**, for people over 60, which has the same validity and price, but gives 30 percent discount.

Other **discounts** on normal fares are for **children** (50 percent discount for 4–12 year-olds) and for large **groups** (10–24 people get 20 percent discount, over 25 people 30 percent discount) – though the group discounts do not apply at Easter, Christmas and from June 25 to the end of August.

Agencies For Italian Rail Tickets

IN THE UK

International Rail Centre, Victoria Station, London SW1 ☎071/834 2345.

Italian State Railways, Marco Polo House, 3–5 Lansdowne Rd, Croydon, Surrey ☎081/686 0677.

Ultima Travel, 424 Chester Rd, Little Sutton, South Wirral, L66 3RB ☎051/339 6171.

Wasteels, 121 Wilton Rd, London SW1 ☎071/834 7066.

IN NORTH AMERICA

CIE Tours International, 108 Ridgedale Ave, Morristown, NJ 07690 ☎201/292-3438 or 800/522-5258.

Council Travel, 205 E 42nd St, New York, NY 10017 ☎212/661-1450. Head office of the nationwide US student travel organisation. Branches in San Francisco, LA, Washington, New Orleans, Chicago, Seattle, Portland, Minneapolis, Boston, Atlanta and Dallas, to name only the larger ones.

Italian State Railways, 666 Fifth Ave, New York, NY 10113 ☎212/697-2100.

Rail Europe, 226–230 Westchester Ave, White Plains, NY 10604 ☎914/682-2999 or 800/438-7245; and branches in Santa Monica, San Francisco, Fort Lauderdale, Chicago, Dallas, Vancouver and Montréal.

Travel Cuts, 187 College St, Toronto, ON M5T 1P7 ☎416/979-2406. Main office of the Canadian student travel organisation. Many other offices nationwide.

By Bus and Coach

On the whole, **buses and coaches** offer little competition to the trains, being generally a shade more expensive and far less frequent. Travelling out from Venice, the only excursion you're likely to do by bus is the trip along the River Brenta. Moving around the mainland, though, there is sometimes no alternative unless you have a car – Ásolo, for instance, has no train connection, and you'll need to take a bus for the great Villa Barbaro at Masèr. Usually the bus station (*Autostazione*) is close to the train station, and even when the terminus is elsewhere, many services call at the train station along their route. Tickets have to be bought before getting on board, either from the bus company's office at the station, or from the nearest agent – their name and address is always shown on the timetable at the bus stop. If you're setting off for a remote place, it's always a good idea to buy your ticket for the return leg at the point of departure, as some villages have just a single outlet which might well be closed when you need it. Services are drastically reduced, or non-existent, on Sunday, and note that lots of departures are linked to school requirements – which sometimes means no services during school holidays.

In contrast, **city buses** are always cheap, usually charging a flat fare of L1000 or thereabouts, and can be a great help to the weary, or if you're staying in accommodation out of town. Again, tickets should be bought before getting on – either from offices at bus terminals and stops, or from *tabacchi* and other shops displaying the company's logo and ticket emblem. Stamp your ticket in the machine on board – inspectors get on board quite regularly.

By Car

Although public transport is adequate for most occasions, there are instances when a **car** is a great convenience. In Venice the most reasonable **car rental** company is *Europcar* (for addresses of firms in Venice, see p.251); you might find slightly better deals in large towns such as Verona, Padua, Vicenza and Treviso, where the car-rental offices congregate around the train station – if you see anything for under L400,000 per week (with unlimited mileage), you've found a bargain. The cheapest way to rent a car in Italy is to arrange the rental in conjunction with your flight or holiday; for travellers from the UK, there's also the option of booking a car through *Holiday Autos*, 25 Savile Row, Mayfair, London W1X 1AA (☎071/491 1111) – they guarantee that their prices cannot be bettered.

Petrol is expensive in Italy, but take your own car and you're entitled to **petrol coupons** (worth 15 percent off) and concessions on the motorway tolls; you can get information on this scheme from the Italian State Tourist Office.

For **documentation** you need a valid driving licence plus an Italian translation (available from the Italian State Tourist Office), and – if you're taking your own car – an international green card of insurance. It's compulsory to carry your car documents and passport while you're driving, and you'll be required to present them if you're stopped by the police. **Rules of the road** are straightforward: drive on the right; at junctions, where there's any ambiguity, give precedence to vehicles coming from the right; observe the speed limits (50kph in built-up areas, 110kph on country roads and on motorways during the week, 130kph on motorways at weekends); and don't drink and drive. If you **break down**, dial ☎116 at the nearest phone and tell the operator where you are, the type of car and your registration number: the nearest office of the *Automobile Club d'Italia (ACI)*, an *AA/RAC/AAA* equivalent, will be informed and they'll send someone to help, though it's not a free service. If you need towing anywhere you can count on it costing a fairly substantial amount, and it might be worth joining *ACI* to qualify for their discounted repairs scheme; write to *ACI*, Via Marsala 8, 00185 Rome.

Chapter 17

Padua and the southern Veneto

Summer in Venice used to be the season for people to leave the city in great numbers, rather than pour into it as they do today. When the temperature rose, the gentry would make for their country retreats along the **Brenta**, which flows into the lagoon at the nearest point on the mainland to the city. Many of these houses still stand, and the finest of them can be visited easily by taking one of the buses that run along the Brenta from Venice to Padua.

Situated a little under forty kilometres west of Venice, **Padua** is the obvious place to seek a room if the hotels of Venice are reaching capacity. It's only half-an-hour's train journey away, accommodation is comparatively cheap, and the city's university guarantees a lively social scene. Moreover, Padua itself has plenty of sights to fill a protracted stay. The **Cappella degli Scrovegni**, for instance, with its astonishing fresco cycle by Giotto, or the **Basilica di Sant'Antonio**, a pilgrimage church which contains some of the finest Renaissance sculpture in the Veneto.

Of the small towns to the **south of Padua** the most enticing are **Monsélice**, which has a superbly restored castle, and **Montagnana**, whose medieval town walls have survived in almost pristine form. And if you need a rest from urban pursuits, the green **Colli Euganei** (Euganean Hills) offer a pleasant excursion, while the **Po Delta**'s

Hostels and hotels in this guide are classified into nine price categories. **Hostels** (① & ②) are classified according to the **high-season cost per person per night**; the **hotel** categories refer to the **minimum** you can expect to pay for **a double room in high season**, excluding the cost of breakfast, which you might not be able to avoid.

① Under L20,000 per person.
② Over L20,000 per person.
③ Under L40,000 per room.
④ L40–60,000 per room.
⑤ L60–80,000 per room.
⑥ L80–100,000 per room.
⑦ L100–150,000 per room.
⑧ L150–200,000 per room.
⑨ Over L200,000 per room.

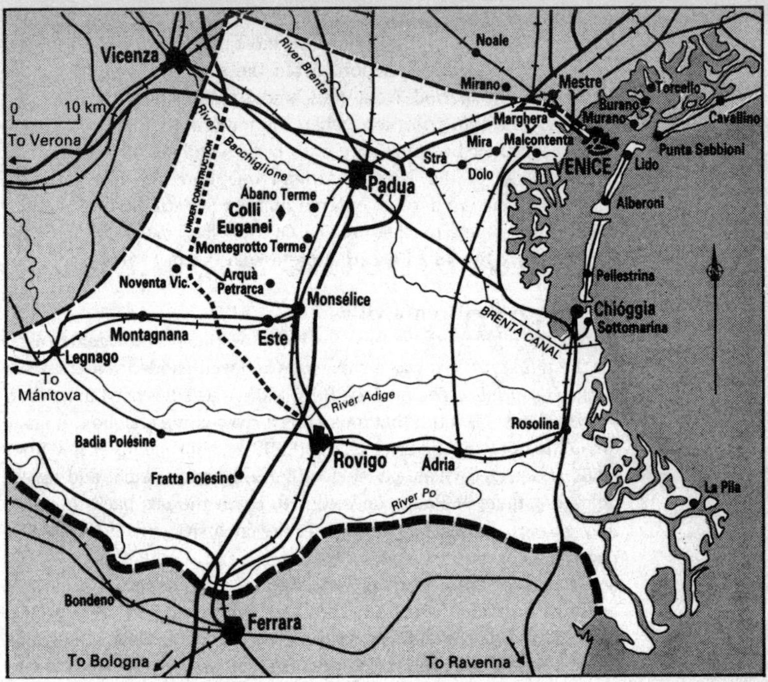

nature reserves and beaches are the quietest stretches of coastline in the area.

The Brenta

The southernmost of the the three main rivers that empty into the Venetian lagoon (the other two are the Sile and Piave), the **Brenta** caused no end of trouble to the earliest settlers on both the mainland and the islands: on the one hand, its frequent flooding made agriculture difficult, and on the other, the silt it dumped into the lagoon played havoc with Venice's water channels. Land reclamation schemes were carried out from the eleventh century, but it was in the fourteenth century that Venice began the large-scale canalisation of the Brenta, an intervention which both reinforced the banks of the river and controlled the deposition of its contents in the lagoon. The largest of the artificial channels, *La Cunetta*, which runs from Stra to Chioggia, was finished as recently as 1896, but by the sixteenth century the management of the Brenta was sufficiently advanced for the land along its lower course, from Padua to the river-mouth at Fusina, to become a favoured building site for the Venetian aristocracy.

Some of these Venetian **villas** were built as a combination of summer residence and farmhouse – most, however, were intended solely for the former function. From the sixteenth century to the eighteenth the period from mid-June to mid-November was the season of the *villeggiatura*, when the patrician families of Venice would load their best furniture onto barges and set off for the relative coolness of the Brenta. Around one hundred villas are left standing: some are derelict, a large number are still inhabited and a handful are open to the public. Of this last category, two are outstanding – the Villa Fóscari and the Villa Pisani.

Getting to the Brenta villas

During the eighteenth century, the mode of transport the gentry used for the *villeggiatura* was a capacious and well-padded vessel known as the *Burchiello*. The modern *Burchiello* – as advertised in a dozen tourist ofices – is a tub that looks like a river-going shoebox. It shuttles tourists along the river at L100,000 a shot, making a few brief stops at selected villas, pausing rather longer for lunch, and finally unloading them at Padua or Venice to catch the bus back to where they started. Lunch and bus ticket are inclusive, you'll be glad to know.

Hoi polloi can get to **Malcontenta** for L1000 on the hourly ACTV **bus** from Piazzale Roma – the trip takes thirty minutes. On your way back, if the first bus that comes along isn't going to Venice, take it as far as Corso del Popolo in Mestre, then cross the road for a #4 to Piazzale Roma – you can do it on one ticket, as it's valid for an hour.

For **Stra**, the Padua bus (which leaves every half hour, takes 50min and costs L3100), goes right past the door and gives you a good view of dozens of villas on the way. They're particularly thick on the ground from **ORIAGO** onwards (16km out of Venice), the most attractive stretch being centred on the elongated town of **MIRA**, shortly after Oriago. The Villa dei Contarini in Mira was one of Henry III of France's ports of call on his visit of 1574, and Byron wrote part of *Childe Harold* in the Palazzo Fóscarini (now the post office), where he lived in 1817–19.

The *Azienda di Promozione Turistica Riviera del Brenta* produces various leaflets on the villas and hotels of the Brenta, most of them aimed at the sort of tourist who finds the *Burchiello* irresistible; their HQ is in the Palazzo Pio, Via Don Minzoni 27, Mira Porte (Mon–Sat 8am–2pm; ☎041/424.973), but the signposted information office a few yards from the Villa Pisani has most of their stuff, and the San Marco tourist office in Venice should supply it too.

The Villa Fóscari

Sometimes known as the Villa Malcontenta, the **Villa Fóscari** at **MALCONTENTA** was designed in 1559 for the brothers Alvise and Niccolò Fóscari by **Palladio**, and is the nearest of his villas to Venice.

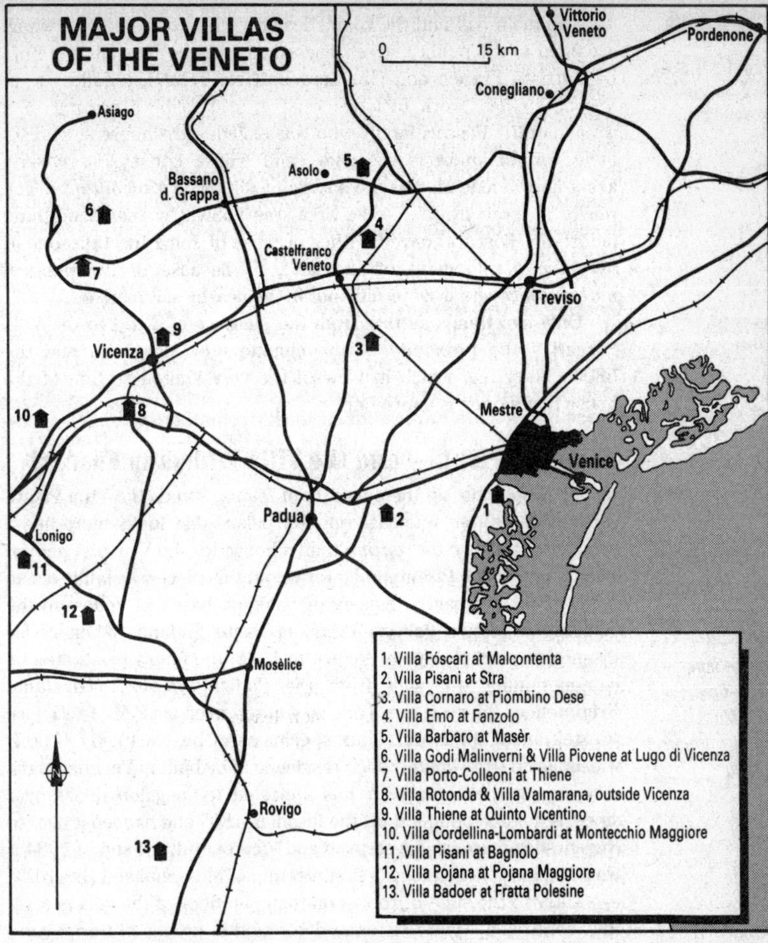

None of Palladio's villas more powerfully evokes the architecture of ancient Rome: the heavily rusticated exterior suggests the masonry of Roman public buildings; the massive Ionic portico alludes to classical temple fronts (which Palladio believed to be derived from domestic architecture); and the two-storey main hall was inspired by the bath complexes of imperial Rome, as was the three-sectioned arched window (a feature known as a thermal window, from the Roman *thermae*). Palladio was practical as well as erudite: to keep the living quarters well clear of the swampy land, he raised them on a high podium, and to keep building costs down he used the cheapest materials that would do the job – look closely at the columns and you'll see that they're made out of hundreds of bricks in the shape of cake slices.

The Villa Fóscari is open April–Oct Tues, Sat and first Sun of each month 9am–noon; L10,000.

The main hall and the rooms leading off it (only some of which are open to the public) were frescoed as soon as the walls were up, by **Battista Franco** and **Giovanni Battista Zelotti**, a colleague of Veronese; their work includes what is said to be a portrait of a woman of the Fóscari family who was exiled to the house as punishment for an amorous escapade, and whose consequent misery, according to legend, was the source of the name *Malcontenta*. The reality is more prosaic – the area was known by that name long before the Fóscari arrived, either because of some local discontent over the development of the land, or because of the political *malcontenti* who used to hide out in the nearby salt marshes.

Only two things detract from the pleasure of a trip to the Villa Fóscari – the proximity of the chimneys of Marghera, and the L8000 entry fee, which in view of the very limited section of the house that's open is exorbitant.

The Villa Pisani – and the Villa Widmann Fóscari

The Villa Pisani and its grounds are open Tues–Sun: June–Sept 9am–6pm; Oct–May 9am–1.30pm; L6000.

At **STRA**, virtually on the outskirts of Padua, stands the **Villa Pisani** (or **Nazionale**), an immense country palace that looks more like a product of the *ancien régime* than a house for the Venetian gentry. The branch of the Pisani family for whom this place was built was an astronomically wealthy dynasty of bankers, based in Venice in the similarly excessive Palazzo Pisani at Santo Stefano. When Alvise Pisani was elected doge of Venice in 1735, the family celebrated by commissioning the villa from the Paduan architect **Girolamo Frigimelica**; later on the work was taken over by **F.M. Preti** (see "Castelfranco" for more bijoux specimens of his work). By 1760 it was finished – the biggest such residence to be built in Venetian territory during the century. It has appealed to megalomaniacs ever since: Napoleon bought it off the Pisani in 1807 and handed it over to Eugène Beauharnais, his stepson and Viceroy of Italy; and in 1934 it was the place chosen for the first meeting of Mussolini and Hitler.

Entry to the suite of rooms on the main floor of the villa is carefully controlled – you're shepherded round in groups of thirty – and most of what you see is unexciting. The house has been stripped of nearly all its original furnishings, and it's as hard to thrill to the eighteenth-century frescoes of smiling nymphs and smirking satyrs that decorate some of the rooms as to the almost blank walls elsewhere. But then there's the **ballroom**, its ceiling covered with a fresco of *The Apotheosis of the Pisani Family*, the last major piece painted by **Giambattista Tiepolo** before his departure for Spain in 1762, at the age of 66. It's a dazzling performance, as full of blue space as it could possibly be without falling apart; and if you're trying to puzzle out what's going on – the Pisani family, accompanied by Venice, are being courted by the Arts, Sciences and Spirits of Peace, while Fame plays a fanfare in praise of the Pisani and the Madonna looks on with appropriate pride. The monochrome frescoes on Roman themes around the musicians' gallery are by Giambattista's son, Giandomenico.

In the **grounds**, the long fish-pond ends in front of a stable-block which might be mistaken from a distance for another grand house. Off to the right (as you look away from the villa) is a peculiar belvedere, resembling a chapel with its dome lopped off; and close by there's an impressive maze – unless a blizzard is blowing, it'll be packed with half a dozen coachloads of Italian schoolkids.

The Villa Widmann Fóscari is open Tues–Sun 9am–6pm; L7000.

A third villa often features on suggested itineraries of the Brenta: the **Villa Widmann Fóscari** at MIRA PORTE, just after Oriago. Built in the early eighteenth century and redecorated fifty years or so later, it's probably a delight for admirers of French Rococo style, but for most people it will only demonstrate by contrast how inventive Tiepolo was.

Padua

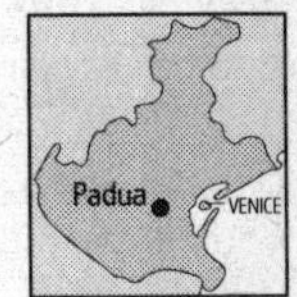

Extensively reconstructed after the damage caused by World War II bombing, and hemmed in by the sprawl which has accompanied its development as the most important economic centre of the Veneto, **PADUA** (PADOVA) is not immediately the most alluring city in northern Italy. It is, however, one of the most ancient and culturally one of the richest, retaining plentiful evidence of its impressive lineage.

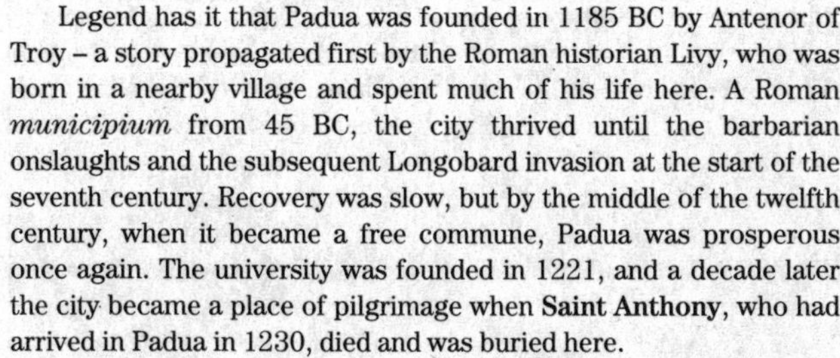

Legend has it that Padua was founded in 1185 BC by Antenor of Troy – a story propagated first by the Roman historian Livy, who was born in a nearby village and spent much of his life here. A Roman *municipium* from 45 BC, the city thrived until the barbarian onslaughts and the subsequent Longobard invasion at the start of the seventh century. Recovery was slow, but by the middle of the twelfth century, when it became a free commune, Padua was prosperous once again. The university was founded in 1221, and a decade later the city became a place of pilgrimage when **Saint Anthony**, who had arrived in Padua in 1230, died and was buried here.

The appalling **Ezzelino da Romano** occupied Padua for two decades from 1237, and then struggles against the **Scaligers** of Verona lasted until the **da Carrara** family established their hold in 1337. Under their domination, Padua's cultural eminence was secured – Giotto, Dante and Petrarch were among those attracted here – but Carraresi territorial ambitions led to conflict with Venice, and in 1405 the city's independence ended with its conquest by the neighbouring republic. Though politically nullified, Padua remained an artistic and intellectual centre: Donatello and Mantegna both worked here, and in the seventeenth century Galileo did research at the university, where the medical faculty was one of the most ambitious in Europe. With the fall of the Venetian Republic the city passed to Napoleon, who handed it over to the **Austrians**, after whose regime Padua was annexed to Italy 1866.

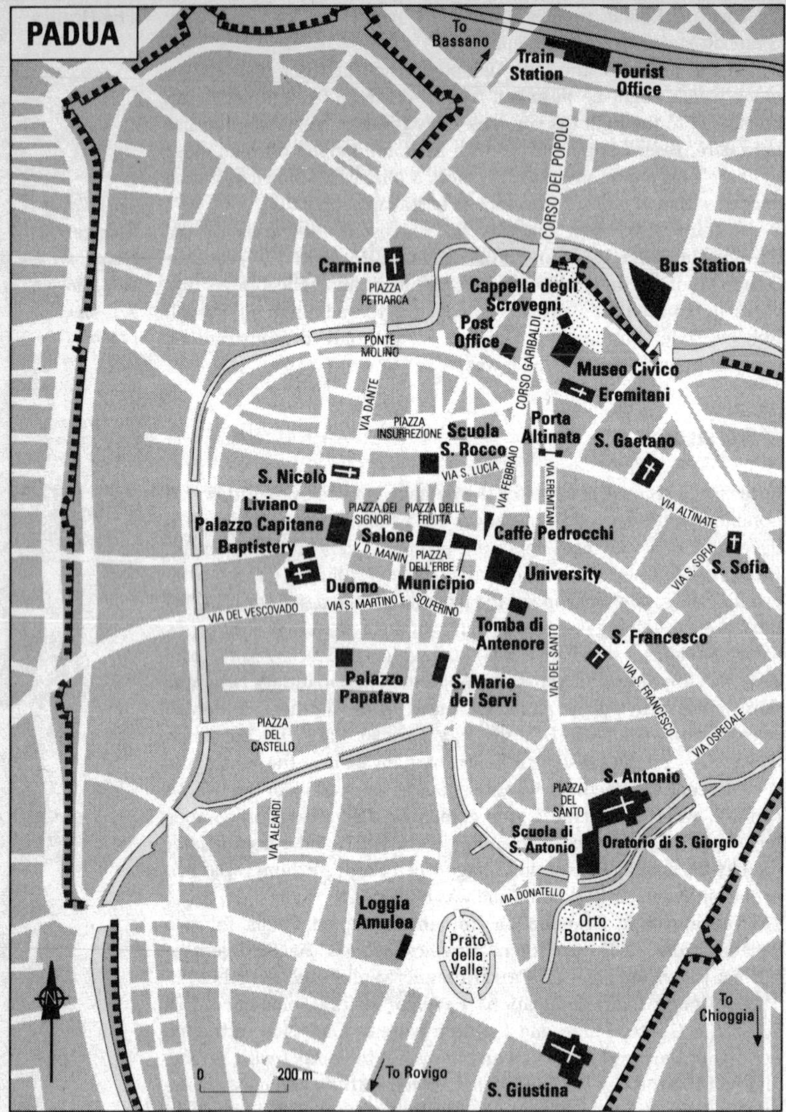

Arrival and accommodation

Trains arrive in the north of the town, just a few minutes' walk up Corso del Popolo from the old city walls. The main **bus station** is at Piazzale Boschetti, immediately north of the walls to the east of the Corso; however, **local buses** for the city and nearby towns such as

Ábano and Montegrotto leave outside the train station. The **tourist office** is at the train station (Mon–Sat 9am–6pm, Sun 9am–noon; ☎049/875.2077); it stocks free maps and lists of accommodation, but does not sell the Padua **biglietto unico**, which costs L10,000 and allows one visit to each of Padua's museums and monuments within one year of purchase – it's available at all these main sites.

A few years ago it was infinitely simpler to find an inexpensive room in Padua than in Venice; it's still the case that the average cost is lower, but availability can be a problem as more and more people use Padua as a base from which to visit its overcrowded neighbour. If you're visiting in high season, be prepared for a slightly protracted search, but don't despair – Padua has around thirty one-star hotels altogether, with singles from L30,000 and doubles from L38,000.

Hotels

Al Cason, Via Fra Paolo Sarpi 40 ☎049/662.636. Large and efficiently run two-star, a few minutes from the station. ⑤.

Al Santo, Via del Santo 147 ☎049/875.2131. One-star right by the Basilica; all doubles have a bathroom. ④.

Bellevue, Via L. Belludi 11 ☎049/875.5547. Decent one-star off the Prato della Valle, with a peaceful courtyard and well-tended rooms, each with private bathroom. ④.

Fagiano, Via Locatelli 45 ☎049/875.3396. Good two-star near the Basilica. ⑤.

Junior, Via L. Faggin 2 ☎049/611.756. Acceptable one-star, close to the station. ④.

Pace, Via Papafava 3 ☎049/8751566. Spacious, clean and friendly place near the Piazza della Frutta. ③.

Sant'Antonio, Via San Fermo 118 ☎049/875.1393. Pleasant two-star, not far from the Ponte Molino, in the northern part of central Padua. ④.

Verdi, Via Dondi dell'Orologio 7 ☎049/663.450. Centrally located one-star. ④.

Hostels and campsites

Ostello Città di Padova, Via A. Aleardi 30 ☎049/875.2219. Padua's *IYHF* hostel is a short walk west of the Prato della Valle – or take bus #3, #8, #12 or #18 from the train station. Very quiet and friendly, but has an 11pm curfew. ①.

Montegrotto Terme, Strada Romana Aponese 104 ☎049/793.400. This is the nearest campsite to Padua – 15km from the city centre, but frequent trains take around 15min; a very upmarket site, it boasts not merely a swimming pool but thermal baths too.

The City

From the train station, the Corso del Popolo and Corso Garibaldi lead south through a gap in the Renaissance city walls towards the centre of the city, passing after a short distance the **Cappella degli Scrovegni**. For many people the **Giotto frescoes** in the Scrovegni are *the* reason for coming to Padua, and the building is frequently full, though the crush is alleviated at crisis periods by a strict time control on large groups.

The chapel was commissioned in 1303 by Enrico Scrovegni in atonement for his father's usury, which was so vicious that Dante allotted him a place in the *Inferno* – he died screaming "give me the keys to my strong box" and was denied a Christian burial. As soon as the walls were built, Giotto was commissioned to cover them with illustrations of the life of Mary, the life of Jesus and the story of the Passion; the finished cycle, arranged in three tightly knit tiers and painted against a backdrop of saturated blue, is one of the high points in the development of European art.

The Cappella degli Scrovegni is open daily: summer 9am–7pm; winter 9am–5.30pm; L8000 for joint ticket with Museo Civico, L3000 for chapel only.

Although Duccio and Cimabue, the two earliest major figures of Italian painting, had done much to relax the stylised, icon-like conventions of painting, it was in the work of Giotto that a consistent humanism first appeared. The Scrovegni series is a marvellous demonstration of this new attention to the inner nature of the figures depicted – the exchange of looks between the two shepherds in the *Arrival of Joachim* is particularly powerful, as are the *Embrace of Joachim and Anna at the Golden Gate* and the *Visit of Mary to Elizabeth*. On occasion even the buildings and landscape have been manipulated to add to the drama for example in the *Deposition*, where a strong diagonal leads the eye straight to the faces of Jesus and Mary.

Beneath the main pictures are shown the vices and virtues in human (usually female) form, while on the wall above the door is the *Last Judgement*, with rivers of fire leading from God to hell, and an angel rolling back the painting to remind us that this is an imaginative scene and not an authoritative vision of eternity. Directly above the door is a portrait of Scrovegni presenting the chapel; his tomb is at the far end, behind the altar with its statues by **Giovanni Pisano**.

The Museo Civico is open daily: summer 9am–7pm; winter 9am–5.30pm.

The neighbouring **Museo Civico**, formerly the monastery of the Eremitani, houses an assembly of fourteenth- to eighteenth-century art from the Veneto, featuring such names as Titian, Tintoretto and Canova: the highpoints, though, are a Crucifixion by Giotto which was once in the Scrovegni chapel, a fine *Portrait of a Young Senator* by Bellini, and a sequence of devils overcoming angels by Guariento. After the paintings, it's a trudge through Etruscan potshards, dull Egyptian and Roman works, dire nineteenth-century paintings and sculpture, and an assortment of coins, medals and other metalwork. There's also a helpful information desk here, which gives out information on Padua's cultural events.

The Eremitani

The nearby church of the **Eremitani**, built at the turn of the fourteenth century, was almost completely wrecked by an allied bombing raid in 1944 and has been fastidiously rebuilt. Photographs to the left of the apse show the extent of the damage, the worst aspect of which was the near total destruction of **Mantegna**'s frescoes of the lives of Saint James and Saint Christopher – during World War

II, only the destruction of the Camposanto in Pisa was a comparably severe blow to Italy's artistic heritage.

Produced between 1454 and 1457, when Mantegna was in his mid-twenties, the frescoes were unprecedented in the thoroughness with which they exploited fixed-point perspective – a concept central to Renaissance humanism, with its emphasis on the primacy of individual perception. Furthermore, Mantegna's compositions had to take into account the low viewpoint of the person in the chapel. The extent to which he overcame these complex technical problems can now be assessed only from the fuzzy photographs and the sad fragments preserved in the chapel to the right of the high altar. On the left wall is the *Martyrdom of St James*, put together from fragments found in the rubble; and on the right is the *Martyrdom of St Christopher* which had been removed from the wall before the war.

The Eremitani is open summer Mon–Sat 8.15am–noon & 3.30–6.30pm, Sun 9am–noon & 3.30–5.30pm; winter Mon–Sat closes 5.30pm, Sun closes 5pm.

To Santa Sofia

Straddling Via Eremitani, the **Porta Altinate** was one of the gates of the medieval city, and bears a plaque recording its violent recapture from Ezzelino da Romano on June 20, 1256. More recent military history is recorded a short way east of here, at Via Altinate 59, in the former residence of Cardinal Pietro Bembo; once the HQ of the Italian Third Army (NE Division) and now the HQ of the artillery, the palace houses the **Museo della Terza Armata** a collection of militaria primarily related to World War I. Continuing past the dull sixteenth-century church of San Gaetano and a scattering of fine houses, you come to **Santa Sofia**, the oldest church in Padua. It dates back to the sixth century, though most of today's beautiful brick-built structure dates from the twelfth and thirteenth centuries. The apse in particular shows Veneto-Byzantine influence, and is reminiscent of the cathedral at Torcello or Santi Maria e Donato on Murano.

The Museo della Terza Armata is open daily 9am–noon & 3–4.30pm; free.

Santa Sofia is open daily 9am–noon & 4–6.30pm.

The university

A short distance south of the Porta Altinate stands the university's main block, the **Palazzo del Bò** – the name translates as "of the Ox", after an inn that used to stand here. Established in September 1221, the University of Padua is older than any other in Italy except that of Bologna, and the coats of arms which encrust the courtyard and Great Hall attest to the social and intellectual rank of its alumni. The first permanent **anatomy theatre** was built here in 1594, a facility that doubtless greatly helped William Harvey, who went on to develop the theory of blood circulation after taking his degree here in 1602. Galileo taught physics here from 1592 to 1610, declaiming from a lectern that is still on show. And in 1678 Elena Lucrezia Corner Piscopia became the first woman to collect a university degree when she was awarded her doctorate in philosophy here – there's a statue of her in the courtyard.

At the moment the Bò is under restoration, and visits have to be arranged by phone (☎049/828.3111); controversy rages over whether the public should be allowed in en masse when the work is finished – the tourist office will have the latest details.

At the back of the Bò there's a minor curiosity, the **Tomba di Antenore**, resting place of the city's legendary founder.

The central squares

The area north and west of the university forms the hub of the city. A little way up from the university, on the left, is the Neoclassical **Caffè Pedrocchi**, which used to be the city's main intellectual salon; it's no longer that, but it does have a multiplicity of functions – chic café, concert hall and conference centre.

Due west of the Pedrocchi, the **Piazza delle Frutta** and **Piazza delle Erbe**, the sites of Padua's daily markets, are lined by bars, restaurants and shops.

The Salone is open Tues–Sun: summer 10am–6pm; winter 10am–4pm; L4000.

Separating them is the extraordinary **Palazzo della Ragione**, or **Salone** as it is more commonly known. At the time of its construction in the 1210s this vast hall was the largest room ever to have been built on top of another storey. Its decoration would once have been as astounding as its size, but the original frescoes by Giotto and his assistants were destroyed by fire in 1420, though some by **Giustio de'Menabuoi** have survived; most of the extant frescoes are by **Nicola Miretto** (1425–40).

Mainly used as the city council's assembly hall, it was also a place where Padua's citizens could plead for justice – hence the appellation *della Ragione*, meaning "of reason". The black stone to the right inside the door, called the *pietra del vituperio* (stone of insults), also played a part in the judicial system: Thomas Coryat recorded that a bankrupt could dissolve some of his debts by sitting on it "with his naked buttocks three times in some public assembly". The gigantic wooden horse with disproportionately gigantic gonads is modelled on Donatello's *Gattamelata*, and was made for a joust in 1466.

Both the Piazza delle Frutta and the Piazza delle Erbe have some attractive buildings around them, as does the **Piazza dei Signori**, which lies a little to the west. At one end of the piazza, beyond the Lombard **Loggia della Gran Guardia** (c.1500) is the **Palazzo del Capitano**, the sixteenth-century headquarters of the city's Venetian military commander, which incorporates the early fifteenth-century **Torre dell'Orologio**, a structure that predates even Venice's clock-tower. At the end of the Corte Capitaniato, beyond the Torre, is the university's arts faculty, the **Liviano**; the frescoes in its upstairs fourteenth-century **Sala dei Giganti** include a portrait of Petrarch.

The Liviano is open Sept–July Sat 3–6pm.

San Nicolò is open daily 8am–noon & 4–7pm.

The road north of the Piazza del Capitaniato runs straight up to the church of **San Nicolò** – basically an altered thirteenth-century building, though it retains an eleventh-century chapel.

The Duomo and Baptistery

Immediately southwest of the Piazza dei Signori is Padua's **Duomo**, an unlovely church whose architect cribbed his design from drawings by Michelangelo; the adjacent Romanesque **Baptistery**, though, is one of the unproclaimed delights of Padua.

The Baptistery is open April–Sept Tues–Sun 9.30am–12.30pm & 2.30–6.30pm; Oct–March Tues–Sat 9.30am–12.30pm & 2.30–5.30pm, Sun 9.30am–12.30pm; L3000.

Built by the Da Carrara clan in the thirteenth century, it's lined with frescoes by **Giusto de'Menabuoi** (c.1376), a cycle that makes a fascinating comparison with Giotto's in the Cappella degli Scrovegni. The influence of Giotto is plain, but in striving for greater naturalism Giusto has lost Giotto's monumentality and made some of his figures awkward and unconvincing. Yet many of the scenes are delightful – the *Marriage at Cana*, for instance – and the vibrancy of their colours, coupled with the size and relative quiet of the building, make the visit memorable. The polyptych **altarpiece**, also by Menabuoi, was stolen in 1972 but quickly recovered, minus some of its wooden framework. Don't overlook the **sepulchre of Fina Buzzaccharini**, one of the Carrara family's most assiduous artistic patrons; she's shown on the front being presented to the Virgin by John the Baptist.

Piazza del Santo and the Gattamelata monument

If you continue trudging south from the Porta Altinate you'll soon find yourself in Via del Santo, where an increasing density of shops selling garishly decorated candles and outsize souvenir rosaries will prepare you for the pilgrim-ensnaring stalls of the **Piazza del Santo**.

The main sight on the piazza is Donatello's **Monument to Gattamelata** ("The Honeyed Cat"), as the *condottiere* Erasmo da Narni was known. He died in 1443 and this monument was raised ten years later, the earliest large bronze sculpture of the Renaissance. It's a direct precursor to Verrocchio's equestrian monument to Colleoni in Venice (and Colleoni was under Gattamelata's command for a time), but could hardly be more different: Gattemelata was known for his honesty and dignity, and Donatello has given us an image of comparative sensitivity and restraint, quite unlike Verrocchio's image of power through force. The modelling of the horse makes a double allusion: to the equestrian statue of Marcus Aurelius in Rome, and to the horses of San Marco in Venice.

The Basilica di Sant'Antonio

Within eighteen months of his death in 1231, Saint Anthony of Padua had been canonised and his tomb was attracting enough pilgrims to warrant the building of the **Basilica di Sant'Antonio**, or **Il Santo**. It was not until the start of the fourteenth century that the church reached a state that enabled the saint's body to be placed in the chapel designated for it. The **exterior** is an outlandish mixture, with *campanili* like minarets, Byzantine domes and Romanesque and Gothic features on the facade and apse.

The Basilica is open daily: summer 6.30am–7.45pm; winter 6.30am–7pm.

The **interior** is similarly heterogeneous: the plan up to the transepts being much like that of Italian mendicant churches, whereas the complex ambulatory with radiating chapels is more like the layout of French pilgrimage churches of the period. Saint Anthony's chapel – the **Cappella del Santo** – is in the left transept, plastered with votive photographs of healed limbs, car crashes survived thanks to the saint's intervention, and other offerings irresistible to the voyeur. The chapel's more formal decoration includes a sequence of nine **panels** showing scenes from Saint Antony's life; carved between 1505 and 1577, they are the most important series of relief sculpture created in sixteenth-century Italy. Reading from the left: Saint Anthony receives his Franciscan habit; a jealous husband stabs his wife, whom the saint later revived; Saint Anthony raises a man from the dead to prove the innocence of his father; he revives a drowned woman (panel by Sansovino); he revives a drowned baby (Sansovino and Minello); he directs mourners to find the heart of a miser in his coffer (Tullio Lombardo); he restores the severed foot of a boy (Tullio Lombardo); a heretic throws a glass which miraculously does not break; and a newborn baby tells of the innocence of its mother (Antonio Lombardo).

Adjoining the chapel is the **Cappella della Madonna Mora** (named after its fourteenth-century French altar statue), which in turn lets onto the **Cappella del Beato Luca**, where Saint Antony's body was first placed: its late fourteenth-century frescoes show scenes from the lives of the Apostles Philip and James the Lesser, including a lovely image of Saint James lifting a prison tower to free a prisoner.

Back in the aisle, just outside the Cappella del Santo, is Padua's finest work by **Pietro Lombardo**, the monument to Antonio Roselli (1467). More impressive still are the high altar's bronze sculptures and reliefs by **Donatello** (1444–45), the works which introduced Renaissance classicism to Padua. Irritatingly, they are often inaccessible, though a word with one of the sacristans may get you a closer view. The neo-Gothic frescoes of the apse, choir and presbytery were begun by **Achille Casanova** in 1903, and took about forty years. Trying to imitate Giotto's use of blue, he ended up turning this end of the Basilica into a gloomy cavern.

The Cappella del Tesoro is open daily 8am–noon & 2.30–7pm.

Built onto the farthest point of the ambulatory, the **Cappella del Tesoro** was designed in the 1690s by **Filippo Parodi**, a pupil of Bernini; its most important relics are from Il Santo himself – his tongue and chin, kept in a head-shaped container.

Most of the back wall of the **Cappella di San Felice**, occupying the right transept, is taken up by a glorious *Crucifixion*, frescoed in the 1370s by Altichiero da Zevio. Other things to seek out are the **monuments to Cardinal Pietro Bembo and Alessandro Contarini** on the nave's second pair of columns, both designed by Sanmicheli in the 1550s with a bust by Danese Cattaneo, and the **tomb of Gattamelata**, in the first chapel on the right.

The south side of the Piazza

To the left as you leave the Basilica are the joined **Oratorio di San Giorgio** and **Scuola di Sant'Antonio**. The Oratorio was founded in 1377 as a mortuary chapel – its frescoes by **Altichiero di Zevio** and **Jacopo Avanzi** were completed soon after. The *Crucifixion* on the altar wall shows the souls of the two thieves being received, one by a devil and one by an angel; the scenes from the life of Saint George on the left wall show not just the customary dragon-slaying, but also the saint being released by angels from a wheel of torture; and the opposite wall is adorned with the wonderfully titled *St Lucy Remains Immoveable at an Attempt to Drag Her with the Help of Oxen to a House of Ill Repute*.

The Oratorio and Scuola are open daily: Feb–March & Oct–Nov 9am–12.30pm & 2.30–4.30pm; April–Sept 8.30am–12.30pm & 2.30–6.30pm; Dec–Jan 9am–12.30pm; L1000.

The **Scuola di Sant'Antonio**, a confraternity run on the same lines as the *scuole* of Venice, was founded soon after Anthony's canonisation, though this building dates only as far back as the early fifteenth century. The ground floor is still used for religious purposes, while upstairs is maintained pretty much as it would have looked in the sixteenth century, with its fine ceiling and paintings dating mainly from 1509–15. Four of the pictues are said to be by **Titian** – *The Jealous Husband Stabbing his Wife*, with an almost insignificant intervention by Il Santo in the background; *St Anthony Reattaching the Severed Foot of a Young Man*; *The Distribution of Blessed Bread*; and the *Newborn Infant Defends the Honour of its Mother*. If any of these are genuine, they would be the earliest known extant works by him. The *Miser's Heart Found in his Treasure Chest* is attributed to Titian's brother, Francesco Vecellio. Some of the other paintings are charming oddities, such as *St Anthony Confronting Ezzelino da Romano* – a perilous diplomatic exercise which may or may not have happened.

Next door to the *scuola*, the **Museo al Santo** is used for one-off exhibitions, often drawing on the resources of the Museo Civico.

A good way to relax from all this art is to stroll round the corner to the **Orto Botanico**, the oldest botanic gardens in Europe. Planted in 1545 by the university's medical faculty as a collection of medicinal herbs, the gardens are laid out much as they were originally, and the specimens on show haven't changed too much either. Goethe came here in 1786 to see a palm tree that had been planted in 1585; the selfsame tree still stands.

The Orto Botanico is open summer 9am–1pm daily plus Mon–Fri 3–6pm; Mon–Sat 9am–1pm in winter; L3000.

The Prato della Valle and Santa Giustina

A little to the south sprawls the **Prato della Valle**, claimed to be the largest town square in Italy; it's a cheerless area, ringed by over-wide roads, and even the summer funfair does little to make it jollier. The greenery in the centre follows the oval plan of the extinct Roman amphitheatre; the two rings of statues commemorate 78 worthy Paduans, both native and honorary.

One side is fronted by the sixteenth-century **Basilica di Santa Giustina** – at 120m long, one of the world's largest churches. A pair of fifteenth-century griffins, one holding a knight and the other a lion, are the only notable adornments to the unclad brick facade; the freezing interior (scarves are worn by the Benedictine monks even when it's warm outside) is offputtingly clinical, with little of interest except a huge *Martyrdom of St Justina* by **Paolo Veronese** (in the apse), some highly proficient carving on the choir stalls, and the sarcophagus which once contained the relics of Luke the Evangelist (in the left transept).

Santa Giustina is open Mon–Sat 7.30am–noon & 3.30–7.30pm, Sun 7am–1pm & 3.30–7.30pm.

Far more appealing are the vestiges of the church's earlier incarnations. In the right transept a stone arch opens onto the **Martyrs' Corridor**, named after a well containing martyrs' bones, now part of the catacombs below the corridor (ask the sacristan for access). This part of the building is a composite of fifth- to twelfth-century architectural fragments, and leads to the **Sacellum di Santa Maria e San Prosdocimo**, burial place of Saint Prosdocimus. He was the first bishop of Padua back in the fourth century, when the church was founded, and is depicted here on a fifth-century panel. The fifteenth-century **old choir** is reached by a chain of corridors from the left-hand chapel of the right transept; the choir stalls are inset with splendid marquetry panels, and the **sacristy** beyond has an amusing painting of *St Maurus Rescuing St Placid from a Lake* by an artist glorying in the name of Toeput.

Eating, drinking and nightlife

As in any university city, there's plenty of choice when it comes to unpretentious bars and restaurants, and the student population guarantees a pretty active after-dark scene.

Catering for the midday stampede of ravenous students, Padua's bars generally produce weightier **snacks** than the routine *tremezzini* – slabs of pizza and sandwiches vast enough to satisfy a glutton are standard. A good variety of stand-up meals is offered at the *rosticceria* in Via Daniele Manin (daily 8.30am–1.30pm & 4–8.30pm), while *La Mappa*, Via Matteotti 17 (closed Sat), offers decent self-service fare.

For a more relaxed session at only slightly greater expense, three of the best cheap **restaurants** are *Da Giovanni* at Via De Cristoforis 1, *7 Teste* at Via C. Battisti 44, and *Al Pero* on Via S. Lucia. On Piazza Cavour, *Pepen* (closed Sun) has a wonderful range of pizzas, with seats on the square in summer. The *Dotto*, Via Squarcione 23, is a superb mid-range restaurant – allow around L60,000 per person. Padua can also boast a trio of really special places, costing an extra L10,000 or so: *Antico Brolo*, Vicolo Cigolo 14 (☎049/664.555; closed Sun); San Clemente, Via Vittorio Emanuele II 142 (☎049/8803.180; closed Sun); and El Toulà, Via Belle Parti 11 (☎049/660.719; closed Sun & Mon).

Padua's student population ensures that the city's **bars** have far longer opening hours than are common in Venice – many don't close until 2am – and that new places spring up as often as established ones revamp their image. Currently trendy are *Alla Ventura*, Via SS. Martino e Solferino, and *Al Coccodrillo*, Riviera S. Benedetto 154. For something a bit more hip, try the devil's grotto ambience of *Lucifer Young*, in Via Altinate.

Being a major university city, Padua has a nightlife which fluctuates in synch with term time; check the posters up around the city, and particularly around the university, for details of music, theatre and such like. Of the local newspapers, the most comprehensive for **listings** is *Il Mattino*. During the summer vacation things tend to be a little somnolent, and Padua's half-dozen regular **discos** are all fairly low-octane places at the best of times: liveliest are *Wag*, Via Savonarola 149, and the flashier *Extra Extra*, Via Ciamician.

Listings

Hitching If you're looking for a long-distance lift, contact *Servizio Autostop*, c/o *Associazione Studenti Universitari di Padova*, Via Zabarella 19 ☎049/657.730.

Hospital Ospedale Civile, Via Giustiniani 2 ☎049/821.111.

Markets General daily markets are held every morning in Piazza delle Erbe, Piazza delle Frutta, Piazza dei Signori and Piazza Capitaniato. Other regular ones are held in Piazzale Azzurri d'Italia (Tues morning), Piazzale Cuoco-Guizza (Wed morning), Via Bajardi-Mortise (Fri morning) and Prato della Valle (all day Sat).

Police Via Santa Chiara ☎049/833.111.

Post office Corso Garibaldi 25 (Mon–Fri 8am–8pm, Sat 8am–noon).

Telephones 24-hour *ASST* booths at Corso Garibaldi 7; alternatively there's the *SIP* office by the Caffè Pedrocchi (8am–9.30pm).

Train information At the station; daily 7am–6.30pm ☎049/875.1800.

The Colli Euganei

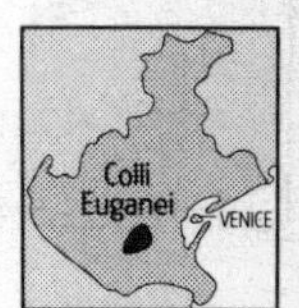

A few kilometres to the southwest of Padua the **Colli Euganei** (Euganean Hills) rise abruptly out of the plains, their slopes patched with vineyards between scattered villages, villas and churches. Between Padua and the hills lie the spa towns of **ÁBANO TERME** and **MONTEGROTTO TERME**, which for much of the year are crowded with people looking for cures or beauty treatment from the radioactive waters and mud baths. It's been like this for centuries, as the names of the towns indicates: *Ábano* comes from Aponeus, a Roman god of healing, while *Montegrotto* is said to derive from "mons aegratorum", meaning "mountain of the infirm". Largely composed of big and expensive modern hotels, these really are places to avoid unless you're hell-bent on trying to poach yourself in the hot springs – the cruellest one bubbles away at 87°C.

A car is a great advantage for exploring the Colli Euganei proper, as buses are few and far between, even to somewhere reasonably popular such as Arquà Petrarca (see below). The villas

The Colli Euganei

The Villa Barbarigo is open May–Sept Mon 2–6.30pm, Tues–Sat 10am–noon & 2–6.30pm, Sun 2–7.30pm; March, April & Oct daily 1.30–5.30pm; L8000.

of the region are its major architectural attractions, but many of them remain in private hands and can only be viewed from a distance. An exception is the **Villa Barbarigo**, at VALSANZIBIO, which is famous for its extraordinary gardens; laid out in 1699, they feature a maze and fantastical Baroque gateways.

While touring the region, look out for the wines with the local DOC seal: a red circle round an image of Donatello's *Gattamelata*. The range includes a Pinot Bianco and Tocai Italico (whites), a Cabernet and Merlot (reds), and a sparkling Moscato.

Arquà Petrarca

Petrarch's house is open April–Sept Sat & Sun 9.30am–12.30pm; L5000.

The gem of the Colli Euganei is the medieval village of **ARQUÀ PETRARCA**, most easily reached by bus from Este or Monsélice. The Carrara family gave the poet **Francesco Petrarca** (Petrarch) a piece of land here on which to realise his dream of a "delightful house surrounded by an olive grove and a vineyard". He spent the last summers of his life (1369–74) in his idyllic home, and this is where he died. Not only does the **house** still stand, but his desk and chair are still intact, as are various parts of the original fabric of the interior – though the frescoes, illustrating his works, were retouched in the seventeenth century. Petrarch's sarcophagus is in the centre of the village, with one epitaph penned by him and another by his son-in-law, who placed it here. The church of **Santa Maria** (founded in the tenth century, altered in the sixteenth) and the **Oratorio della Santa Trinità**, further down the hill, both have interesting fresco fragments.

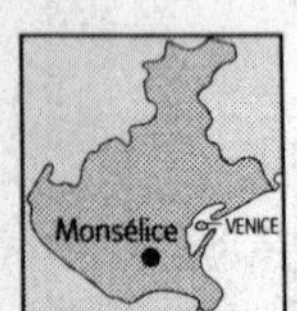

Monsélice

In earlier times **MONSÉLICE** was perched on the pimple of volcanic rock round the foot of which it now winds. Of the five concentric walls that then protected it, all that remains of them and their towers (thanks to nineteenth-century planning) is a small section of the outer ring and a citadel right on the hill's crest. The remnants make a powerful impression though, and the town possesses another fortress which is the equal of any in the Veneto. It's easily accessible from Padua, from where there are nine trains a day.

From the train station, the route to the centre of town crosses the Canale Bisato, from whose bridge you can look back to the **Villa Pisani** (sometimes open for exhibitions), which was a kind of stopover for the Pisani family as they travelled by water from Venice to their estates in Montagnana. The fragmentary town wall leads to the **Torre Civica**, built by Ezzelino da Romano in 1244 and repaired in 1504. Facing the Torre Civica across Piazza Mazzini, just beyond the wall, is the **Loggetta**, a seventeenth-century addition to the **Palazzo del Monte di Pietà**, the facade of which is on the road leading away from the square.

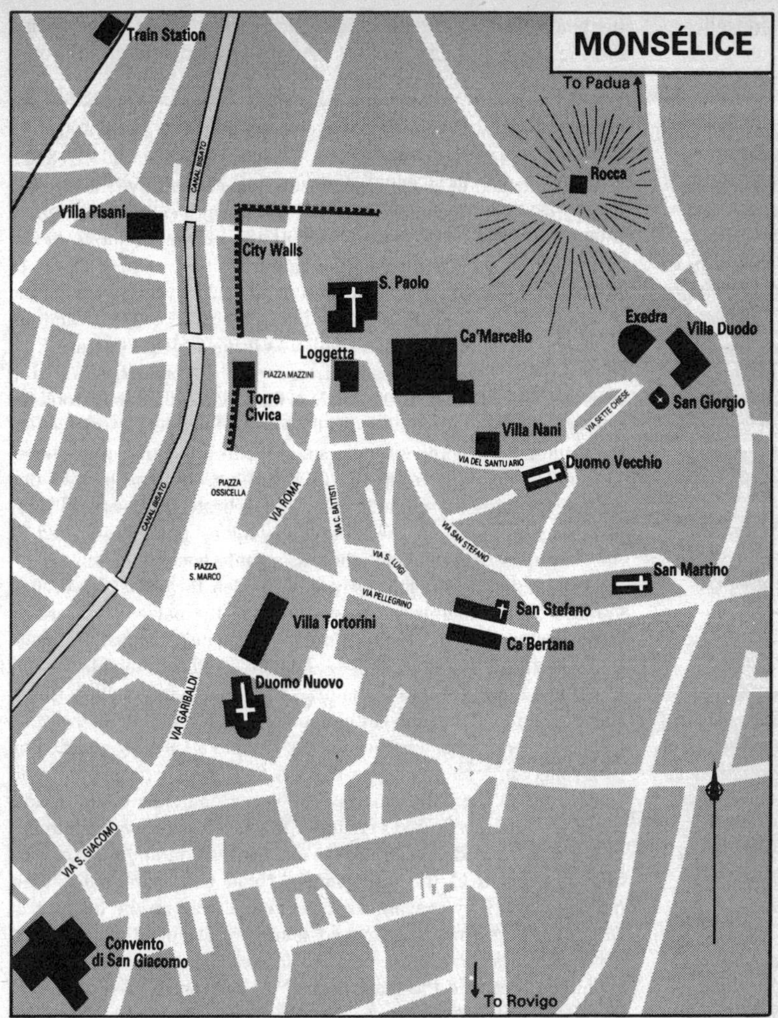

or **Ca' Marcello** as it is more often known. Dating back to the eleventh century, the house was expanded in the thirteenth century by Ezzelino, who added the square tower across the courtyard (the coat of arms was appended after the town came under Venetian rule in 1405). The interior was altered by the da Carrara clan in the fourteenth century, and linking the two main sections is a fifteenth-century bit added by the Marcello family; a library (sixteenth century) and family chapel (eighteenth century) were the only later changes. The castle's immaculate appearance is down to **Count Vittorio Cini**, who inherited the derelict building after it had been in the tender care of the Italian army during World War I, and sank a fortune into restoring it and furnishing each section in the appropriate style.

Guided tours of the Ca' Marcello are held May 1–Nov 11 Tues, Thurs & Sat 9am, 10.30am, 3.30pm & 5pm, Sun 9am & 10.30am, plus 3.30pm & 5pm on second and third Sun of month; L5000.

The tour begins in the **armoury**, three rooms of weaponry occupying the ground floor of Ezzelino's tower. Up from here are the **Marcello family apartments**, an adaption of part of Ezzelino's tower, furnished in sixteenth- and seventeenth-century fashion. The family restyled the **courtyard** in the seventeenth century – dripping with plants and with a well-head in the centre, it looks like a Zeffirelli film set. Up the ramp, a gate leads to the upper storey of the Marcello building, the **anteroom** of which was added to the external wall of Ezzelino's palace and retains the original windows as internal features. The **great hall** was formed by the Carraresi; its fireplace was originally from Ferrara, while the tapestries are from Brussels. The old part of the castle is quite domestic in feel: look for the fourteenth-century painted ceiling in the **Sala del Casteletto**. On the ground floor is the **kitchen**, set out with fifteenth-century furniture and copper plates up to 700 years old. The top part of this section contains the **council hall**, with delicate frescoes and fourteenth-century seating. The library, now minus its books, is used by the University of Padua and others as a conference room.

Continuing up the hill you see on the left the white, featureless **Palazzo Nani**: much more interesting than the palace itself are its steps up the garden (visible through the gate), flanked by mock Roman sculptures and leading to an imitation Roman temple.

The grounds of the Villa Duodo are open daily March–May & Sept–Oct 8am–noon & 1.30–7pm; June–Aug 7am–12.30pm & 3.30–8pm; Nov–Feb 9am–12.30pm & 1.30–7pm.

The **Duomo Vecchio** is the next stop: fourteenth-century fresco fragments and a Romano-Gothic polyptych on the high altar are its principal attractions. Just beyond the Duomo a gateway guarded by two Venetian lions gives onto the *Via Sette Chiese*, a private road leading up to the **Villa Duodo**. The seven churches of the road's name are a domesticated version of the seven pilgrimage churches of Rome, arranged as a line of six chapels leading up to the church of **San Giorgio** at the top. Sinners could earn pardon for their misdemeanours by praying their penitential way up the hill to San Giorgio, where rows of martyred saints are arranged in wood and glass cabinets not unlike old bookcases. The chapels, church, triumphal arch and the main part of the villa were all designed in the late sixteenth century by **Vincenzo Scamozzi**. Now an international centre for the study of hydrology, the villa was commissioned by the son of Francesco Duodo, a hero of the battle of Lépanto; the land was donated by the Venetian state in thanks for services rendered.

It's not possible to go up the steps to the **Rocca** – Ezzelino's citadel right at the summit – as the area is now a nature reserve where rare birds breed.

An alley running round the back of the Duomo leads back to the centre; the most interesting building you'll pass on the descent is the Gothic **Ca' Bertana** in Via M. Carron, which has elegant fourteenth-century windows. There's no need to traipse over to the **Duomo Nuovo** – you'll have seen as much as you need to from the walk up the hill: its only remarkable aspect is its size.

Practicalities

The **tourist office** is in the Loggetta in Piazza Mazzini (Mon–Sat 8.30am–12.30pm & 5–8pm). Best option for **eating** is the trattoria-pizzeria *Al Campiello*, at Riviera G.B. Belzoni 2 (closed Wed); there's a typical range of snacks at *Caffè Grand Italia* in Piazza Mazzini (closed Mon), and at the atmospheric *Enoteca del Castello*, on the way up to the castle at Via del Santuario 22 (closed Mon). There's also a luscious *pasticceria* in Via Pellegrino (closed Tues). If you want to **stay**, try the one-star *Riviera*, Riviera G.B. Belzoni 9 (☎0429/72.591; ④), or the nearby *Cadorno*, Viale Cadorno 62 (☎0429/72.002; ④).

Este

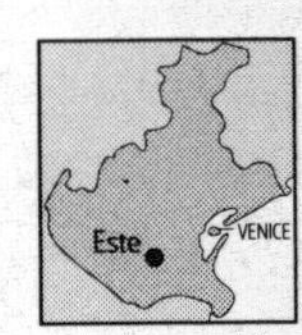

If you're using public transport, just about the best base from which to roam around the Colli Euganei is the ceramics-producing town of **ESTE**, on the southern edge of the outcrop, just a ten-minute train ride from Monsélice (9 daily). Sporadic buses run up into the hills from here and the chief **tourist office** of the Colli Eugenei is in the Piazza Maggiore (Mon–Sat 9am–noon & 4–7pm; ☎0429/3635).

From the train station a road runs straight to the central Piazza Maggiore, passing the blank-faced **Basilica di Santa Maria delle Grazie** (with a fourteenth-century Byzantine *Madonna*) and the Romanesque brick church of **San Martino**. The nearest thing to an alluring building in the Piazza itself is the tatty thirteenth-century home of the *Società Gabinetto di Lettura*, a cultural organisation and archive.

Turning to the right out of the Piazza you come face to face with the walls of the ruined **Castello dei Carraresi**, a fortress founded by the Este dynasty and rebuilt by the da Carrara family in 1340. Material salvaged from the walls was used in the construction of the sixteenth-century palace that now houses the **Museo Nazionale Atestino**. The Veneto's outstanding collection of pre-Roman artefacts is installed on the first floor (burial finds, Bronze Age tools and Iron Age pots), while much of the ground floor is given over to Roman remains. (Roman sites are still being excavated in the western part of the town.) The room devoted to medieval pieces includes a *Madonna and Child* by **Cima** which was once stolen from the church of Santa Maria della Consolazione and is now here for safe keeping. There's also a display of local pottery, a craft that Este has been famous for since before the Renaissance. The castle walls now enclose public gardens – useful on hot summer afternoons when everything is closed.

The Museo Nazionale Atestino is open April–Sept Tues–Sun 9am–1pm & 3–7pm; Oct–March closes 6pm; L4000.

The privately-owned **Villa de Kunkler**, round the back of the castle, was **Byron**'s residence in 1817–18, a stay commemorated by a plaque on the villa's wall. The house actually played a greater part in Shelley's life than Byron's – his daughter Clara fell ill while staying here, and died as a result of being carried by her father on an overnight gallop to see a doctor in Venice. When the Shelleys returned here a few days later, Percy wrote his poem of mourning for past splendour, "Lines Written Among the Euganean Hills".

Leading out of the Piazza Maggiore away from the castle, Via Matteotti passes under the **Porta Vecchia**, a restrained Baroque clock tower built on the site of a much earlier defensive tower. Over the river there's **Santa Maria Consolazione**, a homely church containing nothing of special interest since its Cima painting went to the museum. Turn right instead of going through the tower and you come to the dull sixteenth-century church of San Francesco, beyond which (in the *Quartiere Augusteo*) is the main Roman archaeological site in Este. The **Duomo** (turn right down Via Garibaldi) was rebuilt between between 1690 and 1708 after an earthquake, the oval plan of its Baroque interior anticipating the design of the Pietà in Venice by several decades. The only painting of note is the huge altarpiece of *St Thecla* by **Giambattista Tiepolo**, and even that's not one of his best – maybe because it's set in a scene of pestilence and death, rather than one of his happier, light-filled heavens.

Practicalities

The only one-star **hotel** is the *Leon d'Oro*, Viale Fiume 20 (☎0429/2955; ⑤), but there's a pair of good two-stars charging very similar rates: *Beatrice d'Este*, Via Rimembranze 1 (☎0429/600.533; ⑤), and *Centrale*, Piazza Beatrice 16 (☎0429/3930; ⑤). For **food**, try *Al Gambero*, Via d'Azeglio 6 (closed Sat), or *Da Piero Ceschi*, Piazza Trento 16; the *Leon d'Oro* and *Beatrice d'Este* have restaurants too.

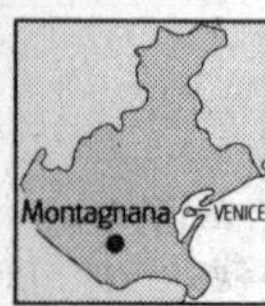

Montagnana

The pride of **MONTAGNANA**, fifteen minutes down the rail line from Este, is its **medieval city walls**, raised by the ubiquitous Ezzelino da Romano after he had virtually flattened the town in 1242. They were later strengthened by the Da Carrara family as Padua's first line of defence against the Scaligers to the west. It was not until the Wars of the League of Cambrai in the early sixteenth century that the battlements were called upon to fulfil their function, and when the hour came they were found wanting – controlled by the Venetians at the start of hostilities, Montagnana changed hands no fewer than thirteen times in the course of the war. After that the walls were not used defensively again. With a circumference of nearly two kilometres and twenty-four polygonal towers spaced at regular intervals, these are among the finest medieval fortifications in the country, and the relatively sparse development around their perimeter makes them all the more impressive. (Appropriately enough, the town is the home of the *Istituto Internazionale dei Castelli*, a centre for historical research on military architecture.)

Montagnana

Gates pierce the walls at the cardinal points of the compass, the entrances to the east and west being further reinforced by fortresses. The **eastern** gate (Porta Padova) is protected by the **Castello di San Zeno**, built by Ezzelino in 1242, with a watchtower to survey the road to Padua. Nearby, the **Museo Civico e Archeologico** displays objects uncovered around the town. On the **western** side, the **Rocca degli Alberi** was built by the da Carrara family in 1362 to keep the roads from Mantua and Verona covered.

The Museo Civico e Archeologico is open Mon–Sat 9am–noon; L1000.

The centre of Montagnana is the Piazza Vittorio Emanuele, dominated by the late Gothic **Duomo**. The most arresting feature of the exterior, its marble portal, was a later addition, possibly designed by Sansovino. **Veronese**'s altarpiece, a *Transfiguration*, is less engaging than the huge anonymous painting of the *Battle of Lépanto* on the left as you enter – it's said to represent accurately the ships and their positions at one point in the battle.

Outside the town, just beyond the Porta Padova, is the **Villa Pisani** by **Palladio** (closed to the public), its magnificent facade at a right angle to the road. It was built as a summer residence and administrative centre for their mainland estates by a branch of the Pisani family of Venice. Also worth looking out for is the elegant facade of the **Palazzo Lombardesco** in Via Matteotti, with its five-lighted window.

Practicalities

The **tourist office** is on the right-hand side of Piazza Vittorio Emanuele (10am–noon & 4.30–7pm, closed Tues & Sun afternoon). For **accommodation** *Locanda Baraldo*, Via San Zeno (☎0429/81.673; ⑤), *Al Turismo*, Via San Antonio 5 (☎0429/81.143; ⑤), and *Ezzelino*, Via Praterie 1 (☎0429/82035; ⑤), are all reasonable hotels. The **youth hostel** is stunning, installed as it is in Rocca degli Alberi (April to mid-Oct; reception 3–11pm; ☎0429/81.076; ①); if you don't have an IYHF card, you can join on the spot.

The cheapest decent **meal** in Montagnana is served at *Pizzeria al Palio* on Piazza Trieste, but for just a little more you can eat delicious home-made dishes at *Da Stona*, Via Carrarese 51 (closed Sun). All the hotels listed have **restaurants** as well. If you're stopping for a picnic in Montagnana, be sure to sample the local *prosciutto*, which is so delicious it's exported all over the world.

Come to Montagnana on the first Sunday in September and you'll see its **Palio** – it may be but a poor relation of the costumed horse races in Siena, but it's enthusiastically performed, and the day finishes with a splendid firework display.

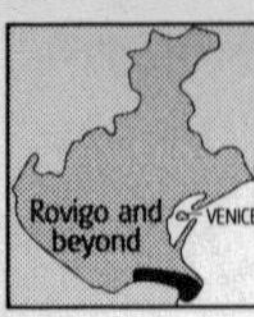

Rovigo and beyond

ROVIGO is the capital of the fertile and often-flooded zone between the Adige and the Po, an area known as the *Polésine* (or "Little Mesopotamia"). Trains on their way to Ferrara and Bologna from Venice call here at least hourly (average journey 90min), crossing another line running east to west – and frankly there's little reason for coming to the town except to change trains. (There's also a two-hourly connection to Chioggia, taking about an hour.) Should you be stuck for a couple of hours waiting for a connection, though, there are a couple of places you could visit. Maps are available from the **tourist office** on the central Piazza Vittore Emanuele (Tues–Sat 9.30am–12.30pm & 4–7pm).

The Pinacoteca is open July & Aug Mon–Sat 10am–1pm; rest of year Mon–Fri 9.30am–noon & 3.30–7pm, Sat 9.30am–noon; free.

Two medieval towers in the centre were part of a castle re-fortified in 954 by the Bishop of Adria when the region was threatened by barbarian invasions. The **Pinacoteca dei Concordi** in Piazza Vittore Emanuele is the city's pride and joy. Eminent artists of the Veneto, in less than breathtaking form, comprise the main part of the collection: Palma il Vecchio, Giambattista Piazzetta and Rosalba Carriera are among those present.

The Polésine museum is open Mon–Sat 8.30am–12.30pm; free.

About fifteen minutes' walk in the same direction is the **Museo Civico delle Civilità in Polésine** in Piazza San Bartolomeo, the main archaeological institute for the area. This is more an assemblage of pieces unearthed by the researchers than a regular museum, and you're shown round by one of the staff, whose informed commentary makes up for the uninspiring display techniques. Items relating to the Polésine's disappearing rural life are exhibited as well – tools of various trades, agricultural implements and so forth.

The only other thing worth hunting out is **La Rotonda**, as La Tempio Beata Vergine del Soccorso, in Piazza XX Settembre, is generally known. An octagonal edifice built in 1594 by **Zamberlan**, a pupil of Palladio, it has a campanile by **Longhena** (1655) and a Baroque high altar of gilded wood.

Fratta Polésine

The Villa Badoer is open Tues–Sun: summer 9am–noon & 3–7pm; winter 10am–noon & 2–5pm; free.

A trip to **FRATTA POLÉSINE**, 18km southwest of Rovigo, will appeal to the more ardent lovers of **Palladio**'s buildings. The **Villa Badoer**, designed in the 1560s, is one of his most eloquent flights of architectural rhetoric, with its distinctive curving colonnades linking the porticoed house to the storage spaces at the side. None of the original furnishings are left, but restorers have uncovered the villa's late sixteenth-century grotesque frescoes by **Giallo**, a recherché Florentine. Two **trains** a day from Rovigo will get you there for the afternoon session.

Adria and the Po delta

Heading **eastward** from Rovigo, trains leave every couple of hours for the Po delta and Chioggia. **ADRIA**, a town of about 20,000 inhabitants, is all that is left of the city from which the Adriatic Sea got its name. It's a sleepy little town sitting on a tributary of the Po some 25km inland now, owing to heavy silting in the lagoon. The only sight is the **Museo Archeologico** in Piazzale degli Etruschi, which has a collection of Greek and Etruscan pieces dating from the time when Adria was a major port.

It's difficult to explore the **Po Delta** properly unless you have a car, though bikes may be hired from *Vittorio Cacciatori* at Via Bologna 1 in PORTO TOLLE – to get there you have to get a bus from LOREO, a couple of train stops after Adria. *Vittorio Cacciatori* also hires out canoes, but if you prefer a less strenuous investigation of the waterways and islets, *Marino Cacciatori*, Via Varsarvia 12, runs half-day cruises in summer for around L12,000 per person – an excellent way to observe the waterfowl and other birds of the delta's nature reserve.

The Po delta's 300 square kilometres of water, swamps and mud flats constitute the finest **birdwatching** region in the country, with the prime sites being centred on COMACCHIO (buses from Venice) and the more southerly PUNTE ALBERETE, both of which lie outside the Veneto in Emilia Romagna. Migratory birds fly into the delta from both north and south, with several wintering species of ducks and waders giving way after April to magnificent herons and egrets – and even, rarely, the exotic glossy ibis.

A few villages around the Veneto sector of the delta tout themselves as seaside resorts. Unfortunately for them, the Po is the filthiest river in Italy, carrying an unspeakable brew of chemical fertilisers and industrial toxins into the northern reaches of the Adriatic. Its annual load of around 250 tons of arsenic, 60 tons of mercury, 20,000 tons of phosphorous and 136,000 tons of nitrates is a major cause of the **algae slicks** that have plagued the resorts of Italy's east coast in recent summers. Faced with a drop in bookings as high as fifty percent, the tourist boards tell everyone that the slime is harmless, blithely dismissing the Ministry of Health's warnings that children, old people, pregnant women, people with skin lesions – in fact, just about anyone who isn't in A1 health – should stay out of the water. The fact is that the precise biochemistry of the algae has still not been determined, as Professor Roberto Marchetti of Milan University has observed – "I have been studying these phenomena for years, but what is occurring in the Adriatic is appalling. It is something we know nothing about." Even if it does turn out to be benign to humans, it still stinks and clings to the skin like glue. And if it were to disappear tomorrow, the water round here would still be foul.

The Museo Archeologico is open daily April–Sept 9am–1pm & 3–7pm; Oct–March closes 6pm; L2000.

Chapter 18

Vicenza, Verona and around

Lying almost midway between Padua and Verona, the orderly and affluent city of **Vicenza** tends to be overlooked in favour of its more charismatic neighbours – passengers getting off at the train station are more likely to be personnel from the local US armed forces base than tourists. Yet the streets of Vicenza form one of the most impressive urban landscapes in Italy, owing largely to the activity of Andrea Palladio – the source of Western Europe's most influential architectural style. Buildings by Palladio and his acolytes are plentiful not only inside the city itself, but also out in the surrounding countryside, where the Venetian and Vicentine nobility built up their farming estates from the sixteenth century onwards.

A few of these **villas** are of interest only to cognoscenti like those who overrun Vicenza during September's architecture conference, but several – such as the **Villa Rotonda** and the Tiepolo-painted **Villa Valmarana**, both on the outskirts – make an impact on the uninitiated and the expert alike. And while Palladianism is the region's distinctive style, it doesn't monopolise the scene. Some of Vicenza's Gothic houses would look fine in Venice, and the **Palazzo Porto-Colleoni at Thiene** is as colourful a pile as you'll find in the Veneto.

Verona is perhaps best known to English speakers as the setting for Shakespeare's *Romeo and Juliet*, and supposed sites of their

Hostels and hotels in this guide are classified into nine price categories. **Hostels** (① & ②) are classified according to the **high-season cost per person per night**; the **hotel** categories refer to the **minimum** you can expect to pay for **a double room in high season**, excluding the cost of breakfast, which you might not be able to avoid.

① Under L20,000 per person.
② Over L20,000 per person.
③ Under L40,000 per room.
④ L40–60,000 per room.
⑤ L60–80,000 per room.
⑥ L80–100,000 per room.
⑦ L100–150,000 per room.
⑧ L150–200,000 per room.
⑨ Over L200,000 per room.

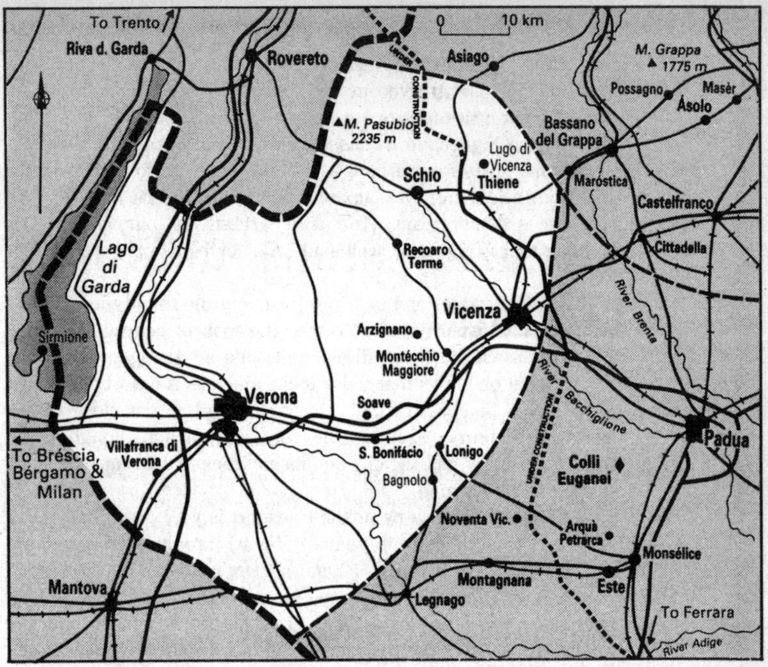

courtship are scattered over the city. Authentic remnants of the city's long and varied past are what makes the place so memorable, though – in particular, the remains of the **Roman** period. Of these, the superb **Arena** is the most prominent, followed by the **Teatro Romano** and various archways and gates. Also high on the list of things to see are the monuments left by the **Scaliger** family, the most celebrated rulers of medieval Verona. Their tombs are masterpieces of Gothic art, and scarcely less impressive is the **Castelvecchio**, once the Scaliger fortress and now home of Verona's civic museum.

More good-quality wine is produced in the Veneto than in any other area of Italy, and the region's most productive vineyards – **Soave, Valpolicella** and **Bardolino** – lie within the hinterland of Verona. Also easily reached from the city is **Lago di Garda**, on the western edge of the Veneto – a resort as popular with southern Austrians and Germans as it is with the Veronese.

Vicenza

Europe's largest centre for the production of textiles, and the focus of Italy's "Silicon Valley", **VICENZA** is a very sleek city – by some estimates, one of the country's richest half-dozen. The wealth isn't as ostentatious as in Milan, but still it can seem that there are as many Mercs and BMWs in town as there are buses, and in one of its backstreets there's a showroom that has Ferraris the way others have Fiats. The discreet Vicentine obsession with style pervades even the local clergy, who invited Italy's designers to improve the look of their priestly attire a couple of years back – prompting entries from big-league names such as Krizia and Laura Biagiotti. Asked what sort of outfit he would be likely to approve, Monsignor Don Giancarlo Santi was anxious not to be too restrictive: "We certainly wouldn't want *Valentino* written on our chests, but anything that is beautiful, well-made and serves its purpose is a gift of God."

Industrial estates and factories form a girdle round the city, and yet modern prosperity hasn't ruined the look of central Vicenza – still partly enclosed by medieval walls, it's an amalgam of Gothic and classical buildings that today looks much as it did when the last major phase of construction came to an end at the close of the eighteenth century. This historic core is compact enough to be explored in a day, but the city and its environs really require a short stay to do them justice.

Getting to Vicenza by public transport is very easy. **Trains** run about every half-hour from Venice (55min) through Padua, and are equally regular from Verona (30min); there's also an hourly service from Treviso (1hr) through Castelfranco Veneto. As with all Italian timetables, there are occasional gaps in the schedule, typically occurring just after the morning rush-hour, when the gap between trains may be twice as long as normal.

Vicenza's history – and Palladio

The early history of Vicenza follows a course familiar in this part of northern Italy – development under Imperial Rome, destruction by Attila, Lombard occupation, attainment of a degree of independence followed by struggles with neighbouring towns, rule by the Scaligers of Verona in the fourteenth century and finally absorption into the Venetian empire in 1404. The fifteenth-century palaces of Vicenza reflect its status as a Venetian satellite, with facades reminiscent of the Canal Grande, but in the latter half of the sixteenth century the city was transformed by the work of an architect who owed nothing to Venice but a lot to ancient Rome, and whose rigorous but flexible style was to influence every succeeding generation – Andrea di Pietro della Gondola, alias **Palladio**.

Born in Padua in 1508, Palladio came to Vicenza at the age of sixteen to work as a stonecutter. At thirty he became the protegé of a local nobleman, Count Giangiorgio Trissino, who directed his architectural training, gave him his classicised name, and brought him into contact with the dominant class of Vicenza. Some of these men were landowners, recently enriched now that peace had returned to the mainland after the War of the League of Cambrai, many were wealthy soldiers, and a decent percentage were well educated – it wasn't unknown for more than 40 of the 100 city councillors to possess doctorates. They turned to Palladio to design houses that would embody their financial and intellectual rank and their corporate superiority to their Venetian rulers. No architect in Western history has been more influential than Palladio, and although much of that influence derives from his *Quattro Libri dell'Architettura* (The Four Books of Architecture) – a survey of building techniques, classical structures and works (built and unbuilt) by himself – his buildings in and around Vicenza have been consistently studied by architects for the last four centuries. Between 1540 and his death in 1580 Palladio created around a dozen palaces and public buildings in Vicenza plus an even larger number of villas on the Vicentine and Venetian farming estates in the surrounding countryside, and the variety of his designs will surprise anyone who associates Palladianism with blandness. Even if you've been inclined to agree with Herbert Read's opinion that "In the back of every dying civilisation there sticks a bloody Doric column", you might well leave Vicenza converted.

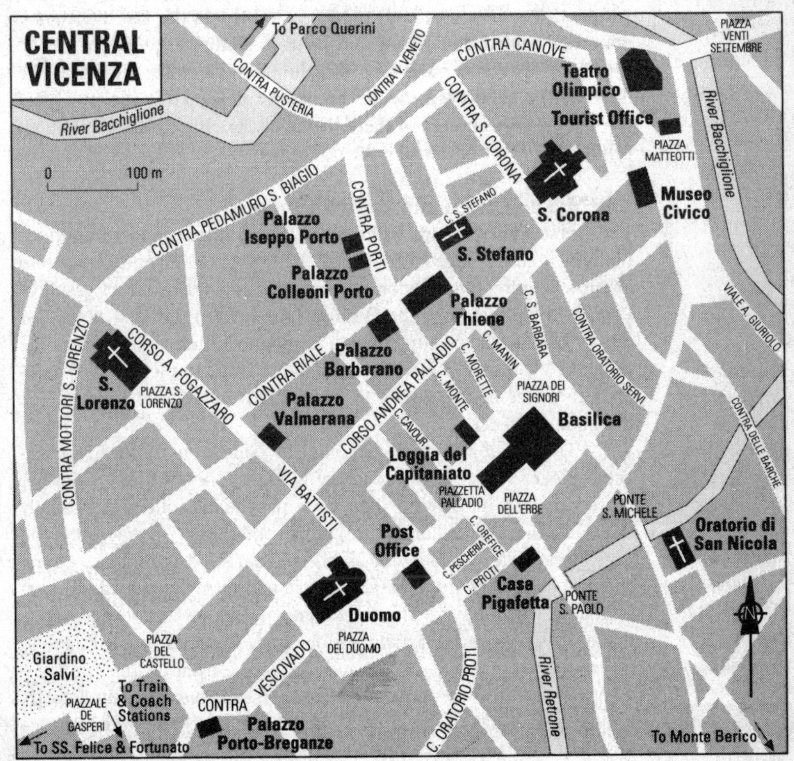

The City

The main street of Vicenza, the **Corso Andrea Palladio**, is a vestige of the Roman street-plan and cuts right through the old centre from the Piazza Castello (overlooked by an eleventh-century tower, once part of the Scaligers' fort) down to the Piazza Matteotti. Cars are banned from the Corso, so the palaces that line it – now all occupied by shops, offices and banks – can be admired with little risk of being killed, although you should keep your ears open for mopeds.

The first major building comes just before the start of the Corso, on the far side of the Piazza Castello – it's the fragmentary **Palazzo Porto-Breganze**, Palladio's last palace in Vicenza. None of Palladio's town houses were completed to plan, but none of the others is as flagrantly unfinished as this one.

Particularly striking on the Corso itself are the following houses: no.13, the **Palazzo Thiene Bonin-Longhare** (by Palladio's follower Scamozzi); no. 38–40, **Palazzo Pagello** (1780); no. 47 **Palazzo Thiene** (fifteenth century); no. 67, **Palazzo Brunello** (fifteenth century – have a look at the courtyard); no. 98, **Palazzo Trissino** (now the town hall; by Scamozzi); no. 147, **Palazzo da Schio** (fifteenth century, restored), which is known as the Ca' d'Oro as it once had gilded decoration and bears a slight resemblance to the Ca' d'Oro in Venice; and no. 163, the **Casa Cogollo**, known as the Casa del Palladio even though he neither designed it (despite what the plaque says) nor lived there. None of the churches on the Corso repays the effort of pushing the door open.

The Museo Civico and Teatro Olimpico

The Corso Palladio ends with one of the architect's most imperious buildings, the **Palazzo Chiericati**. Begun in 1550 and completed about a hundred years later, this commission was a direct result of Palladio's success with the Basilica (see below), being a house for one of the Basilica's supervisors, Girolamo Chiericati. It's now the home of Vicenza's **Museo Civico**, many of whose pieces were gathered together in the 1810s to keep them out of the grasp of the marauding French.

The Museo Civico is open Tues–Sat 9.30am–noon & 2.30–5pm, Sun 9.30am–noon; L3000, combined ticket for Museo Civico & Santa Corona museum L5000.

The ground-floor archaeological collection of locally excavated pieces from the fifth century BC to the seventh AD is neither more nor less interesting than such provincial collections usually are, but the art galleries are more ambitious – especially the *Sezione d'Arte Medievale*, a hi-tech zone of automatic doors, hyper-sensitive environmental controls and ultra-sophisticated presentational techniques. The backbone of the picture collection is made up by Vicentine artists – Montagna, Buonconsiglio, Fogolino (all sixteenth century), Maffei and Carpioni (seventeenth century) – whose work throws up some pleasant surprises without actually knocking you flat on your back. It's the more celebrated names – Memling, Tintoretto, Veronese, Giambattista Tiepolo, van Dyck –

who'll probably make the visit memorable. Mind you, Carpione's emetic bubble-blowing cherub does tend to stick in the mind, as does the ceiling fresco in one of the ground-floor rooms – a comically unflinching depiction of what you'd see if a group of horses steered by a stark naked charioteer flew overhead.

Across the Piazza Matteotti is the one building in Vicenza you shouldn't fail to go into – the **Teatro Olimpico**, the oldest indoor theatre in Europe. Approached in 1579 by the members of the humanist Accademia Olimpica to produce a design for a permanent theatre, Palladio devised a covered amphitheatre derived from his reading of Vitruvius, architect to Augustus, and his studies of Roman structures in Italy and France. In terms of the development of theatre design, the Teatro Olimpico was not a progressive enterprise – contemporaneous theatres in Florence, for example, were far closer to the modern proscenium arch – but it was the most comprehensive piece of classical reconstruction of its time, and the men responsible for it were suitably proud of their brainchild: the toga-clad figures above the stage are portraits of Palladio's clients.

The Teatro Olimpico is open March 16–Oct 15 Mon–Sat 9.30am–12.20pm & 3–5.30pm, Sun 9.30am–12.20pm; Oct 16–March 15 Mon–Sat 9.30am–12.20pm & 2–4.30pm, Sun 9.30am–12.20pm; L5000.

Palladio died soon after work commenced, and the scheme was then overseen by Scamozzi, whose contribution to the design – a backstage perspective of an idealised Thebes – is its most startling feature. As is demonstrated by the theatre's guide (who'll give you a commentary in English on request), the appearance of long urban vistas is created by tilting the "streets" at an angle that demands chamois-like agility from the actors. The building was opened on March 3, 1585, with an extravagant production of *Oedipus Rex* that somehow had 108 performers on its roll-call, and although it later had to share the spotlight with the Teatro Eretenio, today it's once more the only permanent theatre in Vicenza.

The Piazza dei Signori

At the hub of the city, the Piazza dei Signori, stands the most awesome of Palladio's creations – the *Palazzo della Ragione*, known to all but the pedantic as the **Basilica**. Designed in the late 1540s, though not finished until the second decade of the next century, this was Palladio's first public project and secured his reputation. The architect himself, generally regarded as a mild and modest individual, had no doubt as to its merit: "this building can be compared to ancient ones and placed with the most beautiful of the major buildings that have been made by the ancients", he wrote in the *Quattro Libri*. The monumental regularity of the Basilica disguises the fact that the Palladian building is effectively a stupendous piece of buttressing – the Doric and Ionic colonnades, constructed in Istrian stone, enclose the fifteenth-century brick meeting-hall of the city council, an unstable structure which had defied a number of attempts to prop it up before Palladio's solution was put into effect. And if you look closely you'll see that the colonnades aren't quite as regular as they first appear – Palladio had to vary the spaces to accommodate the passageways that go through the lower level. The vast Gothic hall, entered from the upper gallery, is often used for exhibitions, and discussions are taking place about the feasibility of converting the Basilica into an arts centre, but it's early days yet; at the moment the only cultural institution in full-time residence is the *Centro Internazionale di Architettura "A. Palladio"*, the keepers of the sacred flame and organisers of Vicenza's annual architectural conference.

The hall of the Basilica is open Tues–Sat 9.30am–noon & 2.30–5pm, Sun 9.30am–noon; free.

Facing the Basilica across the Piazza dei Signori is a late Palladio building, the unfinished **Loggia del Capitaniato**. Built as accommodation for the Venetian military commander of the city (the *Capitano*), it's decorated with reliefs in celebration of the Venetian victory over the Turks at Lépanto in 1571. Had it been completed, the Loggia would have taken up much of the area now occupied by the terrace of the swish *Gran Caffè Garibaldi*; houses used to join onto the Loggia on that side, but they were demolished in the 1930s. Completing the enclosure of that side of the Piazza is the **Monte di Pietà**, put up in two instalments in the first half of the sixteenth century, which brackets the seventeenth-century church of **San Vincenzo**. The worryingly slender **Torre di Piazza** reached its present altitude in 1444, having been started in the twelfth century and raised in 1311; its clock is claimed to have been the first such public timepiece in Italy. The inescapable Lion of Saint Mark was deposited on top of its column in the mid-fifteenth century, not long after Venice took Vicenza to its bosom; the companion figure of the Redeemer dates from the mid-seventeenth century.

As in the sixteenth century, a daily fruit, vegetable and flower **market** is pitched at the back of the Basilica, in the Piazza dell'Erbe – glowered over by medieval **Torre del Tormento**, once the prison tower. If you're shopping for food, you'll save yourself quite a few lire by dropping down the slope to the shops over the river, where prices tend to be a notch or two lower than within the Basilica's shadow. On Tuesdays a vast general market hits town, spreading along the roads between the Basilica and the Duomo.

In Contrà Pigafetta, just a few yards down the slope from the Piazzetta Palladio, on the Duomo side of the Basilica, there's Vicenza's architectural oddity, the Spanish-influenced **Casa Pigafetta**. Built in 1481, it was the birthplace of Antonio Pigafetta, who set out with Magellan on his voyage of 1519 and kept a record of the expedition. Unlike his leader, Pigafetta lived to see his home town again. If you're puzzled by the street name, *contrà* – sometimes *contrada* – is the Vicentine dialect alternative to *via*.

The Duomo

The **Duomo**, founded before the eighth century but substantially rebuilt chiefly from the fourteenth to the sixteenth century, was bombed to bits in 1944 and carefully reconstructed after the war. It's a gloomy place, notable primarily as one of the few Italian cathedrals to be overwhelmed by its secular surroundings. A polyptych by **Lorenzo Veneziano** (fifth chapel on right) and a *Madonna* by **Montagna** (fourth chapel on left) are the best of its paintings.

Excavations in the crypt have uncovered Roman pavements and parts of a pre-ninth-century basilica, but there's no admission to the public. You can, however, visit the **Criptoporticus** – probably part of a first-century palace – that was unearthed beneath the Palazzo Proti on the other side of the Piazza Duomo. Access is through the door at no. 6, but you first have to apply at the *Centro Touristico Giovanile*, at no. 2.

The Criptoporticus is open Thurs & Sat 10–11.30am.

Santa Corona and Santo Stefano

Far more interesting than the Duomo is the Dominican church of **Santa Corona**, on the other side of the Corso Palladio, at the Piazza Matteotti end. Begun in 1261 to house a thorn from Christ's crown, it has what's said to be the oldest Gothic interior in the Veneto; the thorn itself, a gift from the beatified King Louis IX of France, is sometimes displayed in its fourteenth-century gold reliquary in the chapel on the left of the chancel. Santa Corona is a church that positively welcomes visitors – everything is well labelled and well lit, the sacristan actually volunteers information about the place, and there's even piped Bach and Handel as background music. Here you'll find two of the three superlative church paintings in Vicenza – *The Baptism of Christ*, a late work by **Giovanni Bellini** (fifth altar on left), and *The Adoration of the Magi*, painted in 1573 by **Paolo Veronese** (fourth chapel on right). Also well worth a look are the late fifteenth-century inlaid **choir stalls**, the simple and tranquil **Valmarana Chapel**, added to the crypt in 1576 by Palladio, and the anonymous *Madonna* near the Bellini picture, which includes at its base a view of Vicenza around 1500, added by **Fogolino**. The cloisters of Santa Corona, recently restored, now house a run-of-the-mill Museo Naturalistico-Archeologico.

Santa Corona is open daily: summer 9.30am–12.30pm & 3.30–6.30pm; winter 9.30am–12.30pm & 3–6pm.

The Santa Corona museum is open the same hours as Museo Civico; L3000, or L5000 for combined ticket.

The nearby church of **Santo Stefano** merits a call for the city's third outstanding painting – **Palma il Vecchio**'s typically stolid and fleshy *Madonna and Child with St George and St Lucy*. Getting into Santo Stefano is a bit hit-and-miss; you're likeliest to succeed from 9 to 11am and 4 to 6.30pm.

Contrà Porti and around

The entrance to Santo Stefano faces the most powerful Gothic palace in the city, the **Casa Fontana**, and the immense **Palazzo Negri** – but more intimidating than either is Palladio's rugged **Palazzo Thiene**, on the Corso side of them. Had Palladio's plan been realised, the palace would have occupied the entire block down to the Corso and back to Contrà Porti; in the end, work progressed no further than the addition of this wing to the block built for the Thiene family at the end of the fifteenth century. The facade of the Gothic portion is in Contrà Porti. Palladio was not simply the most inventive architect in the Veneto, he was also the most cost-effective: his columns are usually made of brick covered with a skim of plaster, and as an inspection of the Thiene residence will reveal, his rough-hewn stonework is just cunningly worked brick as well.

There's no better example than Contrà Porti of the way in which the builders of Vicenza skilfully grafted new houses onto old without doing violence to the line of the street: the palaces here span two centuries, yet the overall impression is one of cohesion. At no. 8 is the Gothic **Palazzo Cavalloni**; over the road at no. 11 is Palladio's **Palazzo Barbarano**, designed around 1570 and subsequently tarted up by others; the Thiene palace is followed by the Renaissance **Palazzo Trissino-Sperotti** (no. 14), opposite which is a sweep of Gothic houses, the best being the fourteenth-century **Palazzo Colleoni Porto** (19); next door is Palladio's **Palazzo Iseppo Porto**, designed a few years after the Thiene and a couple of decades before the Barbarano. Luigi da Porto, the author of the story of Romeo and Juliet, died at no. 15 in 1529.

Contrà Porti takes you towards the Pusterla bridge and the **Parco Querini**, the biggest expanse of green in the city; with its backdrop of trees, its avenue of statuary and its tiny decorative hill (populated by ducks, rabbits and peacocks), it reminds you of the picturesque grounds of an eighteenth-century English country house. For those intent on doing a comprehensive Palladian tour, there's a palace by him on this side of the Bacchiglione river too – the **Palazzo Schio-Angaran** at no. 39 Contrà San Marco.

Along Corso Fogazzaro

Connected to Contrà Porti by Contrà Riale (itself not short of grand houses) is Corso A. Fogazzaro, a busy road with a spread of architectural attractions. At the Corso Palladio end is the **Palazzo Valmarana** (no. 16), where Palladio's use of overlapping planes makes the design of the facade legible in the narrow street and at the same time integrates the palace with the flanking buildings. Take a peep at the uncompleted courtyard – the finished section was no more than a third of the projected palace.

San Lorenzo is open daily 6.45am–noon & 3.30–7.30pm.

In the other direction you'll come across the Piazza San Lorenzo, on one side of which stands Francesco Muttoni's Palazzo Repeta, now the *Banca d'Italia*, with the thirteenth-century Franciscan church of **San Lorenzo** opposite. The fourteenth-century marble portal of the west front is the best feature of the church – the dimensions of the interior are impressive, but the church is rather barren in comparison with others of the same period in the Veneto, such as San Nicolò at Treviso or San Zanipolo and the Frari in Venice. **Montagna**'s fresco of the *Beheading of St Paul*, in the chapel on left side of chancel, may once have been stunning, but it's now looking pretty tattered. The cloister is worth a visit, though, even if the monastic calm has given way to the noise of traffic and the neighbouring school.

Further along, where the arcades give out, is the church of **Santa Maria del Carmine**; founded in the fourteenth century but redone in the nineteenth, it has pictures by **Montagna**, **Veronese** and **Jacopo Bassano** which more than compensate for the peculiar decor – although you'll need infra-red vision to make them out on an overcast day.

The fringes of the centre

If the Museo Civico's collection has led to your acquiring a taste for **Francesco Maffei**'s superheated rehashes of Tintoretto, you'll not want to miss the **Oratorio di San Nicola**, which has more paintings by him and his contemporary **Carpioni** than the normal retina can take. Prolonged contemplation of Maffei's delirious altarpiece – *The Trinity* – is strictly for the strong-stomached, but if you want to know what happened to painting in the Veneto after the golden age of the late Renaissance, this is a quick way of finding out.

The Oratorio is open summer Tues, Thurs, Sat & Sun 9.30am–12.30pm, plus Sat 3.30–7pm.

The Oratorio stands by the side of Vicenza's other river, the Retrone, at the foot of its most picturesque bridge, the hump-backed **Ponte San Michele**, built in 1620. You can follow a pleasant loop on the south side of the river by going straight ahead off the bridge to the Piazzola dei Gualdi, then basically following your nose, so that you go past the thirteenth-century gate called the **Portòn del Luzzo** and recross the Retrone by the **Ponte Furo**, from where there's a good view of the Basilica and Torre di Piazza. The long building on the opposite bank is Palladio's unexceptional first project in the city, the **Casa Civena** (c.1540).

Another area just out of the centre that's worth a look is on the far side of the Bacchiglione from the Teatro Olimpico. The bridge leads onto the major traffic confluence Piazza Venti Settembre: the building with porticoes on two facades is the **Palazzo Angaran** – fifteenth century, but rebuilt. In adjacent Contrà Venti Settembre there's the house with the best preserved of Vicenza's exterior frescoes, the fifteenth-century **Palazzo Regaù**.

Don't miss the church of **Santi Felice e Fortunato** either. It's on the opposite side of town, about ten minutes' walk along the Corso of the same name, past the **Giardino Salvi** – a compact little park whose winding gravel paths are punctuated by replicas of great sculptures. Dating back to immediately after the Edict of Constantine (313 AD), the basilica is **the oldest church in Vicenza**, and is approached by a path littered with ancient sarcophagi and architectural fragments. Wrecked by barbarian invaders in 899 and then by earthquakes in 1117, it was largely reconstructed in the twelfth century, and recent restorations have stripped away later accretions to reveal the form of the church at around that period. Remnants of the earliest building have survived – portions of fourth-century and fifth-century **mosaics** have been uncovered in the nave and right aisle, and a door off the right aisle leads into a fourth-century **martyrs' shrine**. Almost as remarkable as the mosaics and *martyrion* is the twelfth-century **fortified campanile**, which now looks as if it might have problems standing up to the next high wind.

Practicalities

The **tourist office** is alongside the entrance to the Teatro Olimpico, at Piazza Matteotti 12 (Mon–Sat 9am–12.30pm & 3–6pm, Sun 9am–12.30pm; ☎0444/320.854); they hand out a map that gives the addresses of all Vicenza's cinemas and sports halls plus details of local transport, a booklet seemingly written by the board of trade, and a very good leaflet on the Teatro. When the office is shut, make use of the *Digiplan* booth next to the piazza's Bar Museo; it looks like a public toilet, but is in fact a computerised information outlet, which will print out directions, phone numbers, accommodation details and so forth, all in English.

For **listings**, pick up a copy of the local papers – *Il Gazzettino* or *Il Giornale di Vicenza*. Culturally the busiest time of the year is from June to August, when there's a glut of concerts, opera productions and plays in town, many of the best being performed in the Teatro Olimpico.

The **post office** is in Piazza Garibaldi, between the Duomo and Basilica; the Corso Palladio is the place for **banks**. For telephones, the SIP offices are at Piazzetta Duomo 1 (daily 8.15am–9.30pm).

Accommodation

Vicenza's one-star **hotels** are nearly all on very noisy roads, above bars and some way out of the centre; best of them is the *Alpino*, Borgo Casale 33 (☎0444/505.137; ④); situated on a quiet residential street near the stadium, it can be reached by bus #3 or #15. Of the two-stars, the *Casa San Raffaele*, Viale X Giugno 10 (☎0444/323.663; ④), has the advantage of a beautiful position on the slope of Monte Bèrico, about half-an-hour's walk from the centre (see p.300). Of the two-stars within a few yards of the Piazza dei Signori, the following are worth trying – *Due Mori*, Contrà Do Rode 26 (☎0444/321.886; ⑤); *Vicenza*, Stradella dei Nodari 5 (☎0444/321.512; ④); and, friendliest of the bunch, *Palladio*, Via Oratorio dei Servi 25 (☎0444/321.072; ④). Wherever you decide to stay, ring ahead to book a room if you're going in summer or early autumn – some places close down in August, and Vicenza's popularity as a conference centre can make it tricky to find rooms, especially in September.

Snacks and restaurants

For a quick **snack**, the best places are *Paninoteca da Renato*, Stradella San Giacomo (between the Corso and Contrà Riale), or *La Cantinota*, Stradella del Garofalino (behind the *Corso* cinema), which offers sandwiches at lunchtimes and self-service meals in the evenings (open until 1am Mon–Fri, 2am on Sat). Another self-service place is *Righetti*, at Piazza del Duomo 3 – but it closes at 9pm and is only open weekdays. If you want to buy your own food, the *alimentari* of the Corso are excellent, especially *Il Ceppo* at no. 196; *Porro*, just south of the Basilica on Contrà Orefice, is also good. If you really want to save money you should head out of the centre across the Retrone, or try along the Corso Santi Felice e Fortunato, where there's a *Despar* supermarket at no. 109.

First recommendation for low-cost **restaurant** eating goes to the *Antica Casa della Malvasia*, Contrà delle Morette 5 (closed Mon) a bustling, roomy inn just off the Piazza dei Signori. The food is variable but cheap, unpretentious and genuinely regional; it has live music on Tuesday and Thursday; it's open till at least 1am on Friday and Saturday; and the bar's excellent too. It's possible to eat more cheaply in central Vicenza – at *Al Bersagliere*, Contrà Pescaria 11 (closed Sun) and *Alla Bella Vicenza*, Contrà G. da Proti – but the *Malvasia* is the one where you'd be tempted to make an evening of it.

Due Mori, Contrà do Rode 26 (closed Wed), and *Da Anna*, Contrà Porta Nova 41 (closed Tues), are big and busy pizzeria-restaurants – fine for pizzas and slightly more elaborate fare, as long as you don't want to linger over your food. Equally popular, but a shade less basic, is the *Vecchia Guardia*, at Contrà Pescheria Vecchia 11 (☎0444/321.231; closed Thurs).

Drifting upmarket a bit more, you might want to try *La Taverna*, in the ground floor of the Basilica (☎0444/547.326; closed Mon), or, up another class, the much-praised *Tre Visi*, Contrà Porti 6 (☎0444/38677; closed Sun & Mon). Local specialities include *baccalà alla Vicentina* (salt cod fried with anchovies and onion), *bigoli con l'arna* (spaghetti seasoned with gravy of roast duck) and *paeta col malgaragno* (turkey with pomegranates).

Bars, cafés and pasticcherie

As for **bars** in the centre of the city, the *Firenze* on Piazzetta A. Palladio is always friendly, as is the *Malvasia* (see above), but the most popular is *Il Grottino*, under the Basilica at Piazza Erbe 2 (closed Sun) – it has a good range of wines, a selection of cold food, and stays open till 2am. The *Big Ben* in Contrà Castello (closed Wed) is a busy pub-style bar, while the *Bar Blu*, Via Ponte San Paolo 2 (closed Mon) has good beer and a small riverside terrace; both these places stay open until 2am too.

There's a range of **cafés** and *pasticcerie* along the Corso and around the Basilica – try the excellent *Soraru*, in the Piazzetta Andrea Palladio, or the *Offelleria della Meneghina*, in Contrà Cavour. You'll find some good ones on Corso Fogazzaro as well. Best **ice creams** in town are at *Tutto Gelato* in Contrà Frasche (between the Basilica and the Duomo), though the huge *Gran Caffè Garibaldi*, on the Piazza dei Signori, runs it close.

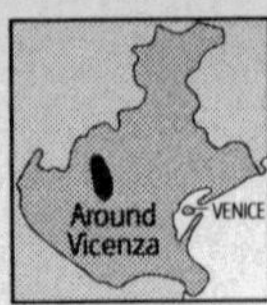

Around Vicenza

The countryside around Vicenza is dotted with hundreds of **villas**, many of them the result of Venice's diversion of money into agriculture in the mid-sixteenth century, as a way protecting the economy against the increasing uncertainties of shipping. The tourist office in Vicenza hands out a booklet and a map plotting the location of all of them, and if you have a hundred thousand lire to spare you can choose between a number of magnificently illustrated tomes on the subject. The trouble is, many of the villas are best seen as glossy photos, because some of the buildings are in the middle of nowhere, some are falling to bits and some of the better-kept specimens are closed to the public. And of those that are open, accessible and in fair condition, some probably won't make much impression on the untrained eye – such as Palladio's **Villa Thiene** at QUINTO VICENTINO (a short journey on the #10 bus) or his **Villa Pojana** at far-flung POJANA MAGGIORE. Yet a number of the villas of wider interest lie within the orbit of Vicenza's public transport network; two of the best, indeed, are to be found right on Vicenza's doorstep, beneath the pilgrimage church of **Monte Bèrico**, the other big attraction of Vicenza's immediate surroundings.

(Other villas of the Veneto are dealt with in the appropriate sections of this guide – for example, "The Brenta", "Masèr", "Castelfranco Veneto".)

Monte Bèrico

Rising behind the rail line, **Monte Bèrico** is seen by everyone who comes to Vicenza, but not actually visited by many, which is a pity as an expedition up the hill has a number of attractions: an amazing view (on a clear day the horizon beyond Vicenza is a switchback of mountain peaks), a clutch of excellent paintings and one of Europe's most famous and imitated buildings.

Buses for Monte Bèrico leave the coach station (beside the train station) on average every ninety minutes; on foot it takes around half an hour from the centre of town. If you decide to walk, the best route is to head for Viale X Giugno (ignoring the road sign that directs you up Viale Dante) and then follow the *Portici*, an eighteenth-century arcade built to shelter the pilgrims on their way up to the church.

In 1426–28 Vicenza was struck by an outbreak of bubonic plague, in the course of which the Virgin appeared twice at the summit of Monte Bèrico to announce the city's deliverance. A chapel was raised on the spot that the Virgin had obligingly marked out for its construction, and it duly became a place of pilgrimage. It was enlarged later in the century, altered again in the sixteenth century, and then, at the end of the seventeenth, replaced by the present **Basilica di Monte Bèrico**. (The facade of the enlarged fifteenth-century version is stuck onto the church's right side.) Pilgrims regularly arrive here by the coachload, and the glossy interior of the church, all gilding and fake marble, is immaculately maintained to receive them. A well-stocked shop in the cloister sells devotional trinkets to the faithful, close to a cash desk displaying the current rates for customised masses and other services.

The sceptical should nevertheless venture into the church for Montagna's *Pietà* (1500), in the chapel on right side of the apse, and *The Supper of St Gregory the Great* by **Veronese** (1572), in the refectory, off the cloister. The latter, the prototype of *The Feast in the House of Levi* in Venice's Accademia, was used for bayonet practice by Austrian troops in 1848 – the small reproduction outside the refectory shows what a thorough job they did on it.

The **Piazzale della Vittoria**, in front of the Basilica, was built to commemorate the dead of World War I; the local lads gather here to find out who's got the loudest car radio, a virility ritual that only slightly detracts from the pleasure of the view across the city.

The Villa Valmarana

Ten minutes' walk away from the Basilica is the **Villa Valmarana ai Nani** – meaning "of the dwarves", after the figures on the garden wall. It's an undistinguished eighteenth-century house made extraordinary by its decoration, a cycle of frescoes by **Giambattista and Giandomenico Tiepolo** which is one of the most gorgeous in the Veneto. To get there, go back to the elbow of the *Portici*, along Via M. D'Azeglio for about a hundred metres, then right into the cobbled Via S. Bastiano, which ends at the Villa Valmarana.

Villa Valmarana is open March 15–April 30 Tues–Sat 2.30–5.30pm plus Wed, Thurs, Sat & Sun 10am–noon; May–Sept Tues–Sat 3–6pm plus same morning times; Oct–Nov 5 Tues–Sat 2–5pm plus same morning times; L5000.

There are two parts to the house. The main block, the six-roomed **Palazzina**, was frescoed with brilliant virtuosity by Giambattista, drawing his heroic imagery from Virgil, Tasso and Ariosto – you're handed a brief guide to the paintings at the entrance. Giambattista also painted one room of the **Foresteria**, the guest wing, but here the bulk of the work was done by his son Giandomenico; his predilections were a little less cerebral than his father's, but his technique was very nearly as accomplished.

La Rotonda

From the Valmarana house the narrow Strada Valmarana descends the slope to **La Rotonda**, unique among Palladio's villas in that it was designed not as the main building of a farming estate but as a pavilion in which entertainments could be held and the landscape enjoyed. Begun in 1566 and finished five years later, it was commissioned by Vicenza-born Paolo Almerico as his retirement home, after years in Rome in the service of the papacy. He chose a hilltop site "surrounded by other most pleasant hills, which present the appearance of a vast theatre" – and Palladio's design certainly makes the most of its centre-stage setting. The combination of the pure forms of the circle and square was a fundamental problem of

Renaissance architecture (Leonardo, Bramante and Michelangelo all worked at it), and the elegance of Palladio's solution led to innumerable imitations – for example Mereworth and Chiswick in England, and Jefferson's rejected plan for the official residence of the US president, a near facsimile of the Rotonda.

The Rotonda is open March 15–Oct 15 Wed 10am–noon & 3–6pm; L5000, including the grounds. The grounds are open all year Tues–Sun same times; L3000.

Only a tour of the lavishly decorated rooms will fully reveal the subtleties of the Rotonda's design, as the interior plan doesn't replicate the symmetry of the exterior. If you're here on a day when the interior's shut, try to get to see Joseph Losey's film of Mozart's *Don Giovanni* – the Rotonda was used as the remorseless seducer's residence. The grounds are open all year, but unless you're an architecture student and really want to scrutinize the walls from point-blank range, the garden can be given a miss, as it's not much more than a belt of grass round the villa.

The Villa Cordellina-Lombardi and Villa Pisani

The Villa Cordellina is open Tues–Fri 9am–1pm, Sat & Sun 9am–noon & 3–6pm; L5000.

A must for Tiepolo fans is the eighteenth-century **Villa Cordellina-Lombardi**, on the outskirts of the small town of **MONTECCHIO MAGGIORE**, 13km to the southwest of Vicenza. Giambattista's frescoes in the entrance hall – *The Clemency of Scipio*, *The Clemency of Alexander* and, on the ceiling, *The Light of Reason Driving out the Fog of Ignorance* – are a touch less exuberant than the later ones at the Villa Valmarana, and show his debt to Paolo Veronese more plainly, but they will still make you feel better about life for the rest of the day.

Montecchio's other attractions, a pair of rebuilt fourteenth-century **Scaliger forts** erected on a ridge overlooking the town, look their best from afar. They were made the strongholds of the Montague clan in Luigi da Porto's *Romeo and Juliet*.

A few **buses** from Vicenza go through Montecchio Maggiore, but there's a glut of services that pass through nearby ALTE CECCATO on their way to Lonigo, Sossano and Noventa Vicentina – get off when you see the huge *Bertozzo* clothes supermarket, then follow the signs for the villa, which is about ten minutes' walk from the road. The journey takes about twenty minutes, through an unrelentingly grim landscape of shops, factories and commercial estates.

The Villa Pisani

The Villa Pisani is open Tues, Fri & Sat 10am–noon & 2–6pm; L7000.

About 20km to the south of Montecchio Maggiore, at **BAGNOLO**, stands Palladio's **Villa Pisani**. Dating from the early 1540s, the Villa Pisani is one of his less sophisticated designs, marking a transition from the traditional fortified villa to the fully classicised projects of the later sixteenth century. The division of the rooms follows a pattern found all over the Veneto: kitchens in the basement, highly decorated living quarters on the next level, and granary space on the upper storey.

Only specialists will get a great deal out of this house, but if you've got a car you might want to give it a look – getting there by public transport involves a bus from Vicenza to LONIGO (almost hourly), then a four-kilometre walk, though at least the hike offers the diversion of a good view of Scamozzi's Villa Rocca-Pisani, a lineal descendant of the Rotonda. The last bus back from Lonigo to Vicenza leaves at 5.45pm. From time to time the Pisani terrace is packed with upper-crust tourists who've paid even more than the customary whack to secure the honour of sipping wine with the boss – so it's wisest to ring ahead to check that the gates aren't chained against the plebs (☎0444/831.104).

Thiene and Lugo di Vicenza

It was only with the ending of the War of the League of Cambrai in 1516 that the landowners of the Veneto were able to disregard defensive considerations when building homes out of the urban centres – prior to that, the great houses of the *terra firma* were a sort of cross-breed between a castle and a palace. The most imposing example of this genre still standing is the **Villa Porto-Colleoni**, built in the 1470s at **THIENE**, a bland textile town 20km north of Vicenza.

Guided tours of the Villa Porto-Colleoni are held March 15–Oct 15 3–5pm; L6000.

The crenellated corner towers, large central block and the encircling protective wall are all features that would have been common in this area in the fifteenth century, although this house, with its facade decorations and ornate Gothic windows, was probably more precious than most. Nowadays the buildings that most closely resemble it are to be found along Venice's Canal Grande (for example the Fondaco dei Turchi) – which is not as strange as it first seems, as they belong to the same family tree, springing from the long-ruined provincial villas of the late Roman Empire. The mandatory guided tour of the interior makes the most of the workaday sixteenth-century frescoes by Giambattista Zelotti and G.A. Fasolo; the plethora of equine portraits is explained by the fact that the Colleoni had a tradition of service in the Venetian cavalry.

To get to Thiene from Vicenza, take the Schio **train**; it leaves virtually every hour, and takes 25 minutes.

Lugo di Vicenza

The Villa Godi Malinverni is open Tues, Sat & Sun: March–May & Sept–Nov 2–6pm; June–Aug 3–7pm; L5000.

The next rung up the evolutionary ladder of the villas of the Veneto is represented 8km to the north of Thiene, on the edge of **LUGO DI VICENZA** (aka Lonedo di Lugo), where you'll find Palladio's first villa – the **Villa Godi Malinverni**, built in 1537–42. The plan of the Villa Godi Malinverni isn't all that different from that of the Villa Porto-Colleoni, but it's been shorn of fortified trappings and is clearly more of a country house than a castle; on the other hand, there's not a feature on the building that refers to the architecture of ancient Rome, and so it could be seen as occupying a position on the evolutionary chain between the Gothic and Renaissance villas.

Professor Remo Malinverni restored the house in the early 1960s, and installed his collection of nineteenth-century Italian paintings in some of the rooms; elsewhere in the building you'll find a fossil museum – neither display can really compete with the sixteenth-century frescoes, some of which show the journeyman **Giambattista Zelotti** on top form.

The Piovene gardens are open daily: summer 2.30–7pm; winter 2–5pm; L3000.

Just above the Godi Malinverni stands the **Villa Piovene**, the central block of which was also built by Palladio around 1540; the Ionic portico was added later in the sixteenth century, and the external staircase and portal came in the eighteenth. Only the nineteenth-century landscaped garden is open to the public.

An infrequent **bus** service runs from Thiene to Lugo, on its way to CALVENE – there's a stop by the Porto-Colleoni.

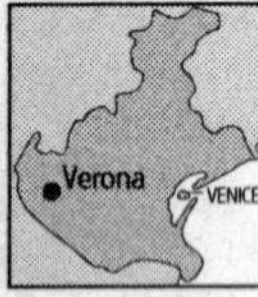

Verona

With its wealth of Roman sites and streets of pink-hued medieval buildings, the easy-going city of **VERONA** has more in the way of historic attractions than any other place in the Veneto except Venice itself. Unlike Venice, though, it's not a city overwhelmed by the tourist industry, important though that is to the local economy. Verona is the largest city of the mainland Veneto, its economic success largely due to its position at the crossing of the major routes from Germany and Austria to central Italy and from the west to Venice and Trieste.

Verona's initial development as a **Roman** settlement was similarly due to its straddling the main east–west and north–south lines of communication. A period of decline in the wake of the disintegration of the Roman Empire was followed by revival under the Ostrogoths, who in turn were succeeded by the Franks – Charlemagne's son, Pepin, ruled his kingdom from here. By the twelfth century Verona had become a city state, and in the following century approached the zenith of its independent existence with the rise of the **Scaliger** family. Ruthless in the exercise of power – they once employed Werner of Urlingea, self-styled "enemy of God and of compassion" – the Scaligers were at the same time energetic patrons of the arts, and many of Verona's finest buildings date from the century of their rule. Both Giotto and Dante were guests of the Scaligers, the latter dedicating his *Paradiso* to Cangrande I, head of the family at the time.

With the fall of their dynasty a time of upheaval ensued, Gian Galeazzo Visconti of Milan emerging with control of the city. Absorption into the Venetian empire came in 1405, and Venice continued to govern Verona down to the arrival of Napoleon. Verona's history then shadowed that of Venice: a prolonged interlude of Austrian rule, brought to an end by the unification of Italy.

Arrival, information and accommodation

Unless you're staying in the youth hostel, the only buses you're likely to need in Verona are the frequent #1 or #8 services (#51 or #58 in the evening) from the **train and bus stations** to the Piazza Brà, site of the Arena and the hub of Verona; buy your ticket before you get on board, from just outside the station.

The main **tourist office** is close to the Arena at Via Leoncino 61 (summer Mon–Sat 8am–8pm, plus Sun 9am–8pm in July & Aug; winter Mon–Sat 8am–7pm; ☎045/592.828). In summer there are additional offices at Piazza Erbe 42 and at the train station (same hours).

Hotels

Al Castello, Corso Cavour 43 ☎045/800.4403. One of the best-situated one-stars. ④.

Armando, Via Dietro Pallone 1 ☎045/800.026. Just about the cheapest rooms within strolling distance of Piazza Brà. ③.

Aurora, Via Pellicciai 2 ☎045/594.717. Two-star hotel, with many rooms overlooking the Piazza delle Erbe. ⑤.

Catullo, Via V. Catullo 1 ☎045/800.2786. Very central one-star, just off Via Mazzini. ④.

Il Torcolo, Vicolo Listone 3 ☎045/800.7512. Nicely turned-out two-star hotel within 100m of the Arena. Extremely welcoming owners – and a favourite with the opera crowds, so book well in advance. ⑤.

Volta Cittadella, Via Volta Cittadella 8 ☎045/800.0077. Another rock-bottom option within the historic centre; midnight curfew. ④.

Hostels and campsites

Ostello della Gioventù, Salita Fontana del Ferro 15 ☎045/590.360. A beautiful old building behind the Teatro Romano; as it's quite a walk from the centre, it's best to take bus #2 or #32 to Piazza Isolo. There's officially a 10.30pm curfew, but there's some flexibility extended to guests with concert tickets. Also has a campsite. ①.

Casa della Giovane, Via Pigna 7 ☎045/596.880. Convent-run hostel for women, with similar curfew to the main hostel. ②.

Campeggio Castel San Pietro, Via Castel S. Pietro 2 ☎045/592.037. Along with the hostel site, this is the most pleasant and convenient place to camp near Verona – take bus #3 or #15 to Via Marsala.

The City

The first impression of Verona is of a city with space. The big lazy curve of the River Adige has carved a wide amphitheatre out of the hills that gives room to look down on the city from within its boundaries, and walking around the city walls, the embankments of the river, and in parts of the very centre, the sense of spaciousness persists. Even in areas where the city is more cramped, the banning of cars from many of the central roads makes Verona a less pressurised place than Padua, for instance, which is a city of comparable size.

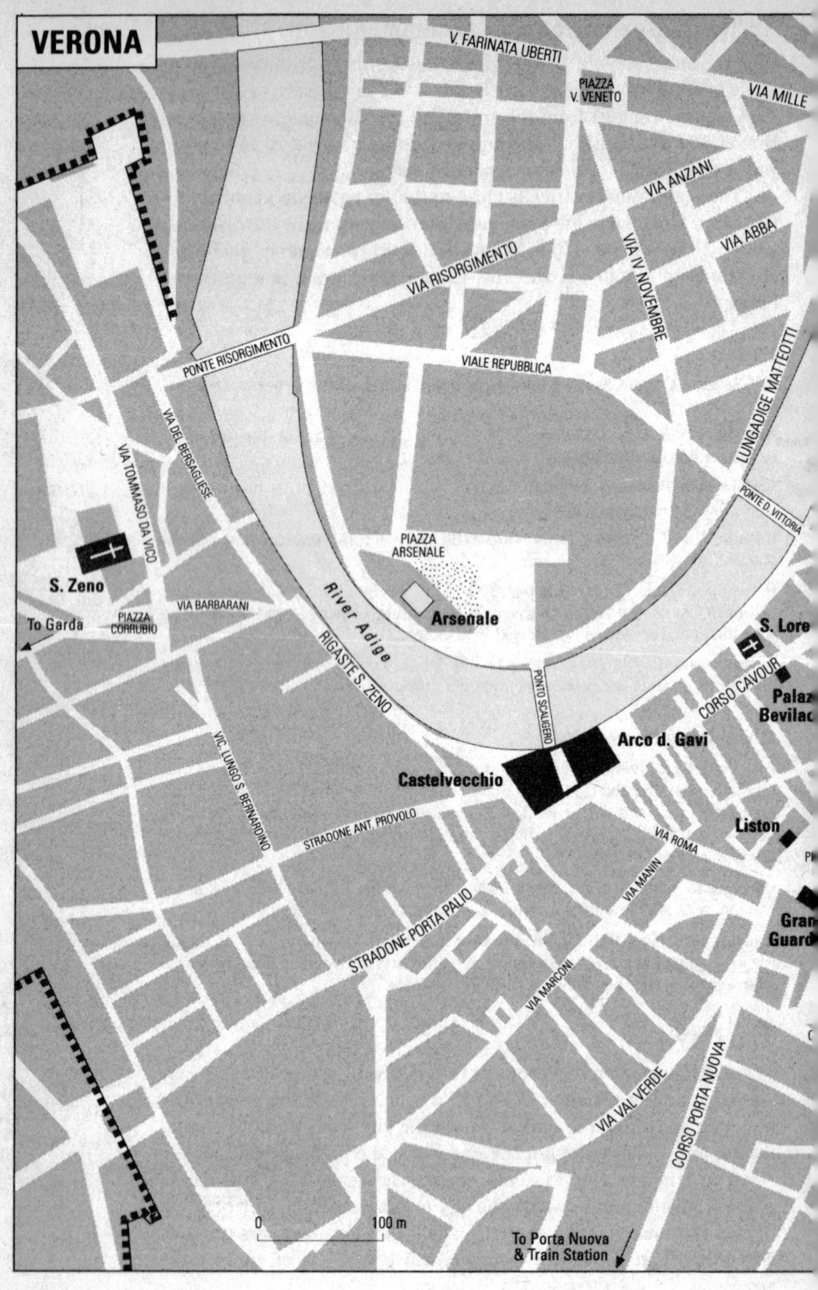
VERONA
V. FARINATA UBERTI
PIAZZA
V. VENETO
VIA MILLE
VIA ANZANI
VIA ABBA
VIA RISORGIMENTO
VIA IV NOVEMBRE
PONTE RISORGIMENTO
VIALE REPUBBLICA
LUNGADIGE MATTEOTTI
VIA DEL BERSAGLIESE
VIA TOMMASO DA VICO
PONTE D. VITTORIA
PIAZZA
ARSENALE
S. Zeno
River Adige
Arsenale
To Garda
PIAZZA
CORRUBIO
VIA BARBARANI
S. Lore
RIGASTE S. ZENO
PONTO SCALIGERO
CORSO CAVOUR
Palaz
Bevilac
Arco d. Gavi
VIC. LUNGO S. BERNARDINO
Castelvecchio
STRADONE ANT. PROVOLO
Liston
VIA ROMA
VIA MANIN
STRADONE PORTA PALIO
Gran
Guard
VIA MARCONI
VIA VAL VERDE
CORSO PORTA NUOVA
0
100 m
To Porta Nuova
& Train Station

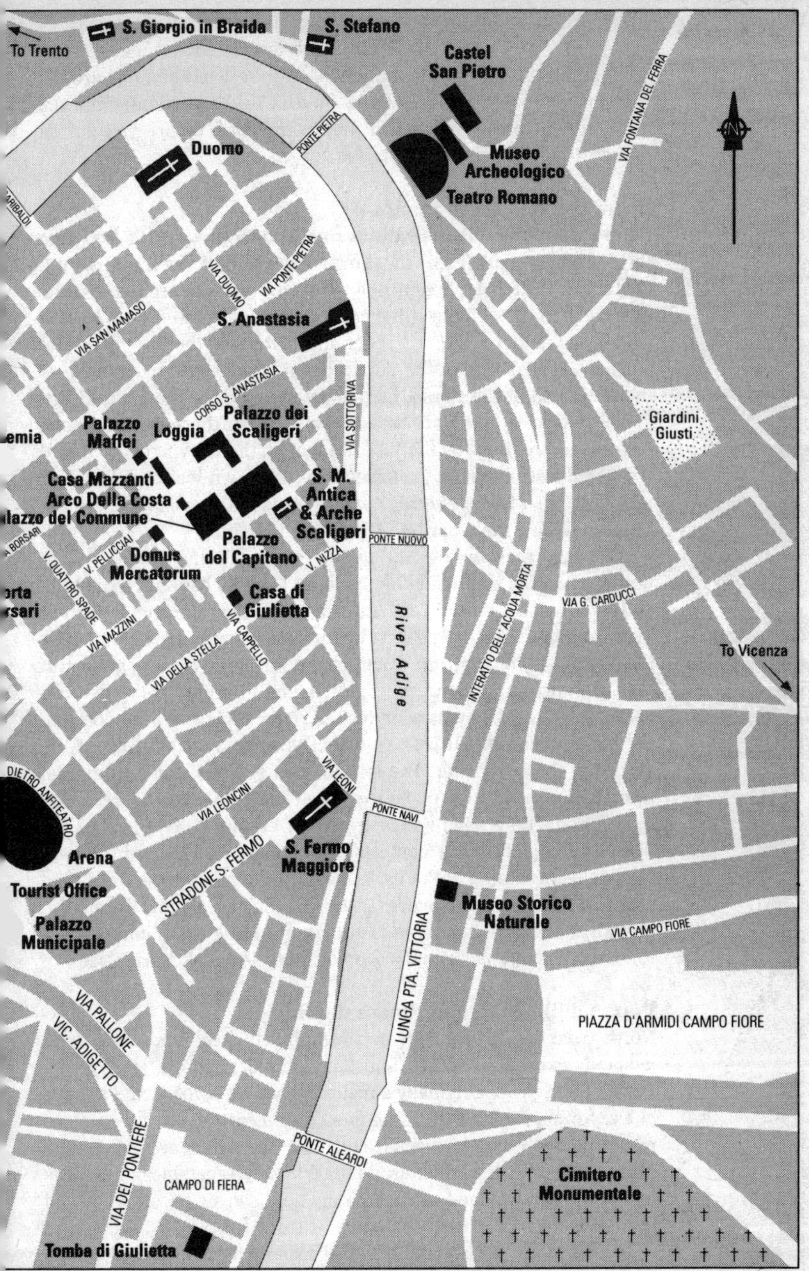

S. Giorgio in Braida
To Trento
S. Stefano
Castel
San Pietro
Duomo
Museo
Archeologico
Teatro Romano
VIA FONTANA DEL FERRA
PONTE PIETRA
VIA DUOMO
VIA PONTE PIETRA
S. Anastasia
VIA SAN MAMASO
CORSO S. ANASTASIA
VIA SOTTORIVA
Palazzo
Maffei
Loggia
Palazzo dei
Scaligeri
Giardini
Giusti
Casa Mazzanti
Arco Della Costa
S. M.
Antica
& Arche
Scaligeri
PONTE NUOVO
Palazzo
del Capitano
Domus
Mercatorum
V. PELLICCIAI
V. QUATTRO SPADE
V. NIZZA
Casa di
Giulietta
River Adige
VIA G. CARDUCCI
INTERATTO DELL' ACQUA MORTA
To Vicenza
VIA MAZZINI
VIA DELLA STELLA
VIA CAPPELLO
DIETRO ANFITEATRO
VIA LEONCINI
VIA LEONI
PONTE NAVI
Arena
S. Fermo
Maggiore
STRADONE S. FERMO
Tourist Office
Palazzo
Municipale
Museo Storico
Naturale
VIA CAMPO FIORE
LUNGA PTA. VITTORIA
VIA PALLONE
VIC. ADIGETTO
PIAZZA D'ARMIDI CAMPO FIORE
VIA DEL PONTIERE
PONTE ALEARDI
CAMPO DI FIERA
Cimitero
Monumentale
Tomba di Giulietta

Traffic restrictions make walking the most efficient way of exploring Verona, and the centre is concentrated enough to make this no great hardship. The only buses you're likely to need are the frequent #1 or #8 services (#51 or #58 in the evening) from the train station to the Piazza Brà; buy your ticket before you get on board, from just outside the station.

From the station to Piazza Brà

Coming from the station or the Verona Sud motorway exit, you pass the Verona's south gate, the **Porta Nuova**, built in the sixteenth century by Michele Sanmicheli (though messed around by the Austrians in the nineteenth century). From Corso Porta Nuova, which begins here, the red roofs and towers of the city stand out against the backdrop of the Torricelle and the Lessini mountains. At the other end of the Corso, battlemented arches of the **Portoni Brà** (1389), formerly part of the city walls, mark the entrance to the historic centre. Built by the Visconti family, the Portoni once carried a covered walk from the Castelvecchio (left down Via Roma) to their residence, of which only the **Torre Pentagona** remains, behind the **Palazzo della Gran Guardia** (1610) on the right.

The Arena is open Tues–Sun 8am–6.30pm; L6000, free on first Sun of month.

Through these arches the mildly chaotic **Piazza Brà** opens up, bordered on the south side by the Gran Guardia (now an exhibition and conference venue), on the east by the nineteenth-century **Palazzo Municipio**, on the west by the **Liston** – the starting point for the Veronese *passeggiata* – and at the far end by the mightiest of Verona's Roman monuments, the **Arena**. Dating from the first century AD, the Arena has survived in remarkable condition, despite the twelfth-century earthquake which destroyed all but four of the arches of the outer wall. The interior was scarcely damaged by the tremor, and nowadays audiences come here to watch gargantuan opera productions where once crowds of around 20,000 packed the benches for gladiatorial contests, mock naval battles and the like. Originally measuring 152m by 123m overall, and thus the third largest of all Roman amphitheatres – after the Colosseum and the amphitheatre at Capua – the Arena is still an awesome sight, and offers a fine urban panorama from the topmost of the 44 pink marble tiers.

Piazza delle Erbe and Piazza dei Signori

North from the Arena, narrow traffic-free Via Mazzini, lined with generally expensive clothes, shoes and jewellery shops, leads to the **Piazza delle Erbe**. Originally a major Roman crossroads and the site of the forum, Piazza delle Erbe is still the heart of the city, a place where people come to meet friends and see who's around. As the name suggests, the market used to sell mainly vegetables; nowadays the range has widened to include clothes, souvenirs, antiques and fast food.

Lined along the square's central axis, and camouflaged by the stalls, are the **Colonna Antica** (a fifteenth-century lantern on a marble pillar), the **Capitello** (a fourteenth-century pavilion where public servants were invested with their office), the fountain of **Madonna Verona** (built in 1368 by Cansignorio della Scala) and finally the column of the lion of Saint Mark, demonstrating Verona's past allegiance to Venice. This specimen is a nineteenth-century copy of one destroyed during the Pasqua Veronese (Veronese Easter), as the city's 1797 uprising against the French is known.

On the left as you look from the Via Cappello end, past the tall houses of the old Jewish ghetto, is the **Domus Mercatorum**, which was founded in 1301 as a merchants' warehouse and exchange and is now a bank and chamber of commerce. At the far end, the Baroque **Palazzo Maffei** has been taken over by shops, luxury apartments and an expensive restaurant; to its left is the fourteenth-century **Torre del Gardello** (1370) and to its right the **Casa Mazzanti**, whose sixteenth-century murals are best seen after dark, under enhancing spotlights.

Moving along this side of the piazza, the **Palazzo del Comune** – a twelfth-century building with Renaissance additions and nineteenth-century alterations – flanks the **Arco della Costa** (Arch of the Rib), the passageway to the Piazza dei Signori. Cynical folklore has it that the whale's rib suspended under the arch will fall if an adult virgin passes underneath.

Piazza dei Signori, sometimes known as Piazza Dante after the grimly pensive statue of the poet in the centre, used to be the chief public square in Verona. Much of the right side is taken up by the **Palazzo del Capitano** (with a splendid gateway by Sanmicheli), which is separated from the Palazzo del Comune by a stretch of excavated Roman street. Facing you as you come into the square is the **Palazzo degli Scaligeri**, residence of the Scaligers; a monument to more democratic times extends from it at a right angle – the late fifteenth-century **Loggia del Consiglio**, former assembly hall of the city council and Verona's outstanding early Renaissance building. The rank of Roman notables along the roof includes Verona's most illustrious native poet, Catullus. For a dizzying view, take a right as soon as you come into the square, and go up the twelfth-century **Torre dei Lamberti**; 83m tall, it's Verona's highest tower. The beautiful Gothic staircase alongside leads to the magistrates' chambers.

The Torre dei Lamberti is open Tues–Sun 8am–6.45pm; L4000 by lift, L3000 on foot.

The Arche Scaligere

Passing under the arch linking the Palazzo degli Scaligeri to the Palazzo del Capitano, you come to the little Romanesque church of **Santa Maria Antica**, in front of which are ranged the **Arche Scaligere**, some of the most elaborate Gothic funerary monuments in Italy. Over the side entrance to the church, an equestrian statue of **Cangrande I** ("Big Dog"; d.1329) grins on the summit of his tomb's pyramidal roof; the statue is a copy, the original being displayed in the Castelvecchio. The canopied tombs of the rest of the clan are enclosed within a wrought-iron palisade decorated with ladder motifs, the emblem of the Scaligers – the family name was della Scala, "scala" meaning ladder. **Mastino I** ("Mastiff"; d.1277), founder of the dynasty, is buried in the simple tomb against the wall of the church; **Mastino II** (d.1351) is to the left of the entrance, opposite the most florid of the tombs, that of **Cansignorio** ("Top Dog"; d.1375). The two who didn't take canine names, **Giovanni** (d.1359) and **Bartolomeo** (d.1304), are at the back.

Sant'Anastasia and the Duomo

Going on past the Arche Scaligeri, and turning left along Via San Pietro, you come to **Sant'Anastasia**, Verona's largest church. Started in 1290 and completed in 1481, it's mainly Gothic, with undertones of the Romanesque. The early fourteenth-century carvings of New Testament scenes around the doors are the most arresting feature of its bare exterior; the interior's highlight is **Pisanello**'s delicately coloured fresco of *St George and the Princess* (in the sacristy), a work in which the normally martial saint appears as something of a dandy.

Via Sottoriva, one of Verona's oldest streets, runs parallel to the Adige beyond Sant'Anastasia; the majority of the houses here date from the Middle Ages, making this one of Verona's most atmospheric areas. Spanning the river and leading over to the Roman theatre, the Roman **Ponte Pietra** was destroyed in 1945 by the retreating Germans, but rebuilt using mostly the original stones and bricks.

Verona's red and white striped **Duomo** lies just round the river's bend. Consecrated in 1187, it has been worked on constantly over the centuries and the campanile is still said to be incomplete, even though the bell-chamber wasn't added until 1927. As a whole it's Romanesque in its lower parts, developing into Gothic as it goes up; the two doorways are twelfth-century – look for the story of Jonah and the whale on the south porch, and the figures of statues of Roland and Oliver, two of Charlemagne's paladins, on the west. The interior has a splendid organ, and fascinating architectural details around each chapel and on the columns – particularly fine is the **Cappella Mazzanti** (last on the right). In the first chapel on the left, an *Assumption* by **Titian** occupies an architectural frame by **Sansovino**, who also designed the choir.

Just to the north of the Duomo is a Romanesque cloister, with fragments of sixth-century mosaic pavement, and the church of Sant'Elena, under which have been uncovered parts of the eighth-century precursor of the Duomo.

The Casa di Giulietta is open Tues–Sun 8am–6.30pm; L5000.

The Casa di Giulietta and San Fermo

South of Piazza delle Erbe runs Via Cappello, a street named after the family that Shakespeare turned into the Capulets – and there on the left, at no. 23, is the **Casa di Giulietta**. Sadly for romantics, the association of the house with Juliet is based on nothing more than its picturesque courtyard and balcony, and even this latter feature is placed, as Arnold Bennett wrote, "too high for love, unless Juliet was a trapeze acrobat, accustomed to hanging downwards by her toes". In fact, although the "Capulets" and the "Montagues" (Montecchi) did exist, Romeo and Juliet were entirely fictional creations; and although bloody feuds were common (the head of one family invited his enemy to a truce-making meal, informing him afterwards that he'd just dined off the liver of his son), there's no record of these two clans being at loggerheads. The cheerless facts notwithstanding, a bronze Juliet has been shoved into a corner of the courtyard, her right breast polished bright by groping hands. The house itself, constructed at the start of the fourteenth century, is in a fine state of preservation, but is largely empty.

There's another spurious "Romeo and Juliet" shrine – the Tomba di Giulietta – in the southwest of the city, in the cloister of the deconsecrated San Francesco al Corso; its hours and entry charge are the same as for the house.

Via Cappello leads into Via Leoni with its Roman gate, the **Porta Romana dei Leoni**, and segment of excavated Roman street, exposed three metres below today's street level. At the end of Via Leoni and across the road stands the red-brick **San Fermo** church, whose inconsistent exterior betrays the fact that it consists of two churches combined. The Benedictines built the original one in the eighth century, then rebuilt it in the eleventh to honour the relics of Saint Fermo and Saint Roch (both supposedly martyred on this site); very soon after, flooding forced them to superimpose another church for day-to-day use, a structure greatly altered in the early fourteenth century by the Minorites. The Gothic upper church may have no outstanding works of art (though the *Annunciation* by Pisanello at the west end is the earliest surviving fresco by the artist), but the numerous fourteenth-century frescoes and the fine wooden keel vault compose a graceful interior – made in 1314, the ceiling is the oldest such vault left in the Veneto. The Romanesque lower church can be entered from the left of the choir; its low vaulting is sometimes obscured by exhibitions.

To the Castelvecchio

After the Arena and the Teatro Romano, Verona's most impressive Roman remnant is the **Porta dei Borsari**, a structure which was as great an influence on the city's Renaissance architects as the amphitheatre. Now reduced to a monumental screen bestriding the road at the junction of Via Diaz and Corso Porta Borsari (west of Piazza delle Erbe), it used to be Verona's largest Roman gate; the inscription dates it at 265 AD, but it's almost certainly older than that.

Along Corso Cavour, which stretches away from the gate, you'll find a couple of minor churches including the Romanesque **San Lorenzo**; the **Palazzo Bevilacqua**, opposite, is an uncharacteristically ornate building by **Sanmicheli**. A short distance further, set back from the road on the right, stands the **Arco dei Gavi**, a first-century Roman triumphal arch; originally raised in the middle of the Corso, it was shifted to its present site overlooking the Adige in 1932. This is the best vantage point from which to admire the

The Castelvecchio is open Tues–Sun 8am–6.30pm; L6000.

Ponte Scaligero; built by Cangrande II between 1355 and 1375, the bridge was blown up by the Germans in 1945 – the salvaged material was used for the plausible reconstruction.

The fortress from which the bridge springs, the **Castelvecchio**, was commissioned by Cangrande II at around the same time, and became the stronghold for Verona's subsequent rulers, all of whom altered it in some way – for example, there's a small fort in the inner courtyard which was built by Napoleon. Opened as the city museum in 1925, it was damaged by bombing in World War II, but opened again after scrupulous restoration in 1964.

The Castelvecchio's collection of paintings, jewellery, weapons and other artefacts flows through a labyrinth of chambers, courtyards and passages that is fascinating to explore in itself. Halfway through the itinerary, you'll come face to face with the equestrian figure **Cangrande I**, removed from his tomb and strikingly displayed on an outdoor pedestal; his expression is disconcerting from close range, his simpleton's grin difficult to reconcile with the image of the ruthless warlord.

Outstanding among the paintings are two works by **Jacopo Bellini**, two *Madonnas* by **Giovanni Bellini**, another *Madonna* by **Pisanello**, **Veronese**'s *Descent from the Cross*, a **Tintoretto** *Nativity*, a **Lotto** portrait and works by **Giambattista and Giandomenico Tiepolo**. The real joy of the museum, however, is in wandering round the fourteenth- and fifteenth-century pieces – beautiful sculptures and frescoes by the often nameless artists of the late Middle Ages.

San Zeno Maggiore

A little over a kilometre northwest of the Castelvecchio is the **Basilica di San Zeno Maggiore**, one of the most significant Romanesque churches in northern Italy. A church was founded here, above the tomb of the city's patron saint, as early as the fifth century, but the present building and its campanile were put up in the first half of the twelfth century, with additions continuing up to the end of the fourteenth century. Its large **rose window**, representing the Wheel of Fortune, dates from the early twelfth century, as does the magnificent portal, whose lintels bear relief sculptures representing the months – look also for Saint Zeno trampling the Devil. Extraordinary bronze panels on the **doors** depict scenes from the Bible and the Miracles of San Zeno, their style influenced by Byzantine and Ottoman art; most of those on the left are from around 1100, most of the right-hand panels dating from a century later.

Areas of the lofty and simple **interior** are covered with frescoes, some superimposed upon others, some defaced by ancient graffiti. Diverting though these are, the one compulsive image in the church is the high altar's luminous *Madonna and Saints* by **Mantegna**. In the apse of the left aisle is a disarming fourteenth-century wooden figure of San Zeno, smiling even more broadly than Cangrande; the saint's tomb is in the beautifully colonnaded crypt beneath the raised choir.

North and east of the Adige

On the other side of Ponte Garibaldi, and right along the embankments or through the public gardens, is **San Giorgio in Braida**, in terms of its art works the richest of Verona's churches. A *Baptism* by **Jacopo Tintoretto** hangs over the door, while the third chapel on the right contains a *Descent of the Holy Ghost* by **Domenico Tintoretto**. The main altar, designed by **Sanmicheli**, incorporates a marvellous *Martyrdom of St George* by **Paolo Veronese**. If you're in need of a place to recuperate or picnic, the piazza in front of the church is your spot, providing a view along the river that must be the most photographed and painted scene in Verona.

It's a short walk along the embankments, past the twelfth-century church of **Santo Stefano** and the Ponte Pietra, to the first-century BC **Teatro Romano**; much restored, the theatre is now used for concerts and plays. When the restorers set to work clearing later buildings away from the theatre, the only one allowed to remain was the tiny church of **Santi Siro e Libera** – built in the tenth century but altered in the fourteenth. Higher still, and reached by a rickety-looking lift, the **Museo Archeologico** (same ticket as the theatre) occupies the buildings of an old convent; its well-arranged collection features a number of Greek, Roman and Etruscan finds.

The Teatro Romano and Museo Archeologico are open Tues–Sun: summer 8am–6.30pm; winter 8am–1.30pm; L5000, free on first Sun of month.

Steps to the side of the theatre lead to the **Castel San Pietro**, built by the Austrians on the site of a Visconti castle which had been destroyed by Napoleon. An uningratiating building, its sole appeal is the view away from it.

If you continue up the road from the Teatro Romano you'll come to the finest formal gardens in Verona, the **Giardini Giusti** on Via Giardini Giusti. Full of artificial waterfalls and shaded corners, the Giusti provides the city's most pleasant refuge from the streets. One last spot on this side of the river might profitably fill an hour or so – the **Museo Storico Naturale**, opposite San Fermo church on Lungadige Porta Vittoria. As well as fossilised mammoths and tigers from local cave sites, the museum has an offbeat section on faked natural wonders – unicorn horns, monstrous animals and the like.

The Giusti is open daily 9am–sunset; L5000.

The Museo Storico Naturale is open 8am–7pm; closed Fri; L2000, free Sun.

Eating, drinking and nightlife

Your money goes a lot further in Verona than it does in Venice: numerous **trattorias** offer full meals for around L20,000 (especially in the Veronetta district, over the river on the east side), while on almost every street corner there's a bar where a glass of house wine (red Bardolino and Valpolicella, white Soave and Custoza) costs as little as L700. **Nightlife** is more varied too, and genuinely goes on into the night, in contrast to Venice's general late-evening shutdown.

Verona

As the Veneto produces more DOC wine than any other region in Italy, it's not surprising that Italy's main wine fair, *Vinitaly*, is held in Verona; it takes place in April, and offers infinite sampling opportunities.

For a non-alcoholic indulgence, sit outside one of the *gelaterie* in Piazza delle Erbe and give a few minutes to an incredible concoction of fruit, cream and ice cream. If you want to follow the trend, the place to make for is *Gelateria Pampanin*, by Ponte Garibaldi.

Restaurants

Ai Preti, Via Acqua Morta 27. Popular *osteria* over in Veronetta district; the pasta and wine are cheap, and musicians often drop by to play. Closes 8pm.

Al Castello, Corso Cavour 43. Good low-cost hotel restaurant, in the centre of the city.

Al Duca, Via Arche Scaligere 2b. The best-value restaurant in the city centre – a genuine, no-frills meal will cost around L15,000.

Arena, Vicolo Tre Marchetti 1. Good pizzeria for a late-night bite, as it's open till 1am. Closed Mon.

Circolo Perbacco, Via Carducci 48. Moderately priced Veronetta restaurant with a very attractive garden. Especially good fish and vegetarian dishes. Closed Wed.

Corte Farina, Corte Farina 4. Another excellent pizzeria that's open till 1am. Closed Mon.

Dal Ropeton, Via S. Giovanni in Valle 46. Located just below the youth hostel, this place does a fine three-course spread for around L25,000. Closed Tues.

Da Salvatore, Corso Porta Borsari 39. Verona's best pizzas. Closed Mon.

Olivo, Piazza Brà. Best pizzas on the city's main square.

Pero d'Oro, Via Ponte Pignolo 25. Another good Veronetta trattoria, serving inexpensive but genuine Veronese dishes. Closed Mon.

Ponte Nuovo, Via Rocca Maggiore 8. In the same district as the *Pero d'Oro*, and with comparable menu. Closed Wed & Sun.

Sayonara, Via S. Maria in Chiavica 5. Very good pizzas, a few seconds' stroll from the Scaliger tombs. Closed Wed.

Bars

Al Carro Armato, Vicolo Gatto 2a. One of the most atmospheric bars in the city, with live music on Thursdays in winter. Open till 2am; closed Wed.

Al Ponte, Via Ponte Pietra. Sip a glass in the garden here and enjoy a marvellous view of Ponte Pietra and the Teatro Romano. Open till 2am; closed Wed.

Antimo, Via Roma 4. University-quarter bar that tends to get busier when the *Campofiore* is closed.

Bottega dei Vini, Vicolo Scudo di Francia. Just off the north end of Via Mazzini, this bar is slightly touristy, but has a selection of wines from all over Italy. Open till midnight; closed Tues.

Campofiore, Via Campofiore. Situated near the university, this is a favourite with Verona's gay population. Open 8am–3pm & 5pm–2am; closed Sun.

Osteria al Duomo, Via Duomo 7a. Best of the city's bars, little changed by twentieth-century fashion, and enlivened on Wednesday afternoons and Friday nights in winter by a traditional singalong. Open 4pm–midnight; closed Tues.

Osteria delle Vecete, Via Pellicciai. Near Piazza delle Erbe, this central bar has a delicious selection of the savoury tartlets known as *bocconcini*, but unfortunately closes at 8.30pm. Closed Sun.

Nightlife

Music and **theatre** are the dominant art forms in the cultural life of Verona. In July and August an opera festival takes place in the **Arena**, always featuring a no-expense-spared production of *Aida*; **big rock events** crop up on the Arena's calendar too – Bob Dylan, Sting, Tina Turner and Joe Cocker have all played it in recent years. (The booking office is in arches 8–9 of the Arena; tickets can only be reserved by post or in person.) A season of ballet and of Shakespeare and other dramatists in Italian is the principal summer fare at the **Teatro Romano**. Some of the Teatro events are free; for the rest, cheapskates who don't mind inferior acoustics can park themselves on the steps going up the hill alongside the theatre. The Teatro's box office also sells tickets for the Arena and vice versa.

Free performances by local dance and theatre groups in May can be surprisingly good, while the June **jazz festival** attracts international names, as does the **Canzone d'Autrice** festival for female singer-songwriters at the end of August.

From October to May **English language films** are shown every Tuesday at the *Cinema Stimate* in Piazza Cittadella. The **disco** scene is much more lively than in Venice, with venues coming and going; look in the local paper, *L'Arena* (there's a copy in every bar), to find out where they are and what days they're open.

The *spettacoli* section of *L'Arena* is the best source of up-to-date information on entertainment in Verona; alternatively, call in at *Musicaviva*, Via Adigetto 6, which sells tickets for most events.

Listings

American Express c/o Fabretto Viaggi, Corso Porta Nuova 11 (Mon–Fri 8.30am–12.30pm & 3–7pm; ☎045/594.700).

Bike rental *Paolo Bellomi*, Via degli Alpini, off Piazza Brà.

Books *The Bookshop*, Via Interrato Acqua Morta 3a, near Ponte Navi. Well-stocked general bookshop with English-speaking staff.

Bus information Piazzale XXV Aprile ☎045/800.4129.

Hospital Ospedale Civile Maggiore, Borgo Trento, Piazza Stefani ☎045/931.111.

Police Lungoadige Porta Vittoria ☎045/596.777.

Post office Piazza Poste, near Ponte Nuovo (Mon–Fri 8.15am–6.30pm, Sat 8.15am–1pm).

Taxis ☎045/532.666.

Telephones *SIP*, Via Leoncino 53.

Train information At the train station, daily 7am–10pm ☎045/590.688.

Chapter 19

The northern Veneto

Lacking a city of Verona's or Padua's appeal, the area extending from the lagoon to the southern edge of the Dolomites is the least visited part of the Veneto – most of those who pass through it are hurrying through to the ski-slopes. Its attractions might be generally on a smaller scale than those of the better-known Veneto towns, but they offer some of the most rewarding day-trips from Venice.

The only real city in the area covered by this chapter is prosperous **Treviso**, just 30km north of Venice. Some of the Veneto's finest medieval buildings and frescoes are to be seen here, and Treviso's centrality to the rail network makes it a good base from which to wander into the crannies of the region. To the west of Treviso, **Castelfranco Veneto** – the birthplace of Giorgione and home of one of his greatest paintings – also sits in the middle of a web of rail lines that runs south to Venice. A hop in one direction brings you to **Cittadella**, an ancient walled town (like Castelfranco itself), while to the north is **Bassano del Grappa**, source of the fiery grappa drink. Two other remarkable old towns lie within a short radius of Bassano: **Maróstica**, famous for its ceremonial chess game played with human "pieces", and **Ásolo**, historically a rural retreat for the Venetian aristocracy, and just a few kilometres from the finest country house in all of Italy – the **Villa Barbaro at Masèr**. A

Hostels and hotels in this guide are classified into nine price categories. **Hostels** (① & ②) are classified according to the **high-season cost per person per night**; the **hotel** categories refer to the **minimum** you can expect to pay for **a double room in high season**, excluding the cost of breakfast, which you might not be able to avoid.

① Under L20,000 per person.
② Over L20,000 per person.
③ Under L40,000 per room.
④ L40–60,000 per room.
⑤ L60–80,000 per room.
⑥ L80–100,000 per room.
⑦ L100–150,000 per room.
⑧ L150–200,000 per room.
⑨ Over L200,000 per room.

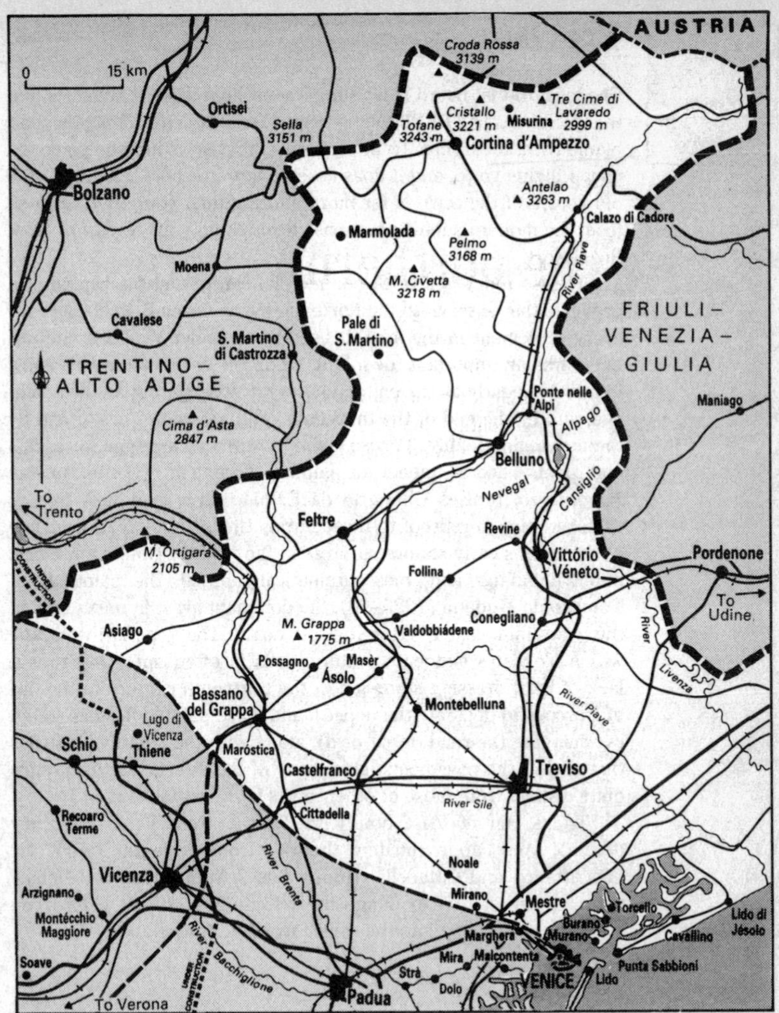

short way to the north of Masèr, lodged on a ridge overlooking the valley of the Piave, **Feltre** boasts another historic centre almost untouched by the last four centuries.

Due north of Treviso, the rail line into the far north of the Veneto runs through **Conegliano**, a town where life revolves round the production of wine, and of the sparkling prosecco in particular. From there a service continues up through **Vittorio Veneto**, with its remarkably preserved Renaissance streets, and on to **Belluno**, in effect the mountains' border post.

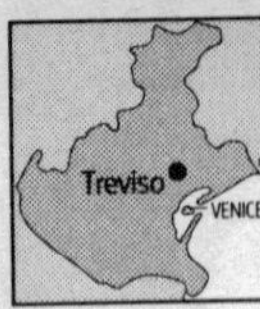

Treviso

The local tourist board is pitching it a bit high when it suggests that the waterways of **TREVISO** may remind you of Venice, but you can't blame them for trying. To most people, Treviso is just the place the cheap flights go to, and it does deserve more respect than that – the old centre of the town is far more alluring than you might imagine from the modern suburbs you pass through on your way to or from the airport.

Treviso today is a brisk commercial centre and the capital of a province that extends to the north almost as far as Belluno. As with every settlement in the area, it used to be under Venetian control, but it was an important town long before its assimilation by Venice in 1389. As early as the eighth century it was minting its own coinage, and by the end of the thirteenth century, when it was ruled by the da Camino family, Treviso was renowned as a refuge for artists and poets, and a model of good government. (Dante, in the *Purgatorio*, praises Gherardo da Camino as a man "left from a vanished race in reproof to these unruly times".) Plenty of evidence of the town's early stature survives in the form of Gothic churches, public buildings and, most dramatically of all, the paintings of **Tomaso da Modena** (1325–79), the dominant artist in north Italy in the years immediately after Giotto's death. The general townscape within Treviso's sixteenth-century walls is often appealing too. A lack of local dressing stone led in the thirteenth century to the use of frescoes to decorate the houses, and these painted facades (often overhanging the road on corbels), along with the lengthy porticoes that shelter the pavements, give many of the streets an appearance quite distinct from those of other towns in the region.

Trains run at least hourly to Treviso from Venice (journey 30min), and approximately hourly from Vicenza (1hr) via Castelfranco and Cittadella. Hourly buses from Padua and Venice arrive at the station in Lungosile Antonio Mattei, just before you cross the river going into the centre from the train station.

The city

Some of the best of these arcades and frescoes are in the main street of the historic centre, **Calmaggiore**, where modern commerce – epitomised by the locally based Benetton – has reached the sort of compromise with the past that the Italians seem to arrange better than anyone else. Modern construction techniques have played a larger part than you might think in shaping that compromise: Treviso was pounded during both world wars, and on Good Friday 1944 around half its buildings were destroyed in a single bombing raid.

The early thirteenth-century **Palazzo dei Trecento** (hall of the town council), at the side of the **Piazza dei Signori**, was one casualty of '44 – a line round the exterior shows where the restoration began.

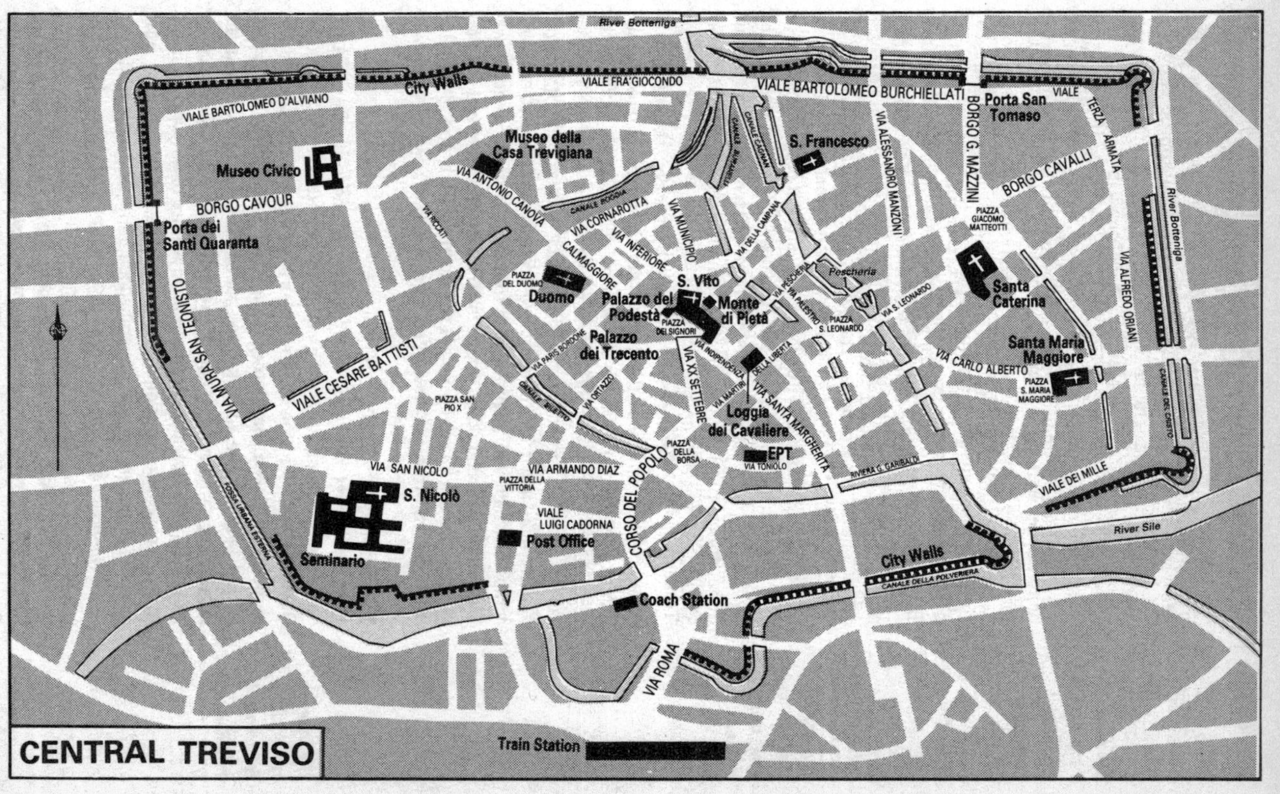

CENTRAL TREVISO
River Botteniga
VIA ALFREDO ORIANI
CANALE DEL CRISTO
River Sile
VIALE DEI MILLE
Santa Maria Maggiore
PIAZZA S. MARIA MAGGIORE
VIA CARLO ALBERTO
Santa Caterina
PIAZZA GIACOMO MATTEOTTI
BORGO CAVALLI
VIALE TERZA ARMATA
Porta San Tomaso
BORGO G. MAZZINI
VIALE BARTOLOMEO BURCHIELLATI
VIA ALESSANDRO MANZONI
VIA S. LEONARDO
Pescheria
PIAZZA S. LEONARDO
VIA PALESTRO
RIVIERA G. GARIBALDI
City Walls
CANALE DELLA POLVERIERA
S. Francesco
CANALE CAGNAN
CANALE BURANELLI
VIA DELLA CAMPANA
VIA PESCHERIA
CALLE LIBERTA
VIA SANTA MARGHERITA
EPT
VIA TONIOLO
Loggia dei Cavalieri
VIA INDIPENDENZA
Monte di Pietà
S. Vito
VIA XX SETTEBRE
PIAZZA DEI SIGNORI
Palazzo del Podestà
Palazzo dei Trecento
VIA MUNICIPIO
VIA INFERIORE
PIAZZA DELLA BORSA
CORSO DEL POPOLO
Coach Station
VIA ROMA
River Botteniga
VIALE FRA' GIOCONDO
VIA CORNAROTTA
CALMAGGIORE
VIA ORTAZZO
VIA ARMANDO DIAZ
VIALE LUIGI CADORNA
Post Office
Train Station
Museo della Casa Trevigiana
VIA ANTONIO CANOVA
Duomo
PIAZZA DEL DUOMO
VIA PARIS BORDONE
CANALE BUFFETTO
PIAZZA DELLA VITTORIA
VIA RICCATI
PIAZZA SAN PIO X
City Walls
VIALE CESARE BATTISTI
VIA SAN NICOLO
S. Nicolò
Seminario
VIALE BARTOLOMEO D'ALVIANO
Museo Civico
BORGO CAVOUR
Porta dei Santi Quaranta
VIA MURA SAN TEONISTO
FOSSA URBANA ESTERNA

Exhibitions are sometimes held in the main hall, which is generally open to the public each weekday from 8.30am to 12.30pm (free entry). The adjoining **Palazzo del Podestà**, with its high tower, is a late nineteenth-century structure, concocted in the appropriate style.

The Monte di Pietà is open Mon–Fri 9am–noon.

Incorporated into the back of this block are three buildings you could easily overlook: the Monte di Pietà (municipal pawnshop) and the churches of San Vito and Santa Lucia. The **Monte di Pietà**, at the end of the small piazza of the same name, is worth a visit for the Cappella dei Rettori, a chapel decorated in the sixteenth century with frescoes, panel paintings and gilded leather. In adjacent rooms you can see the scales used to assess the loans, and pictures by Luca Giordano and Sebastiano Ricci, plus one labelled "attrib. Giorgione", to the understandable embarrassment of the custodians. To get into it, ask at the Cassa di Risparmio della Marca Trivigiana – ring the bell at no. 2, or just go straight up the staircase at no. 5 and ask at one of the counters. The joined medieval churches of **San Vito** and **Santa Lucia** are tucked behind the Monte di Pietà, on the edge of the Piazza San Vito. The latter is the more interesting – a tiny, dark chapel with extensive frescoes by **Tomaso da Modena** and his followers. San Vito has even earlier paintings (twelfth- and thirteenth-century) in the alcove through which you enter from Santa Lucia, but they are not in a good state.

San Vito and Santa Lucia are open daily 9am–noon & 4–6pm.

Another one of Treviso's ancient landmarks, the patricians' meeting-place known as the **Loggia dei Cavalieri**, is close to the Palazzo dei Trecento, down Via Martiri della Libertà. Built in the early thirteenth century and pieced back together after the 1944 air raid, it was decorated first with a brick pattern and grotesque figures, and then with romanticised scenes from the Trojan wars, scraps of which you might be able to make out if you've got hawk-like vision. It's remarkable more for the fact of its survival than for its appearance, but keep your eyes open for it if you're strolling down that way towards the Santa Caterina side of town (see below).

The Duomo

The Duomo is open daily 7am–noon & 3–7pm.

The Duomo of Treviso, **San Pietro**, stands at the end of Calmaggiore, rising above the squall of mopeds on the Piazza del Duomo. Founded in the twelfth century, as were the **campanile** and perpetually closed **Baptistery** alongside, San Pietro was much altered between the fifteenth and nineteenth centuries (when the huge portico was added), and then rebuilt to rectify the damage of 1944. The oldest clearly distinguishable feature of the exterior is the pair of eroded Romanesque lions at the base of the portico; fragments of Romanesque wall are embedded in the side walls too.

The interior is chiefly notable for the **crypt** – a thicket of twelfth-century columns with scraps of fourteenth- and fifteenth-century mosaics (if locked ask sacristan) – and the **Malchiostro Chapel** – with frescoes by **Pordenone** and a much restored *Annunciation* by Titian. Although Pordenone and Titian were the bitterest of rivals, their pictures were commissioned as part of a unified scheme, representing the conception and birth of Christ; the bombs of '44 annihilated the crowning piece of the ensemble – a fresco by Pordenone on the chapel dome, representing *God the Father*. Paintings by **Paris Bordone**, the most famous Treviso-born artist, hang in the vestibule of the chapel and in the sacristy. Other things to search out are the *Monument to Bishop Zanetti* by **Pietro Lombardo**, on the left wall of the chancel, the *Tomb of Bishop Nicolò Franco* by **Lorenzo and Giambattista Bregno**, in the chapel to the left of the chancel, and **Lorenzo Bregno**'s figure of *St Sebastian*, on the west pillar of the left aisle.

San Nicolò

The severe Dominican church of **San Nicolò**, dominating the corner of the old town just over the River Sile from the railway station, upstages the Duomo in every department. Wrapped round several of its massive pillars are delicate frescoes by **Tomaso da Modena** and his school, of which the freshest are the *St Jerome* and *St Agnes* by Tomaso himself, on the first column on your right as you enter. The towering *St Christopher* on the wall of the right aisle, with feet the size of canoes, was painted around 1410, probably by **Antonio da Treviso**. Equally striking, but considerably more graceful, is the composite *Tomb of Agostino d'Onigo* on the left wall of the chancel, created in 1500 by **Antonio Rizzo** (who did the sculpture) and **Lorenzo Lotto** (who painted the attendant pages). Another collaborative work stands on the altar of the Monigo chapel, on the right of the chancel – **Sebastiano del Piombo** painted the upper section and **Lotto** the lower gallery of portraits; the frescoes on the side walls are by fourteenth-century Sienese and Riminese artists. If it's not a sunny day you'll have problems seeing these pictures – the church authorities have fitted intruder alarms, but still haven't got round to any form of illumination.

The figures of Agnes and Jerome are an excellent introduction to Tomaso da Modena, but for a comprehensive demonstration of his talent you should visit the neighbouring **Seminario**, where the **chapter house** is decorated with a series of portraits of members of the Dominican order, executed by the artist in 1352. Although these are not portraits in the modern sense of the term, in that they don't attempt to reproduce the appearance of the men whose names they bear, these paintings are astonishingly advanced in their observation of idiosyncratic reality. Each shows a monk at study in his cell, but there is never a hint of the formulaic: one man is shown sharpening a quill, another checks a text through a magnifier, a third starts back from his desk as if in surprise, and so on.

The Seminario is open Mon–Fri 9am–sunset; free.

The east side

On the other side of town from San Nicolò there's another brilliant fresco cycle by Tomaso da Modena – *The Story of the Life of*

Santa Caterina is open by appointment Tues–Sat 9–11.30am & 2–4.30pm; L2000.

Sant'Ursula. Painted for the now extinct church of Santa Margherita sul Sile, the frescoes were detached from the walls in the late nineteenth century and transported to the Museo Civico. From there they were dispatched in 1979 to **Santa Caterina**, a deconsecrated church maintained for the display of the frescoes by Tomaso and his school, in its Cappella degli Innocenti. To get into the church you have to make an appointment at the Museo Civico (call in person or ring ☎0422/51.337) – so, if you're coming to Treviso for the day and you want to see this extraordinary series, make sure you ring at least one day in advance.

Two other churches in the Santa Caterina quarter are worth a look. To the north of Santa Caterina is the thirteenth-century church of **San Francesco**, which was reopened and restored early this century after years as a military depot. It's an airy building with a high ship's-keel ceiling and patches of fresco, including another vast *St Christopher* and a *Madonna and Saints* by **Tomaso da Modena** in the chapel to the left of the chancel. Close to the door on the right side is the tomb of **Francesca**, **daughter of Petrarch**, who died in 1384, twenty years after **Dante's son**, **Pietro**, whose tomb is in the left transept.

To the south, at the end of one of the most attractive streets in Treviso – Via Carlo Alberto – stands the largely fifteenth-century **Basilica di Santa Maria Maggiore**, which houses the most venerated image in Treviso, a fresco of the Madonna, originally painted by Tomaso da Modena but subsequently retouched.

This is the workshop and market-stall area, a district in which Treviso has the feel of a rather smaller town. The antique sellers and furniture restorers of Treviso even outnumber the Benetton outlets, and it's over this side that you'll see most evidence of them. Trevisans once characterised their town as "gioiosa e amorosa" (happy and amorous), and still insist that there's a "certain sweetness" to life here, to quote a tourist leaflet. You can best appraise the extent to which this sweetness has pervaded the local character by hanging round the stalls in and around the **Pescheria**, which occupies an island in the middle of Treviso's biggest canal. (As in Venice, health regulations dictated the siting of the fish market by a waterway.) For a full-blown display of Trevisan mercantile skills, be here on a Saturday or Tuesday morning, when the the northern part of this quarter, along Viale Bartolomeo Burchiellati and Borgo Mazzini, is overrun by a gigantic **market**.

The Museo Civico is open Tues–Sat 9am–noon & 2–5pm, Sun 9am–noon; L1000.

The museums and city walls

From the historic centre around the Duomo, the recommended route to the **Museo Civico** is along Via Riccati, which has a number of fine old houses – and bicycle fetishists can drool at the window of Colnago, makers of racing machines to the elite of professional road-cycling. The ground floor of the museum is taken up by the archaeological collection, predominantly late Bronze Age and

Roman relics; the picture collection, on the upper floor, is typical of provincial collections all over Italy – acres of hackwork interrupted by a few paintings for which any gallery director would give a year's salary. In this second category are three paintings hanging cheek by jowl in room 9 – a *Crucifixion* by **Jacopo Bassano**, the *Portrait of Sperone Speroni* by **Titian** and **Lorenzo Lotto**'s psychologically acute *Portrait of a Dominican*. Comparing the Titian and Lotto portraits, you can see some justice in Bernard Berenson's contrast between the two – "we might imagine Titian asking of every person he was going to paint: Who are you? What is your position in society? while Lotto would put the question: What sort of person are you? How do you take life?"

Treviso's other public collection, the **Museo della Casa Trevigiana**, is only a couple of minutes away, in Via Antonio Canova. Housed in the fourteenth- to sixteenth-century Casa da Noal, a building that would merit a visit even if it were empty, this is the town's museum of the applied arts – furniture, dolls, architectural decorations, armour, musical instruments and, most impressive of all, wrought-iron work, a local speciality. Not the first place to head for in Treviso, but a definite if you're around for a couple of days.

The Museo della Casa Trevigiana is open Tues–Sat 9am–noon & 2–5pm, Sun 9am–noon; L2000.

The longest unbroken stretch of the **city walls** is in the vicinity of the Museo and Casa Trevigiana, between the Porta dei Santi Quaranta and Porta San Tomaso. The fortification of Treviso was undertaken in 1509, at the start of the War of the League of Cambrai, and the work was finished around 1517, with the construction of these two monumental gates. If you fancy a walk away from the traffic, albeit only ten metres away, the path along the walls is your spot.

Practicalities

The **tourist office** is in the Palazzo Scotti, Via Toniolo 41 (Mon–Fri 8.30am–12.30pm & 5–6pm, Sat 8.30am–noon; ☎0422/547.632); they dispense lists of the town's museums and restaurants, plus a couple of glossies on Treviso's waterways and its frescoed houses. The **post office** is in the Piazzale della Vittoria, over to your left shortly after crossing the river from the train station; for **banks** keep going straight along Corso del Popolo towards Calmaggiore – you'll pass most of them along this stretch.

Accommodation

Although Treviso itself isn't likely to tempt you to stay, you might want to use it as a base from which to strike out into the mainland, or as a fall-back if accommodation in Venice is a dead loss. There are no one-star hotels in the old town. Of the central two-stars, the cheapest is *Al Cuore*, Piazzale Duca d'Aosta 1 (☎0422/410.929; ④), as it's right on top of the main road and rail convergences, to the side of the train station. More comfortable is the *Beccherie*,

Piazza Ancillotto 11 (☎0422/540.871; ④), a pleasant two-star right in the heart of the *centro storico*.

Eating and drinking

Treviso has a number of restaurants with very high reputations and prices to match – the leader of the pack being *El Toulà da Alfredo*, at Via Collalto 26 (☎0422/540.275; closed Sun evening & Mon), where you won't see much change from L100,000. For a splendid range of local dishes, at around L70,000 with wine, try the restaurant of the *Beccherie* hotel (see above; closed Thurs evening & Fri), or the ancient *Al Bersagliere*, Via Barbera 21 (☎0422/541.9888; closed Sat lunchtime & Sun). If that's too steep, the homely *Toni del Spin*, not far from the Duomo at Via Inferiore 7 (☎0422/543.829; closed Sun & Mon lunchtime), is almost as good and around L20,000 cheaper – their risottos are excellent. Also good value, in descending order of cost and quality, are: *All' Oca Bianca*, Vicolo della Torre 7 (closed Wed); the riverside *Al Dante*, Piazza Garibaldi 6 (closed Sat & Sun); *La Tavernetta*, a typical little trattoria at Via Manzoni 46; and the very plain and very cheap *Alla Colomba*, Via Ortazzo 25 (closed Fri).

The most popular **bars and cafés** in Treviso are those clustered underneath the Palazzo dei Trecento; two other good bars are the *Osteria dalla Elsa* on Vicolo San Gregorio, just to the south of the Piazza dei Signori, and *Scandiuzzi Secondo* on Piazza Ancillotto, which serves tasty snacks as well as cheap but fair-quality wine. The polished-chrome cafés of Calmaggiore serve some delicious pastries, but are a bit too slick and not the friendliest places in the Veneto. *Casellato*, Via della Campana 2, just off Piazza San Vito, is just as classy but not quite as chilly. For **ice cream**, the place is the *gelateria* opposite the duomo at Piazza del Duomo 25.

Castelfranco Veneto

In the twelfth century **CASTELFRANCO VENETO** stood on the western edge of Treviso's territory, and from the outside the old town – or **Castello** – looks much as it must have done when the Trevisans had finished fortifying the place against the Paduans. The battlemented and moated brick walls, raised in 1199, run almost right round the centre, and five of their towers still stand, the largest being the Torrione, the clock tower over the north gate. Of all the walled towns of the Veneto, only Cittadella and Montagnana bear comparison with Castelfranco, and the place would merit a call just for its brickwork, even though the Castello is so small that you can walk in through one gate and out through the opposite in three minutes flat. And the place has one other attraction: it was the birthplace of Giorgio da Castelfranco – **Giorgione** – and possesses a painting which on its own is enough to vindicate Vasari's judgement that Giorgione's place in Venetian art is equivalent to Leonardo da Vinci's in that of Florence.

Castelfranco is well connected by **rail** with all parts of the Veneto, but it's most easily approached from Treviso (25min) or Vicenza (40min) – trains run along this line on average once an hour. Connections to Venice (50min) are more sporadic – during working hours it averages out at around one every two hours. In addition there are hourly links to Padua and Bassano, and a train from Belluno every ninety minutes.

The Castelfranco Madonna

Known simply as the **Castelfranco Madonna**, Giorgione's *Madonna and Child with St Francis and St Liberale* hangs in the eighteenth-century **Duomo**, in a chapel to the right of the chancel; the bars of the iron grille across its entrance are far enough apart for you to be able to see the picture clearly, and there's a light-switch to the side (leave donation in nearby box).

The Duomo is open daily 9am–noon & 3–6pm.

Giorgione is the most elusive of all the great figures of the Renaissance: including the Castelfranco Madonna, only six surviving paintings can indisputably be attributed to him, and so little is known for certain about his life that legends have proliferated to fill the gaps – for instance, the story that his premature death in 1510, aged not more than 34, was caused by his catching bubonic plague from a mistress. The paintings themselves have compounded the enigma and none is more mysterious than this one, in which formal abstraction is combined with an extraordinary fidelity to physical texture, while the demeanour of the figures suggests, in the forgivably lush words of one writer – "withdrawal . . . as if their spirit were preoccupied with a remembered dream". Even the identity of the saint accompanying Saint Francis is far from clear: candidates other than Liberale include Saint George and Saint Theodore.

But some facts are known about the picture's origin. It was commissioned by Tuzio Costanza, probably in 1505, to honour his son, Matteo, who had been killed in battle the previous year. The church for which the piece was painted was demolished long ago, and the present arrangement (dating from 1935) differs crucially from that devised by Giorgione's patron, in that the painting was originally placed so that the three figures were looking down at the tomb of Matteo Costanza. Matteo's tombstone is now set into the wall to the left.

After the Giorgione, the only other paintings in the duomo likely to hold your attention are in the **sacristy** – fragments of allegorical frescoes by **Veronese**, removed from the Villa Soranza in the nineteenth century, when the villa was knocked down. The interior of the duomo itself was designed by the local architect **Francesco Maria Preti**, whose major contribution to the landscape of the Veneto is to be seen at the Villa Pisani at Stra (see p.268); the facade is a late nineteenth-century botched job.

Castelfranco Veneto

The Casa Giorgione is open Tues–Sun 9am–12.30pm & 3–6pm; often closed weekday mornings in winter; free.

The rest of the town

Next to the duomo is the enticingly named **Casa Giorgione** – but it contains nothing of note except a chiaroscuro **frieze** in one the first-floor rooms which has been hopefully attributed to Giorgione. The only other interior in Castelfranco that you might want to peep at is the **Teatro Accademico** (Tues–Thurs 9am–noon & 2–6pm, Mon & Fri 9am–noon; free) in Via Garibaldi, opposite the duomo. Designed in the mid-eighteenth century by **Preti**, the auditorium is less modest than you might think from the sober outside.

Practicalities

Tourist information is handled by the **Pro Loco**, at Via Garibaldi 2 (Mon–Sat 8.30am–12.30pm & 3–7pm), which produces a very good free map, annotated with masses of extra practical detail.

The cheapest **rooms** in central Castelfranco are at *Alla Speranza*, a few yards beyond the walls at Borgo Vicenza 13 (☎0423/494.480; ④) – Borgo Vicenza is the continuation of the main street, Via F. M. Preti, on the opposite side of the Castello from the train station. Cheaper still, but about 1km outside the walls, is *All'Antica Priora*, at Borgo Padova 55 (☎0423/491.764; ③).

There are a number of excellent **restaurants** in the town, perhaps the best being *Ai due Mori*, an *osteria* specializing in local dishes; it's inside the walls, in Vicolo Montebelluno, close to the Torrione (☎0423/497.174; closed Wed). A feast at *Ai due Mori* should set you back around L50,000; if this is too much for your budget, there are a few trattorias in Borgo Padova, and a decent one attached to *Alla Speranza*. The large restaurant-pizzeria at the foot of the Torrione, *Alla Torre* (closed Tues), is as good a place as any for pizza, although its restaurant menu is not cheap.

Around Castelfranco

The major attraction within a short radius of **Castelfranco** is the wonderfully preserved Cittadella, which can be easily reached by train, as it's on the Treviso–Vicenza line. Buses and the Venice–Castelfranco *locale* trains stop at the village of **Piombino Dese**, where there's one of Palladio's most influential villas, though the lay person will probably get more pleasure out of the slightly less accessible villa at **Fanzolo**.

Buses from Castelfranco depart from Via Podgora, on the north side of Borgo Vicenza, and from Corso XXIX Aprile, which you cross to go into the Castello when coming from the station.

Cittadella

When Treviso turned Castelfranco into a garrison, the Paduans promptly retaliated by reinforcing the defences of **CITTADELLA**, 15km to the west. The **fortified walls** of Cittadella were built in the first quarter of the thirteenth century, and are even more impressive than those of its neighbour, forming an almost unbroken oval round the town.

You enter the town through one of four rugged brick gateways, built on the cardinal points of the compass; if you're coming from the train station it'll be the **Porta Padova**, the most daunting of the four, flanked as it is by the Torre di Malta. The tower was built as a prison and torture chamber by **Ezzelino da Romano III**, known to those he terrorised in this region in the mid-thirteenth century as the "Son of Satan". Basing his claim to power not on any dynastic or legalistic argument, but solely on the exercise of unrestrained military might, Ezzelino was the prototype of the despotic rulers of Renaissance Italy, and his atrocities earned him a place in the seventh circle of Dante's *Inferno*, where he's condemned to boil eternally in a river of blood.

There's not much else to Cittadella – unless you're entranced by the deer, swans, emus and llamas that constitute the Parco Zoo, under one section of the walls – but it's definitely worth hopping off the train for a quick circuit.

The Villa Emo

Just 8km northeast of Castelfranco is **FANZOLO**, where you'll find one of the best maintained and most sumptuous of **Palladio**'s villas – the **Villa Emo**. In 1556 the Venetian government set up a department called the Board of Uncultivated Properties, to promote agricultural development on the *terra firma* and control subsidies to the landowners. One of the first to take advantage of this campaign was Leonardo Emo, who commissioned the villa from Palladio around 1564, when he switched his financial interests to farming.

The Villa Emo is open Tues, Sat & Sun April–Sept 3–7pm; Oct–March 2–6pm; L6000.

With its central accommodation and administration block, and its arcaded wings for storage, stables, dovecots and so on, the building belongs to the same type as the earlier Villa Barbaro at Masèr, and as at Masèr the main living rooms are richly frescoed. Nobody would make out that **Giambattista Zelotti**'s scenes are a match for Veronese's in the Barbaro house, but neither would anyone complain at having to stare at them every morning over breakfast either – excepting his rubber-necked grotesques.

But the trip does have its minus points. For a start, the entrance fee is inexcusably steep, and getting there isn't easy without a car: some trains from Castelfranco stop at Fanzolo, but so few that the #5 bus is the better option. The return service is so fitful, though, that you either have to zip through the building in twenty minutes or kill three hours there.

The Villa Cornaro

Palladio's villas fall into two broad types: the first is the type designed to be the focus of a large, cohesive farm, and takes the form of a low central block with attached lateral buildings; the second is designed to be the living quarters of an estate which is scattered or where the farming land is unsuitable for building, and takes the form of a tall single building with a freestanding pedimented porch. The Emo and Barbaro houses belong to the first category, and to the second belong the Villa Pisani at Montagnana, the Villa Fóscari at Malcontenta and the **Villa Cornaro**, built in the 1550s at **PIOMBINO DESE**, 9km southeast of Castelfranco. The majestic double-decker portico is the most striking element of the exterior, and when Palladian style was imported into colonial America, this became one of his most frequently copied devices. Unfortunately, the villa's decoration – frescoes by the obscure eighteenth-century artist Mattia Bortoloni – isn't anything to get excited about.

The Villa Cornaro is open May–Sept Sat 3.30–6pm; L4000.

Bassano del Grappa

Situated on the River Brenta where it widens on its emergence from the hills, **BASSANO DEL GRAPPA** has expanded rapidly this century, though its historic centre remains largely unspoiled by twentieth-century mistakes. It's better known for its manufactures and produce, and for the events of the two World Wars (see below), than for any outstanding architecture or monuments. For centuries a major producer of ceramics and wrought iron, Bassano is also renowned for its **grappa** distilleries and delicacies such as *porcini* (dried mushrooms), white asparagus and honey.

Trains run from Venice to Bassano fourteen times daily; the journey takes an hour. **Buses** connect with Masèr (8 daily), Possagno (every 1–2hr), Maróstica (3–5 daily) and Ásolo (Mon–Sat 12 daily, only one bus on Sun).

The town

Almost all of Bassano's sights lie between the Brenta and the train station; go much further in either direction and you'll quickly come to recently developed suburbs. Walking away from the station, the orbital Viale delle Fosse stands between you and the town centre, following the line of the fourteenth-century outer walls. Cross the road, turn right then left to get to Via Da Ponte, which forms a main axis through the centre; the statue is of **Jacopo da Ponte**, leader of the dynasty of Renaissance painters more commonly known simply as the Bassano family.

On the left of **Piazza Garibaldi**, one of the centre's two main squares, the fourteenth-century church of **San Francesco** carries a gold medal plaque in honour of the resistance fighters of World War II; a few fresco fragments remain inside, including an *Annunciation* of 1400 in the porch. The cloister now houses the **Museo Civico**, where the downstairs rooms are devoted to printing – for a long time one of Bassano's chief crafts – and to Roman and other archeological finds. Upstairs is a collection of sixteenth- to eighteenth-century work, including paintings by the **Bassano** family, some huge frescoes detached from a palace in Piazzetta Montevecchio, and a number of plaster works by **Canova**, two thousand of whose drawings are owned by the museum. There's also a room devoted to the great baritone **Tito Gobbi**, who was born in Bassano.

Overlooking the other side of the piazza is the **Torre Civica**, once a lookout tower for the twelfth-century inner walls, now a clock tower with spurious nineteenth-century battlements and windows. Further in the same direction is **Piazza Libertà**, with its seventeenth-century sculpture of San Bassiano, the patron saint of Bassano, and the all-too-familiar winged lion of Venice. Dominating the left hand side of the piazza, the church of **San Giovanni** was founded in 1308 but is now overbearingly Baroque in this relatively delicate city centre; the style continues within. Under the arches of the fifteenth-century **Loggia** on the other side are the frescoed coats of arms of the various Venetian governors of Bassano.

Bassano del Grappa

The Museo Civico is open Tues–Sat 10am–12.30pm & 2.30–6.30pm, Sun 10am–12.30pm & 3–6.30pm; L2000; free guided tour Sun 10.15am.

Bassano del Grappa

From the far right-hand corner, Piazzetta Montevecchio (the original core of the town), its frescoes now faded or removed, leads to a little jumble of streets and stairways running down to the river and the **Ponte degli Alpini**. The river was first bridged at this point in the late twelfth century, and replacements or repairs have been needed at regular intervals ever since, mostly because of flooding. The present structure was designed by **Palladio** in 1568, and built in wood to make the bridge as flexible as possible – floodwater would have demolished an unyielding stone version. Mined by the resistance during the last war, and badly damaged by the retreating German army, it was restored in accordance with Palladio's design, as has been the case with every repair since the day of its completion.

Nardini, a grappa distillery founded in 1779, stands at this end of the bridge; cross over to reach the **Taverna al Ponte**, home of the **Museo degli Alpini**, which also gives a good view of the underside of the bridge. The Alpine soldiers, who crossed the bridge many times during World War I on their way to Monte Grappa and Asiago, saw the bridge as a symbol of their tenacity, and so adopted it as their emblem. They still have strong associations with Bassano, and take part in parades here, looking as though they've just stepped out of some nineteenth-century adventure yarn.

The Museo degli Alpini is open Tues–Sun 8am–8pm; free.

Back on the town side of the bridge again, if you follow Via Ferracina downstream for a couple of minutes you'll come to the eighteenth-century **Palazzo Sturm**, a showcase for the town's famed majolica ware. On the other side of the base of the Ponti degli Alpini, Via Gamba takes you up to the remnants of the **castle**; the huge, blank and none too safe-looking tower was built in the twelfth century by the Ezzelini. The campanile of **Santa Maria in Colle** is a conversion of another tower, while the church itself dates from around 1000; it contains two paintings by **Leandro da Ponte**.

The Palazzo Sturm is open Fri 9am–noon, Sat & Sun 3–7pm; L2000.

Go out of the castle enclosure and round to the right, and spreading round to the right is the **Viale dei Martieri**, named after the resistance fighters who were rounded up in the hills and hanged from trees along here in September 1944. A telescope enables you to get the most out of the views of the Dolomites. To one end is the **Piazzale Generale Giardino**, with its fascist-style memorial to the General, who died 1935; a World War I monument in similar vein stands in the **Parco Ragazzi del'99** below.

If you cut across the town, through Piazza Libertà and south down Via Marinelli or Via Roma, then outside the city walls and right, you can't miss the vast **Tempio Ossario**. Begun in 1908 as a church, its function was changed in 1934, when it became repository of over 5400 tombs, each containing the ashes of a soldier. The major **war memorial**, however, is out of town on **Monte Grappa**. A vast, circular, tiered edifice with a "Via Eroica" leading to a war museum, it holds 12,000 Italian and Austro-Hungarian dead; less a symbol of mourning and repentance than a declaration of future collaboration, it was built by the fascists in 1935. Buses go up there from Bassano during the summer months.

Practicalities

The **tourist office** is opposite the train station at Largo Corona d'Italia 35 (Mon–Sat 9am–12.30pm & 3–6.45pm); their free magazine called *Bassano Mese* gives up-to-date information about the city's facilities and events.

For budget **accommodation**, it comes down to a choice between *Bassanello*, at Via P. Fontana 2 (☎0424/35.347; ③), or *Nuovo Mondo*, Via Vittorelli 45 (☎0424/522.010; ④), a pleasant and central two-star. After that it's a bit of a jump to the *Victoria*, Viale Diaz 33 (☎0424/503.620; ⑤).

As for **food**, the *Antica Osteria*, Via Matteotti 7 (closed Mon) has good bars snacks, while *Combattini*, Via Gamba 22 (closed Sat) is recommended for a full meal, at around L30,000. *Ottocento*, Via San Giorgio 2, is a welcoming *birreria*, though for a late-night drink the most popular spot is *Saiso*, Via Gamba 4 (open till 2am; closed Wed night and Thurs). Of all Bassano's *alimentari*, the one with the fullest range of local delicacies is on the corner of Salita B. Ferracina and Via B. Ferracina; for **grappa**, go to the distillery on the Ponte degli Alpini (8am–8pm; closed Mon) – it sells the best quality stuff and has a bar so you can sample before you select your bottle.

Maróstica

Seven kilometres to the west of Bassano, the walled town of **MARÓSTICA** was yet another stronghold of Ezzelino da Romano III, whose fortress glowers down on the old centre from the crest of the hill of Pausolino. The fortress, the lower castle and the almost intact ramparts that connect them make a dramatic scene, but Maróstica's main claim to fame is the **Partita a Scacchi** – a chess game played every other September with human "pieces".

A **bus** service runs between Maróstica and **Bassano** (3–5 daily; 30min); the stop is outside the lower castle.

The town

Maróstica was run by the Ezzelini for quite a time, the monstrous Ezzelino III being preceded by Ezzelino the Stutterer and Ezzelino the Monk. However, it was a slightly less hideous dynasty of despots, the Scaligers of Verona, who constructed the **town walls** and the **Castello Inferiore** (lower castle): the castle was built by Cangrande della Scala, and the walls by his successor, Cansignorio, in the 1370s. An exhibition of costumes for the *Partita a Scacchi* is now housed in the castle.

The Castello museum is open Sun 2–6pm; L500.

Beyond the castle is **Piazza Castello**, the central square of the town, onto which is painted the board for the **Partita a Scacchi**. The game's origin was an everyday chivalric story of rival suitors, the only unusual aspect being that the matter was decided with chess pieces rather than swords. In 1454 two men, Vieri da Vallonara and Rinaldo d'Angarano, both petitioned the *podestà* of Maróstica, Taddeo Parisio, for the hand of his daughter. Parisio decreed that the matter should be decided by a chess match, with the winner marrying Lionora and the loser being consoled with the prize of Parisio's younger sister – who seems to have had as little say in the proceedings as Parisio's daughter. The game was played with live pieces here in the square, and is re-enacted biennially with great pomp – 500 people in the costume of the time, with music, dancing and fireworks.

The **Doglione**, behind the inevitable lion of Saint Mark, is a much-altered fifteenth-century building; once the castle armoury, it now contains the town library. To the left of it, Via San Antonio runs past the church of the same name to the forgettable church of the **Carmine**, looking like a Baroque palace with the windows missing. A path round to the left of the Carmine winds up through an olive grove to the **Castello Superiore** (upper castle), which was built by Ezzelino III and later expanded by the Scaligers. Most of it is closed for restoration, but the view is marvellous, and the fort does contain a bar. It's only when you're at the top that you realise there's a road up, much less steep than the stony path but longer; if you take this route back down, look out for the cyclists who train on the hill – they whizz through the hair-pins with scarcely a sound to warn of their approach. Near the bottom a little junk shop sells war memorabilia scavenged from the mountains around.

The oldest church in Maróstica, **Santa Maria**, is outside the city walls on the other side – go through the eastern gate, turn left, then second right. Unfortunately it was rebuilt in the eighteenth century, but it has some quirky attractions: modern votive paintings on the ceiling, for instance, and an altarpiece that's a copy of the top half of Titian's *Assumption* in Venice's Frari.

Practicalities

The tourist office is in the lower castle (Mon–Sat 10am–noon & 4–7pm). Maróstica has two **hotels**: the more central is the three-star *Europa* at Via Pizzamano 19 (☎0424/77.842; ⑥), on the first crossroads back towards Bassano; the cheaper *Ponte Campana*, Via Salarola 1 (☎0424/75.160; ④), is about 1km beyond the crossroads. For **food**, there are two good pizzerias at Piazza Castello 42: downstairs, *All'Alfiere* (closed Thurs); upstairs, *La Grieffe* (closed Wed). The best central restaurant is *Dama Bianca*, close to the lower castle at Via Roma 107 (☎0424/75.096; closed Wed); a meal will cost in the region of L35,000, and it's definitely advisable to book at weekends. The *Osteria Madonetta*, just off the main piazza at Via Vajenta 21, is perhaps the most genuine **osteria** in the Veneto – virtually unchanged since it opened in 1904, it looks like someone's shambolic living room. It's run by an old woman and her son, serves the most basic of meals, and sells its wine not from a bar but from an ordinary table set with bottles of red and white wine.

Regular events include first and foremost the **Partita a Scacchi**, played in the second weekend of September on even-numbered years. An exhibition of **cartoonists** specialising in political and social comment takes place in May and June, followed in July and August by a **crafts fair**. An **antiques market** is held the first Sunday of every month.

Possagno

As you approach **POSSAGNO**, a small town lodged at the base of Monte Grappa, one of the strangest sights in the Veneto hits you: a huge temple that rises above the houses like a displaced chunk of ancient Rome. It was built by **Antonio Canova**, one of the dominant figures of Neoclassicism and the last Italian sculptor to be generally regarded as the most accomplished living practitioner of his art. He was born here in 1757, and his family home now houses a magnificent museum of his work. Just as you can't come to grips with Tintoretto until you've been to Venice, so an excursion to Possagno is essential to an understanding of Canova. You can reach Possagno by **bus** from Bassano or Castelfranco Veneto; the first is easier – a fairly regular service that takes an hour.

Shortly after Canova's death in 1822, all the working models that had accumulated in his studio in Rome were transported to Possagno, and here, from 1831 to 1836, an annexe (the Gypsoteca) was built onto the Canova house for the display of the bulk of the collection. A second addition was built in the 1950s, and the Gypsoteca is now one of only two complete displays of an artist's working models in Europe – the other being Copenhagen's collection of pieces by Thorvaldsen.

The Gypsoteca e Casa Canova

The Gypsoteca is open May–Sept Tues–Sun 9am–noon & 3–6pm, Sun 9am–noon & 3–7pm; Oct–April Tues–Sat 9am–noon & 2–5pm; L5000.

The process by which Canova worked towards the final form of his sculptures was a painstaking one, involving the creation of a series of rough clay models (*bozzetti*) in which the general shape would be refined, then a full-scale figure in plaster, and finally the replication of the plaster figure in marble. Preparatory works from all stages of Canova's career are shown in the **Gypsoteca**, and even if you're repelled by the polish of the finished pieces, you'll be won over by the energy and spontaneity of the first versions – such as the tiny terracotta model for the tomb of Pope Clement XIV, or the miniature group of Adam and Eve weeping over the body of Abel.

Canova's range will probably be as much of a surprise as his technique. Among the works collected in the vast main hall, for example, you'll find portraits, images of classical deities, the funerary monument for Maria Christina of Austria (adapted by Canova's pupils for his own tomb in Venice's Frari), and a large *Deposition*, a bronze version of which is to be found in the Tempio (see below). Notions of Canova as a bloodless pedant are dispelled by two overpowering tableaux of violence, each over ten feet high – *Hercules and Lichas* and *Theseus and the Centaur*. More models are kept in the house, but the pleasure of this section of the museum is weakened by Canova's paintings – a parade of winsome Venuses and frolicking nymphs, which will not dispose you to disagree with the artist's own low opinion of his pictorial talents.

The Tempio

The Tempio is open daily: April–Oct daily 9am–7pm; Nov–March 9am–noon & 2–5pm.

Donated to the town to serve as its new parish church, the **Tempio** was designed by Canova with assistance from **Giannantonio Selva** (architect of La Fenice in Venice) and constructed from 1819 to 1830. Both Roman and Greek classical sources were plundered for its composition – the body of the building is derived from the Pantheon, but its portico comes from the Parthenon. The cool precision of the interior is disrupted by a sequence of dreadful paintings of the Apostles, and an appalling altarpiece for which Canova himself was the culprit. To the right is the bronze version of the *Deposition* in the gypsoteca (cast posthumously in 1829), and opposite is the **tomb of Canova** and his half-brother Monsignor G.B. Sartori, with a self-portrait bust to the right. Designed by Canova for a different occupant, this tomb is not the Veneto's only memorial to the sculptor– the other one is in the Frari in Venice. If the sacristan is around, ask him to let you go up to the top of the dome – the view of the Asolean hills and the plain of the Piave is marvellous.

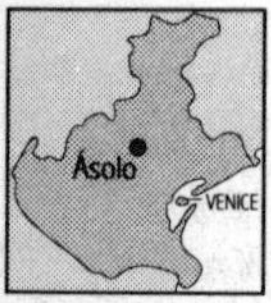

Ásolo

Known as "la Città dai cento orizzonti" (the city with a hundred horizons), the medieval walled town of **ÁSOLO** presides over a tightly grouped range of twenty-seven gentle peaks in the foothills of the Dolomites. Fruit trees and pastures cover the lower slopes of the Asolean hills, and a feature of life in the town itself are the festivals that take place at the various harvest times.

Paleolithic settlements have been found in the region, but the earliest documented settlement was the Roman town called *Acelum*, which thrived from the second century BC until its destruction by Attila. Following resettlement, a succession of feudal lords ruled Ásolo, culminating with the vile **Ezzelino da Romano III**, whose parents were born in the town. Ezzelino wrested Ásolo from the

Bishop of Treviso in 1234, and a network of castles over much of the Veneto shows the extent of his conquests in the years that followed. On his death in 1259 the townspeople of Ásolo ensured that the dynasty died with him by butchering the rest of his family, who were at that time in nearby San Zenone.

The end of the fifteenth century was marked by the arrival of **Caterina Cornaro**; her celebrated court was attended by the likes of Cardinal Bembo, one of the most eminent literary figures of his day, who coined the verb *Asolare* to describe the experience of spending one's time in pleasurable aimlessness. Later writers and artists found the atmosphere equally convivial: Gabriele d'Annunzio wrote about the town, and Robert Browning's last published work – *Asolando* – was written here.

There are regular **buses** to Ásolo from Bassano; if you want to get there from Venice, the quickest route is to take a train to Treviso (there's at least one an hour), where you won't have to wait more than an hour for a bus to Ásolo – in addition to the direct services, all the buses to Bassano go through Ásolo. The bus drops you at the foot of the hill, a connecting minibus taking you up into the town.

The town

The main road into town from Bassano enters the southern Porta Loreggia, with a fifteenth-century fountain on the left and on the right **Casa Freia**, home of the traveller and writer Freya Stark. Via Browning continues up the hill; no. 151, formerly the house of Pen Browning, bears a plaque recording his father's stay in 1889. At the top is the hub of the town, **Piazza Garibaldi**, to the south of which, on the Piazza Maggiore, stands the **Duomo** – not an attraction itself, but containing a couple of good pictures by Jacopo Bassano and Lorenzo Lotto.

Also on the Piazza Maggiore, in the fifteenth-century Loggia del Capitano, is the **Museo Civico**, which has long been in the throes of restoration but should soon be open again. The main interest of the art collection is provided by a pair of dubiously attributed Bellinis, a portrait of Ezzelino painted a good couple of centuries after his death and a brace of large sculptures by **Canova**. More diverting are the memorabilia of Ásolo's residents, especially the portraits, photos and personal effects of **Elenora Duse**. An actress in the Sarah Bernhardt mould, Duse was almost as well known for her tempestuous love-life as for her roles in Shakespeare, Hugo and Ibsen, and she came to Ásolo to seek refuge from public gossip. Although she died in Pittsburgh while on tour in 1924, her wish was to be buried in Ásolo, and so her body was transported back here, to the church of Sant'Anna.

The Teatro Duse occupies part of the **Castello**, most of which has also been under the restorer's trowel for ages. From 1489 to

1509 this was the home of **Caterina Cornaro**, one of the very few women to have played a decisive part in Venetian history. Born into one of Venice's most powerful families, Caterina was betrothed at the age of 14 to the philandering Jacques II, king of the strategically vital island of Cyprus. The prospective groom then prevaricated for a while, until the scheming of his half-sister (who wanted him overthrown) and the Venetian promises of help against the belligerent Turks finally pushed him into marriage. Within a year Jacques was dead, in all likelihood poisoned by Marco Venier, the Venetian governor of Famagusta harbour. A few weeks later Caterina gave birth to a son, after whose christening the Venetian fleet set sail for home. No sooner had the detested Venetians left than the city was taken over by men of the Royal Council, Caterina jailed, and her son handed over to her mother-in-law, Marietta. (Marietta's hatred of Caterina was to an extent due to resentment of the latter's beauty: when Marietta was the mistress of Jacques's father she had been caught making love to him by the king's wife, who bit her nose off in the ensuing melée.)

While Caterina refused to surrender Famagusta to the rebels, news of the insurrection reached the Venetian galleys, who promptly returned and overpowered the city. Their reappearance was a mixed blessing. The death of her son at the age of one was taken by Venier as a cue to propose marriage; spurned, he plotted to kill her instead, but was discovered and hanged. For nine years Caterina resisted Venice's political pressure until at last, in 1489, she was forced to abdicate in order to gain much-needed weapons and ships against a new Turkish attack. Brought back to Venice to sign a deed "freely giving" Cyprus to the Republic, she was given the region of Ásolo as a sign of Venice's indebtedness, and a joust was held on the frozen Canal Grande in her honour. In Ásolo her court was constantly under the eye of the Council of Ten, who dispatched any man rumoured to be her lover for fear that a new dynasty should be started. Eventually Ásolo, too, was taken away from her by the Emperor Maximilian, and she returned to seek asylum in Venice, where she died soon after, in 1510.

Ásolo's ruined medieval fortress, the **Rocca**, is reached by taking Via Collegio up the hill from the back of Piazza Brugnoli (right by Piazza Garibaldi) and going through the Porta Colmarian. You have to be fairly fit to tackle it in the heat of the midday sun, but the views on both sides are worth the sweat. Built on Roman foundations, the Rocca stands 350m above sea level.

Via Canova leads west away from the town centre past Elenora Duse's house (no. 306), near the Porta Santa Caterina. The church of **Santa Caterina** next to the Carabinieri is deconsecrated but open to allow visitors to see its fifteenth-century frescoes. Some way further on, at the junction of the road, is the enchanting fifteenth-century **Lombard house** with allegorical figures carved in soft stone; the architect was Francesco Graziolo, who worked for

Caterina Cornaro. Taking the central of the three roads at this junction you will arrive at the pedestrian Franciscan church of **Sant'Anna**; the **cemetery** on the right, from which there are splendid views, is where Elenora Duse and Pen Browning are buried.

Practicalities

The **tourist office is** in Via Regina Cornaro, close to the Museo (Mon–Sat 10am–noon & 4–7pm); if it's closed, you might find the boss in the bar opposite. They give out a map of the town which is quite handy, even if it isn't exactly a model of clarity.

Accommodation is impossible – two luxury hotels and that's all. Ásolo does have a handful of **bars and restaurants**, though. The large and popular *Caffè Centrale* on Piazza Garibaldi is all right (closed Tues), but not as friendly as the *Enoteca Marcello Agnoletto*, an excellent wine bar in Via Browning (closed Mon) – though it closes as early as 8pm. *La Papessa* in Via Pietro Bembo (closed Wed) has a good range of pizzas plus a few other interesting dishes.

The Villa Barbaro at Masèr

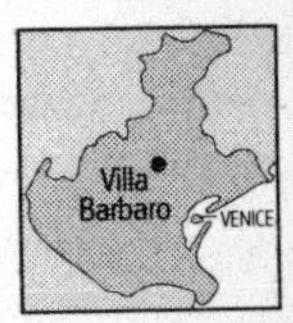

The Villa Barbaro is open March–Oct Tues, Sat & Sun 3–6pm; Nov–Feb Sat & Sun 2.30–5pm; L6000.

Most people come away from the **Villa Barbaro** at **MASÈR**, 7km east of Ásolo, persuaded that this is the most beautiful house in Europe. Touring the villas of the mainland, you become used to discrepancies between the quality of the architecture and the quality of the decoration, but at Masèr you'll see the best of two of the central figures of Italian civilisation in the sixteenth century – **Palladio** and **Paolo Veronese**, whose careers crossed here and nowhere else. If you're reliant on public transport, a visit is best made by bus from Bassano via Ásolo (8 daily), or from Treviso – the services from Treviso to Ásolo all pass the villa.

The villa was built in 1557–58 for Daniele and Marcantonio Barbaro, men whose diverse cultural interests set them apart from most of the other wealthy Venetians who were then beginning to farm the Veneto. Both were prominent figures in the society of Venice. Marcantonio served as the Republic's ambassador to Constantinople and became one of the Procurators of San Marco, a position that enabled him to promote Palladio's scheme for the church of the Redentore. Daniele, the more scholarly of the pair, edited the writings of Vitruvius, wrote on mathematics and perspective, and founded the botanical gardens in Padua; he was also Venice's representative in London and was later elected Patriarch of Acquileia, as well as becoming the official historian of Venice. The association between Palladio and the brothers was very close by the time the villa was built – in 1554 Daniele and Palladio had visited Rome, and they'd worked together on Barbaro's edition of Vitruvius

– and the process of designing the house was far more of a collaborative venture than were most of Palladio's projects.

The interior and the Tempietto

The Villa Barbaro was a working farm in which was embodied a classical vision – derived from writers such as Livy – of the harmony of architectural form and the well-ordered pastoral life. Farm functions dominated the entire ground floor – dovecots in the end pavilions, stables and storage space under the arcades, administrative offices on the lower floor of the central block. It's in the living quarters of the *piano nobile* that the more rarified aspect of the brothers' world is expressed, in a series of **frescoes** by Veronese (1566–68) that has no equal anywhere in northern Italy.

You need to be a student of Renaissance iconography to decode unassisted the allegorical figures in the amazing trompe l'oeil ceiling of the *Hall of Olympus* – the scheme was devised by Daniele Barbaro and centres on the figure of Eternal Wisdom – but an excellent guidebook is on sale in the villa, and most of the other paintings require no footnotes. The walls of the Villa Barbaro are the most resourceful display of visual trickery you'll ever see – servants peer round painted doors, a dog sniffs along the base of a flat balustrade in front of a landscape of ruins, illusory statues throw counterfeit shadows, flagstaffs lean in alcoves that aren't there. At the end of an avenue of doorways, a huntsman (probably Veronese himself) steps into the house through an entrance that's a solid wall – inevitably it's speculated that the woman facing the hunter at the other end of the house was Veronese's mistress. On top of all this, there's some remarkable architectural sculpture by **Alessandro Vittoria**: chimneypieces in the living rooms, figures in the tympanum of the main block, and an ornate **nymphaeum** in the garden at the back. The last incorporates a pond that used to be the house's fish-tank, and whose waters were channelled through the kitchens and out into the orchards.

In the grounds in front of the villa stands Palladio's **Tempietto**, the only church by him outside Venice and one of his last projects – commissioned by Marcantonio a decade after his brother's death, it was built in 1580, the year Palladio himself died. From the outside it's clear that the circular domed temple is based on the Pantheon, but when you get inside you find that the tiny side-chapels give the building a modified Greek-cross plan, thus combining the mathematically pure form of the circle with the liturgically perfect form of the cross. The other surprise of the interior is the richness of the stucco decoration, much of which is again by Vittoria.

There's also a **carriage museum** in the grounds, for which there's an extra entrance charge; it contains a few curiosities – such as a boat-shaped nineteenth-century ice-cream cart with a voluptuous mermaid on its prow – but you'd be better advised giving every spare minute to the villa and Veronese.

Feltre

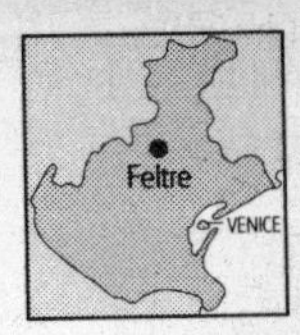

The historic centre of **FELTRE**, spread along a narrow ridge about 20km north of Masèr, owes its beguiling appearance to a disaster. At the outbreak of the War of the League of Cambrai, Feltre declared its allegiance to Venice – and so, when the army of Emperor Maximilian I swept into town in 1509, it was decided to punish Feltre by wiping its buildings and a hefty number of its inhabitants from the face of the planet. The Venetians took care of the reconstruction, and within a few decades the streets had been rebuilt. They still look pretty much as they did when the scaffolding came down. You're not going to find the town crawling with students making notes on the architecture of the Renaissance, but you'll have to travel a long way to get a better idea of how an ordinary town looked in sixteenth-century Italy. And on top of that, there's the beauty of Feltre's position – the Dolomites in one direction, the valley of the Piave in the other. The last stretch of the train journey from the south, along the Piave from Valdobbiádene, is on its own worth the price of the ticket.

There are no direct **trains** to Feltre from Venice, but Feltre is a stop on the **Padua to Belluno** line (12 daily) – you can intercept these trains at Castelfranco. The journey from Padua to Feltre takes ninety minutes, and it's a further thirty to Belluno.

The old town

From the station, down in the modern part of town, the shortest route to the old quarter is to cross straight over into Viale del Piave, over Via Garibaldi and along Via Castaldi, which brings you to the **Duomo** and **Baptistery**, at the foot of the ridge. The oldest section of the much-altered duomo is the fifteenth-century apse; its main objects of interest are a sixth-century Byzantine cross in boxwood – incorporating 52 New Testament scenes – and a tomb by Tullio Lombardo. At the top of the steps going past the side of the baptistery, on the other side of the road, is the painted south gate (1494), from under which a long covered flight of steps rises into the heart of the old town.

You come out by the sixteenth-century **Municipio**, with a portico by Palladio; Goldoni's first plays were performed here in 1730, in a wooden theatre that was redesigned at the start of the nineteenth century and has recently been restored (ask custodian for admission, weekday mornings). Behind the stage-like **Piazza Maggiore** rises the keep of the medieval castello, just below which is the church of **San Rocco** – go round the back for a good view of the mountains. And take a closer look at the carved wall between the steps going up to the church: it's actually a fountain by Tullio Lombardo.

The two Feltrian luminaries facing each other across the square are **Panfilo Castaldi** and Vittorino de' Rambaldoni, usually known as **Vittorino da Feltre** – both unsung heroes of the Renaissance. The former was instrumental in the development of printing in Italy, and according to some he beat Gutenberg to the invention of moveable type; the latter ran a school in Mantua in the first half of the fifteenth century, under the financial patronage of the Gonzaga family, which took in pupils from aristocratic families and unprivileged backgrounds alike, and put them through a regimen in which, for the first time, a broad liberal education was combined with a programme of physical training.

To the left as you look across at San Rocco, the main street of Feltre, **Via Mezzaterra**, slopes down to the fifteenth-century Porta Imperiale. Nearly all the houses here are sixteenth-century, and several are decorated with external frescoes by **Lorenzo Luzzo** (1467–1512) and his pupils. Feltre's most important artistic figure, Luzzo is more widely known **Il Morto da Feltre** (The Dead Man . . .), a nickname prompted by the pallor of his complexion. Having begun with spells in Rome and Florence, Il Morto's career received something of a boost when he was called in to help Giorgione on the Fondaco dei Tedeschi in Venice.

The **Museo Civico**, at the end of Via L. Luzzo, the equally decorous continuation of Via Mezzaterra on the other side of the piazza, contains Il Morto's *Madonna with St Vitus and St Modestus* and other pieces by him, but the building has been undergoing repairs for the last four years, and may not yet be open. If you do manage to get in, you should also discover paintings by Cima and Gentile Bellini, and a display of Roman and Etruscan finds. Il Morto's finest work is generally held to be the fresco of the *Transfiguration* in the **Ognissanti** church; this building is very unlikely to be open in the foreseeable future, but if you want to try your luck, you go out of the Porta Oria, right by the Museo, down the dip and then along Borgo Ruga for a couple of hundred metres.

The Museo Rizzarda is open June–Sept Tues–Sun 10am–1pm & 4–7pm; L2000.

Feltre has another, more unusual museum – the **Museo Rizzarda** at Via del Paradiso 8, parallel to Via Mezzaterra. This doubles as the town's collection of modern art and an exhibition of wrought-iron work, most of it by **Carlo Rizzarda** (1883–1931), the former owner of the house. It might not sound appetising, but the finesse of Rizzarda's pieces is remarkable. The frescoed building at the piazza end of Via del Paradiso is the **Monte di Pietà**, one of the few fifteenth-century buildings to escape the wrath of the Imperial hordes.

Practicalities

You're unlikely to need the Feltre **tourist office**, at Piazza Trento Trieste (Mon–Fri 9am–12.30pm & 3–6pm, Sat 9am–12.30pm), which is just as well, as it's one of the Veneto's less dynamic offices. Neither is it likely that you'll want a **hotel** here, but if you do, it's basically a choice between the two-star *Cavallino* at Via Garibaldi 8

Feltre

(☎0439/81.547; ④), or the three-star *Nuovi Garni* at Via Fornere Pazze 5 (☎0439/2110; ⑥). For **meals**, the *Aurora*, Via Garibaldi 24 (closed Sun), is a cheap and cheerful trattoria.

Conegliano

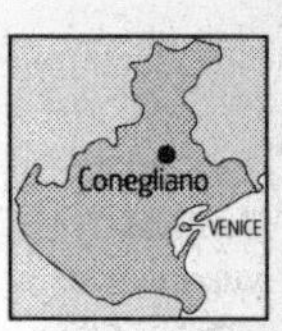

Travelling north from Treviso, it's at the amiable town of **CONEGLIANO**, as the terrain rises towards the mountains, that the landscape ceases to be as boring as a polder. The surrounding hills are patched with vineyards, and the production of wine is central to the economy of the district. Italy's first wine-growers' college was set up in Conegliano in 1876, and today there are a couple of well-established **wine routes** for the tourist to explore: the **Strada dei Vini del Piave**, which follows a looping 68-kilometre course south-east to ODERZO, and the more rewarding **Strada del Prosecco**, a straighter 42-kilometre journey west to VALDOBBIÁDENE. The former takes you through Merlot, Cabernet and Raboso country; the latter passes the Bianco dei Colli, Prosecco and Cartizze producers – the last, a more refined version of Prosecco, could be mistaken for champagne with a small effort of will.

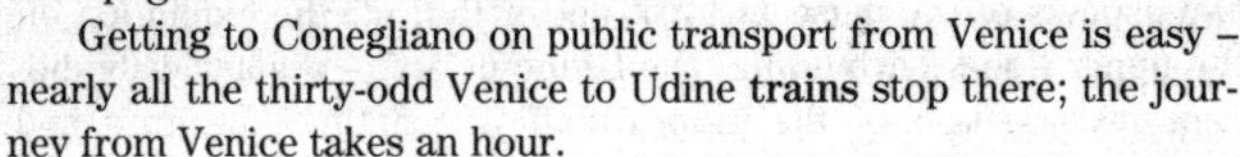

Getting to Conegliano on public transport from Venice is easy – nearly all the thirty-odd Venice to Udine **trains** stop there; the journey from Venice takes an hour.

The town

The old centre of Conegliano, adhering to the slope of the Colle di Giano and presided over by the Castello on its summit (founded in tenth century), is right in front of you as you come out of the station. After crossing the principal street of the modern town (Corso V. Emanuele–Corso G. Mazzini) you pass through a portico and into the original high street – **Via XX Settembre**. Lined with fifteenth- to eighteenth-century houses, this is an attractive street on any day, but to see it at its best you should turn up on a Friday morning, when the weekly **market** sets up camp.

The most decorative feature of Via XX Settembre is the unusual facade of the **Duomo** – a fourteenth-century portico, frescoed at the end of the sixteenth century by **Ludovico Pozzoserrato**, which joins seamlessly the buildings on each side. The interior of the church has been rebuilt, but retains fragments of fifteenth-century frescoes; the major adornment of the church, though, is the magnificent altarpiece of *The Madonna and Child with Saints and Angels*, painted in 1493 by **Giambattista Cima** (c.1459–c.1517), the most famous native of Conegliano.

Alongside the Duomo, at the top of the steps facing the door off the right-hand aisle of the church, is the **Sala dei Battuti** (Hall of the Flagellants), the frescoed meeting place of a local confraternity. (Ask the sacristan for admission.) The pictures are mostly sixteenth-century and depict scenes from the Creation to the Last Judgement, incorporating the weirdest *Ascension* you'll ever see, with Christ half out of the frame and a pair of footprints left behind at the point of lift-off. Individually the frescoes are nothing much to write home about, but the room as a unit is quite striking.

The Cima museum is open Sat & Sun 4–6pm; L1000.

Cima's birthplace, no. 24 Via G.B. Cima, at the rear of the duomo, has been restored and converted into the **Casa Museo di G.B. Cima**. Formally unadventurous, Cima exemplifies the conservative strand in Venetian painting of the early sixteenth century, but at their best his paintings have something of the elegiac tone of Giovanni Bellini's later works. The museum's pictures present clearly his strengths and his weaknesses; not one of them, though, is a painting by Cima – they're all high-class reproductions.

The Museo Civico is open summer Tues–Sun 9am–noon & 3.30–7pm; winter Tues–Sun 9am–noon & 2–5.30pm; L2000.

The **Museo Civico** is housed in the main tower of the reconstructed Castello on top of the hill – reached quickest by the steep Calle Madonna della Neve, which begins at the end of Via Accademia, the street beside the *Accademia* cinema. There are no masterpieces among the paintings (largely workshop of . . . , school of . . ., etc) and the displays of medals, maps, war memorabilia, armour and so forth are no more fascinating than you'd expect. But two aspects of the museum lift it out of the rut: the exhibition on the upper floors devoted to "The Grape in Art" – a maniacally diligent investigation of the grape motif in painting, furniture and jewellery design, glass and silverware, and any other applied art you care to think of; and the view from the roof, after which you'll never look at a Cima painting the same way again.

Practicalities

Conegliano has an extremely helpful **tourist office** at Viale Carducci 32, in front of the station (Tues–Fri 9am–noon & 3–6pm, Sat 9am–noon; ☎0438/21.230). Via XX Settembre has all you'll need in the way of cafés, bars and food shops, and the *Canon d'Oro* at no. 129 (☎0438/34.246; ⑦) is a good three-star **hotel**. If money's tight, you could stay at one of the one-stars a couple of kilometres from the centre of town: *Pare*, Via Vecchia Trevigiana 5 (☎0438/64.140; ④), or the nearby *Dei Mille*, Via Dei Mille 22 (☎0438/61.618; ③). The #1 bus from the train station goes past the *Pare*; both hotels have a trattoria downstairs. The *Canon d'Oro* has a fine **restaurant**, where a meal will cost around L30,000; the fish menu at *Città di Venezia*, Via XX Settembre 77 (closed Sun & Mon), costs about L10,000 less.

Prosecco is the chief wine of the Conegliano district, and its producers compile a list of recommended outlets: two authorised bars to try in the town itself are the *Giardini* café in Piazza Duca d'Aosta and the *Al Montegan Enoteca* in Via Istria. If you want to sample the stuff at source, exploration of the Strada del Prosecco by public transport isn't a problem – **buses** run frequently from Conegliano to Valdobbiádene (1hr), leaving from Piazzale Santa

Caterina (turn left out of train station along Via C. Colombo). For details of both wine routes, ask at the tourist office.

Conegliano has some kind of **festival** – musical, literary, culinary – on each weekend in September, a sequence that's brought to a close on the first weekend of October by the **Dama Castellana**, a gigantic draughts game played with human pieces. Initiated in 1241 to mark a victory over the troops of Treviso, the game is nowadays preceded by a costumed procession and flag-twirling, and followed by a gruelling ritual in which the losers have to shove the winners up the hill to the castle in a cart. In traditional style, fireworks bring the fun to a full stop.

Vittorio Veneto

The name **VITTORIO VENETO** first appeared on the map in 1866 when, to mark the unification of Italy and honour Vittorio Emanuele II, the first king of the new country, the neighbouring towns of Cèneda and Serravalle, which hadn't previously been the best of friends, were knotted together and rechristened. A new town hall was built midway along the avenue connecting the two, and the railway station constructed opposite, in the hope that the towns would grow closer together. To an extent they have, but the visitor emerging from the station still steps straight into a sort of no-man's-land.

Four **trains** a day run direct to Vittorio Veneto from Venice; otherwise it's a short hop **from Conegliano**. There are fifteen northward connections a day from Conegliano (25min) – sometimes these connections are by *Autocorsa*, a coach service on which rail tickets alone are valid. Read the timetable carefully when checking your connection back to Conegliano – if it's an *Autocorsa* you'll probably have to skip over to the bus station behind Piazza del Popolo, which is opposite the train station. From Vittorio Veneto four trains carry on to Belluno (60–90min), and six connect with a Belluno shuttle at PONTE DELLE ALPI. The remaining services chug north from Ponte delle Alpi to Calalzo, in the heart of the eastern Dolomites.

Cèneda

The Museo della Battaglia is open Tues–Sun: May–Sept 10am–noon & 4.30–6.30pm; Oct–April 10am–noon & 3–5pm; L4000.

CÈNEDA, overlooked by the seventh-century Lombard castle of San Martino (now the bishop's residence), is the less appealing of the halves; having a more open situation than Serravalle it has inevitably developed as the commercial centre of Vittorio Veneto. It is, nonetheless, worth a visit for the **Museo della Battaglia** in the sixteenth-century Loggia Cenedese, which is possibly by Sansovino. It's next to the nondescript cathedral, which you get to by turning right out of the station and keeping going until you see the sign for the centre, a fifteen-minute walk. The battle of Vittorio, which lasted from October 24 to November 3, 1918, was the final engagement of

World War I for the Italian army – which is why most towns in Italy have a Via Vittorio Veneto – and the museum is dedicated to the climactic engagement.

The only other building that merits a look in Cèneda is the church of **Santa Maria del Meschio**, where you'll find a luscious *Annunciation* by Andrea Previtali (c.1470–1528), a pupil of Giovanni Bellini. If you turn left off the Cèneda–Serravalle road down Via A. Diaz, instead going right for the cathedral square, you'll come across it quickly.

Serravalle

The Romanesque church of **Sant'Andrea di Bigonzo** will catch your attention as you trudge from Cèneda to Serravalle, at the end of an avenue to the right; it's decorated with Renaissance frescoes, but unless you've a bit of time to spare, content yourself with the view from a distance.

SERRAVALLE, wedged in the neck of the gorge between the Col Visentin and the Cansiglio, is an entirely different proposition from its partner. Once through its southern gate – to the left of which the ruined walls disappear into the trees on the valley side – you are into a town that has scarcely seen a demolition since the sixteenth century. Franco Zeffirelli exploited the place's charm to the full when he used it as one of the locations for his soft-focus *Romeo and Juliet*. Most of the buildings along Via Martiri della Libertà, Via Roma and Via Mazzini, and around the stage-like Piazza Marcantonio Flaminio, date from the fifteenth and sixteenth centuries – the handsomest being the finely painted and shield-encrusted Loggia Serravallese (rebuilt c.1460). This is now the home of the **Museo del Cenedese**, a jumble of sculptural and archaeological bits and pieces, detached frescoes and very minor paintings.

The Museo del Cenedese is open May–Sept 10am–noon & 4–6.30pm; Oct–April 10am–noon & 2–5pm. San Lorenzo is open May–Sept 3–4pm; Oct–April 2–3pm. Both closed Tues; entry to both on same ticket as Museo della Battaglia.

Time is more profitably spent in the churches of Serravalle than in its museum. One of the best-preserved fresco cycles in the Veneto covers the interior of **San Lorenzo dei Battuti**, immediately inside the south gate. Painted around 1450, the frescoes were damaged when Napoleon's lads used the chapel as a kitchen, but restoration subsequent to the uncovering of the cycle in 1953 has rectified the situation.

The **Duomo**, across the River Meschio on the far side of the Piazza Flaminio from the Museo, is a dull eighteenth-century building with a medieval campanile (good view of the gorge from the back) – an altarpiece of *The Virgin with St Peter and St Andrew*, produced in 1547 by **Titian** and his workshop, is the sole reason to go inside.

Behind the apse of the Duomo a flight of steps leads to a path that winds through the woods to the **Sanctuary of Santa Augusta** – go for the walk, not for the building. If you're in town on August 21, the festival of Saint Augusta's martyrdom, you'll be treated to a huge firework display and all-night party. Carry on up Via Roma instead of veering across the Piazza Flaminio, and you'll pass the remnant of the Castello and, eventually, the little church of **San Giovanni Battista** (outside the walls), which has beautiful cloisters. Further on still, and a few yards over the river (take the first right after San Giovanni), is **Santa Giustina**, which contains one of the best funerary monuments in the region – the **tomb** erected in 1336 by Verde della Scala (ie Scaliger) for her husband, Rizzardo VI da Camino, who had been killed in battle. The four praying warriors that support the Gothic sarcophagus were probably purloined from an older pulpit or other such structure.

Practicalities

The **tourist office**, at Piazza del Popolo 18 (Mon–Fri 9am–12.30pm & 3–6pm, Sat 9am–12.30pm), is best for information on the ski resorts and walking terrain around the town (see below).

There are hotels by the train station and in Cèneda, but you'll enjoy Vittorio Veneto more if you stay at the Serravalle end of town. Two minuscule places provide the cheapest **accommodation** here: *Al Postiglione*, Via Cavour 39 (☎0438/556.924; ③), and the extremely friendly *Vecchia Locanda*, a hundred metres up the hill at Via Tommaseo 80 (☎0438/552.121; ③). Best of the plusher accommodation is the three-star *Leon d'Oro*, Via Cavour 8 (☎0438/940.740; ⑥). *Al Postiglione* serves some of the best **food** in town (closed Tues), and the *Vecchia Locanda* (closed Sun) is good too; allow around L30,000 at the former, L25,000 at the latter. *Alla Giraffa*, Piazza Fontana 10, is a popular *gnoccoteca*, offering colossal plates of gnocchi with a variety of luscious sauces. Other places to grab a bite in Serravalle are the *Trattoria alla Cerva* on Piazza Flaminio (closed Tues), or the bar-pizzeria *Al 128* in Via Roma (closed Wed). Upmarket, the restaurant of the *Terme* hotel, on the Serravalle–Cèneda road at Via delle Terme 4 (☎0438/554.345) is also excellent, and should cost around L45,000.

Around Vittorio Veneto

The environs of Vittorio Veneto offer plenty of opportunities for activities more energetic than church crawling. From the centre of the town there are paths leading up into the hills, such as the one that takes you up to Monte Altare, immediately to the west. Further out, there are ski centres on both sides of the gorge to the north of the town, on the ALPAGO and NEVEGÀL slopes. These are the nearest ski resorts to Venice, but are best approached from Belluno, to the north. The **Lago di Santa Croce**, the reservoir which occupies much of the valley floor, is a centre for water-sports. The Vittorio Veneto–Belluno bus skirts the lake.

Progressing up the valley to the west of Vittorio Veneto, the area around the two small lakes of **REVÌNE** is good walking country; the town of Revìne Lago has a campsite with 140 places and a number of inexpensive hotels, and access by public transport from Vittorio Veneto is straightforward. Doughtier individuals can climb up to the head of the valley, past the huge castle of CISÒN DI VALMARINO, to the thirteenth-century Cistercian abbey at FOLLINA, where there are two one-star hotels.

However, the most rewarding area for walkers is to be found to the northeast of Vittorio Veneto – the **Bosco del Cansiglio**, a plateau forested with beech and pine which once was husbanded by the Venetian state as a source of timber for oars. Although the area has been developed as a holiday resort, you can still roam here for hours without seeing a soul. A good base from which to explore this vast expanse of woodland is FREGONA – it has a single one-star hotel plus a few pricier ones, is connected by regular bus to Vittorio Veneto and is close to **Le Grotte del Calieron**, a network of narrow caves scoured out of the rock by an underground torrent.

Belluno

The most northerly of the major towns of the Veneto, **BELLUNO** stands at the point where the tiny River Ardo flows into the Piave, in the shadow of the eastern Dolomites. Once a strategically important ally of Venice, which took the town under its wing in 1404, it is today a provincial capital, and attached more firmly to the mountainous region to the north than to the urban centres to the south – the network of the *Dolomiti-Bus* company radiates out from Belluno, trains run fairly regularly to the terminus at CALALZO, and the tourist office's handouts are geared mostly to hikers and skiers. Many visitors to the town use the place simply for its access to the mountains, and miss out on its attractions – of which there are quite a few, besides its breathtaking position.

At present there's just one **train** a day that runs straight from Venice to Belluno (1.30pm), and only one afternoon train back, but it's just as quick anyway to go via Conegliano (see p.341) – the complete expedition takes just over two hours. You can get to Belluno from Padua as well – there are twelve trains a day, also taking two hours.

The town

Belluno has two quite separate, but adjacent, centres. The hub of the modern town, the spot where you'll find its most popular bars and cafés, is the wide **Piazza dei Martiri** (named after a group of partisans executed in the square by the Nazis in 1944). Off the south side, a road leads to the **Piazza del Duomo**, the kernel of the old town. The sixteenth-century **Duomo** (or Santa Maria Assunta), a Gothic–classical amalgam built in the pale yellow stone that's a distinctive feature of Belluno, was designed by **Tullio Lombardo**; it has had to be reconstructed twice after earthquake damage, in 1873 and 1936. The elegant interior – a long barrel vault ending in a single dome, with flanking aisles – has a couple of good paintings: one by Andrea Schiavone (first altar on right), and one by Jacopo Bassano (third altar on right). From the bell-chamber of the stately **campanile** you get a view that'll have you reeling off the Fujicolour like there's no tomorrow; the tower was designed in 1743 by **Filippo Juvarra**, best known for his rebuilding of eighteenth-century Turin.

Occupying one complete side of the Piazza del Duomo, at a right angle to the Duomo itself, is the residence of the Venetian administrators of the town, the **Palazzo dei Rettori**, a frilly late fifteenth-century building dolled up with Baroque trimmings. A relic of more independent times stands on the right – the twelfth-century **Torre Civica**, all that's left of Belluno's medieval castle. Continuing round the Piazza, in Via Duomo, along the side of the nineteenth-century town hall, you'll find the **Museo Civico**. It's strongest on the work of Belluno's three best-known artists, all of whom were working at the end of the seventeenth and beginning of the eighteenth centuries: the painters Sebastiano and Marco Ricci, and the virtuoso sculptor-woodcarver Andrea Brustolon, who features prominently in Venice's Ca' Rezzonico. For those who prefer a touch less agitation in their art, the placid Paduan artist Bartolomeo Montagna is here as well.

The Museo Civico is open April–Oct Tues–Sat 10am–noon & 3–6pm, Sun 10am–noon; Nov–March Tues–Fri 10am–noon & 3–6pm, Mon & Sat 10am–noon; free.

Via Duomo ends at the **Piazza del Mercato**, a tiny square hemmed in by porticoed Renaissance buildings; until the Venetians shifted the administrative offices to the Piazza del Duomo, this was the nerve-centre of Belluno, and even after the Venetian alterations it remained the commercial centre. Its fountain dates from 1410 and the **Monte di Pietà** (no. 26) from 1501, making it one of the oldest pawnshops in Italy. One of the prime claimants to the honour of being the originator of pawnshops is Martino Tomitani (later Saint Bernardine of Feltre), a Franciscan friar from the village of Tomo, in the vicinity of nearby Feltre. The principal street of the old town, **Via Mezzaterra**, goes down from the Piazza del Mercato to the fourteenth-century Porta Ruga (veer left along the cobbled road about 50m from the end), from where the view along the Piave gorge will provide some compensation if you haven't managed to find the campanile open.

The unprepossessing church of **San Pietro**, just off Via Mezzaterra at the end of Vicolo San Pietro, is worth looking into for pieces by **Sebastiano Ricci** (main altarpiece), **Brustolon** (carved altarpieces on second altars on both sides, and angels over baldachin) and **Andrea Schiavone** (paintings over door and to sides of high altar).

Leaving the Piazza del Mercato in the other direction, you pass through the sixteenth-century **Porta Dojona** and into Piazza Vittorio Emanuele, an extension of the main square of the modern town. Belluno's other major church, **Santo Stefano**, is to the right, on Via

Roma. A bright Gothic building (1486) with banded arches and alternating brown and white columns, it has yet more carvings by **Brustolon** (candelabra by the main altar and, in the left aisle, a Crucifix resting on figures in Purgatory) and restored frescoes by **Jacopo da Montagnana**, painted within a year or so of the church's construction.

Practicalities

The **tourist office**, hidden in an alley off Piazza dei Martiri at Via Psaro 21 (Mon–Sat 8am–1pm), is so dozy that you're better off asking for information at *ASVI Viaggi*, Piazza dei Martiri 27e (Mon–Fri 9am–12.30pm & 3–7pm, Sat 9am–12.30pm).

Accommodation in Belluno is pitched at the skiing fraternity, who generally aren't the type to suffer cash-flow problems. Cheapest **hotel** in town is the *Taverna*, Via Cipro 7 (☎0437/25.192; ④). For more central accommodation, there's a clutch of **hotels** on and just behind Piazza dei Martiri, of which the most reasonable is the *Centrale*, Via Loreto 2 (☎0437/943.349; ⑤). Pick of the central three-stars is *Alle Dolomiti*, Via Carrera 46 (☎0437/941.660; ⑦).

The best **restaurant** at a moderate price is *Al Sasso*, Via del Cansiglio 12 (☎0437/22.424; closed Mon & late June–early July); it serves local specialities at around L30,000 for a full meal, with excellent homemade gnocchi. Two other genuine trattorias are close by: *Da Mara*, Piazza Mazzini 24, and *Moretto*, Via Valeriano 8 (both closed Sun). The *Taverna* hotel has a decent trattoria too. For a **drink**, call in at *Pub Carrera*, Via Carrera 11 (open till 2am; closed Tues).

Mountain excursions

Apart from *Dolomiti Neve* leaflets on the ski resorts of the area, *ASVI* can supply you with details of the **Alte Vie** (High Trails) of the eastern Dolomites – these are six mountain-top routes, up to nearly 200km in length, punctuated by alpine refuges. Most popular is the **Alta Via** no. 1, a north–south route right across the Dolomites from Braies to Belluno. The **Club Alpino Italiano**, at Via Ricci 1, runs several of the refuges, and is another good source of information for intrepid hikers.

If a two-week trek across the vertiginous peaks of northern Italy doesn't appeal, but you feel like a quick burst of alpine exertion, it's best to head south, to the ski centre of NEVEGÀL (11km), easily reached by bus. From there you can take a chairlift up to the *Rifugio Brigata Alpina Cadore*, and then embark on the climb up the mountain ridge to the refuge of **Col Visentin** (1761m), from where you can survey the crags of the Dolomites in one direction, and the waters of Venice in the other. Allow at least two and a half hours for the walk to the refuge.

The train will take you up the Piave valley only as far as Calalzo (10 daily; journey takes 1hr), so you'll probably find the **buses** more useful for trips north. All the **Dolomiti-Bus** services depart from the train station forecourt, and there's an information office there too.

The Contexts

A Brief History of Venice

In the midst of the waters, free, indigent, laborious, and inaccessible, they gradually coalesced into a Republic.

Edward Gibbon

Beginnings

Though the Venetian lagoon supported small groups of fishermen and hunters at the start of the Christian era, it was only with the barbarian invasions of the fifth century and after that sizeable communities began to settle on the mudbanks. The first mass migration was provoked by the arrival in the Veneto of **Attila the Hun**'s hordes in **453**, but a large number of the refugees struck camp and returned to dry land once the danger seemed to be past. Permanent settlement was accelerated a century later, when, in **568**, the Germanic **Lombards** (or Longobards), led by **Alboin**, swept into northern Italy.

A loose conglomeration of island communes arose, each cluster of islands drawing its population from one or two clearly defined areas of the Veneto: the fugitives from Padua went to **Malamocco** and **Chioggia**; the inhabitants of **Grado** mainly came from Aquileia; and Altino supplied many of the pioneers of **Torcello**, **Burano** and **Murano**. Distinct economic, ecclesiastical and administrative centres quickly evolved: Torcello was the focal point of trading activity; Grado, the new home of the Bishop of Aquileia, was the church's base; and Heraclea (now extinct) was the seat of government. The lagoon confederation was not autonomous, though – it owed **political allegiance to Byzantium**, and until the end of the seventh century its senior officials were the **maritime tribunes**, who were effectively controlled by the Imperial hierarchy of Ravenna.

The refugee population of the islands increased steeply as the Lombard grip on the Veneto strengthened under the leadership of **Grimoald** (667–71), and shortly after this influx the confederation took a big step towards independence. This is one of the many points at which Venetian folklore has acquired the status of fact: tradition has it that a conference was convened at Heraclea in 697 by the Patriarch of Grado, and from this meeting sprang the election of the **first doge**, to unify the islands in the face of the Lombard threat. (John Julius Norwich adroitly disentangles the myth in his history of Venice – see *Books*.) In fact, it was not until **726** that the lagoon settlers chose their first leader, when a wave of dissent against Emperor Leo III throughout the Byzantine Empire spurred them to elect **Orso Ipato** as the head of their provincial council.

After a period during which the old system of government was briefly reinstituted, Orso Ipato's son **Teodato** became the second doge in 742. Yet the lagoon administration – which was now moved from Heraclea to **Malamocco** – was still not autonomous. Teodato's relationship to the emperor was less subservient than his father's had been, yet he nonetheless took orders from the capital, and the **fall of Ravenna to the Lombards in 751** did not alter the constitutional relationship between Byzantium and the confederation.

At the close of the eighth century, the Lombards were overrun by the Frankish army of **Charlemagne**, and in **810** the emperor's son **Pepin** sailed into action against the proto-Venetians. Malamocco was quickly taken, but Pepin's fleet failed in its attempt to pursue the settlers when they withdrew to the better-protected islands of **Rivoalto**, and retreated with heavy losses. Now the seat of government in the lagoon was shifted for the second and last time, to Rivoalto, the name by which the central cluster of islands was known until the late twelfth century, when it became generally known as **Venice**. The **Rialto** district, in the core of the city, perpetuates the old name.

From independence to empire

In the **Treaty of Aix-la-Chapelle**, signed by Charlemagne and the Byzantine emperor shortly after Pepin's defeat, Venice was declared to be a dukedom within the Eastern Empire, despite the fact that by now the control of Byzantium was little more than nominal. The traders and boatmen of the lagoon were less and less inclined to acknowledge the precedence of the emperor, and they signalled their recalcitrance through one great symbolic act – **the theft of the body of Saint Mark from Alexandria in 828**. Saint Mark, whose posthumous arrival in Venice was held to be divinely ordained (see the "Basilica di San Marco" entry), was made the patron saint of the city in place of the Byzantine patron, Saint Theodore, and a basilica was built alongside the doge's castle to accommodate the holy relics. These two buildings – the **Basilica di San Marco** and the **Palazzo Ducale** – were to remain the emblems of the Venetian state and the repository of power within the city for almost one thousand years.

By the end of the ninth century the population of the islands of central Venice was increasing steadily. The city was comprehensively protected against attack, with chains slung across the entrance to the major channels and fortified walls shielding the waterfront between the Palazzo Ducale and the area in which the church of Santa Maria Zobenigo now stands. Before the close of the following century, the Venetian **trading networks** were well established – military assistance given to their former masters in Byzantium had earned concessions in the markets of the East, and the Venetian economy was now prospering from the distribution of eastern goods along the waterways of northern Italy .

Slav pirates, operating from the shelter of the Dalmatian coast, were the greatest hindrance to Venetian trade in the northern Adriatic, and in the year **1000** a fleet set out under the command of **Doge Pietro Orseolo II** to subjugate the troublemakers. The successful expedition was commemorated each subsequent year in the ceremony of the **Marriage of Venice to the Sea**, in which the city's lordship of the Adriatic was ritually confirmed. (See the "Lido" entry.) However, although the Doge of Venice could now legitimately claim the title "Duke of Dalmatia", there remained the problem of the **Normans** of southern Italy, whose navy threatened to confine the Venetians to the upper part of the Adriatic. The breakthrough came in the 1080s. In **1081** the Byzantine emperor Alexius Comnenus, himself endangered by Norman expansion, appealed to Venice for aid. The result was a series of naval battles costing thousands of lives, at the end of which Venice had strengthened its shipping lanes, established itself as the protector of the Eastern Empire's seaboard, and earned invaluable commercial rights for its traders. In a charter of 1082, known as the *Crisobolo* (Golden Bull), the emperor declared Venetian merchants to be exempt from all tolls and taxes within his lands. In the words of one historian – "On that day Venetian world trade began".

Venice and the Crusades

In 1095 Pope Urban II called for a Christian army to wrest the Holy Land from the Muslims, and within four years Jerusalem had been retaken by the **First Crusade**. Decades of chaos ensued, which the Venetians, typically, managed to turn to their commercial advantage. Offering to transport armies and supplies to the East in return for grants of property and financial bonuses, Venice extended its foothold in the Aegean, the Black Sea and Syria, battling all the time (sometimes literally) against its two chief maritime rivals in Italy – Pisa and Genoa. While it was consolidating its overseas bases, Venice was also embroiled in the political manoeuvrings between the papacy, the Western Emperor and the cities of northern Italy, the conclusion of which was one of Venice's greatest diplomatic successes: **the reconciliation of Emperor Frederick Barbarossa and Pope Alexander III** in 1177, in Venice.

Now a major European power, Venice was about to acquire an empire. In November 1199 Count Tibald of Champagne proposed a **Fourth Crusade** to regain Jerusalem, which twelve years earlier had fallen to Saladin. It came about that Venice was commissioned, for a huge fee, to provide the ships for the army. In 1202 the forces gathered in Venice, only to find that they couldn't raise the agreed sum. In the negotiations that followed, the doge obtained a promise from the French commanders that the Crusade would stop off to reconquer the colony of Zara, recently captured from Venice by the King of Hungary. No sooner was that accomplished than the expedition was diverted, after Venetian persuasion, to Constantinople, where the succession to the imperial throne was causing problems. The eventual upshot was the **Sack of Constantinople in 1204**, one of the most disgusting episodes in European history. Thousands were massacred by the Christian soldiers and virtually every precious object that could be lifted was stolen from the city, mainly by the Venetians. So vast was the scale of the destruction and murder that a contemporary historian regretted that the city had not fallen instead to the Infidel. Ultimately its consequences were disastrous – not only did no help reach the forces in the Holy Land, but the Eastern Empire was fatally divided between the native Greeks and the barbaric Westerners. The Ottoman conquest of Constantinople in 1453, and the consequent peril of Western Europe, were distant but direct results of the Fourth Crusade. Venice got what it wanted, though – "one quarter and half a quarter" of the Roman Empire was now under its sway, with an almost uninterrupted chain of ports stretching from the lagoon to the Black Sea.

The fourteenth century

The enmities created within the Eastern Empire by the Fourth Crusade were soon to rebound on Venice. The Genoese were now the main opposition in the eastern markets, maintaining a rivalry so violent that some Venetian historians refer to their succession of conflicts as the **Five Genoese Wars**. Genoa's hatred of Venice led to an alliance with the dethroned Byzantine dynasty, whose loathing of the Venetians was no less intense; within months of the Pact of Ninfeo (1261), **Michael Palaeologus VIII** was installed as emperor in Constantinople. Venice now faced a struggle to hold onto their commercial interests against the favoured Genoese.

For the rest of the century, and almost all the fourteenth century, the defeat of Genoa was the primary aim of Venice's rulers. Both sides suffered terrible defeats: at the battle of **Curzola** (1298) 65 ships out of a Venetian fleet of 95 were lost, and 5000 Venetians taken captive; at the Sardinian port of **Alghero** (1353) the Genoese navy lost a similar proportion of its vessels. The climax came with the Fourth War of Genoa, better known as the **War of Chioggia**. Following a victory over the Venetians at Zara in 1379, the Genoese fleet sailed on to Venice, supported by the Paduans and the Austrians, and quickly took Chioggia. This was the zenith of Genoa's power – in August **1380** the invaders were driven off, and although the treaty signed between the two cities seemed inconclusive, within a few decades it was clear that Venice had at last won the battle for economic and political supremacy.

Political upheaval

It was during the Genoese campaigns that the **constitution** of Venice arrived at a state that was to endure until the fall of the Republic, the most significant step in this evolution being the **Serrata del Maggior Consiglio** of **1297**, a measure which basically allowed a role in the government of the city only to those families already involved in it. (See the "Palazzo Ducale" entry.) Not surprisingly, many of those disenfranchised by the *Serrata* resented its instigator, **Doge Pietro Gradenigo**, and when Venice lost its tussle with the papacy for possession of Ferrara in 1309, it seemed that Gradenigo had scarcely a single supporter in the city. Yet the insurrection that came the following year was a revolt of a patrician clique, not an uprising of the people; its leader – **Bajamonte Tiepolo** – had personal reasons for opposing the doge and appears to have wanted to replace the new system not with a more democratic one but with a despotic regime headed by himself. Tiepolo's private army was routed in a battle in the centre of the city, but his rebellion had a permanent effect upon the history of Venice, in that it led to the creation in 1310 of the **Council of Ten**, a committee empowered to supervise matters of internal security. Though the Council was intended to be an emergency measure, its tenure was repeatedly extended until, in 1334, it was made a permanent institution.

The most celebrated attempt to subvert the Venetian government followed a few years later, in **1355**, and this time the malefactor was the doge himself – **Marin Falier**, who ironically had played a large part in the sentencing of Bajamonte Tiepolo. Falier's plot to overthrow the councils of Venice and install himself as absolute ruler seems to have been prompted by his fury at the lenient treatment given to a young nobleman who had insulted him. Exploiting the grievances felt against certain noble families by, among others, the director of the Arsenale, Falier gathered together a group of conspirators, many of whom were drawn from the working class, a section of Venetian society which was particularly affected by the economic demands of the rivalry with Genoa. (Open war had recently broken out again after a long but tense period of truce, and to make the situation worse, the **Black Death of 1348–49** had killed around 60 percent of the city's population.) Details of the planned coup leaked out, Falier was arrested, and on April 17, eight months after becoming doge, he was beheaded on the steps of the Palazzo Ducale.

Terra firma expansion

The sea lanes of the eastern Mediterranean were the foundation of Venice's wealth, but its dominance as a trading centre clearly depended on free access to the rivers and mountain passes of northern Italy. Thus, although Venetian foreign policy was predominantly eastward-looking from the start, a degree of intervention on the mainland was inevitable, especially with the rise in the fourteenth century of ambitious dynasties such as the **Scaligeri** in Verona and the **Visconti** in Milan. Equally inevitable was the shift from a strategy to preserve Venice's commercial interests, to a scheme that was blatantly imperialistic.

The unsuccessful battle for Ferrara was Venice's first territorial campaign; the first victory came thirty years later, when the combined forces of Venice, Florence and a league of Lombard cities defeated the Scaligeri, allowing Venice to incorporate **Castelfranco**, **Conegliano**, **Sacile**, **Oderzo** and, most importantly, **Treviso** into the domain of the Republic. Having thus made safe the roads to Germany, the Venetians set about securing the territory to the west. The political and military machinations of northern Italy in this period are extremely complicated, with alliances regularly made and betrayed, and cities changing hands with bewildering frequency – Treviso, for example, was lost and won back before the close of the fourteenth century. The bare outline of the story is that by **1405** Venice had eradicated the most powerful neighbouring dynasty, the **Carrara** family of Padua, and had a firm hold on **Bassano**, **Belluno**, **Feltre**, **Vicenza**, **Verona** and **Padua** itself. The annexation in **1420** of **the Friuli** and **Udine**, formerly ruled by the King of Hungary, virtually doubled the area of the *terra firma* under Venetian control, and brought the border of the empire right up to the Alps.

Many Venetians thought that any further expansion would be foolish. Certainly this was the view of **Doge Tommaso Mocenigo**, who on his deathbed urged his compatriots to "refrain ... from taking what belongs to others or making unjust wars". Specifically, he warned them against the ambitions of **Francesco Fóscari** – "If he becomes doge, you will be constantly at war ... you will become the slaves of your masters-at-arms and their captains". Within a fortnight of Mocenigo's funeral in 1423, Fóscari was elected as his successor, and Venice was soon on the offensive against the mightiest prince of northern Italy – **Filippo Maria Visconti** of Milan. In the first phase of the campaign nothing except a tenuous ownership of Bergamo and Brescia was gained, a failure for which the Venetian mercenary captain, **Carmagnola**, served as the scapegoat. He was executed in 1432 for treason, and his place taken by Erasmo da Narni, better known as **Il Gattamelata**. The **Treaty of Cremona** (1441) confirmed Venetian control of **Peschiera**, **Brescia**, **Bergamo** and part of the territory of **Cremona**, and by now **Ravenna** was also officially part of the Venetian dominion, but still the fighting did not stop. Peace on the mainland finally came in **1454**, with the signing of a treaty between Venice and the new ruler of Milan, **Francesco Sforza**, Venice's erstwhile ally against the Visconti. Ravenna didn't stay Venetian for long; the rest of its mainland empire, though, remained intact until the coming of Napoleon.

The Turkish threat

The other Italian states might have taken concerted action against Venice had it not been for the fact that the entire peninsula now faced the common threat of the Ottoman Turks, as was acknowledged in the pact drawn up at **Lodi** later in 1454 between Venice, Milan, Naples, Florence and the Papal States. Open conflict between Venice and the Turks had broken out early in the century – the Republic winning the naval battle of Gallipoli in 1416 – but the policy of *terra firma* expansion kept the majority of Venice's warships on the rivers of the north, so reliance had to be placed in diplomatic measures to contain the Turkish advance. They were ineffective. Reports of a Turkish military build-up under the command of the young **Sultan Mahomet II** were not treated with the necessary urgency, and the consequence was that Western troops sent to defend **Constantinople** against the Sultan's army were insufficient to prevent the fall of the city in **1453**.

The trade agreement which the Venetians managed to negotiate with the Sultan could not arrest the erosion of its commercial empire in the East. The Turkish fleets penetrated into the northern Aegean and many times in the last years of the century its cavalry came so close to Venice that the fires from the villages it destroyed could be seen from the top of the Campanile of San Marco. In **1479** Venice was forced to sign away the vital port of **Negroponte** and a batch of other Aegean islands; the defeat of the Venetian navy at **Sapienza** in **1499** led to the loss of the main fortresses of the **Morea** (Peloponnese), which meant that the Turks now controlled the so-called "door to the Adriatic". Virtually the only bright spot in all the gloom came about through the marriage of the Venetian **Caterina Cornaro** to the King of **Cyprus** in 1468. In 1473 the king died, and the ensuing political pressure on the widow paid off in **1489**, when Caterina handed over the island to the government of Venice.

The sixteenth century

In **1494** Italy was invaded by **Louis XII of France**, an intervention which Venice lost no time in exploiting. By playing the various territorial contenders off against each other (mainly France and the Habsburgs), Venice succeeded in adding bits and pieces to the *terra firma* empire, and in 1503 signed a disadvantageous treaty with the Turks so as to be able to concentrate its resources on the mainland. Given the accumulated hostility to Venice, it was a dangerous game, and when the Republic began to encroach on the papal domain in Romagna, it at last provoked a unified response from its opponents. The **League of Cambrai**, formed in **1508** with Pope Julius II, Louis XII, Emperor Maximilian and the King of Spain at its head, pitted almost every power in Europe against the Venetians, in a pact that explicitly declared its intention of destroying Venice's empire as a prelude to conquering the Turks.

The ensuing war began calamitously for Venice – its army was crushed by the French at **Agnadello**, city after city defected to the League, and Venice prepared for a siege. The siege never came, and in the end the conflicting interests of the League enabled the Venetians, through subtle diplomacy, to repossess nearly everything they had held at the start of the war. Nonetheless, when the fighting finished in **1516** many of the cities of the Veneto had been sacked, great swathes of the countryside ruined, and the Venetian treasury bled almost dry.

Worse was to come. Clearly **the discovery of the New World** was going to have significant repercussions for Venice, but the most catastrophic of the voyages of discovery from Venice's point of view was that of **Vasco da Gama**. In September **1499**, da Gama arrived back in Lisbon having reached India by the Cape of Good Hope. The slow and expensive land routes across Asia to the markets and docks of Venice could now be bypassed by the merchants of northern Europe – from the moment of da Gama's return the economic balance of Europe began to tilt in favour of the Portuguese, the English and the Dutch.

In **1519**, with the accession of the 19-year-old **Charles V**, the Habsburg Empire absorbed the massive territories of the Spanish kingdom, and after the **sack of Rome in 1527** the whole Italian peninsula, with the sole exception of Venice, was under the young emperor's domination. Meanwhile, the **Turks** were on the move again – **Syria** and **Egypt** had been taken in **1517**; **Rhodes** had fallen to **Suleiman the Magnificent** in **1522**; and by 1529 the Ottoman Empire had spread right along the southern Mediterranean to Morocco. To survive, Venice had to steer a path between these two empires and France, the other superpower of the period. It did survive, but at a cost. When a combined Christian fleet took on the Turks at **Prevesa** in **1538**, the supreme commander, acting under Charles V's instructions, was so concerned to prevent the Venetians profiting from an allied victory that his tactics ensured a Turkish victory; the Venetians were obliged to accept a punitive treaty shortly after. Even the great allied success at **Lépanto** in **1571** didn't work to Venice's advantage, as the Habsburg commander of the fleet, Don John of Austria, refused to consolidate the Venetian position by sailing east after the victory. In the subsequent negotiations, Venice was forced formally to surrender **Cyprus**, the brutal capture of which by the Turks had been the reason for the allied offensive in the first place.

The seventeenth century

Relations between Rome and Venice were always fractious. Venice's expansion on the mainland was a source of irritation, especially when it turned its attention to areas over which the Vatican claimed sovereignty, but papal animosity was also caused by the restrictions imposed on the pope's authority within the Republic's boundaries, restrictions which led to Venice's being regarded in some quarters as a crypto-Protestant state. The pope was Venice's spiritual overlord, the Venetians agreed, but the doge and his officers were the masters in temporal affairs. The problem for the papacy was that the doge's notion of what constituted temporal affairs was far too broad, and at the start of the seventeenth century, **Pope Paul V** and the Republic came to a head-on clash.

Two incidents provoked the row: Venice's insistence that the pope should routinely approve its candidate for the office of Patriarch; and its determination not to hand over to papal jurisdiction two clerics it had decided to prosecute. Matters came to a head with the **Papal Interdict of 1606** and the excommunication of the whole city. Venice's resistance, orchestrated by the scholar-priest **Paolo Sarpi**, was fierce – the Jesuits were expelled, priests within Venetian territory ordered to continue in their duties, and pamphlets printed putting the Venetian case. One year later the Interdict was lifted, damaging the prestige of the papacy throughout Europe.

No sooner was the Interdict out of the way than the Spanish and Austrian **Habsburgs** entered the fray again. The Austrian branch was the first to cause trouble, by encouraging the piratical raids of the **Uskoks**, a loosely defined and regularly obstreperous community living along the Dalmatian coast. Venice took retaliatory action, Archduke Ferdinand objected, and a half-hearted war dragged on until **1617**, when, under the peace terms, the benighted Uskoks were removed completely from their sea-ports.

The Spanish wing was more devious, attempting, in **1618**, to subvert the Venetian state with a wildly ambitious scheme that has always been known as **The Spanish Conspiracy**. Masterminded by the Spanish Viceroy of Naples, the **Duke of Osuna**, and the Spanish Ambassador to Venice, the **Duke of Bedmar**, the plot involved smuggling a Spanish army into the city in disguised groups of two or three, and then inciting a mutiny among a contingent of Dutch mercenaries already lodged there. Just how convoluted the conspiracy was can be gathered from the fact that its betrayal resulted in the execution of around 300 people.

And then, after half a century of ceasefire, the **Turks** renewed their harassment of the Venetian colonies, concentrating their attention now on the one remaining stronghold in the eastern Mediterranean, **Crete**. The campaign lasted for 25 years, ending in **1669** with the inevitable fall of the island. Even then the war with the Turks was not over – in **1699**, under the military command of **Doge Francesco Morosini**, the Venetians embarked on a retaliatory action in the **Morea** (Peloponnese), and succeeded in retaking the islands. By 1715, however, all the gains had been turned to losses once more, and in the **Treaty of Passarowitz** of **1718** Venice was forced to accept the definition of its Mediterranean empire drawn up by the Austrians and the Turks. It was left with just the Ionian islands and the Dalmatian coast, and its power in those colonies was little more than hypothetical.

Collapse

Venice in the eighteenth century became a political nonentity, pursuing a foreign policy of unarmed neutrality of which one historian wrote "she sacrifices everything with the single object of giving no offence to other states". When the **Treaty of Aix-la-Chapelle** in **1748** confirmed Austrian control of the neighbouring areas of the mainland, the Venetians felt compelled to send ambassadors to the Austrian court in a humiliating attempt to wheedle guarantees of their possessions on the *terra firma*. At home, the economy remained strong, but the division between the upper stratum of the aristocracy and the ever-increasing poorer section was widening, and all attempts to dampen discontent within the city by democratising its government were stifled by the conservative elite.

Politically trivial and constitutionally ossified, Venice was now renowned not as one of the great powers of Europe, but rather as its playground. Hester Thrale observed in 1789 that no other place was "so subservient to the purposes of pleasure", and William Beckford recorded the effects of a life spent between the ballroom and casino – "Their nerves unstrung by disease and the consequence of early debaucheries, allow no natural flow of lively spirits ... they pass their lives in one perpetual doze."

The conflict between Austria and post-revolutionary France quickly brought about the end of the Venetian Republic. Having mollified the Austrians by handing over the Veneto to them, **Napoleon** waited for a pretext to polish off the Republic itself. On 20 April 1797 the Venetians duly provided him with one, by attacking a French naval patrol off the Lido. "I will have no more Inquisitors. I will have no more Senate; I shall be an Attila to the state of Venice," Bonaparte proclaimed; war was declared on Venice, and on May 9 an ultimatum was sent to the city's government, demanding the dissolution of its constitution.

On Friday, **May 12, 1797** the Maggior Consiglio met for the last time. By 512 votes to 20, with 5 abstentions, the Council voted to accede to every one of Napoleon's demands; the vote cast, the last Doge of Venice, **Lodovico Manin**, handed to his valet the linen cap worn beneath the ducal crown, saying – "Take it, I shall not be needing it again." The Venetian Republic was dead.

Within days a provisional democratic council had been formed and there were French troops in the city, many of them occupied with wrecking the Arsenale or stripping the place of its art treasures and shipping them off to Paris. On this occasion, the French didn't stay long, because in the **Treaty of Campo Formio**, signed in October, Napoleon relinquished Venice to the Austrians. They were soon back, though – in **1805** Napoleon joined the city to his Kingdom of Italy, and it stayed under French domination until the aftermath of Waterloo, ten years later. It then passed back to the Austrians again, and remained a Habsburg province for the next half-century, the only break in Austrian rule coming with the **revolt of March 1848**, when the city was reinstituted as a republic under the leadership of **Daniele Manin**, the last heroic figure in Venetian history. The rebellion lasted until **August 1849**, when a combination of starvation, disease and relentless bombardment forced the Venetians to surrender. Liberation finally arrived in the wake of Prussia's defeat of the Austrians at Sadowa in **1866**. Soon after, Venice was absorbed into the Kingdom of United Italy.

To the present

In many respects the Austrians were better for Venice than the French had been. Although the French initiated modernisation schemes such as the creation of public gardens and the cemetery of San Michele, not all of the fifty or so religious buildings and forty palaces which they demolished were destroyed in a good cause; in addition to which, they also wrecked the shipyards and confiscated hundreds of works of art. The Austrians' urban improvements were less ruthless: they filled in some of the more unhygienic canals (the origin of the *rio terrà*), built a rail link with the mainland, and undertook two major, albeit controversial, restoration projects – the Fondaco dei Turchi and the church of Santi Maria e Donato on Murano.

Yet Venice went through most of the nineteenth century in a state of destitution. There were no more government jobs to provide a source of income, and Trieste was the Austrians' preferred port on the Adriatic. By 1820 begging was the main means of support for about one quarter of its population. Families that had once been among the city's wealthiest were obliged to sell their most treasured possessions; the Barbarigo family sold seventeen paintings by Titian to the Czar, for example. Later in the century, even the churches were selling their property to pay for their upkeep. It's been calculated that of the moveable works of art that were to be found in Venice at the fall of the Republic, only 4 percent remains.

Manufacturing activity within the city revived towards the end of the nineteenth century: there were flour mills on Giudecca, glass factories on Murano, lace workshops on Burano, and the 1913 edition of Baedeker described Venice as a "shipbuilding, cotton spinning and iron working centre". The opening of the Suez Canal in 1869 brought a muted revival to the Arsenale docks. Already, though, **tourism** had emerged as the main area of economic expansion, with the development of the **Lido** as Europe's most fashionable resort. It was the need for a more substantial economic base than bathing huts, hotels and a few pockets of industrial production that led, in the wake of World War I, to the development of the industrial complex on the marshland across the lagoon from Venice, at **Porto Marghera**.

By the end of World War I, Venice itself was finished as a maritime centre – battleships had been built in the Arsenale, but the proximity of the enemy forces persuaded the navy to dismantle the docks in 1917 and switch its yards to Genoa and Naples. The new port of Marghera was not a shipyard but a processing and refining centre to which raw materials would be brought by sea. In 1933 a **road link** was built to carry the workforce between Venice and the steadily expanding port, whose progress was a special concern of Mussolini's government. (Venice was the second city in Italy in which organised Fascism appeared; as early as 1919 the local newspaper published an appeal for the formation of fascist squads.) After World War II (from which Venice emerged undamaged) Marghera's growth accelerated even more rapidly. The consequences were not those that had been predicted.

What happened was that the factory workers of Marghera, instead of commuting each day from Venice, simply decamped to the mainland. Housing in Marghera's neighbour, **Mestre**, is drier, roomier, warmer and cheaper to maintain than the apartments in Venice, and as a result the population of Mestre-Marghera is today more than three times that of the historic centre of Venice, which is now around the 75,000 mark. (Immediately after the last war it was around 170,000.) Apart from polluting the environment of the lagoon, Mestre has siphoned so many people of working age from the islands that the average age of Venice's population (44) is now the highest of any major European city. Moreover, the percentage of native Venetians in the city is declining as the place becomes a favourite base or retirement home for the wealthy of Milan, Turin and other more prosperous Italian cities – only the wealthy can afford to maintain the fragile fabric of many of the city's houses, most of which are listed as historic monuments. When a flat is sold in Venice, the odds are now around 2/1 that the buyer will not be a Venetian.

Venice's future?

No city has suffered more from the tourist industry than Venice – over 80,000 people come to the city each day in high season, and around half of those don't even stay a night. Only 8 plumbers are registered in Venice, while the number of souvenir shops has risen to around 400.

Yet Venice at the moment is dependent on tourism, and every year proposals are put forward to break that dependency. A science park, a national library, a conservation and marine technology centre, a national institute for restoration research – all have been suggested as projects which could give Venice a more active role in the life of twentieth-century Italy. Some dismiss such ideas as mere gestures, and prefer to see the recent political shifts in Eastern Europe as the harbingers of Venice's revival. Should political realignment lead to the development of a market economy in these countries, Venice will once again be sitting on a major European trade route – or so the argument runs.

Perhaps the craziest scheme for the renewal of Venice was the proposal that it should be the venue for **Expo 2000**, the trade jamboree that will usher in the new millennium. The project envisaged the drainage of a large part of the lagoon to build the Expo site, and it was anticipated that 45 million people would come to the city over the four months of the show – in other words, four times the city's population daily. Despite the evident idiocy of the idea, it was vociferously championed by Venice-born and Venice-based Gianni de Michelis, then Foreign Minister and, quite coincidentally, owner of a lot of property in the city, where he is known unaffectionately as "The Doge". By a combination of blatant threats and bribery, de Michelis and his brother secured the backing of a majority among the 43 member states of the *Bureau International des Expositions*, and it seemed that the *BIE*'s meeting in June 1990 would be nothing more than a formal ratification of Venice's disastrous application.

But the forces of reason were making themselves heard in the upper reaches of the Italian government. Environmentalists from all over the world lobbied the Italians to reconsider and the upper house of the Italian parliament passed a motion deploring the scheme – as did the European Parliament, by 195 to 14. The near-unanimity of this latter vote was decisive. Two days before the *BIE* meeting the Italian government cancelled the city's application. Hanover will host Expo 2000.

Mr de Michelis's career has followed a downward trajectory since the rejection of his pet project. In the latter half of 1992 a huge bribery scandal broke in Venice. It was alleged that the de Michelis faction of the Socialist party and their Christian Democrat allies had shared out bribes from major civil contractors, splitting the kickbacks on a percentage related directly to the parties' representation on the city council. Known as a **"theorem"**, this system of wealth distribution had been unearthed a few months earlier in

Milan, where it had destroyed the Socialists' reputation for honesty and all but destroyed the career of the party's former Mr Fixit, Bettino Craxi. The Venetian scandal – said to involve some £7 billion worth of contracts – will doubtless do the same to Gianni de Michelis.

It's quite possible that much of the money for the lagoon barrier (see p.375) has found its way into the bank accounts of various politicians. It remains to be seen whether corruption or sound sense will wreck the latest crack-brained idea about how to propel Venice into the twenty-first century. In 1992 Venice was granted metropolitan status, which enabled the town council to apply for central funding for an **urban rail system**. It is now seriously proposed that an underground train line be excavated to link central Venice and the islands of San Giorgio Maggiore, Giudecca, the Lido, San Michele and Murano to the mainland rail network at Marco Polo airport and Mestre. Apologists for the metro project insist that it will enable those of the city's inhabitants who work on the mainland to get quickly to their desks and back home again. Its opponents, led by the conservation group Italia Nostra, argue that the enthusiasm of the Christian Democrats and the Socialists for the train plan has a lot to do with the 700 billion lire set aside for its development, some of which would doubtless percolate into the corridors of the town hall. What's more, they say, the metro will increase the tourist deluge of Venice and undermine the delicate substructures of the city's buildings.

Unfortunately the politicians seem more enamoured of such high-profile schemes than of the more modest proposals emerging from some quarters, most of them based on furthering the city's reputation for crafts and restoration work. When asked to nominate a site for the prestigious European Environmental Agency, the Italian government ignored the overwhelming claim of Venice and instead put forward Milan, which cannot muster the same expertise as a city which exists in a perpetually problematic relationship with the environment. And when asked to give an assurance that the European Centre for the Training of Craftspeople could indefinitely extend its occupancy of the island of San Servolo, the local council demurred – so this unique facility may well be transferred to Germany.

Meanwhile, the councillors plan to deal with the tourism problem by building a massive coach park on the mainland, and setting aside a stretch of the Riva degli Schiavoni for the use of "tourist launches". Massimo Riva, the senator who led the resistance to the Expo plan, has declared that the only hope for Venice is the creation of a new independent agency to run the city, affiliated to no political party and no industrial conglomerates. It is difficult not to agree.

Venetian Painting and Sculpture

After just a day in Venice you notice that the light is softer than that on the mainland and changes more during the course of a day. Reflecting off the water and the white stone facades, it gives shifting impressions of places that would otherwise be shadowed, and adds shimmering highlights to solid brickwork. In view of the specific qualities of Venetian light, it's scarcely surprising that the city's painters emphasised colour and texture rather than structure and perspective. The political and social peculiarities of Venice were equally influential on the development of its art, as will become apparent in the following thumbnail account.

Byzantine Venice

The close political and commercial ties between the early Venetian state and the Byzantine empire (see the "History" section) led to a steady exchange of works of art between the two, and to the creation of the most important work of art from that period – the **Pala d'Oro** on the high altar of San Marco. Begun as a collaboration between Venetian and Byzantine craftsmen, it epitomises the Venetian taste for elaborate decoration and creates the impression of a complex content unified by a dazzlingly rich surface. The *Pala* was later expanded with panels stolen from Constantinople during the sack of 1204, a wholesale plundering which provided Venice with a hoard of artefacts that was to nourish its craftsmen and artists for centuries.

It is notable that the earliest Venetian painter of renown, **Paolo Veneziano** (working from the 1330s to at least 1358), shows far stronger affinities with Byzantine work than with the frescoes created by Giotto at the start of the century in nearby Padua. He generally employs a flat, gold background and symmetrical arrangements of symbolic figures, rather than attempting a more emotional representation of individuals. Two paintings in the Accademia show these characteristics: a *Madonna and Child Enthroned* and a polyptych which achieves the same overall effect as that of the Pala d'Oro – and indeed it was he who was commissioned to paint the **cover of the Pala d'Oro**, now in San Marco's museum.

The first room of the Accademia is full of work displaying this Byzantine indebtedness, and Byzantium remained a living influence in the city up to the seventeenth and eighteenth centuries, sustained in part by the influx of refugees following the **fall of Constantinople** in 1453. The neo-Byzantine *Madoneri* (the main school of the Greek community) are represented in the **Museo Dipinti Sacri Bizantini**, where the paintings show a complete indifference to the post-Renaissance cult of the artist and to notions of aesthetic novelty. The young Cretan **El Greco** (1545-1614) worked with the *Madoneri* for a while, before setting out for fame and fortune in Spain.

Gothic painting and sculpture

Deemed to be relics of a barbaric age, a huge number of Gothic paintings and sculptures were destroyed in the seventeenth and eighteenth centuries. The reinstatement of the Gothic is in large part due to the determination of John Ruskin, whose preoccupation was the Gothic architecture and sculpture of Venice. His meticulous work in **San Zanipolo**, mapping the change from Gothic to Renaissance through a study of the **funerary sculpture**, is still a useful analysis.

San Zanipolo's main apse contains the **tomb of Doge Michele Morosini** (d.1382), described by Ruskin as "the richest monument of the Gothic period in Venice", although its figures (apart from those at the head and foot of the doge) have an awkward, un-Gothic stiffness. More interesting sculpturally is the **tomb of Doge Marco Corner** (d.1368) opposite, which was carved in the workshop of the non-Venetian **Nino Pisano**. Slightly later is San Marco's **rood screen**, by the two brothers **Pierpaolo and Jacobello Dalle Masegne**, who made a study of the work of Pisano and northern European Gothic sculpture. The other high points of Gothic sculpture in Venice are also architecturally related – the **Palazzo Ducale's capitals, corner sculptures** and **Porta della Carta** (though the main figures on the *Porta* are nineteenth-century replicas of fifteenth century originals).

Paolo Veneziano's unrelated namesake, **Lorenzo Veneziano** (working 1356–72) marries a distinctly Gothic element to the Byzantine elements in Venetian painting. The large polyptych in the Accademia is a fine example of his work, showing a roundedness in the face and hands and in the fall of the drapery, and a sinuousness of pose in the figures that suggests the influence of Gothic painters such as Simone Martini of Siena.

Around 1409 **Gentile de Fabriano**, the exemplar of the style known as **International Gothic**, frescoed parts of the Palazzo Ducale with the help of his pupil **Pisanello**. These frescoes are all now destroyed, and the nearest example of Pisanello's work is his *St George* (1438–42) in Verona's church of Sant'Anastasia. Even in this one piece it's possible to see what the Venetians would have found congenial in his art: chiefly an all-over patterning that ties the content of the painting to the picture plane and eschews the illusion of receding space.

The work of Gentile and Pisanello was most closely studied in Venice by **Michele Giambono** (working 1420–62), represented in the Accademia by a *Coronation of the Madonna in Paradise* (1447) and in the church of San Trovaso by *St Chrysogonus* (c.1450). These claustrophobic paintings are of the same date as Padua's frescoes by Mantegna and sculptures by Donatello – Giambono and others in Venice were happily working in a sophisticated high Gothic style at a time when the Renaissance was elsewhere into its maturity.

Early Renaissance painting

Petrarch, who lived in Venice in the 1360s, described the Republic as "a world apart" and nothing illustrates this insularity better than the reception of Renaissance ideas in the city. Venetians were chary of over-emphasising the individual, a tendency implicit in the one-point perspective of Renaissance painting; in addition, the use of abstract mathematical formulas in the depiction of form was alien to the pragmatic Venetian temperament. When the principles of the Florentine Renaissance did belatedly filter into the art of Venice, they were transformed into a way of seeing that was uniquely Venetian.

Key figures in this period of absorption were the **Vivarini** family – **Antonio** (c.1419–c.80), his brother **Bartolomeo** (c.1430–c.91) and son **Alvise** (c.1445–1505). Antonio's work, though still part of the Gothic tradition, marks a shift away from it, with his more angular line and construction of pictorial spaces consistent with the rules of one-point perspective – as in the *Madonna and Child* tryptych in the Accademia, painted in collaboration with Giovanni d'Alemagna. A more humanistic temperament is embodied in the paintings of **Alvise**, manifested less through his depiction of space than through his representation of people. He individualises his figures, giving an emotional charge to narratives which had to that point functioned symbolically. The *St Clare* in the Accademia is an excellent example of his work, establishing an unprecedentedly intimate contact between the saint and the viewer.

The pre-eminent artistic dynasty of this transitional period was that of **Jacopo Bellini** (c.1400–70), once a pupil of Gentile da Fabriano, and his sons **Gentile** (c.1429–1507) and **Giovanni** (c.1430–1516). Jacopo suffered from the anti-Gothic zealotry of later years, and his two major cycles of paintings – at the Scuola di San Marco and the Scuola di San Giovanni Evangelista – were destroyed. From descriptions of these works, it would appear that the two *Madonnas* in the Accademia are rather restrained in their decoration; other pieces by him can be seen in the Museo Correr.

Giovanni is the one that people mean when they refer simply to "Bellini". In the Accademia he's represented by a number of *Madonnas*, a series of allegorical panels and a couple of large altarpieces. Other works around Venice include altarpieces in San Zaccaria, San Pietro (Murano), the Frari, Madonna dell'Orto and San Zanipolo. In the majority of these paintings the attention is concentrated on the foreground, where the arrangement of the figures or a device such as a screen or throne turns the background into another plane parallel to the surface, rather than a receding landscape. That this was a conscious choice which had nothing to do with his perspectival skills is demonstrated by the **San Giobbe altarpiece** (in the Accademia), in which a meticulously worked-out illusionistic space would have suggested the presence of an extra chapel. A fundamental humanism pervades much of Giovanni's output – although these *Madonnas* show an idealised version of motherhood, each possesses an immediacy which suggests to the viewer that this ideal could be attainable.

Meanwhile, **Gentile** was pursuing a form of painting that was also a specifically Venetian Renaissance phenomenon – the *istoria* or narrative painting cycle. At least ten of these were commissioned by public bodies between around 1475 and 1525: the three remaining cycles in Venice are the *Miracles of the Relic of the True Cross* (Accademia), by five artists including Gentile and **Carpaccio**, and the *St Ursula* cycle (Accademia) and the *St George and St Jerome* cycle (Scuola di San Giorgio degli Schiavoni), which are both by Carpaccio. To the modern observer the story line of the *Relic* and *St Ursula* cycles in particular can seem to be naive pretexts for precise renditions of the pageant of Venetian social life and a wealth of domestic minutiae. The details of the paintings were not mere incidentals to the narrative, however – a person hanging out washing or mending a roof would have been perceived as enhancements of the physical reality of the miracle, and not as distractions from the central event.

High Renaissance painting

While these narrative cycles were being produced Giovanni Bellini was beginning to experiment with oil paint, then beginning to displace tempera (pigment in egg yolk) as the preferred medium. Whereas tempera had to be applied in layers, the long drying time of oil allowed colours to be mixed and softened, while its thick consistency enabled artists to simulate the texture of the objects depicted. Close examination of later paintings by Bellini shows he used his fingers to merge colours and soften light, and two of his young assistants at the time – **Giorgione** and **Titian** – were to explore even further the potential of the new material, developing a specifically Venetian High Renaissance style.

Giorgione (1475–1510) seems custom-built for myth: little is known about him other than that he was tall and handsome and he died young (possibly of plague). The handful of enigmatic works he created were innovative in their imaginative self-sufficiency – for instance the Venetian collector Michiel, writing in 1530, was unable to say precisely what the subject was of *The Tempest* (Accademia), perhaps Giorgione's most famous image. His only altarpiece, still in the cathedral at Castelfranco (his home town), isolates the Madonna and the two saints from each other by manipulating perspective and by placing the Madonna against a landscape while the attendant saints stand against a man-made background. Despite the serenity of the individual figures, the painting instils in the viewer a disquieting sense of elusiveness.

Given his long life and huge output, **Titian** (c.1485–1576) is very badly represented in his home town: a *Presentation in the Temple*, a *Pietà* left unfinished at his death, and a couple of minor works in the Accademia; a handful in the Salute; the *Assumption* and *Pésaro Altarpiece* in the Frari, and that's more or less it. (Napoleon made off with a good crop of Titians, including a *Venus* which he hung in his tent; the Louvre now has a fine collection.)

Titian, like Giorgione, used the qualities of oils to evoke a diffuse light and soften contours – in contrast with the contemporaneous art of Rome, the city of Michelangelo, where the emphasis was on the solidity and sculptural aspects of the objects depicted. Artists in Florence were answerable to an imperious ruling family, in Rome they had to comply with the wishes of successive popes, but Titian's success was so great that he could virtually pick and choose from a host of clients from all over the continent, and the diversity of works he produced – portraits, allegories, devotional paintings, mythologies – remains unsurpassed in Western art. The technical range is as impressive as the range of subject matter; the earliest works are highly polished and precisely drawn, but in the later pieces he tested the possibilities of oil paint to their limit, using his bare hands to scrape the canvas and add great gobbets of paint (see the Accademia *Pietà*).

Giorgionesque is an adjective used to describe a number of early sixteenth-century Venetian painters, in reference to the richening of colour popular at the time and to the increasingly "poetic" approach to content. **Sebastiano del Piombo**, who studied under Giovanni Bellini with Titian and Giorgione before moving to Rome in 1611, is one of the artists to whom the term is applied. His altarpiece of **San Giovanni Crisostomo** in the eponymous church is his best work still in Venice. Another is **Palma il Vecchio** (1480–1582); although he was often frivolous in a way that Giorgione and Titian rarely were – ponds of frothy nymphs and the like – his strongest work in Venice is a redoubtable *St Barbara* in Santa Maria Formosa. The most interesting painter of this period and type is **Lorenzo Lotto** (c.1480–1556), represented in the Accademia by the almost metaphysical *Portrait of a Young Man*. The rivalries of other painters eventually drove Lotto from Venice, and it's not too fanciful to see a reflection of the artist's anxieties in his restless, wistful paintings.

Born in 1518, two years after Bellini's death and eight years after that of Giorgione, **Tintoretto** grew up during the period in which the ascendancy of Titian became established. Princes were sending agents to Venice to buy the latest Titian, no matter what the subject, and every visiting dignitary would want to be painted by him. Titian's exploratory attitude to paint and the increasing Venetian receptivity to individual style were both exploited by the energetic and competitive younger artist. The painting that made his reputation, the *Miracle of the Slave* (Accademia; 1548) shows how he learned from Titian's experiments and distanced himself from them. Tintoretto's palette is as rich as Titian's, but is aggressively vivid rather than sensuous, and uses far stronger lighting. And while Titian is concerned with the inner drama of an event, Tintoretto's attention is given to the drama of gesture.

Tintoretto's dynamic style was not universally acclaimed. Pietro Aretino, Titian's close friend and most vociferous champion, disparaged the speed and relative carelessness of his technique, and one member of the **Scuola di San Rocco** said he would give his money towards the decoration of the *scuola*'s building as long Tintoretto was not commissioned. He didn't get his way, and San Rocco's cycle is the most comprehensive collection of paintings by the artist. Dramatic perspectival effects, bizarre juxtapositions of images and extraordinarily fluid brushwork here make the substantial world seem otherworldly – the converse of the earlier *istorie* cycles.

In contrast, the art of **Paolo Veronese** (1528–88), who moved to Venice from Verona in his twenties, conveys worldly harmony rather than spiritual turbulence. This is particularly evident in his work for architectural settings (San Sebastiano in Venice and the Villa Barbaro at Masèr), where he constructed logical spaces which complement the form of the buildings. More urbane than Tintoretto, he nonetheless attracted controversy: in his *Christ in the House of Levi* (Accademia) the naturalistic representation of German soldiers was interpreted as a gesture of support for Protestantism. Veronese's response to his accusers revealed a lot about the changing attitude towards the status of the artist: claiming licence to depict what he wanted, he simply changed the title of the work from *The Last Supper* to the title by which it's now known.

Renaissance sculpture

Venetian **sculpture** in the Renaissance was conditioned by the society's ingrained aversion to the over-glorification of the individual and by the specific restrictions of the city's landscape. Freestanding monumental work of the sort that was being commissioned all over Italy is conspicuous by its absence. The exception to prove the rule, the **monument to Colleoni**, was made by the Florentine artist **Verrocchio**. Venetian sculptors worked mainly to decorate tombs or the walls of churches, and up to the late Renaissance no clear distinction was made between sculptors, masons and architects. Beyond the Renaissance, sculpture was generally commissioned as part of an architectural project, and it's usually futile to try to disentangle the sculpture from its architectural function.

Pietro Lombardo (c.1438–1515) was born in Cremona and went to Rome before arriving in Venice c.1460. His development can be charted in the church of San Zanipolo: his first major monument, the **tomb of Doge Pasquale Malipiero**, is pictorially flat and smothered with carved decoration, but the **monument to Doge Pietro Mocenigo**, with its classicised architectural elements and figures, is a fully Renaissance piece. In true Venetian style the latter glorifies the State through the man, rather than stressing his individual salvation – the image of Christ is easily overlooked. Pietro's sons **Antonio** (c.1458–c.1516) and **Tullio** (c.1460–1532) were also sculptors and assisted him on the Mocenigo monument. Tullio's independent work is less pictorial: his **monument to Doge Andrea Vendramin** (also in San Zanipolo) is a complex architectural evocation of a Roman triumphal arch, though again the whole is encrusted with decorative figures.

Jacopo Sansovino, who went on to become the Republic's principal architect, was known as a sculptor when he arrived in Venice from Rome in 1527. More of a classicist than his predecessors, he nonetheless produced work remarkably in tune with Venetian sensibilities – his figures on the *logetta* of the Campanile, for example, animate the surface of the building rather than draw attention to themselves. **Alessandro Vittoria** was the major sculptor of the middle and later part of the century; originally a member of Sansovino's workshop, Vittoria developed a more rhetorical style, well demonstrated in the figures of *St Jerome* in the Frari and San Zanipolo.

Seventeenth and eighteenth centuries

The High Baroque style in painting and sculpture was largely a Roman phenomenon and the Venetians, whose distrust of Rome led in 1606 to a Papal Interdict (see "History" section), remained largely untouched by it. Suitably enough, the only Venetian interior that relates to Roman Baroque is the **Gesuiti**.

After the hyper-productive **Palma il Giovane**, who seems to have contributed something to the majority of the city's church interiors, it was up to foreign painters – **Johann Lyss** for instance – to keep painting alive in the city. Much the same is true of sculpture: the Venetian **Baldassare Longhena** early in his career turned from sculpture to architecture, leaving the field to the Bolognese **Giuseppe Mazza** (bronze reliefs in San Zanipolo) and the Flemish **Juste Le Court** (high altar of the Salute), although Le Court's Venetian pupil **Orazio Marinelli** (portrait busts in the Querini-Stampalia) did achieve a measure of celebrity. A particularly successful artist towards the end of the seventeenth century was **Andrea Brustolon** of Belluno, best known for his sculptural furniture (Ca' Rezzonico).

The last efflorescence of Venetian art began around the start of the eighteenth century, as Venice was degenerating into the playground of Europe. The highly illusionistic decorative paintings of **Giambattista Piazzetta** (1682–1752) mark the first step and foreshadow the work of **Giambattista Tiepolo** (1696–1777), whose ever-lightening colours and elegant, slightly disdainful Madonnas typified the climate of the frivolous Republic. There's a similarity of mood to most of Tiepolo's work – from the dizzying tromp l'oeil ceiling painted in the Ca' Rezzonico to celebrate a marriage, to the airy *Virgin in Glory* painted for the Carmini.

Another major figure of the period was **Rosalba Carriera** (1675–1758), the first artist to use pastel as a medium in its own right. She was known chiefly as a portraitist, and the Ca' Rezzonico and the Accademia both contain a fine selection of her work – the latter featuring a *Self-Portrait in Old Age* which expresses a melancholy temperament usually suppressed from her pictures. (Incidentally, Carriera was not Venice's only woman artist: Marietta Robusti, Tintoretto's daughter, was known as a fine portraitist and Carriera's contemporary Giulia Lama has a *Judith and Holofernes* in the Accademia.)

By this time, Venetian art was being siphoned out of the city in large quantities, with people such as the English Consul Joseph Smith sending pictures home by the crateful. Aristocrats on the Grand Tour were particularly interested in topographical work – kind of up-market postcards – and in this area the pre-eminent artist was **Canaletto** (1695–1768), whose work was copied and engraved to make further saleable items. Don't be misled into believing he showed the "real" Venice – he idealised the city, changing spatial arrangements in order to suit a harmonious composition and sometimes even altering individual buildings. Canaletto's work in Venice is as sparse as Titian's – there's only one painting by him in the Accademia and a couple in the Ca' Rezzonico.

More sombre is the work of **Francesco Guardi** (1712–93), whose images of the lagoon and imaginary architectural scenes are frequently swathed in atmospheric mist and dotted with a few prophetic ruins. Genre painters were also popular at this time, none more so than **Pietro Longhi** (1708–85), whose wonderful illustrations of Venetian life (painted with a technique that is at best adequate) can also be seen in the Accademia and the Ca' Rezzonico. Longhi's production line was as busy as Canaletto's, as his workshop churned out copies of his most popular paintings to meet demand.

The last word on the painting of the Venetian Republic should be devoted to **Giandomenico Tiepolo** (1727–1804), seen at his best in the cycle of frescoes painted for his home and now installed in the Ca' Rezzonico. Freed from the whims of clients, he produced here a series of images that can with hindsight be seen as symbolic of the end of an era, with Sunday crowds gawping at a peepshow and clowns frittering away their time flirting and playing.

Nineteenth and twentieth centuries

After the fall of the Republic, art in Venice became the domain of outsiders. **Turner**, who visited the city three times, was its supreme painter in the nineteenth century, but as Ruskin said, you'd only have to stay in Venice for a few days to learn about it what Turner had learned. **Whistler, Monet** and **Sargent** were among other visitors. The only Venetian nineteenth-century artist of note is **Frederico Zandomeneghi** (1841–1917), and he decamped for Paris in 1874 to join the Impressionists' circle.

This century the story of art in Venice is no more cheerful. The internationally known artists who stayed as guests of **Peggy Guggenheim** between 1949 and 1979 came and left without making an impact on its cultural life. Every two years the **Biennale** brings in the hot-shots of the international art world, but does little to help young Venetian artists. The few Italian artists who have worked here have not exactly galvanised the city: the painter **Lucio Fontana** lived in Venice in the 1950s, and **Emilio Vedova** – a founder member of the avant-garde groups *Fronte Nuovo* and *Gruppo degli Otto* – taught at the Accademia until his death in the mid-1980s. Today the best-known artists at work in Venice are the video/installation artist **Fabrizzio Plessi** and the American painter **Judith Harvest**.

An Outline of Venetian Architecture

This is just a brief chronology of Venetian architectural styles, intended simply as a means of giving some sense of order to the city's jumble of buildings. For more detailed accounts, refer to the Books section – Deborah Howard's *The Architectural History of Venice* is the best starting point.

Byzantine Venice

Although settlement of the lagoon began as far back as the fifth century, no building has survived intact from earlier than the start of the eleventh century. The very first houses raised on the mudflats were "built like birds' nests, half on sea and half on land . . . the solidity of the earth . . . secured only by wattle-work", according to a letter written in 523 by a Roman official named Cassiodorus. Many of the earliest shelters were only temporary, constructed as refuges from the Barbarian hordes of the mainland and abandoned as soon as the threat had receded, but with the Lombard invasions of the second half of the sixth century, communities uprooted from northern Italy began to construct more durable buildings on the islands. Some of the materials for these buildings were scavenged from Roman temples and dwellings, and a few of these fragments – used over and over again in succeeding centuries – can still be seen embedded in the walls of some of Venice's oldest structures. The great majority of the lagoon buildings were still made of wood, however, and of these nothing is left.

From the twelfth century onwards the houses of the richest families were made from brick and stone; before then, such materials were reserved for the most important public buildings, and so it is that the **oldest structure in the lagoon** is a church – the **cathedral at Torcello**. Founded in 639 but altered in 864 and again, comprehensively, in **1008**, it takes its form from such early Christian basilicas as Sant'Apollinare in Ravenna. The prototypes of the Western Empire influenced other lagoon churches either founded or rebuilt in the eleventh and twelfth centuries – for example **Sant'Eufamia** on Giudecca, **Santi Maria e Donato** on Murano, and **San Giovanni Decollato** and **San Nicolò dei Mendicoli** in central Venice – but the predominant cultural influence on the emergent city was **Byzantium**, on which the lagoon confederation was originally dependent.

Santa Fosca on Torcello and **San Giovanni di Rialto**, traditionally the oldest church in Venice, are Byzantine in their adherence to a Greek-cross plan, but the building in which the Byzantine ancestry of Venice is most completely displayed is the **Basilica di San Marco**. Like the cathedral of Torcello, San Marco was extensively rebuilt in the eleventh century, but the basic layout – an elongated version of the five-domed Greek-cross design of Constantinople's Church of the Apostles – didn't change much between the consecration of the first Basilica in 832 and the completion of the final version in 1094. As much as its architectural form, the mosaic decoration of San Marco betrays the young city's Eastern affiliations – and it was in fact begun, as soon as the shell of the church was completed, by artists from Constantinople.

Byzantium has also left its mark on the **domestic architecture** of Venice, even though the oldest specimens still standing date from the late twelfth century or early thirteenth, by which time the political ties between the two cities had been severed. The high and rounded Byzantine arch can be seen in a number of Canal Grande palaces – the **Ca' da Mosto**, the **Donà** houses, the neighbouring **Palazzo Loredan** and **Palazzo Farsetti**, and the **Fondaco dei Turchi**. All of these buildings have been altered greatly over the years, but paradoxically it's the one that's been most drastically reconstructed – the Fondaco dei Turchi – which bears the closest resemblance to the earliest merchants' houses. Descended from the Roman villas of the mainland, they had an arcade at water level to permit the unloading of cargo, a long gallery on the upper storey, and lower towers at each end of the facade. Frequently they were embellished with relief panels (*paterae*) and insets of multicoloured marble – another Byzantine inheritance, and one that was to last, in modified form, for hundreds of years (for example in the predilection for heraldic devices on the fronts of houses).

Gothic Venice

Building land is scarce in Venice, and the consequent density of housing imposed certain restrictions on architectural inventiveness – ground plans had to make the fullest possible use of the available space (hence the rarity of internal courtyards and the uniformly flat facades) and elevations had to maximise the window areas, to make the most of the often limited natural light. Thus architectural evolution in the domestic buildings of Venice is to be observed not so much in the development of overall forms but rather in the mutations of surface detail, and in particular in the arches of the main facades. Nearly all the rich families of Venice derived their wealth from trade, and the predominant shipping lanes from Venice ran to the East – so it was inevitable that **Islamic features** would show through in Venetian architecture. As the thirteenth century progressed, the pure curve of the Byzantine arch first developed an upper peak and then grew into a type of ogival arch – as at the **Palazzo Falier** near Santi Apostoli, and the **Porta dei Fiori** on the north side of the Basilica. This Islamicised Byzantine shape was in turn influenced in the fourteenth century by contact with the Gothic style of the mainland, so producing a repertoire that was uniquely Venetian.

The masterpiece Venetian Gothic is also the city's greatest civic structure – the **Palazzo Ducale**. Begun in 1340, possibly to designs by **Filippo Calendario**, the present building was extended in a second phase of work from 1423 onwards, culminating in the construction of the most elaborate Gothic edifice in Venice – the **Porta della Carta**, by **Giovanni and Bartolomeo Bon**.

Imitations and variations of the Palazzo Ducale's complex tracery can be seen all over the city, most strikingly in the **Ca' d'Oro**, begun by Giovanni Bon at much the same time as work began on the extension of the Palazzo Ducale. The Ca' d'Oro represents the apex of Gothic refinement in Venice's domestic architecture; for monumental grandeur, on the other hand, none can match the adjoining Gothic palaces on the *Volta del Canal* – the **Palazzi Giustinian** and the **Ca' Fóscari**.

Ecclesiastical architecture in fourteenth- and fifteenth-century Venice is not as idiosyncratic as its secular counterpart – the religious communities who built the churches, affiliated to orders on the mainland, tended to follow the architectural conventions that had been established by those orders. In some of Venice's Gothic churches the old basilical plan prevailed over the cruciform (eg at **Madonna dell'Orto**), but the two most important churches of the period, the immense **San Zanipolo** (Dominican) and the **Frari** (Franciscan), display many of the basic features of contemporaneous churches in the Veneto: the Latin-cross plan, the pointed arches, the high nave with flanking aisles, and the chapels leading off from the transepts. Yet even these churches have distinctively Venetian characteristics, such as the use of tie-beams and the substitution of lath and plaster vaulting for vaults of stone – both necessary measures in a place with no bedrock for its foundations to rest on. In a few Gothic churches the builders capitalised on the availability of skilled naval carpenters to produce elegant and lightweight ceilings in the shape of an inverted **ship's keel** – for example at **Santo Stefano** and **San Giacomo dell'Orio**.

Early Renaissance

The complicated hybrid of Venetian Gothic remained the city's preferred style well into the second half of the fifteenth century, long after the classical precepts of Renaissance architecture had gained currency elsewhere in Italy. The late work of **Bartolomeo Bon** contains classsical elements mixed with Gothic features (for example the portal of **San Zanipolo** and the incomplete **Ca' del Duca**, both from c.1460), but the first architect in Venice to produce something that could be called a classical design was **Antonio Gambello**, with his land gate for the **Arsenale** (1460). Gambello was not a committed proponent of the new ideas, however, and had work on his church of **San Zaccaria** not been interrupted by his death in 1481, it would have resembled a north European Gothic church more closely than any other in Venice.

In the 1470s another dynasty of stonemason-architects succeeded the Bon family as the leading builders in Venice – **Pietro Solari** and his sons **Antonio and Tullio**, otherwise known as the **Lombardi**. Having worked with followers of Donatello in Padua in the 1460s, Pietro Lombardo was familiar with the latest principles of Tuscan architecture, but the chief characteristics of his own work – the elaborately carved pilasters and friezes, and the inlaid marble panels of various shapes and sizes – are not so much architectonic as decorative. The chancel of **San Giobbe**, the courtyard screen of the **Scuola di San Giovanni Evangelista**, the tiny church of **Santa Maria dei Miracoli** and the facade of the **Scuola di San Marco** represent the best of the Lombardi's architecture. Over-ornate though much of their building projects were, their style was closely imitated by numerous Venetian architects: nobody is certain, for example, whether the **Palazzo Dario** (on the Canal Grande) was designed by Pietro Lombardo or one of his "Lombardesque" acolytes.

Antonio Rizzo, a contemporary of Pietro Lombardo, was similarly esteemed as both a sculptor and architect. After the fire of 1483, Rizzo was put in charge of the rebuilding of the entire **east wing of the Palazzo Ducale**, and it was he who designed the **Scala dei Giganti**, a work which displays a typically Venetian delight in heavy ornamentation.

Coducci and his successors

The most rigorous and inventive Venetian architect of the early Renaissance was the man who took over the design and supervision of San Zaccaria after the death of Gambello – **Mauro Coducci** (sometimes spelled **Codussi**). His first commission in the city, the church of **San Michele in Isola** (1469), is not purely classical – the huge lunette and inset roundels are specifically Venetian features – but its proportions and clarity, and the use of classical detail to emphasise the structure of the building, entitle it to be known as the **first Renaissance church in Venice**. Coducci reintroduced the traditional Greek-cross plan in his other church designs (**Santa Maria Formosa** and **San Giovanni Crisostomo**), his impetus coming in part from a scholarly revival of interest in the culture of Byzantium and in part from the work of Renaissance theorists such as Alberti, whose *De Re Aedificatoria* proclaimed the superiority of centrally planned temples. In his secular buildings the influence of Alberti is even more pronounced, especially in his **Palazzo Vendramin-Calergi**, which is strongly reminiscent of Alberti's Palazzo Rucellai in Florence. Coducci was employed by the Venetian nobility, the *scuole* (he designed staircases for both the **Scuola di San Giovanni Evangelista** and the **Scuola di San Marco**) and the religious foundations, yet despite his pre-eminence it was only after archive research in the nineteenth century that he was identified as the author of all these buildings – a fact indicative of the difference between the status of the architect in Renaissance Florence and his standing in Venice.

The economic effects of the War of the League of Cambrai limited the amount of building work in Venice at the start of the sixteenth century, nonetheless it was a period of rapid transformation in the centre of the city: the **Campanile** of San Marco was completed, and the **Torre dell'Orologio** and **Procuratie Vecchie** were built – the last two being commenced to designs by Coducci. In the aftermath of serious fires, major projects were undertaken in the Rialto district as well – notably the **Fabbriche Vecchie** and the **Fondaco dei Tedeschi** – but the architects of the generation after Coducci (who died in 1504) were generally undistinguished. **Guglielmo dei Grigi** designed the **Palazzo dei Camerlenghi** at the foot of the Ponte di Rialto and went on to add the **Cappella Emiliana** to Coducci's San Michele in Isola. **Bartolomeo Bon the Younger** took over the supervision of the Procuratie Vecchie after Coducci's death, and began the **Scuola di San Rocco** in 1515 – a project that was completed by **Scarpagnino** (Antonio Abbondi), the man in charge of the rebuilding of the Rialto markets after the fire of 1514. **Giorgio Spavento**, described by the diarist Marin Sanudo as "a man of great genius", was the most talented architect of this period, and with **San Salvatore** he produced its best church design. By joining together three Greek-cross plans, Spavento created a building which reconciled the long open nave required by modern liturgy with the traditional Byzantine centralised plan.

High Renaissance

The definitive classical authority for the architectural theorists of Renaissance Italy was **Vitruvius**, architect to the Emperor Augustus, and it was in Venice in 1511 that the first printed edition of his *De Architectura* was produced. However, the consistent application of classical models was not seen in Venice until after the sack of Rome by the Imperial army in 1527. A large number of Roman artists then sought refuge in Venice, and it was with this influx that the advances of such figures as Raphael, Michelangelo and Bramante were absorbed into the practice of Venice's architects.

Of all the exiles, the one who made the greatest impact was **Jacopo Sansovino**. Despite his limited architectural experience – he was known mainly as a sculptor when he arrived in Venice – Sansovino was appointed *Proto* of San Marco on the death of Bartolomeo Bon in 1529, a position which made him the most powerful architect in the city, and which he was to hold for the next forty years. From 1537 onwards a group of buildings by Sansovino went up around the Piazzetta, completely changing the appearance of the area: the **Zecca** (Mint) was the first, then the **Loggetta** at the base of the Campanile, and then the most celebrated of all his designs – the **Libreria Sansoviniana**. Showing a familiarity with the architecture of ancient Rome that was unprecedented in Venice, the Libreria is still unmistakeably Venetian in its wealth of surface detail, and the rest of Sansovino's buildings similarly effect a compromise between classical precision and Venetian convention. Thus his palace designs – **Palazzo Dolfin-Manin** (1538) and **Palazzo Corner della Ca' Grande** (1545) – are clearly related to the houses of the Roman Renaissance, but perpetuate the traditional Venetian division of the facade into a central bay with symmetrically flanking windows. Though principally a secular architect, Sansovino did also design churches; the religious buildings by him that still stand are **San Francesco della Vigna**, **San Martino di Castello**, **San Giuliano** and the apse of **San Fantin**.

Of Sansovino's contemporaries, the only one of comparable stature was **Michele Sanmicheli**. More proficient as an engineer than Sansovino, he was employed early in his career by Pope Clement VII to improve the military defences of Parma and Piacenza, and in 1535 was taken on as Venice's military architect. The **Fortezza di Sant'Angelo** (1543), protecting the Lido entrance to the lagoon, was his largest public project, and in addition to this he built two of the most grandiose palaces in the city – the **Palazzo Corner Mocenigo** at San Polo (1545) and the **Palazzo Grimani** (c.1559) on the Canal Grande.

Andrea Palladio, Italy's dominant architect in the second half of the sixteenth century, was based in nearby Vicenza yet found it difficult to break into Venice's circle of patronage. In the 1550s his application for the position of *Proto* to the Salt Office (supervisor of public buildings) was turned down, and his project for the Palazzo Ducale's Scala d'Oro rejected; later schemes for the Ponte di Rialto and the rebuilding of the entire Palazzo Ducale were no more successful. He was never asked to undertake a private commission in the city. The facade of **San Pietro in Castello** was his first contract (eventually built in a much altered form), and it was the religious foundations which were to provide him with virtually all his subsequent work in Venice. Palladio's churches of **San Giorgio Maggiore** (1565) and the **Redentore** (1576) are the summit of Renaissance Classicism in Venice: the scale on which they were composed, the restraint of their decoration, the stylistic unity of exterior and interior, the subtlety with which the successive spaces were combined, and the correctness of their quotations from the architecture of Imperial Rome – all these factors distinguished them from all previous designs and established them as reference points for later churches.

Once Palladio's churches had been finished, the islands of San Giorgio Maggiore and Giudecca presented much the same face to the main part of the city as they do today. The work of his closest follower, **Vincenzo Scamozzi**, brought the landscape of the Piazza very close to its present-day state – it was Scamozzi who completed the Campanile end of the Libreria Sansoviniana and began the construction of the **Procuratie Nuove** in 1582. Another Venetian landmark, the **Ponte di Rialto**, was built at this time; its creator, **Antonio da Ponte**, was also in charge of the repair and redesign of the Palazzo Ducale after the fire of

1577, and designed the new **Prisons** on the opposite bank of the Rio di Palazzo. The bridge connecting the prisons to the Palazzo Ducale – the **Ponte dei Sospiri** (Bridge of Sighs) – was the work of **Antonio Contino** (1600).

Baroque

Although there are a few sixteenth-century Venetian buildings that could be described as proto-Baroque – **Alessandro Vittoria**'s **Palazzo Balbi** (1582), with its encrusted decoration and broken pediments, is one example – the classical idiom remained entrenched for some time as the stylistic orthodoxy in Venice, as is demonstrated by the appointment of the unadventurous **Bartolomeo Monopola** to complete the final stages of the **Palazzo Ducale** in the first decades of the seventeenth century. The colossal **Palazzo Pisani** at Santo Stefano, possibly by Monopola, is further evidence of the city's aesthetic conservatism.

It was not until the maturity of Venice's finest native architect, **Baldassare Longhena**, that the innovations of the Baroque made themselves fully felt. Longhena's early work – for example the **Palazzo Giustinian-Lolin** and the **Duomo** at **Chioggia** (both 1624) – continues the Palladianism of the previous century, but with his design for the votive church of **Santa Maria della Salute** (1631) he gave the city its first Baroque masterpiece. In its plan the Salute is indebted to Palladio's Redentore, but in its use of multiple vistas and devices such as the huge volutes round the base of the dome, it introduces a dynamism that was completely alien to Palladio's architecture. In 1640 Longhena became the *Proto* of San Marco, and between then and his death in 1682 he occupied a position in Venetian architectural circles as commanding as Sansovino's had been. Among his major projects were the completion of the **Procuratie Nuove**, the addition of a grand staircase and library to the monastic complex of **San Giorgio Maggiore**, and the design of two of the Canal Grande's most spectacular palaces – the **Ca' Pésaro** and the **Ca' Rezzonico**.

When compared to much of the work being produced in other parts of Italy at this time, Longhena's brand of Baroque was quite sober. Yet it was the chief exception in his output – the grotesque facade of the **Ospedaletto** – which proved in the short term to be specially influential. Its most direct descendant was **Alessandro Tremignon**'s facade for the church of **San Moisè** (1668), which is choked with sculpture by Heinrich Meyring. **Giuseppe Sardi**'s church of **Santa Maria Zobenigo** (1680) can also be traced back to the Ospedaletto, but on the other hand Sardi's work is equally redolent of the architecture of the sixteenth century – his facade for Scamozzi's **San Lazzaro dei Mendicanti** could be seen as a deliberate rejection of the excesses of the Baroque. His other prominent designs are the **Scuola di San Teodoro** and the facades of **San Salvatore** and **Santa Maria di Nazareth** (the Scalzi), all of them rather routine efforts.

The eighteenth century

The concerted reaction against Baroque began with the work of Sardi's nephew, **Domenico Rossi**. Rossi's facade for the church of **San Stae** (1709) is essentially a neo-Palladian design enlivened by the addition of some exuberant pieces of sculpture, and his rebuilding of the **Palazzo Corner della Regina** is closer to the palace projects of Sansovino than to such works as Longhena's nearby Ca' Pésaro. **Andrea Tirali**, Rossi's exact contemporary (1657–1737), was an even more faithful adherent to the principles of the sixteenth century – the portico he added to the church of **San Nicolò da Tolentino** is strictly classical, and his facade for **San Vitale** is a straight plagiarism of San Giorgio Maggiore. Another church of this period – **San Simeone Piccolo** – is one of the most conspicuous in Venice, standing as it does right opposite the train station. Designed in 1718 by **Giovanni Scalfarotto** (Rossi's son-in-law), its facade and plan are derived from the Pantheon, but the vertical exaggeration of its dome makes it closer in spirit to Longhena's Salute.

The most significant architect of the period was **Giorgio Massari** (1687–1766), whose church of the **Gesuati**, begun in 1726, combines Palladian forms (for example the facade and the arrangement of the interior bays) with understated Rococo details (the ceiling frames). His later church of the **Pietà**, based on Sansovino's destroyed Incurabili church, is more sober in its use of decoration, and his design for the last of the great palaces of the Canal Grande, the **Palazzo Grassi** (1748) is the severest of all his buildings.

The Palladian creed was kept alive in late eighteenth-century Venice through innumerable academic and polemical publications. Two of the leading figures in this movement were **Antonio Visentini** (1688–1782) and Scalfarotto's nephew, **Tomaso Temanza** (1705–89), both of whom taught architecture at the Accademia. Temanza was the more important architect, and his **Santa Maria Maddalena** was the first uncompromisingly Neoclassical building in Venice.

To the present

With the work of **Giannantonio Selva**, a pupil of Visentini and Temanza, Neoclassicism entered its most spare and fastidious phase. His first large scheme was **La Fenice** opera house (1790), where exterior adornment was reduced to the minimum necessary to signify the building's function and importance. Selva's career was undisturbed by the subsequent collapse of the Venetian Republic, and his other main works – the churches of **San Maurizio** (1806) and **Nome del Gesù** (1815) – were created under French rule.

During the second period of French occupation (1806–15) a large number of buildings were demolished to facilitate urban improvement schemes. Four churches were knocked down to make space for the **Giardini Pubblici**, for instance, and by the time the French were ejected by the Austrians a total of nearly 50 religious buildings had been demolished. The most celebrated loss was that of Sansovino's **San Geminiano**, pulled down in 1807 to make room for the construction of the **Ala Napoleonica**, a ballroom wing added to the Procuratie Nuove, which was then serving as a royal palace. In the 1830s the designer of the ballroom, **Lorenzo Santi**, went on to build the now abandoned coffee house (**Palazzetto Bucintoro**) by the Giardinetti Reali, and the **Palazzo Patriarcale**, alongside the Basilica.

Alterations to Venice's network of canals and streets, which had been started by the French with schemes such as the creation of **Via Garibaldi**, were accelerated under Austrian rule. Most of Venice's *rii terrà* (infilled canals) originated in the period of Austrian occupation, and a number of new bridges were constructed at this time too – including the ones at the **Accademia** and **Scalzi**, the first bridges to be put across the Canal Grande since the Ponte di Rialto. It was the Austrians who connected Venice by rail with the mainland (1846), and in 1860 they expanded the train station, demolishing Palladio's church of **Santa Lucia** in the process. And the first major **restoration projects** were carried out under Austrian supervision – at the **Fondaco dei Turchi**, at **Santi Maria e Donato** on **Murano**, and on the north facade of **San Marco**.

Major town planning schemes continued after Venice joined the unified kingdom of Italy. In the 1870s two wide thoroughfares were completed – the **Strada Nova** in Cannaregio and **Calle Larga XXII Marzo** between San Moisè and Santa Maria Zobenigo – and **Campo Manin** was opened up in 1871. The brief industrialisation of central Venice in the late nineteenth century has left behind one prominent hulk – the **Mulino Stucky**, built on Giudecca in 1895. The hotels and middle-class housing developments of the **Lido** – which became a fashionable resort in this period – have outlived the city's industrial sites.

In 1933 Venice was joined by road to the mainland, and five years later the Rio Nuovo was cut from the recently created Piazzale Roma towards the Canal Grande. The chief buildings of the Fascist era are the **fire station** on the Rio di Ca' Fóscari (which continues the Rio Nuovo), and the **Palazzo del Casinò** and **Palazzo del Cinema** on the Lido. Few buildings worth a mention have been put up in Venice since then – the least objectionable are, perhaps, the **train station** (1954) and the **Cassa di Risparmio di Venezia** in Campo Manin, designed in 1964 by **Pier Luigi Nervi** and **Angelo Scattolin**. The density and antiquity of most of Venice's urban fabric makes intervention particularly problematic for the modern architect. Understandable Venetian resistance to new developments, hardened by such insensitive twentieth-century efforts as the extension to the **Hotel Bauer-Grünwald**, adds further difficulties, and accounts for the fact that the two most interesting modern schemes, **Frank Lloyd Wright**'s Ca' Masieri and **Le Corbusier**'s plan for a civic hospital in Cannaregio, never left the drawing-board.

Conservation and Restoration

In 1818 Byron published the fourth section of *Childe Harold's Pilgrimage*, in which is encapsulated the Romantic notion that if Venice isn't actually sinking, then it ought to be:

Venice, lost and won,
Her thirteen hundred years of freedom done
Sinks, like a sea-weed into whence she rose!

Ever since, it's been a commonplace that Venice is doomed to an aquatic extinction. In reality, Venice as an entity was not sinking in Byron's day and is not sinking today – but this is not to say that alarmists have no reason to panic.

The city is threatened by water, by salt, by air pollution and by local subsidence, and faces massive problems of conservation and restoration. The scale of the projects to which this situation gives rise shifts dizzyingly from the restoration of a single painting or architectural detail through to schemes to control the industrialisation of the mainland and the encroachments of the Adriatic. In addition to the intrinsic difficulties of each project, the major interventions prompt interminable arguments about the very purpose of restoration – should Venice be turned into even more of a museum piece, its buildings preserved in the aspic of contemporary restoration techniques, or should parts of the city be razed and rebuilt, reintroducing industry and modern housing? On the one hand, Venice desperately needs the income from tourism, and on the other its population has halved since the war and its houses are in such a state that 45 percent of them don't have adequate bathrooms.

Flooding

On November 4, 1966 the waters of the Adriatic, already dangerously high after two successive high tides had been prevented from receding by gale-force south-easterly winds, were disturbed by an earth tremor. The resulting tidal wave breached Venice's *Murazzi* (the sea walls), and for the next 48 hours the sea level remained an average of six feet above mean high tide – in other words, nearly four feet above the pavement of the Piazza, the lowest point of the city. Venice was left with no power or telephone lines, and buildings were awash with filthy water, mud and oil from broken storage tanks.

Outside Venice, the flooding did not immediately cause extreme concern, partly because floods in Venice were nothing new (at the height of the crisis national radio simply announced "high water in the Piazza San Marco"), and partly because attention was focussed on the same day's disaster in Florence. A reservoir above Florence had become swollen by a month of heavy rain, and in order to relieve pressure on the dam the reservoir gates had been opened, causing a flash-flood that killed several people and caused serious damage – some of it irreparable – to numerous works of art. Nobody was hurt in the Venice flood and no artefacts were lost, but the photographs of water swirling through the doors of San Marco and around the courtyard of the Palazzo Ducale did highlight the perilous condition of the city. When floods almost as bad occurred in the following year, the international campaign to save Venice was already gathering strength, and similarly severe floods in 1979 and 1986 kept the situation in the public eye.

Called the **aqua alta** (high water), the winter flooding of the lower parts of the city is caused by a combination of seasonal tides and persistent south-easterly winds, and has always been a feature of Venetian life. However, in recent years there has been a marked increase in the frequency. Between 1931 and 1945 there were 8 serious *aque alte*; in the 14 years following 1971 there were 49. This may in part be due to slight shifts in global weather conditions, or to the effect of any melting of the polar ice cap, but at least one independent study points the finger firmly at avoidable factors. In a nutshell, the argument is as follows. At the ancient port of Aquileia, at the head of the Adriatic, the height of the Roman wharves relative to the water seems to indicate that there has been no major change in sea level since they were built. Excavations of building foundations in various parts of the city indicate that the notion of a general subsidence is unfounded. Therefore the increased flooding is a local phenomenon related to recent changes in the balance of the lagoon.

It is certainly a fact that the workings of the lagoon have been interfered with in an unprecedented way this century. Land has been reclaimed, both for industrial sites on the mainland and in central Venice itself – around the docks, for instance. At the same time, channels have been deepened to allow modern industrial and commercial vessels to pass through the lagoon, and smaller motor boats within the city also churn up the sea bed and cause erosion. Consequently, both the speed and depth of the tides have been affected.

Bodies such as the centuries-old *Magistrato alle Acque* and the *Consiglio di Nazionale Ricerca Venezia* have studied the workings of the lagoon in detail, and the construction of a **tidal barrier** across the three entrances to the lagoon has often emerged as a possible solution to the problem. In early November 1988 the first component of just such a barrier was towed into place close to the Porto di Lido. Nicknamed **Moisè** (Moses) after the first great manipulator of the waters, it has been put together by the Consorzio Venezia Nuova, a consortium of engineering companies, all eager for international publicity. Around £3.5 billion have been set aside for the project, which basically involves laying eighty steel flaps on the floor of the lagoon, forming a submerged barrage some two kilometres long in total; when the water level rises, the ballast is released from the flaps and the barrier rises to protect the city – or at least, that's the theory.

Predictably enough, the relationship between the government and the consortium has run into difficulties. The official auditors criticised the Consorzio Venezia Nuova for taking a cut of up to 25 percent from contractors, and for ignoring technical criticisms of the barrier's design "for reasons of political opportunism". The original deadline for the completion of Moisè was 1995; latest predictions suggest that 2020 is a more realistic estimate, and many conservationists think that the abandonment of the barrier would be more beneficial to Venice than its completion. Some experts have objected that Moses has been designed as though the waters of the lagoon moved vertically but not laterally – in the event of a sudden tidal surge, they claim, the barrier simply will not be strong enough to resist the push of the water. *Italia Nostra*, Italy's national heritage group, insists that the alteration of the shipping channels and the cessation of land reclamation would be cheaper and more effective responses to the situation, and concludes that "the barrage system will not really solve the basic problems of Venice with its dwindling population and dying lagoon".

Water pollution

A major objection to the barrier is that it will further inhibit the cleansing effects of the tides, already diminished in parts of the lagoon by the creation of firm land out of mudflats. Twice-daily tidal movements and the activity of waste-digesting marine life were enough until fairly recently to keep the water relatively fresh – fresh enough until the 1980s for fastidious Venetians to swim in certain deep spots at high tides.

Much of the **pollution** is the fault of the industrial complexes of Mestre-Marghera, which, though in decline, have dumped thousands of tons of zinc, copper, iron, lead and chrome into the lagoon, creating a toxic sludge so dangerous that nobody has yet devised a safe way of dredging the stuff out. Chemical fertilisers seeping into the water from the mainland add to the accumulation of phosphates in the water, a situation exacerbated by the heavy use of phosphate-rich detergents in Venetian homes. (Although Venice treats its sewage in sumps before emptying it into the sea, all household sinks and baths drain straight into the canals.) Plants, fishes and other forms of marine life are being suffocated by algae that thrive on these phosphates, forming a foul-smelling scum that is thickened by the rotting animal and vegetable matter. When photographs of gondoliers and tourists in face masks brought adverse publicity abroad, it was finally acknowledged that a crisis had been reached, and in 1988 the Ministry of the Environment earmarked £175million to clean up the lagoon – though this too is to be delivered into the hands of a private consortium. Moreover, the town hall has now banned the sale of phosphate-enriched detergents. (Venice's boat-restorers will be pleased about this too: their work has steadily diminished as the bottoms of boats have stayed ever cleaner.)

But local action such as this will still not be enough. Venice's lagoon is threatened by the grossly polluted water of the whole upper Adriatic, into which the Po and numerous other waterways disgorge their effluents. In 1989 the Italian government assigned a sum of £500 million to the cleansing of the Adriatic, but the complexity of the problem is terrifying. It has even been proposed that the techniques used to purify sewage may be actually contributing to the proliferation of the algae by feeding them with vitamin-saturated fluids.

In the 1950s and 1960s Lake Erie was threatened with the same sort of marine disaster as now faces the Venice region; regulations imposed in the 1970s seem to have redeemed the lake. At the most optimistic estimate, if drastic action is taken now , the Po might be a moderately clean river by the end of this century.

Air pollution

The other environmental problem facing Venice is that of **air pollution**, which worsened in phase with the growing industrial complexes on the mainland. Sulphur dioxide combines with the salty and humid air of the lagoon to make a particularly vicious corrosive which eats at brick, stone and bronze alike. An experiment carried out in the 1970s showed that stone covered with pigeon droppings stayed in better condition than stone exposed to the Venetian air. The conversion of domestic heating systems from oil to gas has helped to cut down the amount of sulphur dioxide in the atmosphere, and expenditure on industrial filtration has had an effect too, but Marghera's factories still pump around 50,000 tons of the gas into the atmosphere each year. Some observers point out that the prevailing winds carry the plumes from the Marghera stacks inland, but even though the bulk of the emissions are someone else's problem, the ambient air of Venice was one of the factors the Italian trades union congress had in mind when they christened the city "the capital of pollution".

In the years immediately after the 1966 flood, as Venice attracted ever more attention from outside the country, the city authorities were often criticised for their tardiness in commissioning restoration work on Venice's crumbling stonework. Their cautiousness was to an extent vindicated when it became apparent that the restoration work on Sansovino's Loggetta – initially hailed as an unqualified success – had in fact done as much damage as it had repaired. The resins used to protect the restored marble have now begun to discolour the building, and it may prove impossible to sluice the resins out. A major restoration of the Miracoli church has turned out to be similarly ill-advised, with salt eating at the walls from inside and excreting white crusts onto the marble cladding. The cleaning and strengthening of the Porta della Carta was undertaken with far greater circumspection, and so far it seems that all is well; the lessons learned on that project are being employed on the continuous restoration of the Basilica di San Marco and the Palazzo Ducale.

Subsidence

The industries at Marghera used to threaten Venice from below as well as from above. Drawing millions of gallons of water directly from the ground, they caused a dramatic fall in the water table and threatened to cause the subsidence of the entire city. Calamity was averted in 1973 when the national government built two aquaducts to pipe water from inland rivers to the refineries and factories of Marghera and the houses of Venice.

Local subsidence will continue to be a problem, though. The majority of buildings in Venice are built on wooden pilings driven deep into the mudbanks of the lagoon. Interference with the lagoon's equilibrium has resulted in an increase in the number of extremely low tides as well as the number of floods, and occasionally the water falls so far that air gets at the pilings, causing them to decay. Furthermore, those people unable to afford proper wood-piled foundations would have used rubbish and rubble instead, which through the years slowly compresses. Another crucial factor is the erosive effect of the city's waterbuses: a recent study showed that the foundations of sixty percent of the buildings on the Canal Grande had been damaged by the wash from the vaporetti, and the situation along the Rio Novo (which was created expressly as a short-cut for the water buses) has become so bad that it has now been closed to traffic. Projects to consolidate the houses and churches of Venice will never cease to be necessary: thirteen major sites are currently being consolidated against erosion by the water, including the Lido's Fortezza di Sant'Andrea, which has been lurching forwards owing to the undermining action of the current at its base.

Aid groups

Restoration in Venice is principally a collaborative venture between UNESCO and the city's Superintendancies of Art and of Monuments. The former co-ordinates the fund-raising and restoration proposals from the multitude of aid groups set up in various countries after the 1966 floods; the latter pair oversee the restoration centres in Venice, the cataloguing of endangered buildings and objects and the deployment of restoration teams.

The first top-to-toe makeover for a Venetian building was the restoration of Madonna dell'Orto, undertaken by the British *Italian Art and Archives Rescue Fund* (transformed in 1971 into *Venice in Peril*). The church's facade statue of Saint Christopher was the first Istrian stone sculpture to be cleaned in Venice, and the techniques used were taken up by later restorers. Since then, the organisation has completely restored San Nicolò dei Mendicoli, the Loggetta at the base of the Campanile di San Marco and the Porta della Carta (the ceremonial gateway of the Palazzo Ducale); it's also been a major partner in the restoration of Santa Maria Assunta on Torcello and the Oratorio dei Crociferi, and is at present working on the church of San Giuliano.

Over thirty groups worldwide are now devoted to the rescue of Venice, all of them open to offers of financial help. If you want to make a donation to *ViP*, contact them at 8 St James Place, London SW1 (☎071/495 4023). Their Venice contact is John Millerchip, the British Centre, Campo San Luca, San Marco 4267/a. (Please note: the British Centre is a school for English-speaking children, emphatically not an information source or drop-in centre for homesick Brits.) In the US, the main aid organisation is *Save Venice Inc*, 216 East 78th St, New York, NY 10021.

UNESCO's office in Venice (Piazza San Marco 63) is also used by *Amici dei Musei*, which began as an organisation running cultural courses and guided tours during the winter, and is now also one of the city's main groups for collecting funds and initiating restoration projects. For the most up-to-date information on the state of restoration in Venice, this is the address to approach.

Books

A comprehensive Venetian reading-list would run on for dozens of pages, and would include a vast number of out-of-print titles. Most of our recommendations are in print, and those that aren't shouldn't be too difficult to track down. Wherever a book is in print the UK publisher is given first in each listing, followed by the publisher in the US – unless the title is available in one country only, in which case we have specified which country.

Fiction

Italo Calvino, *Invisible Cities* (Picador/Harcourt, Brace). Characteristically subtle variations on the idea of the City, presented in the form of tales told by Marco Polo to Kublai Khan. No explicit reference to Venice until well past half-way, when Polo remarks – "Every time I describe a city I am saying something about Venice."

Ernest Hemingway, *Across the River and into the Trees* (Panther/Scribner). Hemingway at his most square-jawed and most mannered: our hero fights good, drinks good, loves good, and could shoot a duck out of the skies from the hip at a range of half a mile. Target of one of the funniest parodies ever written: E.B. White's *Across the Street and into the Grill* – "'I love you," he said, "and we are going to lunch together for the first and only time, and I love you very much."'

E.T.A. Hoffmann, *Doge and Dogaressa* (in *Tales of Hoffmann*, Penguin in UK & US). Fanciful reconstruction of events surrounding the treason of Marin Falier, by one of the pivotal figures of German Romanticism. Lots of passion and pathos, narrated at headlong pace.

Henry James, *The Aspern Papers* & *The Wings of the Dove* (both Penguin in UK & US). The first, a 100-page *nouvelle* about the manipulative attempts of a biographer to get at the personal papers of a deceased writer, is one of James's most tautly constructed longer, tales. The latter, one of the three vast and circumspect late novels, was likened to caviar by Ezra Pound, and is likely to put you off James for life if you come to it without acclimatising yourself with the earlier stuff.

Thomas Mann, *Death in Venice* (Penguin in UK & US). Profound study of the demands of art and the claims of the flesh, with the city itself thematically significant rather than a mere exotic backdrop. Richer than most stories five times its length and infinitely more complex than Visconti's sentimentalising film.

Ian McEwan, *The Comfort of Strangers* (Picador/Penguin). Ordinary young English couple fall foul of sexually ambiguous predator. Venice is never named as the locality, but evoked by means of arch little devices such as quotes from Ruskin. A thin Gothic yarn, and extremely predictable.

Marcel Proust, *Albertine Disparue*. The Venetian interlude, occurring in the penultimate novel of Proust's massive novel sequence, can be sampled in isolation for its acute dissection of the sensory experience of the city – but to get the most from it, you've got to knuckle down and commit yourself to the preceding ten volumes. Available in two translations, the Kilmartin/Scott-Moncrieff version, published in three monstrous paperback volumes, and D.J. Enright's revison of that translation, in six hardbacks.

William Rivière, *A Venetian Theory of Heaven* (Sceptre in UK). Pleasant, undemanding story of marital woes and emotional confusion, with expertly evoked Venetian setting. Ideal holiday reading.

Frederick Rolfe (Baron Corvo), *The Desire and Pursuit of the Whole* (Da Capo in UK & US). Transparent exercise in self-justification, much of it taken up with venomous ridicule of the English community in Venice, among whom Rolfe moved while writing the book in 1909. (Its libellous streak kept it unpublished for 25 years.) Snobbish and incoherent, redeemed by hilarious character-assassinations and gorgeous descriptive passages. One of the few books by an Anglophone to be saturated with a knowledge of the place.

Muriel Spark, *Territorial Rights* (Penguin in UK & US). Examination of the wealthy, cultured and venal of Venice. Not one that's going to convince the sceptics that Spark has hidden depths, and even her most devoted admirers wouldn't rate it as one her best.

Michel Tournier, *Gemini* (o/p). Venice is just one of the localities through which the identical twins Jean and Paul (known to their parents as Jean-Paul) are taken in this amazingly inventive exploration of the concept of twinship. It might be flashy in places, yet Tournier throws away more ideas in the course of a novel than most writers dream up in lifetime.

Barry Unsworth, *Stone Virgin* (Penguin/Houghton Mifflin). Yet another story of the uncanny repetitions of history – this time an English expert in stone conservation begins to suspect that his emotional entanglement with a sculptor's wife is a recapitulation of a past liaison. The gobbets of scholarly detail sit uncomfortably alongside the melodrama of the plot.

Jeanette Winterson, *The Passion* (Penguin/Random). Whimsical tale of the intertwined lives of a member of Napoleon's catering corps and a female gondolier. Acclaimed as a masterpiece in some quarters.

Art and architecture

James S. Ackerman, *Palladio* (Penguin in UK & US). Concise introduction to the life, works and cultural background of the Veneto's greatest architect. Especially useful if you're visiting Vicenza or any of the villas.

Patricia Fortini Brown, *Venetian Narrative Painting in the Age of Carpaccio* (Yale in UK & US). Rigorously researched study of a subject central to Venetian culture yet often overlooked in more general accounts. Fresh reactions to the works discussed are combined with penetrating analysis of the ways they reflect the ideals of the Republic at the time. Worth every penny.

Paul Holberton, *Palladio's Villas* (John Murray/Trafalgar Square). Excellent survey of the architectural principles and social environment of the Veneto's greatest architect.

Deborah Howard, *The Architectural History of Venice* (Batsford/Holmes & Meier) and *Jacopo Sansovino: Architecture and Patronage in Renaissance Venice* (Yale in UK & US). The first is by far the best available introduction to the subject in English – a good first acquisition for any serious Venetian library. The analysis of the environment within which Sansovino operated makes the second book of wider interest than you might think – a logical next step after Howard's general survey.

Peter Lauritzen and Alexander Zielcke, *The Palaces of Venice* (o/p). Lauritzen lives in Venice and knows the place as intimately as anyone currently writing. This is a fascinating blend of social and architectural history, and Zielcke's photographs are uniformly good.

Ralph Lieberman, *Renaissance Architecture in Venice* (Abbeville in UK & US). Lieberman illustrates the complex development of architecture in fifteenth- and sixteenth-century Venice through a chronological survey of key buildings, but annoyingly calls a halt at 1540. Authoritative without being pedantic.

John McAndrew, *Venetian Architecture of the Early Renaissance* (o/p). Definitive study of its subject by the only writer to have studied Venice's buildings with anything like Ruskin's concentration. A beautiful book, but expensive even secondhand.

David Rosand, *Painting in Cinquecento Venice* (Yale in UK & US). Covers the century of Giorgione, Titian, Tintoretto and Veronese as thoroughly as most readers will want; especially good on the social networks and artistic conventions within which the painters worked.

John Ruskin, *The Stones of Venice*. Enchanting, enlightening and infuriating in about equal measure, this is still the most stimulating book written about Venice by a non-Venetian. Sadly, the only way to get hold of a full edition is to scour the secondhand bookshops, as the only editions in print are abridgements.

John Steer, *A Concise History of Venetian Painting* (Thames & Hudson in UK & US). Whistle-stop tour of Venetian art from the fourteenth to the eighteenth century. Undemanding, but a useful aid to sorting your thoughts out after the visual deluge of Venice's churches and museums, and the plentiful pictures come in handy when your memory needs a prod.

John Unrau, *Ruskin and St Mark's* (o/p). Ruskin discarded around 600 pages of notes and drawings of San Marco when he came to prepare the text of *The Stones of Venice*; using this material, Unrau has produced a book that is as illuminating about Ruskin as it is about the building. A brilliant selection of watercolours, paintings and photographs complements the text.

History

Fernand Braudel, *The Mediterranean in the Age of Philip II* (Fontana/Harper Collins). Vast, magisterial analysis of the economics and politics of the Mediterranean in the second half of the sixteenth century, with Venice rarely off the stage. Braudel's deployment of masses of raw material (population statistics, contemporary chronicles, trade documents) requires prolonged and unwavering attention.

D.S. Chambers, *The Imperial Age of Venice* (o/p). Concise and fluent account of Venice's heyday and the beginnings of decline, spanning the years 1380–1580. Informative and well illustrated.

David Chambers and Brian Pullen (eds), *Venice: a Documentary History, 1450–1630* (Blackwell in UK & US). A fine anthology of contemporary chronicles and documents, virtually none of which have previously been translated. Invaluable for getting the feel of the city in its heyday.

Robert Finlay, *Politics in Renaissance Venice* (Rutgers in UK & US). Subverts a few received ideas about the political tranquillity of La Serenissima, and is laced with anecdotes about the squabbling, scheming aristocracy. Though not the first book you'd read after your holiday, it explains the mechanics of power in Venice with great clarity.

Christopher Hibbert, *Venice, The Biography of a City* (Grafton/Norton). The usual highly proficient Hibbert synthesis of a vast range of secondary material. Very good on the changing social fabric of the city, and has more on twentieth-century Venice than most others. Excellent illustrations too.

Frederic C. Lane, *Venice, A Maritime Republic* (Johns Hopkins in UK & US). The most authoritative one-volume history of the city in English, based on decades of research. Excellent on the economic infrastructure of the city, and on the changing texture of everyday life.

Jan Morris, *The Venetian Empire: A Sea Voyage* (Penguin in UK & US). Anecdotal survey of the Republic's Mediterranean empire, with excursions on the evidence left behind. More a sketch than an attempt to give the full picture, it bears the usual Morris stylistic imprint.

John Julius Norwich, *A History of Venice* (Penguin in UK & US). Although it's far more reliant on secondary sources than Lane, and nowhere near as compendious – you won't learn much, for example, about Venice's finances – this is unbeatable for its grand narrative sweep.

A Venetian miscellany

Pietro Aretino, *Selected Letters* (o/p). Edited highlights from the voluminous correspondence of a man who could be described as the world's first professional journalist. Recipients include Titian, Michelangelo, Charles V, Francis I, the pope, the doge, Cosimo de' Medici – virtually anybody who was anybody in sixteenth-century Europe.

Joseph Brodsky, *Watermark* (Hamish Hamilton/ Farrar, Strauss & Giroux). Musings on the wonder of being in Venice and the wonder of being Joseph Brodsky, Nobel laureate and friend of the great. Flashes of imagistic brilliance contaminated by neanderthal sexual politics.

Milton Grundy, *Venice: An Anthology Guide* (A & C Black in UK only). A series of itineraries of the city fleshed out with appropriate excerpts from a huge range of travellers and scholars. Doesn't cover every major sight in Venice, but the choice of quotations couldn't be bettered.

Hugh Honour and John Fleming, *The Venetian Hours of Henry James, Whistler and Sargent* (Walker). Few visitors to nineteenth-century Venice were as sensitive to the character of the city as the American triumvirate of James, Whistler and Sargent, and this elegantly written and superbly illustrated book does full justice to their work. One of the most enjoyable books on Venice to be published in recent years.

Henry James, *Italian Hours* (Century/Ecco). Urbane travel pieces from the young Henry James, including five essays on Venice. Perceptive observations on the paintings and architecture of the city, but mainly of interest in its evocation of the tone of Venice in the 1860s and 70s.

Peter Lauritzen, *Venice Preserved* (o/p). Generally optimistic report on the restoration of Venice's paintings and monuments, and the outlook for the future; sometimes contentious, too – Lauritzen doesn't mince his words about Olivetti's part in the "rescue" of the San Marco horses. As with all Lauritzen's books, the pictures are splendid.

Ian Littlewood, *Venice: A Literary Companion* (Murray/Trafalgar Square). Wide-ranging anthology of writings on the city, including many pieces that will be unfamiliar to all but the most scholarly devotees of Venice.

Giulio Lorenzetti, *Venice and its Lagoon* (Lint). The most thorough cultural guide ever written to any European city – Lorenzetti seems to have researched the history of every brick and every canvas. Though completely unmanageable as a guidebook (it even has an index to the indexes), it's indispensible for all those besotted with the place. Almost impossible to find outside Venice.

H.V. Morton, *A Traveller in Italy* (o/p). A mellower book than his earlier *In Search of Ireland* and *In Search of Scotland*, mixing anecdote, observation and history. Concentrates on northern Italy, with a chapter on Verona and two on Venice.

Mary McCarthy, *The Stones of Florence/Venice Observed* (Penguin in UK & US). Entertaining, incisive report, originally written for the *New Yorker*; the briskness is a refreshing antidote to the gushing enthusiasm of most first-hand accounts.

James Morris, *Venice* (Faber/Harcourt, Brace). To some people this is the most brilliant book ever written about Venice; to others it's appallingly fey and self-regarding. But if you can't stomach the style, Morris's knowledge of Venice's folklore provides some compensation.

Mary Stella Newton, *The Dress of the Venetians 1495–1525* (o/p). Specialised academic book accessible to anyone with an interest in fashion, Venetian social history or the art of the period. Official costume, festive costume, the apparel of the visiting foreigners – nothing is missed out except, sadly, the dress of the city's working class.

A.J.A. Symons, *The Quest for Corvo* (o/p). Misanthropic, devious and solitary, Frederick Rolfe was a tricky subject for a biographer to tackle, and Symons's book, subtitled *An Experiment in Biography*, makes the difficult process of writing Rolfe's life the focus of its narrative. An engrossing piece of literary detective work, and a perfect introduction to Rolfe's Venetian novel, *The Desire and Pursuit of the Whole*.

Tony Tanner, *Venice Desired* (Blackwell in UK & US). Scholarly survey of Venice's place in the literary imagination, from Byron and his "sea Sodom" to the cerebral fictions of Sartre and Ezra Pound. Occasionally ponderous but frequently provocative.

Language

Although it's not uncommon for the staff of Venetian hotels and restaurants to speak some English, you'll make a lot more friends by attempting the vernacular. Outside the city, you might by able to get by in English at tourist offices, but life will be considerably easier if you can master at least a few of the phrases below.

Some tips

You'd do well to master at least a little **Italian**, a task made more enjoyable by the fact that your halting efforts will often be rewarded by smiles and genuine surprise that an English speaker should stoop to learn Italian. In any case, it's one of the easiest European languages to learn, especially if you already have a smattering of French or Spanish, both extremely similar grammatically.

Easiest of all is the **pronunciation**, since every word is spoken exactly as it's written, and usually enunciated with exaggerated, open-mouthed

ITALIAN WORDS AND PHRASES

Basics

Good morning	*Buon giorno*
Good afternoon/evening	*Buona sera*
Good night	*Buona notte*
Hello/goodbye	*Ciao (informal; to strangers use phrases above)*
Goodbye	*Arrivederci*
Yes	*Sì*
No	*No*
Please	*Per favore*
Thank you (very much)	*Grázie (molte/mille grazie)*
You're welcome	*Prego*
Alright/that's OK	*Va bene*
How are you?	*Come stai/sta? (informal/formal)*
I'm fine	*Bene*
Do you speak English?	*Parla inglese?*
I don't understand	*Non ho capito*
I don't know	*Non lo so*
Excuse me	*Mi scusi/Prego*
Excuse me (in a crowd)	*Permesso*
I'm sorry	*Mi dispiace*
I'm here on holiday	*Sono qui in vacanza*
I'm English/Scottish/ Welsh/Irish	*Sono inglese/scozzese gallese/irlandese*
I live in . . .	*Abito a . . .*
Today	*Oggi*
Tomorrow	*Domani*
Day after tomorrow	*Dopodomani*
Yesterday	*Ieri*
Now	*Adesso*
Later	*Più tardi*
Wait a minute!	*Aspetta!*
In the morning	*di mattina*
In the afternoon	*nel pomeriggio*
In the evening	*di sera*
Here (there)	*Qui/La*
Good/bad	*Buono/Cattivo*
Big/small	*Grande/Píccolo*
Cheap/expensive	*Económico/Caro*
Early/late	*Presto/Ritardo*
Hot/cold	*Caldo/Freddo*
Near/far	*Vicino/Lontano*
Vacant/occupied	*Líbero/Occupato*
Quickly/slowly	*Velocemente/Lentamente*
Slowly/quietly	*Piano*
With/without	*Con/Senza*
More/less	*Più/Meno*
Enough, no more	*Basta*
Mr . . .	*Signor . . .*
Mrs . . .	*Signora . . .*
Miss . . .	*Signorina . . .* (*il Signor*, *la Signora*, *la Signorina* when speaking about someone else)

clarity. The only difficulties you're likely to encounter are the few **consonants** that are different from English:

c before e or i is pronounced as in **ch**urch, while **ch** before the same vowels is hard, as in **c**at.

sci or **sce** are pronounced as in **sh**eet and **sh**elter respectively. The same goes with **g** – soft before **e** and **i**, as in **g**eranium; hard when followed by h, as in **g**arlic.

gn has the ni sound of our 'o**ni**on'.

gl in Italian is softened to something like li in English, as in sta**lli**on.

h is not aspirated, as in **h**onour.

When **speaking** to strangers, the third person is the polite form (ie *Lei* instead of *Tu* for "you"); using the second person is a mark of disrespect or stupidity. Also remember that Italians don't use "please" and "thank you" half as much as we do: it's all implied in the tone, though if you're in any doubt, err on the polite side.

All Italian words are **stressed** on the penultimate syllable unless an **accent** (´ or `) denotes otherwise, although accents are often left out in practice. Note that the ending **-ia** or **-ie** counts as two syllables, hence *trattoria* is stressed on the i. We've put accents in, throughout the text and below, wherever it isn't immediately obvious how a word should be pronounced: for example, in *Maríttima*, the accent is on the first **i**; similarly the stress in *Pésaro* is not on the **a**, where you'd expect it, but on the **e**. We've omitted accents on some of the more common exceptions (like *Isola*, stressed on the I), some names (*Domenico*), and words that are stressed similarly in English, such as *archeologico* and *Repubblica*.

The **Venetian dialect** virtually qualifies as a separate language, with its own rules of spelling and grammar, and distinctive pronunciation. However, you'll probably encounter it only in the form of the words given in the Glossary below, dialect proper names (which are deciphered in the text) or the occasional shop sign – eg *Venexiana* rather than *Veneziana* .

Some Signs

Entrance/exit	*Entrata/Uscita*
Free entrance	*Ingresso líbero*
Gentlemen/ladies	*Signori/Signore*
WC	*Gabinetto*
Vacant/engaged	*Libero/Occupato*
Open/closed	*Aperto/Chiuso*
Arrivals/departures	*Arrivi/Partenze*
Closed for restoration	*Chiuso per restauro*
Closed for holidays	*Chiuso per ferie*
Pull/push	*Tirare/Spingere*
Out of order	*Guasto*
Drinking water	*Acqua potabile*
To let	*Affítasi*
Platform	*Binario*
Cash desk	*Cassa*
Go/walk	*Avanti*
Stop/halt	*Alt*
Customs	*Dogana*
Do not touch	*Non toccare*
Danger	*Perícolo*
Beware	*Attenzione*
First aid	*Pronto soccorso*
Ring the bell	*Suonare il campanello*
No smoking	*Vietato fumare*

Driving

Left/right	*Sinistro/Destro*
Go straight ahead	*Sempre diritto*
Turn to the right/left	*Gira a destra/sinistra*
Parking	*Parcheggio*
No parking	*Divieto di sosta/Sosta vietata*
One way street	*Senso único*
No entry	*Senso vietato*
Slow down	*Rallentare*
Road closed/up	*Strada chiusa/guasta*
No through road	*Vietato il transito*
No overtaking	*Vietato il sorpasso*
Crossroads	*Incrocio*
Speed limit	*Limite di velocità*

Italian Numbers

1	uno	9	nove	17	diciassette	50	cinquanta	200	duecento
2	due	10	dieci	18	diciotto	60	sessanta	500	cinquecento
3	tre	11	undici	19	diciannove	70	settanta	1000	mille
4	quattro	12	dodici	20	venti	80	ottanta	5000	cinquemila
5	cinque	13	tredici	21	ventuno	90	novanta	10,000	diecimila
6	sei	14	quattordici	22	ventidue	100	cento	50,000	cinquantamila
7	sette	15	quindici	30	trenta	101	centuno		
8	otto	16	sedici	40	quaranta	110	centodieci		

Accommodation

Hotel	*Albergo*
Is there a hotel nearby?	*C'è un albergo qui vicino?*
Do you have a room . . .	*Ha una cámera . . .*
for one/two/three people	*per una/due/tre person(a/e)*
for one/two/three nights	*per una/due/tre nott(e/i)*
for one/two weeks	*per una/due setti-man(a/e)*
with a double bed	*con un letto matrimoniale*
with a shower/bath	*con una doccia/un bagno*
with a balcony	*con una terrazza*
hot/cold water	*acqua calda/freddo*
How much is it?	*Quanto costa?*
It's expensive	*È caro*
Is breakfast included?	*È compresa la prima colazione?*
Do you have anything cheaper?	*Ha niente che costa di meno?*
Full/half board	*Pensione completa/ mezza pensione*
Can I see the room?	*Posso vedere la cámera?*
I'll take it	*La prendo*
I'd like to book a room	*Vorrei prenotare una cámera*
I have a booking	*Ho una prenotazione*
Can we camp here?	*Possiamo campeg-giare qui?*
Is there a campsite nearby?	*C'è un camping qui vicino?*
Tent	*Tenda*
Cabin	*Cabina*
Youth hostel	*Ostello per la gioventù*

Questions and Directions

Where? (where is/ are . . .?)	*Dove? (Dov'è/Dove sono)*
When?	*Quando?*
What? (what is it?)	*Cosa? (Cos'è?)*
How much/many?	*Quanto/Quanti?*
Why?	*Perché?*
It is/there is(is it/ is there . . .?)	*È/C'è (È/C'è . . . ?)*
What time is it?	*Che ora è/Che ore sono?*
How do I get to . . . ?	*Come arrivo a . . . ?*
How far is it to . . . ?	*Quant'è lontano a . . . ?*
Can you give me a lift to . . . ?	*Mi può dare un passaggio a . . . ?*
Can you tell me when to get off?	*Mi può dire scendere alla fermata giusta?*
What time does it open?	*A che ora apre?*
What time does it close?	*A che ora chiude?*
How much does it cost (. . . do they cost?)	*Quanto costa? (Quanto córtano?)*
What's it called in Italian?	*Come si chiama in italiano?*

Travelling

Aeroplane	*Aeroplano*
Bus	*Autobus/pullman*
Train	*Treno*
Car	*Macchina*
Taxi	*Taxi*
Bicycle	*Bicicletta*
Ferry	*Traghetto*
Ship	*Nave*
Hydrofoil	*Aliscafo*
Hitch-hiking	*Autostop*
On foot	*A piedi*
Bus station	*Autostazione*
Railway station	*Stazione ferroviaria*
Ferry terminal	*Stazione maríttima*
Port	*Porto*
A ticket to . . .	*Un biglietto a . . .*
One-way/return	*Solo andata/andata e ritorno*
Can I book a seat?	*Posso prenotare un posto?*
What time does it leave?	*A che ora parte?*
When is the next bus/ train/ferry to . . . ?	*Quando parte il prossimo pullman/ treno/traghetto per..?*
Do I have to change?	*Devo cambiare?*
Where does it leave from?	*Da dove parte?*
What platform does it leave from?	*Da quale binario parte?*
How many kilometres is it?	*Quanti chilómetri sono?*
How long does it take?	*Quanto ci vuole?*
What number bus is it to . . . ?	*Che número di auto bus per . . . ?*
Where's the road to ...?	*Dovè la strada pe ...?*
Next stop please	*La prossima fermata, per favore*

Phrasebooks and Dictionaries

The best of the **phrasebooks** are *Harrap's Italian Phrase Book* , which has useful vocabulary sections and menu readers, and the *Penguin Italian Phrase Book*. Among dictionaries, *Collins* publish a comprehensive series: their *Gem* or *Pocket* dictionaries are fine for travelling purposes, while their *Concise* is adequate for most language needs.

A MENU GLOSSARY

This glossary should allow you to decode any menu; it concludes with a summary of Venetian specialities – for more detail on Venetian food and drink, see p.229.

Basics and Snacks

Aceto	Vinegar
Aglio	Garlic
Biscotti	Biscuits
Burro	Butter
Caramelle	Sweets
Cioccolato	Chocolate
Focaccia	Oven-baked snack
Formaggio	Cheese
Frittata	Omelette
Gelato	Ice-cream
Grissini	Bread sticks
Marmellata	Jam
Olio	Oil
Olive	Olives
Pane	Bread
Pane integrale	Wholemeal bread
Panino	Bread roll
Patatine	Crisps
Patatine fritte	Chips
Pepe	Pepper
Pizzetta	Small cheese and tomato pizza
Riso	Rice
Sale	Salt
Tramezzini	Sandwich
Uova	Eggs
Yogurt	Yoghurt
Zúcchero	Sugar
Zuppa	Soup

Starters (Antipasti)

Antipasto misto	Mixed cold meats and cheese (and a selection of other things in this list).
Caponata	Mixed aubergine, olives, tomatoes and celery.
Caprese	Tomato and mozzarella cheese salad.
Insalata di mare	Seafood salad.
Insalata di riso	Rice salad.
Melanzane in parmigiana	Fried aubergine in tomato and parmesan cheese.
Mortadella	Salami-type cured meat.
Pancetta	Bacon.
Peperonata	Grilled green, red or yellow peppers stewed in olive oil.
Pomodori ripieni	Stuffed tomatoes.
Prosciutto	Ham.
Salame	Salami.

Pizzas

Biancaneve	"Black and white"; mozzarella and oregano.
Calzone	Folded pizza with cheese, ham and tomato.
Capricciosa	Literally "capricious"; topped with whatever they've got in the kitchen, usually including baby artichoke, ham and egg.
Diavolo	Spicy, with hot salami or Italian sausage.
Funghi	Mushroom; tinned, sliced button mushrooms unless it specifies fresh mushrooms, either *funghi freschi* or *porcini*.
Frutti di mare	Sea food; usually mussels, prawns, squid and clams.
Margherita	Cheese and tomato.
Marinara	Tomato and garlic.
Napoli/ Napoletana	Tomato, anchovy and olive oil (and sometimes mozzarella).
Quattro formaggi	"Four cheeses", usually including mozzarella, fontina, gorgonzola and gruyère.
Quattro stagioni	"Four seasons"; the toppings split into four sections, usually including ham, peppers, onion, mushrooms, artichokes, olives and egg.
Romana	Anchovy and olives.

The First Course (Il primo)

Soups

Brodo	Clear broth.
Minestrina	Any light soup.
Minestrone	Thick vegetable soup.
Pasta e fagioli	Pasta soup with beans.
Pastina in brodo	Pasta pieces in clear broth.
Stracciatella	Broth with egg.

Pasta

Cannelloni	Large tubes of pasta, stuffed.
Farfalle	Literally "bow"-shaped pasta; the word also means "butterflies".
Fettuccine	Narrow pasta ribbons.
Gnocchi	Small potato and dough dumplings.
Lasagne	Lasagne.
Maccheroni	Tubular spaghetti.
Pasta al forno	Pasta baked with minced meat, eggs, tomato and cheese.

Pasta (continued)

Penne	Smaller version of rigatoni.
Ravioli	Ravioli.
Rigatoni	Large, grooved tubular pasta.
Risotto	Cooked rice dish, with sauce.
Spaghetti	Spaghetti.
Spaghettini	Thin spaghetti.
Tagliatelle	Pasta ribbons, another word for fettucine.
Tortellini	Small rings of pasta, stuffed with meat or cheese.
Vermicelli	Very thin spaghetti (literally "little worms").

Pasta sauces

Aglio e olio (e peperoncino)	Tossed in garlic and olive oil (and hot chillies).
Arrabiata	Spicy tomato sauce, & chillies.
Bolognese	Meat sauce.
Burro e salvia	Butter and sage.
Carbonara	Cream, ham and beaten egg.
Frutta di mare	Seafood.
Funghi	Mushroom.
Matriciana	Cubed pork and tomato sauce.
Panna	Cream.
Parmigiano	Parmesan cheese.
Pesto	Ground basil, pine nut, garlic and pecorino sauce.
Pomodoro	Tomato sauce.
Ragù	Meat sauce.
Vóngole	Clam and tomato sauce.

The Second Course (Il secondo)

Meat (carne)

Agnello	Lamb
Bistecca	Steak
Cervello	Brains
Cinghiale	Wild boar
Coniglio	Rabbit
Costolette	Chops
Cotolette	Cutlets
Fegatini	Chicken livers
Fégato	Liver
Involtini	Steak slices, rolled and stuffed
Lingua	Tongue
Maiale	Pork
Manzo	Beef
Ossobuco	Shin of veal
Pollo	Chicken
Polpette	Meatballs (or minced balls of anything)
Rognoni	Kidneys
Salsiccia	Sausage
Saltimbocca	Veal with ham
Spezzatino	Stew
Tacchino	Turkey
Trippa	Tripe
Vitello	Veal

Fish (pesce) and shellfish (crostacei)

Acciughe	Anchovies
Anguilla	Eel
Aragosta	Lobster
Baccalà	Dried salted cod
Calamari	Squid
Céfalo	Mullet
Cozze	Mussels
Dattile	Razor clams
Dentice	Dentex (like sea bass)
Gamberetti	Shrimps
Gámberi	Prawns
Granchio	Crab
Merluzzo	Cod
Nasello	Hake
Ostriche	Oysters
Pescespada	Swordfish
Pólipo	Octopus
Ricci di mare	Sea urchins
Sarde	Sardines
Seppie	Cuttlefish
Sgombro	Mackerel
Sógliola	Sole
Tonno	Tuna
Triglie	Red mullet
Trota	Trout
Vóngole	Clams

Vegetables (contorni) and salad (insalata)

Asparagi	Asparagus
Basílico	Basil
Bróccoli	Broccoli
Cápperi	Capers
Carciofi	Artichokes
Carciofini	Artichoke hearts
Carotte	Carrots
Cavolfiori	Cauliflower
Cávolo	Cabbage
Ceci	Chickpeas
Cetriolo	Cucumber
Cipolla	Onion
Fagioli	Beans
Fagiolini	Green beans
Finocchio	Fennel
Funghi	Mushrooms
Insalata verde/ insalata mista	Green salad/mixed salad
Melanzane	Aubergine/eggplant
Orígano	Oregano
Patate	Potatoes
Peperoni	Peppers
Piselli	Peas
Pomodori	Tomatoes
Radicchio	Chicory
Spinaci	Spinach
Zucchini	Courgettes
Zucca	Pumpkin

Desserts (Dolci), Cheeses (Formaggi), Fruit (Frutta) and Nuts (Noce)

Desserts

Amaretti	Macaroons.
Cassata	Ice-cream cake with candied fruit.
Gelato	Ice-cream.
Macedonia	Fruit salad.
Torta	Cake, tart.
Zabaglione	Dessert made with eggs, sugar and marsala wine.
Zuppa Inglese	Trifle.

Cheese

Caciocavallo	A type of dried, mature mozzarella cheese.
Fontina	Northern Italian cheese used in cooking.
Gorgonzola	Soft blue-veined cheese.
Mozzarella	Bland soft white cheese used on pizzas.
Parmigiano	Parmesan cheese.
Pecorino	Strong tasting hard sheep's cheese.
Provolone	Hard strong cheese.
Ricotta	Soft white cheese made from ewe's milk, used in sweet or savoury dishes.

Fruit and nuts

Ananas	Pineapple
Anguria/Coccómero	Water melon
Arance	Oranges
Banane	Bananas
Ciliegie	Cherries
Fichi	Figs
Fichi d'India	Prickly pears
Frágole	Strawberries
Limone	Lemon
Mándorle	Almonds
Mele	Apples
Melone	Melon
Pere	Pears
Pesche	Peaches
Pignoli	Pine nuts
Pistacchio	Pistachio nut
Uva	Grapes

Cooking Terms

Affumicato	Smoked
Al dente	Firm, not overcooked
Al ferro	Grilled without oil
Al forno	Baked
Al Marsala	Cooked with Marsala wine
Al vapore	Steamed
Alla brace	Barbecued
Alla griglia	Grilled
Allo spiedo	On the spit
Arrosto	Roasted
Ben cotto	Well done
Bollito	Boiled
Brasato	Cooked in wine
Cotto	Cooked (not raw)
Crudo	Raw
Fritto	Fried
Grattugiato	Grated
In úmido	Stewed
Lesso	Boiled
Milanese	Fried in egg and breadcrumbs
Pizzaiola	Cooked with tomato sauce
Ripieno	Stuffed
Sangue	Rare
Surgelati	Frozen

Drinks

Acqua minerale	Mineral water
Aranciata	Orangeade
Bicchiere	Glass
Birra	Beer
Bottiglia	Bottle
Caffè	Coffee
Cioccolata calda	Hot chocolate
Ghiaccio	Ice
Granita	Iced coffee- /fruit-drink
Latte	Milk
Limonata	Lemonade
Selz	Soda water
Spremuta	Fresh fruit juice
Spumante	Sparkling wine
Succo	Concentrated fruit juice with sugar
Tè	Tea
Tónico	Tonic water
Vino	Wine
Rosso	Red
Bianco	White
Rosato	Rosé
Secco	Dry
Dolce	Sweet
Litro	Litre
Mezzo	Half
Quarto	Quarter
Salute!	Cheers!

Venetian Specialities

Antipasti e Primi

Acciughe marinate	Marinated anchovies with onions.
Bigoli in salsa	Spaghetti with butter, onions and sardines.
Brodetto	Mixed fish soup, often with tomatoes and garlic.
Castraura	Artichoke hearts.

Granseola alla Veneziana	Crab cooked with oil, parsley and lemon.
Pasta e fasioi	Pasta and beans.
Prosciutto San Daniele	The best quality *prosciutto.*
Risotto di mare	Mixed seafood risotto.
Risotto di cape	Risotto with clams and shellfish.
Risotto alla sbirraglia	Risotto with chicken, vegetables and ham.
Risotto alla trevigiana	Risotto with butter, onions and chicory.
Sopa de peoci	Mussel soup with garlic and parsley.

Secondi

Anguilla alla Veneziana	Eel cooked with lemon and tuna.
Baccalà mantecato	Salt cod simmered in milk.
Fegato veneziana	Sliced calve's liver cooked in olive oil with onion.
Peoci salati	Mussels with parsley and garlic.
Risi e bisi	Rice and peas, with Parmesan and ham.
Sarde in saor	Marinated sardines.
Seppie in nero	Squid cooked in its ink.
Seppioline nere	Baby cuttlefish cooked in its ink.

Dolci

Frittole alla Veneziana	Rum- and anise-flavoured fritters filled with pine nuts, raisins and candied fruit.
Tiramisù	Dessert of layered chocolate and cream, flavoured with rum and coffee.

Glossary of Italian Words and Acronyms

Italian Words

ANFITEATRO Amphitheatre.

AUTOSTAZIONE Bus station.

AUTOSTRADA Motorway.

BELVEDERE A look-out point.

CAPPELLA Chapel.

CASTELLO Castle.

CENTRO Centre.

CHIESA Church.

COMUNE An administrative area; also, the local council or the town hall.

CORSO Avenue/boulevard.

DUOMO/CATTEDRALE Cathedral.

ENTRATA Entrance.

FESTA Festival, carnival.

FIUME River.

LAGO Lake.

MARE Sea.

MERCATO Market.

MUNICIPIO Town Hall.

PALAZZO Palace, mansion or block (of flats).

PARCO Park.

PASSEGGIATA The customary early evening walk.

PIAZZA Square.

PONTE Bridge.

SANTUARIO Sanctuary.

SENSO ÚNICO One-way street.

SOTTOPASSAGGIO Subway.

SPIAGGIA Beach.

STAZIONE Station.

STAZIONE FERROVIARIA Train station.

STAZIONE MARÍTTIMA Ferry terminal.

STRADA Road/street.

TEATRO Theatre.

TEMPIO Temple.

TORRE Tower.

TRAGHETTO Ferry.

USCITA Exit.

VIA Road.

Venetian Words

CALLE Main alleyway.

CAMPO Square, generally named after a church.

CAMPIELLO Small square.

CORTE Courtyard.

FONDACO (or FONTEGO) Warehouse/hostel used by foreign traders.

FONDAMENTA Pavement along a stretch of water.

PISCINA Former site of a pool.

PUNTA Point, the extremity of an island.

RAMO Small side street.

RIO (pl. Rii) Canal.

RIO TERRÀ Infilled canal.

RIVA A major *fondamenta*.

RUGA Usually a main shopping street.

SACCA Inlet.

SALIZZADA (or Salizada) Main street of a parish. Means "paved street" – originally only main thoroughfares were paved.

SOTTOPORTICO (or Sottoportego) Small alleyway running under a building.

Acronyms

AAST Azienda Autonoma di Soggiorno e Turismo (local tourist office).

ACI Italian Automobile Club.

APT Azienda Promozionale Turismo; equivalent to the AAST.

DC Democrazia Cristiana; the Christian Democrats.

EPT Ente Provinciale di Turismo (provincial tourist office).

FS Italian State Railways.

IVA Imposta Valore Aggiunto (VAT).

MSI Movimento Sociale d'Italia; the Fascist party.

PDS Partito Democratico della Sinistra; the former communist party.

PSI Partito Socialista d'Italia; the Socialist Party.

RAI The state TV and radio network.

SIP Italian state telephone company.

SS Strada Statale; major carriageway.

Glossary of Artistic and Architectural Terms

AMBULATORY Corridor round the back of the altar formed by a continuation of the aisles

APSE Recess at the altar end of a church.

ARCHITRAVE The lowest part of the entablature.

BALDACHIN Canopy over an altar or tomb.

BAPTISTERY Chapel for baptisms, often detached from church.

BAROQUE Dynamic architectural and sculptural style of seventeenth century and early eighteenth century.

CAMPANILE Bell-tower, sometimes detached.

CAPITAL Top of a column.

CHANCEL Part of church containing the altar and sanctuary.

CHOIR Part of church in which the service is sung; often raised or screened, usually near the altar.

CRYPT Burial place, usually under the choir.

CUPOLA A dome.

ENTABLATURE The part above the capital on a classical building.

EX-VOTO Painting or some other object presented as thanksgiving to a saint.

FRESCO Painting applied to wet plaster so that pigments are absorbed into the wall.

FRIEZE Decorative strip along top of wall or on an entablature.

ICONOSTASIS Screen between the sanctuary and nave in Eastern churches.

LUNETTE Semicircular panel above a door or window.

NAVE Central space in a church, usually flanked by aisles.

PANTOCRATOR An image of Christ, portrayed with outstretched arms in the act of blessing

PIANO NOBILE Main floor, usually the first.

POLYPTYCH Painting or carving on several joined wooden panels.

PORTICO The covered entrance to a building.

ROCOCO Florid eighteenth-century style.

RELIQUARY Receptacle for a saint's relics.

ROMANESQUE General term for plain architectural style of eleventh century to late thirteenth century.

ROOD SCREEN Screen between sanctuary and nave, bearing a rood (crucifix).

RUSTICATION Large blocks of stone with deep joints, or brick designed to simulate them.

SANCTUARY Area immediately surrounding the high altar.

STELE Inscribed stone slab.

STUCCO Heavy plaster made from water, sand, lime and powdered marble, used for decorative work.

TESSERA Small square piece of stone or glass used in mosaics.

TRACERY Geometrical or patterned stonework.

TRANSEPT Part of church at ninety degrees to the nave.

TROMPE L'OEIL Painting designed to trick the viewer into seeing a three-dimensional image.

TRIPTYCH Painting or carving on three joined panels.

TYMPANUM Panel enclosed by lintel of a door and the arch above it.

Index of Names

General Index

NOTES

NOTES

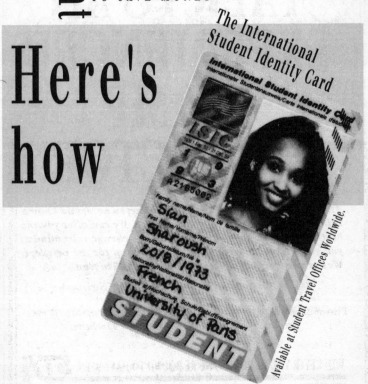